D0841258

♔ ROLEX

Rolex Submariner Date. Chronometer in steel and 18 ct gold.

John Bull

OFFICIAL ROLEX RETAILER BAHAMAS

284 Bay Street, **Nassau**, Tel: (242)322-4253
• Crystal Court at Atlantis, Tel: (242)363-5821
• Marsh Harbour, Abaco

Family Float Plan!
Old Port Cove Style

"Palm Beach County's Ultimate Yachting & Sportfishing Facilities"

OUR FAMILY OF MARINE BUSINESSES PROVIDE ONE STOP BOATING FUN.

- 400 WET STORAGE SLIPS TO 150+ FT • 200 DRY STORAGE RACKS TO 32+ FT • RECIPROCAL SECURE DOCKAGE AT THREE LOCATIONS • PRIVATE YACHT CLUB PRIVILEGES • FUEL DISCOUNTS • CLEAN BOAT YARD, KNOWLEDGEABLE STAFF • REFERRAL PROGRAM CREDITS • ON-SITE CAR RENTALS • BOAT U.S. PARTICIPATING MARINAS • PERSONAL STORAGE LOCKERS

Old Port Cove Marina

Beautiful North Palm Beach Marina

New Port Cove Marine Center & Boat Yard

Power In Tune With Nature
HONDA MARINE
Palm Beach County's Only Authorized
Honda Sales & Service Center.

In Palm Beach County, File Your Family Float Plan With Our One Stop Boating Family!
Spectacular Service for 25 Years and Growing.

THESE BENEFITS AVAILABLE TO YOU THROUGH YOUR IN-HOUSE CHARGE ACCOUNT AT
ALL THREE HOME PORTS:

Beautiful **North Palm Beach Marina**
New Port Cove Marine Center & Boat Yard

561-626-4919   **561-844-2504**

Old Port Cove Marina
561-626-1760

www.opch.com   email: marinas@opch.com

"Gateway to the Caribbean"

400 slips with accommodations to 250 ft.

Everything you could ask for, a full service marina on Government Cut.

- Texaco Star Port, fuel and pump-out facilities
- Dockmaster tower with state-of-the-art weather service
- Bay walk overlooking the port
- Excellent security
- Heated swimming pool
- Lighted parking

- Bathrooms & showers
- Laundry facilities
- Hopkins-Carter Marine Hardware, bait & tackle
- Suzanne's Market, gourmet grocery, wine, beer, ice
- Monty's Raw Bar
- Monty's Fine Dining
- Retail shops

- Tarpoon dive shop
- Reward II drift fishing
- Sportfishing charters
- Yacht and charter brokerages
- Europa Seakruz, dining bands, full casino

World famous Ocean Drive closeby.

MARINA
In the heart of South Beach

300 Alton Rd. • Miami Beach, FL 33139
(305) 673-6000 • Fax (305) 538-1780
Monitoring Channel 16
See our website www.miamibeachmarina.com

Managed by RCI Marine, Inc.

A true yachtsman's resort.

Introducing the Marina at Atlantis,
Opens December, 1998.

On an island of endless wonders – aptly named Paradise. In the shadow of a magnificent palace that isn't just on the water but is *of* the water. There is a marina where the finest vessels in the world find uncompromised shelter and unmatched luxury. The legend of Atlantis is no longer long ago and far away. It is here. Now. 63 full-service slip

Bahamas.

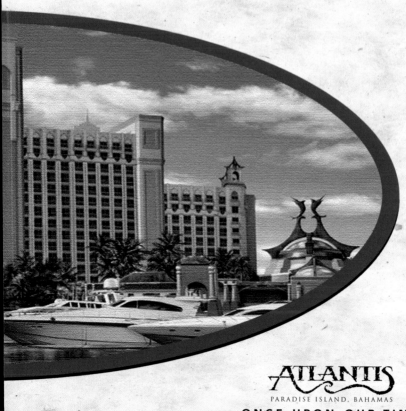

ATLANTIS
PARADISE ISLAND, BAHAMAS
ONCE UPON *OUR* TIME.

accommodating yachts up to 200 feet with full access to Atlantis' world-class restaurants, night clubs and casino, as well as the world's largest marine habitat, nine pools, golf, tennis and every other distraction Paradise Island has to offer. For information or slip reservations, call 1-800-ATLANTIS or 242-363-6068.   www.sunint.com/atlantis

32 NEW BOAT SLIPS

TURTLE • COVE • MARINA

Friendly Service • Quantity Fuel Discount
Free Video on Provo

- Port of Entry
- R.O. Water & Ice
- Diesel & Gas
- 6' Draft at Low Tide
- Cable TV
- 220-110V
- Hotel, Restaurants, and Bars at Docks
- Laundry Nearby
- Doctors & Clinic
- Recompression Chamber
- Diving on Site
- Casino & Golf

FOR INFORMATION:
PROVIDENT LTD.
P.O. BOX 594 PROVIDENCIALES
TURKS & CAICOS ISLANDS
BRITISH WEST INDIES
(649) 946-4303
FAX (649) 946-4326

We honor VISA, MasterCard, and American Express

TURTLE • COVE • MARINA
ON VHF CHANNEL 16 (649) 941-3781
PROVIDENCIALES "PROVO"
TURKS & CAICOS ISLANDS • BRITISH WEST INDIES

Yes, you can have it all...
...only in **Fort Lauderdale!**

Three great locations...One great city... and a new facility for Mega Yachts!

Cooley's Landing

Fort Lauderdale announces the opening of its new Las Olas Docks, specifically designed to accommodate mega yachts.

Boaters can now choose from three affordable marinas offering amenities including ample deep water dockage, dockside parking, along with water, electric, phone jacks and Cable TV/HBO at each slip. Plus, each marina is located near some of Fort Lauderdale's most popular attractions.

NEW LAS OLAS DOCKS
• 52-slip marina for mega yachts
• Comfort station with restrooms, showers, laundromat and small meeting facility
• Vacuum sewage pumpout facilities
• Daily dockage and temporary anchorage area for small boats
• Gated security

• Next to Fort Lauderdale Beach, Beach Place, clubs and restaurants

COOLEY'S LANDING
• 30 slips and three boat launches
• Comfort station with restrooms, showers and laundromat
• Sewage pumpout connections at each slip
• On-site security
• Near the Broward Center for the Performing Arts, Museum of Discovery & Science, and Las Olas Riverfront

NEW RIVER DOWNTOWN
• 100 slips with full utilities
• Fueling site and two pumpout stations
• Roving security
• Located on the City's Riverwalk
• Pavilions and picnic areas
• Near Las Olas Boulevard shops, galleries and restaurants

New River Downtown

City of Fort Lauderdale Marine Facilities
2 South New River Drive East
Fort Lauderdale, FL 33301
Ph: (954) 761-5423 • Monitor VHF Chs. 9 & 16
Web: http://ci.ftlaud.fl.us/marinas
E-mail: webmaster@ci.ftlaud.fl.us

Make Plans Now! Call 1-800-FTL-DOCK

THE ISLAND WITHIN.

Welcome to the Yacht Club & Marina at South Florida's luxurious Turnberry Isle Resort & Club. As a marina guest, all the amenities usually reserved exclusively for club members are at your command. The 119-slip marina, directly off the Intracoastal Waterway, accommodates vessels up to 200 feet, and features 30, 50 and 100-amp 3-phase electric service, cable television, two phone lines, mail service, showers, restrooms, and ice, plus a ship's store, Crew's Lounge and 24-hour security. And our European-trained staff redefines the meaning of excellent service. Slip inside the island within.

24 Tennis Courts.
Multi-surface facilities
host many tournaments
and pros including
resident pro, Fred Stolle.

4 Pools, 1 Ocean.
Refresh yourself as you
relax at the Ocean Club,
the Country Club or the
Yacht Club.

2 Golf Courses.
2 Robert Trent Jones
courses surrounded
by tropical gardens and
winding waterways.

Turnberry Isle Resort & Club

A RAFAEL HOTEL

19999 West Country Club Drive, Aventura, Florida 33180. Call: (305) 932-6200 or (800) 223-6800.

MEMBER OF:

The Leading Hotels of the World

RAFAEL HOTELS & RESORTS WORLDWIDE: AVENTURA / NEW YORK / BERMUDA / GENEVA / DÜSSELDORF / MUNICH / COURCHEVEL / BAGNOLS
BOWRAL / BORA BORA / PHUKET ISLAND/ BALI / MOYO ISLAND / PAMILICAN ISLAND / KUALA LUMPUR / YANGON

What passed by your window today?

When cruising The Abacos, stop by and tie up at The Bluff House Beach Hotel's marina. We can offer you a friendly, helpful smile as well as dockage and electricity along with showers, gasoline, diesel, water and ice. Our "Palms Beach Club" will serve you a great lunch with daily specials and tropical cocktails to cool you off after your voyage and our newly restored air-conditioned Main House will create elegant candle-lit dinners. We can also help you to rent a golf cart or scooter to look around our island and visit the historic and picturesque village of New Plymouth. Call us on VHF 16.

fine dining in our panoramic diningroom

our secluded talcum-powder beach

the island's only junkanoo parties

air-conditioned, luxury suites

Bluff House Beach Hotel

Green Turtle Cay, Abaco, Bahamas
Tel.:(242) 365-4247, ext. #226
Fax:(242) 365-4248
online: http://oii.net/BluffHouse
email: BluffHouse@oii.net

Refuel with Texaco

• **Southern** Coverage from the Georgia-Florida line south to the Keys, then up the west coast of Florida and across the Gulf to Brownsville, Texas. Also includes the St. Johns River, the Okeechobee and Tennessee-Tombigbee waterways, and the Bahamas.

• **Mid-Atlantic** Coverage of the entire Chesapeake Bay and the Intracoastal Waterway from Mile 0 in Norfolk, south to the Georgia-Florida line. Also includes the Delmarva Coast and the Outer Banks of North Carolina.

• **Northern** Coverage from Cape May, New Jersey, to Eastport, Maine, as well as Long Island Sound and the Connecticut River. Also includes the scenic Triangle Loop Cruise up the Hudson River, through Lake Champlain, the Erie Canal and across Lake Ontario.

The yachtsman's trusted companion for over 50 years.

All the information you need—in three updated volumes.
• Marina Listings
• Cruising Tips
• Anchorages
• Mariner's Handbook
• Bridge Clearances and Schedules
• Navigational Hazards
• Shoreside Attractions

New in Southern 1999 edition:
Cruising to Cuba
Tarpon Fishing
Conquering Mal de Mer

Now Available:
1999 Southern edition	$36.95
1999* Mid-Atlantic edition	$36.95
1999**Northern edition	$36.95

*Available December 1998
**Available March 1999

WATERWAY GUIDE®

A PRIMEDIA Intertec Publication

1-800-233-3359

Welcome to the Palm Beach's BEST Full Service Marina & Resort

With Guest Quarters & Restaurant

24 Hour Service

Where the Season Never Ends!

NO MARINA IS CLOSER TO THE GULF STREAM

· Open 24 hours a day, 365 days a year · Everything for the Angler & Boat ·
· Bait, Tackle, Fuel, food & Ice · Transient & Seasonal Dockage ·
· Guest Accommodations with Efficiencies, Pool & BBQs ·
· Perfect Place to Stay before going to, or coming from, the Bahamas ·
· Just minutes from the Gulf Stream · Located just North of the Palm Beach Inlet ·
· The very finest Sportfishing Charter Fleet on the East Coast ·
· IGFA member MET Weight Station · Weekly Sunset Celebrations · Water Taxi ·
Boat Rentals · Summer Kids Camp · Seawall Aquarium · and much more!

The **Sailfish**
Marina & Resort

98 Lake Drive · Palm Beach Shores · FL 33404

Call **(561) 844-1724** or **1-800-446-4577**

VHF 16 & 68 · Fax: 561-848-9684
www.sailfishmarina.com

Present this ad and receive a free Charter Fleet T-Shirt

TEXACO

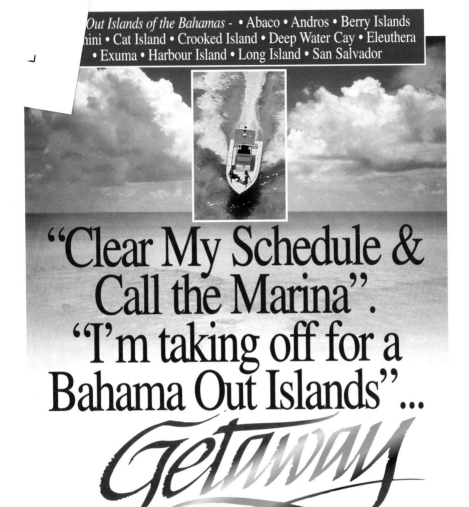

Out Islands of the Bahamas - • Abaco • Andros • Berry Islands
•Bimini • Cat Island • Crooked Island • Deep Water Cay • Eleuthera
• Exuma • Harbour Island • Long Island • San Salvador

"Clear My Schedule & Call the Marina". "I'm taking off for a Bahama Out Islands"...

Getaway

ABACO
Abaco Beach Resort/Boat Harbour
800-468-4799 Fax 242-367-2819
Bluff House Beach Hotel
242-365-4247 Fax 242-365-4248
Club Soleil Resort & Marina
242-366-0003 Fax 242-366-0254
Conch Inn Resort & Marina
242-367-4000 Fax 242-367-4004
Green Turtle Club & Marina
242-365-4271 Fax 242-365-4272
Guana Beach Resort & Marina
242-365-5133 Fax 242-365-5134
Hope Town Hideaways
242-366-0224 Fax 242-366-0434
Sea Spray Resort Villas & Marina
242-366-0065 Fax 242-366-0383
Spanish Cay Inn & Marina
888-722-6474 Fax 561-655-0172
Treasure Cay Hotel Resort & Marina
800-327-1584 Fax 242-365-8362

ANDROS
Andros Lighthouse Yacht Club
242-368-2305 Fax 242-368-2300
BERRY ISLANDS
Great Harbour Cay
800-343-7256 Fax 242-367-8115
BIMINI
Bimini Big Game Fishing Club
800-737-1007 Fax 242-347-3392
Bimini Blue Water
242-347-3166 Fax 242-347-3293
CAT ISLAND
Hawk's Nest Resort & Marina
242-342-7050 Fax 242-342-7051
ELEUTHERA
Palmetto Shores
242-332-1305 Fax 242-332-1305

For Complete Crusing Information on the Marina's of the Bahamas Out Islands contact us today!

EXUMA
Exuma Fantasea
242-336-3483 Fax 242-336-3483
Staniel Cay Yacht Club
242-355-2024 Fax 242-355-2044
GRAND BAHAMA
Deep Water Cay Club
242-353-3073 Fax 242-353-3095
Lucayan Marina Village
242-373-8888 Fax 242-373-7630
HARBOUR ISLAND
Harbour Island Club & Marina
242-333-2427 Fax 242-333-2427
Valentine's Yacht Club & Inn
242-333-2142 Fax 242-333-2135
LONG ISLAND
Stella Maris Resort Club
800-426-0466 Fax 242-338-2052
SAN SALVADOR
Riding Rock Resort & Marina
800-272-1492 Fax 242-331-2020

OUT ISLANDS PROMOTION BOARD
1-800-Out-Islands
(954)359-8099 • Fax (954)359-8098 • www.bahama-out-islands.com • e-mail: boipb@ix.netcom.com

**MINISTRY OF TOURISM
NASSAU IN THE BAHAMAS**

OFFICE OF THE THE MINISTER

Dear Boating Enthusiasts:

For years, visiting boaters and sporting enthusiasts alike have enjoyed the beauty of The Islands of The Bahamas and, from Bimini in the north to Inagua in the south, lovers of the sea have marvelled at our unique treasures.

As more and more persons become interested in the ecological environment and the preservation of our natural resources, the clean, clear waters of our archipelago are in demand more than ever.

To make cruising through The Bahamas even more inviting, each year, our tourism office in Miami organizes escorted boating flings for novice sailors while the more adventurous boaters chart their own course to individually explore our 700-island chain.

Whatever your reason for selecting The Bahamas, we are grateful and happy. We hope that when you return home, you will share your experiences with family and friends and trust that you, too, will agree that in The Islands of The Bahamas, "It Just Keeps Getting Better"!

Hon. C.A. Smith, M.P.
Minister of Tourism

EDITOR'S MESSAGE

A number of changes of interest to boaters have occurred this past year in New Providence and Grand Bahama. A second bridge now spans Nassau Harbor. On Paradise Island is the new, enormous Atlantis resort/marina complex. At West End in Grand Bahama, extensive renovation and expansion is transforming the old Jack Tar Marina property into the impressive new Old Bahama Bay. Businesses otherwise serving the marine community proliferate in the Out Islands as well.

Fortunately, the remote natural beauty of the Out Islands remains, stunning when you encounter it. It is still possible to cruise the Bahamas and frequently enough find yourself an anchorage off one of the loveliest little-known beaches of the world -- so many of which exist throughout these hundreds of islands and cays. It's regrettably true that cruise-ship companies now control Gorda Cay (which Disney Cruise Lines has renamed Castaway Cay) and Little San Salvador (which Holland-America Westours now calls Half Moon Cay), in addition to the old news at Great and Little Stirrup Cays at the north end of the Berries. It sometimes seems to us that these once pristine islands have been surgically tooled into soulless perfection to meet the expectations of popular fantasy, like Stepford Wives.

As always, input we get from our readers is invaluable to us. It's often the information we get from you that tips us off to happenings, changes, and other goings-on throughout the islands. We wouldn't know much of this as *soon* as we do without you. Keep those letters and postcards coming!

Also, be sure to look for us at our new web site at *yachtsmansguide.com*. We'll be looking for you there too.

Meredith Helleberg Fields

Regional Correspondents

• David Ralph (Marsh Harbour, Abaco) • Basil Minns (George Town, Exuma)

Contributors: Ruth Albury, BASRA, Terry Bain, Stephen Carner, Judd Clarence, D. Valerie Gray, Gary L. Hein, John Jones, Kenneth R. Kalasky, Bill Keefe, Steven C. Jewell, Chris Lloyd, David Pinder, SEARCH, George W. Shaw, Peg Thompson, Carolyn and Nick Wardle, Cindy Weatherford, James and Cheri Williamson

Meredith Helleberg Fields, Editor
TROPIC ISLE PUBLISHERS, INC.

For additional books or sketch charts, contact: Tropic Isle Publishers, Mailing and Shipping Office, P.O. Box 610938, North Miami, FL 33261-0938 (telephone 305/893-4277). Send $34.95 for each additional copy. Florida residents add appropriate state sales tax. Add $5.00 for postage and handling on orders outside the continental United States.

Letters to the Editor (*mail or fax only, please*): Tropic Isle Publishers, Editor's Office, P.O. Box 15397, Plantation, FL 33318 (fax 954/321-0806).

For advertising rates and information, contact: *In The Bahamas* Helen Phillips, P.O. Box N-208, Nassau, Bahamas (telephone 242/324-1184); *In the U.S.* Advertising Coordinator, Tropic Isle Publishers, P.O. Box 281, Atlantic Highlands, NJ 07716 (telephone 732/291-7222).

Copyright ©1998 by Tropic Isle Publishers, Inc., P.O. Box 281, Atlantic Highlands, NJ 07716. All rights reserved. Reproduction in any form, including office copying machines, in whole or in part, without written permission is prohibited by law.

The "official guide" of The Bahamas Ministry of Tourism

CAUTION

While this book has been prepared based on the information available at the time of publication, the publisher disclaims all liability for any errors or omissions. **The publisher further disclaims all warranties, expressed or implied, as to the quality, merchantability or fitness of this book for any particular purpose.** *The navigator is warned not to place undue reliance on the accuracy and completeness of the sketch charts, pilotage directions, soundings, or other information contained herein, or on their continuing validity in light of constantly changing conditions.*

All sketch charts are updated from time to time; for changes consult the current edition of the Yachtsman's Guide to The Bahamas. Readers are urged to report any changed conditions, errors, or discrepancies to the editor, so that future editions can reflect such information. Suggestions for the improvement of the next issue must be received by June 1, 1999.

ISBN 0-937379-22-0

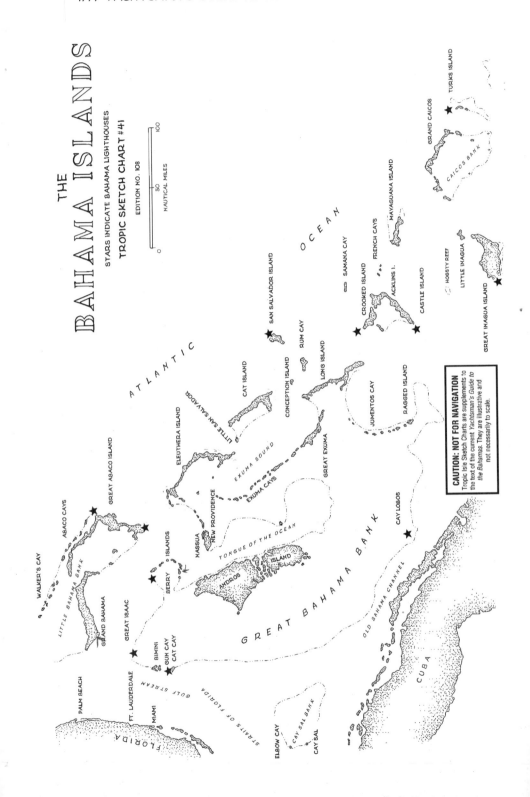

THE BAHAMA ISLANDS

STARS INDICATE BAHAMA LIGHTHOUSES

TROPIC SKETCH CHART #41

EDITION NO. 108

MAUTICAL MILES

0   50   100

CAUTION: NOT FOR NAVIGATION

Tropic Isle Sketch Charts are supplements to the text of the current *Yachtsman's Guide to the Bahamas*. They are illustrative and not necessarily to scale.

CONTENTS

Additional Information

IMPORTANT INFORMATION

WHAT YOU MUST KNOW BEFORE USING YOUR YACHTSMAN'S GUIDE

The Yachtsman's Guide to The Bahamas will be your invaluable cruising companion. Since we began publishing this Guide in 1951, it has accompanied thousands of yachtsmen as they cruised these islands. From the outset, we've been greeted year after year with enthusiastic response as the "indispensable" cruising guide to this area. As happy as all this makes us, nobody's perfect, and we feel it's important to emphasize a few things:

• **The *Guide* alone is insufficient for navigation.** Always use it in conjunction with navigational aids such as government charts and publications. Even with the annual updating that adds to or corrects much of the text, the Guide can never be considered "complete." Each year we visit several island areas, and we get useful information from other sources about certain waters and islands, but by no means can we get all possible information about all of the islands every year. There will always be important information that we do not have and therefore cannot include.

• **The Tropic Isle charts in this book are in fact sketch charts, which means they are for illustrative purpose only.** Position on the sketch charts should be considered approximate, including land features, navigational aids and markers, depths, hazards, and landmarks. The limited scale of our sketch charts precludes the plotting of every individual rock, coral head, or obstacle. Therefore, shown routes must be used with caution. Pilotage by eye is always essential in The Bahamas. Sketch charts should always be used with reference to the corresponding text and the appropriate government charts for clarification.

You definitely cannot draw a GPS waypoint onto one of our sketch charts, and from that point derive a course or another waypoint by using our scale or compass rose. To attempt this is a sure way to get into trouble. Use government charts for these purposes, but realize that many government charts are based on very old surveys and may contain considerable errors. See section "Navigation fixes" in chapter entitled "What the Skipper Should Know."

• **You cannot accurately lay out courses or measure distance or direction on our sketch charts.** Use government charts for this purpose. As explained above, our sketch charts are not necessarily to scale.

• **Distances stated in text or shown on sketch charts are often estimates and should be considered approximate.** They were worked out before the advent of GPS or Loran, and may be eyeball estimates or measured on government charts. Very frequently GPS measurements will be different from distances stated in this Guide. See section "Charts and text directions in this Guide" in chapter entitled "What the Skipper Should Know."

• **The Guide is written for the responsible skipper and crew.** Your own experience, training, competence, and caution are essential. Bahamian waters present a variety of navigational challenges, and because of this they are not a place for novices. We provide information that will make your cruise pleasant, but we cannot give you all the information you need to make it safe.

• **Remember that in shallow or reef-strewn waters, you must**

proceed slowly and keep a good lookout (at the bow in a sailboat for best visibility). The sun must be high and behind you. Above all, never attempt such tricky passages when visibility is in any way diminished. Having a GPS on board does not in any way change this.

• **Where sandbanks are a factor, it must be remembered that they shift constantly and that channels meander.** Be aware that although a sketch chart may indicate a channel existed, shifting sands may block the channel completely or change the depths at any time.

• **It must be remembered that cuts or passages exposed to the open ocean can be impassable in adverse wind or heavy swells.** A dangerous swell can exist without any wind.

• **Be aware that all man-made markers, whether government or privately maintained, cannot be absolutely reliable.** We do our best to ascertain the position of all markers, but constantly changing and unpredictable conditions make it impossible to guarantee the continuing validity of our information.

• **The prominence of landmarks in general cannot be guaranteed.** Even over short periods of time, they can disappear, change color, and be made comparatively less conspicuous. For example, casuarina trees, which proliferate throughout The Bahamas, grow and multiply quickly and can also disappear suddenly if someone gets ambitious with a chain saw. Therefore they cannot be considered reliably consistent landmarks from year to year, and they can also be expected to obscure or reveal other landmarks rather quickly.

• **To avoid confusion and unnecessary elaboration, we do not attempt to describe every new feature that might be called a landmark.** Although we like to know about these, we feel that areas that are already recognizable will not benefit from additional and excessive detail.

• **At the risk of stating the obvious, we must remind you that the courses shown in this Guide can only approximate where boats of suitable draft have made successful passage.** Since our sketch charts are not necessarily to scale and are of too small scale to show all dangers, and since the difference between danger and safety in shallow or reefy water may be a matter of a few inches, the prudent mariner must take our courses for what they are, and realize that changed conditions or a slight offset from what was for others a safe passage may be critical.

• **In general, we make no attempt at completeness in showing dangers that are significantly removed from the course lines in our text or on our sketch charts.**

• **We are a small company providing a resource network for the skipper's use and participation. We catch some of our mistakes but not all.** We do use information from volunteers and from other sources, not all of which can be verified in time for the next edition. We encourage our readers to report any changes to us as soon as they become aware of them.

• **Inasmuch as new information appears in each annually updated Guide, all previously published editions must be considered obsolete.**

• **The prudent mariner will not rely solely on any single aid to navigation.** Always cross-check information with frequently updated sources such as your charter company's briefings, notices to mariners and other government publications, local knowledge and, of course, what your own eyes tell you. Remember that in these remote waters, a great many reefs and other hazards to navigation are uncharted. Used judiciously with the navigational resources available to you, your *Yachtsman's Guide* will enrich your cruising experience and enjoyment immeasurably.

INTRODUCTION TO THE BAHAMAS

Within a mere 50 miles of Florida's coastline lies entrance to The Bahamas, a 700-mile-long archipelago of pure crystal, bathed in the brilliance of perennial summer. The Bahamas seem to have been specially designed by a kind act of Providence as a boatman's paradise. An extensive chain of islands, cays (pronounced *keys*), and reefs, most of which are uninhabited, The Bahamas lie between the latitudes of 20°56' and 27°25' N, and the longitudes of 71°00' and 79°20' W, and have a land area of approximately 5400 square miles. For the most part they are low and rocky, surrounded by coral reefs and sandbanks through and around which channels lead into the most perfect harbors and coves imaginable. But it isn't on land where the yachtsman finds the greatest pleasure, but on (or in) the crystal-clear water, which ranges in color from a translucent midnight blue off soundings to the palest of blues and bottle greens close inshore. Then there are the beaches, remote and dazzling white or pale pink, with coral sand as fine as powder. The bordering coconut palms and scrub serve merely to

SUN POWER DIESEL

50 YEARS of QUALITY SERVICE. 1949-1999

- 24-Hour Mobile Service
- Extensive Inventory of Parts, Engines & Generators
- Free Live-aboard Docking during Repairs
- Full Service Marina ■ 30 Ton Travel Lift

Detroit Diesel • Caterpillar • Cummins • John Deere • Onan • Kohler • Westerbeke
Yanmar • Lehman • Perkins • Universal • Mercruiser • Fischer-Panda

DETROIT DIESEL

KOHLER GENERATORS

YANMAR

Onan

Cummins

WESTERBEKE

CAT

ON NEW RIVER at 413 S.W. 3rd AVE., FORT LAUDERDALE, FL 33315
FT. LAUDERDALE *(954) 522-4775* • MIAMI (305) 947-1459 • FAX *(954) 760-7155*
E-mail: sunpower@icanect.net   Visit our Website at: www.sunpowermarine.com

emphasize the brilliance of the water.

Historically The Bahamas are of great interest to the seaman. In 1492 Columbus made his first landfall in the New World here, although the precise location is avidly debated by Columbus scholars (San Salvador and Samana Cay are most frequently named). The islands were peopled by peaceable Lucayans, who lived by fishing and agriculture. The Spaniards ended their idyllic existence by transporting the Lucayan population to forced labor in mines and plantations of Hispaniola. The Bahamas remained almost uninhabited until an unsuccessful colonization attempt was made by the Eleutherian Adventurers.

Pirates and "boucaniers" soon found The Bahamas ideal for forays against merchant shipping, notably the rich Spanish merchants homeward bound from the Main by way of the Straits of Florida or the Windward Passage. This scourge was finally routed by Captain Woodes Rodgers, first Royal Governor of The Bahamas, although isolated settlements continued to depend on wrecking as their livelihood. Today many cays, creeks, and island freight boats bear the names of infamous freebooters.

Planters arrived on the southern islands as early as the mid-1600s, importing slave laborers from Africa to work on small plantations that never achieved much success. When the American War of Independence ended, several northern Bahamian islands were settled by Loyalists who also brought slaves, increasing the ratio of slaves to owners in The Bahamas to about 3 to 1. Although many settlements were abandoned after the Emancipation Act in 1833, their ruins can still be found. The descendants of slaves comprise the majority of Bahamians today.

The first real prosperity the islands knew came in 1861 when they became one of the principal staging bases for Confederate blockade runners, but at the end of the Civil War the grand homes and warehouses tumbled into decay. During the 1920s, with Prohibition declared in the United States, a similar economic rise-and-fall occurred as bootlegging enriched a number of Bahamian merchant families and stimulated a brief boom in land investment.

Two world wars and the Prohibition Era in the United States brought The Bahamas full into the 20th century and created conditions that led to majority rule. After World War II The Bahamas began promoting tourism, which meant that all Bahamians felt the impact of world change. This change took its inevitable turn on July 10, 1973, when the Bahama Islands became independent after 300 years as a British Colony.

Recommended reading. Some books listed here are difficult to find in bookstores but might be found in libraries. Many shops in larger Bahamian towns carry books of Bahamian history, literature, and lore, including children's books about the islands. Try bookshops in Nassau, the Loyalist Shoppe in Marsh Harbour, the Sandpiper in George Town, and out-island resort shops.

Abaco Life, Caribe Communications (P.O. Box 1366, Fort Lauderdale, FL 33302). Colorful quarterly publication features the Hub of Abaco area.

The Abaconian (David and Kathleen Ralph, Publishers, P.O. Box 551, Marsh Harbour, Abaco.) Monthly local newspaper, informative and fun to read.

Atlas of the Commonwealth of The Bahamas, Ministry of Education, Nassau, Bahamas, 1976, Kingston Publishers, Ltd. (Kingston, Jamaica). Excellent companion to the *Yachtsman's Guide.*

Artist on His Island, A Study of Self-Reliance, Randolph W. Johnston, Little Harbour Press, Box 530, Marsh Harbour, Abaco. Diary of this remarkable family's search for, and life on, their own island.

Bahamian Anthology, College of The Bahamas, Macmillan Education, 1983. Poetry, stories, and plays by Bahamian writers.

Bahamas: In a White Coming On, Dennis Ryan, 1981, Dorrance (Ardmore, Pa.). Delightful book of Bahamas-inspired poetry.

Bahamas Handbook and Businessman's Manual, Etienne Dupuch, Jr. Publications (Nassau). Annually published current state of the islands.

Birds of New Providence and the Bahama Islands, The P.G.C. Brudenell-Bruce, Collins (London). Bahamas supplement to Peterson's classic *Field Guide to the Birds.*

Birder's Guide to the Bahama Islands, White, Anthony W., 1998, American Birding Association, Inc. (Colorado Springs). Information-packed island-by-island guide for birdwatchers, with maps, color photos, bird checklist, and list of other observable wildlife.

A Book of Shells and *A Game of Shells,* MacTaggart, Cécile E. Environmentally friendly, delightfully written guide to shell collecting in The Bahamas, for children and adults. Color photos. The shell identification game includes a sand timer and card storage box (fun for cruising with kids).

The Conch Book: All You Ever Wanted to Know About the Queen Conch from Gestation to Gastronomy, Dee Carstarphen, 1982, Pen & Ink Press.

Eleuthera: The Island Called Freedom, Everild Young, Regency Press, London. Reprint of 1966 edition. Interesting, affectionate account of Eleuthera's history and eccentricities, including description of the island in the 1960s.

Ephemeral Islands, The: A Natural History of The Bahamas, David G. Campbell, 1978, Macmillan Education. First comprehensive natural history of The Bahamas in over 70 years, a cornerstone of Bahamas conservation.

Flora of the Bahama Archipelago, Including the Turks and Caicos Islands, Drs. Donovan and Helen Correll, 1983, Lubrecht & Cramer (Monticello, N.Y.). Detailed description of 1369 Bahamian plants with over 700 superb drawings.

Florida Sportsman, Wickstrom Publishers, Miami. Monthly magazine covers The Bahamas and Caribbean islands in "Tropical Sportsman" feature.

Gourmet Bahamian Cooking, Marie Mendelson and Marguerite Sawyer, Best-Way Publishing (Iowa City, Iowa). Excellent book on Bahamian cookery.

Guide to Corals and Fishes, Idaz Greenberg, Seahawk Press (Miami). Color illustrations of many species of coral with an excellent section on reef fish. Available in waterproof edition.

A History of the Bahamas, Michael Craton, 1986, San Salvador Press (Ontario, Canada). Bahamian history through 1985, emphasis on politics.

Homeward Bound. A History of the Bahamas Islands to 1850, Sandra Riley, 1983, Island Research (Miami, Florida). Detailed, highly readable history, with emphasis on Abaco in the Loyalist plantation era.

Man-O-War, My Island Home, Haziel L. Albury, Holly Press. History of Man of War Cay, with unusual sketches of early Bahamian buildings and boats.

Nassau Historic Buildings, S. Russell, Bahamas National Trust. Photographic history of Nassau's interesting landmarks.

Native Trees of The Bahamas, Jack Patterson and George Stevenson (Hope Town, Abaco, Bahamas.) Handy manual to over 200 trees and plants.

Out Island Doctor, Cottman and Blassingame, Landfall Press (Dayton, Ohio). An appealing account of Out Island people and customs through the eyes of a sailing doctor.

Out Island Portraits, Ruth Rodriquez, Out Island Press. An excellent record of life in four Out Island communities in the decade following WW II.

Pilot's Bahamas & Caribbean Aviation Guide, Aviation Book Co. A must for the private pilot. Annually published.

Sailing Directions, The Caribbean Sea, Pub. #144, D.M.A. Written for deep-draft vessels, includes an excellent section on climatology.

Salute to Friend and Foe, Sir Etienne Dupuch, The Tribune (Nassau). Companion work to earlier volume on Sir Etienne's life.

Shallow Water Sponges of the Western Bahamas, Felix Wiedenmeyer, Birkhauser Verlag, (Stuttgart, Germany). Comprehensive book on sponges with an extensive, illustrated glossary.

South to the Caribbean: How to Carry Out the Dream of Sailing Your Own Boat to the Caribbean, Bill Robinson, 1982, W.W. Norton.

Southern Boating Magazine (Miami). Features frequent updates on the islands and an annual Bahamas special issue.

Story of The Bahamas, The, Dr. Paul Albury, Macmillan (London). An accurate history of The Bahamas up to Independence.

Times of the Islands, Times Publications Ltd (Providenciales, Turks and Caicos). Colorful quarterly magazine features people, events, history, and new developments in the Turks and Caicos Islands.

Tribune Story, The, Sir Etienne Dupuch, Ernest Benn (London). Sir Etienne's struggle to maintain The Bahamas' second daily newspaper.

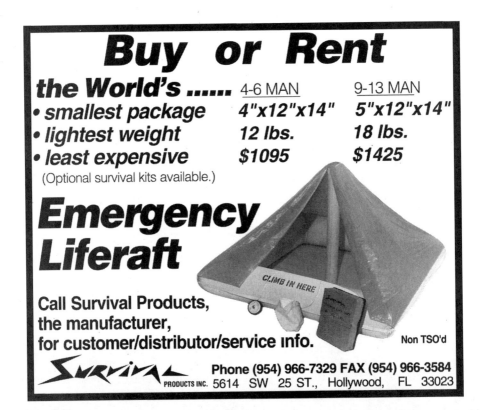

Buy or Rent

the World's ......

	4-6 MAN	9-13 MAN
• smallest package	4"x12"x14"	5"x12"x14"
• lightest weight	12 lbs.	18 lbs.
• least expensive	$1095	$1425

(Optional survival kits available.)

Emergency Liferaft

CLIMB IN HERE

Non TSO'd

Call Survival Products, the manufacturer, for customer/distributor/service info.

SURVIVAL PRODUCTS INC.

Phone (954) 966-7329 FAX (954) 966-3584
5614 SW 25 ST., Hollywood, FL 33023

WHAT THE SKIPPER SHOULD KNOW

Cruising The Bahamas is not like cruising United States waters. Markers and beacons are few and may be missing or out of place. Shoals, coral heads, and other obstructions and hazards are common and, for the most part, unmarked. Consequently, piloting requires more preparation and concentration. It is necessary to use a variety of techniques not often needed in U.S. waters, where there are usually reliable navigational aids at strategic locations. Used properly, GPS is useful; improperly used it can be dangerous. There are already many instances where overreliance on GPS has been the cause of serious trouble. The problem may be compounded by use of government charts, which are based on very old surveys and may contain errors.

For the safety of their boats and crews, yachtsmen planning to cruise the islands should do their "homework" before getting under way. They should understand the effect that changing tides can have on their vessels as well as their itineraries. They should know their knots as well as the idiosyncrasies of their engine room. A copy of Chapman's *Piloting, Seamanship & Small Boat*

MORE POWER TO YOU and your BOAT!!!

Established 1950

South Florida's Most Complete
MARINE ELECTRIC SPECIALISTS

Marine Industries Association of South Florida

EQUIPMENT

Wire & Cable (Spooled or Cut)
Battery Chargers
Shorelines & Adaptors
Circuit Breakers

Switches
Converters/Inverters
Enclosures
Panel Meters
Wiring Devices

Light Fixtures
Custom Panels
Transformers
Corrosion Control

SERVICES

Computerized Engraving
Electrical & Corrosion Surveys
Repairs
Modifications
New Installations

Ward's Marine Electric, Inc.

630 S.W. Flagler Ave., Ft. Lauderdale, FL 33301 • Phone: (954)523-2815 • 1-800-545-9273
Bus. Fax (954) 523-1967 • Order Fax (800) 297-8240
www.wardsmarine.com • E-mail: info@wardsmarine.com

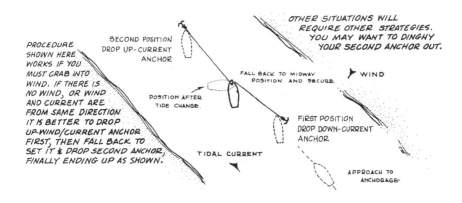

Handling should be a familiar and close companion.

Anchoring. There will be many occasions when you must set two anchors. The most common are when anchoring in a small basin where swinging room is limited or when anchoring in a tidal flow.

The accompanying diagram indicates the procedure most commonly used. While moving up current, drop your down-current anchor at the desired position, permitting the rope to run free and being careful not to foul the keel or propeller. Continue upstream until you have reached the position at which you intend to drop your up-current anchor. Set the first anchor and drop your second anchor immediately, then fall back on the current to a position midway

Fernandez Bay anchorage, Cat Island. (Tropic Isle photo)

between the two, setting the up-current anchor and cinching up on both. Thus, when the tidal current changes, the bow will remain in one spot while the stern swings to the current and wind.

Good seamanship prescribes employment of a chain leader on all rope anchor rodes. We strongly suggest donning mask and snorkel to inspect your result. If in doubt, dive down and set your anchor by hand to avoid a breakout.

An anchor light should always be displayed between sunset and sunrise.

The boat. One of the best ways to enjoy the real essence of The Bahamas is by sea in a boat capable of crossing the Gulf Stream and the banks. Whether sail or power, a draft of 4 to 6 feet is fine. More than 6 feet of draft is often too much to explore many places among the cays. Heavy winds and seas are not uncommon, so boats of 30 to 40 feet or more help make life comfortable. However, there are lots of people who cruise through the islands in smaller boats, both power and sail. This is particularly true during the summer months when winds tend to be lighter. Small craft should have a minimum length of 25 feet, twin engines (sailboats, an auxiliary), a VHF radio, and a minimum cruising range of 125 miles. Boats unable to meet these requirements should travel in the company of larger craft. Whatever boat you choose, remember that the Gulf Stream and many long passages between islands are sea voyages and the going can get heavy fast. Your boat and all its equipment must be in good shape, and you must have on board all the proper safety and navigation equipment.

Bicycles and motorcycles aboard. Bicycles, motorcycles, and scooters aboard visiting yachts may be required to be licensed at the yacht's port of entry. This includes Bahamian insurance, plates, inspection costs, and a customs import duty. If they are to be brought ashore, they are subject to customs duty or bond in the form of a cash deposit or a locally recognized banker's guarantee. If you aren't prepared to include these costs (which can be considerable) in your cruising budget, leave your shoreside transportation at home. As a tourist, you may drive in The Bahamas with your U.S. driver's license.

Charts and text directions in this _Guide_. We've had people ask us some questions recently indicating that they intend to use the _Guide_ as their sole source of information, or that they are trying to extract a degree of precision from it that just isn't there. _This is dangerous,_ so we want to explain what kind of publication we intend the _Guide_ to be. Do not try to use it for more than what we intend. You must supplement the _Guide_ with _all_ possible sources of

Kamalame Cay Beach (Staniard Creek, Andros). (Tropic Isle photo)

information that are available to safely cruise the remote, relatively uncharted waters of The Bahamas.

What is our definition of the *Yachtsman's Guide to The Bahamas?* It is a compendium of general, often approximate, but still valuable information collected from many sources over many years. It is annually updated, but never fully up to date. Scale, distance, and courses, whether shown on sketch charts or stated in the text, should be considered approximate. They were worked out before the advent of GPS or Loran, and may be eyeball estimates or measured on government charts. Very frequently GPS measurements will be different from distances stated in the *Guide*. Sketch charts are called "sketch charts" because they are more akin to sketched directions than to navigational charts. Wherever we say a course is on a certain heading, we mean it is *approximately* on that heading. Whenever you plan a long passage where there will not be landmarks along the way, you should without fail work out your courses on government charts. In addition, you should also routinely double-check even our short courses on government charts, against landmarks and bottom features. We're not infallible, and many of the courses, since they are shown as magnetic, may be a few degrees off due to increased variation over time, or because your compass and ours do not match, or because we were affected by undetected currents while measuring the courses (which we can only do occasionally), or for any number of other reasons. Finally, wherever distances stated in the text are critical, realize they may be estimates.

When using the *Guide* it is essential that you keep watch, think about what is happening, and make necessary corrections where reality doesn't seem to match what we say or show. Remember that our sketch charts are not all updated every year, and depths, hazards, landmarks, navigation aids, etc., can change without our knowing it. If you can't see, you can't keep a good watch. If you don't know the area, and visibility is or will be obstructed by weather conditions or darkness, don't go. With the information we give, you definitely cannot hook the autopilot to the GPS or Loran and go below for a nap.

Overall, the *Guide* is analogous to directions you might give someone about how to go to the store from your house. You'd give approximate headings, distances, and landmarks — for example: "Go out the driveway, turn north. Stay on that road for about 2 miles. When you see a pond on your right, you'll come

---

Special Note to Readers Regarding Sketch Charts

Sketch charts are updated from time to time. For changes consult the current edition of the Yachtsman's Guide to the Bahamas. *We call upon the visitor's spirit of good seamanship to aid his fellow travelers by reporting additions and discrepancies to us. Watch for: changes in depths, shoals, or channels, or submerged objects or obstructions (new uncharted, or those that have vanished). Report pilings and landmarks that are new or have vanished, distinctive smokestacks, towers, spires, tanks, antennas, missing or off-station buoys, lights not operating. Any easily distinguishable feature may prove useful in piloting. Please report your observations to the editor (see title page for address). Your special contribution will be appreciated by all who follow.*

LOOK FOR US AT YACHTSMANSGUIDE.COM

to a stop sign. Turn right and go about another mile and you'll see the store. Turn right into the street just before it and park behind it." Everything here is approximate, but it does the job. It would be silly to *exactly* measure distances on your odometer and make the turns just when the suggested mileages came up. If you did, you might drive right into the pond, or try to turn into the store where there is no street and end up in someone's living room. *You must use your eyes when navigating and match the approximate to what you see.*

A related problem we've been hearing, in spite of the fact that no one should be under way at night, is that people are coming to grief entering one harbor or another after dark. If you don't know how to do this, don't do it. It is very confusing in settled weather and nearly impossible in bad weather. If you should find yourself in such a position and you can't sort it out, stay in deep water for the night and enter when daylight comes. Do not "just give it a try." Lots of people end up on the rocks, some not very close to what they thought they were aiming for. There is not much help available at night. Plan ahead. Having GPS on board does not in any way change our advice here.

Depths stated on our sketch charts are based on experience dating back many years. They are updated from time to time to the extent that information is available. But storms and time do cause sandbanks to shift and depths of water to change. The wise mariner will be extremely cautious when the sketch chart depths, modified by information from the tide tables, approximate the draft of his vessel — otherwise he may find himself unexpectedly aground.

Enlargements of the sketch charts in 11x17-inch format, from the current edition of the *Guide*, are available for your convenience. See the complete list at the end of this book.

Charts (Government). Government charts are available or can be ordered through most marine stores. N.O.S. and nonclassified D.M.A. charts may be ordered from Distribution Branch N/CG33, National Ocean Service, Riverdale, MD 20737-1199. Telephone orders may be placed (VISA and MasterCard accepted) by calling (301) 436-6990. The Better Boating Association's Chart Kit includes reproductions of N.O.S. charts of The Bahamas

~ The Original ~

WATERPROOF CHARTS inc.

Full Color CHARTS for the BAHAMAS
Call for Free Catalog
1-800-423-9026
Visit our web site: *www.waterproofcharts.com*

as well as color aerial photos. It's available at marine stores or can be ordered by writing the BBA, Box 407, Needham, MA 02192.

The following charts, printed by the U.S. Government, are recommended for Bahamas cruising. Asterisks (*) indicate small-scale charts that, when combined, include all of the Bahama Islands and are best for navigation.

N.O.S.

Charts	Areas Covered
11013*	Florida, Cuba, Bahamas
11460*	Florida, Gulf Stream, Bimini

D.M.A.

Charts	Areas Covered
11461	Straits of Florida, Southern Part (Loran-C)
25720*	Turks & Caicos to Dominican Rep. N. Coast (Loran-C)
26240*	Crooked Island Passage to Cabo Maisi (Loran-C)
26253	Mira Por Vos, Wide Opening, Clarence Town
26255	Ragged Island Anchorage, Raccoon Cut
26256	Jumentos Cays: Nurse Channel
26257	Highborne & Wax Cay Cuts, Ragged Island Harbour, Golding Cay
26260*	Caicos Islands and Adjacent Passages (Loran-C)
26261	Turks Island Passage and Mouchoir Passage
26262	Grand Turk Island: Western Approaches, Southwest Anchorages
26263	Mayaguana Island, Abraham's Bay, Plana Cays, Hogsty Reef
26267	Great, Little Inagua, Matthew Town, Man of War Bay
26268	Passages between Acklins Island, Haiti, and Caicos Islands (Omega)
26279	Eleuthera Island to Crooked Island Passage (Omega)
26280*	Eleuthera Island to Crooked Island Passage (Loran-C)
26281	San Salvador Approaches, Cockburn Town
26282*	AUTEC — Andros and Exuma Sound Operating Area
26284	Cat, Conception Islands, Rum Cay, Port Nelson
26286	Elizabeth Harbour and Approaches, George Town
26288	Bird Rock to Mira Por Vos Passage
26299	Little Bahama Bank to Eleuthera (Omega)
26300*	Little Bahama Bank to Eleuthera (Loran-C)
26303	Tongue of the Ocean, Southern Part (Loran-C)
26304	AUTEC Sites: Deep Creek, High Point Cay, Pipe Cay
26305	Eleuthera and Northern Exuma Sound (Loran-C)
26306	Cays to Eleuthera: Douglas and Fleeming Channels
26307	Eleuthera Island: Northwestern Part, Central Part
26308	Tongue of the Ocean: North Part, Andros to Exuma Cays (Loran-C)
26309	New Providence Island
26312	AUTEC Sites: Andros Town, Salvador Pt., Big Wood Cay, Golding Cay
26316	AUTEC, Andros Town
26319*	Northern Part of the Straits of Florida and Northwest Providence Channel (Omega)
26320	Northern Part of the Straits of Florida and Northwest Providence Channel
26321	Hope Town and Approaches
26323	Freeport Area Approaches, Freeport Harbour, Riding Point
26324	Anchorages and Harbours, Great Bahama Bank: Great Isaac Anchorages
26328	Berry Islands
27040	Old Bahama Channel to Ragged Island

C.I.T.E.S. (Convention of International Trade in Endangered Species). The Bahamas government is a signatory of the C.I.T.E.S. Treaty, a convention against international trade in endangered species.

Communications. Telephone communications are efficient throughout the islands, and calls can easily be made between the islands and internationally (many Batelco offices also offer fax services). Cellular service is available from Batelco throughout practically the entire northern Bahamas and on down through the Exumas and Cat Island to Long Island. You should confirm or reconfirm with your own cellular service company whether they have a working roaming agreement with Batelco. If this seems to be affirmative, it would then be wise to confirm what you think you've found out with Batelco. This whole subject is a moving target, so be prepared to be confused. There have been recent problems in The Bahamas with cloning and theft of cellular service. We have experienced this. Of course, most Out Island settlements have telephone stations where calls can be made to Nassau and the rest of the world.

When dialing direct into The Bahamas or dictating a telephone number to an overseas operator, the area code (242) should be used. To the States, AT&T's USADIRECT service is available at many phones. Dial 1-800-872-2881 and a U.S. operator will answer. You can then easily call collect or by credit card.

Batelco Phone Cards (debit cards sold in denominations of $5, $10, and $20) can be purchased throughout The Bahamas and at many marinas. One of these might be a good thing to have, since many public phones (at times the only phone in the settlement) are now for debit-card use only. In other places where long lines form at regular pay phones, a debit phone is often available. There is no refund for leftover credit, but the cards are valid indefinitely.

A growing number of establishments throughout the islands will receive e-mail and allow you to send e-mail, either free or for a nominal charge. Since this

Batelco station, Guana Cay. (Tropic Isle photo)

is an emerging development, we cannot with any completeness list where you can find these services other than to advise you to check with your marina or tap into the local knowledge.

Yachtsmen who double as Ham operators are especially fortunate in that they can enjoy daily communications while they cruise the more remote islands. Cruising and shoreside Hams gather at 0745-0845 daily on 7268 kHz, then stand by at 1000, 1200, 1400 and 1600 EST. Ham operators should have a U.S. or their own country's license, as well as a Bahamas license when operating in the islands. Well before your cruise (one writer recommends at least 10 weeks ahead of time or more to be sure), write for a Bahamas reciprocal license to the Radio Licensing Dept., Bahamas Telecommunications Corp., P.O. Box N 3048, Nassau, Bahamas. Send a copy of your current license, a copy of passport identification page or birth certificate, and a money order for $6.00 (personal checks are no longer accepted and you can only renew one year at a time). A Bahamas license must be renewed annually.

The Bahamas Amateur Radio Society (BARS) 2-meter repeater in Nassau operates on 146.640 (down 600 to transmit). There's also a 2-meter repeater in the Treasure Cay area operating on 145.210 (down 600 to transmit). BARS meets every Sunday on 7140 kHz at 0830. Visitors are welcome to participate.

Pleasure craft cruising the islands should be equipped with a VHF radio with the required marine channels. Most shoreside facilities stand by on Channel 16. Some shoreside installations still use DSB ship-to-shore radios, and stand by on 2182 kHz and 2738 for extended conversations. Considering the sophisticated telephone communications in The Bahamas, an SSB radio is not a necessity unless the vessel intends to remain in the more remote reaches of the Out Islands and must maintain long-distance communications.

There is a cruiser's net around the Marsh Harbour area on VHF 68 at 8:15 a.m. It begins with a broadcast of the weather, and then opens up for a half hour for the exchange of all kinds of information useful to yachtsmen.

Conservation and recreation. The Bahamas National Trust, a nongovernmental, nonprofit, self-funded organization, is the official body charged with

Laughing Gulls, Green Turtle Cay. (Tropic Isle photo)

Warderick Wells, part of the Exuma Cays Land and Sea Park. (Tropic Isle photo)

the management of The Bahamas' National Park System. The Trust was established by an Act of Parliament in 1959 for places of historic interest and natural beauty. All yachtsmen are invited to visit and enjoy the parks and to join the Trust in its efforts to preserve the parks for future generations. Marine parks administered by The Bahamas National Trust include Exuma Cays Land and Sea Park, Peterson Cay National Park (Grand Bahama), and Pelican Cays Land and Sea Park (Abaco).

The Trust has issued regulations prohibiting capture of any marine life within National Park boundaries. By so doing, these parks will become a safer haven where marine animals can live unmolested and perpetuate their own stocks. The Trust hopes that parks throughout The Bahamas will begin serving as marine nursery areas or replenishment areas for the rest of the archipelago.

For further details contact: Bahamas National Trust, P.O. Box N-4105, Nassau, Bahamas; telephone (242) 393-1317 or 393-2848.

Costs and credit cards. The variety and fluctuation in prices of dockside services make it impossible for us to project firm prices for the upcoming year at our deadline. In general, however, dockage can range from very reasonable in the Out Islands to the equivalent of stateside prices and higher at the larger marinas in Nassau, Freeport, or even Marsh Harbour. Expect to pay prices for fuel in Nassau that are moderately higher than in the U.S., and substantially more in the out islands. Water too can range from free to about 40 cents a gallon. If your budget is tight, you'd be wise to call ahead at about the time you plan to be in the islands to get an accurate idea of these things.

Most over-the-counter items, such as food, repair, and maintenance materials, are imported from the U.S. and 33.5 percent import duty plus shipping costs have been paid on them. Thus their counter price in The Bahamas is 50-60 percent over that of the same item purchased stateside. Note: The

LOOK FOR US AT YACHTSMANSGUIDE.COM

Bahamian dollar is on par with the U.S. dollar.

Acceptance of credit cards in the islands is left up to the individual dealer. Call or write ahead of time to be sure. It is not uncommon for merchants in the islands to add a surcharge of 5% to credit-card purchases. Also, when we last visited, US$100 bills were becoming increasingly difficult to use because of an increase in counterfeiting.

Distances. Owing both to the clarity of the atmosphere and the lowness of the land, distances are apt to be deceptive. As a rule you will sight the average cay at a distance of 4-5 miles. Those with trees or hills rising to about 50 feet can be seen 7-8 miles away, while those of 100-foot height will usually be visible at 10-12. Fog in The Bahamas is almost unknown, but can form infrequently during the winter months.

Draft. Since the Bahama Banks are shallow, the less your vessel draws, the better. A yacht drawing only 3-4 feet can go almost anywhere. Many have cruised among the islands drawing 7 or 8 feet and by awaiting the tide have precluded themselves from few of the more attractive harbors. Of course, vessels carrying that much draft could lie in comfort outside and explore the shallower passages by dinghy.

Where our text shows depths at marinas and docks (either alongside or in the approaches) that are close to your draft, you should confirm directly with the marina that you can be accommodated. We measure where we can, but marinas also supply us with figures and sometimes these may be overstated.

Drugs. Possession of any unprescribed drug is illegal in The Bahamas, and will result in heavy fines and possibly jail sentences.

Firearms. Personal firearms are permitted aboard visitor yachts entering Bahamian waters as a part of ship's equipment for a period of three months,

H. M. Prison, Simms, Long Island (and the usual suspect). (Tropic Isle photo)

after which a certificate must be obtained from the Commissioner of Police. All firearms, and an *accurate* count of the amount and type of ammunition aboard must be declared when entering and listed on the ship's transire (see chapter on Customs and Immigration: Entering Bahamian Ports). They must remain on board the vessel for the duration of its stay in Bahamian waters, and protected from theft under lock and key. These regulations are strictly enforced. If even the slightest discrepancies are found, you are subject to arrest.

Fishing, spearfishing, and hunting rules. *Bahamian fisheries laws are subject to change. For current information at the time of your visit, check with Bahamian customs officials at your port of entry or write the Dept. of Fisheries at P.O. Box N-3028, Nassau, Bahamas. The following information is correct as of our press date.*

Foreign vessels may not engage in any commercial fishing transaction in Bahamian waters. Also, be aware that the following regulations apply not only to serious sportfishermen manning boats equipped with tuna towers, but also to anyone cruising The Bahamas who as much as drops a line over the side.

Sportfishing. We list only a summary of rules most relevant to the average fisherman, as of our press deadline. Current rules and regulations are summarized on the back of the required fishing permit, and a complete list of current sportfishing regulations is available from the Director of Fisheries, Department of Fisheries, P.O. Box N-3028, Nassau, Bahamas, or to The Bahamas News Bureau, 19495 Biscayne Blvd., Suite 809, Aventura, FL 33180.

A permit is required for visiting vessels to engage in sportfishing, at a cost of $20 per trip or $150 per year for vessels on which not more than six reels will be used. Vessels on which more than six reels will be used require a permit costing $10,000 annually. Permits are available at port of entry. The use of a spear, fish trap, or net other than a landing net is prohibited unless authorized by and endorsed on the permit issued.

Sportfishing tournament directors must have written approval from the Department of Fisheries to organize or hold a sportfishing tournament in The Bahamas.

Bag limits. The bag limit for kingfish, dolphin, and wahoo is six fish per person on the vessel, comprising any combination of these species. Any other migratory fish caught, unless they are to be used, must be returned to the sea alive and not unnecessarily injured. Bag limits for other fishery resources are 20 pounds of scalefish, 10 conch, and 6 crawfish per person at any time (within season). The above amounts may also be exported by the vessel upon leaving The Bahamas.

The capture, possession, or molesting of coral, turtles, or marine mammals is prohibited.

Spearfishing. When using spearfishing apparatus, a Hawaiian sling is the only device permitted to discharge a missile underwater. Spearfishing is prohibited within one mile off the coast of New Providence, one mile off the southern coast of Freeport, Grand Bahama, and 200 yards off the coast of all Out Islands.

SCUBA. The use of SCUBA or air compressors to aide in the harvest of fishery resources is prohibited.

Conch. The taking of conchs with shells that do not have a well-formed flaring lip is prohibited.

Eating Your Catch: Caution Regarding Ciguatera

We strongly caution the visitor not to eat larger species of fish such as amberjack or barracuda and other bottom feeders (in many areas, this includes blackfin grouper, yellowfin grouper, red snapper, jack fish, hogfish, and perhaps shellfish). These have been known to cause **ciguatera poisoning,** *a serious disease that can result in lasting nerve damage, coma, and even death. A nerve poison generated by a dinoflagellate that feeds on coral reefs is passed on to fish that ingest the dinoflagellates. The fish is unharmed, but the poison accumulates in its system as it ages (thus the larger the fish, the more toxic it is to eat). There is no way to determine if a fish is toxic or not, and no way to detoxify an affected fish (cooking or freezing are ineffective). If you eat a toxic fish you will experience nausea, vomiting, diarrhea, and stomach cramps 3-10 hours later, usually accompanied by weakness, joint and muscle pain, and tingling around the nose and mouth. Medical aid should be sought immediately if you develop these symptoms after eating fish.*

Be prepared to identify any fish you catch and plan to eat (tuna, dolphin, and wahoo are said to usually be safe) — but in any case you must still rely on local knowledge as to which fish are safe to eat in any particular geographic area, as this varies from place to place throughout the islands.

Crawfish. Crawfish season opens August 1 and closes March 31. The minimum harvestable size limit is 3-1/4 inches carapace length or 5-1/2 inches tail length. The possession of "berried" (egg-bearing) females is prohibited.

Scalefish. The capture of bonefish by net is prohibited, as is the purchase or selling of bonefish. Catching of grouper or rockfish weighing less than 3 pounds is also prohibited.

Hunting. Foreign visitors are prohibited from hunting in The Bahamas, the sport being limited to Bahamian citizens, permanent residents, and persons who have lived in The Bahamas 90 days or more. In The Bahamas the penalties for taking birds out of season, or from restricted areas, are severe. The yacht or vehicle, personal effects, equipment, and stores thereon may be seized. The government sells these items at public auction, keeps half of the proceeds, and pays the other half to the persons giving information leading to the conviction.

Additional regulations pertaining to Sea Parks. The taking by any means of any marine life, whether living, dead, or fossilized, is prohibited in all Sea Parks, designated by the Bahamas National Trust.

Flag etiquette. Once you have entered The Bahamas and officially cleared with the boarding officer, the quarantine flag should be replaced by the courtesy flag and flown for the duration of the yacht's visit in The Bahamas. It should be flown from the starboard shroud or hoist on all masted vessels and from the bow staff on motor yachts.

Flight connections. For yachtsmen planning to rendezvous with crew members in the islands, a number of U.S.-based airlines fly daily to Nassau, Freeport, Treasure Cay, Marsh Harbour, Rock Sound, Governor's Harbour, George Town, with lesser service to a number of other destinations. Pan Am Air Bridge (formerly Chalk's International Airlines, with the same fleet of Grumman

Mallards) flies from Fort Lauderdale to Bimini, Paradise Island, and Walker's Cay and from Miami to Bimini and Paradise Island. Bahamasair connects with most of the Out Islands through Nassau, and there are several private charter businesses.

Garbage disposal. *Never throw garbage into the quiet anchorages of the islands, where it will attract scavengers.* Food scraps that could serve as fish food should be disposed of while under way, outside any anchorage. Boaters who toss plastic bags or 6-pack rings overboard are creating a disastrous situation for turtles and sea birds. Turtles mistake the floating bags for Portuguese man-of-war, which they sometimes feed on, and birds get their beaks and necks caught in the rings. Carry your garbage with you, depositing it at your next marina or settlement. If there are no marinas or disposal units immediately available, abide by the old rules: break all bottles and punch cans at both ends, and then dispose of them in deep water, *not* on the banks or along the reefs. Again, food scraps that can serve as fish food should be disposed of while under way either on the banks or in deep water. Plastics should be crushed and saved for when you reach the next disposal unit, no matter how far in the future that will be. Never throw plastic overboard to inevitably litter the beaches, and never leave bagged garbage or litter of any sort on an uninhabited island.

Whatever we say here now, don't be surprised to see constant and big changes regarding garbage and its disposal in The Bahamas. This is a growing problem, and there will be different requirements in different locations to cope with a bad situation. There are already heavy consequences for anyone who disregards these. And, while we're on the subject, letting your dog poop all over the beaches is also a way to make yourself extremely unpopular.

Gulf Stream. The courses given in the chapter on Approaches to The Bahamas are based on a Gulf Stream current of 2.5 knots, but sometimes it may be more and sometimes less. The wise mariner must be able to figure these courses for himself in order to factor in up-to-the-minute conditions. GPS, loran, radar, or a good direction finder are useful backups.

Holidays and special events. It's wise to be aware of the various holidays celebrated in The Bahamas to anticipate business closings, attend some of the festivals and special events, or avoid overtime fees while clearing customs. The Bahamas celebrates New Year's Day, Good Friday, Easter Monday, and

BEL AIR
TRANSPORT, INC.

1560 S.W. 23rd Street
Fort Lauderdale, FL 33315
Phone & Fax
(954) 524-0115

· Servicing all of the islands in the
  Bahamas, Turks & Caicos
· Servicing Florida and the Keys
· Individual service, 24-hour standby
· Twin engine Piper Chieftain,
  Air-conditioned

· FAA approved, Commercial license, highly
  insured, experienced trained pilots
· Pickup services from Palm Beach, Miami or the
  West Coast of Florida
· Scheduled flights to the Berry Islands from
  Fort Lauderdale International Airport

Christmas on the traditional dates. Bahamians also celebrate Whit Monday (the seventh Monday after Easter), Labour Day (the first Friday in June), Independence Day (annually on July 10), Emancipation Day (the first Monday of August), Discovery Day (October 12), and Boxing Day (the day after Christmas). A complete schedule of holidays and special events, as well as the dates of many upcoming fishing tournaments, regattas, and races not available at our press deadline, will be available from the Bahamas Tourist Office, 19495 Biscayne Blvd., Suite 809, Aventura, FL 33180 (phone 305-932-0051).

Many small resorts and some businesses in the islands close during September and early October. If your itinerary depends on any such destination, you're advised to check ahead.

Lighthouses and beacons are maintained by The Bahamas government. However, due to the vastness of the area and the number of lights to be maintained, at any given time some lights will not be working or may have flashing patterns varying from those noted on charts or in this text. (See also the list of Batelco towers on page 39.)

The Bahamas Lighthouse Preservation Society, founded in 1995, is dedicated to preservation of traditional hand-wound, kerosene-burning Bahamian lighthouses. Three lighthouses (in Hope Town, San Salvador, and Great Inagua) are the only such operating lighthouses remaining in the world, and the Society works to maintain museum-quality restoration and display of each. Donations or volunteer assistance would be welcome support for this worthwhile

1-888-LIFEFLT
Critical Care Helicopter Transport

Next vacation, take along some peace of mind.

LifeFlight® is the critical care helicopter which provides expert medical care while transporting sick, injured and disabled newborns, children or adults.

- Highly-skilled staff
- Advanced medical equipment
- Operates throughout South Florida and the Caribbean
- Available 24 hours a day for emergency and non-emergency transport
- Accommodates up to two patients

LifeFlight®

**1-888-LIFEFLT
305-663-6859**

MIAMI CHILDREN'S HOSPITAL

Mount Sinai MEDICAL CENTER

®LifeFlight is the registered trademark of Hermann Hospital Foundation, Houston, Texas.

BATELCO Towers

Many of the following Batelco towers appear on our sketch charts as hollow stars. Batelco has plotted those that don't appear on our sketch charts on charts of such small scale that we cannot yet determine their geographic positions precisely enough to plot them on our larger-scale sketch charts. This list, provided us by Batelco, summarizes locations of their towers, whether plotted on our sketch charts or not. Towers over 50 feet should be lighted at their tops with red lights with fixed or flashing patterns. The taller towers have one or more additional steady red lights at intermediate levels.

Bimini: Alice Town (100'), Cat Cay (50'), Bailey Town (82')

Berry Islands: Bullocks Harbour (235'), Chub Cay (200')

New Providence: Delaporte (200'), Lyford Cay (160'), Coral Harbour (160'), Defence Force Coral Harbour (100'), Soldier Road (260'), Soldier Road (225'), Poinciana Drive (200'), East Street (80'), Perpall Tract (150'), Perpall Tract (150'), Perpall Tract (80'), Perpall Tract (80')

Grand Bahama: Bassett Cove (420'), Eight Mile Rock (200'), Freeport (200'), Grand Cay (275'), McLeans Town (200'), Pinders Point (100'), South Riding Point (225'), Sweetings Cay (60'), Water Cay (50'), West End (150')

Abaco: Cedar Harbour (50'), Cherokee Sound (255'), Coopers Town (200'), Crossing Bay (80'), Crossing Rock (40'), Cocoa Bay (80'), Fox Town (200'), Green Turtle Cay (100'), Guana Cay (50'), Hope Town (40'), Man of War Cay (40'), Marsh Harbour (200'), Marsh Harbour (250'), Mores Island (200'), Sandy Point (260'), Treasure Cay (200'), Casuarina Cay (60'), Gorda Cay (Castaway Cay) (60')

Andros: Cargill Creek (100'), Fresh Creek (225'), Kemps Bay (150'), Mangrove Cay (100'), Mars Bay (100'), Mastic Point (100'), Nicholl's Town (255'), Red Bays (50'), Staniard Creek (200')

Eleuthera: Governor's Harbour (180'), Governor's Harbour (59'), Green Castle (240'), Harbour Island (40'), Hatchet Bay (265'), Lower Bogue (200'), Rock Sound (100'), Savannah Sound (200'), Spanish Wells (120'), Tarpum Bay (200')

Exuma: Barraterre (150'), Black Point (100'), Bock Cay (100'), Farmers Hill (40'), George Town (105'), George Town (180'), Highborne Cay (260'), Lee Stocking Island (60'), Little Farmer's Cay (260'), Rolleville (260'), Rudder Cut Cay (50'), Staniel Cay (260'), Williams Town (200')

Long Island: Clarence Town (60'), Deadman's Cay (200'), Simms (200'), Stella Maris (50'), Hog Cay (50')

Cat Island: Arthur's Town (200'), Hawks Nest (50'), The Bight (235')

Little San Salvador: West Bay (Half Moon Cay) (60')

San Salvador: Cockburn Town (59'), Cockburn Town (150'), Dixon Hill (60'),

Rum Cay: Port Nelson (200')

Crooked Island: Cabbage Hill (82'), Cabbage Hill (200'), Cabbage Hill (59')

Acklins Island: Spring Point (70'), Spring Point (70'), Spring Point (235')

Mayaguana: Abraham's Bay (70'), Abraham's Bay (70'), Abraham's Bay (70'), Abraham's Bay (225'), Betsy Bay (105')

Inagua: Matthew Town (70'), Matthew Town (70'), Matthew Town (59'), Matthew Town (50')

endeavor. Contact the Lighthouse Society at 242-366-0282, or write to Dave Gale, President, Bahamas Lighthouse Preservation Society, Hope Town, Abaco, Bahamas.

Law enforcement. All visitors to these islands are subject to Bahamian law. *The Royal Bahamas Defence Force* is charged with protecting its population, fishing grounds, and ecology from foreign predators, and has the authority to inspect any boat, plane, or activity for illegal action, products, or equipment. In addition to its 42-acre main base, HMBS Coral Harbour, located at the site of the former Coral Harbour Hotel and Marina in New Providence, the Royal Bahamas Defence Force also operates a Southern Satellite Base, HMBS Matthew Town, in Matthew Town, Inagua. Defence Force patrol boats and planes patrol sensitive areas on a continuous schedule. Visitors who want to know the firing practice procedure at Coral Harbour, New Providence, or to report suspicious activities, should call (242) 322-4436 or 325-5127. Both lines are open around the clock. Keep in mind when you sight a Defence Force Patrol Boat that they are on station for your protection, as well as to patrol for poachers and drug runners. They monitor VHF 16, and the skippers are fine seamen who would be glad to share their local knowledge with cruising visitors.

Medical facilities and emergencies. In the event of a medical emergency at sea, call the Coast Guard on 2182 SSB or call BASRA on VHF 16 (telephone 242-322-3877), and they will arrange for emergency air transport to the nearest medical facility. Patients requiring special or intensive care will be taken to Doctors Hospital (242-322-8411) or Princess Margaret Hospital (242-322-1039), both in Nassau, or Rand Memorial Hospital in Freeport (242-352-6735). Most of the populated islands throughout The Bahamas maintain local clinics, staffed by doctors or nurses, to take care of medical emergencies. LifeFlight's critical care helicopter, based at the Miami Children's Hospital, is fully medically equipped and available around the clock for emergency and non-emergency transport throughout South Florida and The Bahamas. Call 1-888-LIFEFLT or 305-663-6859. Also, a private ambulance service, National Air Ambulance, operates out of Fort Lauderdale International Airport and will transport patients from The Bahamas to the United States. Remember that in the more remote islands, you may be largely on your own.

Every boat cruising The Bahamas should carry a complete first-aid kit and a comprehensive medical book with first-aid information. Since medical facilities can be few and far between in some areas and emergencies can occur at any time, yachtsmen must be prepared for self-reliance. Shop around for a medical book that is organized for easy reference, addresses the specific treatment of marine mishaps, and suggests the contents of a good first-aid kit.

Mosquitoes and sand flies are at their worst when the wind dies and you're tied to a wharf or anchored close to land, especially with mangroves nearby. Best to anchor off, install fans over bunks where possible, and *carry a good supply of repellent*. There are harbors and anchorages from the northernmost Abacos all the way down to Great Inagua and the Turks and Caicos where hordes of mosquitoes and sand flies will eat you alive. You'll regret it if you arrive at one of these unprepared.

Navigational fixes. A properly compensated compass is a must, and a hand-bearing compass is most helpful for obtaining fixes and as a backup to the main compass. A lead line or electronic depth sounder is a necessity.

GPS is the thing now, and we are getting requests to print GPS waypoints. We don't for several reasons, the simplest being this: you *must* have appropriate government charts on board, with which you can figure any waypoint you need with a straightedge in a matter of seconds. However, it's important to know that many government charts are based on very old surveys and may contain considerable errors, so be careful to build a safety factor into waypoints you obtain. One way to do this is to figure waypoints a mile or more safely seaward of your objective, and then adjust and proceed based on what you see.

We are continually hearing of people coming to grief entering various cuts or other tight spots using GPS and apparently not using their eyes. This is crazy. Under no circumstances, even with perfect waypoint information, is it safe to enter such places navigating only by GPS. Even though GPS can be very accurate, it can still be inaccurate enough to put you in trouble. Add to this the errors in many government charts of The Bahamas, and the chances of something going wrong are substantial. You should not rely solely on any single aid to navigation, and since your own eyes are perhaps your most important navigational aids, you should not be under way, particularly in a tight place, if visibility is in any way diminished.

Loran-C must be used with care in The Bahamas. The time differences on the navigational charts are in error. The physical location of the southeast chain of Loran-C stations tends not to favor accurate fixes in the islands (Whiskey and Zulu slaves are the best). However, if you have Loran-C and have obtained your own readings at a given location, you should be able to return to the same spot without difficulty. (We have had *some* reports of poor repeatability.)

Comments from Loran-C and GPS users are most welcome.

Navigation rules. The American buoyage system (red-right-returning) is generally used in The Bahamas. In the Turks and Caicos, changeover to red-right-returning was recently completed. However, wherever these changes are made, there is often some confusion of systems for awhile, so beware.

Passing oncoming traffic is usually according to the U.S. system (port to port) but local skippers accustomed to driving on the left sometimes exercise this habit afloat, confusing the visitor in confined channels. Operators of some of the high-speed local boats are not aware of any rules at all, sometimes even running

PHONE: 954-527-0040
TOLL FREE: 888-527-1158
FAX: 954-527-4960

LAUDERDALE MARINE CENTER   2001 S.W. 20th St. Ft. Lauderdale, FL 33315

• 100+ FLOATING SLIPS
• BOATS UP TO 150 FT.
• 2 TRAVEL LIFTS (70/100 TON)
• 200 TON LIFT (COMING SOON)
• DO IT YOURSELF YARD
• DRY STORAGE YARD
• NO FIXED BRIDGES

• LOCATED ON NEW RIVER
• HURRICANE HOLE
• VISIT OUR SISTER MARINA IN MARYLAND:
  BALTIMORE MARINE CENTER
• QUALITY CONTRACTORS ON SITE
• TOP SECURITY
• ALL ELECTRIC INCLUDING 3 PHASE

at night without lights. With these possibilities in mind, pilot your craft through congested areas in a defensive manner, and exercise caution at all times. The 5-6 m.p.h. (or lower) harbor and channel speed is enforced in the more populated island settlements. In Hope Town, the limit is 3 m.p.h.

Pets on board. The importation of domestic pets into The Bahamas is under the jurisdiction of the Department of Agriculture. All animals must have an import permit. To obtain an application for a permit to import, write to the Director, Department of Agriculture, P.O. Box N-3704, Nassau, Bahamas (telephone 242/325-7413; fax 242/325-3960. Upon completion of this application return it along with a $10 permit processing fee in the form of an International Money Order or Postal Order, made payable to the Public Treasury (personal checks are not accepted). Send it Registered Air Mail to the above address. Following these procedures as outlined will greatly reduce the time it will take to obtain your permit, but it is suggested that you allow at least 30 days' processing time when mailing in your completed application along with your fee.

In addition to the permit, a veterinary health certificate along with all vaccination and other requirements listed on the import permit (including any Convention or International Trade in Endangered Species of Wild Animals of Plants [C.I.T.E.S.] documentation necessary) is required for entry. These papers are presented to the Customs or Agricultural Officer when clearing port of entry. A customs charge may be required.

If you plan to bring a pet, be aware that veterinary services are limited in The Bahamas. Here we list licensed private veterinarians of whom we've been informed.

• *New Providence:* Dr. Dawn Wilson, Veterinary Outpatient Care (242)

Pet on board. (Tropic Isle photo)

328-5635; Dr. Gary Cash, Palmdale Veterinary Clinic (242) 325-1354, emergencies (242) 324-7462; Dr. Patrick Balfe, Eastern Veterinary Clinic (242) 325-2818, weekend emergencies (242) 325-6961; Dr. Basil Sands, Central Animal Hospital (242) 325-1288

   • *Grand Bahama:* Dr. Allan Bater, Freeport Animal Clinic (242) 352-6521; Dr. Valentino Grant, Community Animal Hospital (242) 351-3647

   • *Marsh Harbour:* Dr. Owen Hanna, Community Animal Hospital (242) 367-DOGS; emergencies (242) 351-DOGS. Office hours are Thursday and Friday from 9 a.m. to 5 p.m.

   Last but not least, and it's worth repeating: letting your dog poop all over the beaches is a way to make yourself extremely unpopular.

   Pilotage. Two distinct types of pilotage are necessary when cruising Bahamian waters. The first is normal, deep-water pilotage when traversing the deep sounds and channels that separate many of the island groups, where soundings reach 1000 fathoms or more. The two most important things to remember about deep-water pilotage are: (1) the tides, as a rule, set directly onto and off of the banks, so that at night when the boat's exact position cannot always be accurately fixed, it is wise to give the edge of any bank a wide berth; and (2) the edge of any bank drops away abruptly, so you cannot always rely on the sounding lead to warn you of impending danger.

   Banks pilotage is quite a different story and takes some practice to master. Since the water is seldom deeper than 3-4 fathoms and frequently considerably less, the bottom is visible at all times. Pilotage is done entirely by eye, judging depth by the color of the water (see examples on page 60 showing water depths). It follows, therefore, that at night in most localities it is unwise for the stranger to be under way. The same thing applies in overcast weather or when the sun is low and ahead. The best conditions for crossing a bank are clear weather with the sun high and behind you. Dangers can then be seen at a considerable distance. The Great Bahama Bank between Bimini and Cat Cay and the Northwest Channel Light is almost free from coral heads, but crawfish trap floats can be a hazard to navigation in this area.

   A Bahamian pilot who has spent his life in and about these unusual shades of blue and green can, while perched high on your vessel's bow, call out the depths ahead as accurately with more speed and cover a wider area than your most sophisticated electronic gear. However, with careful concentration, it takes but a short cruise or two to acquaint you with most of the bottom characteristics. A basic point to remember: over a constantly shallowing bottom the color pales in relation to the diminishing depth. Consider the water as a clear, pale-blue filter; the thicker (deeper) it is, the darker it will appear. This filter will have the same effect over any color of bottom; a mottled black-brown and yellow coral head ringed with white sand will blend to blue-black ringed in a lighter blue at depths.

   Coral heads might be found in many places on the banks, even if they're not shown on charts or sketch charts, or mentioned in this *Guide. It would be very dangerous to assume you can pass over coral heads, even if you might have found, at one time or another, that you can pass over some of them.* At times coral heads will be encountered in an area covered with dark grass. These are harder to spot, but frequently they are surrounded by a ring of white

VHF Emergency Calling Stations in The Bahamas

Location	Call Sign	Channel	Hours	Range
Nassau	BASRA	16, 22A	0900, 1700	50
Nassau	Nassau Harbour Control	16	24	50
New Prov.	RBDF	16	24	50
Bimini	BASRA Bimini	16	0700-2100	30
Gr. Bahama	BASRA Freeport	16, 68, 84, 86	0700-2200	70
Abaco Cays	BASRA Man of War Cay	16	0700-2100	30
Abaco Cays	BASRA Hope Town	16	0700-2100	30
Great Abaco	BASRA Marsh Harbour	16	0700-2100	30
Great Abaco	BASRA Little Harbour	16	0800-1800	20
Eleuthera	BASRA Spanish Wells	16	0800-1730	20
Eleuthera	BASRA Governor's Hbr	16	0800-1730	20
Exuma Cays	BASRA Black Point	16	0800-1800	30
Exuma Cays	BASRA Staniel Cay	16	Daylight Hrs	20
Great Exuma	BASRA George Town	16	0800-2100	40
Cat Island	BASRA Hawksnest	16	0900-2300	40
Long Island	BASRA Clarence Town	16	0900-1700	30
Long Island	BASRA Sunseeker	16	0700-2100	50
Crooked Island	BASRA Landrail Point	16	0730-2100	20

sand, which according to local lore is kept clean by the fish that inhabit the head. Therefore, when sailing over a grassy bottom avoid such circular white patches on principle. Also remember that small clouds passing across the face of the sun will cast shadows on the water that look exactly like rocky patches. Unless you are sure they are shadows, avoid them. An electronic depth finder is useful; a lookout above the deck, in the ratlines, or on the wheelhouse roof is essential. Sunglasses with polarizing lenses eliminate most of the surface glare of the water, and are a helpful aid in reading the depth of the water.

The color photographs on page 62 showing water depths indicate a sprinkling of typical situations. Whether you decide to sail through the color or merely admire it, you will agree that nowhere in the world is there a more breathtaking and beautiful "aid to navigation."

With the foregoing, the phenomenon of "fish muds" should be mentioned. These muds, which sometimes extend for more than 2 miles, are caused by enormous schools of fish, (usually bonefish, shrimp, pinfish, or sailors choice) feeding on the bottom, thus stirring up the marl. As food they attract shark, so never swim near a fish mud. Seen from a short distance, the muds have the appearance of a shallow white sandbank. They occur in depths up to 5 fathoms.

Rescue. The Bahamas Air-Sea Rescue Association (BASRA) is composed of numerous boats, aircraft, and an enthusiastic membership of volunteers who share daily duty in the principal towns and settlements of the islands, standing by during various hours to serve in an emergency. BASRA works in cooperation with the U.S. Coast Guard, so if you require assistance, call the Coast Guard on VHF or 2182 kHz or the Nassau Marine Operator on VHF 27 or 2198 kHz or 2182 kHz and state your position and circumstances. BASRA maintains its own building at the west end of Malcolm Park in Nassau. The officer on duty stands by from 9 a.m. to 5 p.m. on 2182 kHz and VHF 16 and 22A (Nassau telephone [242] 325-8864). If an emergency situation arises outside these hours, you may call the Police Answering Service at (242) 322-3877 and they will contact the duty officer. In Freeport, standby frequency is VHF 16 (Freeport telephone [242] 352-5458). In the event that a cruising visitor is needed for emergency at home, BASRA will try to contact any pleasure craft cruising The Bahamas.

For emergency VHF traffic only, if you fail to reach an answering party on channel 16, try channel 22A to reach BASRA headquarters in Nassau through BASRA's automatic repeater link (or, if in the vicinity of New Providence, you can switch to U.S. Channel 22A to try to reach the Royal Bahamas Defence Force). Within a 50-mile radius of Freeport, try channels 86 or 84. Other automatic repeater stations are now in operation at Chub Cay in the Berry Islands (temporarily not in operation at this writing) and Highborne Cay, Exuma, each with a receiving range of about 50 miles in all directions, depending on your set. If you can't contact any of these or the emergency stations mentioned here, try calling the marine facilities nearest to you. *Note: Chub Cay Marina monitors VHF 68, not 16.*

Remember that most of these operations are voluntary in The Bahamas and that there can be no guarantee that these listed will be monitoring the frequency at the time of your call. For additional safety, try to maintain daily contact with a friend or boating acquaintance while on an extended cruise. *Be aware that while cruising The Bahamas, you will to a large extent be on your own.* This is yet another good reason to never be under way at night.

Only dire circumstances such as a fire or sinking justify a Mayday call. A Sécurité call should be made if the craft is lost, out of fuel, having engine trouble, or experiencing similar mishaps.

Marcus Mitchell at Sampson Cay in the Exumas has a 100-foot salvage

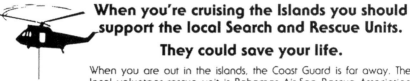

When you're cruising the Islands you should support the local Search and Rescue Units.

They could save your life.

SEARCH

When you are out in the islands, the Coast Guard is far away. The local volunteer rescue unit is Bahamas Air-Sea Rescue Association (BASRA). They need your money to be ready to help you.

SEARCH (Search and Rescue Charitable Foundation), a U.S. tax-exempt foundation, is devoted to improving and expanding all the volunteer search and rescue units in the Caribbean and the Bahamas.

Send your TAX-DEDUCTIBLE donation today to:

SEARCH
901 S.E. 17th Street, Suite 205, Fort Lauderdale, FL 33316

❑ I wish to make a tax-deductible donation to SEARCH of $50/$100/more ($_____) My check is enclosed. Please send my contributor's certificate and recognition decal to my address below.
❑ Please send more information.

NAME_____ DATE_____

ADDRESS_____

CITY_____ STATE_____ ZIP_____

Yacht's name/Aircraft Type and Reg. No. _____

Please make checks payable to SEARCH and mail this form with your generous donation.

YOUR MONEY SAVES LIVES — MAYBE YOURS.

A COPY OF THE OFFICIAL REGISTRATION AND FINANCIAL INFORMATION MAY BE OBTAINED FROM DIV. OF CONSUMER SERVICES BY CALLING 1-800-HELP-FLA, WITHIN FLA. REGISTRATION DOES NOT IMPLY ENDORSEMENT, APPROVAL OR RECOMMENDATION BY THE STATE.

vessel equipped to handle any type of salvage situation in The Bahamas and beyond, as well as a seaplane for emergencies. He has saved a significant number of people who found themselves in dire straits. Contact him at (242) 355-2034 or call *Sampson Cay* on VHF 16.

Security. The U.S. Coast Guard advises owners of yachts cruising in The Bahamas and Caribbean to be very careful about taking on hitchhikers and paid hands by thoroughly checking their references and background. Even a rescue at sea should be approached with caution, and a "Float Plan" should be filed with someone who could report to the proper authority if arrival is overdue.

Remember that by most North American standards The Bahamas is an underdeveloped country, and a significant economic gap exists between tourists and many Bahamians. Private yachts can represent a great deal of wealth to some islanders so, to avoid creating temptation, we caution you against leaving your vessel unattended while anchored in Nassau Harbour or at any harbor wharf that does not have some sort of security patrol. Take the same safety precautions ashore in The Bahamas that you would elsewhere, particularly in the larger population centers; crime is not unknown.

Tides. Once in the islands, you must reckon with the tides. The wise mariner will be extremely cautious when depths shown on government charts, in this text, on sketch charts, or in the tide tables are at all close to the draft of his vessel — otherwise he may find himself unexpectedly aground, perhaps on something hard. The tide tables in the back of this *Guide* are as accurate as possible, but they are only approximate as to any particular place. Also note that low tides vary as much as a foot or more in height, depending on the phase of the moon, its distance from earth, and its relation to the sun. In addition to moon and sun there are many other factors, including wind and local geography, that cause time and height differences in the tide at any particular place. Depths shown on our sketch charts are based on experience dating back many years. They are updated from time to time to the extent information is available — but information of this kind will by nature be less than perfect, and storms and time do cause things to change.

Water safety. Sharks and barracuda are unpredictable and should be treated with respect. To be safe, never swim alone and never swim far from shore or the boat. Never tease or annoy a shark or barracuda. Avoid swimming over grass, as this is where smaller fish feed, attracting larger fish. Never swim in murky water or at night, as the fish can then see you but you can't see them. Avoid wearing shiny objects while in the water as barracuda have been known to be attracted to them. If you have speared a fish, get it out of the water as soon as possible, as its blood will attract larger fish.

The rules governing water skiing in The Bahamas parallel those of the United States: do not ski in congested areas, maintain an observer, and never "buzz" anchored yachts, as someone might be swimming close by.

Wrecked vessels. All vessels wrecked or stranded beyond repair or salvage should be reported immediately to the Port Controller, Port Department, P.O. Box N-8175, Nassau, Bahamas; phone 322-8832.

CUSTOMS AND IMMIGRATION

Entering Bahamian Ports

Ports of Entry. The following are ports of entry in The Bahamas. Vessels may not enter at places other than those listed.

- **Abaco:** Walker's Cay, Spanish Cay (customs facilities temporarily closed at this writing), Green Turtle Cay, Treasure Cay, Marsh Harbour.
- **Andros:** Morgan's Bluff, San Andros, Fresh Creek, Congo Town.
- **Berry Islands:** Great Harbour Cay, Chub Cay.
- **Bimini:** Alice Town (North Bimini).
- **Cat Cay:** Cat Cay.
- **Eleuthera:** Harbour Island, Spanish Wells, Governor's Harbour, Rock Sound, Cape Eleuthera (Note: Customs facilities at Cape Eleuthera were closed at this writing).
- **Exuma:** George Town (Government Dock in Elizabeth Harbour).
- **Grand Bahama:** West End, Freeport Harbour, Port Lucaya Marina, Lucaya Marina Village, Xanadu Marina.
- **Inagua:** Matthew Town.

First in Service

Dedicated To a tradition of
Quality Craftsmanship and Service

Power • 70 Ton Travelift • Sail

Mechanical Repairs
Electrical Repairs
Repower Gas & Diesel
Electronics Service

Air Conditioning/Refrigeration
Carpentry/Restoration
Sandblasting
Fiberglass Repairs

Welding & Fabrication
Painting
Refinishing
Rigging

First Full Service Boatyard on the New River

CHINNOCK MARINE INC.

954-763-2250

518 W. LAS OLAS BLVD., FT. LAUDERDALE, FL 33312
Toll-Free (888) 763-2250 • Fax (954) 763-2294 • E-Mail: Chinnock@marineweb.com
Visit our web site at: http://www.marineweb.com/marina/chinnock

- **Long Island:** Stella Maris.
- **New Providence:** Nassau (any yacht basin).
- **San Salvador:** Cockburn Town.
- **Cat Island:** Smith Bay or New Bight (airport).

Customs and immigration procedure. All vessels arriving into Bahamian waters must enter immediately with both customs and immigration officials at the nearest port of entry listed above, whether or not the time of arrival will incur overtime charges. An exception to this is if conditions preclude safe approach to a port of entry. Under these circumstances, you must plan to enter as soon as feasible, even though doing so might mean incurring overtime charges. If conditions are such that you are forced to anchor out or tie up, and your entry is delayed, make every effort to inform customs/immigration or the dockmaster at your port of entry of your situation. If, for any reason, you fail to report for clearance within 24 hours of arrival into Bahamian waters, you will be subject to penalties and the vessel is liable to seizure and forfeiture. When nearing the selected port of entry a quarantine (yellow) flag must be flown. No goods may be unloaded, and no contact may be made with the shore other than tying up, until the vessel has been granted practique by custom and immigration officials.

To clear immigration in The Bahamas, visitors generally need a valid passport. However, U.S. citizens may, as an alternative, produce a valid original birth certificate or voter's registration card, which must be accompanied by a valid driver's license with photo. These are the requirements according to The Bahamas Immigration Department at this writing, but keep in mind that these rules are subject to change, so it might be a good idea to have a passport or birth certificate with you as well as one of the other forms of identification.

In the case of a pleasure craft with no dutiable cargo, the captain will fill out duplicate copies of Maritime Declarations of Health, Inwards Report for pleasure vessels, crew/passenger lists and immigration cards.

The captain of the vessel, upon request, would then be given a cruising permit for the vessel, which is good for up to 12 months. This permit is issued at a cost of $10. Two additional extensions to the initial 12 months can applied for and may be granted at a cost of $500 for each request. When these have expired, you must leave The Bahamas or pay duty.

For additional requirements for sportfishing boats, see section on Fishing, Spearfishing, and Hunting Rules in the chapter on What the Skipper Should Know.

If you are arriving by commercial airline and returning by boat, we suggest purchasing a round-trip air fare in the United States, using half of it to fly to The Bahamas. Leave the return reservation open, and when you return on private craft, you may either turn in the unused portion for a refund or use it for a future trip, depending on the airline. You might want to check with your carrier first regarding their policy (some are difficult to pin down with refund requests after you've cancelled your ticket). If you leave your boat in The Bahamas to make a return trip home by air, be sure to take with you a copy of cruising permit (the original must stay aboard the boat). You will be allowed back into The Bahamas without a return ticket out again if you can show your cruising permit.

An International Maritime Declaration of Health (in duplicate), in lieu of a Bill of Health, is accepted from yachts arriving in The Bahamas. Smallpox vaccination certificates and cholera inoculation certificates are required only if the yacht is arriving directly from an infected area.

During normal working hours, from 9:00 a.m. to 5:30 p.m., Monday through Friday, no charge other than the clearing officer's transportation costs is made for clearance of pleasure craft at designated entry points. If you arrive outside these hours, however, the dockmaster of the port of entry must summon Bahamas Customs and Immigration. If the officers are called between 6:00 a.m. and 10:00 p.m. on Saturday, charges will be made on the basis of time and one-half of the officer's salary (1 hour minimum) plus transportation charges for each. If the officers are called to clear a yacht on Sunday or a holiday, or between the hours of 10:00 p.m. and 6 a.m. on any day, the charge is made on the basis of double-time, plus transportation costs for each officer; pro rata is permissible for groups of vessels. If the port of entry maintains both a customs officer and an immigration officer, both will be required to clear the vessel. If only one of the departments is represented, that officer will clear for both. In any event, ask for a receipt for services rendered.

If these overtime clearing and transportation charges seem excessive by stateside standards, reduce your expenses by entering within business hours, and at a port of entry where the docks lie within walking distance of the customs office, for example, Bimini or Green Turtle Cay.

Rules regarding importation of boats and parts. As of autumn 1997, the rate of duty on pleasure vessels of less than 150 gross tons but not less than 30 feet in length, is 5% (with additional stamp duty of 1%). Pleasure vessels of less than 150 gross tons but more than 100 feet in length likewise now are subject to a 5% duty rate (with additional stamp duty of 1%). Boats of 150 gross tons or more are duty-free. (For boats of less than 30 feet, the duty is 22.5% (with the additional 7% stamp duty). Owners of foreign-registered vessels (including U.S.) may keep them in The Bahamas for one year without paying duty and may extend this one-year stay for up to three years by paying a fee of $500 per year after the first.

Spare parts imported for installation on vessels under a temporary cruising permit are duty-free. You must show your cruising permit to qualify for this. If spare parts are imported as cargo, a 7% stamp duty is applicable.

There is an exemption of customs duty on pleasure vessels of not less than 23 feet in length imported as cargo for temporary use and entered at a port of entry in any other part of The Bahamas as previously designated by the Comptroller for the entry, being vessels which the Comptroller is satisfied are to be reshipped out of The Bahamas.

Departing and Entering U.S. Ports

This information covers, in brief, the needs of the owner/master of a pleasure vessel. If you are not sure of the status of your vessel, call the nearest U.S. Customs or Immigration Office, or if abroad, the U.S. Consulate.

Departing U.S. ports. Yachts and pleasure craft owned by U.S. citizens that are state-numbered and documented by the U.S. Coast Guard are not required to obtain formal clearance at the customs house before departing the U.S. All foreign-owned and foreign-flag vessels must obtain formal clearance with U.S. Customs before departing the U.S. Operators of private vessels of 30 feet or more in length are required to complete Customs Form 339 (Annual Processing Fee Decal Request) and display the subsequently provided decal on the side window of the vessel. The decal number will be required when you report your arrival to customs upon your return to South Florida. If the decal is not obtained prior to departure for a foreign location, upon his return the vessel operator will be directed to the nearest customs office to purchase a decal within 48 hours of arriving in the U.S. A Customs User Fee Decal costs $25 and may be purchased at the following locations during business hours Monday through Friday:

• U.S. Customs Service, Port of Miami, 1500 Port Blvd., Miami, FL 33132; (305) 536-5786

• U.S. Customs Service, Port Everglades, 1700 Spangler Blvd., State Road 84 & U.S. 1, Port Everglades, FL 33316; (954) 356-7240

• U.S. Customs Service, 4 East Port Road, Suite 104, Riviera Beach, FL 33404; (561) 844-4393

• U.S. Customs Service, 4430 East Adamo Drive, Suite 301, Tampa, FL 33605; (813) 228-2385

• U.S. Customs Service, 301 Simonton St., Room 105, Key West, FL 33040; (305) 296-5411

If there are aliens aboard, call the immigration office for further instructions. If you have aboard or intend to take along any plants, seeds, or cuttings, you should contact the nearest office of the Plant Protection and Quarantine Division of the Department of Agriculture. If you have animals or birds that will be returned to the U.S., contact the same office. These instructions apply only to pleasure craft and not to any vessel used for commercial purposes. To determine your status, call the customs office before you depart from the U.S.

Entering U.S. ports. New, simplified reporting requirements for small vessels were announced by the U.S. Customs Service in May 1994, eliminating the need for boaters to proceed directly to formerly specified reporting stations. According to the new regulations, boaters arriving from foreign locations must report, immediately upon first landfall (that is, arriving at land, not just sighting it) from any telephone, using one of three toll-free numbers:

1-800-432-1216
1-800-458-4239
1-800-451-0393

Only the master or owner of the vessel may disembark to make his report of arrival. All others must remain on board until clearance has been granted.

When you call for clearance, have the following information at hand:

• Vessel name and registration number
• Vessel owner name
• Vessel commander name and date of birth
• Passenger names and dates of birth
• Foreign ports or places visited and duration of stay
• Total value of all acquisitions and purchases made
• Customs User Fee decal number, if one has been issued

Customs officials will issue a clearance number to the vessel operator if clearance is granted. If not, the vessel operator will be instructed to await further action such as an inspection or examination.

Masters of vessels who fail to report immediately to customs will be liable for a civil penalty of $5,000 for their first violation and $10,000 for each subsequent violation. Any vessel utilized in connection with any such violation will be subject to seizure and forfeiture.

These are the rules and regulations as of our press deadline, but they are always subject to change. For updates or additional information, write the Port Director of Customs, U.S. Customs, Miami International Airport, P.O. Box 59-2061 AMF, Miami, FL 33159; or call (305) 536-5786.

The U.S. Customs Service encourages yachtsmen to report suspicious smuggling activity that they observe by calling 1-800-BE-ALERT, open 24 hours a day. The anonymity of all callers will be protected.

Importation of crawfish. All crawfish must conform to size limitations, that being the carapace must measure *more* than 3 inches in length. Since the rules regarding crawfish importation are subject to frequent change, the Florida Marine Patrol strongly recommends for your convenience that you bring in your crawfish whole (not separated) to avoid questions of legality. In open season (August 6 through March 31), the limit is 6 per person or 24 per boat, whichever is greater (two persons in a boat can possess 24; six persons can possess 36). On August 1, 1994, Florida crawfish were designated a restricted species, and for numbers in excess of the recreational bag limit a Florida Salt Water Products License (SPL) is required with a crawfish endorsement *and* a restricted species endorsement. No egg-bearing females may be taken, and eggs may not be stripped from a lobster. Persons returning from The Bahamas with more than the recreational bag limit must be in possession of appropriate receipts or bills of sale showing that the crawfish were purchased in a foreign country.

If any person takes crawfish in The Bahamas and returns with them to the U.S., the burden of proof is on that person to show that the crawfish came from The Bahamas. Bahamian recreational limit is six lobsters per person, and U.S. vessels are not allowed to harvest commercial quantities of lobster in The Bahamas. If you violate Bahamian law (see section on "Fishing, spearfishing and hunting rules" in *What the Skipper Should Know* for Bahamian crawfish regulations) and then make a border crossing into the U.S., it may be a violation of the Federal Lacey Act. Persons returning from The Bahamas by boat should proceed directly to the dock and not stop to fish or dive in Florida waters. If they are found fishing or diving in Florida waters, the legal presumption is that their entire catch came from Florida waters.

These rules were established by the Florida Marine Fisheries Commission and are enforced by the Florida Marine Patrol. If in doubt as to your status in regard to these rules, call the Florida Marine Patrol's Miami office at (305) 795-2145 or 1-800-DIAL-FMP (342-5367) before entering as violations are subject to heavy fines.

Thunderstorm approaches Great Guana Cay. (Tropic Isle photo)

WIND AND WEATHER

Nassau's all-year average air temperature is 77°F. The difference between maximum and minimum daily temperature is about 12° in all months of the year. The difference in mean temperature between the six coldest and six hottest months is a mere 8°. However, there are seasons in The Bahamas, winter and summer, which consist of two distinct weather patterns.

Winter weather. The winter weather pattern begins between November and January with a norther, an outbreak of cold, continental high-pressure air that interrupts the normal easterly flow of water-tempered air. Northers occur throughout the winter and typically start with the wind veering to the south and southwest. When the cold front arrives, the wind shifts suddenly to northwest, then works through north and blows itself out from northeast. In midwinter this cycle takes several days, and in spring only 24 hours. Winds vary from brisk sailing breezes to winds of 20-25 knots to anchor-rattlers.

A "rage" is a year-round phenomenon, but is more frequent in winter. Common in the Abacos, Nassau, Eleuthera or any other place exposed to the open sea, swells break heavily across various entrances to harbors and banks from the open ocean. Rages can be caused by oncoming cold fronts or offshore Atlantic storms. A rage can occur in beautiful weather, with no wind, caused by a disturbance so far distant that the weather that causes it never directly affects the islands. These rages can be spectacular; they are also extremely dangerous.

LOOK FOR US AT YACHTSMANSGUIDE.COM

Nassau and Miami regularly broadcast weather forecasts. By following the weather in the eastern United States you can get even earlier warning and some idea of the severity of a coming norther. After a Midwestern blizzard, when gale warnings go up south of Cape Hatteras, when South Carolina and Georgia report low temperatures, another norther is likely in the offing for The Bahamas. When the cold reaches northern Florida, it's only 12 hours from Nassau and even less from Grand Bahama and Abaco. The more severe the weather in the U.S., the colder and windier it's likely to become in the islands.

Most northers are dry, but some arrive with frontal rain or thunder squalls. A quarter of Nassau's annual rainfall of 50 inches comes from such showers. Typically the sky is deep blue, half-flecked with cotton-ball clouds that let sun shine brightly for eight hours a day.

Except for occasional anchor-draggers, storms with winds of over 34 knots are rare in winter. However, the captain of one of the fuel tankers that plies the islands told us of a phenomenon he has noticed around the northwest Little Bahama Bank in winter: northers sometimes seem to gain strength (perhaps from the Gulf Stream) and reach whole gale force with enough frequency that he thought we should mention it. So — follow the forecasts and beware if the wind veers to south.

Normal wind speeds are 5-15 knots, the lower figure more likely near

Dog day afternoon in Hope Town. (Tropic Isle photo)

shore, the higher over open water. Though Nassau shows calms in 7.5% of its daylight observations, there are few calms over open water in winter. A gust at sunrise is followed by a steady breeze that increases gradually until early afternoon. At sunset the wind often lessens and backs a point or two. Winds from northeast, east, and southeast account for two-thirds of all winter winds, with northeast and east winds outnumbering southeast winds three to one.

Summer weather. The summer weather pattern, ruled entirely by an easterly flow of maritime air, begins in May after the last norther. Winds from northeast, east, and southeast account for four-fifths of all summer winds, east and southeast winds now outnumbering northeast winds three to one. Winds are lighter in summer (5-12 knots), and calms at night are frequent. In August and September 12% of daytime observations at Nassau show calms. The sun still shines brightly for an average of 8 hours daily; puffy cumulus clouds still cover about half of the daytime sky.

Fed by updrafts over land or over shallow water, some of these dumpling clouds grow into towering thunderheads. They grow leisurely, are visible from a long way off, and move so slowly that you can sail around them or outrun them under power. They let go with fireworks, sound effects, and hailstone-sized drops over a small area, but usually without malicious winds. The bulk of Nassau's rainfall, which is 6 inches during each of the six summer months, comes from such showers.

The fuel-tanker captain mentioned above also told us that in his experience, in summer, the area around the northwest Little Bahama Bank down to

STUART YACHT

450 SW SALERNO ROAD, STUART, FL 34997
561 / 283-1947   PALM BEACH 561 / 747-1947   Fax 561 / 286-9800
G.N. Burdick, President / General Manager

Custom Yacht Design and Construction in Modern Composite Materials. Full Service Yacht Repair & Refinishing. Major Refits and Repowering. Sailboat Rigging and Refitting. Metal Fabrication - S/Steel and Aluminum. Electronics. Generators. Refrigeration & Air Conditioning. Water Makers.

★★★★★★★★★★

BROKERAGE OFFICE AT THE
STUART CORINTHIAN YACHT CLUB
TEL 561 / 283 - 9400 FAX 561 / 286 - 2494

★★★★★★★★★★

AWLGRIP

E-MAIL: syb@stuartyacht.com   INTERNET: http://www.stuartyacht.com
AMERICAN BOAT & YACHT COUNCIL, SOCIETY OF NAVAL ARCHITECTS & MARINE ENGINEERS.
MARINE INDUSTRIES ASSOCIATION, AMERICAN BOAT BUILDERS & REPAIRERS ASSOCIATION

Bimini produces more waterspouts than most others.

Several times during each summer the normal pattern is interrupted by an "easterly wave," the weatherman's name for a trough of low pressure in the trade wind belt. There is no change in temperature, but the pressure drops, humidity rises, and the atmosphere becomes unstable and ridden with thunderstorms. A mild easterly wave drifting over you with the prevailing wind merely brings more frequent showers. A severe wave passes in band after band of showers, with overcast skies and perhaps drizzle in between, and calms followed by gusty winds for as long as three days. Even while they are still hundreds of miles from land, these waves are carefully watched by weathermen because some develop into tropical depressions, areas of circular winds up to 35 knots. If the surface wind speed increases they become revolving tropical storms. With wind speeds of above 64 knots they are hurricanes.

Over many years the number of such storms over the North Atlantic, including the Caribbean and the Gulf of Mexico, averages seven per year. The probability of a storm in June, July, and November is one every other year; for August, September, and October it is two a year. But averages are not to be trusted; as few as two and as many as 21 tropical storms have been recorded in one year.

Storms of the early season tend to pass well south of The Bahamas. Skippers in the islands don't consider June and July dangerous months, but in August they are wary. In September and October they expect some storms that might threaten The Bahamas. Early reports from weather satellites, planes, and ships, and observation from hurricane hunter patrols let the weather bureau warn boatmen of storms in the making or on the move. These storms travel slowly at first, 8-10 knots perhaps, so warning of any danger usually comes early. Perhaps twice during a hurricane season, all craft are advised to seek shelter.

Keep in mind that a "rage" is a year-round phenomenon that can affect any area exposed to the open ocean. Although more common in winter, rage conditions with dangerous breaking swells can occur at any time during the year. (There is more information on rages in the preceding section on Winter Weather.)

Out Island weather. The Out Islands, though as far from end to end as South Carolina is from New York City, all have about the same climate. Most

Hurricane Andrew left the Current Club in rubble in 1992. (Tropic Isle photo)

Hurricane Caution

A number of long-term weather forecasters predict a period of increased hurricane activity affecting the United States and Caribbean, caused by changing oceanic circulation patterns, that could last for the next 20 years. Keep in mind that after a severe storm, aids to navigation may be missing, off station, or changed in other ways, and some depths and channels may be affected, perhaps never again to be the same. Local knowledge and an observant eye could be particularly important to you for some time after a storm passes through.

---

figures given for Nassau will serve for any of the islands.

Temperatures in the entire area are not very different from Nassau readings, but many northers stall or dissipate before even reaching George Town in the Exumas. Compared with Nassau, there are more northeast winter winds in Abaco and more southeast winds in the Exumas and the southern islands.

Weather reports. There are several radio facilities that add another safety factor to cruising. Broadcast times are subject to change during the year.

• Radio Bahamas ZNS 1, Nassau, 1540 kHz on the dial and carrying 20,000 watts, is on the air 24 hours. ZNS 1 broadcasts weather forecasts during regular newscasts, with weather updates at intervals throughout the day. ZNS 2, 1240 on the dial, 1000 watts, also broadcasts local weather throughout the day and carries the ZNS 1 weather program network. In Grand Bahama, Radio Bahamas northern service, ZNS 3 at 810 kHz, 1000 watts, carries Grand Bahama weather at intervals throughout the day and also broadcasts the weather broadcast from Nassau after national news broadcasts. You can also pick up ZNS-FM (107.9) from the repeater in Great Exuma.

• In The Bahamas, you can dial 915 by telephone (also reachable through marine operator) for a brief weather forecast from the Meteorological Service in Nassau, updated three times daily and available 24 hours a day.

• Nassau Marine Operator, Channel 27, broadcasts the latest weather information regularly on every even hour 24 hours a day and will also read it on request.

• Silbert Mills at Admiral Yacht Haven in Marsh Harbour broadcasts weather reports daily at 0815 on the cruiser's net.

• Wherever lots of cruising boats are gathered, like the Hub of Abaco or George Town, there usually springs up a cruiser's net, or someone takes it upon him/herself to rebroadcast weather reports via VHF. Check local knowledge.

• WOM (Fort Lauderdale High Seas Radiotelephone Service) broadcasts the National Weather Service information for the South Atlantic, Caribbean, and Gulf of Mexico areas on the following schedule: ITU channels 403, 802, 1206, 1601, and 2215 at 1300 and 2300 UTC. Note that channels listed for WOM are international frequency designators. Free literature about High Seas Radiotelephone Service is available; call 954-587-0910. Visitors are welcome at their facility at 1340 NW 40th Ave. in Fort Lauderdale.

• WEAT from West Palm Beach, 850 kHz, gives the NOAA marine forecast for Jupiter Inlet to Key Largo at 7:17 a.m., Monday through Saturday.

Spring shower and sunshine. (Tropic Isle photo)

• Miami Beach Coast Guard, SSB A3J, gives weather at 1150 and 2350 EST at 2670 kHz. Special broadcasts are made for boating safety and selected Notices to Mariners over VHF-FM Channel 22 at 0830 and 1830 EST.

• National Weather Service Coral Gables KHB-34, 162.55 MHz, and West Palm Beach KEC-50, 162-475 MHz, broadcast weather and marine information continuously on VHF radio. These stations are regularly heard in the closer Bahama islands. MF, Miami Radio Beacon, 365 kHz, broadcasts aircraft weather continuously.

• For the sailor cruising southeast from George Town in the Exumas, (out of range for the above broadcasts) station 4 BEH (Cap Haitien) 1030 kHz, offers world news and U.S. Weather Bureau Forecasts in English at 0700 (EST) Monday through Saturday.

• When cruising in the Out Islands, the most reliable sources of weather information are the Offshore Broadcasts from the USCG Station NMN in Portsmouth, Virginia. A good SSB communications receiver with the following frequencies is required. Frequencies and times (Z or UTC) are:

4426.0	6501.0	8764.0	13089.0	17314.0
0500	0500	0500	1130	1730
0930	0930	0930	1600	
	1130	1130	1730	
	1600	1600	2200	
	2200	2200	2330	
		2330		

Cruising Facilities Index

This information is supplied to us by the facilities themselves. What they say is available may be a bit imaginative at times, so, if something is important to you, we advise that you phone ahead to make sure they can provide what you need.

Facilities are listed in the order they appear in the Guide's text. For depth information, consult the text or contact the facility directly for availability. *Berths* indicate approximate number of berths. *Elec* indicates Electricity; *reps* indicate repairs. References *Groc* (Groceries), *Accom* (Accommodations), *Rest* (Restaurant), *Doc* (Doctor), *Dent* (Dentist) or *NC* (Nurse/Clinic) indicate availability nearby (walking distance or short taxi ride) if not on site . The notation *cba* indicates "can be arranged." For propane availability only, *TR* indicates taxi-ride distance.

Bimini/Cat Cay
Weech's Bimini Dock (242-347-3028) Berths 15, Engine reps (cba), Water, Ice, Elec, Showers, Groc, Laundry, Accom, Rest, Doc, NC

Sea Crest Hotel and Marina (242-347-3071) Berths 18, Engine reps, Propane, Water, Ice, Elec, Showers, Groc, Laundry, Accom, Rest, Doc, NC

Bimini Big Game Fishing Club & Hotel (242-347-3391) Berths 100, Gas/Oil, Diesel, Engine reps (cba), Water, Ice, Elec, Showers, Groc, Laundry, Accom, Rest, Doc, NC

Bimini Blue Water Resort (242-347-3166) Berths 32, Gas/Oil, Diesel, Engine reps (cba), Electronic reps (cba), Propane, Water, Ice, Elec, Showers, Groc, Laundry, Accom, Rest, Doc, NC

Cat Cay Yacht Club (954-359-8272) Berths 72, Gas/Oil, Diesel, Water, Ice, Elec, Showers, Groc, Laundry, Rest, Doc, NC

Berry Islands
→**Chub Cay Club** (242-325-1490) Berths 96, Gas/Oil, Diesel, Engine reps (cba), Water, Ice, Elec, Showers, Groc, Laundry, Accom, Rest

Great Harbour Cay Marina (242-367-8005) Berths 80, Gas/Oil, Diesel, Water, Ice, Elec, Showers, Groc, Laundry, Accom, Rest, Doc, NC

BERRY Isl. Club 7ft water 130ft - 877 795 1613

New Providence
East Bay Yacht Basin (242-394-1816) Berths 25, Gas/Oil, Diesel, Engine reps (cba) Propane, Water, Ice, Elec, Showers, Groc, Laundry, Accom, Rest, Dent, Doc, NC

The Marina at Atlantis (242-363-6068) Berths 63, Gas/Oil, Diesel, Hauling facilities, Engine reps (cba), Hull reps, Electronic reps (cba), Propane (TR), Water, Ice, Elec, Showers, Groc, Laundry, Accom, Rest, Dent, Doc, NC

Nassau Yacht Haven (242-393-8173) Berths 100, Gas/Oil, Diesel, Engine reps (cba), Electronic reps (cba), Propane, Water, Ice, Elec, Showers, Groc, Laundry, Accom, Rest, Dent, Doc, NC

Bayshore Marina (242-322-8232) Berths 150, Gas/Oil, Diesel, Hauling facilities, Hull reps, Water, Elec, Groc, Accom, Rest, Dent, Doc, NC

Nassau Harbour Club Hotel & Marina (242-393-0771) Berths 65, Diesel, Engine reps (cba), Electronic reps (cba), Propane, Water, Ice, Elec, Showers, Groc, Laundry, Accom, Rest, Dent, Doc, NC

Brown's Boat Basin (242-393-3331) Berths N/A, Gas/Oil, Diesel, Hauling facilities, Engine reps, Hull reps, Propane (TR), Water, Ice, Elec, Groc, Laundry, Accom, Dent, Doc, NC

Hurricane Hole Marina (242-326-3600) Berths 45, Diesel, Hauling facilities, Engine reps, Hull reps, Electronic reps, Propane, Water, Ice, Elec, Showers, Groc, Laundry, Accom, Rest, Dent, Doc, NC

Paradise Harbour Club and Marina (242-363-2992) Berths 20, Engine reps (cba), Electronic reps (cba), Propane (TR), Water, Ice, Elec, Showers, Groc, Laundry, Accom, Rest, Dent, Doc, NC

Lyford Cay Club Harbour (private) (242-362-4131) Berths 76, Gas/Oil, Diesel, Engine reps (cba), Electronic reps (cba), Propane (TR), Water, Ice, Elec, Showers, Groc, Laundry, Rest, Doc, NC

Grand Bahamas
Old Bahama Bay Marina (formerly Jack Tar) (242-346-6211) Berths (under reconstruction,

planned to be 100 in 1999), Gas/Oil, Diesel, Propane (TR), Water, Ice, Elec, Showers, Groc, Laundry, Rest, Doc, NC (development/expansion in progress; call ahead for facility update)

Harbour Hotel and Marina Berths 21, Gas/Oil, Diesel, Water, Elec, Groc, Laundry, Rest, Doc, NC

Xanadu Beach Resort and Marina (242-352-6783) Berths 60, Gas/Oil, Diesel, Engine reps (cba), Electronic reps (cba), Propane (TR), Water, Ice, Elec, Showers, Groc, Laundry, Accom, Rest, Dent, Doc, NC

Running Mon Marina (242-352-6834) Berths 28, Gas/Oil, Diesel, Hauling facilities, Engine reps, Hull reps, Propane, Water, Ice, Elec, Showers, Groc, Laundry, Accom, Rest, Dent, Doc, NC

Ocean Reef Yacht Club (242-373-4662) Berths 52, Engine reps (cba), Electronic reps (cba), Water, Ice, Elec, Showers, Laundry, Accom, Rest, Dent, Doc, NC

Lucayan Marina Village (242-373-7616) Berths 150, Gas/Oil, Diesel, Engine reps (cba), Electronic reps (cba), Propane (TR), Water, Ice, Elec, Showers, Groc, Laundry, Accom, Rest, Dent, Doc, NC

➤ **Port Lucaya Marina** (242-373-9090) Berths 100, Gas/Oil, Diesel, Engine reps (cba), Hull reps, Propane (TR), Water, Ice, Elec, Showers, Groc, Laundry, Accom, Rest, Dent, Doc, NC

Abaco

Walkers Cay Hotel and Marina (242-352-5252) Berths 75, Gas/Oil, Diesel, Water, Ice, Elec, Showers, Groc, Laundry, Accom, Rest, NC

Grand Cay-Island Bay Front Hotel (242-359-4476) Berths 15, Gas/Oil, Diesel, Water, Ice, Elec, Groc, Laundry, Rest, Accom, NC

Fox Town Shell Service (242-365-2046) Berths 4, Gas/Oil, Diesel, Water, Groc, Laundry, Rest

Spanish Cay (242-365-0083) Berths 70, Gas, Diesel, Engine reps (cba), Electronic reps (cba), Propane (TR), Water, Ice, Elec, Showers, Laundry, Accom, Rest, (Doc, NC at Cooper's Town)

Cooper's Town Shell (242-365-0161) Berths 6, Gas/Oil, Diesel, Engine reps (CBA), Elec reps (CBA), Propane (TR), Water, Ice, Elec, Showers, Groc, Laundry, Accom, Rest, Doc, NC

Murray's Service Station (ESSO) (Cooper's Town) (242-365-0039) Gas/Oil, Diesel, Engine reps (cba), Electronic reps (cba), Propane, Water, Ice, Elec, Showers, Groc, Laundry, Accom, Rest, Doc, NC

Abaco Yacht Services Ltd. (Green Turtle Cay) (242-365-4033) Berths 3, Hauling facilities, Engine reps (cba), Hull reps (ltd), Elec reps (cba), Water, Ice, Elec, Showers, Groc, Laundry, Accom, Rest, NC

Other Shore Club (Green Turtle Cay) (242-365-4195) Berths 15, Gas/Oil, Diesel, Engine reps (cba), Water, Ice, Elec, Showers, Groc, Laundry, Accom, Rest, NC

Roberts Dock and Cottages (Green Turtle Cay) 242-365-4105) Berths 4, Water (ltd.), Elec, Groc, Laundry, Accom, Rest, NC

Black Sound Marina (Green Turtle Cay) (242-365-4531) Berths 15, Engine repairs (cba), Water, Ice, Elec, Showers, Groc, Laundry, Accom, NC

Bluff House Beach Hotel and Marina (Green Turtle Cay) (242-365-4247) Berths 20, Gas/Oil, Diesel, Engine reps (cba), Electronic reps (cba), Propane (TR), Water, Ice, Elec, Showers, Groc, Laundry, Accom, Rest, Dent, Doc, NC

Green Turtle Club & Marina (Green Turtle Cay) (242-365-4271) Berths 35, Gas/Oil, Diesel, Engine reps (cba), Electronic reps (cba), Propane (TR), Water, Ice, Elec, Showers, Groc, Laundry, Accom, Rest, Dent, Doc, NC

Dolphin Marine (Green Turtle Cay) (242-365-4262) Berths N/A, Hauling facilities, Engine reps, Groc

Treasure Cay Hotel Resort & Marina (242-365-8250) Berths 150, Gas/Oil, Diesel, Engine reps (cba), Electronic reps (cba), Water, Ice, Elec, Showers, Groc, Laundry, Accom, Rest, Dent, Doc, NC

Guana Beach Resort (242-365-5133) Berths 22, Water, Ice, Elec, Showers, Groc, Accom, Rest, NC

Orchid Bay Yacht Club & Marina (Guana Cay) (242-365-5175) Berths 32, Gas/Oil, Diesel, Engine reps (cba), Electronic reps (cba), Water, Elec, Showers, Groc, Laundry

NOTE TO CRUISING FACILITIES

Please send updates for the 2000 Guide (mail or fax only) to the Editor, Yachtsman's Guide to the Bahamas,, P.O. Box 15397, Plantation, FL 33318; FAX 954-321-0806. Include name of contact, address, and telephone and FAX numbers. We must recieve it before August 1999.

Edwin's Boat Yard (Man of War Cay) (242-365-6006) Berths N/A, Hauling facilities, Engine rep (cba), Hull reps, Electronic repairs (cba), Propane, Water, Elec, Showers, Groc, Laundry, Accom, Rest

Man-O-War Marina (Man of War Cay) (242-365-6008) Berths 26, Gas/Oil, Diesel, Engine reps (cba), Electronic reps (cba), Water, Ice, Elec, Showers, Groc, Laundry, Accom, Rest, Dent, Doc, NC

Conch Inn Marina (Marsh Harbour) (242-367-4000) Berths 75, Gas/Oil, Diesel, Engine reps, Electronic reps, Propane, Water, Ice, Elec, Showers, Groc, Laundry, Accom, Rest, Dent, Doc, NC

Mangoes Marina (Marsh Harbour) (242-367-4255) Berths 30, Engine reps (cba), Electronic reps (cba), Propane (TR), Water, Ice, Elec, Showers, Groc, Laundry, Accom, Rest, Dent, Doc, NC

Harbour View Marina (Marsh Harbour) (242-367-2182) Berths 40, Gas/Oil, Diesel, Engine reps (cba), Electronic reps (cba), Propane, Water, Ice, Elec, Showers, Groc, Laundry, Accom, Rest, Dent, Doc, NC

Triple-J Marine (Marsh Harbour) (242-367-2163) Berths 26, Gas/Oil, Diesel, Propane (TR), Water, Ice, Elec, Showers, Groc, Laundry, Accom, Rest, Dent, Doc, Berths 26, Engine reps (cba), Electronic reps (cba), Propane, Water, Ice, Elec, Showers, Groc, Laundry, Accom, Rest, Dent, Doc

Abaco Beach Resort & Boat Harbour (Marsh Harbour) (242-367-2158) Berths 182, Gas/Oil, Diesel, Engine reps (cba), Electronic reps (cba), Propane (TR), Water, Ice, Elec, Showers, Groc, Laundry, Accom, Rest, Dent, Doc, NC

Marsh Harbour Marina (Marsh Harbour) (242-367-2700) Berths 50, Gas/Oil, Diesel, Engine reps (cba), Electronics reps (cba), Propane, Water, Ice, Elec, Showers, Groc, Laundry, Accom, Rest, Dent, Doc, NC

Lighthouse Marina (Hope Town) (242-366-0154) Berths 6, Gas/Oil, Diesel, Hauling facilities, Engine reps, Hull reps, Water, Ice, Elec, Showers, Laundry, Accom, Rest, NC

Hope Town Marina (Hope Town) (242-366-0254) Berths 12, Water, Ice, Elec, Showers, Groc, Laundry, Accom, Rest

Hope Town Hideaways Marina (Hope Town) (242-366-0224) Berths 12, Electronic reps (cba), Water, Ice, Elec, Showers, Groc, Laundry, Accom, Rest

Abaco Inn (Elbow Cay) (242-366-0133) Berths 0 (Med-style Docking), Ice, Accom, Rest, Doc, NC

Sea Spray Resort (Elbow Cay) (242-366-0065) Berths 24, Gas/Oil, Diesel, Engine reps (cba), Electronic reps (cba), Propane (TR), Water, Ice, Elec, Showers, Groc, Accom, Rest, Doc, NC

Andros

Morgan's Bluff Esso (242-329-2519) Gas/Oil, Diesel, Ice, Water, Rest

Kamalame Cay Marina (formerly Ting'Um Quay Marina) (Staniard Creek) (242-368-6281) Berths 3, Gas/Oil, Diesel, Engine reps (cba), Electronic reps (cba), Propane, Water, Ice, Elec, Showers, Groc, Accom, Rest, Doc, NC (development/expansion in progress; call ahead for facility update)

Lighthouse Club and Marina (Andros Town) (242-368-2305) Berths 17, Gas/Oil, Diesel, Engine reps (cba), Propane, Water, Elec, Showers, Groc, Laundry, Accom, Rest, Dent, Doc, NC

Eleuthera

Spanish Wells Yacht Haven (242-333-4255) Berths 35, Gas/Oil, Diesel, Propane, Water, Ice, Elec, Showers, Groc, Laundry, Rest, Dent, Doc, NC

Spanish Wells Marine & Hardware (242-333-4122) Berths 10, Gas/Oil, Diesel, Hauling facilities (up to 30' boat), Engine reps (ltd.), Hull reps (minor), Electronic reps (cba), Propane, Water, Ice, Elec, Groc, Laundry, Accom, Rest, Doc, NC

R & B Boat Yard (formerly Pool's Drydock) (Spanish Wells) (242-333-4462) Berths N/A, Hauling facilities, Engine reps (cba), Hull reps, Electronic reps (cba), Propane, Groc, Accom, Rest, Doc, NC

Valentine's Yacht Club & Inn (Harbour Island) (242-333-2142) Berths 38, Diesel, Propane , Water, Ice, Elec, Showers, Groc, Laundry, Accom, Rest, Doc, NC

Harbour Island Club & Marina (242-333-2427) Berths 32, Gas/Oil, Diesel, Engine reps (cba), Electronic reps (cba), Propane (TR), Water, Ice, Elec, Showers, Groc, Laundry, Accom, Rest, Doc, NC

Marine Service of Eleuthera (242-332-0186) Gas (nearby)/Oil, Diesel, Hauling facilities, Engine reps, Hull reps, Propane, Water, Ice, Elec, Groc, Laundry, Accom, Rest, Dent, Doc, NC

Cape Eleuthera Marina (242-334-6312) Berths 28, Gas/Oil, Diesel, Engine reps (cba), Propane (TR), Water, Elec

Davis Harbour Marina (242-334-6303) Berths 18, Gas/Oil, Diesel, Propane (TR), Water, Ice, Elec,

Continued on page 63

Always within reach!

COAST STATIONS

CELLULAR LOCATIONS

VHF (Channel 16)

West End
GRAND BAHAMA
Freeport
Fox Town
BIMINI
Basset Cove
Coupers Town
CH 27
Treasure Cay
BERRY ISLANDS
Marsh Harbour
Bullock's Harbour
ABACO
TRANSMIT 2522 KHZ
RECEIVE 2126 KHZ
CH 27
Sandy Point
TRANSMIT 2582 KHZ (SSB)
RECEIVE 2186 KHZ (SSB)
Nicholl's Town
Harbour Island
Fresh Creek
ANDROS
NASSAU
Lower
Bogue
Hatchet Bay
Cargill Creek
Governor's Harbour
ELEUTHERA
Kemp's Bay
Green Castle
Exuma
Cays
Highbourne Cay
Staniel Cay
CAT ISLAND
Little Farmer's
Cay
New Bight
George Town
Rolleville
SAN SALVADOR
William's Town
RUM CAY
LONG ISLAND
Simms
Clarence Town
CROOKED ISLAND
ACKLINS
Ragged Island
MAYAGUANA
LITTLE INAGUA
GREAT
INAGUA
Matthew Town

COAST STATION FREQUENCIES: (TRANSMIT - RECEIVE)
NASSAU MARINE (SSB) 2522 KHZ (UPPER) - 2126 KHZ (UPPER)
NASSAU MARINE VHF CH27 161.960 KHZ - 157. 350 MHZ
EIGHT MILE ROCK MARINE VHF CH27 161.950 MHZ 157.350 MHZ
DISTRESS & CALLING 2182 KHZ

We keep you in touch with the world
For further information call:
IN NASSAU 242-328-0990 • IN FREEPORT 242-352-3500 • FROM THE FAMILY ISLANDS 1-242-300-1234
FAX: 242-328-0966 • e mail: bmrkt@batelnet.bs

SAVE MONEY!...Use the **Bahamas Direct Prepaid Card** to call from The Bahamas to anywhere in the world.

CUT OUT AND REDEEM THIS COUPON FOR YOUR **FREE PREPAID CARD** AT ANY BATELCO CENTRAL TELEGRAPH OFFICE.

Bahamas Direct
PREPAID CARD

YG98

READING THE DEPTH OF THE WATER BY ITS COLOR

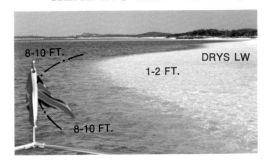

◀ The obvious deep water which carries 8-10 feet lies to the left of the shallow sand, the edge of which is steep, forming an ideal soft place to careen a vessel for a bottom scrub.

The shallow coral head off the port ▶ bow joins with the shallower brown bar which extends off to the right. Round the head and keep the bar well off to port.

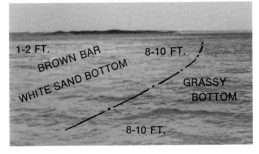

Enter the harbour entrance channel over the green water and grassy patch squarely between the shallow rocky bars. ▶

◀ Stay over the deeper sand and grassy patches while rounding the shallow brown bar on the port hand.

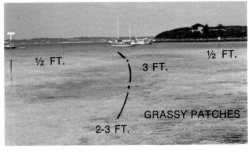

Enter this channel over the darker ▶ blue water between the sand bars. Note that the deeper water further up the channel lies close under the land.

Editor's Note: The flag in the above photographs is the club burgee of the Bahamas Out Island Squadron.

◀ Negotiate this dredged channel slowly as the bottom is hard marl with occasional grassy patches. Stay equi-distant between the tidal flat over the darkest green water.

Continued from page 60

Showers, Groc (TR), Laundry, Accom (TR), Rest (TR), Dent, Doc, NC

Exuma
Highborne Cay Marina (242-355-1008) Berths 30, Gas/Oil, Diesel, Water, Ice, Elec, Groc, Laundry, Accom

Compass Cay Marina Ltd. (242-355-2064) Berths 11, Engine reps (cba), Electronic reps (cba), Water, Ice, Electricity, Groc (ltd.), Accom (house rental)

Sampson Cay Club (242-355-2034) Berths 25, Gas/Oil, Diesel, Engine reps, Hull reps, Ice, Elec, Groc, Laundry, Accom, Rest

Staniel Cay Yacht Club (242-355-2024) Berths 12, Gas/Oil, Diesel, Engine reps (cba), Electronic reps (cba), Propane, Water, Ice, Elec, Groc, Laundry, Accom, Rest

Happy People Marina (Staniel Cay) (242-355-2008) Berths 7, Engine reps (cba), Electronic reps (cba), Propane, Water, Ice, Elec, Showers, Groc, Laundry, Accom, Rest, Nurse and clinic

Farmer's Cay Yacht Club & Marina (242-355-4017) Berths 4, Gas/Oil, Diesel, Engine reps, Electronic reps, Propane, Water Ice, Elec, Showers, Groc, Accom, Rest, NC

Exuma Docking Services (George Town) (242-336-2578) Berths 40, Gas/Oil, Diesel, Engine reps (cba). Electronic reps (cba), Propane, Water, Ice, Elec, Showers, Groc, Laundry, Accom, Rest, Dent, Doc, NC

George Town Marina (Master Harbour, Red Shank Cays) Hauling facilities, Hull reps

Long Island -
Stella Maris Marina (242-338-2055) Berths 12, Gas/Oil, Diesel, Hauling facilities, Engine reps, Hull reps, Electronic reps, Propane (TR), Water, Ice, Elec, Showers, Groc, Laundry, Accom, Rest, Doc, NC

Harding's Supply Center (Salt Pond) (242-337-3333) Berths 4, Gas/Oil, Diesel, Engine reps, Electronic reps (cba), Propane (TR), Ice, Groc, Accom, Rest, Doc (10 mi.), NC (10 mi.)

Clarence Town Dock (242-357-1004) Berths 5, Gas/Oil, Diesel, Engine reps (cba), Electronic reps (cba), Propane (TR), Ice, Elec, Groc, Laundry, Rest, Dent, Doc, NC

Cat Island
Hawk's Nest Resort & Marina (242-342-7051) Berths 8, Gas/Oil, Diesel, Engine reps (cba), Electronic reps (cba), Water, Ice, Elec, Showers, Laundry, Accom, Rest, Doc, NC

San Salvador
Riding Rock Inn Resort & Marina (242-342-7050) Berths 8, Gas/Oil, Diesel, Engine reps (cba), Electronic reps (cba), Water, Ice, Elec, Showers, Groc, Laundry, Accom, Rest, Doc, NC

Rum Cay
Sumner Point Marina Berths 18, Gas/Oil, Diesel, Engine reps (cba), Hull reps, Electronic reps (cba), Water, Ice, Elec, Groc, Laundry, Rest

Turks and Caicos Islands
Flamingo Cove (Grand Turk) (649-946-2227) Berths 8, Oil, Diesel, Engine reps (cba), Hull reps, Electronic reps (cba), Propane (TR), Water, Elec, Accom, Rest, Dent, Doc, NC

Texaco Caribbean Inc. (Grand Turk) Gas, Diesel

Sea View Marina (Cockburn Town) (649-946-3245) Berths 3, Gas/Oil, Diesel, Hauling facilities, Engine reps, Electronic reps, Propane, Water, Ice, Elec, Showers, Groc, Laundry, Accom, Rest, NC

Pinnacle Fuel Suppliers Ltd. (Cockburn Town) (649-946-3283) Gas/Oil, Water (cba)

Turtle Cove Marina (Provo) (649-946-5600) Berths 32, Gas/Oil, Diesel, Engine reps (cba), Electronic reps (cba), Propane (TR), Water, Ice, Elec, Accom, Rest, Dent, Doc, NC

Caicos Marina and Shipyard (Provo) (649-946-5600) Berths 12, Diesel, Hauling facilities, Engine reps (cba), Hull reps, Elec reps (cba), Propane (TR), Water, Ice, Elec, Showers, Groc, Laundry, Accom, Rest

Leeward Marina (Provo) (649-946-5000/553) Berths 17, Gas/Oil, Diesel, Engine reps (cba), Electronic reps (cba), Propane, Water, Ice, Elec, Groc (TR), Laundry, Accom, Rest, Dent, Doc, N/C

Diving Facilities Index

Most yachtsmen keep masks and snorkels aboard, not just for underwater boat maintenance and checking their anchors, but because the Bahama islands offer almost limitless undersea exploring possibilities. You might just want to snorkel around on the surface; certainly the shallow water of The Bahamas provides some of the best snorkeling territory in the world. Or, if you're scuba-certified, there are all kinds of dives: drift dives, wreck dives, reef dives, dramatic drop-off dives. There are shallow coral reefs alive with brilliant parrotfish, angelfish, and triggerfish. Friendly grouper swim about close to the bottom, near caves and rocks. Vertical walls drop thousands of feet to the ocean floor, lined with a descending parade of spectacular sea life.

We recommend that you dive with a guide from one of the many dive concessions throughout the islands. Tank refills are usually available, and some shops rent underwater photo equipment and have photo labs that will develop your film. If you aren't certified, most of the dive resorts offer instruction with certification.

Remember that it is illegal to use or import any type of trigger-actuated spear gun. The use of a Hawaiian sling is allowed only with mask, fins, and snorkel and *not* with scuba.

In a dive-related medical emergency, contact BASRA for immediate local assistance. There are recompression chambers at UNEXSO in Freeport, Grand Bahama; AUTEC, Andros; Providenciales, Turks and Caicos; and at the NOAA Diving/Hyperbaric Center on Virginia Key in Miami. If the Miami chamber is needed, call either of these 24-hour numbers: U.S. Coast Guard (305) 536-5611 or Dade County Emergency Rescue (305) 271-8996. They will contact the chamber and necessary doctors to be ready for your arrival.

Following is a list of many of the dive facilities available in The Bahamas. Some shops rent equipment only to those divers going on their tours, so check ahead about your particular needs. The location of the shop is noted if the mailing address does not supply that information. "All equipment" denotes mask, fins, snorkels, BC (buoyancy compensator), regulator, tank, pac, and weight belt.

NOTE TO DIVING FACILITIES

We need any updates of information for our diving facilities index for the next (2000) Yachtsman's Guide to the Bahamas *no later than* **June 1, 1999.** *Please send (mail or fax only) revisions to the Editor,* Yachtsman's Guide to the Bahamas, *P.O. Box 15397, Plantation, FL 33318; FAX 954-321-0806. Include name of contact, address, and telephone and FAX numbers.*

ABACO

BRENDAL'S DIVE SHOP INTERNATIONAL LTD., Green Turtle Cay, Abaco, Bahamas. Contact: Brendal Stevens. Instruction: Certification and Resort. Tours: Group and Custom. Rent all equipment. Sales, airfills.

DIVE ABACO, P.O. Box AB 20555, Marsh Harbour, Abaco, Bahamas. Location: Conch Inn Marina. Contact: Keith Rogers. Instruction: Certification and Introductory lessons. Tours: Group and Custom. Rent all equipment, some sales. Airfills.

MAN-O-WAR MARINA, Man of War Cay, Abaco, Bahamas. Contact: Tommy Albury. Tours: Custom. Rent tanks and weights. Sell snorkels and some dive equipment. Airfills.

TREASURE CAY DIVE CENTER, c/o Treasure Cay Services. 2301 S. Federal Highway, Fort Lauderdale, FL 33316. Location: Treasure Cay Beach Hotel. Contact: Elliott Aronowitz. Instruction: Resort. Tours: Group. Rent all equipment. Airfills.

WALKER'S CAY DIVE SHOP, c/o Walker's Cay Hotel, 700 SW 34th St., Fort Lauderdale, FL 33315. Location: Walker's Cay Hotel. Contact: Gary Adkison or Barry Albury. Instruction: Certification and Resort. Tours: Group and Custom. Rent all equipment. Airfills.

ANDROS

SMALL HOPE BAY LODGE, P.O. Box 21667, Fort Lauderdale, FL 33335. Location: Fresh Creek. Contact: Peter Douglas. Instruction: Certification and Resort. Tours: Group and Custom. Equipment rental with dive. Airfills.

BIMINI

BIMINI UNDERSEA ADVENTURES, P.O. Box 21766, Fort Lauderdale, FL 33335. Location: Alice Town. Contact: Bill and Nowdla Keefe. Instruction: Certification and Resort. Tours: Group and Custom. Rent all equipment. Airfills.

(Minitour photo)

ELEUTHERA

ROMORA BAY CLUB, P.O. Box 7026, Boca Raton, FL 33431. Location: Harbour Island. Contact: Jeff Fox. Instruction: Certification and Resort. Tours: Group. Rent all equipment. Airfills.

VALENTINE'S DIVE CENTER, P.O. Box 1, Harbour Island, Eleuthera, Bahamas. Contact: Rose Liva or Bob Beregowitz. Instruction: Certification through Instructor. Tours: Group and Custom. Rent and sell all equipment. Airfills.

EXUMA

SAMPSON CAY CLUB, P.O. Box SS-6247, Nassau, Bahamas. Contact: Marcus Mitchell. Instruction: Resort. Tours: Custom. Airfills

EXUMA DIVE CENTRE, George Town, Exuma, Bahamas. Contact: John and Connie Dey. Instruction and equipment rental.

GRAND BAHAMA ISLAND

GRAND BAHAMAS WATERSPORTS, P.O. Box F-43819, Freeport, Grand Bahama, Bahamas. Contact: Fred Riger. Instruction: Certification, Resort, Divemaster. Tours: Group and Custom.

UNDERWATER EXPLORERS SOCIETY (UNEXSO), P.O. Box F-42433, Freeport, Grand Bahama, Bahamas. Instruction: Certification, Checkout dives, and Resort. Tours: Group and Custom. Rent and sell all equipment. Airfills.

LONG ISLAND

STELLA MARIS INN, P.O. Box SM-105, Long Island, Bahamas, Instruction: Certification and Resort. Tours: Group and Custom. Rent all equipment, some sales. Airfills.

NEW PROVIDENCE

BAHAMAS DIVERS (1976) CO. LTD., P.O. Box SS-5004, Nassau, Bahamas. Location: Nassau Yacht Haven. Instruction: Certification and Resort. Tours: Group and Custom. Rent and sell all equipment. Airfills.

SUNSKIFF DIVE CENTER, P.O. Box N-142, Nassau, Bahamas. Location: Coral Harbour. Contact: Chrys Cheong or Monty Doyle. Instruction: Certification and Resort. Tours: Group and Custom. Rent all equipment. Airfills.

DIVER'S HAVEN, P.O. Box N-1658, Nassau, Bahamas. Contact: Wenzel Nicolls. Instruction: Certification. Tours: Group and Custom. Rent and sell all equipment. Airfills.

NASSAU SCUBA CENTRE, P.O. Box 21766, Fort Lauderdale, FL 33335. Location: Coral Harbour. Contact: Neal Watson. Instruction: Certification and Resort. Tours: Group and Custom. Rent all equipment. Airfills.

STUART COVE'S DIVE SOUTH OCEAN, P.O. Box CB13137, Nassau, Bahamas. Location: South Ocean Golf and Beach Resort. Contact: Stuart Cove. Instruction: Certification and Resort. Tours: Group and Custom. Rent and sell all equipment. Airfills.

DIVE, DIVE, DIVE, LTD., P.O. Box N-8050, Nassau, Bahamas. Location: Coral Harbour. Instruction: Certification and Resort. Tours: Group and Custom. Rent and sell all equipment. Airfills.

SAN SALVADOR

RIDING ROCK INN, c/o Out Island Service Co., 1170 Lee Wagener Blvd., Suite 103, Fort Lauderdale, FL 33315. Location: Riding Rock Inn Resort & Marina, Cockburn Town. Instruction: Certification and Resort. Tours: Group and Custom. Rent all equipment.

TURKS AND CAICOS

BLUE WATER DIVERS, P.O. Box 124, Grand Turk, Turks and Caicos, BWI. Contact: Mitch Rolling. Instruction: Certification and Resort. Tours: Group and Custom. Rent and sell all equipment. Airfills.

ART PICKERING'S PROVO TURTLE DIVERS, P.O. Box 219, Turtle Cove Marina, Provo, Turks and Caicos, BVI. Location: Ocean Club Condos and Turtle Cove Inn, Provo. Contact: Art Pickering. Instruction: Certification and Resort. Tours: Group and Custom. Rent and sell all equipment. Airfills.

SEA EYE DIVING, P.O. Box 67, Grand Turk, Turks and Caicos, BWI. Locations: Hotel Kittina and Duke St. Contact: Cecil Ingham. Instruction: Certification and Resort. Tours: Group and Custom. Rent and sell all equipment. Airfills.

DIVE PROVO, P.O. Box 350, Provo, Turks and Caicos, BWI. Locations: Turquoise Reef Resort and Casino, Grace Bay. Instruction: Certification and Resort. Tours: Group and Custom. Rent and sell all equipment. Airfills.

FLAMINGO DIVERS, P.O. Box 322, Provo, Turks and Caicos. Location: Turtle Cove Landing. Instruction: Certification and Resort. Tours: Group and Custom. Rent and sell all equipment. Airfills.

Doesn't the Kalik truck deliver to the dock? (Salt Pond, Long Island) (Tropic Isle photo)

RADIO FACILITIES

COMMERCIAL BROADCAST

Nassau Broadcasting

Station ZNS I •*ID Code* ZNS 1 • *Tr* 1540 kHz • *Loc* 25:05N 77:22W • *Hrs EST* 24 hrs • *Remarks* Reports at intervals during regular broadcasts

Station ZNS II •*ID Code* ZNS II • *Tr* 1240 kHz • *Loc* 25:05N 77:22W • *Hrs EST* 24 hrs • *Remarks* Also reports at intervals

Station ZNS III (Freeport) • *ID Code* ZNS III • *Tr* 810 kHz • *Loc* 26:32N 78:41W • *Hrs EST* 24 hrs • *Remarks* Also reports at intervals

MARINE FACILITIES

Nassau Marine Operator • *ID Code* C6N3 • *Tr/Rec* VHF 27 • *Loc* 25:05N 77:22W • *Hrs EST* 24 hrs • *Remarks* Weather forecasts, even hrs

Nassau Marine Operator • *ID Code:* C6N3 • *Tr/Rec* 2182 kHz • *Loc* 25:05N 77:22W • *Hours EST* 24 hrs • *Remarks* International distress

Nassau Radio • *ID Code* C6N3 • *Tr/Rec* VHF 16

Nassau Marine Operator • *ID Code* C6N2 • *Tr/Rec* 2522/2126 kHz • *Loc* 25:05N 77:22W • *Hrs EST* 24 hrs •   Weather forecasts at even intervals

Marsh Harbour (Abaco) • *ID Code* Call Marsh Harbour Operator • *Tr/Rec* 2582 kHz/2106 kHz • *Loc* 26:33N 77:03W • *Hrs EST* 0730-1930

Freeport (Grand Bahama) • *ID Code* Call Freeport Harbour Control • *Tr/Rec* VHF 16 • *Loc* 26.31N 78:40W • *Hrs EST* 24 hrs • *Remarks* International Distress

Freeport (Grand Bahama) • *ID Code* Call BASRA Freeport • *Tr/Rec* VHF 16, 86, 84 • *Loc* 26:30N 78:46W • *Hrs EST* 0800-2200 • *Remarks* International Distress

Grand Turk Marine Operator • *ID Code* VSI • *Tr/Rec* 2182 kHz • *Loc* 21:28N 71:09W • *Hrs EST* 0100-0120 • *Remarks* For medical advice, request services of Turks Is. Health Officer

(Grand Turk Marine Operator) • *ID Code* VSI • *Tr/Rec* 2590 kHz • *Loc* Same as above • *Hrs EST* 1500-1520

(Grand Turk Marine Operator) • *ID Code* VSI • *Tr/Rec* VHF 16 • *Loc* Same as above • *Hrs EST* 1900-1920

Great Inagua • *ID Code* Call BASRA Great Inagua • *Tr/Rec* 2182 kHz, 2638 kHz, 2738 kHz • *Loc* 20:58N 73:40W • *Hrs EST* 0730-1930 • *Remarks* International Distress

RADIO BEACONS

Note: *We get many reports about radio beacons that are not working. Be prepared for this eventuality. Many that are working provide only a weak output, and reception is often difficult; adjusting up or down may help.*

Chub Cay • *ID Code* Z C C • *Tr* 302 kHz • *Loc* 25:25N 77:53 W

Governor's Harbour • *ID Code* G H B • *Tr* 224 kHz • *Loc* 25:17N 76:20W

Freeport • *ID Code* Z F P • *Tr* 209 kHz • *Loc* 26:33N 78:42W • *Remarks* At entrance to harbour

Fort Lauderdale (FL) • *ID Code* P J N • *Tr* 242 kHz • *Loc* 26:08N 80:13W

Grand Turk • *ID Code* G T • *Tr* 232 kHz • *Loc* 21:28N 71:08W

Great Inagua • *ID Code* Z I N • *Tr* 376 kHz • *Loc* 20:59N 73:40W

Hillsboro Inlet (FL) • *ID Code* Q • *Tr* 299 kHz • *Loc* 26:15N 80:05W

Jupiter Inlet (FL) • *ID Code* J • *Tr* 294 kHz • *Loc* 26:57N 80:04W • *Remarks* 20 min-30 min and 50 min-60 min

Marsh Harbour • *ID Code* Z M H • *Tr* 361 kHz • *Loc* 26:31N 77:05W

Miami, Government Cut • *ID Code* U • *Tr* 322 kHz • *Loc* 25:46N 80:08W

Miami Intl. Airport • *ID Code* M F • *Tr* 365 kHz • *Loc* 25:48N 80:23W

Nassau Int'l Airport • *ID Code* Z Q A • *Tr* 251 kHz • *Loc* 25:02N 77:28W

Palm Beach Intl Airport • *ID Code* P B • *Tr* 356 kHz • *Loc* 26:41N 80:11W

Perrine (FL) • *ID Code* P R R • *Tr* 266 kHz • *Loc* 25:36N 80:32W

Providenciales • *ID Code* P V • *Tr* 387 kHz • *Loc* 21:41N 72:15W

Rock Sound • *ID Code* R S D • *Tr* 348 kHz • *Loc* 24:54N 76:10W

San Salvador • *ID Code* S S J • *Tr* 281 kHz • *Loc* 24:04N 74:13W

South Caicos • *ID Code* S C • *Tr* 260 kHz • *Loc* 21:30N 71:31W

Treasure Cay • *ID Code* Z T C • *Tr* 233 kHz • *Loc* 26:44N 77.22W

Walker's Cay • *ID Code* Z W C • *Tr* 280 kHz • *Loc* 27:16N 78:23W

A—ALPHA	• —		S—SIERRA	• • •
B—BRAVO	— • • •		T—TANGO	—
C—CHARLIE	— • — •		U—UNIFORM	• • —
D—DELTA	— • •		V—VICTOR	• • • —
E—ECHO	•		W—WHISKEY	• — —
F—FOXTROT	• • — •		X—RAY	— • • —
G—GOLF	— — •		Y—YANKEE	— • — —
H—HOTEL	• • • •		Z—ZULU	— — • •
I—INDIA	• •		0—ZE-RO	— — — — —
J—JULIET	• — — —		1—WUN	• — — — —
K—KILO	— • —		2—TOO	• • — — —
L—LIMA	• — • •		3—TREE	• • • — —
M—MIKE	— —		4—FOWer	• • • • —
N—NOVEMBER	— •		5—FIFE	• • • • •
O—OSCAR	— — —		6—SIX	— • • • •
P—PAPA	• — — •		7—SEVEN	— — • • •
Q—QUEBEC	— — • —		8—AIT	— — — • •
R—ROMEO	• — •		9—NIN-er	— — — — •

• THIS IS THE ROYAL BAHAMAS DEFENCE FORCE •

RBDF ships are easily recognized. All are painted the traditional naval grey, with white pennant numbers painted on their sides. Their crews wear uniforms; either working blues, tropical whites, or green camouflage battle dress. They will be armed with automatic weapons and/or pistols. The names of the patrol craft are:

PO1 HMBS Marlin 103' Patrol Boat
PO3 HMBS Yellow Elder 108' Patrol Boat
PO4 HMBS Port Nelson 108' Patrol Boat
PO5 HMBS Samana 108' Patrol Boat
P10 HMBS San Salvador II 95' Patrol Boat
P11 HMBS Fort Fincastle 95' Patrol Boat
P27 HMBS Inagua 60' Patrol Boat
A01 HMBS Fort Montague 90' Supply Craft
HMBS P34 40' Patrol Boat
HMBS P38 45' Patrol Boat
HMBS P42 40' Dauntless Search & Rescue
HMBS P43 40' Dauntless Search & Rescue
HMBS P41 27' Challenger Boston Whaler
HMBS P110 21' Impact Boston Whaler
HMBS P111 21' Impact Boston Whaler
HMBS P112 19' Wahoo
HMBS P113 19' Wahoo

Note: HMBS stands for Her Majesty's Bahamian Ship.

The Royal Bahamas Defence Force is a vibrant, multi-mission force that has been described as the "best little navy in the Caribbean." It became a legal entity on 31 March 1980, with the passing of the Defence Act, but was active since 1978 working with marine police, whom it superseded. After independence in July 1973, it became apparent that a sovereign nation with the second longest coastline in the Caribbean (2,200 nm) and 700 islands and cays sprawled over 100,000 square miles of sea, would need to keep a maritime presence in that vast area to protect its interest. The Defence Force is required to not only protect the Commonwealth of The Bahamas, but to combat fish and crawfish poaching, illegal immigration, drug smuggling, and of course, to provide aid and succor wherever and whenever required to boaters visiting The Bahamas.

HARDWARE An assortment of 17 coastal and inshore patrol craft makes up the Defence Force fleet. Quick mobilization and the ability for rapid deployment are the operating principles of the squadron. Two fixed wing aircraft, a Cessna Golden Eagle 421 C and a Cessna Titan Ambassador 404, constitute the Air Wing and are used chiefly for reconnaissance, maritime air patrol in support of surface craft, SAR and transportation.

PERSONNEL Manpower is just under 900, including 61 officers and 99 women under the command of a Bahamian Commodore. Because of the multiplicity of tasks, Defence Force personnel train at some of the finest establishments in the world, among them Britannia Royal Naval College in England and the US Coast Guard Officer Candidate School, Yorktown, Virginia.

MISSIONS In addition to its maritime law-enforcement duties, the guiding mission of the Defence Force is the preservation of the free and tranquil use of the waters of The Bahamas for the thousands of boaters who visit The Bahamas annually. The jewelled waters of The Bahamas also lure criminals seeking to abuse the geography of The Bahamas to traffic drugs, and the Defence Force is constantly on patrol to search assiduously, identify positively and deal vigorously with offenders. These efforts, in tandem with local law-enforcement agencies and the United States Coast Guard and Customs, have succeeded in making The Bahamas such a "heat" area that traffickers have steadily abandoned The Bahamas for alternative routes.

BOARDING AND SEARCH The above scenario means that it will be necessary to board your boat to ascertain that you are eligible for the time-honoured right of innocent seafarers to roam the seas at will. Rest assured that the boarding party will be polite and endeavor not to alarm you in any way, but it is standard procedure and a necessary precaution for them to carry small arms. As an excerpt from the 1992-93 edition of the Defence Force magazine *Defender* explains: "Safety is the prime concern of every boarding officer and the boater should keep in mind that the arms carried by the boarding party are not to intimidate but protect." On completion, you will be asked to sign a boarding certificate to attest that the boarding was done correctly and any search carried out was done politely and in the presence of the owner or a person nominated by him or the skipper. As a result of bilateral agreements with the United States, Defence Force personnel conduct joint patrols with US Customs in the Bimini area and seariders are stationed on Coast Guard cutters to give them jurisdiction in Bahamian territorial seas.

If you have any queries on boarding procedures, direct them to: The Commander Defence Force, Defence Force Headquarters, P.O. Box N-3733, Nassau, Bahamas, Tel. (242) 323-3691, Fax (242) 328-8912; The Commanding Officer, HMBS Coral Harbour, P.O. Box N-3733, Nassau, Bahamas, Tel. (242) 362-1818, Fax (242) 362-1374; The Squadron Commanding Officer, HMBS Coral Harbour, P.O. Box N-3733, Nassau, Bahamas, Tel. (242) 322-4436.

If the reader should care to report any suspicious event or activity, please do so as soon as possible. Time tends to confuse the message and firsthand reports are always the most accurate.

The Royal Bahamas Defence Force wishes you many years of happy boating in The Bahamas and is always ready to serve, aid, or assist you in any way it can as you travel throughout the many islands of The Bahamas.

The Royal Bahamas Defence Force

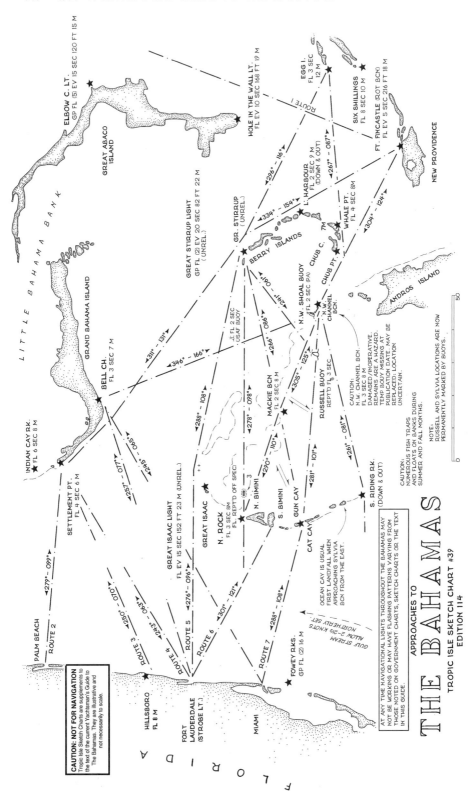

Approaches to The Bahamas

D.M.A. Charts: 26300, 26308, 26309, 26319, 26320, 26321, 26323, 26324. N.O.S. Charts: 11013, 11460. Tropic Isle Sketch Charts: Sets B, C, D, 39, 42.

The Gulf Stream. Under normal conditions an allowance of about 2.5 knots should be made for the drift of the Gulf Stream at any point off the South Florida coast. The table on the following page reflects this figure. Please note that we do not include courses across the Gulf Stream for boats under speeds of 10 knots. The slower the boat, the more any Gulf Stream variation will affect the accuracy of a course calculated for average conditions, and we feel that the potential error resulting from the varying velocities of the stream and that of the direction and intensity of the wind makes calculation of a course for slower boats inadequate. Every responsible skipper who plans to take a vessel across the Gulf Stream, or for that matter cruise anywhere in The Bahamas, must be able to plot a course with government charts, using vector diagrams when necessary to factor in actual current and wind conditions at the time of passage.

The surface velocity of the Gulf Stream is sometimes decreased by strong northerly winds. Under these conditions there may be almost no northerly drift at all. In moderate winds from the east, south, or west, the Gulf Stream will be comparatively smooth, but in fresh to strong winds from the northwest, north, or northeast, a big sea soon builds up. Owners of small craft should wait for fair conditions before leaving the Florida coast for the short run across.

Warning: Use Extreme Caution in the Vicinity of Northwest Channel Beacon

Northwest Channel Beacon, hit by a large boat several years ago, shows only jagged barely-above-water remains that are not easy to see and are a hazard. Until recently there was a temporary buoy about 100-200 feet north of the old structure, but just before our press deadline, we received several letters reporting the temporary buoy missing. So now Northwest Channel Beacon is a dangerous ruin, and there is nothing to warn you off it. This is a very dangerous situation.

We continue to use the words "Northwest Channel Beacon" with the hope that at some time in the future the beacon structure actually will be rebuilt to replace the dangerous jagged ruins of the old structure. Now we also hope that at some time the temporary buoy might be replaced. Be prepared for any eventuality.

MAGNETIC COURSES FOR SPEEDS INDICATED

Route	Naut. Miles	From Florida to The Bahamas					From The Bahamas to Florida				
		Direct	10 kts	15 kts	20 kts	25 kts	Direct	10 kts	15 kts	20 kts	25 kts
2 Palm Beach West End	56	099	114	109	106	105	279	265	269	272	273
3 Hillsboro West End	65	070	083	079	076	075	250	237	241	244	245
4 Fort Laud West End	69	063	075	071	069	068	243	231	235	237	238
5 Fort Laud. Gt. Isaac	54	096	111	106	103	102	276	261	266	269	270
6 Fort Laud. Bimini	48	121	134	130	128	126	301	288	292	294	296
7 Miami Gun Cay	45	108	122	117	115	114	288	274	279	281	282

Slow craft and sailboats: Leave from a departure point far enough south that you won't have to fight the stream the whole way over. An evening departure will get you to a Bahamas landfall by morning, and if something goes wrong, you'll still have the whole day to work it out. You should know how to work out crossing vectors so you can make corrections on the fly, because the vagaries of the stream can affect slow boats in not entirely predictable ways. It is probably a good idea to motorsail because the better a speed you can make good, the easier everything will be. Watch out for traffic at night, because there's a lot of it, and lots of it is big and fast.

Route 1: Comparatively few yachts approach The Bahamas from the north. Those that do, having crossed the Gulf Stream somewhere south of Hatteras, are advised to stand well to the east of the Little Bahama Bank, which extends in a northwest-southeast direction for 132 miles. From the bank's northwest corner at Matanilla Shoal, where no light is located, the Bahama Bank is unlighted until Walker's Cay, 40 miles to the east, where there is a 250-foot mast with a flashing red light. Southeast from there the cays and settlements are clearly visible under most conditions with major lights on Elbow Cay (vis 15 m) and Hole in the Wall (vis 19 m) on Great Abaco within 45 miles of each other. At times a strong tidal set is experienced on the east coast of Abaco. This current sets either northwest or southeast and is reported to attain a velocity of up to 3 knots. It is therefore prudent, especially in a sailing vessel, to give this coast a good offing between Elbow Cay and Hole in the Wall. On the southern side of the Northeast Providence Channel are two problematical 12-mile lights, the one on Man Island down and out for several years, and the other on Great Egg Island unreliable, as are many lights throughout these islands.

Route 2: *Lake Worth Inlet (Palm Beach) to West End and Nassau, or the Abacos.* This route cuts directly across the Gulf Stream. Yachts may go into West End, which is a port of entry for The Bahamas, but some will prefer to run down the southwest coast of Grand Bahama to Lucaya or across the Northwest

Providence Channel to Great Stirrup Cay, where anchorage may be found in Panton Cove (Great Harbour) in 9 feet of water. The distance from Great Stirrup Cay to Nassau is 50 miles. The total distance from Florida to Nassau on this route is about 189 miles.

Route 3: *Hillsboro Inlet (Pompano Beach) to West End and Nassau or the Abacos.* This route takes advantage of the northern drift of the Gulf Stream.

Route 4: *Port Everglades (Fort Lauderdale) to West End and the Abacos.* This route is favored by yachts leaving from Fort Lauderdale for the Abacos as it takes advantage of the Gulf Stream.

Route 5: *Port Everglades (Fort Lauderdale) to Great Isaac Light, Great Stirrup Cay, and Nassau.* This route also cuts directly across the Gulf Stream and has the advantage of a 23-mile light (recently reported unreliable) to pick up at Great Isaac. The next leg, to Great Stirrup, parallels the northern side of the Great Bahama Bank, and thence to Nassau as in Route 2.

Route 6: *Port Everglades (Fort Lauderdale) to Bimini.*

Route 7: *Departing Government Cut from Miami to Gun Cay, thence over the Great Bahama Bank to Northwest Channel Beacon (see caution, page 73), and Nassau.*

Routes 6 and 7 are two of the most popular routes, especially for power craft and for sailing yachts not exceeding a 5-foot draft. If, having entered at Bimini, you wish to continue on across the Great Bahama Bank to Northwest Channel Beacon (*see caution, page 73*), it is necessary to return to the deep water west of Bimini and run south 9 miles in deep water west of the bank,

CRUISING GUIDE

TO THE

Florida Keys

$19.95

New 10th Edition!

• PLACES TO GO
• THINGS TO SEE
• DETAILED CHARTS
• WEATHER INFO
• AERIAL SATELLITE PHOTOS
• UNDERWATER ACTIVITIES

Send $19.95 to:
    Tropic Isle Publishers
    P.O. Box 610938
    North Miami, FL 33261-0938

Add $3 Postage & Handling for orders inside the U.S., $5 for orders outside the U.S.
Florida residents add applicable Sales Tax.

With Florida West Coast Supplement
CONTENTS: PLACES TO GO, THINGS TO SEE, AERIAL SATELLITE PHOTOS, MARINAS, 42 DETAILED CHARTS, WEATHERS & TIDE INFORMATION.

reentering onto the bank via Gun Cay Cut.

To enter Gun Cay Cut from the west, approach Gun Cay Lighthouse on an easterly course to keep well clear of the shoal that extends northward from the north end of North Cat Cay (see sketch chart B-1, Bimini-Cat Cay). Approach within 200 yards and then turn to starboard, rounding the south end of Gun Cay close-to. Follow the coast until the light bears approximately northwest; you will then be in 12-18 feet of water.

If bound for Cat Cay, then turn again to starboard and stay on a line between Gun Cay Light and the light at the entrance of Cat Cay Harbour. Avoid the sandy shoal (4 feet or less at low water) that has in recent years been working out from the banks toward Gun Cay Cut. If bound east across the banks to Russell buoy and Northwest Channel Beacon (*see caution, page 73*), follow this same route toward Cat Cay Harbour, but about 300 yards short of its entrance head northeast, then east to work your way around the north side of the shoal area (visible even in less than ideal conditions) which lies just north and east of the marina breakwater. Once around, you can take up the 101° course to Russell buoy. Here, you should avoid the bar working east toward Gun Cay Cut by passing to its south. This route takes you south of the shoal area reported building in recent years south and east of Bimini and should be able to carry 5 feet at low water through the area, although lower low waters and certain wind conditions, or a combination of the two could leave considerably less water here. Sand banks, which you must avoid, continue to build in this area. You must know the state of the tide, keep a good lookout, and navigate carefully by eye to stay clear of them. Once onto the banks, you will be in 9 feet of water or better. Note: In crawfish season avoid tethered floats of traps on the bank extending from Gun Cay to Northwest Channel Beacon (*see caution, page 73*).

We have eliminated the route via Sylvia buoy because of shoaling there.

The tides on the banks flow in a northeast-southwest direction and are affected by the wind. In light winds, a way to ascertain tidal drift in this area is to stop several times while crossing the bank to check your drift over the bottom, and then compensate for it.

Because of increasing traffic of small, commercial vessels carrying freight between Florida and Nassau, the route via North Bimini, Russell buoy, Northwest Shoal and Northwest Channel Beacon is busy day and night. Do not anchor in these sea lanes at night as many of these vessels run without lights and lack

"Just head east, Mavis, he sez to me. There's a place on the beach where they serve wonderful conch fritters. You can't miss it, he sez. This is the last time I take to the water without my Guide!"

Yachtsman's Guide to the Bahamas

Over 450 pages of indispensable (useful, and accurate) information

Call (305) 893-4277

Or write to: Tropic Isle Publishers
P.O. Box 610938, North Miami, FL 33261-0938

alert lookouts at the wheel. If yours is a slow vessel and you must anchor for the night, do so a mile or so south of either Russell buoy or Northwest Channel Beacon, well out of the sea lanes and with a bright anchor light. In these areas expect a strong surge at the change of the tide, especially south of Northwest Channel Beacon.

Northwest Channel Beacon (*see caution, page 73*) should be left to starboard when proceeding eastward. The course from Northwest Channel to Nassau fairway buoy is 122°, 49 miles all in deep water. Stops can be made at Chub Cay, Frazer's Hog Cay, or Bird Cay anchorages. The distance from Gun Cay to Nassau on this route is about 110 miles.

A way to discern whether you are north or south of the course when approaching the vicinity of Northwest Channel Beacon: The bottom north of the course is generally grassy; to the south it tends to be brown. There is a quick flashing buoy on the point of the bank 2 miles northwest of Northwest Channel Beacon (*see caution, page 73*) to warn yachtsmen of that shoal area. (We are constantly receiving information from our readers that this buoy is off station or that its light is out. Consider its position approximate, and don't count on its light.) Pass well south of this buoy.

Caution: If you are proceeding westbound from Northwest Channel Beacon (see caution, page 73) to Cat Cay or the Gun Cay Cut at night, do not confuse the very brightly illuminated Ocean Cay, 12 miles south of Gun Cay, for Gun Cay. As emphasized previously, we do not advocate cruising at night across the banks. However, for those who do, the lights of Ocean Cay

ᗏᗏᗏTHE LAUDERDALE MARINA, INC. ᗏᗏᗏ

1900 S.E. 15th St., Ft. Lauderdale, FL 33316 · (954) 523-8507 · Fax (954) 524-5225
· Miami (305) 949-2303

Bahama Bound?

CITGO

MARINE FUELS

Complete One Stop Service.
Diesel, Gasoline, Oil Changing.
Pump Out Facility. Full Marine
Supply and Ship's Store.
★
Open 7 Days
★
Complete Fishing
Supplies/Bait
★
Dive Air · Dry Ice
★
15th Street Fisheries
Restaurant

Over 50 years of service to yachtsmen.
Our proximity to Port Everglades makes us the ideal spot
for that pre-dawn jump to the Bahamas.

VHF CH.16 & 9

Authorized dealer for
Boston Whaler · Albemarle Sport Fishing
Johnson · Yamaha · Mercury
Complete Parts & Service

could be a misleading hazard or, for the experienced boatman, a valuable landmark.

For boats drawing up to 8 feet, there are two alternate entrances onto the bank, which are indicated on sketch chart 39 (Approaches to The Bahamas). Entering via North Rock at the north end of the Biminis, be aware of the Moselle Bank which lies northwest of North Rock. Take North Rock to starboard, and continue east for about 2 miles, or far enough to pass north of the 6-foot shoal area lying just south of the course line. Then steer 110° for the 30 miles to a point north of Mackie Beacon. Here, alter course to 125° to pass just south of Northwest Shoal Buoy, at which point you can continue on a course of 101° for the final 4 miles to Northwest Channel Beacon (*see caution, page 73*). (Note: We've had letters from time to time informing us that the light at North Rock was off spec, one letter reporting an 8-second interval rather than the 3 seconds shown on government charts and on our sketch chart. When and if Bahamian authorities tend to this, they will probably put it back to 3 seconds, so be prepared for either of these possibilities or, perhaps just as likely, something else.)

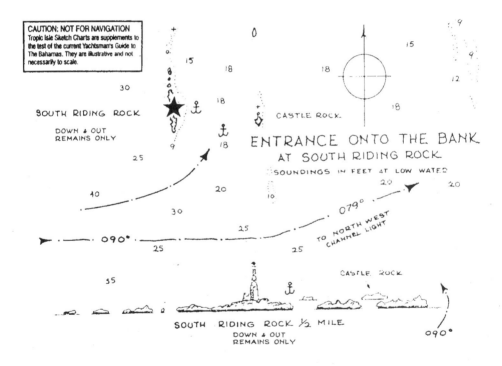

The entrance onto the bank immediately south of **South Riding Rock** is straightforward also. The open area between the light and Castle Rock, one-half mile to the east, provides a calm-weather anchorage with poor holding for small boats. Continuing to the east, carry on that heading until abeam of Castle Rock before taking up 079° for the 55-mile leg to Northwest Channel Beacon (*see caution, page 73*).

BIMINI AND THE
GREAT BAHAMA BANK

D.M.A. Charts: 26319, 26320, 26324. N.O.S. Charts: 11013, 11460. Tropic Isle Sketch Charts: 39, B-1.

The northwestern tip of the Great Bahama Bank extends north to latitude 26°08' N and is separated from the island of Grand Bahama by the Northwest Providence Channel. The bank is covered by a depth of water ranging from 9 to 20 feet with a few shoal patches, some of which dry at low tide.

At the northwest corner of the bank is Great Isaac Island, in the center of which stands the white lighthouse of Great Isaac Light (recently reported unreliable). The island itself is three-quarters of a mile long and lies in an east-northeast to west-southwest direction with an elevation of about 40 feet. Temporary anchorage can be found under its lee. Shoals extend both southwest and east-northeast of Great Isaac. They should be given a wide berth, as the tide sets onto them.

Along the western side of the bank, a chain of cays and reefs extends in a roughly north and south direction. Some have navigable channels between them for vessels of shallow draft. However, as previously mentioned, the best routes onto the bank are at North Rock, Gun Cay Cut, and South Riding Rock. Along the edge of the bank from South Riding Rock up to Great Isaac Light is

Hemingway display at the Compleat Angler. (Fields photo)

PLEASE NOTE: *For a description of* **Batelco towers in
all areas and their light characteristics**, *please check page
39 of this Guide.*

---

one of the world's prime sportfishing areas. At various times of the year, marlin, bluefin tuna, sailfish, bonito, dolphin and kingfish are plentiful. The juxtaposition of the Gulf Stream and the banks also offers good diving and snorkeling.

Bimini (Tropic Isle Sketch Chart: B-1), like many islands set between civilization and remoteness, has for centuries attracted opportunists and eccentrics. It's a good hideout and jumping-off point. Pirates, wreckers, Confederate blockade runners, rum-runners and smugglers have in the past brought waves of prosperity in and as quickly out of town. The famous and infamous have escaped to Bimini where, they think, no one will be watching. Ernest Hemingway pursued gin and shark-shooting here in the 1930s, and in the late 60s, Adam Clayton Powell lived in Bimini with his mistress. Hemingway and Powell are both remembered with fondness by older Biminites. A Fountain of Youth of sorts is alleged to exist in the woods of South Bimini (Ponce de Leon did stop at Bimini in his quest for everlasting youth, but if he sampled the waters here, they didn't do the job). And every year the Quest for Atlantis expedition convenes here to explore the Bimini Road, hundreds of large flat boulders about 15 feet underwater off Paradise Point, north of Alice Town. They believe this suspiciously uniform formation might be a fallen Atlantean temple.

The island of **North Bimini** is about 7 miles long and is extremely narrow and flat. Most of the island is less than 700 feet in width, and nowhere does it have an elevation greater than 15-20 feet above sea level. The main settlement and sportfishing center is **Alice Town.**

At this writing, the 281-foot LF radio tower on South Bimini, which was the best approach landmark, is down. Do not let Batelco towers in Alice Town or Bailey Town confuse you. Approach South Bimini on a course of about 85° for a point approximately one-third of the distance from the south end of South Bimini to the south end of North Bimini. Stay in good water until you see the shallow sandbars and other obstructions that lie off South Bimini's western shore and do not proceed through these until you find a range consisting of two orange and white striped poles on the beach. This will lead you in through the entrance channel on a heading of 80°. As you pass through, take care to avoid the shallow sandbar to port and the rocky brown bar to starboard. Shifting sands caused by prolonged high winds and strong tides are known to rearrange the shallow sandbars here, so keep your eye out. Once inside, follow the channel, about 4.5

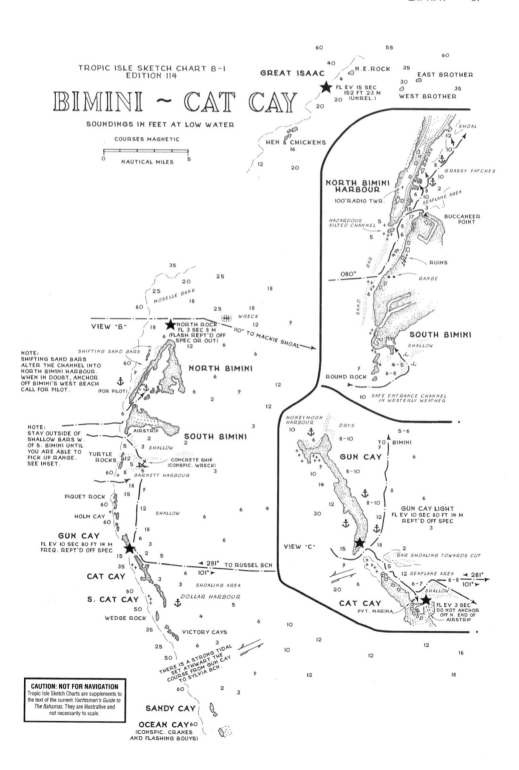

TROPIC ISLE SKETCH CHART B-1
EDITION 114

BIMINI ~ CAT CAY

SOUNDINGS IN FEET AT LOW WATER

COURSES MAGNETIC

0   NAUTICAL MILES   5

GREAT ISAAC

60   55   60

40   N.E.ROCK   35   EAST BROTHER

4   30

★ FL EV 15 SEC   WEST BROTHER   35
152 FT 23 M   20
(UNREL.)

HEN & CHICKENS
16

12   20

SHOAL
12
10
GRASSY PATCHES
10
NORTH BIMINI   2
HARBOUR   8
100'RADIO TWR.   6   SEAPLANE AREA

HAZARDOUS   5   BUCCANEER
SILTED CHANNEL   17   POINT
8
5   6

RUINS

080°   RANGE

SOUTH BIMINI
SHALLOW

4-5
9   6-8

ROUND ROCK   10   SAFE ENTRANCE CHANNEL
IN WESTERLY WEATHER

35
20   25
25   18
MOSELLE BANK   18
60   25   18
18   WRECK   9

VIEW "B"   18   ★ NORTH ROCK   12
FL 3 SEC 8 M   110° TO MACKIE SHOAL
6 (FLASH REPT'D OFF
SPEC OR OUT)
12   4

SHIFTING SAND BARS
NOTE: 60   9   6
SHIFTING SAND BARS
ALTER THE CHANNEL INTO   NORTH BIMINI   12
NORTH BIMINI HARBOUR.   6
WHEN IN DOUBT, ANCHOR   ⚓   2   9
OFF BIMINI'S WEST BEACH   (FOR PILOT)
CALL FOR PILOT.   12

HONEYMOON
HARBOUR   DRYS   5-6
NOTE: 10   ⚓   TO
STAY OUTSIDE OF   AIRSTRIP   3   6   8-10   BIMINI
SHALLOW BARS W.   2   SOUTH BIMINI   9   8-10   6
OF S. BIMINI UNTIL   3   SHALLOW   GUN CAY
YOU ARE ABLE TO   TURTLE   12   8-10
PICK UP RANGE.   ROCKS   5   CONCRETE SHIP   10
SEE INSET.   60   8   (CONSPIC. WRECK)   3   14   8
18   BARNETT HARBOUR   12   8
PIQUET ROCK   15   30   8-10
60   12   SHALLOW   6   12
HOLM CAY   60   18   GUN CAY LIGHT   3
FL EV 10 SEC 80 FT 14 M
GUN CAY   18   3   REPT'D OFF SPEC
FL EV 10 SEC 80 FT 14 M   2   6   VIEW "C"   15   ★   18   2
FREQ. REPT'D OFF SPEC   15   5   BAR SHOALING TOWARDS CUT
CAT CAY   35   281° TO RUSSEL BCN   9   5   12   SEAPLANE AREA   281°
101°   6-7   6-8   101°
6   SHOALING AREA   20   SHALLOW
S. CAT CAY   DOLLAR HARBOUR   CAT CAY   ★
60   ⚓   5   PVT. MARINA   FL EV 3 SEC
WEDGE ROCK   50   4   6   10   DO NOT ANCHOR
OFF N. END OF
35   VICTORY CAYS   3   AIRSTRIP
25   6   12   12   16
50   THERE IS A STRONG TIDAL   10
SET ATHWART THE   12
COURSE FROM GUN CAY   9   12
TO SYLVIA BCH.   18
60   2   3

CAUTION: NOT FOR NAVIGATION
Tropic Isle Sketch Charts are supplements to
the text of the current Yachtsman's Guide to
The Bahamas. They are illustrative and
not necessarily to scale.

SANDY CAY

OCEAN CAY 60
(CONSPIC. CRANES
AND FLASHING BOUYS)

feet LW, that parallels the beach into Bimini Harbour, avoiding the shoal that extends out from the northwestern point of South Bimini across from the south point of North Bimini. *Cautions: 1) Never attempt this channel in strong onshore conditions. 2) Watch out for cruise-ship moorings, which are not particularly prominent and may have gear trailing from them.*

Caution: A strong tide, ebb and flood, runs through Bimini Harbour. Also, Pan Am Air Bridge (formerly Chalk's Airlines) operates two or three flights daily to and from Miami from their ramp inside the entrance channel, and their seaplanes use most of the harbor for takeoffs and landings. Keep a watchful eye aloft and don't anchor in their operating area.

Immediately inside **Bimini Harbour**, an abandoned three-story beige hotel lies to port, while the dredged entrance to the Buccaneer Point Canal lies to starboard. Next to your port as you proceed are the Pan Am Air Bridge seaplane ramp, pink-and-aqua terminal building, and customs office for passengers. Don't attempt to tie up here, as the water is quite shallow. Instead, tie up at one of the marinas, yellow flag flying, and ask the dockmaster for the necessary forms for customs and immigration clearance. These should be completed and taken by the skipper to the customs and immigration headquarters, the two-story pink building next to the government dock, north of Weech's Bimini Dock. The only anchorage in the harbor is toward the north end, off the Bimini Big Game Fishing Club. The channel must be left clear for boat traffic and seaplane arrivals and departures.

Proceeding north up the harbor from the seaplane ramp, taking care not to stray off to starboard (where the water shoals rapidly) and passing the blue Sea View disco, restaurant, and lounge, the next docks are not usable (Brown's Marina is no longer in business, although the hotel, under new management, is undergoing renovation). Next door is Freddy Weech's Bimini Dock and Bay View Rooms with accommodations for 15 boats as well as ice, electricity, and

North Bimini Harbour. (Tropic Isle photo)

showers. Freddy's son Hank is manager/owner, and Morris Bowleg is the dockmaster.

North of Weech's are the government dock and Customs House. Just beyond, the Sea Crest Hotel and Marina has 18 slips, showers, 30 and 50-amp electricity, freshwater showers and washdown, and ice. Across the street from the marina, the hotel has air-conditioned rooms and suites with TVs available at reasonable rates. The surrounding balconies offer lovely views of the ocean and bay. Sportfishing, bonefishing, and diving excursions can be arranged. The marina manager is Alfred Sweeting; Michael Murphy is the dockmaster.

The next facility north, the Bimini Blue Water Resort has dock space for 32 yachts and all marine and fishing services available. Bimini Blue Water monitors VHF 68. There's an attractive dockside pool and patio next to the marina. Across the street up the hill are Blue Water Resort's accommodations, Marlin Cottage and the Anchorage Guest House, with spotless airy rooms and a cozy bar. The Anchorage restaurant, the home of famed fisherman and Hemingway cohort Michael Lerner in the 1930s, has good food, cheerful decor, and a bright ocean view. They will prepare tasty box lunches if you order a day ahead.

Further up the waterfront, the 100-slip Bimini Big Game Fishing Club offers all petroleum products and fishing services, along with about everything else you might need, in its self-contained complex. The club monitors VHF 16. Curtis Carroll is the marina manager and Don Smith is dockmaster. The Gulfstream Restaurant serves breakfast and dinner, and an island-style lunch is

SEA CREST

HOTEL AND MARINA

Located in North Bimini's famous Hotel & Marina District, Sea Crest offers the "Best in Island Accommodations." From beautiful guest rooms & suites with Ocean & Bay views to the modern Marina facilities, Sea Crest has come to be known as "Bimini's Best Deal."

Hotel: AC & Color T.V., beaches, restaurants, night spots. **Marina:** Fresh water showers & washdown, 30 & 50 AMP electric, ice. **Charter Arrangements:** Sport, Bone & Reef fishing, Diving/Snorkeling... 1/2 day/full day & group rates available.

Special Off Season Rates
Available October - February

We monitor VHF Ch. 68

P.O. Box 654 / Bimini, Bahamas

For Res: 1-242-347-3071
Marina: 1-242-347-3477
Fax: 1-242-347-3495

served at the New Sports Bar. There are at least two bars on the premises, a gift shop, a liquor store, and the only tennis courts on the island. The Big Game Club is headquarters for the Bimini branch of BASRA. Boats in distress should call *BASRA-Bimini* on VHF 16.

On Bimini, as on many of the Out Islands, fresh water is scarce. Distilled water is sold for upwards of 40¢ per gallon. The dock water is brackish but fresh enough for washing down the boat, taking a shower, or even washing clothing.

Sportfishing tournaments are scheduled frequently throughout the year and very popular, so it's a good idea to reserve slips or rooms ahead of time, Arrangements for fishing guides or charters can be made through most of the marinas. It's not hard to find a bonefishing guide — including Bonefish Ansil, Bonefish Ben, Bonefish Bill, Bonefish Cordell, Bonefish Ebbie, Bonefish George, Bonefish Jackson, Bonefish Ray, Bonefish Rudy, Bonefish Sammie ... well, you get the idea. They can supply equipment and bait, and you bring along the comestibles. Bonefishing is fun for children, and the guides will make sure they have a good time.

Although you can easily get around Alice Town on foot, it's fun to rent a scooter or bike to explore the rest of the island. Sam Brown's Bimini Buses monitor VHF 68 and run up and down King's Highway for $3 each way. You'll recognize them from the 20 or so bumper stickers stuck on the windows.

Propane, kerosene, and alcohol are usually available at Brown's Supply Store, about a mile and a half north of the Big Game Club. It's on the Bimini Bus route, handy if you're planning to lug a tank of propane. Limited fishing and marine supplies are sold at Bimini's General Store, next to Weech's. Laundry arrangements can be made through the larger marinas. The post office is in the government building north of Bimini Big Game, along with the commissioner's office, the police station, and the local Defence Force unit. The Royal Bank of Canada is next to the Sea Crest Hotel. Shops sell duty-free perfume, liquor, and jewelry as well as T-shirts, souvenirs, and sundries.

We've been impressed by how Alice Town has brightened up its appearance in the last few years — fresh paint in cheerful Caribbean colors, cleaned-up streets, and a new straw market. There's a pretty little town library with neatly kept books and three long shelves full of *National Geographics*. Schoolchildren like to gather here in late afternoon. Money is being raised to support the ongoing restoration of the abandoned post office building (the two-story balconied building near the straw market) for use as a museum of Bimini history.

Groceries on King Street include Watson's Supermarket (terrific fresh-baked coconut, banana, and raisin bread) and Jontra's Super Market. C.J.'s Deli has good ice cream and milk shakes, sandwiches, burgers, and snacks. Opal's on the hill near the Bimini Big Game Club serves a good Bahamian lunch popular with locals. Burger Queen, next to the Big Game Club, caters to fishermen with takeout food, and both the Big Game Club and the Anchorage will prepare box lunches with advance notice. Excellent seafood is served at the Red Lion Pub and Restaurant.

In this fisherman's town, many places open early for breakfast and plenty of bars stay open late, including the graffiti-decorated End of the World bar with its sand floor and rows of donated well-worn BVDs and other underthings drooping from the roof beams. The Compleat Angler Hotel, famous for its collection of Hemingway memorabilia, was the first fishing club in The Bahamas when it was built in the 1930s and is the hub of Bimini night life with a calypso band and unbridled revelry most nights. If you stay up long enough you can go directly to Captain Bob's for breakfast starting at 6 a.m. The Captain also serves lunch, including sandwiches to go, and he and his wife Bonita will prepare dinner by special request (and they're excellent cooks).

There's a long, uncrowded beach on the west side of the island, a few minutes' walk over the hill from the harbor, near the Anchorage. The best beach on the island, however, is probably the one up at Paradise Point, where boats might anchor during the day when weather conditions are favorable. A large mansion built in Art Deco style, the result resembling a cruise ship crossed with a wedding cake, overlooks the beach. Built in the 1950s by George Lyons, who allegedly invented the hub cap, the house is locally called Rockwell House from a period when it was owned by Rockwell International. At present it houses the Bimini Bay restaurant, run by Basil and Antoinette Rolle. It's a gorgeous setting for dinner, with windows all around overlooking the ocean, genteel furnishing, and sincere hospitality. You can call them on VHF 68 to make reservations, and they can arrange for your transportation from and back to Alice Town.

SCUBA divers and snorkelers can explore a variety of drop-offs, wrecks, and shallow reef dives in the Bimini island area. Many of the reefs have mooring buoys installed for dive use only (anchorage is discouraged to protect sea life). Offshore between the north end of Bimini and Paradise Point are the aforementioned underwater rocks of the Bimini Road, as well as the broken-up sunken remains of an old English vessel, referred to as the English Wreck, in about 17 feet of water. Along the same reef line, Hawksbill Reef, Rockwell Reef, and

End of the World Bar. (Fields photo)

Lobster Reef, in 45 feet of water, are dense with colorful tropical fish and lobsters. La Chance Rocks (locally known as Three Sisters Rocks), off Paradise Point, offer good snorkeling. A favorite dive of visitors is Off The Wall — down 130 feet to peer into a 2,000-foot deep-blue drop-off. The 150-foot-long Bimini Barge is sunk 95 feet at the edge of the Continental Shelf, an attraction for both deep-water and reef fish. Between Bimini and Cat Cay is the wreck of the concrete ship *Sapona* in 15 feet of water. Built by Henry Ford, it has served variously as private club, rumrunner's storehouse in the 20s, and bomb-practice target for the U.S. Navy during WW II. This is a good snorkeling spot, as are nearby Turtle Rocks. Further south, Tuna Alley, right off Cat Cay, and Victory Reef, south of South Cat Cay, have spectacular coral formations and lots of marine life to observe. Bill and Nowdla Keefe at Bimini Undersea Adventures in Alice Town can supply equipment, directions, and advice. Their dive headquarters will relocate to Bimini Blue Water Marina in late 1998.

When entering the Buccaneer Point Canal, on **South Bimini** across from the seaplane ramp, take care to stay in the deeper green water. Enter only in good light with an eye on the bottom, as we've riled the sand here at low tide.

Between Bimini Harbour and Gun Cay, a distance of 9 miles, there are a number of small rocky cays that should be given a good berth at night, as the flood tide sets onto them. It is possible to carry 5 feet down the inside from South Bimini to Gun Cay, the only shallow area being immediately east of Turtle Rocks, where there is only 6 feet at low water. There is no longer a pole beacon in the vicinity of Picquet Rock, marking the south side of the entrance to Barnett Harbour, and it seems unlikely to be replaced. One-half mile onto the bank is the hulking wreck of the concrete ship *Sapona*, a good landmark visible from a great distance.

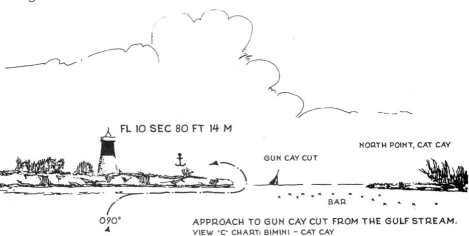

FL 10 SEC 80 FT 14 M

NORTH POINT, CAT CAY

GUN CAY CUT

BAR

090°

APPROACH TO GUN CAY CUT FROM THE GULF STREAM.
VIEW "C" CHART: BIMINI – CAT CAY

Gun Cay, just northwest of Cat Cay, is easily recognizable by its lighthouse. On the northwest tip of Gun Cay is a cove called Honeymoon Harbour with a lovely beach, a nice fair-weather anchorage.

When making for **Gun Cay Channel** bound either for the bank or Cat

Yachtsman's Guide to the Virgin Islands

Over 300 pages of indispensable information including 16 pages of full color aerial photos.

Yachtsman's Guide to the Bahamas

Over 450 pages of indispensable information

- The most complete guides available for cruising the Bahamas and Virgin Islands.
- Profusely illustrated with our beautiful hand-drawn sketch charts, landfall sketches and photographs.
- Detailed island by island profiles and things to do ashore.

Sketch Charts also available separately in 11"x17" format. Call or use order form in the Guide.

Call (305) 893-4277

Or write to:
Tropic Isle Publishers
P.O. Box 610938
North Miami, FL 33261-0938

"Someday, Father, I shall write great guides for yachtsmen. Sailors like us will never wander aimlessly again. That is... if we ever get back. Sir, will we soon see land?"

Cat Cay - one of the finest marinas in the Bahamas

and one of the most beautiful...

Cat Cay lies just twelve miles south of Bimini on one of the main routes across the Bahama Bank. We welcome visiting yachtsmen.

Of course, the Cat Cay marina offers quality fuels, fresh water, 110-220 electric power, cable TV and ice. You can dine al fresco at our lovely restaurant overlooking the marina. We serve delicious fish, seafood, chops, steaks, sandwiches, and salads. To re-supply your provisions we have a small, well-stocked island grocery store.

For those who like shopping, our Cat Cay Boutique is famous for both casual and elegant resort wear, gifts and accessories for men, women and children.

As you may know, most of our island is private, for members only. But if you book a yacht rendezvous your group can play our challenging golf course, swim in our pool or play tennis. You can drive a golf cart (no cars here!) past our hidden estates or lose yourself walking our miles of empty beaches.

Dock with us. Dine with us. Rendezvous with us. For a small fee, you can stop here just to clear customs. It's easy and quite convenient. For more information, contact our Fort Lauderdale office at 954-359-8272 or the island at 242-347-3565. We monitor VHF channel 16. Stop at Cat Cay and discover why we are called one of the finest marinas in the Bahamas.

PHOTOGRAPH COURTESY OF FOREST JOHNSON PHOTOGRAPHY AND THE BOYS & GIRLS CLUB OF BROWARD COUNTY

The wreck of the Sapona. *(Fields photo)*

Cay, the route is described as Route 7 in the previous chapter, Approaches to The Bahamas.

If you prefer to cross the bank via Sylvia buoy, turn to the northeast when within 200-300 yards of the entrance to Cat Cay Harbour, and follow the edge of the very conspicuous sandbank around until the Gun Cay lighthouse bears 296°. Then take up its reciprocal 116° for Sylvia buoy. As mentioned previously, there is shoaling on this route and we do not recommend it.

APPROACH TO CAT CAY FROM GUN CAY CUT

Cat Cay (Tropic Isle Sketch Charts: 29, B-1) lies about one mile southeast of Gun Cay Light. On approaching you will see the little Cat Cay lighthouse at the end of the breakwater. Inside, the Cat Cay Yacht Club docks can accommodate 72 vessels with up to 8 feet draft. With the exception of July 4, when members fill the marina to capacity, visiting yachtsmen are welcome to clear

Honeymoon Harbour. (Tropic Isle photo)

Gun Cay. (Tropic Isle photo)

customs here and use marina facilities, including a fuel dock, commissary, liquor store, laundry, showers, ice, electricity, and dockside cable hookups. The Nauticat Restaurant and Pub serves lunch and dinner (trousers and shirts with sleeves are required for men for indoor evening dining). Although the rest of the island is reserved for members, Cat Cay can be a convenient jumping-off point for the rest of The Bahamas. The marina fee of $25 for clearing customs and immigration is waived if you stay at the marina overnight. The club's airstrip runs south from the lighthouse, and management requests that yachts not anchor off the north end of the strip where they would obstruct that end of the aircraft traffic pattern. A fully equipped clinic on Cat Cay serves visiting yachtsmen as well as

Cat Cay. (Tropic Isle photo)

club members. Helicopter evacuation to the United States of the seriously ill or injured can be arranged.

Dollar Harbour, which lies to the east of South Cat Cay's southern tip (see D.M.A. Chart 26324) gives good protection in winds from east-northeast to almost south by way of west, but can be uncomfortable in strong winds from east or southeast. There is 12-18 feet of water with good holding ground, but a strong tidal current sets through this anchorage.

Nine miles south of Cat Cay lies **Ocean Cay,** the by-product of an aragonite sea mining operation. The cay, which is presently about 40 acres in size, will eventually grow up to 200 acres. With its cranes and various loading paraphernalia, the island is a handy landmark for cruising yachtsmen. Ocean Cay is a bulk material handling facility and as such can offer no services or accommodations to yachtsmen. It may, however, provide assistance and sheltered water to vessels in distress. Extreme caution should be exercised when entering the harbor from the Gulf Stream and when crossing the water that lies to the east of the island, since dredging operations will continue in that area.

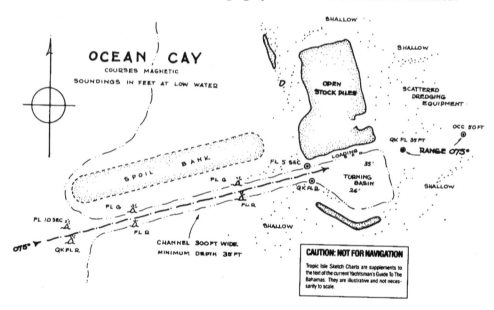

A farther chain of small, scrub-covered or barren cays extends 18 miles south of Cat Cay to **South Riding Rock,** on which stands what remains of an old light. **Orange Cay,** 18 miles south of South Riding Rock, is a small, barren cay rising to about 13 feet above sea level. The radar beacon that stood here is reported to have fallen down. From Orange Cay, the edge of the Great Bahama Bank runs south to 24°11' and then trends in a south-southeasterly direction to the Old Bahama Channel, which narrowly separates the bank from Cuba. Along the edge of the bank are isolated shoals and wrecks.

LOOK FOR US AT YACHTSMANSGUIDE.COM

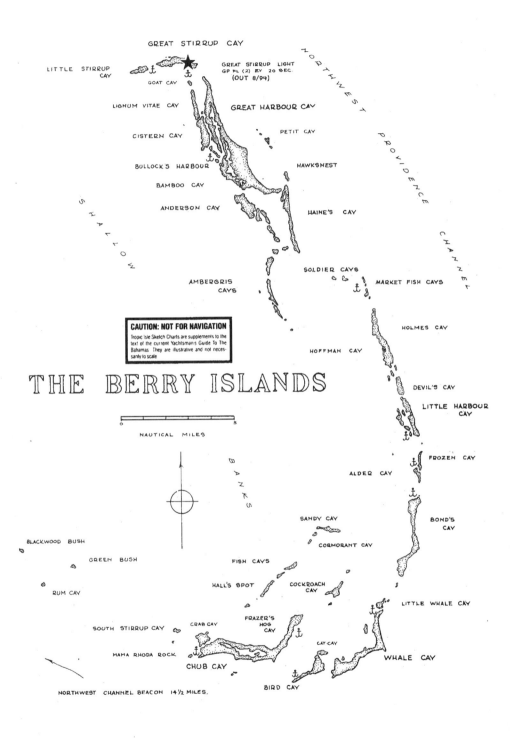

THE BERRY ISLANDS

CAUTION: NOT FOR NAVIGATION

Tropic Isle Sketch Charts are supplements to the text of the current Yachtsman's Guide To The Bahamas. They are illustrative and not necessarily to scale.

BERRY ISLANDS

D.M.A. Charts: 26299, 26300, 26308, 26319, 26320, 26328. Tropic Isle Sketch Charts: C-1, C-2, C-3, C-4.

The Berry Islands, a stirrup-shaped chain of cays and islets along the northeastern edge of the Great Bahama Bank between latitudes 25°50' N and 25°22' N, are bounded on the north and east by the Northwest Providence Channel and on the south by the Tongue of the Ocean. Among these roughly 30 large cays and numerous small ones are many good harbors and anchorages.

The bank to the west is mostly shallow and cannot be navigated except by shoal-draft vessels on the tide. A number of channels do exist, however, and we have plotted those used by local fishermen, in the hope that use of these channels might save smaller craft from going outside in adverse weather. Local knowledge is advisable for these passages, at least for the first time. Competent guides are available at Bullocks Harbour and the Chub Cay Club.

Because most yachts en route to Nassau approach the southern Berry Islands by way of Bimini, Cat Cay, and the Great Bahama Bank, the area descriptions that follow begin with the southern Berrys and proceed north.

Departing Northwest Channel Beacon (see caution, page 73) en route to Nassau, with a stopover at **Chub Cay,** travel 14.8 nautical miles to a point just south of Mamma Rhoda Rock, which lies immediately west of Chub Point. Then proceed north between the two, being careful to avoid the reef south of Mamma Rhoda Rock, into Chub Cay Marina.

In winter there is good protection for shoal-draft vessels in Mamma Rhoda Channel; however, make provisions for the strong tidal flow that passes through. Entering, there is a bar between the south end of Mamma Rhoda Cay and the point on which stands the lighted range that guides you into the marina. This is good for only about 5 feet on the tide. The anchorage, which is off the damaged

Chub Cay Marina. (Tropic Isle photo)

> **PLEASE NOTE:** For a description of **Batelco towers in all areas and their light characteristics**, please check page 39 of this Guide.

dock on the left side as you enter, has depths of 5 feet at low water. Beyond this point the water shallows.

There is good anchorage in 6-7 feet in the cove formed by Chub Point. A draft of 4.5 feet can get farther into the cove, off the sandy beach, and so escape some of the surge that swings in around the point. (We have a letter from a reader saying this anchorage has been scoured out, and holding is not very good. So check that your anchor is dug in.) This anchorage gives protection in winds from north through east to southeast but is untenable in winds from south to northwest. Do not anchor near the channel that heads in on the red-lighted 35° range; it must be kept clear for the surprisingly large vessels that enter the marina at all hours, dependent on the tide. Consider your scope and be sure you cannot swing into the approach, because large vessels cannot deviate from the channel.

Approaching the Chub Cay Marina, you must avoid the reefs south of Mamma Rhoda Rock. Remain .75 mile south of Mamma Rhoda Rock and Chub Point until you can approach the marina entrance of a course of 35°. If you shortcut this approach, you can be on the heads south of Mamma Rhoda Rock and in trouble. As you get closer and see the actual range, be on it. Once safely by Mamma Rhoda and its reefs, the entrance channel (6 feet at low water) is straightforward as indicated on sketch chart C-3 (Southern Berry Islands). Chub Cay is a port of entry for The Bahamas. The customs office is at the airstrip, so if you arrive late and the customs officers are busy with arriving planes, you're likely to have to pay overtime. In addition, if you go to Chub Cay's docks to clear customs and don't take a slip for the night, you'll be charged $25 by the club (this will be credited if you do stay overnight at the docks).

Chub Cay Club is a private resort with all facilities available to registered guests. Proximity to the Great Bahama Bank and the Tongue of the Ocean accounts for Chub Cay's fame as a sportfishing resort, and there's also a beautiful uncluttered beach — making the resort a great all-around destination as well as a convenient stopping-off point. Contact dockmaster Gerreth Roberts on VHF 68 for slip assignments or marina information; VHF 71 (the club office) should be used only for questions regarding store hours, restaurant reservations,

Chub Cay Marina. (Tropic Isle photo)

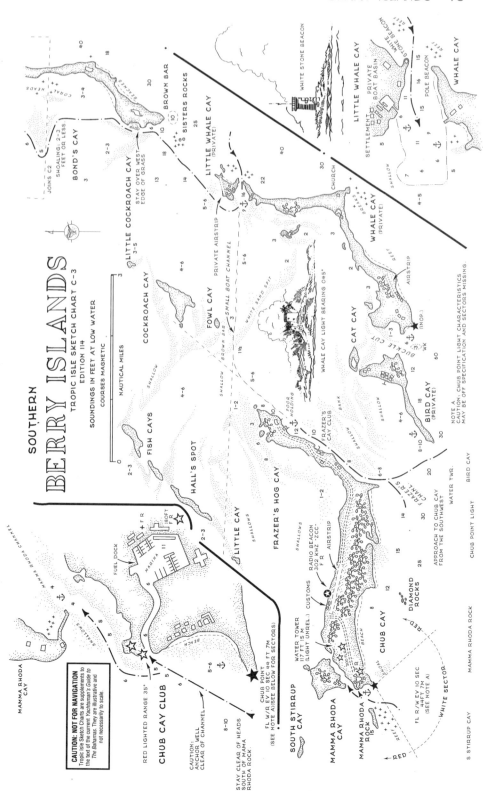

SOUTHERN

BERRY ISLANDS

TROPIC ISLE SKETCH CHART C-3

EDITION 114

SOUNDINGS IN FEET AT LOW WATER

COURSES MAGNETIC

NAUTICAL MILES

CAUTION: NOT FOR NAVIGATION
Tropic Isle Sketch Charts are supplements to
the text of the current Yachtsman's Guide to
The Bahamas. They are illustrative and
not necessarily to scale.

Whale Cay Light. (Tropic Isle photo)

accommodations, and similar administrative matters. You're most likely to make contact once you're beyond the light at the point and nearing the entrance to the club itself. All dock facilities are available with electricity, cable TV and water. The club's restaurant serves excellent Bahamian specialties. Groceries, liquor, and gifts are sold in the Island Shoppe.

A bit east of the airport, the Frazer's Hog Cay Resort (not to be confused with the Frazer's Cay Club), offers peaceful accommodations in a natural environment. There is a beachside grill and open-air restaurant, a pub, gift shop.

From Chub Point en route to Frazer's Channel, be sure to pass to the south of Diamond Rocks and don't confuse the mouth of Frazer's Creek (1.5 miles north of Diamond Rocks) with Frazer Channel, which is a mile farther east.

The approach to **Frazer's Hog Cay** can be made on any course from 050° through north to 330° to the southeast point of the island. The channel entrance lies between the sandbar and a position 150 feet off the point. The next few yards beyond the point are the shallowest, about 6-7 feet at low water. Wind and lunar conditions can change this one way or the other, and you may have to feel your way around a bit to find the deepest channel. From here on you should see a dark-water channel over a grassy bottom running parallel to the shore. If the depth of 6-7 feet at the start is a tight fit, or the channel farther on is difficult to read, call the Frazer's Cay Club on VHF 16 for guidance. *(Note: The Frazer's Cay Club is no longer under its prior management, and we have been unable to ascertain what, if anything, is going on here at this writing.)* The best holding ground is 1000 yards beyond the Frazer's Cay Club dock (200

Frazer's Hog Cay Resort

**A totally peaceful island environment where you can
enjoy a natural Bahamian experience.**

· Beachside Dining · The Driftwood Bay Pub · Gift Shop ·
· Watersports, Volleyball, Fishing & Diving ·
· Spectacular Clear Aquamarine Waters ·

On Chub Cay at the Southern Tip of the Berry Islands Chain.

P.O. Box N-3199, Nassau, Bahamas
Phone: 242-328-8952 Fax: 242-356-6086
E-mail: fhcresort@bahamas.net.bs

WHALE POINT LIGHT (FL. EV. 4 S.)
70 FT VIS. 8M.(U) BR'G 045°
(DOWN & OUT)

BEACH

HOUSE

⚓ 6FT

yards off the small beach) and on up to the northeast end of the island in 18-24 feet. (Readers have recently reported to us that the bottom in this channel is scoured and difficult for anchoring; others report that it is fine. Be prepared for either possibility.)

Bird Cay, to the east of Frazer's Hog Cay, is private property. This cay, one of the most extensively developed in The Bahamas, has great stands of casuarina, citrus, and coconut groves with several luxurious homes, roadways, gardens, village green, and public buildings. The usual anchorage at Bird Cay is off the white stone quarry at the southwest end in about 9 feet. It is subject to an uncomfortable surge in southeasterly weather.

Whale Cay is reportedly being developed by Canadian interests. Midway in the bay lies a sunken barge awash at low water. Because of the ever-present surge we do not recommend this as an overnight anchorage.

Little Whale Cay was previously owned by Wallace Groves, founder of Freeport, Grand Bahama, and is an excellent example of what can be done with such an island in the way of landscaping. There is an elaborate aviary with scores of semi-rare birds including flamingos, peacocks, golden pheasant, and many species of duck and geese. There is an airstrip and harbor. Little Whale Cay is a private residence, and landing is not permitted.

There is a good anchorage between Little Whale and Whale Cays, the entrance carrying about 12 feet at low water (see sketch chart C-3, Southern Berry Islands). Take care to avoid the shallow rocky reef in the entrance. It can be passed on either side, but it is advisable to follow the track passing north of it, shown on the sketch chart. A pole beacon stands on the north point of Whale Cay and there is a white stone tower on Little Whale Cay. The entrance is between these two markers, but much closer to the latter. The entrance is open

Anchorage between Little Whale and Whale Cays. (Tropic Isle photo)

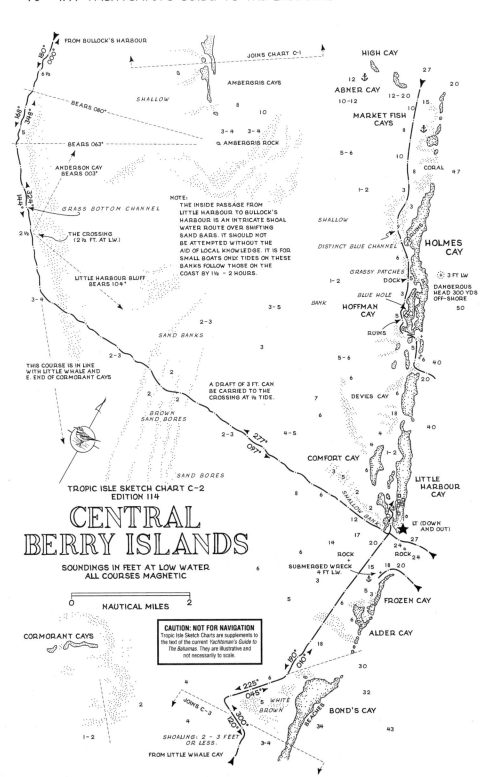

FROM BULLOCK'S HARBOUR

JOINS CHART C-1

HIGH CAY

AMBERGRIS CAYS

ABNER CAY

SHALLOW

MARKET FISH CAYS

BEARS 080°

BEARS 063°

AMBERGRIS ROCK

ANDERSON CAY BEARS 003°

GRASS BOTTOM CHANNEL

CORAL

NOTE:
THE INSIDE PASSAGE FROM
LITTLE HARBOUR TO BULLOCK'S
HARBOUR IS AN INTRICATE SHOAL
WATER ROUTE OVER SHIFTING
SAND BARS. IT SHOULD NOT
BE ATTEMPTED WITHOUT THE
AID OF LOCAL KNOWLEDGE. IT IS FOR
SMALL BOATS ONLY. TIDES ON THESE
BANKS FOLLOW THOSE ON THE
COAST BY 1½ – 2 HOURS.

THE CROSSING
(2½ FT. AT L.W.)

SHALLOW

DISTINCT BLUE CHANNEL

HOLMES CAY

GRASSY PATCHES

DOCK

3 FT LW

LITTLE HARBOUR BLUFF
BEARS 104°

BLUE HOLE

DANGEROUS
HEAD 300 YDS
OFF-SHORE

HOFFMAN CAY

BANK

RUINS

SAND BANKS

A DRAFT OF 3 FT. CAN
BE CARRIED TO THE
CROSSING AT ½ TIDE.

THIS COURSE IS IN LINE
WITH LITTLE WHALE AND
E. END OF CORMORANT CAYS

BROWN
SAND BORES

DEVIL'S CAY

277°
097°

SAND BORES

COMFORT CAY

**TROPIC ISLE SKETCH CHART C-2
EDITION 114**

CENTRAL
BERRY ISLANDS

LITTLE
HARBOUR
CAY

SHALLOW BANK

SOUNDINGS IN FEET AT LOW WATER
ALL COURSES MAGNETIC

LT (DOWN
AND OUT)

ROCK

ROCK

0   2
    NAUTICAL MILES

SUBMERGED WRECK
4 FT L.W.

FROZEN CAY

CORMORANT CAYS

CAUTION: NOT FOR NAVIGATION
Tropic Isle Sketch Charts are supplements to
the text of the current *Yachtsman's Guide to
The Bahamas*. They are illustrative and
not necessarily to scale.

ALDER CAY

180°
010°

225°
045°

JOINS C-3

300°
120°

WHITE
BROWN

BOND'S CAY

BEACHES

SHOALING: 2 – 3 FEET
OR LESS.

FROM LITTLE WHALE CAY

Frozen and Alder Cays. (Tropic Isle photo)

on an east-west bearing. The holding ground is good and there is usually a surge only in strong easterly winds.

Bond's Cay is privately owned. It is shoal close under its western shore, and readers in a catamaran drawing 2 feet, 10 inches, report having touched sand bottom attempting the banks passage west of this cay. They did not report date and time, so there may be less water than this.

Frozen and Alder Cays (Tropic Isle Sketch Charts C-2, C-4) are almost joined together and anchorage can be found in their lee in 6-18 feet. Alder Cay, the southernmost of the two, is covered with vegetation while Frozen Cay is almost barren. Birdwatchers will enjoy a visit to these cays, which are a natural bird rookery. The early morning and twilight air fills with many species of tern, while coastal rocks are spotted with nesting brown noddys, and an occasional pelican can be seen circling the shoreline. Frozen and Alder Cays are private property; visits ashore are by invitation only. The southern end of Frozen is being heavily developed, with extensive private docks. We are told that dredging for the goings-on here may have shoaled some of the approach to the inner harbor between the cays. Also, there is a new line of pilings from the southwest point of Frozen across the narrows to Alder. We don't know what these will become.

The anchorage where the cays overlap has been reported shoaling and grassy, but boats drawing up to 4 feet or a little more can work their way in and find a pleasant anchorage. Don't go too far toward the head of the harbor.

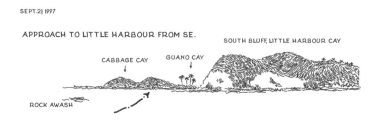

SEPT.21 1997

APPROACH TO LITTLE HARBOUR FROM SE.

SOUTH BLUFF, LITTLE HARBOUR CAY

CABBAGE CAY   GUANO CAY

ROCK AWASH

Little Harbour Cay (Tropic Isle Sketch Charts: C-2, C-4) has one of the best and prettiest harbors in the Berry Islands. In the inner harbor, available to yachts drawing up to 6 feet, there is complete protection. The approach to Little Harbour, between Frozen Cay and Little Harbour Cay, is wide, but a dangerous rock, awash at half tide, exists in the channel. It is easy to discern, as any sea or

Little Harbour Cay harbor. (Tropic Isle photo)

swell breaks heavily on it. In entering, you may pass the rock on either side, but the best water lies close under the point of Little Harbour Cay. From this point you may steer direct for the south point of Cabbage Cay, where the harbor will soon open up to starboard.

A rocky shoal carrying 5-6 feet at low water extends for a short distance east of the south point of Cabbage Cay, and should be given a wide berth when turning into the harbor as the flood tide sets strongly onto it.

The best anchorage in the harbor is east of the north end of Cabbage Cay in about 18 feet of water over a sandy bottom (we've had a recent report that the sand here is thin and holding difficult; as always, it's wise to check your anchor). North of this, toward the small detached cay, the bottom becomes rocky and the holding poor. Continuing northward up the east side of the cay, watch your depths and stay in deep water.

Little Harbour Cay is high and thickly covered with vegetation. Since the demise of the sponging industry, what was once a thriving settlement has shrunk to the Darville family of nine (as well as dogs, pigs, and peacocks), who live on the hill above the dock. For permission to land at the dock, contact Chester Darville on VHF 68. You can leave your boat here under Chester's supervision; he'll look after it and can pick you up or drop you off at Chub Cay or Great

Chester Darville's dock and Flo's Conch Bar & Restaurant. (Tropic Isle photo)

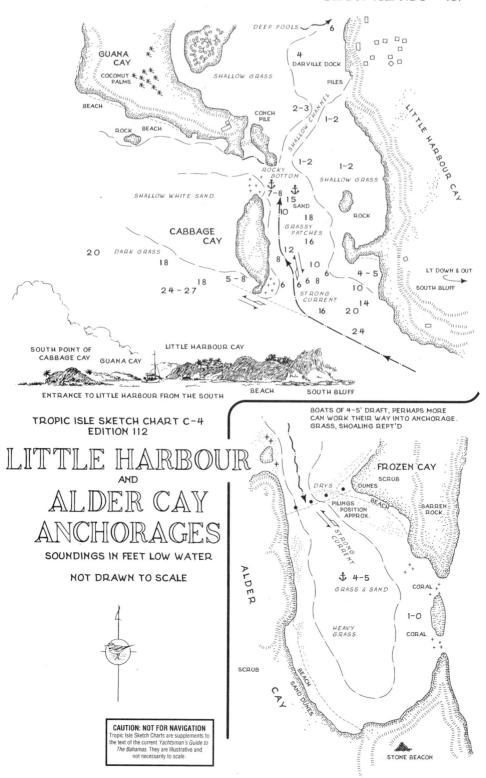

DEEP POOLS   6

GUANA CAY

COCONUT PALMS

BEACH

ROCK   BEACH

SHALLOW GRASS

CONCH PILE

DARVILLE DOCK

PILES

LITTLE HARBOUR CAY

2-3

1-2

SHALLOW CHANNEL

1-2

1-2

ROCKY BOTTOM

SHALLOW WHITE SAND

7-8   15
10   SAND
10   18
GRASSY PATCHES   16

SHALLOW GRASS

ROCK

CABBAGE CAY

20   DARK GRASS
18

12

8

10   6

4-5

10

LT DOWN & OUT

SOUTH BLUFF

18
24-27   18
5-8   6   6   6   8
STRONG CURRENT
16   20   14

24

SOUTH POINT OF CABBAGE CAY   LITTLE HARBOUR CAY
GUANA CAY
BEACH   SOUTH BLUFF

ENTRANCE TO LITTLE HARBOUR FROM THE SOUTH

TROPIC ISLE SKETCH CHART C-4
EDITION 112

LITTLE HARBOUR
AND
ALDER CAY
ANCHORAGES

SOUNDINGS IN FEET LOW WATER

NOT DRAWN TO SCALE

BOATS OF 4-5' DRAFT, PERHAPS MORE CAN WORK THEIR WAY INTO ANCHORAGE. GRASS, SHOALING REPT'D

FROZEN CAY

SCRUB
DUNES
DRYS   BEACH
PILINGS
POSITION APPROX.
BARREN ROCK

STRONG CURRENT

ALDER

4-5
GRASS & SAND

CORAL

1-0

CORAL

HEAVY GRASS

SCRUB

CAY

BEACH
SAND DUNES

STONE BEACON

CAUTION: NOT FOR NAVIGATION
Tropic Isle Sketch Charts are supplements to the text of the current *Yachtsman's Guide to The Bahamas*. They are illustrative and not necessarily to scale.

Holmes, Hoffman, and Devil's Cays. (Tropic Isle photo).

Harbour Cay for arrival or departure. Flo's Conch Bar & Restaurant serves lobster in season, outstanding conch and fish, burgers, beer, and mixed drinks. All meals require three hours' notice and dinner reservations must be made by 3 p.m., preferably earlier (call on VHF 68). Fresh bread can be ordered. Do not disturb the privately owned houses, garden areas, and fruit groves on the island.

The banks passage north, past **Comfort, Devil's, Hoffman, and Holmes Cays,** as indicated on sketch chart C-2 (Central Berry Islands), is intricate, with a 3-foot controlling depth, and should not be attempted without local assistance. The same applies, of course, to the high water passage for small boats to Bullocks Harbour, which has an even shallower controlling depth (see sketch charts C-2 and C-1, Northern Berry Islands). There is an anchorage in the lee of **White Cay** between Devil's and Hoffman Cays. To reach it, enter midway between the southernmost of some rocks that trail south from White Cay and the north tip of Devil's Cay. There are some reefs off the north tip of Devil's, but if you stay center in the good water, the entrance is wide and deep. Once through the cut, turn north and anchor off the beach on the west side of White Cay. In addition to this, while flying over this area, we've seen boats anchored just north of the southwest point of Hoffman Cay. From the air, we could not tell what the depth and bottom were; however, the boats were monohull sailboats.

The bight between the **Ambergris Cays** and the **Market Fish Cays** is fairly deep, ranging from 6-18 feet. Fishing hereabouts is reported to be good.

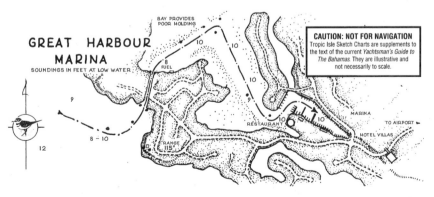

Great Harbour Cay (Tropic Isle Sketch Chart: C-1) is the largest of the

Entrance channel into Great Harbour Cay Marina. (Tropic Isle photo)

Berry Islands and the location of Bullocks Harbour settlement. Running a course of 180°, enter the bank 200 yards off the southwest tip of Little Stirrup Cay. Continue on 180° for a distance of about 2.5 miles in 10-20 feet of water, paralleling an easily visible sandbank until you've passed west of the red-and-white triple-pile outer mark "BH." (This mark used to be Ra Ref and Mo {A}, but was neither when we were there most recently.) Then turn onto approximately 110° for the well-marked 5.5-mile course (6-8 feet LW over sand and grass) from the outer mark into the Bullocks Harbour area. On this 110° heading the 235-foot Batelco tower of Bullocks Harbour will be just off your port bow. The marks along this course change a bit from time to time, but they're usually red-right-returning, sometimes numbered and with arrows, sometimes not. In addition to the marks, there is a range, which is only visible very close in and hard to spot in the vegetation, that will put you on a 115° heading to a point just south of the harbor entrance. Enter the harbor through a straightforward 80-foot cut with a reported controlling depth of 8 feet. The swing bridge that once blocked the entrance is no longer there. Once through the entrance, the channel to the marina is usually marked conventionally.

Great Harbour Cay Marina has 86 slips for boats of up to 12 feet draft, full marina services, RO and fresh water, laundry, showers, ice, grocery and liquor

The Yacht Club, Great Harbour Cay Marina. (Tropic Isle photo)

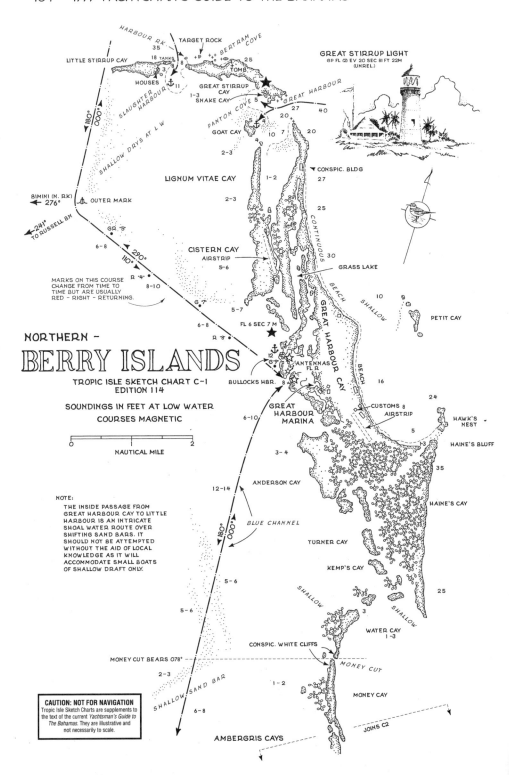

GREAT STIRRUP LIGHT
GP FL (2) EV 20 SEC 81 FT 22M
(UNREL.)

NORTHERN –

BERRY ISLANDS

TROPIC ISLE SKETCH CHART C-1
EDITION 114

SOUNDINGS IN FEET AT LOW WATER
COURSES MAGNETIC

NAUTICAL MILE

NOTE:
THE INSIDE PASSAGE FROM
GREAT HARBOUR CAY TO LITTLE
HARBOUR IS AN INTRICATE
SHOAL WATER ROUTE OVER
SHIFTING SAND BARS. IT
SHOULD NOT BE ATTEMPTED
WITHOUT THE AID OF LOCAL
KNOWLEDGE AS IT WILL
ACCOMMODATE SMALL BOATS
OF SHALLOW DRAFT ONLY.

MARKS ON THIS COURSE
CHANGE FROM TIME TO
TIME BUT ARE USUALLY
RED – RIGHT – RETURNING.

CAUTION: NOT FOR NAVIGATION
Tropic Isle Sketch Charts are supplements to
the text of the current *Yachtsman's Guide to
The Bahamas*. They are illustrative and
not necessarily to scale.

Great Harbour Cay Marina. (Tropic Isle photo)

stores, boat cleaning and repair, freshwater pool and bar, yacht and sportfishing charters, and limited golf. Dockmaster Rufus Pritchard can supply fresh bread. Gas, diesel, and oil are at the fuel dock, between the cut and the marina. Restaurants include the Tamboo Club, The Wharf, or several local restaurants and bars. Beach villas or townhouses with private docks are available (advance reservations are suggested). Elorne Rolle has a gift shop called the Happy People at the marina, where he also rents motorbikes, bikes, boats, and jeeps. With reasonable notice, you may arrange fishing charters from deep-sea and bottom fishing to bonefishing by contacting Percy Darville. Great Harbour Cay Marina monitors VHF 68.

If you have not cleared customs and immigration, hoist your quarantine flag upon entering and notify the dockmaster so that customs officials can be summoned from the airport.

Right near the marina, the casual Great Harbour Yacht Club bar and grill has a nice varied menu from seafood, sandwiches, and hamburgers to salads. Meals are served alfresco, and you can jump in the swimming pool. The proprietors are Paul and Janet Rich.

A post office and clinic are in the government administration building in the settlement of Bullock's Harbour. Several grocery stores sell fresh produce, canned goods, and frozen meats, and many homemakers bake fresh bread for sale. Meals are served at the Watergate Bar & Restaurant and you can get food to go from Coolie Mae's Takeaway. The Backside Lounge serves drinks with a nice sunset view. The new White Water Restaurant and Bar serves breakfast, lunch, and dinner daily. On the beach side near the airport is a breakfast and lunch bar called The Beach Club, where proprietors Mama and Papa T serve great burgers, sandwiches, and drinks. In front of the Beach Club and the neighboring villas is an anchorage with plenty of water less than 100 yards off the magnificent beach. Entrance is between Petit Cay and Hawk's Nest through water so crystal-clear that starfish are visible on the sandy bottom 24 or more feet below. You'll be protected from winds almost southeast through west to

Great Stirrup Cay. (Tropic Isle photo)

almost northwest.

Great Stirrup Cay, at the north end of the Berry Islands, is important for two reasons: it is the entrance to Great Harbour (not to be confused with Great Harbour Cay Marina), and a government lighthouse stands there. This light is painted white and guards the south end of the Northwest Providence Channel. The approach and entrance to Great Harbour (between the east end of Great Stirrup Cay and the north end of Great Harbour Cay) is quite straightforward, being roughly southwest, keeping midway between the two points as rocky shoals extend from Great Stirrup.

Panton Cove provides a convenient anchorage, snug in northerly winds. It is important to stay close to the shore as you enter, in 6-8 feet of water. Beware of the submerged sailboat hull that lies in shallow water on the bottom between Snake Cay and the inner point. The deck section of the same boat is visible 50-70 feet to the east of the hull. North of Snake Cay in Panton Cove is a dock where you can tie your dinghy and a path that leads to the Great Stirrup lighthouse, the old U.S. Tracking Station, and the cruise facilities at Bertram's Cove.

Approach the south, or inner point of Great Stirrup and follow the shore

Cruise-ship facility, Bertram Cove. (Tropic Isle photo)

Cruise ship off Little Stirrup Cay. (Tropic Isle photo)

along closely, about 50-75 feet off, keeping in the green water. Shallow sand and grass bars extend where N.O.S. Chart 26258 gives 6-9 feet. Proceed in curving slightly to the west until nearly south of the small, scrub-covered Snake Cay, which lies due south of the lighthouse. You may anchor there in 5 feet at low water. Westward the water shoals to 3 feet. Quite a strong tidal current runs through this anchorage and two anchors are advised if there are more than two boats here. There is excellent protection from northwest-north-northeast and southeast winds. Little surge seems to find its way into this anchorage. Better protection from westerly winds as well as some refuge from cruise-ship aggravation will be found under the cliffs of Goat Cay, about 50 yards off in 9 feet of water.

Both Great Stirrup Cay and Little Stirrup are regular day stops for two cruise lines. We have a recent letter from a reader warning that the cruise ships' mooring buoys are unlighted and a hazard when visibility is bad. Bertram Cove, on the north side of Great Stirrup Cay, is a good day anchorage but no place to be caught in a norther. The cove, named for a British survey-ship commander buried here, would be idyllic but for the steady stream of hundreds of cruise-ship guests ferried to shore to purchase baskets, T-shirts, and other souvenirs.

Slaughter Harbour lies between Great and Little Stirrup and provides good cover except in northerly weather. The entrance to Slaughter Harbour is 8 feet but deepens just beyond. Watch for small rocks in the water just off the east tip of Little Stirrup as you approach Slaughter Harbour. There is 15-18 feet inside. This being a Royal Caribbean Cruise Lines destination, the anchorage is now anything but peaceful. We have letters describing it as a "beehive of activity" and telling that "any private vessel anchored becomes the focal point for jet skiers and the parasailing boat." So if it's confusion you came here for, this is one place to find it.

Little Stirrup Cay is low and rocky, with two large ponds in its center.

NEW PROVIDENCE ISLAND

TROPIC ISLE SKETCH CHART D-1
EDITION 11¼

SOUNDINGS IN FEET AT LOW WATER

NAUTICAL MILES

WHEN APPROACHING NEW PROVIDENCE FROM THE NORTH-WEST
LYFORD CAY WATER TOWER IS USUALLY THE FIRST LANDFALL.

PROMINENT HOTELS
PARADISE ISLAND

PARADISE I. LT.

FORT FINCASTLE WATER TWR.
FL 5 SEC 216 FT. 16 M

NASSAU HARBOUR ENTRANCE SE 3 MILES

FROM SPANISH WELLS
228° — 048°

CHUB RK. LT
FL EV 5 SEC 25 FT 4 M
(OUT 9/94)

PORGEE RK. LT.
FL 3 SEC 23 FT 5 M

300° - 120°
FROM BEACON CAY
EXUMA CAY

EAST END POINT
FL 6 SEC 27 FT 8 M
(OUT 9/94)

287°

MONTAGU BAY

PORT NEW
PROVIDENCE

MARKED
CHANNEL

PARADISE ISLAND

MAST
500 FT
FL R

NASSAU
260'
FL R

PARADISE ISLAND LT
FL W/R EV 5 SEC 66 FT
(UNREL)

FT. FINCASTLE

GREEN RANGE
LIGHTS 151'

302°
122°

TO NORTHWEST
CHANNEL

LONG
CAY

SILVER CAY

ARAWAK
CAY

2 NS
1540KHZ
1240KHZ

MAST
500 FT
FL R

CORAL WORLD
TOWER
BRIDGE

CABLE
BEACH

DELAPORTE PT.
(ORANGE ROOFS)

NORTH CAY

LAKE
KILLARNE

160' FL R

100' FX R

CORAL
HBR.

233°

MAST
500 FT
FL R

NASSAU INTERNATIONAL AIRPORT
RADIO BEACON
"ZQA" 251 KHZ

GR & W ROT. BCN.

FRESH CREEK

SOUTHWEST BAY

APPROACH TO LYFORD CAY HBR.

LYFORD CAY
WATER TWR.
FL R 185 FT

CLIFTON
PIER
(COMMERCIAL)

ROYAL BAHAMAS DEFENSE FORCE GUN
PRACTICE RANGE EXTENDS 9 MILES WEST
AND 8½ MILES SOUTH

LYFORD CAY

WEST BAY

SIMMS POINT

GOULDING CAY LT
FL 2 SEC 36FT 8M
(DOWN & OUT 9/94)

CAUTION: NOT FOR NAVIGATION
Tropic Isle Sketch Charts are supplements to
the text of the current Yachtsman's Guide to
The Bahamas. They are illustrative and
not necessarily to scale.

NEW PROVIDENCE

D.M.A. Charts: 26300, 26306, 26308, 26309, 26319, 26320. N.O.S. Chart: 11013. Tropic Isle Sketch Charts: Set D.

Although New Providence is one of the smallest of the inhabited islands of The Bahamas, it is by far the most important and the center of Bahamian economic and social life. Twenty-one miles long and only 7 miles wide, the island has a population of over 170,000. Scrub and pine woods cover much of the poorly soiled interior, but the coastline blooms with luxurious residential areas, resort apartment-hotel complexes, and modern developments. Yachtsmen should be aware that the entire north shore of New Providence is a protected area where spearfishing is forbidden within a mile from shore.

Nassau Harbour: As you approach Nassau's main (western) harbor entrance (between **Paradise Island Light** and Silver Cay breakwater) from the northwest, your first landfall will probably be the Lyford Cay water tower in Nassau and the Atlantis resort's 24-story buildings on Paradise Island. East of the water tower, about halfway to the harbor entrance, are the prominent orange-roofed white buildings of Delaporte Point development. East of these and still about 3 miles west of the harbor entrance is Cable Beach, easily identifiable by the wildly colored Nassau Marriott Resort and Crystal Palace Casino. About a mile offshore, between Delaporte Point and the harbor entrance, are three small cays with dangerous reefs west of and between them. Easternmost of these is Silver Cay. The entrance into Nassau Harbour is between Silver Cay breakwater (which runs east from the cay itself for more than a half mile) and the breakwater that runs westward from the Paradise Island Light (now painted all white). (*Note:* The big Halloween storm of 1991 broke through a section of this latter breakwater. Don't confuse the break, which remains unrepaired at this writing, for the entrance.) Do not mistake the prominent Coral World tower (it often flies a large Bahamian flag), southwest of Silver Cay and just off the northwest corner of Arawak Cay, for the less prominent Paradise Island Light. A few yachtsmen have even mistaken the bridge connecting Coral World to Arawak Cay for the

CROCODILES

WATERFRONT BAR & GRILL

TELEPHONE 323-3341

EAST BAY STREET, P.O. BOX N-233, NASSAU, BAHAMAS

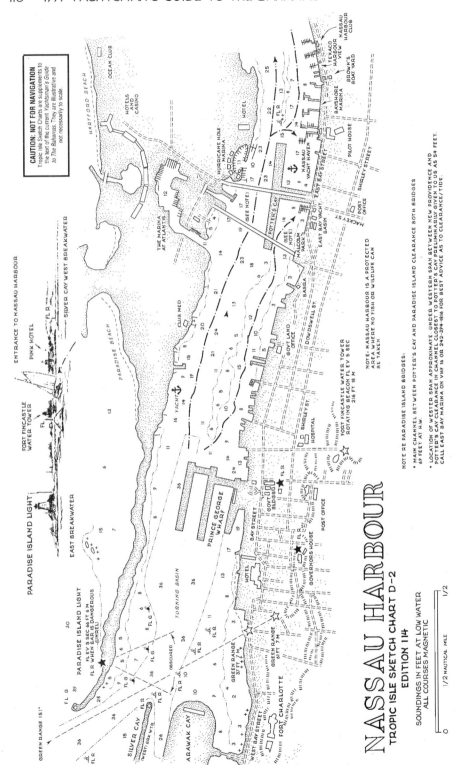

CAUTION: NOT FOR NAVIGATION
Tropic Isle Sketch Charts are supplements to the text of the current *Yachtsman's Guide to The Bahamas*. They are illustrative and not necessarily to scale.

NASSAU HARBOUR
TROPIC ISLE SKETCH CHART D-2
EDITION 114

SOUNDINGS IN FEET AT LOW WATER
ALL COURSES MAGNETIC

0   1/2 NAUTICAL MILE   1/2

NOTE: NASSAU HARBOUR IS A PROTECTED AREA WHERE NO FISH OR WILDLIFE CAN BE TAKEN

NOTE RE PARADISE ISLAND BRIDGES:

• MAIN CHANNEL BETWEEN POTTER'S CAY AND PARADISE ISLAND CLEARANCE BOTH BRIDGES 69 FEET AT H.W.

• LOCATION OF WESTER SPAN APPROXIMATE. UNDER WESTERN SPAN BETWEEN NEW PROVIDENCE AND POTTER'S CAY CLEARANCE IN CHANNEL CLOSEST TO POTTER'S CAY PRELIMINARILY GIVEN TO US AS 54 FEET. CALL EAST BAY MARINA ON VHF 16 OR 242-394-1816 FOR BEST ADVICE AS TO CLEARANCE/ TIDE.

PLEASE NOTE: For a description of **Batelco towers in all areas and their light characteristics**, please check page 39 of this Guide.

Paradise Island Bridge. (The June 1996 issue of the SEARCH newsletter reported a recent sinking resulting from this confusion; it happens.) The two bridges may be somewhat the same shape but are nowhere near each other in scale or location.

If you approach the harbor entrance at night (not a good idea at this or any other Bahamian harbor entrance) you'll find it extremely confusing even in the best of circumstances. Probably the first thing you'll notice, approaching from the northwest in favorable weather, is the green-and-white rotating beacon at the airport. East of that, the Nassau Marriott Resort and Crystal Palace Casino complex on Cable Beach, about 3 miles west of the harbor entrance, is lit up at night as garishly as it is painted. The Coral World tower and bridge are usually floodlit, at least during the early part of the night. Once offshore of the harbor entrance, you should be able to recognize the Fort Fincastle water tower's rotating beacon. Although this is a navigation mark, it's hard to pick out among the bright city lights and other towers all over the island. The green leading range lights will only be visible once you are lined up with them just outside the harbor.

PHILLIPS SAILMAKERS

SAILMAKERS   LOCATED ON EAST SHIRLEY STREET

CRUISING & RACING SAILS

Repairs and new sails, Dacron, Mylar, Kevlar, Ripstop Nylon, Vivatex

MARINE CANVAS

Bimini tops, awnings, cushions, dodgers, sail covers, sail bags

P.O. Box N-208 • Nassau. Bahamas • (242) 393-4498 • Fax (242) 394-7412 • VHF 16 ... call Fandango

---

FREEZING POINT LTD.

MARINE AIR CONDITIONING & REFRIGERATION
....*Increasing the Comfort of Life*
★ Ice Machines ★ Coolers & Freezers ★
★ Air Conditioning & Refrigeration ★

★ **CRUISAIR AUTHORIZED DEALERS** ★
★ **MARINE AIR AUTHORIZED DEALERS** ★
★ **AQUA AIR** ★ **SEA RECOVERY** ★

Phone (242)325-3589 Fax (242)356-5271
Montrose Ave. & Harley St. P.O. Box SS6537 Nassau, Bahamas

PARADISE ISLAND LIGHTHOUSE E.S.E.

Paradise Island Light is very weak (it may be out altogether), and you must remember that a breakwater extends well westward of it. The low western end of Paradise Island itself has few lights on it, and could be mistaken for the harbor entrance by looking across it to the town and cruise ships in the distance.

As mentioned earlier in this *Guide*, entering harbors at night is very confusing in settled weather but nearly impossible in bad weather with limited visibility, a windshield covered with spray, and you and/or your crew panicked. If you should find yourself in such a predicament and can't sort it out, stay in deep water for the night and enter when daylight comes. Don't attempt to "just give it a try," — a mistake here will put you in serious trouble. *All this should be avoided by planning your passage so as to arrive during daylight.* Again we

East Bay Yacht Basin

Nassau, Bahamas – Tel/Fax (242)394-1816

Shell Products   **Showers**
Washers   **Security**
Dryers   SAIL WELL-GO SHELL!   **Deep Water**
Ice   **Elec. 30 &**
R/O Water   **50 Amp**

Personalized Service   Lowest Rates   VISA

MasterCard

SOUTH SIDE OF HARBOUR (NOW) BETWEEN BRIDGES
Quiet Waters ⚓ FREE From Harbour Traffic Wakes

CALL - VHF Channel 16
     For New Bridge Height Clearance & Info.

Bud Geiselman

HURRICANE HOLE MARINA

PARADISE ISLAND, THE BAHAMAS

- New docks for yachts of any size and draft
- Electricity - 110, 220, 440 volts
- Shell Gasolines, Diesel Oil and Marine Lubricants
  All-day fuel service on Sundays and Holidays
- Fresh Water and Ice
- 24-hour security
- Laundry facilities
- Modern showers and dressing rooms
- Swimming pool and poolside bar
- American Express, Visa and MasterCards accepted
- Near to restaurants, shopping, supermarkets,
  casinos and banks

Shell
Quality fuels
that run the
nation

TEL.(242) 363-3600 • FAX:(242) 363-3604 • VHF 16

P.O. Box SS-6317, Nassau, The Bahamas

"Nassau's Finest Marine Center"
Lightbourne Marine

- Quicksilver Inflatables
- Perkins Diesel Engines
- ITT Jabsco Pumps
- Par Products
- Racor & Fram Filters
- Woolsey/Z-spar Paints
- Electronics
- Fishing Tackle
- Cleaning Products
- Fiberglass Products
- Marine Hardware
- Boating Accessories
- Tools
- Coca-Cola Products
  at factory prices
- Haul & Launch to 25ft
- Oil & Esso Gasoline

OUR FACTORY-
TRAINED
TECHNICIANS
SERVICE OUTBOARD
MOTORS, DIESEL
ENGINES AND
GENERATORS

MERCURY OUTBOARDS

merCruiser

KOHLER MARINE GENERATORS

AWLGRIP

LIGHTBOURNE MARINE The Friendly Ones

EAST BAY STREET (east of Paradise Island Bridge)
Tel: 809-393-5285/393-5549 • Fax: 809-393-6236
P.O. Box N-4894, Nassau, Bahamas

MARLIN *Marine* LTD.

The Finest
Marine Store in
The Bahamas!

- OMC Parts
- Penn, Shimano
- Fenwick Rods & Reels
- Berkley & Ande Lines
- O'Brien Ski Equipment
- Cressi Sub Diving Gear
- Pettit Paint
- Rubbermaid
- Charts
- G.P.S., Depth Finders
- VHF Radios
- Marine Hardware

- Lubricants
- Foul Weather Gear
- 3M, Starbrite
- Anchors
- Rope
- Perko & Tempo

BOSTON WHALER

EVINRUDE OUTBOARDS

CONTENDER

OMC SERVICE

LOGIC

Located on East Bay Street
1/4 mile east of the bridge
Ph (242) 393-7873, 393-3874
Fax (242) 393-0066

BAYSHORE MARINA

NASSAU • BAHAMAS

Transient Dockage   24hr Security

Monthly Dockage   Haul & Launch

Weekly Dockage   Power Wash

Dry Storage   Bottom Painting

Only Full Service Marina Gas & Diesel   **ESSO**

Located on East Bay Street • Ph (242) 393-8232
Fax (242) 393-0066

Starpower

"Powerboat adventure has been fuelled by Texaco for over 100,000 miles.

We need performance every single day.

Texaco delivers..."

Captain Nigel Bower
of Powerboat Adventure

StarPort Locations:
Conch Inn, Abaco
Green Turtle Cay, Abaco
Guana Cay, Abaco
Man-O-War, Abaco
Sea Spray, Abaco
Sandy Point, Abaco
Treasure Cay Hotel & Marina, Abaco
Bimini Big Game Club, Bimini
Chub Cay Club, Berry Islands
Harbour view, Nassau
Rum Cay
Turtle Cove Marina, Providenciales
Valentine's Marina, Harbour Island, Eleuthera

Star Port ®

Welcome to Nassau's most complete and sought-after Hotel & Marina

- Owner Operated
- 50 air-conditioned guest rooms with color T.V. and direct phone
- Newly renovated Restaurant and Bar overlooking marina
- Fresh water
- Swimming pool and patio deck downstairs
- Satellite T.V.

- 65-slip marina, to over 150 feet with cable T.V.
- Monitor VHF 16
- Water and electrical lines (110 & 220; 3-phase available)
- Esso diesel fuel
- Fresh Water
- Security
- Laundry facilities, token-operated
- Our own 110,000 sq. ft. shopping mall opposite the hotel

The Out Islands Experience With the Convenience of Nassau

MAJOR CREDIT CARDS ACCEPTED

NASSAU HARBOUR CLUB HOTEL
AND MARINA
P.O. Box SS5755, Nassau, Bahamas
Telephone (242) 393-0771/2/3, Fax (242)393-5393

 QUALITY PETROLEUM PRODUCTS
www.mosko.com

Shell Marinas in the Bahamas and the Turks & Caicos Islands

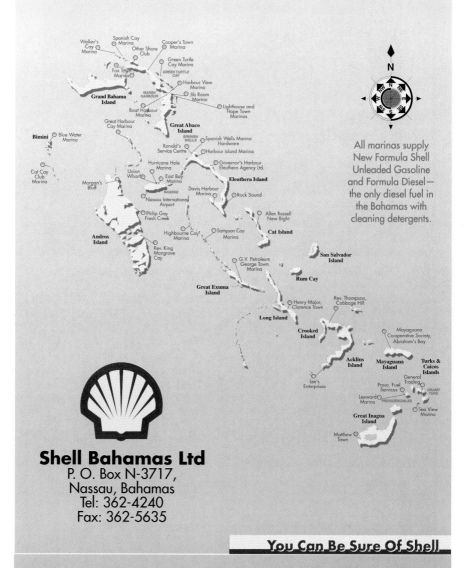

All marinas supply New Formula Shell Unleaded Gasoline and Formula Diesel—the only diesel fuel in the Bahamas with cleaning detergents.

Shell Bahamas Ltd
P. O. Box N-3717,
Nassau, Bahamas
Tel: 362-4240
Fax: 362-5635

You Can Be Sure Of Shell

remind you of the recent breach in the breakwater running westward from Paradise Island Light. If it remains unrepaired, looking through it at night could be confusing.

Under heavy weather conditions, when the bar is breaking, the entrance channel is too dangerous. The best protection then is usually found under the west end of New Providence off Clifton Pier.

The entrance channel itself is well buoyed and straightforward. The harbor, with a depth of 36 feet, will accommodate the world's largest cruise ships. As of early 1990, a new cruise-ship berthing area has been added outside the old facilities in the harbor. Its outer (north) side is parallel to the old outer mole and 175 yards further out into the harbor. Add to this distance the beam of a cruise ship, and barely 200 yards are left to pass between Paradise Island and the north edge of the ship facilities off Prince George Wharf.

The big change in Nassau Harbour this year is the construction of a second bridge to Paradise Island just west of the original bridge. This new bridge is to have the same clearance over the main channel between Potters Cay and Paradise Island as the old bridge, namely 69 feet at high water. Between Potters Cay and New Providence, the highest point is under the span closest to Potters Cay, and there are to be two pilings as lateral markers to delineate the channel under this span; these may or may not ever be painted or otherwise marked to indicate they are navigational marks, but that's what they are. Our best information at our deadline is that under this span the bridge will have 54 feet clearance at high water at the point in the channel closest to Potter's Cay. (The

SUNPOWER MARINE LTD

DISTRIBUTORS FOR

Johnson OUTBOARDS
MOTORS & ACCESSORIES

JOHNSON & EVINRUDE
Parts and Accessories
Sales & Service
Hynautic Steering Systems
*Propane Tank Refilling
Wednesday mornings at 7am*

SERVICE

BAY STREET, JUST WEST OF BASRA
(242) 322-2500 • (242) 325-2313
(242) 328-8945 • FAX (242) 328-8944
P.O. Box N-663, Nassau Bahamas

Nassau Harbour with bridge construction and location visible near end of Potter's Cay. (Tropic Isle photo)

bridge was still under construction when we were in Nassau this spring, and the spans between New Providence and Potter's Cay had not yet been placed. Correct official information as to the height here is, for some strange reason, hard to come by.) You must pass under this section to reach the East Bay Yacht Basin, and it may turn out there's a bit more clearance than the 54 feet we state. If you have any questions, or your need is for a greater clearance, straighten things out before trying to pass through by calling East Bay Yacht Basin on VHF 16 or by telephone at 242 394-1816. They should be able to help with tides and clearances.

    Sailing vessels with spars too tall for the main spans of these bridges wishing to tie up at any of the marinas east of the bridges must enter the harbor via Chub and Porgee Rocks (see sketch chart D-3, Eastern Approaches to

ATLANTiC ⌃CAT

Atlantic Equipment & Power Ltd.
For all of your marine engine needs.
PARTS • SALES • SERVICE
Fuel Filtration • Electronic Engine Repair
Nassau: (242)323-5701 • E-mail: aep@bahamas.net.bs
Freeport: (242) 352-5981 or 5987

Nassau Harbour). The tide runs strong through the Chub and Porgee Rocks channel but the controlling depth (10 feet) and the straightforward approach make it an easy one. Once in the harbor and tied up at one of the marinas, if you have not already entered officially at another port, hoist your quarantine flag and await a visit from customs.

All vessels, including pleasure craft, are required to clear with Nassau Harbour Control when entering, departing, or changing positions within the confines of Nassau Harbour. Nassau Harbour Control is operative 24 hours daily. Call them on VHF 16, switching to a working channel per instructions. When switching to a working channel on your VHF in the Nassau area, please stay off channel 12, which is the call-up channel for boats loading and unloading passengers at Prince George Wharf.

The tide sets toward the east in the harbor on the flood. At times, in the vicinity of Potter's Cay, it reaches a velocity of 2.5 knots. It is advisable to check your tides before entering. When docking in Nassau Harbour, do not spare the spring lines, and tie off to the adjoining slip when possible. Unless your boat has plenty of power and you are familiar with the strong tides in the harbor, we caution you against backing out of your slip against the tide. Auxiliaries especially should take note of this as many a visiting sailboat attempts this tricky maneuver each year, only to end up crosswise with a broken mizzen, ripped shrouds, or a few cracked ribs, to say nothing of the damage to nearby boats.

Because of heavy traffic in Nassau Harbour, the office of the Port Controller has restricted the areas available for anchorage (see sketch chart D-2, Nassau Harbour). At present, due to the expanded cruise ship facilities, there really aren't many anchorages in the harbor. In whatever remain, the holding is poor. You'd be well advised to make reservations at one of the marinas here before your arrival to be sure you'll have someplace to tie up.

Some notes of caution: We have had reports of thieves robbing boats in Nassau Harbour at night, so you may want to tie up at a marina in any event, for security. Take the same safety precautions ashore in Nassau that you would in any large population center; crime is not unknown.

Also, be extremely careful operating in Nassau Harbour, especially at night. We have reports of unlighted boats being operated carelessly at high speeds in the harbor. These pose a serious threat of which you should be aware.

Nassau, the capital city, is the ideal base for cruising through the islands,

HAULING & GENERAL HULL REPAIRS

BROWN'S BOAT BASIN

ESSO

P.O. Box N-716, Nassau, Bahamas
TEL. 393-3331 or 393-3680 Fax 393-1868

The Marina at Atlantis in development, May 1998. (Tropic Isle photo)

with modern marinas, yacht chandlers, fuel, ice, and supplies of all kinds.

Between the bridges, adjoining Potter's Cay Causeway, is East Bay Yacht Basin, offering all services to 25 boats of moderate size. Willie Meadows is the marina manager.

West of both bridges is another new addition to Nassau Harbour, the new Marina at Atlantis, scheduled to open on December 12, 1998, as part of the new Hollywood-epic scaled Atlantis resort. Sixty-three slips, accommodating yachts up to 220 feet, give complete shelter from wind and tide, with an access channel good for up to 11 feet at low water. All marine services will be available, including fuel, water, ice, electricity, and showers. Yachtsmen are welcome to sample the considerable amenities of Atlantis: 40 restaurants, bars, and nightclubs, the largest casino on the island (50,000 square feet), the world's largest outdoor aquarium, 11 pool areas (as well as a 5-story Mayan temple with water slides and an "archeological dig" revealing the lost continent of Atlantis), golf, tennis and more.

Nassau Yacht Haven, which lies immediately east of Potter's Cay, has complete services and slips for 100 yachts. A major refit to the docks and shore power supply, including new pedestals, has been completed. Fuel, water, ice, electricity, showers and laundry are available, and nearby are whatever repair facilities you might need as well as groceries, hotels, and restaurants. Mail can be forwarded to the dockmaster and held for your arrival. Bahama Divers, on the premises, sells diving equipment and supplies, and charter fishing boats are available at the docks. Topside, the Poop Deck restaurant and bar has for years been a hangout for yachtsmen and locals.

Just east of Yacht Haven, Bayshore Marina offers 150 berths at its modern docks. Gas, diesel and ice are available and major credit cards are accepted. There are hauling facilities for up boats up to 40 feet. Marlin Marine is right here

Nassau Yacht Haven. (Tropic Isle photo)

with their well-found ship's chandlery and boat sales. Across the street, Lightbourne Marine has a large selection of marine hardware and boating supplies. Next door, Nautical Marine sells and services outboards.

Farther east is the hospitable Nassau Harbour Club Hotel and Marina, which will accommodate 65 yachts, with diesel, water, electricity, and laundry facilities. On the upper level of the club there is a restaurant, and downstairs a bar and grill. Fifty rooms are available and there's a swimming pool. Across the street from the marina, a colonial-style shopping center includes one of City Markets' excellent grocery stores, as well as a bank, pharmacy, travel agency, hardware store, liquor store, beauty salon/spa, and just about anything else you might need.

Between Nassau Harbour Club and Brown's Boat Basin is the Harbour View marina, with all Texaco fuels available. Slips are available for transients, with water, ice, electricity, showers, laundry, a convenience store, and other

Nassau Harbour Club. (Tropic Isle photo)

Hurricane Hole Marina. (Tropic Isle photo)

services. The marina is managed by Hubert Bethel.

Brown's Boat Basin, immediately east of Bayshore Marina, offers gas and diesel fuels and repairs to hulls and machinery. Ice and water are available. Robert Brown is the man in charge.

Hurricane Hole Marina, across the harbor on Paradise Island, offers the good protection of 61 slips well out of the tide for drafts of up to 9 feet. Low-water limiting depth in the entrance is 8 feet. A 300-foot dock on the harbor side of the basin can accommodate vessels of well over 100 feet with drafts up to 10 feet. All petroleum products, ice, and satellite TV hookups are available. Ed Munroe is the dockmaster. There's a nice harborside swimming pool with a poolside bar and grill. Recent development in and around the marina complex include Portside at Hurricane Hole condominiums and also Hurricane Hole Plaza, which includes a marine store, The Blue Marlin Restaurant, a liquor store, bank, and some nice shops.

Paradise Harbour Club and Marina. (Tropic Isle photo)

The first marina on Paradise Island when you come in from the east, located opposite Fort Montagu, is the Paradise Harbour Club and Marina (PHC), which also offers hotel and condo rental facilities with luxury amenities that include cable TV and a large swimming pool with waterfall and jacuzzi. Twenty slips ranging from 30 to 200 feet are offered for short or long-term rental, and there is scheduled water-taxi service to downtown Nassau. PHC monitors VHF 16 and working channel 8. Anthony Hall is the dockmaster. The Columbus Tavern waterfront gourmet restaurant, located on top of the marina, serves fine food from 7 a.m. until 11 p.m. daily and can provide catering service to yachts as well as hotel room service.

The Royal Nassau Sailing Club and the Nassau Yacht Club are both located near Fort Montagu at the eastern end of the harbor.

Sunpower Marine, just west of BASRA on Bay Street, specializes in sales, repairs, and maintenance of outboard motors. In the Out Island Traders Building east of the bridge, Ingraham's Marine stocks marine hardware and accessories. Phillips Sailmakers, in the shopping mall just east of the Shirley Street Post Office, handles racing and cruising sails and specializes in repairs. Orders for sail bags, sail covers, and boat awnings can also be filled, and pickup and delivery can be arranged. They monitor VHF 16: call *Fandango*.

Mail can be sent to yachtsmen c/o General Delivery at either the General Office or Shirley Street Post Office, both in Nassau. The Shirley Street location is less hectic and within easy walking distance of the East Bay area. In the shopping plaza just east of the Shirley Street Post Office is the telecommunica-

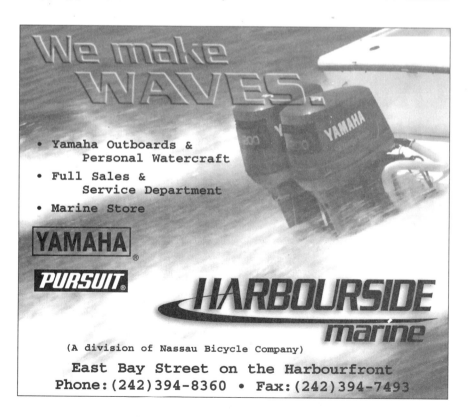

We make WAVES.

- Yamaha Outboards & Personal Watercraft
- Full Sales & Service Department
- Marine Store

YAMAHA
PURSUIT.

HARBOURSIDE marine

(A division of Nassau Bicycle Company)
East Bay Street on the Harbourfront
Phone: (242) 394-8360 • Fax: (242) 394-7493

tions station. Luden Limited will hold mail for yachtsmen who wish to replenish their liquor supply, do their laundry, and check their correspondence in one stop.

Nassau offers much of interest ashore and afloat. In the harbor, some of the largest cruise ships in the world come and go daily, with live music and general hoopla heralding their arrival. Freighters unload their enormous cargos, and at Potter's Cay, mailboats carrying supplies and passengers to and from the out islands line the dock. Power and sailing yachts of every description and port of call pass by continuously during the daylight hours, and it's not unusual for a cruising boat to run into one or more good friends on their way to other islands or returning home. Many of the houses and public buildings in town are picturesque and historic, some in genteel disrepair and others refurbished and freshly painted. Along the waterfront, the mellow smell of age and humidity mingles with the pungent odor of fish and conch being cleaned, the fumes of diesel fuel and auto exhaust, and whiffs of the flowering trees and shrubs that thrive all over town. There's sand and dust kicked up around construction and renovation sites, where collectors have found old bottles, musket balls, and other treasures from times past. The two-story open-air Straw Market, between Bay Street and the waterfront, is always crowded with tourists bargaining with vendors for straw baskets and hats, shell jewelry, T-shirts, wood carvings, and other island crafts. Also on Bay Street, in the Vendue House, the Pompey Museum features exhibits of Bahamian art and photography, many devoted to the ideal of freedom and the history of slavery and emancipation in The Bahamas. (Pompey was a Bahamian hero who led a slave revolt against

DAMIANOS REALTY CO. LTD.

ESTATES CLUB
THE ART OF MARKETING PROPERTY.

Realtors since 1945

Specializing in the Sale of:

Private Islands

Estates • Houses • Condominiums • Commercial Properties
Lyford Cay • Cable Beach • Paradise Island
Port New Providence • Family Islands

*Accelerated consideration for Permanent Residence status
for home buyers spending $500,000. or more.*

East Shirley Street, P.O. Box N-732, Nassau, N.P., The Bahamas
Tel: (242) 322-2305 Evenings: (242) 324-3993 Fax: (242) 322-2033

SEA FROST®

Refrigeration and Freezer Systems for Boats

The Cool Choice

To The Bahamas And Beyond!

Sea Frost, 372 Route 4, Barrington, NH, USA 03825
603-868-5720// Fax: 603-868-1040

web site: www.seafrost.com   e-mail: seafrost@worldnet.att.net

CRUISE THROUGH OUR AISLES

While cruising through our Islands, we invite you to let City Markets and Winn-Dixie provide you with complete one stop shopping. We carry a full line of groceries, snacks, meat and produce. And if you're on the go, visit our Deli for that fast carry-out meal or choose a party platter from our wide array of delicious meats and cheeses.

PHONE US WITH YOUR ORDER! WE WILL DELIVER TO YOU FREE FOR ORDERS OF $100 OR MORE.

In Nassau, visit our City Markets location at the Harbour Bay Shopping Center, walking distance from the Harbour Bay Club Marina on East Bay Street. For phone orders at this location call **393 - 6060**.

Or visit our other City Market locations at the Lyford Cay Shopping Center, walking distance from the Lyford Cay Marina. For phone orders at this location call **362 - 4283**.

Hdqts. 393-2830

THE MEAT PEOPLE

Other convenient City Markets locations:
• Independence Shopping Centre • Market Street • Village Road • Cable Beach Shopping Centre • Rosetta Street • Sea Grape Shopping Centre • South Beach.

FREEPORT

THE LOW PRICE LEADER.

Grand Bahama - Stop by Winn-Dixie at the Downtown Shopping Center or phone us at **352-7901**. Or visit our new store at the Lucaya Shopping Center or phone **373 - 5500**.

plantation-owner Lord Rolle on Exuma in the 1700s). Just off West Bay Street is a new pirate museum worth checking out.

The Bahamian government recently gave duty-free status to most items of tourist expenditure, including perfumes, cameras, watches and clocks, china, crystal, leather goods, table linens, and liquor. You'll find notable savings compared to years past in the shops on and around Bay Street. John Bull's elegant store is one of the best known, with a wide variety of the finest watches and other luxury items. The Nassau Shop also carries a comprehensive selection of duty-free goods.

Traffic is often at a standstill along the narrow one-way streets, especially at lunchtime — in fact, a traffic reporter now broadcasts updates on the radio. If you want to explore you're best off walking or at least hiring a cab driver who knows the shortcuts. Fares are regulated and meters are required, so if your driver claims to have a broken meter and seems particularly interested in whether this is your first visit to Nassau, beware. Most cab drivers, however, are friendly, honest, and good guides. The cheapest travel alternative is to catch one of the jitneys that travel frequently around the city.

There are many good places to eat in town or within a taxi ride's distance. A pleasant ride about nine miles out on West Bay Street, the Traveller's Rest is famous for fresh cracked conch and "smudder" grouper, and the Seagrape boutique and gift shop on the premises sells Bahamian art and Androsia print clothing. In town, the Crocodile's Waterfront Bar & Grill offers good fresh seafood, Bahamian dishes, hamburgers, and salads, as well as a daily happy hour.

It's worthwhile on Paradise Island to visit the grounds of the exclusive Ocean Club, once home of eccentric multimillionaire Huntington Hartford and now an Atlantis facility. Here the Versailles Gardens, loosely modeled after those in France, include an assortment of statues ranging from giants David Livingstone and Franklin D. Roosevelt, to scattered ardent gods and goddesses, to Faust and Mephistopheles. Overlooking the gardens is the Cloisters, a French monastery purchased by William Randolph Hearst years ago, disassembled and shipped to America, and then bought by Hartford and rebuilt here. People, especially rich ones, do strange things.

There are many things to see and do in and around Nassau if you take the time to explore. While you're here you might want to check out the nightlife. On Paradise Island and Cable Beach are miles of sprawling luxury hotels and enormous casinos that will leave you dazzled if not dazed, featuring elaborate floor shows with pyrotechnics, wild animals, magicians, and statuesque women of regal carriage wearing relentless smiles, stacks of eyelashes, and little else.

There are few anchorages around the coast of New Providence of interest to yachtsmen with the exception of **West Bay** (see sketch chart D-5, Western New Providence). This bay is at the extreme western end of the island and is well protected from the prevailing winds. It is sheltered from the north by Lyford Cay and to some extent from the west-northwest by **Goulding Cay** and a series of coral reefs. Holding is reported poor in this sand over rock, and it is pretty much surrounded by private property. The entrance is from the west-northwest between Simms Point and Goulding Cay. A draft of 7 feet can be carried in at

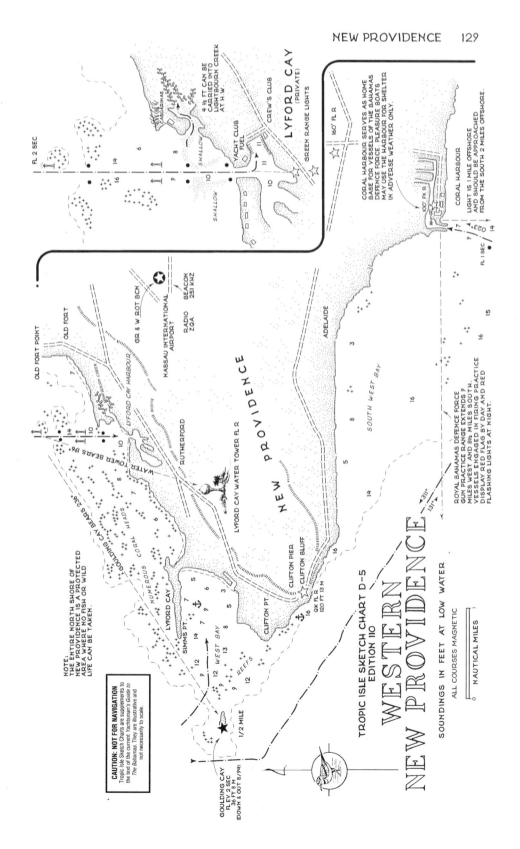

NOTE:
THE ENTIRE NORTH SHORE OF
NEW PROVIDENCE IS A PROTECTED
AREA WHERE NO FISH OR WILD
LIFE CAN BE TAKEN.

CAUTION: NOT FOR NAVIGATION
Tropic Isle Sketch Charts are supplements to the text of the current Yachtsman's Guide to The Bahamas. They are illustrative and not necessarily to scale.

TROPIC ISLE SKETCH CHART D-5
EDITION 110
WESTERN
NEW PROVIDENCE
SOUNDINGS IN FEET AT LOW WATER
ALL COURSES MAGNETIC
NAUTICAL MILES

OLD FORT POINT
OLD FORT

GR & W ROT BCN
NASSAU INTERNATIONAL
AIRPORT
RADIO
ZQA
BEACON
251 KHZ

LYFORD CAY HARBOUR
WATER TOWER BEARS 196°
RUTHERFORD
LYFORD CAY WATER TOWER FL R

NEW PROVIDENCE

GOLDING CAY BEARS 236°
NUMEROUS
CORAL HEADS
LYFORD CAY
SIMMS PT.
WEST BAY
REEFS

GOULDING CAY
FL EV 2 SEC
36 FT 8 M
(DOWN & OUT 8/94)
1/2 MILE

CLIFTON PT.
CLIFTON PIER
CLIFTON BLUFF
QK FL R
120 FT 13 M

ADELAIDE

SOUTH WEST BAY

331°
131°

ROYAL BAHAMAS DEFENCE FORCE
GUN PRACTICE RANGE EXTENDS 9
MILES WEST AND 8½ MILES SOUTH.
VESSELS ENGAGED IN FIRING PRACTICE
DISPLAY RED FLAG BY DAY AND RED
FLASHING LIGHTS AT NIGHT.

LYFORD CAY
(PRIVATE)

CASUARINAS
4½ FT CAN BE
CARRIED INTO
LIGHTBOURN CREEK
AT H.W.
YACHT CLUB
FUEL
CREW'S CLUB
SHALLOW
SHALLOW
GREEN RANGE LIGHTS
FL 2 SEC

160' FL R

CORAL HARBOUR SERVES AS HOME
BASE FOR VESSELS OF THE BAHAMAS
DEFENCE FORCE. PLEASURE BOATS
MAY USE THE HARBOUR FOR SHELTER
IN ADVERSE WEATHER ONLY.

100 FX R
CORAL HARBOUR
LIGHT IS 1 MILE OFFSHORE
AND SHOULD BE APPROACHED
FROM THE SOUTH 2 MILES OFFSHORE.
FL 1 SEC

Lyford Cay Club marina. (Tropic Isle photo)

low water, but keep a good lookout for isolated coral heads.

The Lyford Cay Club and its Lyford Cay Yacht Harbour (see sketch chart D-5, Western New Providence) lie to the east of **Lyford Cay.** Lyford Cay Club management writes that the 10-foot entrance channel is once again well marked. Lyford Cay Club is private, but visiting yachts are welcome to the harbor. Facilities include fuel, electricity, showers, water, ice, laundry, and yacht monitoring. Nearby is a shopping center with a bank, hardware store, art gallery and liquor store. Contact the harbormaster from 8 a.m. until 5 p.m. on VHF 16. Space can be tight, so call ahead.

Before it closed in 1972, **Coral Harbour** was one of the finest marinas in The Bahamas. The harbor and marina are now a restricted area owned by the Bahamian government and used as headquarters for the craft of the Royal Bahamas Defence Force. Certain authorized boats may pass through the harbor to the canal waterways, keeping to the northern side of the harbor and proceeding at slow speed. Otherwise, boats may only use the harbor to seek shelter from adverse weather conditions and should report arrival to the Defence Force Duty Operations Officer for berthing instructions.

All vessels cruising the Coral Harbour area should be aware that the Defence Force operates a surface gun practice firing range here on a frequent schedule. The range, rectangular in shape, extends 9 miles to the west of the harbor entrance and 8.5 miles south. Vessels engaged in firing practice display a red flag by day and red fixed or red flashing lights at night; shore units display a red flag on the northern side of the harbor entrance. In addition, marine warnings are broadcast regularly on VHF 16 while the facility (i.e., the range) is in use. Pleasure craft cruising this area should maintain course and speed and if firing commences, clear the area at the earliest possible moment.

In heavy weather from the north or northwest when the Nassau Bar is dangerous, shelter can be found under Clifton Bluff in 16-24 feet (see sketch chart D-5, Western New Providence). This anchorage is in South West Bay.

For the most part the south and east coasts of New Providence are shoal and studded with reefs. Be familiar with government charts of these areas; we recently had a letter from someone who ran aground on a rocky spot just east of New Providence. **Rose Island, Athol Island, Green Cay,** and **Salt Cay** offer excellent day and weekend cruising for small boats based in Nassau. Green Cay and Sandy Cay are private property and landing is not permitted.

The numerous anchorages indicated on sketch charts D-3 (Eastern Approaches to Nassau Harbour) and D-4 (Rose Island) are recommended for yachts of moderate size under prevailing weather conditions. There are also

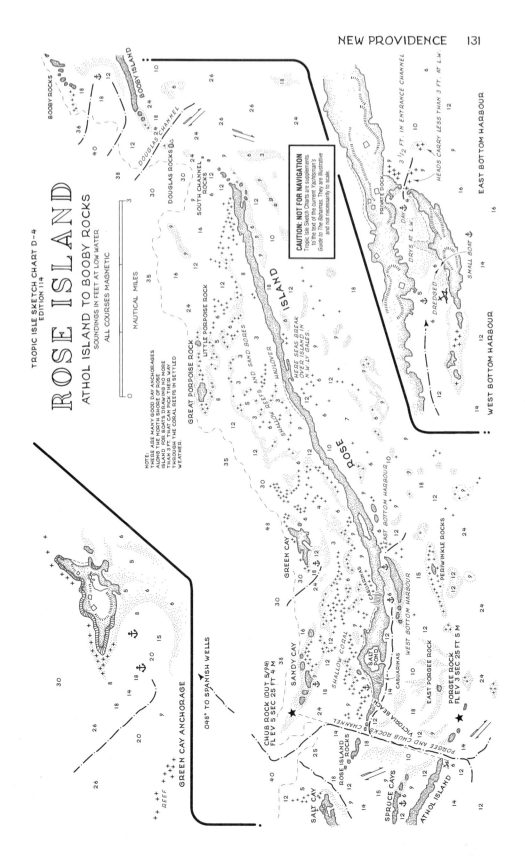

TROPIC ISLE SKETCH CHART D-4
EDITION 11.4

ROSE ISLAND

ATHOL ISLAND TO BOOBY ROCKS

SOUNDINGS IN FEET AT LOW WATER

ALL COURSES MAGNETIC

NAUTICAL MILES

CAUTION: NOT FOR NAVIGATION
Tropic Isle Sketch Charts are supplements
to the text of the current Yachtsman's
Guide to The Bahamas. They are illustrative
and not necessarily to scale.

NOTE:
THERE ARE MANY GOOD DAY ANCHORAGES
ALONG THE NORTH SHORE OF ROSE
ISLAND FOR BOATS DRAWING NO MORE
THAN 3 FT. THAT CAN PICK THEIR WAY
THROUGH THE CORAL REEFS IN SETTLED
WEATHER.

BOOBY ROCKS

BOOBY ISLAND

DOUGLAS CHANNEL

DOUGLAS ROCKS

SOUTH CHANNEL ROCKS

3 1/2 FT. IN ENTRANCE CHANNEL

HEADS CARRY LESS THAN 3 FT. AT L.W.

EAST BOTTOM HARBOUR

PRIVATE DOCK

DRY'S AT L.W.

DRY'S AT L.W.

SMALL BOAT

DREDGED

WEST BOTTOM HARBOUR

GREAT PORPOISE ROCK

LITTLE PORPOISE ROCK

SAND BORES

SHALLOW REEFS AND

HAULOVER

ROSE

ISLAND

HERE SEAS BREAK
OVER ISLAND IN
N W'LY GALES

EAST BOTTOM HARBOUR

PERIWINKLE ROCKS

GREEN CAY

CASUARINAS

WEST BOTTOM HARBOUR

SHALLOW CORAL

SANDY CAY

SALT POND

CASUARINAS

EAST PORGEE ROCK

PORGEE ROCK
FL EV 3 SEC 25 FT 5 M

GREEN CAY ANCHORAGE

REEF

048° TO SPANISH WELLS

CHUB ROCK (OUT 5/94)
FL EV 5 SEC 25 FT 4 M

ROSE ISLAND
ROCKS

VICTORIA BEACH

PORGEE AND CHUB ROCKS CHANNEL

SALT CAY

SPRUCE CAYS

ATHOL ISLAND

some nice day anchorages along the north shore of Rose Island for small boats that can pick their way through the coral reefs in settled weather.

Eastern entrance to Nassau Harbour. Leaving Nassau Harbour by the eastern entrance, avoid the series of shallow patches that extend eastward from Potter's Cay three-quarters of a mile in a narrow belt down the center of the harbor. Several high-water channels carrying 6 feet or better exist through this shallow area, but if you draw 5 feet or more it is best to stay in the deep water.

The main channel through the length of Nassau Harbour lies between Paradise Island and Potter's Cay under the highest spans of the Paradise Island Bridges. From Potter's Cay, heading eastward and keeping the shallow area mentioned above to starboard, the deepest water lies on the northern side of the channel, about 8-9 feet at low water over a grassy bottom. A shallow rocky shoal extends northeast about 300 yards from the vicinity of Fort Montague, and must be avoided. There is now an airport on the southeast corner of Paradise Island, and planes taking off toward the east will pass low over the light in the Narrows. The seaplane ramp has also moved here from its old location west of the bridge, so watch for seaplane traffic.

If departing Nassau Harbour via **The Narrows,** vessels drawing more than 5.5 feet should proceed to a position one-quarter mile south of Salt Cay before altering course eastward. A shallow sandbank runs out a short distance south from the tower standing on the eastern end of Salt Cay. From there proceed into the Northeast Providence Channel, leaving Chub Rock to starboard, or into the anchorage under Sandy Cay.

Proceeding eastward, but not through the Narrows, a very good lookout must be kept for coral patches that lie to the south of Athol Island. While most of these are deep, some carry less than 6 feet at low water. It is not possible to give set courses for this area. Although the bottom is composed mainly of dark grass, most of the heads are encircled with a ring of white sand that helps to make them visible. In general, the better water lies about one-quarter mile south of the Athol shore to a position one-quarter mile south of Porgee Rocks. Once you have passed Porgee Rocks, you should have no difficulty.

Shallow sandbanks lie on both sides of Chub and Porgee Rocks Channel, but they are easily seen and the water between them is deep. Again, a strong tidal current exists here.

In approaching the eastern entrance to Nassau Harbour from the southeast, **Porgee Rocks** may be difficult to pick up against the changing shoreline as you come north. A good way to make this approach is to steer for the large clump of trees on the western end of Rose Island on a 320° heading. (Two large clumps of trees on Rose Island are visible for 10 miles or more; be sure to use the western and higher clump in these directions.) Whichever route you use to return from the Exumas, you must avoid the foul ground off the east end of New Providence (see DMA 26306). When the center span of the Paradise Island Bridges bears about 287°, turn in on that heading, taking Porgee Rocks about one-quarter mile to starboard, and follow sketch chart D-3 (Eastern Approaches to Nassau Harbour) in from there. Years ago the highest point in Nassau was the Fort Fincastle water tower, but now the towering hotels on Paradise Island are higher and visible for a considerable distance.

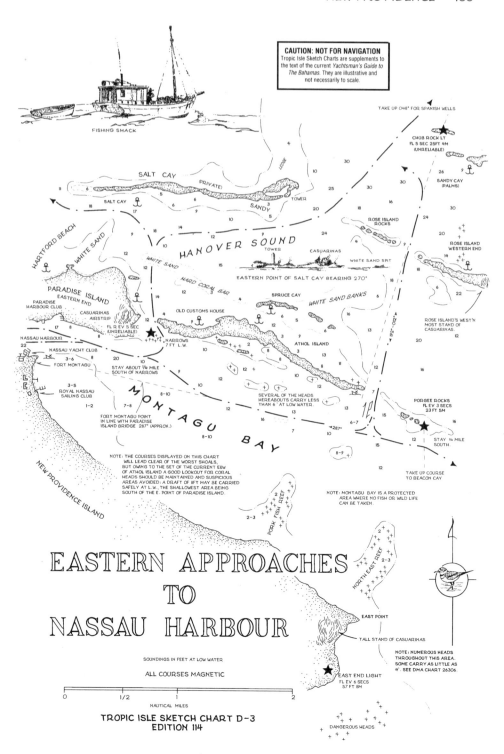

CAUTION: NOT FOR NAVIGATION
Tropic Isle Sketch Charts are supplements to the text of the current *Yachtsman's Guide to The Bahamas*. They are illustrative and not necessarily to scale.

TAKE UP 048° FOR SPANISH WELLS

CHUB ROCK LT
FL 5 SEC 25FT 4M
(UNRELIABLE)

SANDY CAY
(PALMS)

FISHING SMACK

SALT CAY
(PRIVATE)

LEDGE

SALT CAY

SANDY

TOWER

ROSE ISLAND
ROCKS

ROSE ISLAND
WESTERN END

HARTFORD BEACH

WHITE SAND

HANOVER SOUND

TOWER   CASUARINAS

WHITE SAND SPIT

EASTERN POINT OF SALT CAY BEARING 270°

WHITE SAND

HARD CORAL BAR

SPRUCE CAY

WHITE SAND BANKS

ROSE ISLAND'S WEST'N
MOST STAND OF
CASUARINAS

PARADISE ISLAND
Eastern End

PARADISE
HARBOUR CLUB

CASUARINAS
AIRSTRIP

OLD CUSTOMS HOUSE

FL R EV 5 SEC
(UNRELIABLE)

NARROWS
7 FT L.W.

ATHOL ISLAND

NASSAU HARBOUR

NASSAU YACHT CLUB

FORT MONTAGU

STAY ABOUT ¼ MILE
SOUTH OF NARROWS

3-6

20

3-5
ROYAL NASSAU
SAILING CLUB

1-2

7-8

8-10

SEVERAL OF THE HEADS
HEREABOUTS CARRY LESS
THAN 6' AT LOW WATER.

PORGEE ROCKS
FL EV 3 SECS
23 FT 5M

STAY ¼ MILE
SOUTH.

MONTAGU BAY

FORT MONTAGU POINT
IN LINE WITH PARADISE
ISLAND BRIDGE 287° (APPROX.)

8-10

287°

TAKE UP COURSE
TO BEACON CAY

NOTE: THE COURSES DISPLAYED ON THIS CHART
WILL LEAD CLEAR OF THE WORST SHOALS,
BUT OWING TO THE SET OF THE CURRENT EBW
OF ATHOL ISLAND A GOOD LOOKOUT FOR CORAL
HEADS SHOULD BE MAINTAINED AND SUSPICIOUS
AREAS AVOIDED. A DRAFT OF 8FT MAY BE CARRIED
SAFELY AT L.W., THE SHALLOWEST AREA BEING
SOUTH OF THE E. POINT OF PARADISE ISLAND.

NOTE: MONTAGU BAY IS A PROTECTED
AREA WHERE NO FISH OR WILD LIFE
CAN BE TAKEN.

NEW PROVIDENCE ISLAND

PORK FISH REEF

2-3

NORTH EAST REEF

EAST POINT

TALL STAND OF CASUARINAS

EASTERN APPROACHES
TO
NASSAU HARBOUR

NOTE: NUMEROUS HEADS
THROUGHOUT THIS AREA.
SOME CARRY AS LITTLE AS
4'. SEE DMA CHART 26306.

SOUNDINGS IN FEET AT LOW WATER

ALL COURSES MAGNETIC

EAST END LIGHT
FL EV 6 SECS
57 FT 8M

0   1/2   1   2

NAUTICAL MILES

DANGEROUS HEADS

**TROPIC ISLE SKETCH CHART D-3
EDITION 114**

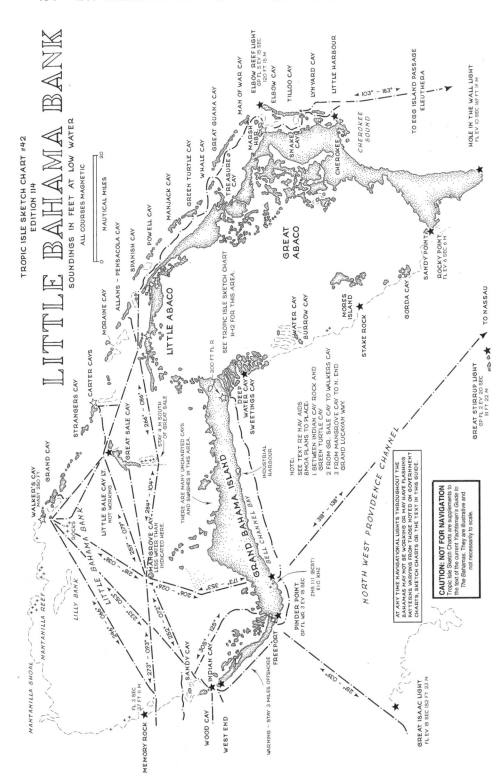

Grand Bahama

and the Little Bahama Bank

D.M.A. Charts: 26299, 26300, 26319, 26321, 26323. Tropic Isle Sketch Charts: B-2, 42, Set H.

Most northerly of The Bahamas, the Little Bahama Bank is considered one of the finest cruising grounds in the western hemisphere, with its hundreds of islands and superlative fishing. From **Matanilla Shoal** at the northwest corner, the bank extends in a great arc southeastward to Little Harbour Bar, a distance of 155 miles. Thence the rugged coast of Great Abaco continues for 31 miles further to Hole in the Wall, southernmost point of the bank.

On the west coast of Abaco at Sandy Point, 15 miles to the north of Hole in the Wall, the bank continues again and trends north-northwest past Gorda Cay and remote Mores Island to the southeastern tip of Grand Bahama. The south and west coasts of Grand Bahama are steep-to and rocky. From West End Point it is 45 miles back to Matanilla Shoal.

The northeastern side of the bank is fringed by a chain of cays and reefs, where you will find some of the most beautiful scenery and picturesque settlements in The Bahamas. There are three large islands in this group: Grand Bahama, Great Abaco, and Little Abaco. There are settlements and many new developments. At the same time a large number of the cays are still uninhabited and you may, if you wish, be just as remote as in the Exuma Cays.

Grand Bahama (Tropic Isle Sketch Charts: 42, B-2, 3, 4, 5) is the fourth largest island in The Bahamas, covering 430 square miles, about 65 miles long and 7 miles wide. The land is low and in some places swampy; dense pine forest covers higher ground. The north coast from a bit east of West End to its extreme southeastern point is mangrove swashes and creeks where only shoal-draft vessels, with local knowledge, may penetrate. Off this coast for considerable distance are rocky bars and scores of small cays and swashes that don't appear on any chart. The south coast of Grand Bahama is steep-to and should given wide berth by sailboats, as it becomes a dangerous lee shore in southerly winds.

Grand Bahama is about to experience something of a boom as Hutchison Port Holdings has already spent $78 million building the new Freeport Container Port, with plans to expand it further into the largest transshipment

---

PLEASE NOTE: For a description of **Batelco towers in all areas and their light characteristics**, please check page 39 of this Guide.

TROPIC ISLE SKETCH CHART B-2
EDITION 114

WEST END

GRAND BAHAMA

SOUNDINGS IN FEET AT LOW WATER

ALL COURSES MAGNETIC

NAUTICAL MILES

RECOMMENDED APPROACH TO THE L. BAHAMA BANK FOR
5-6FT DRAFT. AREAS OF ROCK & LEDGE. GOOD LIGHT REQUIRED.

CAUTION: NOT FOR NAVIGATION
Tropic Isle Sketch Charts are supplements to
the text of the current *Yachtsman's Guide to
The Bahamas.* They are illustrative and
not necessarily to scale.

4 - 4 ½ MILE

3-5

SHALLOW

SANDY CAY-PRIVATE
(PROMINENT STAND
OF CASUARINAS)

6-8   3-5

NOTE:
WHEN WORKING SOUTHWEST FROM
MANGROVE CAY THE TALL TREES
ON SANDY CAY ARE RAISED BEFORE
WOOD CAY OR WEST END.

NOTE:
WORKING NORTHEAST FROM
INDIAN CAY RK. SET COURSE
TO PASS MARKS AS SHOWN.
ONCE PAST BARRACUDA SHOAL
MAINTAIN SAME COURSE UNTIL
SANDY CAY BEARS DUE WEST
BEFORE TAKING UP A COURSE
FOR WALKER'S CAY, MANGROVE
CAY, OR GRAND LUCAYAN WWY.

3-5

BARACUDA SHOAL
FL 4 SEC

½ MILE

5

SHALLOW
4

CHURCH BANK

SHALLOW - DRYS

7-9

SHALLOW

5-7

STRONG TIDAL SE

7-9

14

5

STAY 100 YDS OFF

6

WOOD CAY

8

18   14

8

ROCKY BAR

FL R 4 SEC

10

8

BAR

GRASSY PATCHES

6

5-6   GOODWILL CH.

OLD BAHAMA BAY
MARINA

10

5 6

18-20 DAY MK

INDIAN CAY RK.
FL 6 SEC 40 FT 8M
(UNREL.)

YACHT
BASIN

CREEK IS
OFF-LIMITS
TO VISITORS

INDIAN CAY

SHALLOW WHITE BANK

3-4

DOCKMASTER

(SEE NOTE)   NORTH PT.

OLD BAHAMA BAY MARINA

3-4

CROSS BAY
TEMP. ANCH.
(POOR HOLDING)

215' TWR
FR OVER FR

3-4   3-5   2   3

CONSPIC.
WATER TWR

FL 4 SEC 32 FT 6M

CUSTOMS

4

COMM
OFF PINK
BLDG

3-4

SHALLOW

SETTLEMENT
GOV'T. WHARF

PINK BUILDING
TANKS

GOV'T.
WHARF

4-5

SETTLEMENT PT.

AIRSTRIP

3

4-5

STAY OVER WHITE SAND

NOTE:
PLANS CALL FOR
REMOVAL
OF 215 FT TOWER

180°

APPROACH TO WEST END VICINITY FROM GULF STREAM

INDIAN CAY ROCK
FL 6 SEC
(UNREL)   INDIAN CAY

TO MARINA

Old Bahama Bay Marina. (Tropic Isle photo)

port in the Western Hemisphere. Hutchison, along with the Grand Bahama Development Corporation, is also heavily involved in hotel and resort development, and has purchased properties throughout the Freeport/Lucaya area. You can expect to see big changes here over the next several years, and as they occur, there will be landmarks that disappear or change their appearance, and new ones that sprout up where there had been none.

West End West End (Tropic Isle Sketch Chart: B-2). The former Jack Tar Marina and surrounding property are under new ownership and management. This property is now known as Old Bahama Bay, and the marina is the Old Bahama Bay Marina. Work is progressing very rapidly to enlarge and modernize the marina as well as raze the old resort and redevelop the area into a new residential community and luxury resort. Strategic location on the extreme northwestern tip of Grand Bahama, at the western edge of the Little Bahama Bank, makes the Old Bahama Bay Marina a convenient port of entry for yachts bound for the Abaco Cays. As time goes by, Old Bahama Bay, with its many amenities, will itself be a destination. The Old Bahama Bay Marina will remain open during renovation, continuing as a port of entry, with slips, fuels, water, electricity, telephone, etc., but be prepared to encounter work in progress. Where changes are imminent, such as here, we advise you to check ahead of time as to navigation marks and availability of facilities important to you. Call the marina at 242 346-6251. Use VHF 16 for help entering and docking instructions.

(Note: In the following text we describe Old Bahama Bay and its approach as they were at publication time for this edition of the Guide. More changes are planned, so be prepared to see differences.)

Old Bahama Bay, new entrance. (Tropic Isle photo)

Harbour Hotel and Marina, West End. (Tropic Isle photo)

In a daylight approach to the marina, the conspicuous water tower is the best landmark. There is presently also a 215-foot tower on the Old Bahama Bay property with fixed red lights top and midpoint. Plans call for this to be removed, so it may or may not be there. In addition, this tower is frequently hit by lightning, so even if it is there, it may not be functioning. If you are approaching at night (a practice we strongly discourage anywhere in The Bahamas), this tower, if there and working, will be your first landfall. If it's out or gone, you're pretty much on your own, because the Indian Cay Rock and Settlement Point Lights are unreliable. There are plans to put a light atop the water tower, but when this may happen we can't say.

The approach here has been changed considerably. The new approach is through the old commercial harbor entrance, and the old marina entrance has been closed. Do not try to cut your approach (or departure) short; you must approach from deep water straight into the entrance channel. Then you should have 13 feet all the way in. If, departing, you do not get to deep water before turning up toward Indian Cay, or if you try to run in too close from Indian Cay down to the marina entrance, you'll be on a ledge. Once inside the marina, the rest of the harbor will have from 8-10 feet. Phase 1 of the development plan calls for about 75 slips to be completed in the old marina area by the end of summer 1998. Also at this stage there are plans for a 50-room hotel and a restaurant/bar. Phase 2 will add new slips, docks and breakwaters in the area just inside the entrance to the harbor. The ultimate plan is for about 180 slips sized to accommodate yachts up to 175 feet. Also, canals will be dug for future house sites and, as they say, much much more. There is a lot of acreage here and the location is unique; money and time could bring very big changes.

Between Settlement Point and North Point (West End Point on some charts), there is a day anchorage in 30 feet of water in Cross Bay. Holding is poor in thin white sand over rock and there is shelter only in winds from northeast to east. If you're anchored here and the wind is onshore, you and your boat will probably wind up onshore too.

In West End settlement there is the Harbour Hotel and Marina. This is accessible through the Goodwill Channel which is good for about 3-4 feet at low

Freeport Harbour. (Tropic Isle photo)

water. When we were working on this edition, this channel was unmarked, so you'll need a favorable tide and good light to eyeball your way in. The jetties surrounding the marina are unfinished to their full height, and so do not yet offer the protection they will when complete. There are 21 slips in the marina, a nice restaurant/bar, the Harbour Bay Watch, nine hotel rooms, a laundromat, electricity, water, diesel, and gas. As always, it's a good idea to call ahead to be sure anything you really need will be available. In town there is a telephone station, doctor, and grocery. Kerr's Bakery has good raisin bread. The Seaside Bakery stands by on VHF 16, has a taxi, and will deliver. The Star Hotel, built in 1946, was the island's first hotel and is now a bar and restaurant. Other places to eat include Yvonne's Cafe (great conchburgers) and the Village Tavern. On Saturday nights an informal street fair serves food on the waterfront. If you have four or more people and reasonably priced good Swiss-Bahamian cooking with an ocean view is what the crew is clamoring for, the Buccaneer Club will send

Bradford Grand Bahama. (Tropic Isle photo)

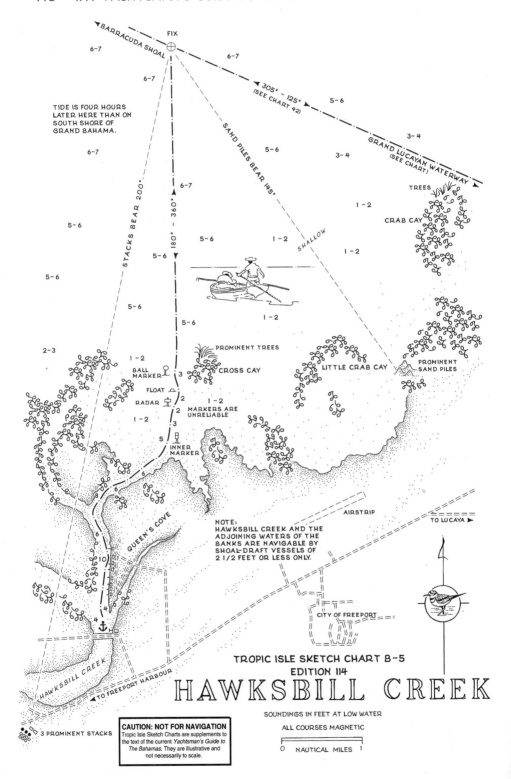

TROPIC ISLE SKETCH CHART B-5
EDITION 114

HAWKSBILL CREEK

SOUNDINGS IN FEET AT LOW WATER

ALL COURSES MAGNETIC

O   NAUTICAL MILES   1

CAUTION: NOT FOR NAVIGATION
Tropic Isle Sketch Charts are supplements to
the text of the current *Yachtsman's Guide to
The Bahamas*. They are illustrative and
not necessarily to scale.

NOTE:
HAWKSBILL CREEK AND THE
ADJOINING WATERS OF THE
BANKS ARE NAVIGABLE BY
SHOAL-DRAFT VESSELS OF
2 1/2 FEET OR LESS ONLY.

TIDE IS FOUR HOURS
LATER HERE THAN ON
SOUTH SHORE OF
GRAND BAHAMA.

BARRACUDA SHOAL

FIX

305° - 125°
(SEE CHART 42)

GRAND LUCAYAN WATERWAY
(SEE CHART)

SAND PILES BEAR 145°

STACKS BEAR 200°

180° - 360°

SHALLOW

TREES

CRAB CAY

PROMINENT TREES

CROSS CAY

LITTLE CRAB CAY

PROMINENT
SAND PILES

BALL
MARKER

FLOAT

RADAR

MARKERS ARE
UNRELIABLE

INNER
MARKER

QUEEN'S COVE

AIRSTRIP

TO LUCAYA ►

CITY OF FREEPORT

HAWKSBILL CREEK

TO FREEPORT HARBOUR

3 PROMINENT STACKS

a bus to pick you up. The ride is worth it.

On the western elbow of Grand Bahama's south shore is the extensive commercial enterprise known as **Freeport** (D.M.A. Charts: 26320, 26323. Tropic Isle Sketch Charts: B-3, 42). **Freeport Harbour** can accommodate oceangoing vessels seeking refuge from heavy weather. Bradford Marine has opened a branch yacht repair facility here called Bradford Grand Bahama. A 150-ton Travelift is capable of hauling boats up to 120 feet. Bradford can do all manner of repairs here including fiberglass, welding, propeller and shaft.

Freeport is a port of entry for The Bahamas with the customs and immigration office adjoining that of the port director. However, as it's a commercial port, it's preferred that private yachts clear customs and immigration at the Lucayan Marina Village, Port Lucaya Marina, or Xanadu Marina.

When approaching Freeport Harbour from the south, keep a sharp lookout for the offshore tanker berths that lie southeast of the harbor entrance. Pleasure craft may not anchor in Freeport Harbour, but may tie up for up to 4 hours at no charge to clear customs and immigration. Obtain berthing assignments and request customs and immigration by calling Freeport Harbour Control on VHF Channel 16. If you stay longer than four hours, dockage and harbormaster's fees will be charged from time of arrival. Minimum fee for vessels up to and including 45 feet for 24 hours, or part thereof, is $1.00 per foot.

Freeport Harbour was formed from the south end of **Hawksbill Creek** and is separated from the north end by two causeways. The north end of the creek opens onto the Little Bahama Bank and is accessible only to small boats on the tide. Controlling depth just north of the north entrance is a mere 2 feet at low water, but 5-8 feet are offered in the blue-water channels inside. A number of Freeport residents live along the eastern side of the creek and their docks reach into the channel. Best to favor the east side along here. There are several ocean holes in the creek where fishing is excellent.

For the 9 miles east of Freeport Harbour to Bell Channel (Lucaya), give the coast at least a one-mile berth. Stay at least 1.5 miles off after you pass the entrance to Running Mon Marina. Staying over a depth of 100 feet or more will keep you at a safe distance, but if your depth sounder shows less than that, you're dangerously close to the many rocky patches that lie quite far out. Ship mooring buoys, dive markers, and other marks placed on the reef and farther out nearly to the 100-foot contour are dangers you must watch for. This is especially true west of Bell Channel. Some of these are reported to look exactly like the Bell Channel sea buoy, so be sure of your position before you enter. Marks such as these can be placed or removed at any time, so be prepared for the various possibilities. *Caution: With the exception of Freeport Harbour, all of the entrance channels along this stretch of coast are comparatively shallow and should not be negotiated in strong southeast through westerly conditions.*

The entrance channel to Xanadu Marina lies 5 miles east of Freeport Harbour, and is identifiable by the white pyramid on top of the Xanadu Beach and Marina Resort tower building. The approach channel, which carries a minimum of 6 feet at low water, is marked by a lighted sea buoy, flashing white, which lies approximately one-half mile offshore. The marina has 70 slips and can accommodate boats up to 200 feet long. Power, water, ice, TV, telephone, and

FREEPORT~LUCAYA

TROPIC ISLE SKETCH CHART B-3

EDITION 114

SOUNDINGS IN FEET AT LOW WATER
ALL COURSES MAGNETIC
THIS CHART NOT DRAWN TO SCALE

3 – 4 MILES TO DOWN TOWN
FREEPORT, SHOPPING MALL,
INTERNATIONAL BAZAAR AND
CASINO.

NOTE: THE DISTANCE FROM
BELL CHANNEL BAY TO THE
GRAND LUCAYAN WATERWAY
IS ABOUT 4½ MI.

ZNS 1 1 1 (BCST)
1040KHZ

PETERSON CAY 1¼ MI.

GP FL (2)
5 SEC.
(UNREL.)

GRAND LUCAYAN WATERWAY

345°

16

7

CONTINUOUS REEF

TO AVOID REEFS STAY 1 MI. OFFSHORE

CONTINUOUS REEF

STAY 1½ MI. OFFSHORE

FORTUNE BAY

LUCAYAN MARINA VILLAGE

BELL CHANNEL BAY

12

FL G

FL R

PORT LUCAYA
MARINA

CONTINUOUS REEF

STAY 1½ MI. OFFSHORE

345°

FL G o FL R

16

FL W
(UNREL.)

SILVER POINT

OCEAN REEF YACHT CLUB

345°

RUNNING MON
MARINA

CONTINUOUS REEF

STAY 1 MI. OFFSHORE

FREEPORT HARBOUR
5 MILES

XANADU BEACH AND MARINA RESORT

FL W
FL G
6 FL R

REEF

345°

14

BELL CHANNEL
FL 3 SEC 36 FT 7 M

12

12

12

REEF BREAKS

345°

FL R

FL G
6–8

12

BELL CHANNEL BAY

LUCAYAN
MARINA
VILLAGE

12

TWR.

PORT LUCAYA
MARINA

LUCAYAN BEACH
RESORT & MARINA

PORT LUCAYA
RESORT
& YACHT CLUB

REEF
BREAKS

LIGHT

TOWER

CHANNEL
ENTRANCE

REEF BREAKS

SEA BUOY
(UNRELIABLE)

ENTRANCE TO BELL CHANNEL BAY NORTH 1½ MI.

WHITE BEACH

CAUTION: NOT FOR NAVIGATION
Tropic Isle Sketch Charts are supplements to
the text of the current Yachtsman's Guide to
The Bahamas. They are illustrative and
not necessarily to scale.

FREEPORT
HARBOUR

SILOS

BASIN

BASIN

RANGE
FL W

30

32

BASIN

43

BASIN

CANAL

BRADFORD
GRAND
BAHAMA

WHARF
10 FT
HIGH

AERO Q.W. 20 M

FL R

30

RESTAURANT

FL 4 S 2M

FL G

FL R

FL R

120°

LIGHTED AND
UNLIGHTED OFFSHORE
TANKER BERTHS HERE.

Port Lucaya

MARKETPLACE & MARINA

Ideal Warm Winter Berthing

First-class facilities with trained friendly and professional staff. Only minutes away with daily air service from South Florida. For special long-term rates and full information package, call Jack Chester or Karen Pinder at (242) 373-9090 or fax (242) 373-5884.

All the Fun in One Wonderful Place

Across from Lucayan Beach • Diving • Snorkeling • Watersports • 85 Shops & Waterfront Restaurants • Live Music • Nightly Casino & Golf 7 minutes away • Beautiful Yacht Club with Grand Piano Bar, Mini-Cinema, and Outdoor Dining Terrace.

Grand Bahama Island – Just 70 miles from South Florida.

Bell Channel
Entrance
Outer Red & White Buoy
LAT. 26°29'95"N / LONG. 78°38'62"W.

Port Lucaya
Marketplace
Shops, Restaurants
& Bars

Port Lucaya
Resort & Hotel

Keep port to
Port Lucaya

High Speed
Fuel Dock

Central Wing

Garden Wing

Port Lucaya
Marina
Home of the Big Yachts
& the small ones too!

Website: www.portlucaya.com or E-mail: port@batelnet.bs

Gateway To The Bahamas

- 100 Slip Full Service Marina (Phase 1 Opening January '99)
- Dockage for Vessels up to 120'
- Fuel Dock (Diesel, Gas and Oil)
- New Deep Water Entrance Channel
  (13' controlling depth in channel, 8' to 10' dockside)
- Lighted and Marked Entrance Channel
- Official Port of Entry - Customs and Immigration On-Site
- Customs House Restaurant and Lounge (Opening Spring '99)
- Shower and Laundry Facilities
- Electrical Power (30, 50, 100 AMP), Cable T.V. and Phone Jacks
- Dive Shop
- Convenience Store
- 50 Cottage Style Suites (Opening in '99)
- Freshwater Pool and Secluded Beaches
- World Class Big Game, Reef and Bone Fishing
- Premier Island Resort Community with Ocean Front and
  Deep Water Canal Lots
- American Express, Visa and Mastercard Accepted

OLD BAHAMA BAY

An Island Resort Community

West End, Grand Bahama Island
242-346-6500 • VHF Channel 16

Xanadu Marina (in background) and Running Mon Marina (foreground). (Tropic Isle photo)

fuel are available. Full room service is available to boats along with laundry and shower facilities, tennis, a freshwater pool, a beach, restaurant, hotel, and dive concession. The marina is protected by 24-hour security. Keithlin Russell is the marina manager. Xanadu Marina is a port of entry.

The entrance to Running Mon Marina and Resort begins about one-half mile farther east, outside the continuous reef. It isn't marked except by two channel markers flashing red-right-returning just seaward of the jetties. A small group of condos that look like neatly piled shoeboxes, four high on each other, right on the white beach just east of the eastern jetty, is a good landmark. Controlling depth is 5-6 feet at low water, although we do have reports that it may be less. Call the marina for guidance, if necessary. There are slips for 66 boats, with all marine services, utility hookups, showers, a laundromat, a sportfishing fleet, 40-ton travel hoist, and good protection in all weather. There is also a nice, reasonably priced hotel, with a restaurant serving breakfast, lunch, and dinner. Running Mon Marina is not a port of entry.

Continuing east, outside the continuous reef, stay 1.5 miles offshore with your depth finder showing at least 100 feet of water as far as Bell Channel. About halfway between the turn in toward Running Mon Marina and Bell Channel is the entrance to the Ocean Reef Yacht Club. It is between two jetties, just off the end of which is a pair of marks with red and green lights. There is a controlling depth of 6 feet into the marina, which offers 52 slips accommodating boats up to 180 feet, electricity, water, ice, showers, cable and satellite TV, resort

Ocean Reef Yacht Club (Tropic Isle photo)

Ocean Reef Yacht Club. (Tropic Isle photo)

facilities, and rental cars. There are luxury villas or suites for rent and packages available for long-term dockage with security. Transient yachts are welcome.

As you continue east toward Bell Channel, keeping 1.5 miles offshore, a good landmark is the white beach in front of Riviera Towers, about 2 miles west of the channel. As you near the red-and-white vertically striped sea buoy with a

Set your course to:
26.29:22 N
78.39:50W

Located between Bell Channel
& Running Mon Marina

Please inquire for your
Membership

Ocean Reef Yacht Club ...*Freeport/Lucaya's newest and most complete marina & resort! Conveniently located on the south beach, we're close to the Lucayan Casino. Stunning new 1;2, & 3-bedroom suites & villas for rent. Electronic security system. Pamper yourself in serene luxury at Ocean Reef...you'll enjoy it!*

- 52 DOCK SLIPS UP TO 140'
- 6' MINIMUM WATER AT LOW TIDE
- 110/220 V (3PH.) ELECTR. SERVICES
- SATELLITE TV (HBO, SHOW & OTHERS)
- MODERN BATHROOMS & SHOWERS
- SHUTTLE SERVICE

- POOL & JACUZZI
- SNACK BAR
- DBL. TENNIS COURT
- GOLF PRIVILEGES
- WASHERS & DRYERS
- TELEPHONE & FAX

For more information:
Phone (242) 373-4662/4661
WE MONITOR VHF CH.16 • FAXSIMILE (242) 373-8261

Bell Channel Bay (Port Lucaya to the left, Lucayan Marina Village to the right. (Tropic Isle photo)

flashing white light, which marks the entrance to Bell Channel, we advise you to beware of and don't be confused by cruise-ship mooring buoys and other marks on the drop off and further out near the 100 foot contour. The yellow cruise ship moorings are about half a mile west of the sea buoy. Other marks come and go, and some might be similar to the sea buoy, so be sure to enter at the sea buoy and not something else. Between the sea buoy and the jetties are intermediate fixed posts, flashing green to port and red to starboard to guide you through a shallow area. The channel (5-6 feet at low water, with dredging to 8 feet planned) is about 345° from the sea buoy to the Bell Channel jetties.

Having cleared the channel and entered Bell Channel Bay, you have two marinas to choose from. If you parallel the shore to starboard, you'll see the Lucayan Marina Village open up straight ahead. Or, if you turn to port and round the first "peninsula" off the port bow, you'll be at Port Lucaya Marina.

The Lucayan Marina Village's totally renovated docks offer about 130 slips accommodating yachts up to 170 feet. Fuel, electricity, water, phone, and satellite TV are available at every slip, and ice, bait, and sodas are sold on the dock. Next to the docks are some of the grandest showers and laundry facilities you'll find anywhere. Customs and immigration officials can clear you either at the fuel dock or at your slip. The marina setting is peaceful and beautifully landscaped, with everything spic-and-span. Two swimming pools, a pool bar, and the Ferry House Restaurant at the shuttle landing are available to marina guests. A 30-passenger shuttle takes marina guests over to the other side of Bell Channel Bay to the Port Lucaya Marketplace, UNEXSO, the Dolphin Experi-

Lucayan Marina Village. (Tropic Isle Publishers)

Port Lucaya. (Tropic Isle photo)

ence, a casino (not in operation at this writing) and a beach. Yachtsmen who stow their golf bags just in case the opportunity arises are welcome to play at the affiliated Lucayan Golf Club. You can contact dockmaster Thomas Lockhart on VHF 16.

Port Lucaya Marina has over 100 slips accommodating yachts up to 175 feet in length with fuel, water, electricity, cable TV, and phones at each slip. Sodas, bait, and tackle are sold on the fuel dock. To clear customs, call the marina office on VHF 16 so that a customs officer can be available. Senior dockmaster Ryan Knowles or assistants Chris or Johnny stand by on VHF 16. Half of the slips are in the tranquil Sea Garden wing, around the hotel, with a swimming pool, jacuzzi, open-air bar, and restaurant. Remaining slips are on the waterfront at the lively Port Lucaya Marketplace, with over 80 shops, 18 international bars and restaurants (a contributor recommends Zorba the Greek as delicious and reasonable), and nightly live music and dancing in Count Basie Square. The new Port Lucaya Yacht Club has a grand-piano bar, restaurant, mini-cinema and bar lounge, and an open garden terrace overlooks the marina basin. Beaches and a casino are within walking distance. Marina guests are offered food, laundry, cleaning, and general maid services, as well as courtesy transportation to and from the airport and a Winn Dixie. Nearby restaurants include the Bell Channel Inn for excellent traditional Bahamian cooking and hospitality, and the family-run China Café, recommended by a contributor for "superfresh" food and the young chef's own sweet-and-sour sauce.

The Underwater Explorers Society (UNEXSO), in Lucayan Harbour, is a complete scuba school including a library, photo lab, museum, pub, and recompression chamber. They can be reached on VHF 19.

The city of Freeport lies 5 miles inland from Freeport Harbour. At Freeport International Airport, just north of the city, daily flights are scheduled from New York, Miami, Fort Lauderdale, Palm Beach, and Nassau. Freeport and most of its surroundings are immaculately groomed and spacious. The focal point of the city is the International Bazaar, where imported bargains are available at innumerable little shops and restaurants built in the architectural traditions of their respective nations. West of the bazaar are the distinctive Moorish turrets of the Princess Casino. The sister Princess hotels are examples of grand proportion Las Vegas-style, with lavish shows and restaurants. Out of town on

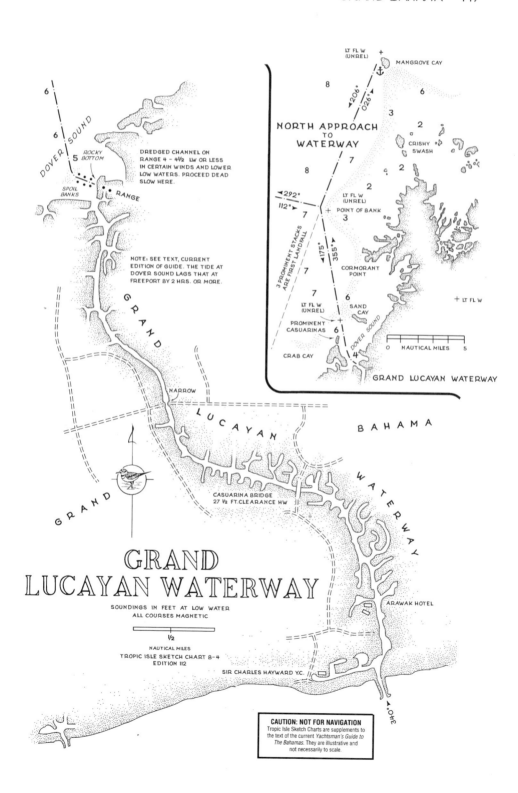

DREDGED CHANNEL ON
RANGE 4 - 4½ LW OR LESS
IN CERTAIN WINDS AND LOWER
LOW WATERS. PROCEED DEAD
SLOW HERE.

NOTE: SEE TEXT, CURRENT
EDITION OF GUIDE. THE TIDE AT
DOVER SOUND LAGS THAT AT
FREEPORT BY 2 HRS. OR MORE.

DOVER SOUND

ROCKY
BOTTOM

SPOIL
BANKS

RANGE

NARROW

GRAND

LUCAYAN

BAHAMA

WATERWAY

CASUARINA BRIDGE
27 ½ FT. CLEARANCE HW

GRAND

ARAWAK HOTEL

GRAND LUCAYAN WATERWAY

SOUNDINGS IN FEET AT LOW WATER
ALL COURSES MAGNETIC

½

NAUTICAL MILES
TROPIC ISLE SKETCH CHART 8-4
EDITION 112

SIR CHARLES HAYWARD Y.C.

NORTH APPROACH
TO
WATERWAY

LT FL W
(UNREL)

MANGROVE CAY

206°
026°

8

6

3

2

CRISHY
SWASH

7

8

2

292°
112°
7

LT FL W
(UNREL)
POINT OF BANK

2

3 PROMINENT STACKS
ARE FIRST LANDFALL

175°

355°

3

7

CORMORANT
POINT

7

6

SAND
CAY

LT FL W

LT FL W
(UNREL)

PROMINENT
CASUARINAS

6

CRAB CAY

DOVER SOUND

4

GRAND LUCAYAN WATERWAY

0   NAUTICAL MILES   5

340°

CAUTION: NOT FOR NAVIGATION
Tropic Isle Sketch Charts are supplements to
the text of the current *Yachtsman's Guide to
The Bahamas.* They are illustrative and
not necessarily to scale.

Southern entrance to the Grand Lucayan Waterway

Queen's Highway are some delightful places to eat, including The Buccaneer and Harry's American Bar, both serving an unusual variety of Bahamian specialties on the oceanfront. At the Lucayan National Park, observation decks overlook part of the world's longest charted cavern system. There is a self-guided trail through the park's woodlands.

The **Grand Lucayan Waterway** places Freeport squarely on the main route from South Florida to the Abaco Cays. A handy addition for Abaco cruising buffs in search of a few day's respite among Freeport's wonders en route, this 7.5-mile canal bisects Grand Bahama at a point 4.5 miles east of Bell Channel Bay. It offers the protection of a variety of canals and anchorages to relieve the monotony of the long cruise across the Little Bahama Bank. Work has been completed in Dover Sound and on any shallow spots in the waterway proper. There is now at least 5 feet at low water all the way through the land cut, but there is still a place in Dover Sound, between the poles leading in to the range at the north end of the waterway, that carries only 4 to 4.5 feet at mean low water. Boats drawing more than this will have to await the tide to pass through. Proceed at dead slow through this shallow dredged portion. If you only go "sort of slow" your boat will squat and plow the water right out of the trough, and you will make it even shallower for yourself. *It is important to realize that under certain wind and lunar conditions, which cause lower low waters, there can be considerably less water here.* Remember that the tide at Dover Sound lags that at Freeport by 2 hours or more. The Casuarina Bridge in the waterway is fixed and allows clearance of only 27 feet at high water.

Vessels arriving from Florida should clear customs at one of Grand Bahama's official ports of entry, then proceed east outside the continuous reef to enter the canal at its southern terminus. From offshore, the lighted entrance is identified by the single high-rise Arawak Hotel, a good landmark about a mile inshore that is recently reported somewhat obscured by casuarinas. Due to the vast expanse of navigable water that this channel opens to the sea, tidal currents of 2.5 knots, both ebb and flood, should be allowed for. We recommend entering here following high or low slack, at least for the first time.

On your port, as you enter the waterway, is the site of the old Sir Charles

Dredged channel at Dover Sound. (Tropic Isle photo)

Hayward Yacht Club, which has not been in operation in recent years and so offers no facilities, but there is excellent protection in westerly conditions here. A U.S. group is now planning to develop a hundred or so canal homes here, so look for activity and changes as this gets underway.

The main canal is 250 feet wide for over half its length, then narrows to 150 feet for the remaining half at the north end. All side canals are identified by their narrower width of 100 feet. The Port Authority requests that a 5-knot cruising speed be maintained in the waterway.

To aid your approach from the north to the northern end of the waterway, three new lights on poles, each flashing white, have been placed. *(Caution: In spite of the fact that these marks are supposed to be lit, don't try this passage when visibility is poor for any reason. It's not that easy, and these lights are often out.)* Proceeding from north to south: (1) pass west of the light at Mangrove Cay, (2) pass west of the light on the point of bank, and (3) pass close to, either side, of the light between Sand Cay and the prominent casuarinas at the north end of Crab Cay. From here, a course of about 150° for about 1.5 miles will bring you toward the outer, lighted pair of the series of poles that mark both sides of the dredged channel leading into the range at the north end of the waterway. Proceed slowly, because these are hard to find from any distance, and if you miss, the water outside the dredged channel is very shallow over a hard bottom.

The approach to the waterway from Mangrove Cay on the Little Bahama Bank is indicated on sketch charts B-4 (Grand Lucayan Waterway) and 42 (Little Bahama Bank). As you proceed southwest from Mangrove Cay on the 200° heading for the 10 miles to the point of bank, your first landfall, about dead ahead, will be the three refinery stacks at Freeport Harbour. On the 175° heading approaching the light between Sand and Crab Cays, be careful to give the narrow sandbank that extends west of Sand Cay ample berth to port. When in the well-marked, dredged channel, proceed slowly and stay center channel, on the range, until through the inner lighted pair of marks. The course then doglegs to starboard quite close to the seawall. Parallel to the seawall are two final marks, which you leave to starboard as you head south into the waterway.

One and one-quarter miles east of the southern entrance to the Grand Lucayan Waterway you will come to Peterson Cay, a protected land/sea park, where Freeport yachtsmen congregate for holiday picnics. Here, under the watchful eye of The Bahamas National Trust, the visitor will find a small but uniquely beautiful range of coral gardens where fish, marine animals, and plant

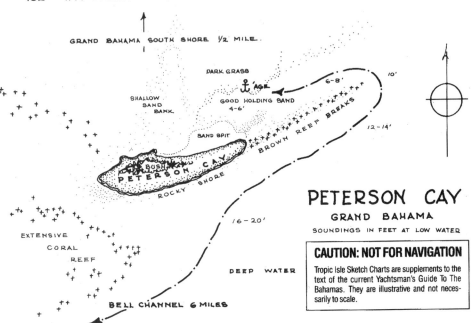

PETERSON CAY

GRAND BAHAMA

SOUNDINGS IN FEET AT LOW WATER

CAUTION: NOT FOR NAVIGATION

Tropic Isle Sketch Charts are supplements to the text of the current Yachtsman's Guide To The Bahamas. They are illustrative and not necessarily to scale.

life may be closely observed. There is a fair weather anchorage (5 feet at low water) off a sparkling sand beach just off the northeast end of the island. To gain the anchorage, be careful to round the brown bar that extends 300 yards northeast.

Fifteen miles farther east and identified from offshore by its conspicuous white spoil banks is a dredged harbor facility designed to accommodate supertankers. This is usually pretty deserted now, but if caught in strong onshore winds along here, you could probably find adequate refuge inside, although it could also prove to be an uncomfortable dust bowl. We do have a letter from a reader who tells of having taken refuge here and being very well treated by "the authorities" here.

Seventeen miles farther east is **Deep Water Cay,** marked Carrion Crow Harbour on D.M.A. Chart 26320. The nearest landmark is the fixed light on **Sweeting's Cay,** 3 miles to the southwest (unreliable). Controlling depth into the anchorage is limited to 4 feet at low water over the bar and over the rocky patch at the southeast end of Sam Lang Cay.

The Deep Water Cay Club is open from mid-September through mid-July. Reservations are essential. This is a spectacular bonefishing club with oceanfront cottages, a lovely dining/club room, beautiful grounds, and white sand beaches for anyone who'd like to give the fish a day's rest. The nearby flats are practically endless. Expert guides, most of whom have been here for many years, will find fish for you and, just as important, keep you from getting lost in the intricate maze of waterways. Three moorings are available and yachtsmen are welcome to dine ashore. Marine supplies and facilities are very limited — this is a bonefish club.

Routes across the Little Bahama Bank. (Tropic Isle Sketch Charts: 42, B-2). To cruise from West End eastward it is necessary to depart by the way

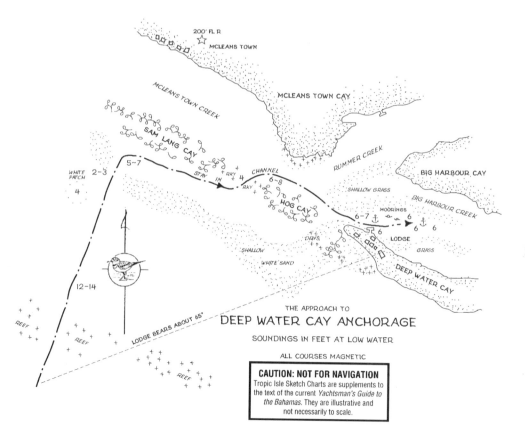

200' FL R
MCLEANS TOWN

MCLEANS TOWN CAY

MCLEANS TOWN CREEK

SAM LANG CAY

RUMMER CREEK

BIG HARBOUR CAY

WHITE PATCH 2-3   5-7

STAY IN   RKY 4 CHANNEL
RKY   6-8

4

HOG CAY

SHALLOW GRASS

BIG HARBOUR CREEK

MOORINGS
6-7   6   6   6

6-7   6

LODGE

DRYS   GRASS

SHALLOW

WHITE SAND

DEEP WATER CAY

12-14

THE APPROACH TO
DEEP WATER CAY ANCHORAGE

SOUNDINGS IN FEET AT LOW WATER

ALL COURSES MAGNETIC

REEF
REEF

LODGE BEARS ABOUT 65°

REEF

CAUTION: NOT FOR NAVIGATION
Tropic Isle Sketch Charts are supplements to
the text of the current *Yachtsman's Guide to
the Bahamas*. They are illustrative and
not necessarily to scale.

Deep Water Cay. (Tropic Isle photo)

you entered, then enter the bank again three-quarters of a mile to the north at **Indian Cay Rock,** as indicated on Sketch Chart B-2 (West End). Entering here, pass about 150 yards north of the light tower (unreliable), between a pair of marks (the mark on the north side of the channel was missing when we overflew it recently). Beginning where these marks are meant to be, the channel is supposed to be marked through to Barracuda Shoal as indicated on the sketch chart. However, when we flew over recently there was only one mark between the mark at Indian Cay Rock and Barracuda Shoal. (This doesn't give you much to work with for an area where knowing how much you're being set one way or the other is important. And, of course, not much will have to happen to cause there to be no marks, so be prepared for the eventualities.) This channel will carry about 5-6 feet at low water and has a rocky bottom. Having passed Barracuda Shoal day mark, continue on the same heading that brought you through the channel until Sandy Cay bears due west before taking up a new heading for your desired destination. It is important through this channel to be aware of the strong currents that will sweep you one way or another, regardless of what your compass tells you. If you don't compensate, you may end up aground, perched on something very rocky. *Caution: If the marks should for some reason disappear again, we'd advise, as we did while they were missing, that you enter onto or leave the bank by another route. There is a shallow rocky bar north of the channel at Indian Cay Rock. Without marks, you must navigate here by eyeball, and bad light and tidal rips will often make this impossible. In addition, with no marks for reference, strong currents in the area can sweep you onto rocky bottom and lots of trouble.*

Deeper-draft vessels (over 5 feet), including island freighters that ply the waters between Palm Beach and the Abaco Cays, enter the bank by way of **Memory Rock.** The best water here lies about 2-2.5 miles south and southeast of the light (unreliable). To avoid the shallow sand bores (3-6 feet at low water) that lie 3 miles east-southeast of the light, enter the bank on an easterly heading, passing about 2 miles south of the light (see DMA 26320). Continue on this heading until the light bears 295°, at which time you can take up the appropriate heading for either Walker's Cay or Mangrove Cay (see sketch chart 42, Little Bahama Bank).

Still another entrance onto the bank can be made 4.5 miles northwest of Sandy Cay. There are, on this route, areas of shallow rock and ledge. *Don't try it without good light and a knowledge of how to read the water.* Once through, you can proceed on to Mangrove Cay and points east. **Sandy Cay** is a pretty island densely planted with coconut palms and casuarinas. A beach and small house are located toward its eastern end. Sandy Cay is privately owned and trespassers are not welcome. The cay can be seen from a distance of 7-8 miles.

Mangrove Cay might provide some lee, but you'll have to stand well off on the west side where it's very shallow for at least 250 yards out. On the east you may be able to work in a bit closer. All around are isolated heads, so exercise caution. Extending from the cay to and beyond the lighted pole to the north is a shallow rocky bar, and on the south side rocky bars and shallows extend south to Grand Bahama. On the beach at the south end of the cay is a small crashed plane that, from a distance, looks like a Cherokee Six, a good little cargo carrier.

From Mangrove Cay you may pass either north or south of Great and Little

Proposed Marks for the Little Bahama Bank

For the fourth year, the Bahama Marina Operator Association continues to have a plan to place marks on the Little Bahama Bank. If the rate at which they're executing this plan is any indication of how these marks will be maintained once in, you shouldn't count on them. Some marks incorporated into the plan as already existing are, in fact, already missing, so things are deteriorating already before they've even begun. Here we give what information we have in case this all comes to be. The following description of the scheme, enclosed within quotation marks, was given us by a representative of the Bahama Marina Operators Association. Except for a few clarifications and changes in punctuation and capitalization for readability, it is verbatim:

"#1 Pole: 2 red triangles to be attached to the first starboard pole in the Indian Cay channel.

#2 Pole: 2 red triangles to be attached to the second pole in that channel.

#3 Pole: to be placed as near opposite to Barracuda Shoal on the south side of the channel. 2 red triangles and a radar reflector to be attached.

#4 Pole: to be placed halfway to Mangrove Cay on a direct line to the pole at its northern point. 2 red triangles and a radar reflector to be attached.

#5 Pole: 2 red triangles to be attached to the existing marker pole just north of Mangrove Cay. Light but no radar reflector.

#6 & #7 Poles: to be places equal distance apart in a direct line to the next pole at Great Sale Cay. 2 red triangle and a radar reflector on each pole.

#8 Pole: to be placed approx. 1.5 miles northwest of the north end of Great Sale Cay, on the edge of the bank. 2 red triangles and a radar reflector to be attached.

#9 Pole: to be placed ON Sale Cay Rocks with 2 red triangles and a radar reflector.

10 Pole: to be placed approx. 1 mile south of the sand bar at Carters Bank. 2 red triangles and a radar reflector. Another pole to be placed .5 mile north of #10 with a yellow light, and 2 green squares marked with a hazard warning.

#11 Pole: to be placed 1.5 miles north of the Hawksbill Cays on a heading for Crab Cay. 2 red triangles and a radar reflector to be attached.

#12 Pole: to be placed ON Centre of the World Rock. 2 red triangles (no radar reflector) to be attached. Another pole and yellow light to be placed ON Veterans Rock (this is a real hazard to ships). Another pole and yellow light to be placed by the south end of the sand bank off No Name Cay.

Additional Markers on Alternate Routes

#6S Pole: 2 red triangles to be placed on the existing pole south of Mangrove Cay on route to the Lucayan Waterway.

#7S Pole: 2 red triangles to be placed on the second existing pole going to the Lucayan Waterway.

#7W Pole: to be placed at Double Breaster Bar with a light and 2 red triangles.

#6W Pole: to be placed 2 miles north of Triangle Rocks with a light and 2 red triangles. A second pole to be placed approx. .5 mile northeast of #6W, marking the edge of the sand bar with 2 green squares with a hazard warning and a yellow light.

Lastly, it is proposed to place two channel marker poles halfway between Memory Rock and Sandy Cay, approx. .5 mile apart. Both poles would have lights on them. This would give a safe entrance onto the banks if people did not want to come via West End and Indian [Cay] Rock. The poles would have one

Continued on following page

Continued from preceding page

green square and one red triangle attached.

The lights would have solar panels and enough metal to remove the need for a radar reflector. The triangles signs are 48-inch Daymark red with reflective borders and numbers. The square signs are 36-inch Daymark green with a diamond shape inside the border. In the diamond there will be a hazard warning."

Yachtsmen with the necessary skills, adequately equipped boats, and the requisite government charts can find their way to the Abacos without these proposed marks. Those without proper skills, boats, and equipment shouldn't be tempted, because parts of the trip are reasonably long sea voyages that can be made even more difficult by bad weather. Also, the proposed lighted marks should not be taken to mean travelling at night is safe; it is not.

Marks throughout the islands are often missing, inoperative, or off specification, and there is no good reason to think these proposed marks, if placed, will be better maintained. Don't depend on marks that might not be there. Some of the proposed marks are to be positioned where no other distinct landmarks are in sight, so if they are gone, or never placed, there will be nothing. Be aware of the various possibilities.

Sale Cays. The northern route carries the best water and is quite straightforward. If you choose the southern route, take care to avoid the shoals that extend almost 4 miles south off the southern point of Great Sale Cay.

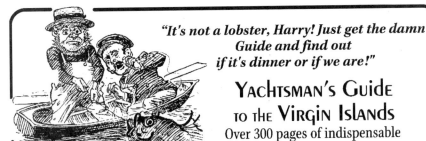

"It's not a lobster, Harry! Just get the damn Guide and find out if it's dinner or if we are!"

YACHTSMAN'S GUIDE TO THE VIRGIN ISLANDS

Over 300 pages of indispensable information including 16 pages of full color aerial photos.

YACHTSMAN'S GUIDE TO THE BAHAMAS

Over 450 pages of indispensable information

- The most complete guides available for cruising these waters.
- Profusely illustrated with our beautiful hand-drawn sketch charts, landfall sketches and photographs.
- Detailed island by island profiles and things to do ashore.

Call (305) 893-4277
Or write to: Tropic Isle Publishers
P.O. Box 610938, North Miami, FL 33261-0938

Walker's Cay. (Tropic Isle photo)

ABACO CAYS

D.M.A. Charts: 26299, 26319, 26320, 26321. Tropic Isle Sketch Charts: 42, Set H.

To avoid confusion, the Abaco Cays are described here from north to south, assuming that the yachtsman has crossed the Little Bahama Bank from West End, Grand Bahama, or by way of Memory Rock to Walker's Cay.

Note: In the area around Walker's Cay, Grand Cays, and Fox Town, VHF radio is used as a local "telephone" system and Channel 68 is used as a hailing and emergency channel. It is monitored by BASRA-Freeport for this reason. While in the area, please try to refrain from using Channel 68 as much as possible.

Walker's Cay (Tropic Isle Sketch Chart: H-1) is the northernmost island of The Bahamas with the exception of Jump Off Rocks, which lie one mile to the northwest. There are three approaches to Walker's Cay, indicated on sketch chart H-1 (Walker's Cay to Carter Cay). The most straightforward is from the south and westward of the bank, which lies south of the area between Walker's Cay and Grand Cays. Arriving from the bank to the west point of Tea Table Cay, follow the stake markers into the marina. Depths into the marina can be shallower than shown at lower low waters and in certain wind conditions. It's a good idea to call the marina for instructions before entering for the first time. They stand by on VHF 16 and 68, but try them on 16 first.

Walker's Cay Hotel and Marina stands high on the cay with a magnificent

LONG WHITE BEACH   HARBOUR   CLUB

WALKER'S CAY FROM TEA TABLE CAY.

20°

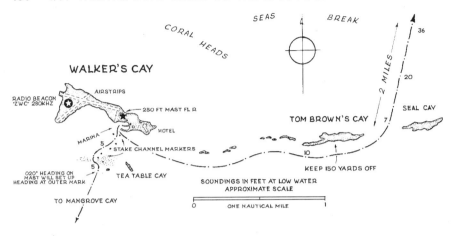

view, particularly over the shallow banks to the west and south where the colors are breathtaking. The resort is frequented by divers and sportfishermen (in 1992, a record 828-pound blue marlin was caught here). The approach to the marina has a controlling depth of 4.5 feet, and the marina itself has space for 75 boats with up to a 7-foot draft. All petroleum products and marina services are available. Tony Knowles is the dockmaster; Gary Adkinson is marina manager as well as dive manager. The airstrip and customs offices are within walking distance. The hotel includes a restaurant and bar with entertainment and dancing, a card and game room, two swimming pools, and tennis courts. At the marina there's a dive shop, commissary, and The Lobster Trap bar/restaurant. Laundry service is available through the hotel. Visiting yachtsmen may use all facilities. Hotel rooms and villas are available for overnight stays.

WALKER CAY BEARING WNW. (APPROACHING FROM GRAND CAYS)

If bound for Grand Cays, you may proceed by the northern or outer channel that lies south of **Tom Brown's Cay** and south of the rocks that extend west-northwest from Grand Cays. This route is deep but beset by reefs and sand bores. It can also be choppy when the ebb is setting eastward against the wind.

Grand Cays are an archipelago of islands covering a considerable area. Much of the water within the group is shallow, but there is a very good harbor adjacent to the settlement. There are also nice beaches on the ocean side.

GRAND CAYS SETTLEMENT

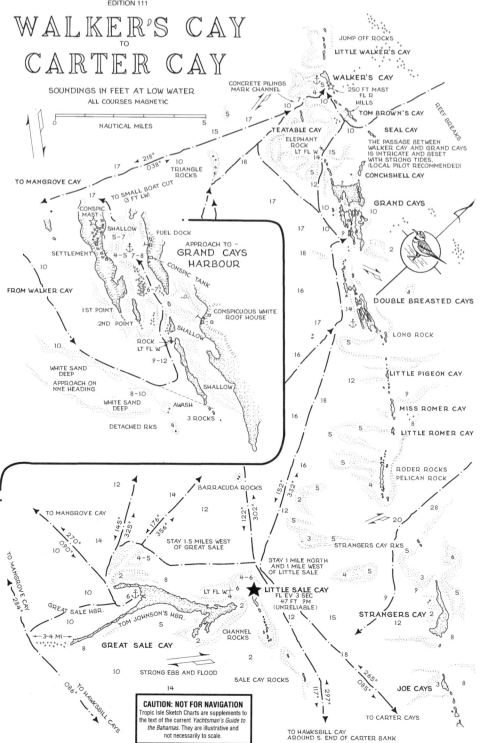

TROPIC ISLE SKETCH CHART H-1
EDITION 111

WALKER'S CAY
TO
CARTER CAY

SOUNDINGS IN FEET AT LOW WATER
ALL COURSES MAGNETIC

NAUTICAL MILES
0   5

JUMP OFF ROCKS
LITTLE WALKER'S CAY

CONCRETE PILINGS
MARK CHANNEL

WALKER'S CAY
250 FT MAST
FL R
HILLS
TOM BROWN'S CAY

SEAL CAY

TEATABLE CAY
ELEPHANT
ROCK
LT FL W

THE PASSAGE BETWEEN
WALKER CAY AND GRAND CAYS
IS INTRICATE AND BESET
WITH STRONG TIDES.
(LOCAL PILOT RECOMMENDED)

CONCHSHELL CAY

REEF BREAKS

218°
038°

TRIANGLE
ROCKS

TO MANGROVE CAY

GRAND CAYS

TO SMALL BOAT CUT
(3 FT LW)

CONSPIC
MAST

SHALLOW
5-7

FUEL DOCK

SETTLEMENT

4-5 7-8

APPROACH TO -
GRAND CAYS
HARBOUR

CONSPIC TANK

DOUBLE BREASTED CAYS

FROM WALKER CAY

1ST POINT

2ND POINT

6-7

CONSPICUOUS WHITE
ROOF HOUSE

LONG ROCK

ROCK
LT FL W

SHALLOW

9-12

LITTLE PIGEON CAY

WHITE SAND
DEEP

APPROACH ON
NNE HEADING

MISS ROMER CAY

SHALLOW

8-10

WHITE SAND
DEEP

AWASH

3 ROCKS

LITTLE ROMER CAY

DETACHED RKS

RODER ROCKS
PELICAN ROCK

BARRACUDA ROCKS

152°
332°

122°
302°

STRANGERS CAY RKS

TO MANGROVE CAY

145°
325°

176°
356°

STAY 1.5 MILES WEST
OF GREAT SALE

270°
090°

STAY 1 MILE NORTH
AND 1 MILE WEST
OF LITTLE SALE

STRANGERS CAY

TO MANGROVE CAY

284°

GREAT SALE HBR.

LT FL W

LITTLE SALE CAY
FL EV 3 SEC
47 FT 9M
(UNRELIABLE)

TOM JOHNSON'S HBR.

3-4 MI

GREAT SALE CAY

CHANNEL
ROCKS

086° TO HAWKSBILL CAYS

STRONG EBB AND FLOOD

SALE CAY ROCKS

JOE CAYS

117°
297°

265°
085°

TO CARTER CAYS

CAUTION: NOT FOR NAVIGATION
Tropic Isle Sketch Charts are supplements to
the text of the current *Yachtsman's Guide to
the Bahamas*. They are illustrative and
not necessarily to scale.

TO HAWKSBILL CAY
AROUND S. END OF CARTER BANK

Grand Cays harbor. (Tropic Isle photo)

Mangrove-bordered creeks wind tortuously inside, while in the broader sounds and lagoons, shallow flats are the home of innumerable bonefish. A reader reports that a new "huge, tall radio antenna" is visible for miles and a new black water tank with a white top near Rosie's is another good landmark. We have not yet seen these, and so are unable to plot them on our sketch chart.

The entrance to Grand Cays Harbour is somewhat intricate, so we suggest that if a local guide is available, his services be employed. A few boats from the settlement are usually fishing outside and the men are always willing to assist.

The entrance to the harbor lies at the southeastern end of the cays, between a long, thin cay with three rocks off its southeast point, and the smaller cay southwest of it. (See sketch chart H-1, Walker's Cay to Carter Cay.) The approach is on an approximately 90° course for the east point of the long thin cay, taking care to give the above-water rocks and the submerged bars west-northwest of Double Breasted Cays a good berth. As you approach more closely, you'll see two detached rocks about 300 yards south of the point of the long cay. A short distance to the west of these is a sunken rock, sometimes awash. Leave all these rocks to starboard. On the port side of the channel a point of white sand makes out toward the rocks, but this is deep and you can pass over it. From a position abreast of the rocks, about off the center of the long cay, steer for the center of the long cay. When 50-75 yards off its shore, turn to port. From this position the harbor will be open and a detached rock will be visible at the west end of the cay. Run in parallel to the shore, leaving the rock to starboard. On a continuation of the shore are two small cays and a small white bar to be left to starboard. From here favor the north side of the channel, as another white bar (rock) lies off the eastern tip of the large, bush-covered cay. Leave this to port. Now, leave one more small bar to starboard, and then leave the long, white bar plainly visible beyond the mangroves to port. You will now have a good 8-9 feet of water to the anchorage.

An anchorage on white marl in 6-9 feet at low water can be found in one of the small coves opposite the settlement or off the settlement dock in 6-7 feet. In the anchorage off the dock, keep over white water, as the grass to the north is shallow. In both cases the holding ground is good, but two anchors are advised because a moderately strong tidal current runs through the harbor.

About 400 people live in this friendly, helpful settlement. Many work at

Walker's Cay or as fishermen. The town is fun to explore, with meandering sidewalks, clusters of shy, smiling children, and pretty views. Street lights have been added to newly improved roads. The Island Bay Front Hotel has air-conditioned rooms and dock facilities for perhaps 15 smaller-to-medium-sized boats, with water, gas, diesel, water, and ice. On the premises, Rosie's Place serves good Bahamian food in the air-conditioned dining room with adjoining disco and bar. Other good places to eat are Eddie Cooper's Hilltop View Restaurant and Lounge, the New Palms Bar and Restaurant, or Ali Rolle Runway 87 Snack Bar. For provisions, try L&S Restaurant and Grocery or Father and Son Grocery and Drug. Fresh bread is sold at Ena's Bakery and Ida Cooper's Bakery and Dry Goods. There's a telephone station and clinic. About every 10 days, an island freighter makes the round trip from Grand Cays to Nassau.

Grand Cays is a safe and quiet harbor, a good base for fishing of all kinds, including game, bone, and reef, or for day trips around this mini-cruising area. Reliable guides for the area are Andy Hield, Gerald Rolle, Willard Munnings, Cardinal Albury, Leslie Edgecombe, and Myer Albury. BASRA contacts at Grand Cays are Boss, who answers to *Love Bone,* and Rosie, who answers to *Love Train,* on channels 68 or 16.

Double Breasted Cays. These cays, which form another archipelago of innumerable islands and rocks, are nothing less than fabulous. Line upon line of cays of all shapes and sizes enclose flats, sandbanks, and beaches through which deep channels run. Exploring by dinghy may indicate you can bring in the mother vessel. On a bright day the colors are as brilliant as you will find anywhere in The Bahamas. Stay in deep water and approach the island on a northerly course. Six feet runs up close to the shore, and an anchorage protected from west through north to east may be found.

Miss Romer Cay lies 2.5 miles east-southeast of Double Breasted Cays. Between are many above-water rocks and bars with no pass between them. This cay is low, rather flat, and covered with brush and small trees. A white sandbank lies a short distance south of it.

Roder Rocks are in reality two small scrub-covered cays and a large number of rocks, all around which is shoal water.

Barracuda Rocks are three small rocks about 3.5 miles northwest of

"It's not a lobster, Harry! Just get the damn Guide and find out if it's dinner or if we are!"

YACHTSMAN'S

Guide to the Virgin Islands

Over 300 pages of indispensable information including 16 pages of full color aerial photos.

Call (305) 893-4277

Or write to: Tropic Isle Publishers
P.O. Box 610938, North Miami, FL 33261-0938

landmark when proceeding either east or west across the bank north of Sale Cay.

Little Sale Cay lies a short distance north of Great Sale Cay and is surrounded by an area of shallow water extending about a mile west of the island. The cay is comparatively high (44 feet), and has steep cliffs at its northwest end.

Great Sale Cay is the largest cay in the area, measuring some 5.5 miles in length. It is low, flat, and marshy. **Great Sale Harbour** provides good shelter in winds from west-southwest through north to southeast, a good haven if you're overtaken by a norther in this vicinity. It is also a useful stop when bound across the bank to or from West End.

In the harbor itself the deepest water, 7-9 feet over mud and grass, is in the center on the eastern side. Along the western side, which is thickly fringed with mangroves, there are extensive grassy banks, between which anchorage in 4 feet can be found. A draft of 6-7 feet can be carried up to the northern end of the harbor, where the holding ground is good. Upon entering you may see what appear to be extensive white banks; don't be misled, as these are bonefish muds.

Should you anchor here on a quiet evening, it is worthwhile to row as quietly as possible along the edge of the mangroves, in the shallow water toward the western point. There you will see all manner of fish: sand sharks drowsing peacefully on the warm mud, rays swimming slowly with graceful undulations of their "wings" or sleeping half buried in the marl, hordes of gray snappers and grunts weaving in and out of mangrove roots while bonefish feed on the flats, and probably a school of young barracuda patrolling in fan formation, their long snouts and sharp, black eyes barely beneath the surface.

On the east coast of the island another harbor, known as Tom Johnson's Harbour, is largely shallow, but a lee can be found in winds from west and northwest within its confines.

Off the south point of Great Sale Cay shallower water extends southward for some distance. If leaving Great Sale Harbour in the morning when the light is against you, take great care in rounding the point to the eastward. Keep a berth of at least 4 miles if your vessel is deep-draft, and look out for grassy banks.

LONG WHITE BEACH   HILL WITH TREES

STRANGERS CAY   BEARING N.W^N

Stranger's Cay is a large, pretty cay with a number of fine beaches. Unfortunately, shoal water extends for some distance offshore, and the approach is between a maze of sandbanks. We suggest that, unless you are bent on exploration and are carrying a very shoal draft, you do not attempt to reach this cay except with a reliable guide. Some of the banks in this area are in the form of gigantic horseshoes with the bow, or convex part, pointing to the southwest. The "shoe" itself is formed of a shallow sand bore but a few yards across, while deep water lies in the center. If cruising close under the cays here, it's easy to find yourself in such a trap. After searching for miles around the edge looking for an exit, you'll find you must return by the way you came in.

Joe Cays, of which there are three with several off-lying rocks, are also guarded by shallow white sandbanks through and around which deep channels may be found. The center cay is of medium size, rather flat, and thickly covered with small trees. It has two beaches.

Carter Cays (Tropic Isle Sketch Chart: H-2) consist of four large and medium-sized cays, several smaller cays, and countless rocks. Several of the cays are relatively high. To the west, south, and southeast are extensive sandbanks, all plainly visible. On the "back" side of the cays (that is, to the north), the water is deep. There are two harbors. At the main one between Big and Little Carter Cays there is a small seasonal settlement. The other harbor, the Safety Hole, is entered from the north side of Big Carter. Approaching the main harbor from the south, you'll see a white sand bore. The entrance channel on a white diamond marker range leads you in over patches of grass close east of the bore in 4 feet low water and into the harbor. Never anchor in the main channel, as a very strong tidal current sluices through. Steer over to the eastern side where you may see a local fishing boat off the settlement. Here you may anchor in from 5-14 feet with fair holding ground. This harbor gives protection from all but north-northwest winds, when it may become uncomfortable. Under these conditions, when the Safety Hole cannot be attempted, local fishermen take their vessels to a bay on the south coast of the central cay, about one mile to the west.

To gain the **Safety Hole,** leave by the northern entrance of the main harbor, which is deep and clear of obstructions. Proceed west along the north coast of Big Carter Cay. The entrance to the Safety Hole is concealed from the eastward until you are upon it. It is narrow and a very strong tidal current runs through it both ebb and flood. It carries 4 feet at low water with much deeper water inside. Favor the western side, taking care to avoid the bar that extends

The Safety Hole. (Tropic Isle photo)

CHANNEL RKS

SALE CAY RKS

TO LITTLE SALE CAY

18

16

14

265°
085°

14

JOE CAYS

10   12

10

10

14

14

14

BIG CARTER CAY

LITTLE CARTER CAY

117°

297°

180°
000°

WHEN ENROUTE TO CARTER
CAY FROM THE EAST, AVOID
CARTER CAY BANK BY
PROCEEDING AS IF TO LITTLE
SALE CAY, TURNING IN ON
CARTER CAY WHEN IT BEARS
DUE NORTH.

CARTER BANK
PLAINLY VISIBLE,
REPORTED
EXTENDING
S' WARD.

14

14

14

9   3

6

4

4

4

6

4

CARTER
CAY
BANK

6

4

4

2

GROUPER ROCKS

**TROPIC ISLE SKETCH CHART H-2
EDITION 114**

CARTER CAY
TO
ALLAN'S~PENSACOLA CAY

SOUNDINGS IN FEET AT LOW WATER
ALL COURSES MAGNETIC

TO A POINT 4 MI
SW OF GREAT SALE CAY

12

1 WEST END
BARS

2

14

FROM 6.5 M.
W. OF WEST END
OF LITTLE ABACO
(SEE TEXT)

9·10

POOR
HOLDINGS

8·10

CONSPIC. PALM

7

CAVE
CAY

4

5·6

DRYS

152°   332°

BAR

SPENCE ROCK

5

4

4

CASHES CAY

WEST END ROCKS

266°
086°

12

110°
290°

VETERAN SHOAL
BREAKS

STAKE
MISSING

5-6

14

14

THE HAULOVER

PEAR CAY

CROWN HAVEN

TRADE WINDS HOTEL

TWR FL R

BREAST CAY

PATTON CAYS

0   NAUTICAL MILES   5

6

5-6

12

18

10

5

FOX
TOWN

MAST
FLR

LITTLE ABACO

CAUTION: HAZARD
VETERAN SHOAL IS AWASH
AT H.W. AND DIFFICULT TO
SEE IN POOR LIGHT

LOCAL KNOWLEDGE IS ADVISED
ON THIS ROUTE AT LEAST
FOR THE FIRST TIME

20

16

STRONG

18

SEE DMA 26320

18

STRONG

POOR HOLDING

22

HAWKSBILL CAYS

6

MOUNT HOPE

WOOD CAY

TO CRAB CAY

16

16

TO CRAB CAY

273°
093°

18

250°
070°

CAUTION: NOT FOR NAVIGATION
Tropic Isle Sketch Charts are supplements to
the text of the current *Yachtsman's Guide to
The Bahamas.* They are illustrative and
not necessarily to scale.

SAFETY HOLE

12

BIG CARTER CAY

20

12

TIDE
RIP

THIN
SHALLOW
SAND BORE

12

6-8

035°

STRONG CURRENT
10 EDGE 12

20
5

GRASS

RANGE

SAMMY'S
CAY

3

VIEW "A" LITTLE CARTER CAY

CARTER CAY
AND ANDCHORAGE
EDITION 110

10

PAW PAW CAYS

16

14

PAW PAW ROCKS

14

12

FISH CAY ROCKS

12

8

FISH CAYS

9

15

10

9

9

MORAINE CAY

3

12   8

BREAKS

20

STRONG

4

16

9

9

UMBRELLA CAY

14

9

GUINEMAN CAY

14

ALLANS PENSACOLA CAY

12

CENTER OF THE
WORLD ROCK

from the eastern side of the inlet. There is room for one boat; we suggest using the usual two anchors. The settlement is inhabited for some months of the year by a small community of fishermen from Crown Haven on Little Abaco.

Grouper Rocks is a cluster of one large and several small rocks standing halfway between Carter Cays and the Paw Paw Cays. They are surrounded by shallow banks and can be seen clearly from the deep water to the south.

Paw Paw Cays are four smallish islands and several rocks, some moderately high and all thickly covered with scrub and small trees. There are some beaches, but the water around them is shallow. Paw Paw Rocks lie about 2 miles east of the Paw Paw Cays and may be passed slowly in deep water to the east, if you are bound for the Fish Cays.

The largest **Fish Cay** is sporadically visited by fishermen. The second cay as you proceed southeast is the smallest and is irregular in shape, with a number of hillocks. The southeast point of this cay and the northwest point of the third cay overlap slightly, forming a quiet pool with moderately deep water. However, a hard white bar speckled with brown coral makes out in a northwesterly direction from the northwest point of the latter, and care must be taken to pass around the end of it. This is a quiet-weather anchorage only. Both the third and fourth cays are long, flat, and fairly low. They are divided by a narrow cut through which only dinghies may pass. Both are covered with small trees and palmetto, and both have sandy beaches on the north side. Deep water from 12-20 feet runs close to their southern shore. Between the southeast Fish Cay and Moraine Cay is an extensive area of shallow white sand on which there are a few coral patches. Along the edge of this bank there is 12-18 feet of water, at first over dark grass and then over white sand.

Moraine Cay is an interesting little island which, in good weather, is worth a visit. It is privately owned, and the owner requests that visitors not bring or leave garbage ashore, and that they dispose of conch or crawfish shells in deep water far from shore and respect the wildlife that abides here. The cay is roughly T-shaped with good beaches on its southwest and southeast sides. The southwest beach is shallow and available only to dinghies, but a fair-weather anchorage in 6 feet over grass about 20 yards offshore can be found off the southeast beach. Off the southeast end of Moraine Cay are another small, scrub-covered cay and two isolated rocks. Having detoured Fish Cay Bank, you can approach on a northerly bearing for the center of the island. Extending southeast from Moraine Cay is a shallow and dangerous reef that breaks in all but the calmest weather. It should be left to the north and given a wide berth.

UMBRELLA CAY BEARING N W 1 1/2 MILE

Umbrella Cay, with fine white sand beaches, lies one mile northwest of Guineaman Cay. Anchorage can be found under its lee in 9 feet, but it will be uneasy in a strong wind. The holding here is less than the best.

Guineaman Cay is narrowly divided by a cut from the northwest end of

Hurricane harbor at Allan's/Pensacola Cay. (Tropic Isle photo)

Allan's Cay. It is small and low, and the approach to the sandy bay on the southwest side is shoal.

Allan's/Pensacola Cay: Within living memory these were two separate cays, but a hurricane filled the narrow channel between them and it is now covered with bush and grass. The harbor thus formed is the easiest of access north of Green Turtle Cay. We have taken 6.5 feet draft in at low water, but a few shallow grassy spots must be avoided.

Pensacola Cay is 3 miles long, the northwest end low and rising in a series of small hills toward the southeast end, which is distinguished by high, gray cliffs. The southeastern end of Allan's/Pensacola Cay is privately owned. However, here lies a completely landlocked hurricane harbor lined with mangroves. Four feet can be carried through its narrow channel at high water by keeping the south shore of the channel close aboard. Watch for a small, rocky shoal to port where the channel narrows. Sand fleas abound inside.

North Coast of Little Abaco (Tropic Isle Sketch Charts: 42, H-2, H-3). About 300-400 yards from the west end of Little Abaco, a deep cove behind some small rocks provides a good, temporary anchorage and shelter for a yacht of moderate draft. From here east to the Pear Cays, the coast continues low, and

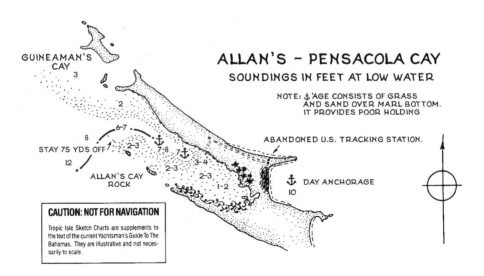

although there is generally deep water (8-9 feet) close to the rocky shore, there are also many off-lying rocks up to at least 200 yards offshore, often awash or submerged. It's best to stay about a half mile offshore. Closer approach to the coast should be made cautiously, in good light. North of the west end of Little Abaco, be aware of the West End Rocks and associated shallow areas shown around them on government charts. Further east, Veteran Shoal (sometimes marked with a tiny stake, sometimes not, and in either case hard to see except at LW) and the 6-foot patch just northeast of it lie about 3 miles northwest of the haulover. When passing south of Veteran Shoal, stay at least a half mile off to avoid a shallow rocky area around it, in which, on a calm day, you can see beautiful sea gardens. A reader tells us he spotted a coral head no more than 2 feet underwater about one-quarter to one-half mile southwest of Veteran Shoal.

PEAR CAY ROCK

The **Pear Cays** are a group of 7-8 small, bush-covered cays and innumerable rocks. There are shoal patches for about one-half mile north of them. There is also a 4-foot patch, which we haven't seen, shown on government charts about 1.5 miles on a bearing of 340°T from the westernmost end of the Pear Cays. We also have a recent letter advising of a reef with less than 5 feet of water on top of it a little more than a half mile east of the easternmost Pear Cay. Keep a good lookout.

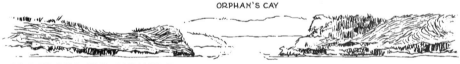

ORPHAN'S CAY

THE HAULOVER, FROM THE NORTH

The Haulover lies immediately south of the Pear Cays. It is a very narrow cut not over 20 feet in width, through which the tidal current runs like a sluiceway in either direction, except at slack. It was cut in the early 1940s for the benefit of local fishermen who worked both sides of Little Abaco and preferred not to detour around West End to do so. Although the cut is narrow and carries only 5 feet, local smacks are taken through under sail alone. The channels south of the cut are intricate and should not be attempted without a local pilot.

TIRE MARKER

ROCK WITH BEACON OFF W. POINT, HAWKSBILL CAY

The **Hawksbill Cays** provide the only shelter on this coast from winds from northwest-north-northeast. On the north coast of these cays are several pretty little beaches and coves, but they must be approached with caution. To gain the anchorage, approach the westernmost rock with the stake and tire beacon on it from the north, taking it to port about 150 yards off. From this point, continue on a SSE heading for about .25 mile until you can head eastward, south of a line of above-water rocks, to the anchorage south of the small beach at the western end of the island. There you will have 6 feet at low water. There are scoured-out spots and also spots with some grass where you can hold. You may have to move around to find good anchorage, and you might want to dive to check your anchor. There are several shallow bars in the area, easily visible in good light.

HAWKSBILL CAYS, WEST | 1/2 MILES

Fox Town, the first refueling port east of West End, lies due south of Hawksbill Cay at the west end of Little Abaco. From the outlying rocks off Hawksbill Cay a course of approximately 160° will take you past the Hawksbill anchorage to the line of four brush-covered rocks that separate Fox Town anchorage and docks from the banks. Access to the inner anchorage and the government pier is between the third and fourth rocks (counting from right to left). Inside, there is good holding in water adequate for yachts drawing about 4 feet. (We were told there is an 8-foot hole inside of the third and fourth rocks, but we haven't seen this.) At the government pier, which can accommodate vessels up to 4 feet at low water, fuels are delivered by truck. There is a 4.5-foot channel into Merlin McIntosh's Fox Town Shell east of the easternmost brush-covered cay, then direct to the dock marked with a Shell flag. This dock will accommodate 3.5 feet at low water. Gas and diesel are available. Call *Fox Town*

Fox Town Shell. (Tropic Isle photo)

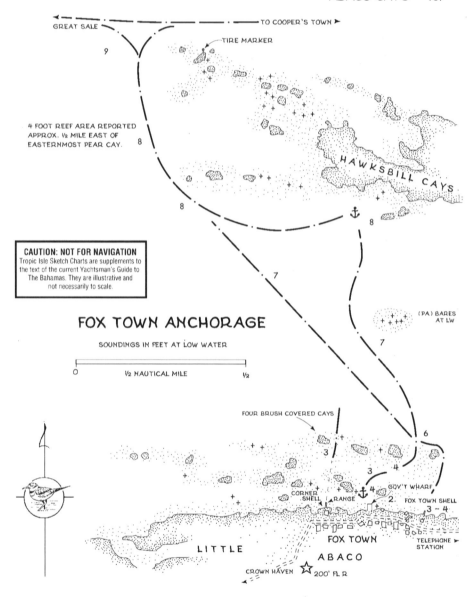

FOX TOWN ANCHORAGE

SOUNDINGS IN FEET AT LOW WATER

CAUTION: NOT FOR NAVIGATION
Tropic Isle Sketch Charts are supplements to
the text of the current Yachtsman's Guide to
The Bahamas. They are illustrative and
not necessarily to scale.

Shell Service on VHF 16. Gersil Edgecombe, manager, will be happy to guide you in if you need help. Ashore Merlin and his wife Millie operate a small hotel and restaurant serving delicious seafood and cracked conch. If you proceed between the first and second rocks, you will see a range ashore that brings you to Daniel Parker's Corner Shell. This channel will carry about 3 feet at LW and the dock will accommodate about 3 feet LW on the outer end.

Fox Town is a pretty settlement with a good restaurant overlooking the harbor, a dry-goods store, a shady park, and a telephone station up the road.

Daniel Parker's Corner Shell, with back range mark. (Tropic Isle photo)

Any of the town's friendly little boys will be glad to show you around. For a taste of Bahamian nightlife, stop by Reflections, between Fox Town and Crown Haven.

Center of the World Rock lies 2 miles offshore in the vicinity of **Wood Cay.** The settlement of **Cedar Harbour** is shallow and available to craft drawing not more than 4.5 feet on top of the tide. Here fuel can also be carried or dispensed by truck, and there is a telephone station.

Little Abaco is joined to Great Abaco by a narrow causeway one mile south of Angel Fish Point.

Comfortable anchorage may be found in the lee of **Crab Cay.** Avoid the shoal, rocky ledge that lies more or less parallel to Crab Cay's southwest side and anchor in about 8 feet of water just southwest of Angelfish Point and the southeast end of Crab Cay. Or you can anchor, again in about 8 feet, between the southeast end of Crab Cay (avoiding the rocky ledge) and the small cays to the south. The water shoals to 3-4 feet and possibly less, in toward these small cays, and to the east toward Great Abaco.

ALANS – PENSACOLA CAY

HOG CAYS LOOKING WEST FROM
ANCHORAGE WEST OF SE HOG CAY.

Hog Cays are covered in brush. Scale and crawfishing are good in this area, and there are some beautiful beaches on Big Hog Cay. A draft of 7 feet can be taken in close to the southwesternmost cay. There are some cottages on Prince Cay and the cay just east of it.

The marina at **Spanish Cay** is toward the southeast end, on the sound side. A breakwater will give good protection in most conditions except possibly in winds from southwest to north. When we were there recently, we were told that the various services offered in the marina were somewhat sporadic; we'd advise calling ahead to be sure that whatever you might need is available. The marina restaurant, the Point House, was open for breakfast and lunch, with

Spanish Cay. (Tropic Isle photo)

drinks served until 6 p.m. The marina stands by on VHF 16; their telephone number is 242 365-0083. Spanish Cay is at this writing temporarily closed as a port of entry.

To enter the harbor at the northwest end, which has a shoal approach but about 9 feet inside over a grassy bottom with poor holding, round Squashes Cay, at which point you'll see the approach on a southeasterly heading. This is sometimes marked with stakes and should be good for 5 feet at high water. There is good calm-weather anchorage anywhere under the lee of the cay in about 9 feet.

Between Spanish Cay and Powell Cay is a bank that must be avoided by making a detour toward the mainland.

Cooper's Town is the largest settlement at the north end of Great Abaco. The principal economy is based on crawfish, conch and scalefish. The Cooper's Town Community Clinic is one of the most modern in The Bahamas, with dental, X-ray, laboratory, and 24-hour emergency services. There's also a museum here of local history.

Cooper's Town Shell, at the north end of town, can accommodate at LW 6-9 feet at the seaward portion of the fuel dock and 4-5 feet farther in. All petroleum products, water, ice, electricity, and showers are available. Medious Edgecombe and his son, Medious Jr., who run the fuel dock, monitor VHF 16; call *Cooper's Town Shell*. On site are a small convenience store, a liquor store, a small marine store and some hardware supplies. Hours are 8 a.m. to 11:30 p.m. Reachable when he's in town, Anthony Edgecombe can do gas or diesel mechanical repairs. Capt. Edward Rolle, Medious' cousin, knows this area well and can help you locate a guide if you need one.

The dock at Murray's Service Station, a bit more than a half mile south of

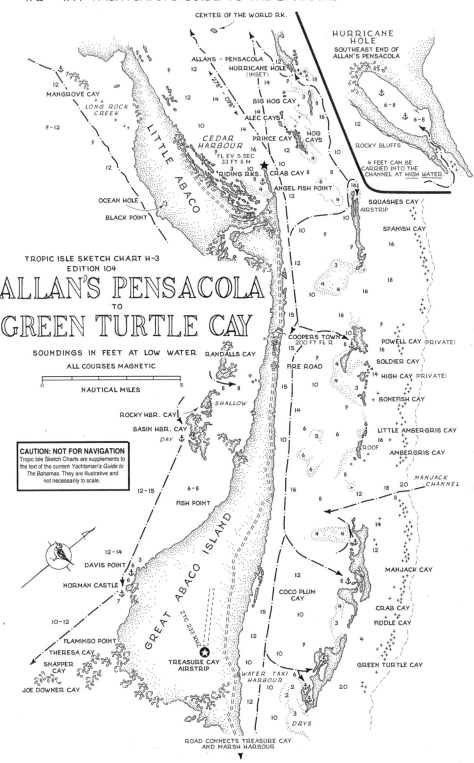

CENTER OF THE WORLD RK.

HURRICANE HOLE
SOUTHEAST END OF
ALLAN'S PENSACOLA

ALLANS - PENSACOLA
HURRICANE HOLE
(INSET)

MANGROVE CAY
LONG ROCK CREEK

BIG HOG CAY
ALEC CAYS
HOG CAYS
PRINCE CAY

CEDAR HARBOUR
FL EV 5 SEC
33 FT 8 M
RIDING RKS.
CRAB CAY

ROCKY BLUFFS

4 FEET CAN BE
CARRIED INTO THE
CHANNEL AT HIGH WATER

ANGEL FISH POINT

OCEAN HOLE
BLACK POINT

LITTLE ABACO

SQUASHES CAY
AIRSTRIP

SPANISH CAY

TROPIC ISLE SKETCH CHART H-3
EDITION 104

ALLAN'S PENSACOLA
TO
GREEN TURTLE CAY

SOUNDINGS IN FEET AT LOW WATER

ALL COURSES MAGNETIC

NAUTICAL MILES

COOPERS TOWN
200 FT FL R

POWELL CAY (PRIVATE)

RANDALLS CAY

FIRE ROAD

SOLDIER CAY
HIGH CAY (PRIVATE)

BONEFISH CAY

SHALLOW

ROCKY HBR. CAY
BASIN HBR. CAY
DAY

LITTLE AMBERGRIS CAY

ROOF
AMBERGRIS CAY

MANJACK
CHANNEL

CAUTION: NOT FOR NAVIGATION
Tropic Isle Sketch Charts are supplements to
the text of the current *Yachtsman's Guide to
The Bahamas*. They are illustrative and
not necessarily to scale.

FISH POINT

DAVIS POINT
NORMAN CASTLE

MANJACK CAY

GREAT ABACO ISLAND

COCO PLUM
CAY

CRAB CAY
FIDDLE CAY

FLAMINGO POINT
THERESA CAY
SNAPPER CAY
JOE DOWNER CAY

ZTC 233 KHZ

TREASURE CAY
AIRSTRIP

WATER TAXI
HARBOUR

GREEN TURTLE CAY

DRYS

ROAD CONNECTS TREASURE CAY
AND MARSH HARBOUR

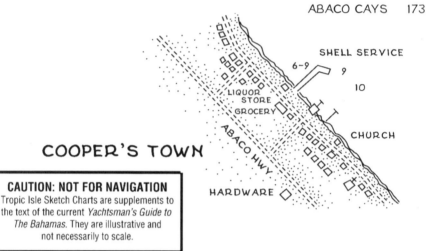

COOPER'S TOWN

CAUTION: NOT FOR NAVIGATION
Tropic Isle Sketch Charts are supplements to
the text of the current *Yachtsman's Guide to
The Bahamas.* They are illustrative and
not necessarily to scale.

the Shell pier, has all Esso products and water. The gas dock will accommodate drafts of 8-10 feet LW. Alfred Murray, who runs the fuel dock, monitors VHF 16; call *Murray's Service Station.* He's a good source of local knowledge and can help you locate a guide if you need one. Adjacent to the dock is Murray's Laundromat and Murray's General Store for marine supplies and hardware.

Grocery stores are within walking distance, and in town are a telephone station and two bakeries, Rosalie's and Princess'. Aunt Evie sells bread from her blue house on Front Street about 50 yards south of the government dock. Just south of Cooper's Town Shell, the Conch Crawl bar/restaurant serves Bahamian fare and seafood from 9 a.m. until 12 p.m. The proprietor is Noel Bootle. Less than ten minutes away is Gelina's Pizza, run by hospitable Angelina Cooper. Evl's Place, owned and operated by Evelyn and Anthony Cooper, was praised at length by a contributor for Evelyn's delicious fresh sautéed grouper and other specialties. The mailboat calls weekly.

Powell Cay is privately owned and as yet uninhabited. It has one of the prettiest beaches to be found hereabouts and also some of the hungriest mosquitoes. The cay is fairly high (100 feet) and shaped like an *L,* the upright extending south and protecting the anchorage to some extent from southeasterly winds. The best anchorage is off the two plainly visible high bluffs. A draft

*"It's not a lobster, Harry! Just get the damn Guide and find out
if it's dinner or if we are!"*

YACHTSMAN'S
Guide to the **Virgin Islands**
Over 300 pages of indispensable information
including 16 pages of full color aerial photos.

Call (305) 893-4277
Or write to: Tropic Isle Publishers
P.O. Box 610938, North Miami, FL 33261-0938

Powell Cay. (Tropic Isle photo)

of 6 feet can be taken close in, about 75-100 yards off. The holding ground is grassy. The approach to the anchorage is on a northeast bearing to avoid the bank that extends southwest. There is a path to the cay's eastern beaches that starts from a point just a short distance east of the pier.

The **Ambergris Cays** lie 3 miles southeast of Powell Cay. Both have attractive beaches, but the southernmost and larger of the two is privately owned and developed into a small estate. A large area of very shoal water lies both to seaward and on the western sides of the Ambergris Cays, which at low water are joined by a rocky bar that dries.

Manjack Cay and **Crab Cay** must be taken together, as they virtually join at low water. Both cays have irregular coastlines with many deep bays and creeks, wonderful places for dinghy explorations. The best anchorage lies in the deep cove formed by the two cays. Here a white streak, which appears shallow but is not, runs across the entrance to this anchorage. A draft of 6.5 feet can be taken well in toward the shore.

Green Turtle Cay (Tropic Isle Sketch Charts: H-3, H-6) has an uneven coastline with deep bays, sounds, and delightful beaches. The island is 3 miles long, 1.5 miles wide, and in places rises to a height of over 80 feet. It is possible to anchor off the cement dock at the northwest end of New Plymouth settlement in 7-9 feet over grass. The town wharf has been rebuilt in a smaller version. There is a good dinghy tie-up area and there are ladders. Settlement Creek carries only 3 feet at low water and has limited space for anchoring. While we do not recommend it as an anchorage, it is possible for yachts drawing up to 6 feet to approach the village at Settlement Creek at high water. The channel is narrow but well marked. Don't get caught in here on a falling tide, or you'll be aground.

Some useful information for boats cruising throughout this general area: taxis on the mainland monitor VHF 6, most facilities at the airport monitor VHF 88, and the Green Turtle ferry along with most marinas and restaurants monitor VHF 16.

New Plymouth is a neat, prosperous, and picturesque settlement whose economy is based on crawfish, scalefish, fruit, and tourism. It is a port of entry, with a post office, two marine hardware stores, and several well-stocked shops. Curry's Food Store has a dinghy dock right on the harbor, with 4 feet at high water. You can buy food supplies at Sid's or Lowe's, both near the government dock. Above Lowe's Food Store, the Island Restaurant serves great food in a convivial atmosphere. The Plymouth Rock package store also has snacks, homemade sweets, and some Bahamian artwork for sale. Atop the highest hill, the Batelco station monitors VHF 16 and has a fax service. Barclay's Bank is open Tuesdays and Thursdays from 10 a.m. to 2 p.m. Floyd Lowe's water taxis make the 2-mile trip to Abaco on a regular schedule, where you can get a taxi to the airstrip. The Nassau mailboat calls weekly.

A government doctor visits New Plymouth on Thursdays (although at times he's off island and does not follow this schedule). The telephone number of the Green Turtle Cay Nurse's Clinic is 365-4028.

Laura's Kitchen is recommended for lunch or dinner (her cracked conch

New Plymouth. (Tropic Isle photo)

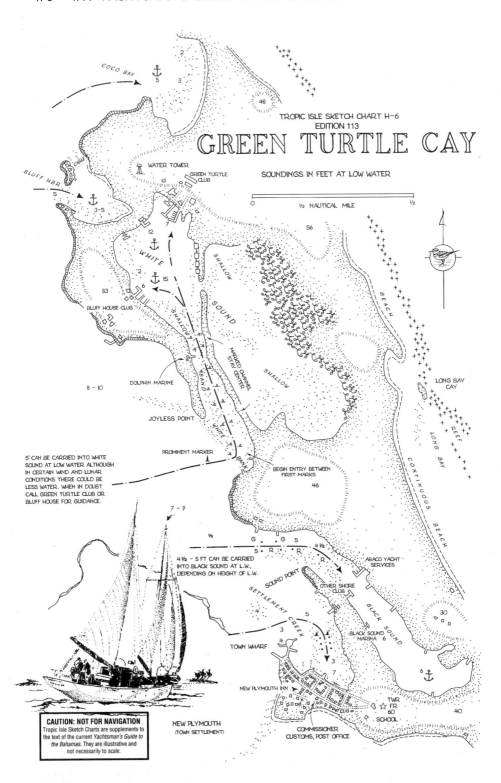

TROPIC ISLE SKETCH CHART H-6
EDITION 113

GREEN TURTLE CAY

SOUNDINGS IN FEET AT LOW WATER

0   ½ NAUTICAL MILE   ½

COCO BAY

BLUFF HBR.

CABLE

WATER TOWER

GREEN TURTLE CLUB

WHITE

SOUND

SHALLOW

SHALLOW

SHALLOW

BEACH

BLUFF HOUSE CLUB

DOLPHIN MARINE

8 - 10

JOYLESS POINT

PROMINENT MARKER

MARKED CHANNEL STAY CENTER

ISLAND

WHITE

SOUND

BANK

LONG BAY CAY

REEF

LONG BAY

CONTINUOUS BEACH

BEGIN ENTRY BETWEEN FIRST MARKS

46

5' CAN BE CARRIED INTO WHITE SOUND AT LOW WATER ALTHOUGH IN CERTAIN WIND AND LUNAR CONDITIONS THERE COULD BE LESS WATER. WHEN IN DOUBT CALL GREEN TURTLE CLUB OR BLUFF HOUSE FOR GUIDANCE.

7 - 9

½

4½ - 5 FT CAN BE CARRIED INTO BLACK SOUND AT L.W., DEPENDING ON HEIGHT OF L.W.

G · G 5
5 · R · R
R

4½
R

ABACO YACHT SERVICES

SOUND POINT

OTHER SHORE CLUB

SETTLEMENT CREEK

TOWN WHARF

BLACK SOUND

BLACK SOUND MARINA 6

30

NEW PLYMOUTH INN

TWR FR 60

SCHOOL

40

CAUTION: NOT FOR NAVIGATION
Tropic Isle Sketch Charts are supplements to the text of the current *Yachtsman's Guide to the Bahamas*. They are illustrative and not necessarily to scale.

NEW PLYMOUTH
(TOWN SETTLEMENT)

COMMISSIONER
CUSTOMS, POST OFFICE

New Plymouth waterfront. (Tropic Isle photo)

is especially good). Laura and her family operate the restaurant out of their home, where she was born. Across the street, the Shell Hut carries cards, gifts, and souvenirs. At the Sand Dollar Shoppe, you can buy Abaco-hand-crafted jewelry, sportswear, T-shirts, and souvenirs. The Blue Bee Bar and, next door, the Sea Garden Club, have similar convivial atmospheres. The Rainbow Restaurant serves excellent local and continental cuisine, with takeout available. Ole B's sells deli sandwiches and ice cream, and you can pick up baked goods or a bite to eat at McIntosh Takeaway. The Rooster's Rest Pub and Restaurant, just outside of town on the hill near the Batelco station, is a popular night spot

The
OTHER SHORE CLUB
and *Marina*

GREEN TURTLE CAY, ABACO, BAHAMAS

A very restful, refreshing stop for the cruising yachtsman!
An ideal setting with a friendly, informal atmosphere.

Excellent accomodations include comfortable housekeeping cottages, swimming pool, and complete marina facilities. Only a five minute walk to picturesque New Plymouth and well stockted stores. Also served by Treasure Cay Airport, with daily flights from Florida. Water Taxi meets all flights.

SAIL WELL – GO SHELL!

2 docks – main dock is located on Black Sound, one of the most protected harbours in the Abacos. Marine fuels, dockside electricity, showers, ice. Bone fishing and reef fishing with professional guide.

Send for full-color brochure

OTHER SHORE CLUB and MARINA
Float Markers
Channel Depth 6' M.L.W.
Black Sound
Village of New Plymouth

New Plymouth. (Tropic Isle photo)

and home base of the Gully Roosters, who play there on Friday and Saturday nights. At the head of Settlement Creek, the Wrecking Tree serves breakfast, lunch, and dinner, beer and mixed drinks, and baked goods including fine coconut bread. Sunday special is souse, described by our research team's appreciative gourmand as chicken broth with two or three chickens thrown in per serving. The New Plymouth Inn, over 130 years old, offers more formal dining atmosphere in the building that once served as the "French Exchange" for all imports arriving in Abaco by sailing ship. The food is excellent, and accommodations are first-rate.

The Albert Lowe Museum, housed in a 150-year-old residence next to the commissioner's office, was lovingly restored by artist Alton Lowe and displays his own paintings as well as his father's ship models. The museum's outstanding collection of Green Turtle Cay photographs dates back to Abaco's earliest days.

BLACK SOUND MARINA
MARINA
PHONE/FAX 242-365-4531

Black Sound Marina
Green Turtle Cay

In beautiful seclusion you can enjoy a relaxing escape at Black Sound Marina including:

➢ 7' at low tide
➢ Showers & laundromat
➢ Leave your boat up to three years
   (Cruising permit extended for 2nd and
   3rd year at $500 PA.)
➢ Wet storage up to 70'
➢ Newest at Green Turtle Cay

Abaco Yacht Services. (Tropic Isle photo)

Next door at the Loyalist Rose Shoppe you can buy gifts and locally written books. The Loyalist Memorial Garden, built with funds raised by the New Plymouth Historical Society, is a recommended visit. A life-sized sculpture of two young women, one black and one white, dominates the center of the garden. Bronze busts of prominent Bahamian citizens are arranged around the area.

The entrance into **Black Sound**, dredged and marked, is available for 4.5 feet at low water, more or less, depending on the height of low water. The shallow spot is as you work your way in and turn a bit to starboard, before reaching Abaco Yacht Services' dock; here the channel is about 4.5 to 5 feet over soft muddy bottom for a short distance, then it deepens again. The sound, which is quiet, is considered a hurricane harbor, with some holes up to 15 feet over deep grass inside. Check your anchor and don't count too heavily on your Danforth. On the eastern shore, just inside, is Abaco Yacht Services, a full-service, do-it-yourself, spic-and-span boatyard and a good place to store your boat. The 50-ton travel lift can accommodate boats of 20-foot beam. Three slips are available, with water, ice, electricity, showers, and laundry service. Yard manager Everette Roberts, formerly of the Nassau Port Authority, monitors VHF 16.

Also conveniently located on Black Sound, the Other Shore Club has dockage for 15 boats and fuel, water, ice, dockside current, and showers. Guests are welcome to use the saltwater pool. Shoreside accommodations here are very pleasant and the management — Allan and Trudy Andrews, daughter Babs and son Cleve — is about the most informal and friendliest you could find. Dockmaster Kevin McIntosh is also head man of the popular Gully Roosters band. Arrangements for fishing charters can be made, and town is a 5-minute walk away.

On the same side and about 200 yards in from the Other Shore Club, the

Green Turtle Cay, Black Sound in foreground. (Tropic Isle photo)

Black Sound Marina has 15 slips offering 7 feet at low water and accommodating boats up to 55 feet in length. At the end of the dock is space for boats up to 140 feet (or a number of boats adding up to that length). Electricity, water, ice (block and cube), a laundromat, and showers are available, as well as long-term wet storage and docking for transients. Guests are welcome to use the picnic tables, barbecues, and hammocks. Reggie Curry is dockmaster; you can reach him at 242-365-4531 or via VHF 16.

Also on the same side as the Other Shore Club, Roberts Docks and Cottages offers dockage up to 65 feet with electricity (daily, weekly, and monthly rates available), short and long-term wet storage, and cottages and efficiency apartment rentals. Linton's Beach and Harbour Cottages offer beachside rentals with a private dock for guests only.

The entrance channel into **White Sound** has been dredged and we've measured it at 5 feet, possibly a bit more, at low water. However, there will be many low tides with less water than this, some associated with full and new moons, others not. Additionally, some winds will lower the water. Proceed carefully, and enter on a rising tide. Boats drawing less than 5 feet have been on hard bottom in this entrance. *If this channel could pose any problem for you, we advise you to call the Green Turtle Club or Bluff House on VHF 16 for tidal information and entering instructions.* Right outside the entrance there is a marker with a sign; pass just south of this. On entering, be sure to begin at the beginning, and stay as mid-channel as possible between the red and green marks; this dredged channel is 30 feet wide, and there is a big difference between being in it and out of it.

At White Sound are two resorts catering to yachtsmen, each with its own special but different charm and both with excellent restaurants. Atop an 80-foot hill with a spectacular view of the surrounding ocean and banks, the Bluff House Beach Hotel and Marina Village has beachfront or hillside villas and rooms available. There are 20 slips at their docks in White Sound or you can pick up one of their moorings there. Fuel, water, ice, electricity, and showers are available at these docks, or you could instead get gas, diesel, ice and water outside at their fuel/dinghy dock on the Abaco Sound side (5.5 feet available alongside the dock at LW), just under the club. The beach club on the bay side

White Sound approach. (Tropic Isle photo)

White Sound, looking southeast: Green Turtle Club docks to lower left and Bluff House docks to upper right. (Tropic Isle photo)

has a snack bar and convenient dinghy dock. (Note: At this writing, plans are under way that include dock renovation, replacement, and expansion and new facilities for marina guests, including a restaurant and bar, commissary and chandlery, self-service laundry, showers, and more. Call the Bluff House at 242-365-4247 for current information.) Dinner at Bluff House's elegant restaurant is popular among yachtsmen for good food and sociability. Reservations are requested; call on VHF 16. On some evenings there's live music. At the head of White Sound is the Green Turtle Club, with room at its docks for up to 35 boats of draft up to 8 feet draft. Water, fuel, electricity, TV hookups, ice, showers, and a chandlery are available. The club also has moorings in White Sound. Accommodations range from waterfront villas to poolside suites. The harborside bar is a lively meeting spot, and the dining room on the waterfront serves dinner by candle light. Reserve for dinner before 5 p.m. on VHF 16. The Gully Roosters band, of great local fame, entertain weekly. Around the early part of July, in conjunction with both Bahamian and American Independence Days and Regatta Time in Abaco, the Bluff House and/or the Green Turtle Club host or otherwise participate in a number of special events. Contact them for details.

Dolphin Marine, located on the west side of the entrance channel into White Sound, is an Evinrude/Johnson and Hydrasport/Boston Whaler dealer/distributor and also handles repairs. Four OMC-trained mechanics are on staff, and a large stock of boats, engines, and parts are kept on hand. Dry boat storage is available. Under the same management is the new Outboard Shop in Marsh Harbour. John Robertshaw is the man to see.

Pelican Cay lies between No Name Cay and Green Turtle Cay. It has a good beach and can be identified by its dense stand of coconut palms. In the usual bright sunny weather Pelican is the typical South Sea island, with the vivid colors of the bank in the foreground and the deeper greens and blues of the reef and ocean beyond. On the barrier reef the swell breaks in cascades of dazzling white foam. Pelican Cay is private property and visits ashore are by invitation only.

No Name Cay is private property. There is a good anchorage off the northwest corner of the cay in 9 feet. A strip of deep water runs down close to the shore, but rocky shoals extend from most of the headlands. There are several

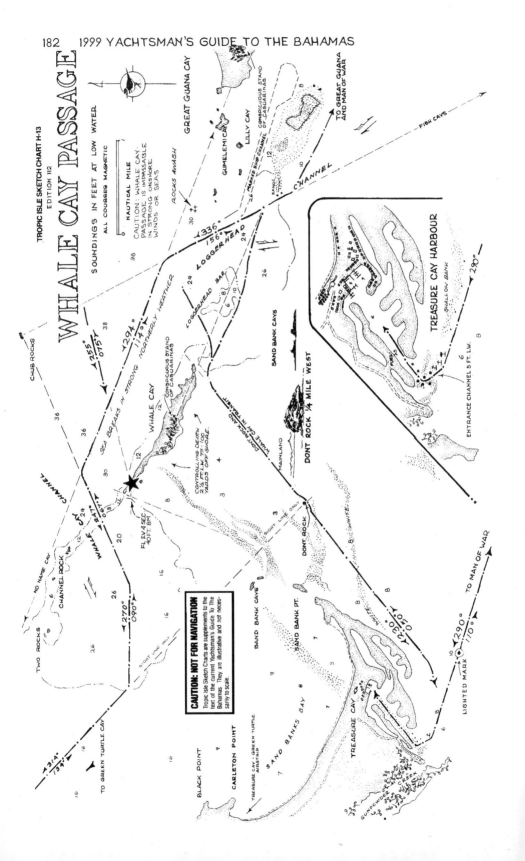

WHALE CAY PASSAGE

TROPIC ISLE SKETCH CHART H-13
EDITION 112

SOUNDINGS IN FEET AT LOW WATER

ALL COURSES MAGNETIC

NAUTICAL MILE

CAUTION: WHALE CAY
PASSAGE IS IMPASSABLE
IN STRONG ONSHORE
WINDS OR SEAS

CAUTION: NOT FOR NAVIGATION

Tropic Isle Sketch Charts are supplements to the text of the current Yachtsman's Guide to The Bahamas. They are illustrative and not necessarily to scale.

GREAT GUANA CAY

TO GREAT GUANA
AND MAN OF WAR

FISH CAYS

LILLY CAY

GUMELEMI CAY

CONSPICUOUS STAND
OF CASUARINAS

26 MARSH SHIP CHANNEL

ROCKS AWASH

CHANNEL

TREASURE CAY HARBOUR

SHALLOW BANK

ENTRANCE CHANNEL 5 FT. L.W.

LOGGERHEAD

LOGGERHEAD BAR

SAND BANK CAYS

DONT ROCK ¼ MILE WEST

MAINLAND

WHALE CAY

CONSPICUOUS STAND
OF CASUARINAS

CONTROLLING DEPTH
2⅓ FATHM. 75 YARDS OFF SHORE

DONT ROCK

SIGHT LINE IN TRANSIT

WHALE CAY IN TRANSIT

SEA BREAKS IN STRONG NORTHERLY WEATHER

CHUB ROCKS

FL EV 4 SEC
40 FT. BM

WHALE

CHANNEL

NO NAME CAY

CHANNEL ROCK

TWO ROCKS

SIGHT LINE IN LINE

SAND BANK CAYS

SAND BANK PT.

SAND BANKS BAY

TO MAN OF WAR

LIGHTED MARK

BLACK POINT

CARLETON POINT

TREASURE CAY - GREEN TURTLE
AIRSTRIP

TREASURE CAY

GUNPOWDER CREEK

TO GREEN TURTLE CAY

Note Regarding Whale Cay Passage

Cruise-ship operations here have long since ceased. In spite of a well-marked (but deteriorating) approach for the cruise ship, we have, over recent years, continued to include our old directions for this section of the Whale Cay Passage in case the cruise-ship marks should cease to be adequate. This is likely to become a reality. Our old directions rely on natural landmarks, and the resulting courses differ somewhat from the cruise-ship approach. If you use our directions exclusively, the cruise-ship marks, spoil banks and islands become hazards that must be avoided. Marks, depths, and bottom geography and characteristics will probably change here over the next years, so it is essential that you use your eyes and head as you work your way through this entire area.

lovely beaches and the still fishing is good.

Whale Cay Passage: *Caution: The passage outside Whale Cay should never be attempted in strong onshore winds, particularly from the north or northeast, or in a rage sea (caused by offshore ocean swells), as the sea breaks in the passage seaward of Whale Cay and also right across all the cuts northwest and southeast of Whale Cay. Always wait for fair weather and calm seas. Remember, there can be rage conditions without any apparent wind.* (You can get advice as to conditions in Whale Cay Passage by talking to Everette Roberts at Abaco Yacht Services on VHF 16).

Proceeding south from Green Turtle Cay, steer west from the anchorage for about one-half mile, then alter course to 134° until the north end of Whale Cay bears 090°. Then you may steer for it for about a mile, or until Chub Rocks bear 067°. Then steer for them. This will place you in about 14 feet of water, midway in the channel between Channel Rock and the north end of Whale Cay, where ocean swells sometimes break in untenable conditions. Chub Rocks, which lie 1.5 miles offshore, can be seen in any weather. If you are bound out into the ocean, you can pass them on either side.

Caution: Never pass close to the west end of Whale Cay, where there are dangerous swells even in settled weather. Never underestimate the Whale Cay Passage; several boats and lives have been lost here in recent years.

Continuing out Whale Cay Passage toward Chub Rocks, when on a line between No Name Cay and Gumelemi Cay (294°-114°) steer 114° toward Gumelemi Cay until Chub Rocks bear 336°, then steer the reciprocal (156°) into Loggerhead Channel onto a course for the northwesternmost of the Fish Cays. You must give the rocks awash, one-half mile to port, ample berth. Just west of the spoil banks south of Gumelemi Cay, two large, unlighted posts make a range for the cruise-ship approach described later. If continuing toward the Fish Cays, be sure to pass west of these posts to avoid the spoil area. If the posts disappear, you still must work your way around the west end of the shallows. Unlighted marks such as these posts and many other marks in this area are one good reason you should not be under way at night here or elsewhere in The Bahamas.

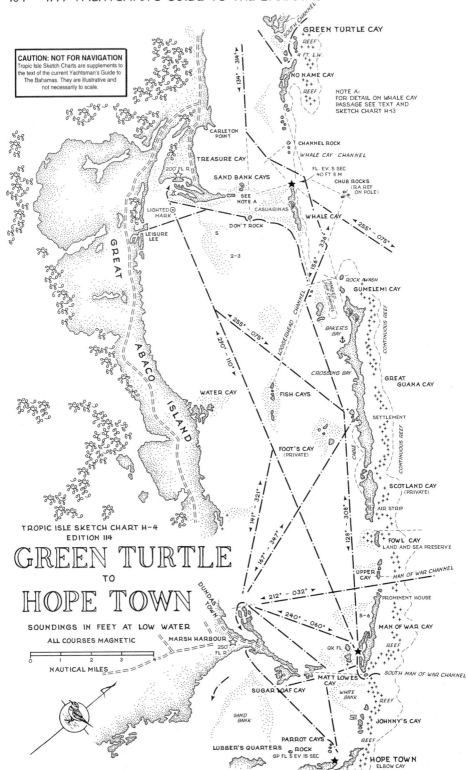

CAUTION: NOT FOR NAVIGATION
Tropic Isle Sketch Charts are supplements to
the text of the current Yachtsman's Guide to
The Bahamas. They are illustrative and
not necessarily to scale.

GREEN TURTLE CAY

SOUTH CHANNEL

REEF
+ + +
4 FT. L.W.

NO NAME CAY

REEF
+ +

NOTE A:
FOR DETAIL ON WHALE CAY
PASSAGE SEE TEXT AND
SKETCH CHART H-13

131°
134°

CARLETON
POINT

CHANNEL ROCK

WHALE CAY CHANNEL

TREASURE CAY

200' FL R

SAND BANK CAYS

FL. EV. 5 SEC
40 FT 8 M

CHUB ROCKS
(RA REF
ON POLE)

SEE
NOTE A

CASUARINAS

WHALE CAY

255° - 075°

LIGHTED
MARK

DON'T ROCK

336°

LEISURE
LEE

5

156°

ROCK AWASH

2-3

GUMELEMI CAY

MARKED
SHIP CHANNEL

255° - 075°

290° - 110°

BAKER'S
BAY

CROSSING BAY

GREAT
GUANA CAY

WATER CAY

FISH CAYS

SETTLEMENT

CABLE

FOOT'S CAY
(PRIVATE)

SCOTLAND CAY
(PRIVATE)

AIR STRIP

321°

128° - 308°

141°

167° - 347°

FOWL CAY
LAND AND SEA PRESERVE

**TROPIC ISLE SKETCH CHART H-4
EDITION 114**

UPPER
CAY

MAN OF WAR CHANNEL

GREEN TURTLE

DUNDAS
TOWN

PROMINENT HOUSE

212° - 032°

5-6

TO

HOPE TOWN

240° - 060°

MAN OF WAR CAY

MARSH HARBOUR

250'
FL R

QK FL

REEF

SOUNDINGS IN FEET AT LOW WATER

ALL COURSES MAGNETIC

SOUTH MAN OF WAR CHANNEL

0   1   2   3   4

NAUTICAL MILES

MATT LOWES
CAY

WHITE
BANK

REEF

SUGAR LOAF CAY

SAND
BANK

JOHNNY'S CAY

REEF

PARROT CAYS

LUBBER'S QUARTERS

ROCK
GP FL 5 EV 15 SEC

HOPE TOWN
ELBOW CAY

GREAT

ABACO

ISLAND

Spoil island, Whale Cay Passage. (Tropic Isle photo)

A rocky patch known as Loggerhead Bar, carrying from 6-10 feet, lies about one-third mile southeast of Whale Cay. It should be avoided, as the swell builds up steeply over the bar and tends to break.

There was extensive dredging at the northwest end of Great Guana Cay to accommodate the cruise ship that used to call here from Florida. What were spoil islands are subsiding fast, and the surrounding shallow banks, also deposited by the dredge (some of which used to be islands), are being moved by the currents from their original position, which was generally on a line that bears about 300° on the southeast tip of Whale Cay. The farthest northwest portion of all this is now a very shallow bank that lies southwest of Gumelemi Cay. The remainder of the spoil, now a single island with a healthy stand of young casuarinas surrounded by a large area of shallow banks, trails off from here for almost a mile toward the southeast.

The approach for the cruise ship is at this writing still well marked and on a course of about 150°. As opposed to our old course of 156°, which points you toward the northwesternmost Fish Cay, this marked channel takes you from a point just west of Chub Rocks on a course that heads you toward the *southeasternmost Fish Cay*. In addition to the lateral marks on this leg of the cruise ship's approach, there is a range on the two large unlighted posts (mentioned above) just west of the spoil banks southwest of Gumelemi Cay. If you intend to pass west of the spoil banks, be sure to pass west of these range posts or you'll be in the shallow spoil area. Short of the range, and northwest of the spoil islands, the incoming cruise-ship approach doglegs to port between the spoil banks and the northwest end of Great Guana Cay. At the time of our most recent visit, the lateral marks for these channels were of various types: some buoys, some driven piles with and without dayboards, some lighted, some not. (We repeat, you should not be under way at night here or elsewhere in The Bahamas.) The type of mark used throughout this facility seemed to change indiscriminately in the past, and marks may now begin to disappear. So be ready for anything. In the turning basin, the perimeter of which is at this writing still clearly marked, are several large mooring buoys. Some of them look water-logged and may soon sink if nothing is done to maintain them — more potential hazards left from this abandoned operation. We recently noticed that one of them had broken loose and was on the beach in Baker's Bay.

You can follow the ship channel through the turning basin and into Baker's Bay to the anchorage or, staying far enough off the southeast point of Baker's Bay for good water, move on down toward Marsh Harbour or Man of War Cay. Or if you want to avoid the cruise-ship anchorage, continue in on the 156°

course, making sure to leave the spoil banks, their surrounding shallows, and the previously mentioned range far enough to port to stay in deep water. When clear, turn south of the spoil banks onto a course to pass between Foot's Cay and the rocks west of the point at Guana Cay settlement.

Don't Rock Passage is negotiable only by small boats in good light at rising tide near high water. Local knowledge and the ability to navigate by eyeball are essential. Constantly shifting sand causes channels to meander, often completely blocking the passage and making the area impossible to chart.

Caution: Don't Rock Passage is never a usable alternative to Whale Cay Passage in northerly weather, heavy seas, or rage conditions. The swells in such conditions will work their way in, where they steepen, break, and can slam a boat down on hard bottom with disastrous results.

Whale Cay (D.M.A. Charts: 26320, 26322. Tropic Isle Sketch Charts: H-4, H-13). Although about 1.5 miles long, Whale Cay is low, rising to a height of 30 feet at its northwest end. It has some good beaches. In settled weather, small craft drawing no more than 2 feet can pick their way through along the lee (south) shore of Whale Cay, staying generally about 75-150 yards offshore; this takes wiggling and eyeballing, but it's doable.

Carleton Point, the site of Abaco's first settlement, lies at the north end of the Treasure Cay property. A plaque here recognizes its historical significance. In September 1783, Loyalist refugees from New York City settled near this point hoping to recapture the glory of the British Empire in Abaco. They named the settlement Carleton after Sir Guy Carleton, British commander-in-chief in North America. The town failed to prosper. Settlers fought among themselves, and within six months most had left to found Marsh's Harbour about 20 miles down the coast. Soon thereafter, Carleton ceased to exist.

Treasure Cay Hotel Resort & Marina lies on the mainland southwest of Whale Cay. For help entering and information regarding tides and depths, call the dockmaster on VHF 16. The entrance channel is well marked and straightforward as indicated on sketch chart H-13 (Whale Cay Passage). It carries about 5 feet at low water, depending, as with all low-water figures, on the height of low water for the particular day.

In the anchorage inside, a fee for anchoring entitles you to use of all the marina facilities. You might instead pick up one of the new moorings installed here. (*Caution:* We have a letter from a reader telling us that at low water, in a boat drawing 5 feet, he hit a concrete block — perhaps an old mooring — in the anchorage.) Facilities at the marina include dockage for 150 yachts, all marine fuels and services, bait, showers, and laundry service.

In the marina complex there is a pool, bar, restaurant, market, post office, telephone, charter operation, and dive shop. On resort grounds is a golf course. Marine and garden-view hotel rooms or villas on the beach are available. Dr. Wilson keeps limited hours in the new Corbett Medical Centre (on the street behind the grocery store) Monday through Saturday — on Wednesday, he's "gone fishin'." His office monitors VHF 83A, and his telephone number is (242) 365-8288 (if no one answers, try 365-8286). The Treasure Cay Marine Store carries the latest edition of this *Guide* as well as Tropic Isle sketch charts. Bill's Canvas makes biminis and bags, and does sail repairs. Little Switzerland sells

> **PLEASE NOTE:** *For a description of* **Batelco towers in all areas and their light characteristics,** *please check page 39 of this Guide.*

china, crystal, jewelry, and watches. Next door, the Harbour Shop sells Androsia batik sportswear and swimwear. The marina-view Spinnaker restaurant is open for all meals, with a bar called The Tipsy Seagull. Florence's Bakery and Ice Cream Parlor is good for sweet rolls and coffee in the morning and a return trip for dessert after dinner. A short ride west of the marina are Macy's Cafe and the Touch of Class restaurant/disco.

Leisure Lee is on mainland Abaco, 2.5 miles southeast of Treasure Cay. It is easily recognized by the conspicuous houses. The owners report a channel dredged to 7 feet leads in from a slatted tower on an off-lying cay. A range on shore aids entry to a series of inland canals which they report are dredged to 8 feet. The owners welcome you to look around.

Great Guana Cay (Tropic Isle Sketch Chart: H-4), which is one of the longest in the Abaco group, has perfect white sand beaches that stretch for miles on both ocean and bank sides. The formerly pristine anchorage in Baker's Bay was until recently a cruise-ship destination with dock and entertainment complex for passengers. The anchorage at the southeast end of Baker's Bay is about the same as it was, but the scenery has been altered by the now defunct cruise-ship operation. These facilities, optimistically named Treasure Island, are now a wasteland, although Treasure Cay, their parent, seems to consider them worthwhile enough to warn in an advertisement in the June 1997 issue of *The Abaconian*, that they have an armed security guard with dog ready to apprehend and prosecute you to the "fullest extent of the law" if you're found trespassing.

In Crossing Bay, just southeast of Baker's Bay, there is a new resort called Guana Seaside Village. On a property that runs from the ocean to the sound, they have two beaches, a freshwater pool, and an 8-room hotel. Lunch and

Treasure Cay Marina. (Tropic Isle photo)

> **Caution:** There are a number of unburied electrical cables in the areas of Marsh Harbour, Guana Cay, Hope Town, Man of War Cay, and Scotland Cay. Be careful not to foul them. If you do, contact BASRA for advice.

dinner are available, and there are showers and a laundry. There is a dock with limited draft available at this writing, and dredging is planned.

The anchorage off Guana Cay settlement is pleasant in prevailing conditions with winds out of the east, but becomes untenable in any kind of a blow if the wind swings much south of east. Holding is less than the best because of a grassy bottom. A draft of 6.5 feet can be taken well into the cove. Guana Beach Resort's dock, parallel to the government dock, offers 22 slips in 6 feet at low water. The best protection, however, is in the harbor west of the resort, where they have a dinghy dock for visitors. The 15-room resort offers indoor and outdoor dining and a freshwater swimming pool. Fuel, water, ice, showers, and groceries are available.

On the point on the east side of the cove is a large new dock built for Orchid Bay Yacht Club and Marina, a new "planned island community" being developed there. The full-service 32-slip marina, with fuel, water, ice, electricity, showers, and laundry, is open to visiting yachts. Homesites overlooking the beach or bay are for sale, and a restaurant and accommodations are planned for late 1999. Chris Albury is marina manager.

Guana Cay settlement is small, modest, and picturesque, with coconut palms and casuarinas growing along a crescent beach at the head of the cove. You can replenish provisions at Guana Harbour Grocery and Fig Tree Wine and Spirits. There are some souvenir/sundry shops on the waterfront road. P & J

Guana Cay settlement harbor. (Tropic Isle photo)

Variety sells straw hats, gifts, and boat hardware and housewares. There's a telephone station and a post office, and the mailboat calls weekly. Follow the signs up a hill to the east side of the island, where Nippers Beach Bar and Grill perches high on a bluff with a breathtaking view of the ocean and beach below. Ferry service is available from Guana Cay to Man of War Cay and Marsh Harbour.

Foots Cay, about one mile south of Great Guana Cay, is privately owned. It has a house on it that is visible and conspicuous from the south. About 2 miles west-southwest of Foots Cay are the **Fish Cays,** some of which are covered with stunted vegetation. Anchorage is in 9-12 feet over white sand or grass on either side of these cays.

Scotland Cay has good beaches on its north shore and an anchorage in good water under its lee. Scotland Cay. There's good soil here that was once cultivated, but in recent years the cay has blossomed as a private resort with a number of vacation houses and an airstrip at the cay's eastern end.

Fowl Cay Preserve lies immediately southeast of Scotland Cay. Visitors are invited to enjoy the flora and undersea life here. Spearfishing or taking of coral formations is prohibited; anchor carefully with regard for the beauty below.

North Man of War Channel (Tropic Isle Sketch Charts: H-4, 5, 7.) This entrance through the outer reef to the shelter of the cays is wide, deep, and straightforward except during very strong onshore winds or during a rage, when all channels are impassable. The one danger in this channel is a submerged rock of considerable area approximately one-quarter of the distance between the northwest end of Man of War Cay and the next small, rocky cay (Upper Cay) to

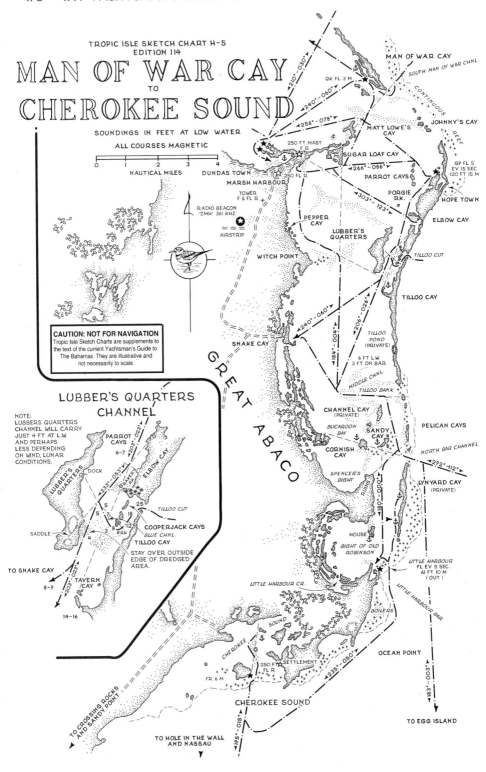

TROPIC ISLE SKETCH CHART H-5
EDITION 114

MAN OF WAR CAY
TO
CHEROKEE SOUND

SOUNDINGS IN FEET AT LOW WATER

ALL COURSES MAGNETIC

NAUTICAL MILES

RADIO BEACON
"ZMH" 361 KHZ

AIRSTRIP

CAUTION: NOT FOR NAVIGATION
Tropic Isle Sketch Charts are supplements to
the text of the current Yachtsman's Guide to
The Bahamas. They are illustrative and
not necessarily to scale.

LUBBER'S QUARTERS
CHANNEL

NOTE:
LUBBERS QUARTERS
CHANNEL WILL CARRY
JUST 4 FT AT L.W.
AND PERHAPS
LESS DEPENDING
ON WIND, LUNAR
CONDITIONS.

PARROT
CAYS
6-7

DOCK

LUBBER'S
QUARTERS

SADDLE

TO SNAKE CAY
8-9

TAVERN
CAY

14-16

ELBOW CAY

25
TILLOO CUT

5
5   7   18
8   12
RK
COOPERJACK CAYS
BLUE CHNL.
TILLOO CAY

4

STAY OVER OUTSIDE
EDGE OF DREDGED
AREA.

GREAT ABACO

MAN OF WAR CAY
SOUTH MAN OF WAR CHNL.
QK FL 3 M

JOHNNY'S CAY

MATT LOWE'S
CAY

250 FT MAST
F R

SUGAR LOAF CAY

GP FL 5
EV 15 SEC
120 FT 15 M

DUNDAS TOWN
250 FT R
250 FL R

PARROT CAYS

MARSH HARBOUR

TOWER
F & FL R

PORGIE
RK.

HOPE TOWN

PEPPER
CAY

LUBBER'S
QUARTERS

ELBOW CAY

WITCH POINT

TILLOO CUT

TILLOO CAY

SNAKE CAY

TILLOO
POND
(PRIVATE)

6 FT LW
3 FT ON BAR

MIDDLE CHNL.
TILLOO BANK

CHANNEL CAY
(PRIVATE)

BUCAROON
BAY

SANDY
CAY

PELICAN CAYS

CORNISH
CAY

NORTH BAR CHANNEL

SPENCER'S
BIGHT

LYNYARD CAY
(PRIVATE)

HOUSE

BIGHT OF OLD
ROBINSON

LITTLE HARBOUR
FL EV 5 SEC.
61 FT 10 M
(OUT)

LITTLE HARBOUR CR.

BOILERS

LITTLE HARBOUR BAR

OCEAN POINT

CHEROKEE
SOUND

LITTLE HARBOUR
SOUND

250 FT
FL R

CHEROKEE
SETTLEMENT

FR 6 M

TO CROSSING ROCKS
AND SANDY POINT

CHEROKEE SOUND

TO EGG ISLAND

TO HOLE IN THE WALL
AND NASSAU

the northwest. While this rock may be passed on either side in calm weather, yachts are strongly advised to leave it to port (or the southeast) on entering as at some states of the tide and during fresh onshore winds the swells tend to break heavily between it and the end of Man of War Cay.

Approaching North Man of War Channel from the ocean, locate the break in the reef that bears approximately north-northeast from the northwest end of Man of War Cay, and steer in on a course of 212°, keeping in the dark water. This will take you a little north of midway between Man of War Cay and Upper Cay. A strong tide runs through this channel, sometimes creating a rip on the ebb as it runs out against a fresh trade wind. North Man of War Channel is far safer than South Man of War Channel, which should be avoided unless accompanied by local knowledge.

If bound south for Man of War Cay or Hope Town, you'll find deep water fairly close to the west coast of Man of War Cay over a dark grass bottom. Avoid the areas of white water that extend from the land in one or two places. The area west of Upper Cay and Fowl Cay is largely shoal with banks and rocky bars.

Man of War Cay (Tropic Isle Sketch Charts: H-4, 5, 7, 14) is a lovely island with some beautiful ocean beaches and hospitable people, a worthwhile stop on any yachtsman's itinerary. This cay is one of the most interesting in The Bahamas and has two of the best harbors, safe in any weather. The entrance is at the southwest side of the cay on the lee side, and carries 5 feet at low water.

The channel entrance is narrow and requires careful pilotage. There is a small, rocky point on the northwest side of the channel just after you pass the

MAN-O-WAR MARINA

Man-O-War Cay, Abaco, Bahamas
Phone 242-365-6008 Fax 242-365-6151

OFFICE & SHOWERS

SMALL BOAT STORAGE

LAUNDRY

CANADIAN IMPERIAL BANK of COMMERCE

To TOWN

FUEL DOCK

DINGHY DOCK

BAR-B-Q GAZEBO

PLAY GROUND

DIVE and GIFT SHOP

PAVILION RESTAURANT

StarPort

MAN-O-WAR MARINA is situated in the main harbour at Man-O-War Cay at the center of the settlement. The docks, equipped with separately metered electricity and water, can handle yachts drawing up to 8'. Cubed and block ice, extra-clean showers and laundry facilities are available on shore. Renowned for safety and tranquility, boat owners can leave their boats in the marina's capable hands while repairs are made. The easily accessible fuel dock serves fresh, filtered Texaco products from 7:00am to 12:00pm, 1:00pm to 5:00pm daily (3:00pm on Sunday). On the premises are the Man-O-War Dive Shop equipped with scuba compressor, tanks, a complete line of dive gear, gifts, garments and basic marine supplies, and the Pavilion, a delightful open-air restaurant, serving lunch and dinner.

Man-O-War Marina. (Tropic Isle photo)

light. Once inside, the channel, plainly visible under most light conditions, divides and heads off at right angles toward each of the two harbors. Watch that the currents don't set you out of the channel.

All petroleum products and services, including mechanical, refrigeration, and cosmetic repairs, prop changes, underwater work and repairs, and a dive shop, are available at the 26-slip Man-O-War Marina. Vessels drawing up to 8 feet can lie alongside. Tommy and Gina Albury are the folks in charge. The fuel dock is right on the harbor. At the marina is a pavilion where lunch and dinner are served (grilled steak, ribs, and fish are weekend specials).

At its new headquarters a short walk south of Man-O-War Marina is Albury's Ferry Service, a fleet of water taxis providing scheduled daily service around the Marsh Harbour/Hope Town/Man of War/Guana Cay area. Charters can be arranged; call them on VHF 16.

Yachtsmen may leave garbage in the large bins down the road past the Sail Shop, at what is locally referred to as "the point." There is a dock here from which garbage is barged to Marsh Harbour for disposal. If you're docked in the Man-O-War Marina, they'll take your garbage as part of the service they offer. If not, they'll charge a dollar per bag to leave it there.

Edwin's Boatyard #1. (Tropic Isle photo)

GREEN TURTLE

CLUB AND MARINA

★ ★ ★ ★ ★

Rare flavour and atmosphere captured for the discerning yachtsman on an unspoiled island with a historic settlement of old world charm.

Situated at the head of a magnificent sheltered harbour with easy access. Sandy rock-free marked channel – 6' minimum at low water.

Harbourside Clubhouse with restaurant and bar. Candlelit dinners of fine cuisine from freshly caught fish, lobster and conch to prime steaks. Luxury rooms and harbour villas with private docks. Superb beaches. Large hillside swimming pool and pool bar.

Fully Equipped Marina

- 240v/120v, 30/50 amp outlets
- Cable TV with 8 premium channels
- Ice, water, and bait
- Gas and diesel, multiple filtered (dirt and water free)
- Boat, Scooters & golf cart rental available
- Marina store, commissary & grog shop
- Showers, coin-operated laundry

New Facilities Include:

- Full Service PADI Resort Association Dive Center

PLEASE INQUIRE ABOUT PRIVILEGES AND DISCOUNTS FOR OUR YACHT CLUB MEMBERS.

WWW.GREENTURTLE.COM

Yachts Call VHF Radio Channel 16
For further information call or write:
(242) 365-4271 • (242) 365-4272 FAX

SHELL BAHAMAS

GREEN TURTLE CAY • ABACO • BAHAMAS

In the Bahama Out Islands, It Just Doesn't Get Better Than This.

We've blended the relaxed, laid back attitude of the Out Islands with the most breathtaking waterfront location you can imagine.

Welcome to Abaco Beach Resort & Boat Harbour.

- Deluxe beachfront rooms and two bedroom cottages with fully equipped kitchens
- Full service marina accommodating yachts up to 200 feet
- Air-conditioned restaurant and bar overlook the turquoise bay
- Tennis, watersports, scuba diving, fishing, and nearby golf
- Two sparkling freshwater pools, one with a swim-up bar
- Shopping on site and nearby

ABACO BEACH
RESORT
&
Boat Harbour

For information,
call your travel agent or
800-468-4799 or 242-367-2736.
www.greatabacobeach.com
E-mail: abrandbh@batelnet.bs

DISTRIBUTORS AND DEALERS IN THE ABACOS

DOLPHIN MARINE
GREEN TURTLE CAY
ABACO
TEL. 242-365-4262

THE O/B SHOP
MARSH HARBOUR
ABACO
TEL. 242-367-2703

SEAHORSE MARINE
HOPE TOWN
ABACO
TEL. 242-366-0023

ISLAND MARINE
PARROT CAY
ABACO
TEL. 242-366-0282

ROBERTS MARINE
GREEN TURTLE CAY
ABACO
TEL. 242-365-4249

FULL RANGE OF RELIABLE
JOHNSON & ADVANCED EVINRUDE MOTORS
IN STOCK 2 HP THRU 250 HP
AT LOWER THAN U.S. PRICES

FULL RANGE OF JOHNSON & EVINRUDE PARTS IN STOCK
FACTORY TRAINED MECHANICS & RELIABLE SERVICE

DRY STORAGE AVAILABLE

BOSTON WHALER/HYDRA-SPORTS/CAROLINA SKIFF

ORCHID BAY

Yacht Club & Marina
Great Guana Cay, Abaco, Bahamas

Chart Your Course for Orchid Bay;
You May Never Want to Leave.

Settle into your slip. Then just settle down. There are 10,000 beautiful bays in the Bahamas. The difference is, you can now call this one home.

Orchid Bay offers a full service marina, exclusive beachfront and bayside homesites. There are even plans for a seaside restaurant overlooking the Sea of Abaco.

Orchid Bay features:

- Beachfront and Bayside homesites for sale
- Full service marina
  (with laundry and showers)
- Accommodations up to 7 1/2 ft. draft
- 32 slips
- 50 and 30 amp electrical service
- 24 hour weather monitoring service
- Quality Texaco products

Orchid Bay Yacht Club & Marina
Great Guana Cay, Abaco, Bahamas
(242) 365-5175 • Fax (242) 365-5166

Boats are built at several yards at Man of War Cay. Willard and Benny Albury turn out beautiful fiberglass runabouts prized throughout The Bahamas. They are also a dealer for Mercury-Mariner outboards. Edwin's Boat Yard consists of Edwin's #1 and Edwin's #2, the two largest yards on the island, with the only marine railways, and also Jay's sail loft at yard #2. Edwin's does first-rate work and repairs of practically any type — you won't find better anywhere. Obviously they're busy, so it's best to call ahead (they've been busier than ever with boaters' increased reliance on GPS). In recent years, Edwin's has built a winner and two contenders for the annual Family Islands Regatta. One of the most illustrious sailing vessels built here is the 70-foot topsail schooner *William H. Albury*. She represented The Bahamas in the Tall Ships Race and Operation Sail '76.

Joe Albury builds distinctively designed sailing dinghies. His unique half-models, finely crafted wooden furniture, and nautical accessories are on display at his studio on the harbor shore. Here you will also find an excellent selection of books on The Bahamas, including these *Guides* and Tropic Isle sketch charts.

Ena's Place serves sandwiches, fresh lemonade, and iced tea from 10:30 a.m. to 9 p.m. Albury's Harbour Store has a fine selection of fresh fruits, vegetables, and frozen goods. Next door, Sally's Seaside Boutique sells tropical clothing and gifts. Albury's Bakery and Lola's Bakery are both good. Duffle bags, yachting jackets, hats, and other handsome accessories (but no longer sail repairs) are made by Uncle Norman Albury's industrious family at their Sail Shop on the harbor next to Edwin's Boat Yard #1. We use their small drawstring bags to store camera lenses, radios,

EDWIN'S BOAT YARD

Your Full Service Yard on Man 'O War Cay
Hauling up to 65' or 50 tons
Painting • Welding • Carpentry • Mechanical Work
SAIL LOFT ON PREMISES
Sails • Sail Repairs • Rigging • Splicing
Canvas Tops & Covers

(242) 365-6006 I • (242) 365-6007 II • VHF CHANNEL 16

Johan Van Olden Barneveldt *at Edwin's Boat Yard. (Tropic Isle photo)*

GPS, and assorted stuff. No stop at Man of War is complete without a visit here.

Up the hill, Man'O'War Grocery has a full selection of supplies. Nearby are gift shops, a telephone station and a post office. Sheila's Deli sells conch fritter batter, pies, and jam. Edison Albury runs Bel-Ena, a department store of sorts with T-shirts and sundries. In Kathy Hura's studio in the center of town, her paintings and crafts are displayed with work by other local artists. Across the street, Mary's Corner Store sells gifts and straw goods; proprietor Haziel Albury is the former postmaster as well as author of the highly recommended *Man-O-War, My Island Home (A History of an Outer Abaco Island).* For hair overhauls, try Carmen Albury's shop, Bahama Waves. There is a clinic in town, and the mailboat calls weekly. The Canadian Bank of Commerce is open Thursday from 10 a.m. to 2 p.m.; the Royal Bank of Canada is open Friday from 10 a.m. to 1:00 p.m.

Man of War is an extraordinarily peaceful and self-contained little town, with narrow streets used mostly by pedestrians and townspeople on motorbikes. Many houses look newly painted, brilliantly colored in the sun. Paths are lined with coconut palms, orange trees, or sea grapes shedding scarlet leaves if the season is right, and graceful dinghies and runabouts rest ashore in the shade. Children ride bicycles into the twilight hours, and on many evenings church services are heartily amplified (no lambs could stray here for lack of God's Word). Later at night it's dead quiet but for wind rustling the palms.

Man of War Cay is a dry settlement where spirits are not sold at stores or restaurants. Visitors are expected to wear appropriate clothing while ashore; scant bikinis are out of place on Man of War streets.

Man Of War to Marsh Harbour (Tropic Isle Sketch Charts H-5, 14). This is a direct deep-water passage of 4 miles, good for a draft of 9 feet at low water. Pass northwest of Garden Cay, and as you leave it behind, steer about 230° for a group of white houses. This is Dundas Town.

Do not pass Marsh Harbour outer point closer than 300 yards, as a rocky shoal lies slightly to seaward. Cross Fanny Bay and round the inner point, then enter the harbor following closely along the small cays and northern shore in about 12 feet of water.

From Man of War Cay to Hope Town is a distance of only 4 miles, but at high tide all but shoal-draft vessels must round the shallow bank extending southwest between the two. East of this bank are a number of small cays, the largest of which is Johnny's Cay.

En route to Hope Town from Man of War, you will pass **Matt Lowe's Cay** to starboard. There is a nice little anchorage off a beach on its western side.

Marsh Harbour (Tropic Isle Sketch Charts: H-5, 8), one of the easiest harbors to enter, provides good shelter in all but strong westerly winds. Vessels of 9 feet can be taken into the government wharf at low water. Upon entering and running up under the northern shore, proceed until the wharf bears about south, then alter course across the harbor and enter between the stakes. The dockmaster can supply fresh water for a small charge. Continuing on under the bluff as indicated in sketch chart H-8 (Marsh Harbour), there is 6-7 feet low water to the center of the harbor where the holding ground, grass over mud, is good. Take care to avoid the large, abandoned anchor (indicated on the sketch chart); it has only 2 feet over it at low water. Sometimes it is marked, sometimes not.

The Conch Inn Marina, at the harbor's southeast corner, has berths for 75 yachts, although the eastern side of the eastern dock is occupied by a charter company. There is up to a 7-foot depth at the docks over a soft bottom. Some space is available for boats up to 100 feet. A channel marked with red and green

Marsh Harbour. (Tropic Isle photo)

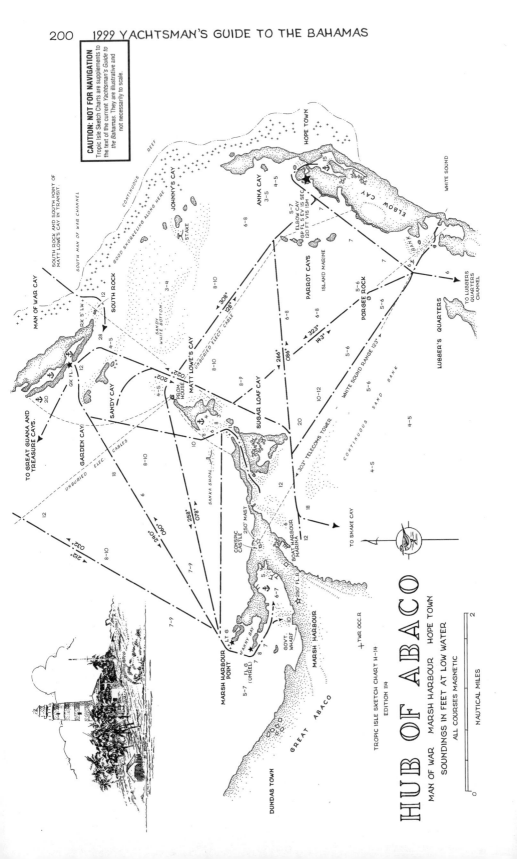

CAUTION: NOT FOR NAVIGATION
Tropic Isle Sketch Charts are supplements to the text of the current *Yachtsman's Guide to the Bahamas.* They are illustrative and not necessarily to scale.

HUB OF ABACO

MAN OF WAR   MARSH HARBOUR   HOPE TOWN

SOUNDINGS IN FEET AT LOW WATER

ALL COURSES MAGNETIC

TROPIC ISLE SKETCH CHART H-114
EDITION 114

NAUTICAL MILES

floats leads to the fuel dock. In 1994 a large boat hit a submerged object in the mooring field in this vicinity, and was holed. Stay in the channel. Rooms are available, a grocery is planned, and the Conch Inn Cafe has happy hours on Monday and Thursday. The Guana Cay ferry leaves four times daily from the marina. A short walk to the east, the Island Breezes Motel has eight spic-and-span air-conditioned rooms available at reasonable rates.

Just a few steps west on the waterfront, in the thick of things, is Mangoes Restaurant, Marina, and Boutique, owned by Bo and Libby Roberts. The restaurant is well known for its sophisticated menu and pleasant atmosphere. At the patio bar you can get lunch and drinks from 11:30 on, and there's a fine happy hour Tuesday nights from 5-7 p.m. at the Cabana Bar and live music that night. The boutique carries clothing, jewelry, watches, and local crafts. Mangoes has a marina with 30 slips offering all services except fuel. Monthly marina rates are available. There's a dinghy dock for restaurant customers. Wally's Place, the pink restaurant operated by Wally Smith across the street, is a very popular spot with excellent food and frequent live music. There's an interesting selection of resort wear, jewelry, and crafts in the boutique.

Just west of Mangoes is Harbour View Marina, attended by Hubert and Barbara Bethel, with 40 slips, fuel, water, ice, showers, and a laundromat. Across from the marina is Sapodilly's bar and grill, run by Brenda and Steve Mitchell. Lunch, dinner, and Sunday brunch are served, with live music in the evenings. The Tiki Hut is now located on its own dock just west of the Harbour View Marina. Dinghy in for lunch or dinner; the Tiki Hut serves Bahamian and American food from burgers to steak. Guy Toothe is the proprietor.

Triple J Marine has dockage for 26 boats, gas and diesel fuel, ice, water, electricity, showers, and a laundromat. The store stocks boat supplies and parts, fishing gear and diving equipment, and copies of this *Yachtsman's Guide*. The boutique offers a large variety of gift items, beachwear, souvenirs and jewelry. Triple-J Marine Electronics sells, services, and repairs electronic and electrical equipment. You may use the floating dinghy dock (being rebuilt at this writing) and dispose of garbage in the dumpster behind the marine store. Just west of the Triple J dock, Long's Landing has fresh seafood for sale. Within walking distance are bakeries and takeaways selling Bahamian food.

The government Union Jack dock is west of the Triple J pier and east of the

Beautiful Colonial Building

Open Tuesday through Saturday for
Lunch & Dinner
11:30 am - 3:00 pm   6:00 pm - 9:00 pm
Bar Open 11:00 am -(until closing)

Boutique Open
Tuesday - Saturday 9:00 am - 9:00 pm
Live Music by Estin
Wednesday and Saturday Evenings

FOOD • DRINK • GIFTS
We Monitor CH 16 V.H.F.

On the Marsh Harbour Waterfront • (242) 367-2074

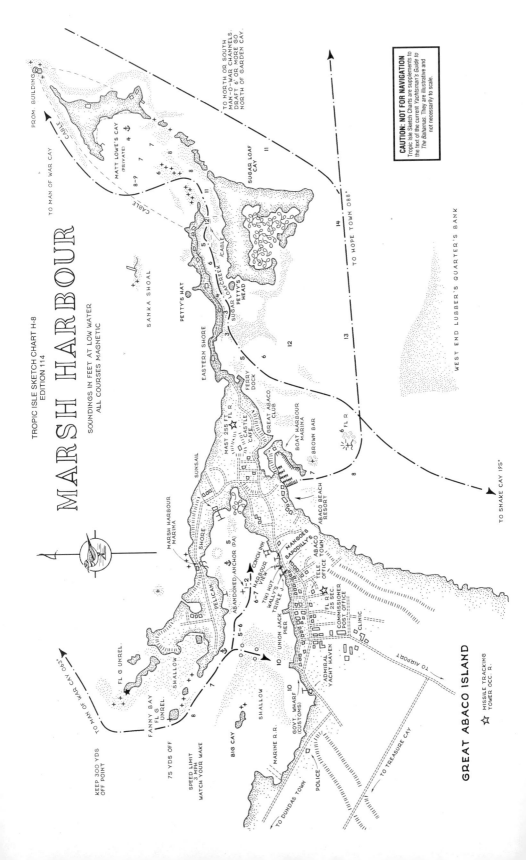

government customs wharf. You can leave your dinghy here while you shop.

West of the customs wharf, Admiral Yacht Haven has 26 slips with up to 5-6 feet LW alongside. Services include water, power, and showers. There's a Pizza Hut on site. This is on the west side of town, where excellent restaurants include Mother Merle's, Alfonza's Bayview, and Cynthia's Kitchen.

Across the harbor under the conspicuous (especially after dark) yellow and white building is the full-service Marsh Harbour Marina and Jib Room Restaurant. The marina location enjoys cooling southeast summer breezes and good protection from winter northerlies. The two-story Jib Room offers its famous BBQs two nights a week, always with music and dancing. Sunday night is steak night, and Wednesday night is for ribs (chicken and lobster are also available). The Mermaid Reef snorkeling area is a short walk up the road. The Castle Cafe, in the castle on the hill just east of the harbor, serves lunch from 11 a.m. to 5 p.m. The menu includes good burgers and steaks, homemade soups, sandwiches, salads, pizza, and pasta; nothing is fried. The view is beautiful. Proprietors are Monica Nyderak (who is also the cook) and Gail Cottman, daughter of *Out Island Doctor* author Evans Cottman.

Immediately east lies Sunsail's fleet of bareboat yachts. Sunsail does not operate a public marina but will accommodate yachtsmen in an emergency.

Abaco Wholesale will deliver provisions free to your dock (call them on VHF 16). Solomon Brothers and the Golden Harvest supermarket are other good grocery sources, and there are several bakeries in town. In Memorial Plaza, Cultural Illusions offers a wide variety of Bahamian crafts including hurricane glass lamps from Nassau, teas and Souse Packs, Androsia fabrics, jams, herbs, soaps, painted poinciana pods, dolls made of fish floats, and jewelry, sculpture,

Triple J Marine

26 SLIP FULL SERVICE MARINA AND MARINE STORE

Metered 250V/50A Electric Service
Showers • Laundromat • Water • Ice

Esso *Esso Gasoline and Diesel Fuel*

Marine Electronics

Factory Authorized Sales, Service and Repair for:

FURUNO™ **ICOM**™ **SIMRAD**™
A KONSBERG Company

and Others • FCC Licensed, Factory Trained Technician

Boaters Boutique

Pool and Beach Wear
Jewelry and Gifts
Souvenirs
Androsia Fabric
Island Music
Tapes and CD's

Marine Store
On the Waterfront
Boating Equipment
Marine Hardware
Fishing Tackle

Dock Open Sundays & Holidays 8- 12   Store: Mon - Fri. 8 - 5 and Sat. 8 - 12
Phone 242-367-2163 • Fax 242-367-3388 • Dock 367-2287 • VHF Ch. 16

Marsh Harbour Marina. (Tropic Isle photo)

and paintings by local artists. Kimberly Sturrup runs the shop.

Marsh Harbour is growing. If you look, you can find just about anything you might need. Tools, hardware supplies, lumber, propane, and welding services are available. There's a post office, telephone station, banks, coin laundries, modern drugstores, and even a one-hour photo lab. There are doctors, a resident dentist, and a government clinic. Accommodations range from resort-style to small inns and efficiencies. Several airlines provide daily service to Nassau and Florida, the Nassau mailboat calls weekly, and freighters service Marsh Harbour from Palm Beach on a weekly schedule. To get a taxi in Marsh Harbour, call "Any taxi in the vicinity of ..." on VHF 6. Practically before you've finished speaking, about a dozen taxi drivers will cut in and begin a heated discussion about who's

GOLDEN HARVEST
SUPERMARKET
A DIVISION OF ABACO MARKETS LTD.

NEWLY RENOVATED • LARGE VARIETY OF PRODUCTS

COMPLETE GROCERY LINE

• CHOICE MEATS
• FRESH FRUIT & VEGETABLES
• DAIRY PRODUCTS & FROZEN FOODS
• FAMOUS BRAND NAMES

See It, Touch It, Taste It, its the Golden Harvest way!

Queen Elizabeth Dr. • Marsh Harbour, Abaco
Tel: (242) 367-2310 • Fax: (242) 367-2322

Conch Inn Marina & Hotel

For The Finest Service In The Abacos

- 75 slips including deep water large yacht berths
- Transient and long term dockage
- 30, 50 & 100 amp facilities and cable TV services
- Good fresh water, ice and showers
- Full service diesel, gas and oil fuel dock
- Proximity to Marsh Harbour's shopping & business center
- Nine air conditioned, harbour-view rooms with phones
- Fresh water swimming pool
- Marsh Harbour's only dive shop
- Mini market on site
- Laundry facilities
- Mail drop off/Fax service

Plus the **Bistro Mezzamore** restaurant & bar for fabulous Bahamian and Italian cuisine, breakfast, lunch and harbourside dining by candlelight.

We monitor VHF 16
For more information or bookings contact:

P.O. Box AB-20469
Marsh Harbour, Abaco, Bahamas
Phone: (242) 367-4000
Fax: (242) 367-4004

For yacht charter reservations
in the U.S. and Canada call
1-800-535-7289
(727) 535-1446

WE LOOK FORWARD TO TAKING YOUR LINES

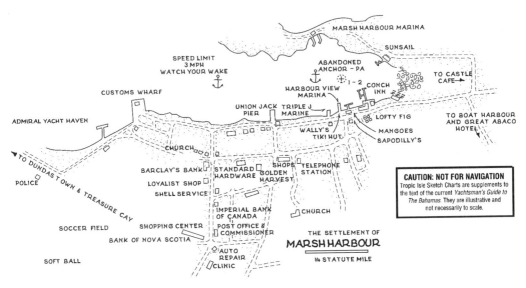

CAUTION: NOT FOR NAVIGATION
Tropic Isle Sketch Charts are supplements to the text of the current *Yachtsman's Guide to The Bahamas.* They are illustrative and not necessarily to scale.

THE SETTLEMENT OF
MARSH HARBOUR
¼ STATUTE MILE

going to pick you up — it's a regular feeding frenzy.

Marsh Harbour was established in the late 1700s when dissidents from the settlement of Carleton left to form their own community at "Marsh's" Harbour. In the late 1800s and early 1900s, when sponging and shipbuilding were at their peak, Marsh Harbour was one of the busiest and most prosperous settlements in The Bahamas, but with the decline of sponge fishing after World War I, the settlement's economy almost collapsed and many inhabitants left to look for work in Nassau. In the 1950s, an agricultural project was initiated, with hundreds of acres cultivated to supply fresh farm produce to the Abaco district and Nassau. This and the growth of tourism have helped to establish present-day Marsh Harbour as the commercial center of Abaco's widespread settlements, with roads connecting with Sandy Point to the south, and Treasure Cay, Cooper's Town, and Fox Town to the northwest. Citrus farming is an emerging industry here, with B. G. Harmon Company's 10,000-acre plantation outside of town.

Marsh Harbour East Side. Sugarloaf Creek, running under Marsh Harbour's eastern shore, used to be a convenient anchorage, but the profusion of docks running out from the houses on the north side, new underwater electric cables serving the private houses on Sugarloaf Cay, and heavy traffic through the creek make this no longer so. Passing through the creek, the best water lies along the north side. On Sugarloaf Cay, work on private homes and docks continues, so look out for changes here. Proceed at slow speed in this area not only for the sake of the boats moored along the north side of the creek, but also so you can

Sugarloaf Creek. (Tropic Isle photo)

Abaco Beach Resort and Boat Harbour. (Tropic Isle photo)

read the water. About halfway between the west end of Sugarloaf Creek and Boat Harbour Marina is the terminal for Albury's Ferry Service.

High on the eastern slope of Marsh Harbour, overlooking its own beach, the Abaco Beach Resort & Boat Harbour offers an unmatched view across Abaco Sound and the cays to the east. On the same property, just east of the hotel, is the 182-slip Boat Harbour Marina. They can handle boats up to 150 feet with 30, 50, and 100-amp and 3-phase power, and TV and telephone hookups at each slip. Complete marine services are available, and use of the pool and tennis courts is included for all marina guests. There's a grocery store, liquor store, boutique, bicycles, and the marine store at Little Switzerland, all on the property. Anglers, a waterfront bar/restaurant supervised by Chef Dietmar Uiberreiter, serves breakfast, lunch, and dinner, with evening entertainment. The marina office, managed by Kevie Thomas, handles reservations, messages for visiting yachts, emergencies, and a mail drop. They can also arrange repairs, maintenance, and cleaning services. The entrance to the harbor is clearly marked, but if you need help, call dockmaster Cecil Ingraham on VHF 16. Penny Turtle is still here to greet friends old and new. Stafford Patterson's Sea Horse Boat Rentals is here, with boats, bikes, and snorkeling gear available. The marina is also the Marsh Harbour base for Florida Yacht Charters and Sales' charter fleet and the Abaco base for the World Association of Yacht Clubs.

Approaching the **Parrot Cays** from Marsh Harbour, keep North Parrot Cay, which has a wooden platform off its north end on your starboard hand. Located on the middle cay is Dave Gale's Island Marine.

Hope Town (Tropic Isle Sketch Charts: H-5, 9, 14). A draft of 7 feet at high water may be carried from a position approximately 300 yards northeast of North Parrot Cay on a bearing of 150°. Proceed in on that bearing and turn to port to parallel Elbow Cay's shore about 100 yards off, as indicated on sketch chart H-9 (Elbow Cay). Upon sighting **Eagle Rock,** with its prominent yellow house, turn slowly to starboard, being careful to give the shallow bar a wide berth, until the white pole and post range is in line. Then go in on it, on a bearing of 148°. As you approach the shore, the channel turns sharply to starboard. From there you can proceed down the center of the channel to the harbor and anchor in 12-18 feet. Remember that the harbor speed limit of 3 m.p.h. is enforced.

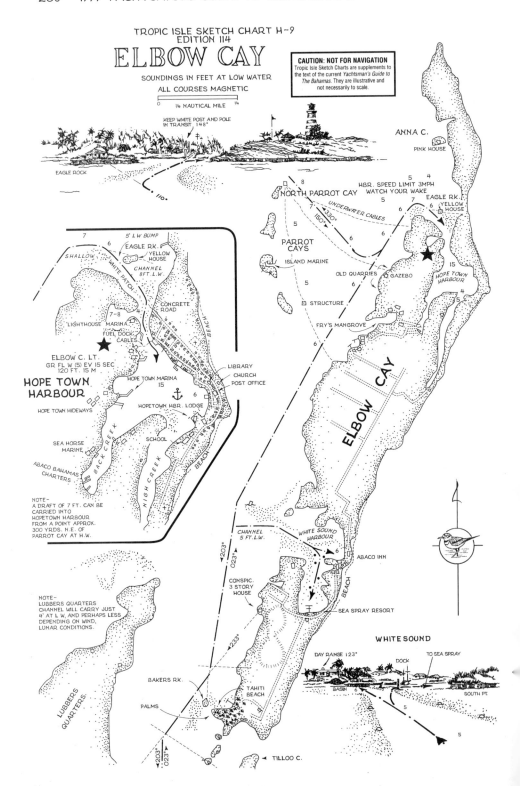

TROPIC ISLE SKETCH CHART H-9
EDITION 114

ELBOW CAY

SOUNDINGS IN FEET AT LOW WATER

ALL COURSES MAGNETIC

0   ¼ NAUTICAL MILE   ¼

CAUTION: NOT FOR NAVIGATION
Tropic Isle Sketch Charts are supplements to
the text of the current *Yachtsman's Guide to
The Bahamas.* They are illustrative and
not necessarily to scale.

KEEP WHITE POST AND POLE
IN TRANSIT 148°

ANNA C.

PINK HOUSE

EAGLE ROCK

110°

HBR. SPEED LIMIT 3MPH
WATCH YOUR WAKE

NORTH PARROT CAY

UNDERWATER CABLES

EAGLE RK.
YELLOW
HOUSE

150°   330°

PARROT
CAYS

ISLAND MARINE

OLD QUARRIES   GAZEBO

HOPE TOWN
HARBOUR

STRUCTURE

FRY'S MANGROVE

7   5' LW BUMP

EAGLE RK.
YELLOW
HOUSE

SHALLOW   WHITE PATCH   CHANNEL
8 FT. L.W.

7-8   CONCRETE
ROAD

'LIGHTHOUSE' MARINA

FUEL DOCK
CABLES

BEACH

ELBOW C. LT.
GR FL W (5) EV 15 SEC
120 FT. 15 M

LIBRARY
CHURCH
POST OFFICE

HOPE TOWN
HARBOUR

HOPE TOWN MARINA   15

HOPE TOWN HIDEWAYS

HOPETOWN HBR. LODGE

SEA HORSE
MARINE

BACK CREEK

SCHOOL

ABACO BAHAMAS
CHARTERS

HIGH CREEK

BEACH

ELBOW CAY

NOTE-
A DRAFT OF 7 FT. CAN BE
CARRIED INTO
HOPETOWN HARBOUR
FROM A POINT APPROX.
300 YRDS. N.E. OF
PARROT CAY AT H.W.

CHANNEL
5 FT. L.W.

WHITE SOUND
HARBOUR

ABACO INN

023°

BEACH

NOTE-
LUBBERS QUARTERS
CHANNEL WILL CARRY JUST
4' AT L W, AND PERHAPS LESS
DEPENDING ON WIND,
LUNAR CONDITIONS.

CONSPIC.
3 STORY
HOUSE

SEA SPRAY RESORT

WHITE SOUND

DAY RANGE 123°   TO SEA SPRAY

DOCK

LUBBERS QUARTERS

BAKERS RK.

PALMS

TAHITI
BEACH

BASIN

SOUTH PT.

203°   023°

TILLOO C.

203°   023°

Dinghy race, Hope Town. (Tropic Isle photo)

Anchoring is no longer allowed in Hope Town Harbour. You must use moorings, go to a marina, or anchor outside the harbor. Call *Hope Town Marina, Lucky Strike,* or *Abaco Bahamas Charters* for moorings, and do it as early as possible, because the entire harbor is often full. A no-discharge rule is now enforced here, as it should be.

The only place to get fuel in Hope Town Harbour is Lighthouse Marina, on your starboard just inside the harbor mouth. All petroleum products and dockside services are available, as well as a marine store. The marina manager monitors VHF 16 during business hours.

The long dock 300 yards south is Hope Town Marina, with 14 protected slips in 7.5 feet at low water. Here, Club Soleil's bar/restaurant features continental and Bahamian specialties, and a Sunday brunch as well. Six hotel rooms are available and there's a freshwater pool.

LIGHTHOUSE MARINA
& *Marine Hardware Store*

★ *Fuel*
★ *Dockage 110/220*
★ *Ice*
★ *Clean, hot showers*
★ *Water (filtered)*
★ *Laundry*
★ *Pressure cleaning*
★ *Bottom painting*
★ *Dry boat storage*
★ *Mechanic*

Sail Well
Go Shell

Hope Town Marine, Ltd.
Hope Town, Abaco, Bahamas
(242) 366-0154
VHF Ch. 16

Yamaha Outboards • Stand-By Generator
• House Rentals Including Boat

Hope Town Harbour. (Tropic Isle photo)

Next door to Club Soleil, Hope Town Hideaways' new marina has 12 deep-water slips accommodating boats up to 70 feet, with metered electricity and filtered water. Pretty air-conditioned two-bedroom villas overlook the harbor, with full kitchens, decks, and maid service. For guests there is a freshwater swimming pool, a coin laundry, and ice. The grounds are landscaped with tropical fruit trees and exotic flowers. Proprietors Peggy and Chris Thompson are happy to share their knowledge of the area both at sea and ashore with guests.

Abaco Bahamas Charters, Ltd., operated by Evans Wilhoyte, was the first bareboat fleet in The Bahamas. Their fleet of sailing yachts is headquartered on the harbor's west creek. The west creek is known as Back Creek. Also here is Sea Horse Marine, Stafford Patterson's OMC dealership and boat rental operation.

Fishing around Hope Town is excellent. Maitland Lowe is a fishing guide, and Robert Lowe, Truman Major, and Will Key operate offshore sportfishing boats. Contact them via VHF 16.

Hope Town, with its red-and-white-banded lighthouse, is the most photo-

Out Islands Finest Vacation Homes and Waterfront Properties. Rentals & SALES. New Marina.

HOPE TOWN HIDEAWAYS

1 Purple Porpoise Place
Hope Town, Abaco, Bahamas

Chris and Peg Thompson, Proprietors
Phone: 242-366-0224 • Fax 242-366-0434
Website: www.hopetown.com

graphed harbor in The Bahamas. The lightkeeper usually welcomes visitors for a spectacular view of the surrounding area, but remember that these men tend the light all night, and during daytime hours they entertain you on their own time. Visiting hours for most Bahamas lighthouses are from 9 a.m. to 5 p.m. This lighthouse is one of the few remaining manned lighthouses in The Bahamas, with a Fresnel (bulls-eye) lens that focuses, magnifies, and directs the light from a kerosene vapor lamp outward, where it is visible up to 20 miles offshore. The lens floats in a pool of mercury to keep it level and eliminate friction. The rotating mechanism must be rewound by hand every hour and a half. The lighthouse is worth the climb, not only for the view, but also to see and appreciate this beautiful apparatus.

Since its founding in the late 1700s by Loyalists, until about 30 years ago, Hope Town had been all but isolated from the rest of the world and so preserved a distinct character. Many local surnames date back through generations of seafarers and boatbuilders. The village is remarkably serene. Vehicles must be left on the edge of town, with only delivery and garbage trucks permitted inside. Potcakes nap wherever there's shade. Residents take pride in their homes, many of which are decorated and named with individuality and wit. Detail includes intricate openwork and lovely hand-carved signs and edging. Tropical trees and flowers thrive everywhere, from elaborate gardens to rows of porch pots. There's a library, drug store, telephone station, beauty shop, marine/engine repair shop, and hardware and liquor stores. At the head of the inner public dock, a building over 100 years old houses the post office upstairs and, downstairs, the

HOPE TOWN - ABACO - BAHAMAS

PHONE 242-366-0280 · FAX 242-366-0281

The Bahamas has the last three hand-wound kerosene-burning lighthouses in the world – we're proud of our maritime heritage. Under the threat of their automation, we founded, in 1995, the...

Bahamas Lighthouse Preservation Society

...a non-profit historical and educational society dedicated to their museum quality maintenance.

You are welcome to visit the Elbow Reef Lighthouse at Hope Town or the beautiful lighthouses at San Salvador and Great Inagua. For $25 (more if you like) you may join us, and receive our newsletters, helping us to preserve these beautiful symbols of maritime history, of which no other country can boast. Please make checks payable to:

Bahamas Lighthouse Preservation Society
General Delivery, Hope Town, Abaco, Bahamas

Hope Town firehouse. (Tropic Isle photo)

Dolphin and Whale Museum. Ship's laundry can be handled through the marinas. Yachtsmen can bring trash in plastic bags to the government dock on Mondays, Wednesdays, and Fridays between 8:30 and 9:30 a.m. to a blue truck, the "Hope Town Queen," for disposal. Place your bags in the back of the truck. Make sure the hours and location haven't changed before you set off with garbage in hand. Rum barrels placed around the village are only for incidental trash like cups, cans, or tissues. They are not for boaters' garbage.

The tiny Wyannie Malone Historical Museum, in one of Hope Town's oldest houses, is crammed with manuscripts, photographs, and artifacts of Hope Town history. Local ancestries, pottery and ship's china recovered by wreckers, and household antiques are here; it feels as intimate as exploring someone's attic. Souvenirs and locally crafted gifts are sold at The Ebb Tide, Tanny Key's Native Touches, Kemp's Souvenir Center, and Edith's Straw Market. Vernon's Grocery/Upper Crust Bakery sells baked goods, fresh and frozen meats, vegetables, and seafood. Bethel's Store, on the waterfront, has a good grocery selection and is the Hope Town LP gas agent (ask for Willard Bethel).

Hope Town Harbour Lodge, with its lovely harbor view, has a poolside patio overlooking the reefs and ocean beach to the east. Reservations are requested for the popular Sunday champagne brunch. Harbour's Edge, on the harbor shore near the inner, public dock, serves lunch and dinner, with a daily happy hour from 5:00 to 6:00 p.m. They sell ice and have a pool table and satellite TV. Another good place to eat on the waterfront is Cap'n Jack's restaurant and bar, for Bahamian-style breakfast, lunch and dinner. There's a children's menu and a salad bar. Rudy's Place, nestled in the woods in the center of the island, serves excellent Bahamian dishes. Rudy will provide transportation from Hope Town upon request. Dinner reservations are requested by 6:00 p.m.

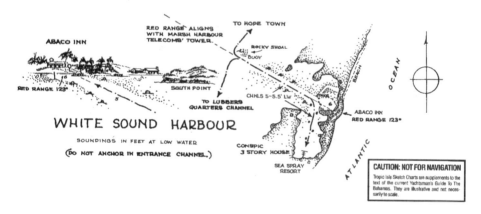

A little farther south on Elbow Cay lies **White Sound,** which is entered on the Abaco Inn's red, lighted range (123°). The entrance channel is marked with buoys and is good for 5-5.5 feet at low water. (Note: The inn is closed in September and October, and during these months the range may or may not be lit.) Shoreside under the inn is a dock which management tells us is good for 6 feet at low water. Dockage is free for patrons. When approaching White Sound Channel, you can call the inn on VHF 16 for assistance. Visiting yachtsmen who dine at the restaurant are welcome to the beach and pool.

The Abaco Inn seems beautifully isolated on its narrow strip of land, but

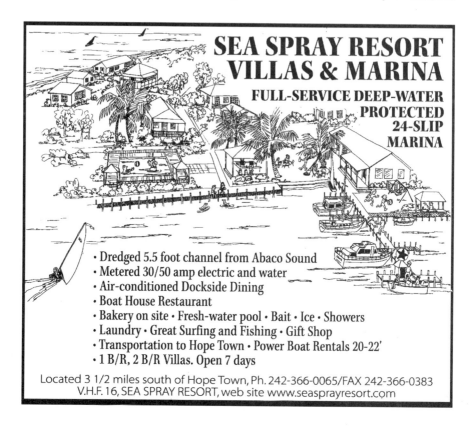

SEA SPRAY RESORT VILLAS & MARINA

FULL-SERVICE DEEP-WATER PROTECTED 24-SLIP MARINA

- Dredged 5.5 foot channel from Abaco Sound
- Metered 30/50 amp electric and water
- Air-conditioned Dockside Dining
- Boat House Restaurant
- Bakery on site · Fresh-water pool · Bait · Ice · Showers
- Laundry · Great Surfing and Fishing · Gift Shop
- Transportation to Hope Town · Power Boat Rentals 20-22'
- 1 B/R, 2 B/R Villas. Open 7 days

Located 3 1/2 miles south of Hope Town, Ph. 242-366-0065/FAX 242-366-0383
V.H.F. 16, SEA SPRAY RESORT, web site www.seasprayresort.com

White Sound. (Tropic Isle photo)

is actually within a good walk's distance from town. On the west side are clear water and sandy beaches; to the east, surf pounds at ledges of coral rock. The inn has nice rooms, a saltwater pool, and a gourmet restaurant serving breakfast, lunch, dinner, and Sunday brunch. The staff is cordial and the menu outstanding.

At the south end of White Sound Harbour is Sea Spray Resort & Villas, operated by Ruth and Monty Albury. The 50-foot wide entrance channel has lateral stakes (red-right-returning). Most of the channel is about 50 feet wide, but as with all dredged channels, it's best to stay center as much as possible. Management tells us that the channel is dredged for 5.5 feet at low water, but this can vary depending on the height of low water for the particular day. Sea Spray's marina has fuel, electricity, water, boat rentals, rental villas, a freshwater pool, and a gift shop. Homemade bread and pies are prepared at Belle's Bakery. The Boat House Restaurant, serving Bahamian and American cuisine, is open for breakfast, lunch and dinner. Most Hope Town restaurants will pick up patrons for dinner in the White Sound Area. This is a lovely place to headquarter your boat and enjoy this part of the Abacos.

Lubbers Quarters Channel (Tropic Isle Sketch Chart: H-5). There is a channel which, at low water, will be tight for boats drawing any more than 4 feet, from Hope Town, inside the Parrot Cays, and south between Elbow Cay and Lubbers Quarters. This route is obstructed in places by shallow sandbanks, particularly in the vicinity of Tilloo Cut, but if you can negotiate it, it saves considerable distance. Upon departing Hope Town, go south to a position just west of the outer mark for the channel into White Sound. From that point steer toward Baker's Rock at the west end of Tahiti Beach on a heading of 203°. The Parrot Cays will be dead astern on this heading. Baker's Rock is a flat cay, about 50 yards in diameter, with no structures or trees. Then when abeam of the point on Elbow Cay just north of Baker's Rock, turn toward the saddle between the two southernmost hills on Lubbers Quarters on a heading of about 233°. (The

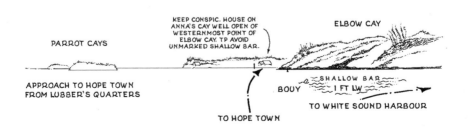

Yahoe's Sand Bar. (Tropic Isle photo)

saddle now appears to be the second dip against the skyline from the south end of Lubbers Quarters, because tree growth has formed what appears to be another saddle, but is not. If you are on a course of 233° and the conspicuous 3-story house on Elbow Cay is right on your stern bearing 53°, you're aimed at the saddle.) Continue on this course until you are abeam of the southernmost Cooperjack Cay (houses), at which point you will be about two-thirds the distance between Elbow Cay and Lubbers Quarters. Here alter to port to 203° toward a point just west of the westernmost point of **Tavern Cay**. Watch for the deep blue, rectangular dredged area off the Abaco Ocean Club dock; if on course you should pass over its eastern edge. (See inset, sketch chart H-5, Man of War Cay to Cherokee Sound.) When abeam of the south point of Lubbers Quarters, turn toward Snake Cay (about 240°, white sand banks on shore). You can continue on this heading all the way to Snake Cay, or until Lubbers Quarters' south point is again abeam, at which time you can take up 206° for the western end of Tilloo Bank.

On Lubbers Quarters itself is a new restaurant/beach bar by the name of Yahoes Sand Bar. Here, chef Hans Hinrichsen serves elegant continental and Caribbean cuisine using local produce and fresh catch of the day. There are full moon parties, BBQ buffets, and a boater's bar serving exotic tropical drinks with music and dancing (all in and around a large yurt roofed with old sails). There's a nice little beach where you can sit and quaff a few. Call *Yahoes* on VHF 16 for reservations (they're closed on Mondays). Yahoes is easy to find; you'll see it near the dredged area as you turn south from the 233° leg southbound through Lubbers Quarters Channel. You can tie up at their small boat harbor.

Tilloo Cay is 4 miles long and rather narrow. There are attractive beaches on its southwestern shore. The dredged pond offered a narrow anchorage in about 5 feet in its center, but there is now a sign at the entrance that states:

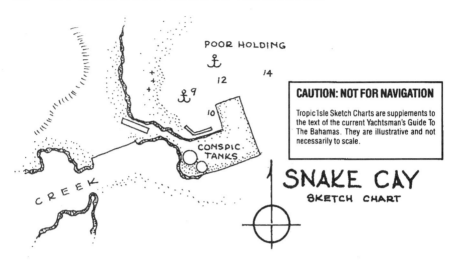

POOR HOLDING

CAUTION: NOT FOR NAVIGATION

Tropic Isle Sketch Charts are supplements to the text of the current Yachtsman's Guide To The Bahamas. They are illustrative and not necessarily to scale.

SNAKE CAY
SKETCH CHART

"Dredged channel/No anchoring inside/By order of the Commissioner, Marsh Harbour." Because of poor holding, this is not a safe haven in bad weather. The entrance, which is good for a little over 4 feet, is usually marked. North of it is a rock with a stake on it which is *not* one of the entrance marks. The entrance lies just north of the shoal which runs north a short distance from the little cay that forms the western side of the pond. South of this cay is a false entrance that dries at low water. Once through the entrance and into the middle of the pond, turn south. Do not turn north.

The coast south from Marsh Harbour East Side (Tropic Isle Sketch Chart: H-5) From Marsh Harbour East Side the best water (12-15 feet) lies along the shore, about 200 yards off a line of small above-water rocks, until you come to Pepper Cay, the largest of the small cays and the only one with any vegetation.

To clear the rocky reef extending east from Witch Point, you must pass midway between the south end of Lubbers Quarters and Witch Point. From a position 300 yards east of Pepper Cay, alter course for the south end of Lubbers Quarters (123°). Don't alter course again until the break between Matt Lowe's Cay and Sugarloaf Cay bears 004°. Then steer the reciprocal course 184°.

Snake Cay has an industrial wharf that is completely rotting away; do not go near it. There is poor holding in the tiny harbor inside, so best avoid this area altogether.

Pelican Harbour (Tropic Isle Sketch Charts: H-5, 10) which has deep water, lies west of the Pelican Cays and extends to the mainland at Spencer's Bight. In days gone by, large vessels entered at North Bar Channel to load lumber. Its pilotage is straightforward.

North Bar Channel is the one used by the mailboat on her weekly run to Abaco. This channel is wide and deep, carrying 16-18 feet at low water. The approach is on a west-northwesterly course, about midway between the north end of Lynyard Cay and Channel Rock. If trees on Sandy Cay are not trimmed, they can obscure the post on Cornish Cay that is the back mark of the range shown on sketch chart H-10 (North Bar Channel). *Sometimes when Little Harbour Bar is impassable, North Bar Channel can be run and vice versa, but*

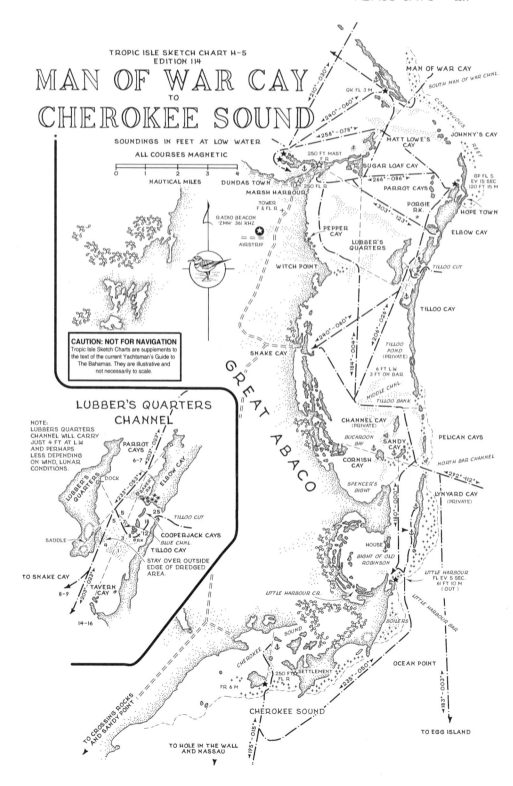

TROPIC ISLE SKETCH CHART H-5
EDITION 114

MAN OF WAR CAY
TO
CHEROKEE SOUND

SOUNDINGS IN FEET AT LOW WATER

ALL COURSES MAGNETIC

NAUTICAL MILES

0 1 2 3 4

MAN OF WAR CAY
SOUTH MAN OF WAR CHNL.
CONTINUOUS REEF
JOHNNY'S CAY
QK FL 3 M
240°-030°
240°-060°
258°-078°
MATT LOWE'S CAY
250 FT MAST F R
DUNDAS TOWN
MARSH HARBOUR
250 FL R
SUGAR LOAF CAY
266°-086°
PARROT CAYS
303°-123°
PORGIE RK.
GP FL 5 EV 15 SEC 120 FT 15 M
HOPE TOWN
TOWER F & FL R
RADIO BEACON "ZMH" 361 KHZ
AIRSTRIP
PEPPER CAY
LUBBER'S QUARTERS
ELBOW CAY
WITCH POINT
TILLOO CUT
TILLOO CAY
240°-060°
206°-026°
184°-004°
TILLOO POND (PRIVATE)
6 FT L.W 3 FT ON BAR
MIDDLE CHNL.
TILLOO BANK
SNAKE CAY

CAUTION: NOT FOR NAVIGATION
Tropic Isle Sketch Charts are supplements to the text of the current Yachtsman's Guide to The Bahamas. They are illustrative and not necessarily to scale.

CHANNEL CAY (PRIVATE)
BUCAROON BAY
SANDY CAY
PELICAN CAYS
CORNISH CAY
NORTH BAR CHANNEL
292°-112°
SPENCER'S BIGHT
LYNYARD CAY (PRIVATE)
180°-000°
RUINS
HOUSE
BIGHT OF OLD ROBINSON
LITTLE HARBOUR FL EV 5 SEC. 61 FT 10 M (OUT)
LITTLE HARBOUR CR.
LITTLE HARBOUR BAR
BOILERS
OCEAN POINT
183°-003°
SOUND
CHEROKEE
250 FT FL R
SETTLEMENT
235°-050°
FR 6 M
CHEROKEE SOUND
TO EGG ISLAND
195°-015°
183°-003°
TO HOLE IN THE WALL AND NASSAU

GREAT ABACO

LUBBER'S QUARTERS CHANNEL

NOTE:
LUBBERS QUARTERS CHANNEL WILL CARRY JUST 4 FT AT L.W. AND PERHAPS LESS DEPENDING ON WIND, LUNAR CONDITIONS.

PARROT CAYS
6-7
203°-023°
235°-055°
ELBOW CAY
LUBBER'S QUARTERS
DOCK
25
TILLOO CUT
5
5
SADDLE
8
3
12
RK
COOPERJACK CAYS
BLUE CHNL.
TILLOO CAY
STAY OVER OUTSIDE EDGE OF DREDGED AREA.
4
TO SNAKE CAY
8-9
203°-023°
TAVERN CAY
14-16

TO CROSSING ROCKS AND SANDY POINT

neither should be attempted when the seas break right across. Sometimes, during rage conditions, you must beware of heavy seas that can work their way well in through the break between South Pelican Cay and the north end of Lynyard Cay, making the south end of Pelican Harbour at least nerve-wracking, and perhaps dangerous.

With good light, pleasure craft drawing no more than 6 feet can negotiate Pelican Harbour and round Tilloo Bank with little difficulty (see sketch chart H-10, North Bar Channel). The narrowest part of the channel lies a few hundred yards west of the Middle Channel (whose marker is now missing) and is bordered by Tilloo Bank on the north and two conspicuous white sandbanks on the south, the westernmost of which carries only 4 feet at low water.

North Bar Channel passes into the **Pelican Cay Land and Sea Park,** founded by The Bahamas National Trust to help preserve the natural beauty of this area of cays and seabed. Yachts are requested not to drop their anchors in the coral formations. Friends of the Environment, with contributions of time and money from various individuals and The Bahamas National Trust, has placed five half-ton moorings, with buoys of varying colors and sizes, for boats 25 feet or less, just east of Sandy Cay reef. Larger boats should anchor elsewhere in Pelican Harbour and use their dinghies to visit the reef. (Do not anchor to the east of Sandy Cay Reef, because the holding is very poor. If you do, the park officer will ask you to move.) You have to be careful here because, as noted above, heavy seas can work into Pelican Harbour, causing problems with the moorings and making mooring here dangerous. Laws prohibit spearfishing and the destruction

We welcome you to Abaco and invite you to enjoy our sun, sea and sand. Please take home beautiful memories and colorful photographs, but leave our precious live shells, sea fans, and starfish for future visitors to enjoy. We ask that everyone remember one universal fact: "We do not own this planet, we are just passing through."

Membership is open to all; contact Harbour View Grocery or Island Marine in Hope Town

Friends of the Environment

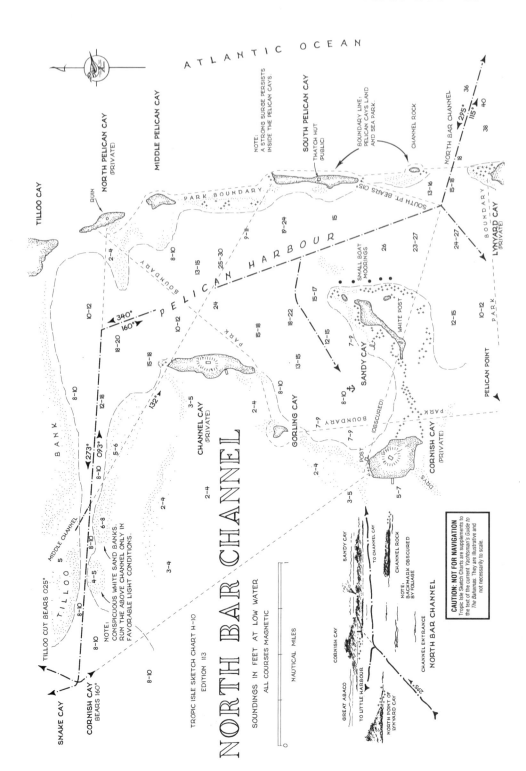

ATLANTIC OCEAN

TILLOO CAY

NORTH PELICAN CAY
(PRIVATE)

MIDDLE PELICAN CAY

RUIN

SOUTH PELICAN CAY

THATCH HUT
(PUBLIC)

NOTE:
A STRONG SURGE PERSISTS
INSIDE THE PELICAN CAYS.

BOUNDARY LINE:
PELICAN CAYS LAND
AND SEA PARK.

CHANNEL ROCK

NORTH BAR CHANNEL

36
295°
115°
40
38
18
15-18

PARK BOUNDARY

13-16

SOUTH PT. BEARS 015°

BOUNDARY

LYNYARD CAY
(PRIVATE)

PARK

2-4
8-10

9-11
9-24
15

13-15
25-30

24

10-12

10-12

24-27

PELICAN HARBOUR

26
23-27

SMALL BOAT
MOORINGS

12-15
10-12

15-17
WHITE POST

18-22
15-18

12-15

13-15

18-22

7-9

8-10

SANDY CAY

PELICAN POINT

(OBSCURED)

7-9

POST

CORNISH CAY
(PRIVATE)

DRY'S

PARK BOUNDARY

7-9

GORLING CAY

2-4

3-5

5-7

2-4

CHANNEL CAY
(PRIVATE)

2-4

2-4

3-5

2-4

3-4

2-4

BANK

10-12

18-20

15-18

12-18

8-10

8-10

340°
160°

PELICAN HARBOUR

132°

273°
093°

5-6

6-8

8-10

4-5

8-10

8-10

8-10

MIDDLE CHANNEL

TILLOO 5

8-10

TILLOO CUT BEARS 025°

SNAKE CAY

CORNISH CAY
BEARS 160°

NOTE:
CONSPICUOUS WHITE SAND BANKS.
RUN THE ABOVE CHANNEL ONLY IN
FAVORABLE LIGHT CONDITIONS.

CAUTION: NOT FOR NAVIGATION
Tropic Isle Sketch Charts are supplements to
the text of the current Yachtsman's Guide to
The Bahamas. They are illustrative and
not necessarily to scale.

NORTH BAR CHANNEL

TROPIC ISLE SKETCH CHART H-10
EDITION 113

SOUNDINGS IN FEET AT LOW WATER
ALL COURSES MAGNETIC

NAUTICAL MILES

SANDY CAY

TO CHANNEL CAY

CHANNEL ROCK

NOTE:
BACKMARK OBSCURED
BY FOLIAGE

CORNISH CAY

GREAT ABACO

TO LITTLE HARBOUR

NORTH POINT OF
LYNYARD CAY

CHANNEL ENTRANCE

NORTH BAR CHANNEL

or removal of any plant or animal life, corals, sea fans or gorgonians, bird life or eggs. Dumping of litter or waste is also prohibited. These laws, enforceable with heavy penalties on conviction, have been written to insure the preservation of the Pelican Cay Park for the enjoyment of all. Call *Park Officer* on VHF 65A if you have questions about the Park.

Caution: A heavy surge sometimes exists in Pelican Harbour, especially along the lee of the Pelican Cays. Beaching dinghies and skiffs on the sand beaches hereabouts can be dangerous.

Cornish Cay is private property. Visits ashore are by invitation only.

Lynyard Cay has a white house surrounded by casuarinas about one mile south from the north end. It is visible all around. There is a nice anchorage in the lee of Lynyard off either the first or second sandy cove from the south end. There is 9 feet of water over a grassy bottom close to the beach, and some protection in most winds from any direction. An area of shoal water lies west of Lynyard Cay about halfway along its length. To get to the anchorages, pass this to port (bound south), and then alter course toward the sand beaches at the south end of the cay. The houses on Lynyard Cay are private residences and visits ashore are by invitation only.

Bridges Cay is private property, and visits ashore are by invitation only. The water north of the cay carries no more than one foot at low water. The prominent house at the southern end of the cay is a good landmark.

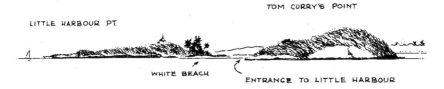

LITTLE HARBOUR PT

TOM CURRY'S POINT

WHITE BEACH

ENTRANCE TO LITTLE HARBOUR

Little Harbour (Tropic Isle Sketch Charts: H-5, 11). Yachts drawing over 3 feet must wait for the tide to enter Little Harbour, but it's well worth it. A draft of 6 feet can just barely be taken in at high water, depending on the height of high water. Upon entering, keep centered in the channel between the land masses on either side. Ahead is a white sand patch extending from the inner east side of the harbor entrance. The deepest water lies between the floats, which are marked red-right-returning, but time, sun, and marine growth tend to change these colors and you may have to do a bit of figuring to decide which is which. Once through you'll have 7-10 feet to the anchorage off the center of the beach.

Little Harbour is almost circular in shape with a white sand beach running two-thirds around it. The holding ground is good, although you should take care to set your anchor, and there is protection from winds of any direction. If you prefer a mooring, inquire at Johnston Studios on VHF Channel 16. On the western side are high rocky cliffs with some interesting caves. The ocean side is also high, giving protection from prevailing winds. You might see turtles swimming around the anchorage. Observe but don't disturb them.

Little Harbour has long been the home of sculptor Randolph Johnston and his talented family. Randolph Johnston died at the age of 88 in 1992. His monumental bronze sculptures such as *Monuments to Bahamian Women, Sir*

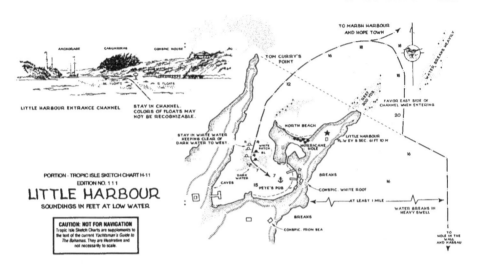

LITTLE HARBOUR ENTRANCE CHANNEL STAY IN CHANNEL. COLORS OF FLOATS MAY NOT BE RECOGNIZABLE.

PORTION - TROPIC ISLE SKETCH CHART H-11
EDITION NO. 111

LITTLE HARBOUR

SOUNDINGS IN FEET AT LOW WATER

CAUTION: NOT FOR NAVIGATION
Tropic Isle Sketch Charts are supplements to the text of the current Yachtsman's Guide to The Bahamas. They are illustrative and not necessarily to scale.

Milo Butler, and others can be seen in Rawson Square in Nassau, and his book, *Artist on His Island, A Study in Self-Reliance,* is an inspiring account of a man who left convention behind to pursue an artistic vision. His son Peter continues to maintain the studio, shop, and foundry on the water's edge, where he casts his own marine sculpture and gold jewelry. His large sculptures of dolphins and other sea creatures have been erected in Palm Beach and other American cities. Visiting hours are generally 10:00 a.m. to 1:00 p.m. and 2:00 to 4:00 p.m., except Sundays. Pete's Pub sometimes serves food and drink.

The Johnstons as well as other residents would appreciate your not disposing of refuse overboard, as all such trash ends up on their lovely beaches. As on all small islands, garbage disposal is a problem and the Johnstons are in no position to provide such a service for the hundreds of yachtsmen who anchor

Little Harbour. (Tropic Isle photo)

here. They request that visitors take trash to one of their commercial layovers for disposal.

Little Harbour's cliff, north beach, reef, and harbor are all protected under The Bahamas National Trust. Spearfishing, removal of flora and fauna, removal of turtles or their eggs, or disturbing nesting birds is prohibited.

Once in Little Harbour it is worthwhile spending a day or two exploring the innumerable small cays and beaches of Little Harbour Creek by dinghy. There is first-rate fishing around the "boiling holes," found mainly in the shallows among the small rocky cays. These are very deep holes in the limestone that are connected underground to the ocean and only a few yards in diameter. The name "boiling holes" derives from the flood tide boiling up through them. Inside and around the boiling holes are many species of fish, ranging from small grunts up to 60-pound grouper.

Little Harbour Bar is an excellent entrance *in normal weather* to the sound that lies between Great Abaco and the cays. *Caution: Never attempt this passage in a rage or in strong onshore winds when a heavy sea is running. In such conditions, North Bar channel, 3 miles to the north, may be safer.*

Little Harbour Bar is clear, wide, and deep (16 feet at low water) but should still be negotiated with care, according to the following directions. Approaching Little Harbour Bar from the south, stand off the coast not less than one mile until Little Harbour Point and Tom Curry's Point are in transit. (See sketch chart of Little Harbour.) They will then be bearing roughly 305°. Alter course to port to keep them on this bearing until in mid-channel between the point and the line of breakers on the reef that extends south from Lynyard Cay. Then alter course to north, running parallel to the land for about 400 yards, in order to clear the reef that extends for about 300 yards north from Little Harbour Point. You will then be in 18-24 feet. As you alter course, rounding the reef, to your port a cove behind the lighthouse will open up. This will be easily recognized by the white sand beach and a group of coconut palms in the eastern corner. This is not a good anchorage as a surge runs in around the corner and makes it uneasy. Carry on into the landlocked pool behind.

The coast from Little Harbour Bar to Cherokee. An offing of at least one mile is desirable and will clear all dangers, but care must be taken to give The Boilers a good berth. This reef, which breaks heavily in all but the calmest weather, is about 1.25 miles south of Little Harbour.

Caution: Neither Cherokee Sound nor the anchorage behind Chero-kee Point can be entered in anything but fairly calm conditions.

The anchorage under Cherokee Point is usable only under light conditions, so it can't necessarily be considered a refuge for sailors bound north from Nassau or Eleuthera who find Little Harbour Bar and North Bar Channel impassable. A deep reef trends in a southwesterly direction from the point, and if you attempt to cross it under strong conditions you might be pounded down on it. Also the anchorage itself could have a dangerous surge. In favorable conditions, however, this can be a comfortable anchorage over good holding sand.

Behind the settlement, a mile north of **Cherokee Point,** is an extensive body of shoal water known as **Cherokee Sound.** In it there is a small, all-weather anchorage, three-quarters of a mile from the settlement, that is

CAUTION: NOT FOR NAVIGATION

Tropic Isle Sketch Charts are supplements to the text of the current Yachtsman's Guide To The Bahamas. They are illustrative and not necessarily to scale.

A SKETCH CHART

CHEROKEE SOUND

SOUNDINGS IN FEET AT LOW WATER

APPROXIMATE SCALE

NAUTICAL MILE

ALL COURSES MAGNETIC

ONCE THROUGH OUTER REEF LINE UP POLE WITH CENTER OF LIGHTHOUSE AND MOVE IN TOWARD DUCK CAY ON THIS HEADING UNTIL APPROX. 100 YDS FROM SHORE. THEN TURN TO STBD AND PASS ABOUT 50 YDS FROM SHORE BETWEEN POINT AND BAR TO SE MARKED AS AWASH.

protected on all sides by shallow sandbanks. The entrance to this channel is through a break in the outer reef, and should never be attempted in anything but flat sea conditions and good light. We recommend a local pilot's aid, at least for the first time. Lie off Cherokee Point or Duck Cay and call *Cherokee Radio* on VHF 16. Ask for a pilot and someone will come out to guide you in.

To approach the channel entrance, pass through the outer reef on a 007° heading, keeping the east point of Duck Cay and the west end of Point of Spit in line. As you near Duck Cay, tend southeastward of the breaking reef south of Duck Cay until the pole marker and the center of the lighthouse on Duck Cay are in transit. Approach Duck Cay with these leading marks in transit until approximately 100 yards from shore. Then turn to starboard, passing about 50 yards from shore between the southeast point of Duck Cay and a bar which is awash at low water southeast of the point. Carry on past the east end of Duck Cay on a course of about 020° in 5-6 feet, low water, and continue on this course to where the conspicuous sandbar and the grassy patches meet (2 feet at low water). This marks the beginning of the dredged inner channel which appears black. It is possible to anchor in the channel in about 6 feet just east of Duck Cay if you can find one of the places with good holding. The rest is rock.

By following the blue channel (4 feet at low water) around Point of Spit Cay, you can gain the inner anchorage (6-8 feet low water) immediately west of Riding Cay. From here it is a three-quarter mile dinghy ride at high water or ankle-deep hike at low water south to the settlement.

The picturesque, tidy community of Cherokee, once famed for boatbuilding, is well worth a visit in normal good weather. The village can be visited by road from Marsh Harbour. Benny Sawyer has several of the largest Spanish Wells offshore fishing smacks to his credit. Clifton Sawyer is another helpful Cherokee resident. For sandwiches or bread, ask for Diane Sawyer, who bakes out of her home. There's a post office and a Batelco station whose operator monitors VHF 16. Nearby, a monument honors Cherokee fishermen lost at sea. The well-stocked Cherokee Food Fair also carries a small selection of clothing, housewares, and gifts. There's a limited supply of fresh fruit in season. Try some of the delicious mammoth watermelon. When Cherokee residents finally got electricity in 1995 and were no longer dependent on candle power and generators, the *Abaconian*'s Cherokee correspondent, Lee Pinder, wrote: "... now that we have electricity and street lights, the birds sing all night through ... we are not complaining, their serenades are certainly preferable to sounds of traffic, with ambulance and police sirens heard in bigger cities."

On Casuarina Point, on the mainland overlooking Duck Cay in Cherokee Sound, is a new establishment called Different of Abaco. Here proprietor Nettica

Cherokee. (Tropic Isle photo)

Cherokee waterfront. (Tropic Isle photo)

Symonette offers 8 rooms, a restaurant, a museum, and a natural aquarium. Bonefishing on both the bight and east side of Great Abaco, snorkeling, and deep-sea fishing can all be arranged.

The coast between Cherokee and Hole in the Wall is for the most part steep-to and completely devoid of shelter. For 9 miles in the vicinity of Guineaman Bay and Crossing Rocks there are off-lying shoals, but in making the passage from Hole in the Wall to Little Harbour Bar, yachtsmen are advised to give the coast a wide berth, owing to the strength and uncertainty of the currents there. The sketch chart shows the only anchorage on this stretch to be at Hole in the Wall, where shelter can be found in winds from west through north to northeast. It should be regarded merely as a temporary anchorage. There are reports of people fouling their anchors here.

Hole in the Wall lighthouse's old mechanism has been dismantled and the light is now automated, to the chagrin of the Bahamas Lighthouse Preservation Society. BASRA's automatic VHF radio repeater station located in the light-house was not operating at our deadline.

Hole in the Wall to Nassau. From a position 5 miles east of Hole in the Wall Light, this is a straightforward, deep-sea passage of 47 miles on a course of 205°. The passage can be shortened by stopping off at Royal Island or Spanish Wells. Under normal conditions none of these passage present any particular difficulty. Northbound, however, you must keep in mind that in strong onshore winds (those from northeast/east/southeast), or rage conditions, the passages through the reefs at Little Harbour, or North Bar Channel, or other Abaco entries may be impassable.

A word of warning: Between Hole in the Wall and Elbow Cay a northerly

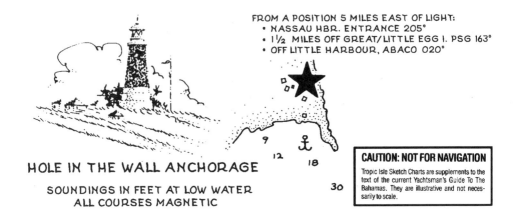

FROM A POSITION 5 MILES EAST OF LIGHT:
- NASSAU HBR. ENTRANCE 205°
- 1½ MILES OFF GREAT/LITTLE EGG I. PSG 163°
- OFF LITTLE HARBOUR, ABACO 020°

HOLE IN THE WALL ANCHORAGE

SOUNDINGS IN FEET AT LOW WATER
ALL COURSES MAGNETIC

CAUTION: NOT FOR NAVIGATION
Tropic Isle Sketch Charts are supplements to the text of the current Yachtsman's Guide To The Bahamas. They are illustrative and not necessarily to scale.

or southerly set is occasionally experienced. The cause of this set is unknown as it appears to bear no relation to the tides, nor does it always exist.

Bound north: Egg Island to Hole in the Wall. Whether leaving Spanish Wells or Royal Island Harbour by day or night, it is safe and easy to pass midway between Great and Little Egg Islands. The minimum depth is about 12 feet. Stand out 1.5 miles on a west course to give the corner of Egg Reef a good berth, and then set a course of 343° to a position 5 miles east of Hole in the Wall Light. The light tower on Great Egg Island is visible for 8 miles in daylight. Hole in the Wall lighthouse can be seen from about 15 miles.

Hole in the Wall lighthouse. (Tropic Isle photo)

WEST COAST OF GREAT ABACO

D.M.A. Charts: 26299, 26300, 26319, 26320. Tropic Isle Sketch Chart: H-12.

Among the scores of cays large and small, there are many anchorages and harbors in the Bight where protection can be found from any winds. Pilotage, except in a very few places, is straightforward, the scenery diversified and the fishing superb. A draft of 6 feet could be carried throughout the area described in this section, although vessels drawing over 6 feet are advised to approach from the west, by way of Mores Island, rather than from the north. By the western approach 9-10 feet could be carried safely. Tides in the Bight vary from 1 to 1.5 hours later than on the east coast.

In the Bight, as the whole area is known, you're very much on your own. It is little frequented, even by fishing smacks. There is no settlement on the west coast of the mainland for about 50 miles between Cooper's Town at the north and Sandy Point at the south. However, the Disney Cruise Line has transformed Gorda Cay into a cruise-ship destination called Castaway Cay, "Disney's Own Private Island." With thousands of passengers released ashore weekly, the once-pristine quality of this area has vanished. Disney magic.

The Bight of Abaco may be gained from the north around the tip of Little Abaco, from Sandy Point toward the south, or it can be approached by way of any of the numerous passages along the edge of the bank between Gorda Cay and the southeast point of Grand Bahama. Here we give directions for the Bight commencing at the northern approach, working down the west coast of Great Abaco to Sandy Point, and returning north by way of the outer cays that lie on the edge of the Northwest Providence Channel.

There are two routes around the **western end of Little Abaco** (Tropic Isle sketch charts H-2, H-12). Both lead to the Cave Cay-Spence Rock Passage, which carries about 3.5-4 feet at LW, so once around, this becomes the controlling depth.

The deeper route around, safe for up to 6 feet at low water, lies to the west of the West End Bars, about 6.5 miles west of West End, the westernmost tip of Little Abaco. The second route around, good for 2-3 feet at low water (not easy, local knowledge essential), is usable only with good light; it is a difficult channel to see and a mistake will put you on a rocky bottom. This route lies about 300 feet off the west end of Little Abaco, and transits shallow rock and reef that extend some distance westward of Little Abaco. Careful eyeball navigation is required here.

Having successfully crossed the bar, you'll be in deeper water, at which point you must again choose between two routes, both of which require some feeling around. You may either proceed down in the deeper water to Cave Cay, being careful to avoid the shallow water off the western end of West End Cay

TROPIC ISLE SKETCH CHART H-12
EDITION 114

THE BIGHT OF ABACO

SOUNDINGS IN FEET AT LOW WATER

0   5   10   15
NAUTICAL MILES

CARTER CAY

FISH CAYS
MORAINE CAY
PAW PAW CAYS

ALLAN'S-PENSACOLA CAY

WEST END ROCKS   20
VETERAN ROCK   14
HAWK'S BILL CAY
SPANISH CAY
THE HAULOVER
WEST END   FOXTOWN   COOPERS TOWN
(SEE TEXT)   CROWN HAVEN   POWELL CAY
LITTLE ABACO
POOR HOLDING   PATTON CAYS
8-10   CAVE CAY   CASHE'S CAY   MANGROVE CAY   BLACK POINT
9-12   RANDALL'S CAY   MANJACK CAY
BREAST CAY   ROCKY HARBOUR CAY
CROSS CAYS   8-10   SPENCE ROCK   JONES ROCKS
7-9   20   BASIN HARBOUR CAY   GREEN TURTLE CAY
12-15
DAVIS POINT   WHALE CAY
GRAND BAHAMA (EAST END)   NORMAN CASTLE   GREAT GUANA CAY
200' FL R   12-14   18-20   GREAT   TREASURE CAY
DEEP WATER CAY   JOE DOWNER CAYS   MAN OF WAR CAY
SWEETINGS CAY   MARSH HARBOUR
FL EV 6 SEC 25 FT M   ELBOW CAY
FANNY CAY   200' FL R   GP FL (5) EV 15 SEC
EAST END BUSH   120 FT 15 M
7-10   RED SHANK CAY   14-16   WOODENDEAN CAYS   14
10
WATER CAY   16-18
BURROWS CAY   12-14   MASTIC POINT   NORTH BAR CHANNEL
30   FOUL GROUND   12-16   LITTLE HBR.
12-14   200' FL R
HARD BARGAIN   10-12   MORES ISLAND   BIG MANGROVE
LILLY CAY   10   8-10   250 FL R
BLACK ROCK   7   CRAB CAY   CHEROKEE SOUND
CHANNEL CAY   THOMAS CAY   (CONSPIC WHITE ROOFS)
FL EV 2 SEC 32 FT 6 M   TOP CAY   SOUTHERN CAY
(UNREL)
ENTER APPROX   CEDAR CAYS
100 YARDS SOUTH OF   DINGHY DOCK AT ROAD   GUINEAMAN
OR APPROX. ¼ NORTH   IS JUST A SHORT WALK   CROSSING ROCKS
OF LIGHT. (SEE TEXT)   8-10   FROM OCEAN BEACH.
ENTER GOOD LIGHT ONLY
LONG ROCKS   10-12   TONY CAY
CRAB CAY   3-4
GORDA CAY   FOUL GROUND   SANDY POINT
30   7   260' FL R
ROCK POINT
FL EV 6 SEC 35 FT 10 M   HOLE IN THE WALL
FL EV 10 SEC 168 FT 19 M

B I G H T   O F   A B A C O

G R E A T   A B A C O   T H E   M A R L S

N O R T H W E S T   P R O V I D E N C E   C H A N N E L

SEA WOOD BARS

CAUTION: NOT FOR NAVIGATION
Tropic Isle Sketch Charts are supplements to
the text of the current Yachtsman's Guide to
The Bahamas. They are illustrative and
not necessarily to scale.

AT ANY TIME NAVIGATIONAL LIGHTS THROUGHOUT THE
BAHAMAS MAY NOT BE WORKING OR MAY HAVE FLASHING
PATTERNS VARYING FROM THOSE NOTED ON GOVERNMENT
CHARTS, SKETCH CHARTS OR THE TEXT IN THIS GUIDE.

> **PLEASE NOTE:** For a description of **Batelco towers in all areas and their light characteristics**, please check page 39 of this Guide.

(especially a factor if you chose the close-in route around the west end of Little Abaco), or you can turn to port and pass through the narrow but deep channel that runs between West End and West End Cay. Don't try the latter course unless the light is good and you can read the water; the flats on either side are very shallow. From West End, Cave Cay will be visible on a bearing of 110°.

Cave Cay covers considerable acreage, is comparatively high in places, and has a deeply indented coastline. Years ago there was a small settlement on its eastern coast, but after a damaging hurricane the government moved the community to the mainland, founding Crown Haven. On the north coast of Cave Cay the water is 8-9 feet deep almost up to the rocks, over a hard bar bottom. A bit farther offshore it is a good deal deeper. Off the northwest corner of the island is a small detached mangrove-covered cay and a series of small above-water rocks that ring an almost enclosed lagoon.

A good anchorage in 8 feet can be found west of the small cay, although a better one, in deeper water and greater protection, can be found north of the low rocky head in the first bay to the south. Again, as is the case in all bays on this coast, the water shallows so you can't get far inside. From the bays farther south, rocky bars extend westward. Opposite the low cliffs, however, deep water runs right into the shore. Good water runs close down the east coast of Cave Cay, but the large bay and creek where the settlement once stood are shallow.

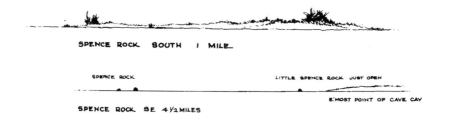

Proceeding south from West End toward **Spence Rock,** the deep-water channel lies between Cave Cay and Cashe's Cay. The only obstruction in this channel is a brown bar almost midway between the two cays.

Cashe's Cay is not as large as Cave Cay, but is equally covered with vegetation and trees. The best anchorage off the west coast is at the southwest corner close to the rocks in 8-10 feet.

Bound for the east or south, you must go by way of Spence Rock. This passage should not be attempted in bad light conditions or without local knowledge. Leaving the south end of Cashe's Cay, steer approximately south-southeast until you sight the rock. Spence Rock is low but unmistakable once you have seen it (see sketch). Continue to steer toward Spence Rock, keeping it fine on the port bow until within one mile of it. The above channel offers about 4 feet at low water. Never try to pass east of Spence Rock. Once past, you are in deep water providing you gave the rocks extending south from it ample berth. Continuing east, steer to pass one-half mile south of Breast Cays and Patton Cays, which are low and covered with scrub.

On approaching Mangrove Cay, stay south of the shallow coral and rock bar that extends west-southwest toward the Breast Cays. You can take 5 feet between this reef and Mangrove Cay into the white beach on the mainland.

MANGROVE CAY ENE 3 M.

Mangrove Cay is low, flat, and thickly covered with brush and mangroves. A fair anchorage will be found under the western side in 6-7 feet about 300 yards offshore. In northerly winds you can either run in under the mainland or, rounding the shallow bar that protects the anchorage from the south, anchor close under the southern shore in 10-12 feet over a grassy bottom.

Mangrove Cay eastward: There is ample water close along the south coast of Mangrove Cay, but another reef extends eastward from its southwest corner. Steering for Black Point, you are in 12 feet all the way. The mainland hereabouts is high rolling countryside with thick pine woods. From here to Randall's Cay the water continues deep and free from dangers. Sisal was once

DARK PINE FOREST

090°

BLACK POINT FROM MANGROVE CAY 4M.

Randall's Cay is a long, undulating island with jagged peaks. Off the high cliffs lie many detached rocks. Between the south point of Randall's Cay and the north point of Rocky Harbour Cay lies Big Cut. In the center of this cut and slightly to the west of it are the twin Jones Rocks. In entering, these can be passed on either side.

Rocky Harbour Cay is somewhat similar in appearance to Randall's Cay, but it is not so high. Deep water, 12-18 feet, can be carried in close to the shore in most places.

Basin Harbour Cay is the most spectacular cay in the whole of the Bight.

BASIN HARBOUR CAY 120° 2M

Almost everywhere, except on its eastern side, deep water (18-20 feet) runs up to the limestone cliffs that rise as high as 50 feet. A vessel can stand in so close that a man standing on her deck may touch the rocks. Many of the prominent headlands around the coast have been sculptured by wind and weather into forms resembling gargoyles. There are two excellent harbors, Basin Harbour and East End Harbour. Basin Harbour is entered between two imposing headlands, has a fairly uniform depth of 5.5 feet at low water except under the northern point, where it reaches 5-6 feet. The bottom is uniformly hard rock. A gray-and-white house is located on the eastern headland, and there is another building on the other side. **East End Harbour,** which has two entrances, contains deeper water. There is an uncomfortable surge in both these harbors during strong southeasterly conditions, at which time Randall's Cay anchorage would be a wise alternative. On the eastern side of the island, luxuriant vegetation runs down to the water's edge, and in places it is low and swampy. On the flats to the east lies the wreck of the sloop *Chase*. Today she is an aquarium for the scores of gray snapper who have adopted her. Basin Harbour Cay is a perfect headquarters from which to fish and explore the area.

The passage from **Basin Harbour Cay to Norman Castle** can be made in deep water steering a direct course to Davis Point, which can be identified by the bald hill and the heavy fall of rock at its extreme end. In the bay to the south of Davis Point is a good anchorage in 6-7 feet with protection in prevailing conditions under the cliffs.

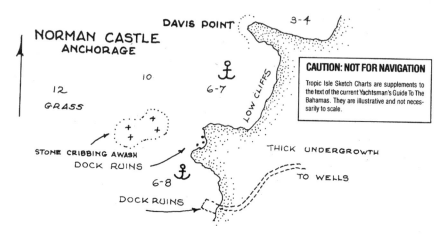

The old settlement of Norman's Castle was at the south end of this bay. Once a busy logging camp, it was abandoned in 1929. Lumber was shipped to U.S. ports in large, three-masted schooners, among them the *Bahamas*, *Abaco*, *Wyefax*, and *Caterina*. Few traces of the settlement remain and the only inhabitants now are wild horses and hogs. A few traces of the old dock might be seen, where it ran out in a westerly direction to deep water. Caution is advised for yachts drawing over 4 feet because of the few steel girders that project from the bottom to within 3-4 feet of the surface. They are in the vicinity of two large piles of stones that lie offshore west of the southern point of the headland.

DAVIS POINT FROM THE NORTH

North Joe Downer Cay is long and quite high, thickly covered with brush and small trees. It has several beaches. A hard bar runs out to the west for some distance from the north end of this cay carrying 3-6 feet of water. A vessel drawing 4-5 feet could pick her way into an anchorage off the south end, but a careful lookout for shallow patches must be maintained.

South Joe Downer Cay is rather higher and has more beaches. From its southern point a rocky bar makes out in a southwesterly direction for perhaps three-quarters of a mile. A stake marks its extremity but, if you draw over 4.5 feet, give the marker a good berth. There is good water from the north side of this shoal to an anchorage close to the cay. You may also carry 5-6 feet south of it on a 040° bearing to an anchorage off the small cay next south of South Joe Downer Cay. A draft of 6 feet can be taken in far enough to obtain shelter from the bar in westerly winds. Another bar extends one mile off the south end.

Joe Downer Cays to Woolendean Cays. Between these are many small cays and rocks. A draft of 4-5 feet can be carried fairly close inshore if you avoid the isolated bars that should be easily seen. About one mile off you will have 10-12 feet of water.

The **Woolendean Cays** stretch for about 9-10 miles and consist of several long, low islands thick with scrub and palmetto. On the northernmost cay, a crawfish station operates from October to March. It comprises about a dozen thatched huts at the north end of the island. There is a long beach of yellow sand on the west coast. The best anchorage here is due west of the huts at the north end in 5-6 feet, about 300 yards offshore. A channel leading in toward the mainland carrying 6 feet LW exists north of this cay on a 075° direction. Shallow Water Point, a separate cay, can be identified by a group of casuarinas on it.

MASTIC POINT - SOUTH ¾ M

Mastic Point is high at its western end and has a thick clump of casuarinas on it. Another dense casuarina growth is further inland to the east. Unfortunately the Bight on the north side of Mastic Point is shallow, but an anchorage can be found about one-quarter mile offshore with the point bearing 120° in 7 feet hard rock bottom. About one-half mile farther off you have 12-14 feet.

SANDY POINT - LIGHT 'TOWER'

Mastic Point to Sandy Point is a run of 21 miles that must be doglegged around the Sarah Wood Bars, which extend northward from Sandy Point for about 5 miles. We suggest a course of 209° from a position one mile off Mastic Point for 15 miles to a position 4 miles from Gorda Cay, which will be clearly in sight, as will be Sandy Point. From here steer 166° to a position about a half to three-quarters of a mile off the main dock at Sandy Point, and then steer into the dock on a course of 72°. You must avoid a 2-3 foot bar just north of the last leg into the dock. Your course into the dock should be good for 5 feet. The flood tide in this area sets to the east and northeast. Should you find yourself carried eastward within sight of the Sarah Wood Bars, work your way around their western edge. The best water lies in the direction of Gorda Cay. For the most part the Sarah Wood Bars are white rock speckled with brown coral and sea fans.

The approach to the **Sandy Point** town dock on a course of 72° for half to three-quarters of a mile is good for a draft of about 5 feet at low water. Sandy Point is a picturesque settlement shaded by an extensive plantation of coconut palms. The people here earn much of their living from the sea, and it isn't unusual to find boats at anchor or careened in the creek for overhaul and repair. A good local contact is Captain Ernest Dean, owner and former skipper of the mailboat. Groceries, fresh produce, and meats are available at E & E Department Store or Florence Grocery. You can get gas for your outboard at Theophilus Thompson's Esso station/hardware store just up from the town dock. Pete & Gay's Guest House, at the head of the dock, serves meals and has air-conditioned rooms with TVs. It's a popular place with visiting fishermen. Proprietors are Ruben "Pete" Dean (Capt. Ernest's brother) and his wife Glacie "Gay" Dean; the manager is their nephew Stanley J. White. The food here, served family style, is outstanding (try the conchburgers). Nancy's Seaside Inn serves stewfish, boilfish, and other Bahamian dishes. Popular bars include the Beach Inn Club on the creek side, and the Crystal Palace, which also serves food. A bit out of town toward the airport, Oeisha's Resort has air-conditioned rooms and a bar, restaurant, and disco. There's a telephone station in town and a post office adjacent to the commissioner's office. Mail is carried weekly to Nassau via mailboat. The government clinic is open from 9 a.m. to 1 p.m. on weekdays (weekends and holidays for emergencies only).

A bit east of Sandy Point, a considerable area of woodland wilderness has been set aside as a sanctuary to facilitate the breeding requirements of the Bahama parrot, an endangered species that is now increasing in numbers.

There are two anchorages at Sandy Point. That used in normal weather

Sandy Point harbor. (Tropic Isle photo)

is an open roadstead and lies west of the settlement dock in 6-7 feet over grass about 200 yards offshore. Both north and south of this anchorage the water shallows and the holding ground is poor.

A shallow white sandbank runs out in a westerly direction from Sandy Point in the vicinity of the light tower for a considerable distance. When shifting from the roadstead anchorage into the creek it is necessary to round its western point. The channel into the creek, available to craft drawing 6 feet at high water, runs close along the northern edge of this bank. The channel is rather narrow, with extensive flats to the north and the shallowest area at its outer, or western part.

Anchorage may be found in the mouth of the creek over patches of grass in 5 feet at low water or in the creek itself in slightly deeper water over hard gravel. The deep channel (6 feet at low water) runs for about 1.5 miles between the mainland of Sandy Point and a large mangrove swash which gives almost perfect protection from all directions. A very strong tidal current runs through the creek and two anchors are necessary, both because of the tidal current and the lack of swinging room. Any yacht drawing 4.5 feet or over is advised to employ a local pilot when entering the creek for the first time.

A contributor notes that, when approaching Rock Point or Sandy Point at night, the lights of Sandy Point settlement are a distinct landmark, and that these lights can obscure the visibility of Rock Point light.

Rock Point, 2 miles south of Sandy Point, has an area of shoal water around it and should be given a reasonable berth. A light marks the dangerous submerged reef that lies a short distance to seaward of Rock Point.

Sandy Point to Gorda Cay. We remind you of the changes, discussed at the beginning of this chapter, that have taken place on and around Gorda Cay as the Disney Cruise Line has transformed it into "Castaway Cay." We still have received no information as to what restrictions, if any, have been placed on the activities of private yachts or whether there will be any facilities for them. Information that appears here is about Gorda Cay as it was when we visited in 1996, but be prepared for changes. Among other things, it's likely that navigation marks, permanent or temporary, may be placed.

Gorda Cay is just visible from Sandy Point at a distance of 8 miles. Most yachtsmen prefer to make this passage in deep water along the edge of the bank where trolling is excellent. It's possible, though, to remain on the bank and, by keeping west of the Sarah Wood Bars, approach Gorda Cay from the east in 9-12 feet. A few shallow bars will be met along here.

One-half mile off the east coast of Gorda Cay there is 9 feet of water, but as you approach the northern end of the island the water shoals considerably and a half tide would be necessary to take a draft of 4.5 feet around the end of Crab Cay and into the northern anchorage. The west coast of Gorda Cay is steep-to and deep, except in the Bight. **Gorda Cay** is highest toward its southern end and has two harbors. One harbor lies in the deep bight at the southwest end of the cay, and is open to the south and southeast, but is protected by very shallow banks that prevent any real sea from making up. Boats drawing no more than 4 feet can enter through the southernmost of the two narrow cuts. The second anchorage lies on the north side of the cay off a white sand beach. It is reached by rounding the northwest point of the off-lying cay at a distance of about 100 yards. In the northern bay there are a few shallow sandbanks. Anchorages can be found in 6-8 feet, but the waters here usually kick up in strong northerly conditions. Gorda Cay is private property and visits ashore are by invitation only.

BEACH EXTENDS AS SAND BAR

GORDA ROCK NW ¼ M.

Gorda Cay to Mores Island. Gorda Rock is large with sparse vegetation, one mile north of Gorda Cay. On the eastern side are a small cove and beach which extend in the form of a shallow bank far to the east. You must pass west of Gorda Rock where, when bound north, temporary anchorage can be found in good water north of the rock and sandbar.

Long Rocks can be passed on either side but it is better to keep offshore in deep water, as the edge of the bank becomes increasingly infested with heads. Greatest care must be taken not to approach the edge of the reef too closely both

Gorda Cay. (Tropic Isle photo)

north and south of Channel Cay for shallow reefs extend for a considerable distance along the edge of soundings.

To approach **Mores Island**, pass south of **Channel Cay** (locally called Stake Cay), which has a light tower. (A reader has written to tell us of an uncharted lighted mark near the reef line southeast of Channel Cay. If it remains there, don't let it confuse you.) Although many yachts seem to use the south side, a mailboat captain told us he was entering north of Channel Cay because of an uncharted sunken rock near the channel south of the light. He did not describe his entry in detail. See D.M.A Chart 26320, which does not encourage one to use his entry, and as always, keep a good lookout for obstructions. Once past Channel Cay, a direct course good for 6 feet may be steered for the north end of Mores Island. The principal settlement, **Hard Bargain**, lies about one-half mile from the north point on the west coast. It is identified by a conspicuous white house. Anchorage can be found in 10 feet over grass about 200 yards offshore. At the foot of the town dock is Sheva Jones' Cool Spot. You can also get something to eat at N & J or Sea View (only Sea View serves beer). Rooms are available at Gator's Inn in The Bight or Tom's Inn near the airport.

Mores Island covers considerable area and rises at its northern end to 110 feet. It is thickly covered with brush and trees. Besides Hard Bargain, there is a second village known as The Bight. These picturesque settlements together have more than 1,000 people. Gas is available at the end of the concrete pier at the north side of the settlement of Hard Bargain, with a dinghy landing on the south side of the pier. A *Guide* contributor describes Queenie's one-room store as well stocked with groceries, including fresh produce, flour, pasta, and notions. He added that Queenie assisted them elegantly dressed in a gold lamé dress and a turban. There are a few other facilities, some supplies, and a telephone station.

The anchorage off Hard Bargain is comfortable in prevailing winds, but if you must seek shelter from winds between southwest and north, there is deep

Mores Island waterfront. (Tropic Isle photo)

water around the north point of the island and as far down the east coast as the first beach. On the north coast under the high conical hill are two mangrove creeks. The north creek offers good shelter but is reported to have a controlling depth at the mouth of about 3.5 feet at low water. The entrance to the south creek is reported shoaled with mangrove sprouts growing across the mouth.

Mores Island to Burrows Cay. This passage may be made by returning to Channel Cay and running northwest along the edge of the bank approaching Burrows Cay from the southwest, or by proceeding across the bank direct. The first passage is straightforward if you stay out in deep water to avoid the heads along the edge. On the second, equally easy but much shorter, you meet with two sand shoals that show up clearly from the dark, grassy bottom. The first is about 1.5 to 2 miles northwest of Mores Island. The shoals' narrow ridges almost dry, but there is 8-10 feet between them. The second, about 3 miles farther on, is deeper. Both can be easily detoured.

Up to the south end of **Burrows Cay** you can carry 12-15 feet. However, on a close approach keep a sharp lookout for coral heads that lie on a 150° bearing 1-1.5 miles from its south end. A strong tidal current runs along here, the ebb sweeping out of the Bight in a southwesterly direction.

Burrows Cay has a single conspicuous palm (we are told by one of our readers it is a Washingtonian palm) on its southwest point. The cay is low with cliffs along its coast except at the northeast end, where there is a small beach. Very deep water runs close to the rock off the southwest point of the island, but on the northwest corner is a very shallow bar. About 4 feet could be taken between the cay and the bar, but it would be safer to detour the bar to the north. An anchorage in 6 feet over a hard bottom will be found off the beach. There is no passage except for dinghies between Burrows Cay and Water Cay.

Water Cay derives its name from the small well of fresh water at its southwest end. It will be found a few yards inshore from the end of the beach on the northern side. The cay is long and very low with some stunted vegetation, sea grapes, coco plums and palmetto. There are long beaches on both sides, off which conch are prolific. An anchorage can be found under the north coast in 5-6 feet. Deep channels run northeastward on both sides of these cays.

Red Shank Cay lies 4 miles north of Water Cay. This is a small island thickly covered with scrub and mangroves. A beach on its northwest side extends southwest for one-half mile in the form of a narrow sandspit that seldom covers completely. There is a crawfish station at its northern end.

Red Shank Cay to Spence Rock. From this cay the bank that lies off the southeast coast of Grand Bahama can be followed around in deep water (12-18 feet). The Grand Bahama coast and its off-lying cays are clearly visible all the way. On approaching Spence Rock, Cave Cay will be the first landfall sighted. Take care in identifying Spence Rock; it has a wedge-shaped formation that should not be difficult to recognize.

We would advise yachts drawing over 6 feet to proceed into the Bight of Abaco by way of Mores Island. Vessels drawing less than 6 feet may safely enter by way of West End (Little Abaco). It must be remembered that the Spence Rock Passage with its 4-foot controlling depth at low water must be negotiated. See text above, and Sketch Charts H-12 and H-2.

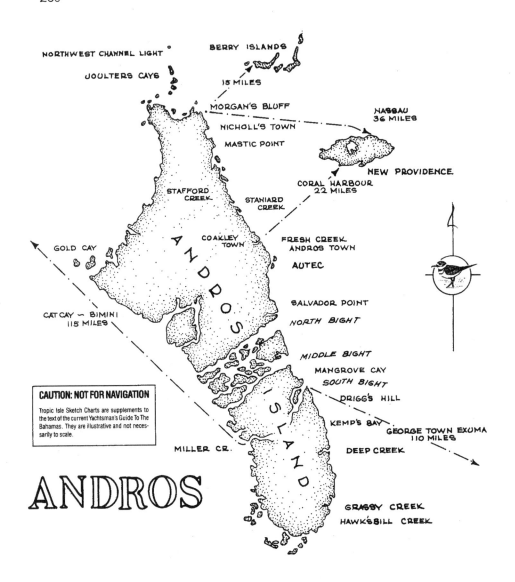

ANDROS

D.M.A. Charts: 26257, 26299, 26300, 26303, 26308, 26312, 26316, 26319, 26320, 27040. N.O.S. Charts: 11013, 11461. Tropic Isle Sketch Charts: F-1, 2,3,4.

The island of Andros, at its nearest point only 20 miles west of New Providence, is the largest of The Bahamas group and has a strange, otherworldly charm all its own. Much of the island is water; almost all of the dozens of creeks have narrow shoal inlets from the sea that widen into vast areas of shallow water

> **PLEASE NOTE:** For a description of **Batelco towers in all areas their light characteristics**, please check page 39 of this Guide.

and swamp. Some connect with freshwater lakes, and several meander tortuously from coast to coast. Few are navigable, with the exception of the Bights. North, Middle, and South Bights pass through to the western shore of Andros, which is uninhabited.

Most of Andros is covered with forests of pine and hard woods including mahogany, horseflesh (used in modern shipbuilding), and lignum vitae, sometimes known as "sailor's cure" because its sap provided the most effective cure for syphilis known until the 1900s. Bird life too is far more prolific than on the other islands and so, unfortunately, is insect life. Bring heavy-duty repellents (horse flies are locally called "doctor flies" because their bites sting like injections). Of animal life there is not much except a few wild hog.

In some remote areas of Andros, where superstition still holds sway, it isn't difficult to credit the local belief in *chickcharnies,* a form of pixie, leprechaun, or gremlin. Chickcharnies are tiny birdlike beings with huge eyes who, when not employed in mischief, nest in pine trees. It is unwise to irritate a chickcharney.

Paralleling the east coast of Andros is one of the longest barrier reefs in the world. This off-lying reef is over 140 miles in length and has few openings that are not blocked by the inner reef. Only the most straightforward and safest channels through these reefs are indicated on the sketch charts in this *Guide.* There are several prominent wrecks on these reefs which appear from a distance to be boats at anchor, so sailor beware.

The lane of water between the reef and the land varies in width from a few hundred yards to 2 miles or more, and is liberally sprinkled with shallow bars, sandbanks, and coral heads. With local knowledge, good light and, in places, high tide, it's possible to carry a draft of 4 feet inside the reef from one end of the island to the other, with a few exceptions. Remember that sketch charts in this *Guide* are of such small scale that the courses shown only roughly approximate what the real courses should be. The depths shown indicate what we've found over the years, but in many places you'll have to do some searching to find them, and since change is constant, there may not be as much water as indicated. This area should not be attempted by anyone unaccustomed to piloting by eye. Competent guides can be found in any of the major settlements.

The Tongue of the Ocean, bordering the east coast of Andros, is more than 1,000 fathoms deep. The Tongue and the coastal areas of Andros are noted for an ample supply of game fish, including marlin, sailfish, tarpon, bonefish, barracuda, grouper, snapper, and rockfish.

CONSPIC WHITE ROOFS

MORGAN'S BLUFF   270°   2 MILES

Commercial harbor, Morgan's Bluff. (Tropic Isle photo)

From a point off Nassau Harbour entrance, the most direct route to Andros is to cross to **Morgan's Bluff** (named after the celebrated pirate). The course is 282°, distance 37 miles. This trip can be shortened by running down the north coast of New Providence to West Bay 13 miles, anchoring there in good shelter and leaving early next morning to cross the Tongue of the Ocean. From Goulding Cay to Morgan's Bluff is 297° a distance of 26 miles. On either route the first sign of land is a tall stand of trees in the vicinity of Mastic Point, bearing about 240°. As the land rises above the horizon, Morgan's Bluff appears as three detached humps. Enter through the buoyed channel immediately north of the bluff. There is no continuous reef off Morgan's Bluff.

On the inside of the Bluff itself, the New Providence Barge takes on its cargo of fresh water to complement the lean supply in Nassau. From the barge wharf a long white sand beach borders the anchorage where you will be protected from winds from northeast-south-west, but there may be a surge. West of the anchorage is a small commercial harbor where yachts are neither prohibited nor desired. The wharf has a rough face and no electricity is available,

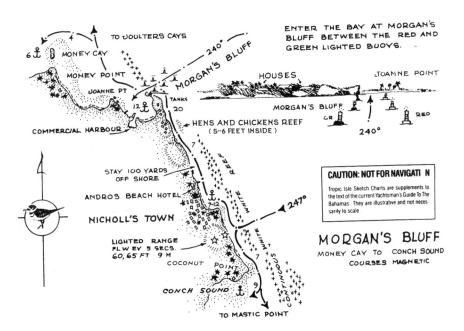

but Patrick Romer, who will give that "Esso service with a smile and any information that will make your cruise happy," sells Esso fuels here and has water and ice. Just a step from Patrick's is Wilmore Lewis' little bar and restaurant, Willy's Water Lounge, where Bahamian-style lunch, supper, sometimes fish fries, and possibly breakfast souse by arrangement is served. Contact Allan Russell or the Prate Brothers for rental cars. Down the road behind Willy's is a parklike grassy area where a woman named Rebecca has a bar in her home. About 200 yards from the beach just off the road, a sign marks the location of "Henry Morgan's Cave," where one contributor found "a nice colony of bats." This commercial harbor area is not beautiful, but it is convenient and has the only fuel available on Andros until Fresh Creek.

If you're caught by a norther at Morgan's Bluff, you can find a good anchorage in the lee of Hog Cay. To get there, run westward to a point just north of Joanne Point, then steer approximately 320° for a position one-half mile east of Hog Cay. A casuarina tree will be conspicuous at about the center of the island. Steer in for this and then follow the dark channel around the shore to the south side. A reddish-appearing bar lies off the southeast side. You will find 6 feet of water and good shelter. A crawfish station is active here in season.

Another good harbor in northerly conditions is **Lowe Sound,** west of Money Point. It is reported to have barely 4 feet in the entrance at high water but considerably more inside. Lowe Sound was once an anchorage popular with sponging vessels. In the 1926 hurricane, several schooners anchored here were carried by rising tide and wind far into the pine ridge. The little village is friendly and pretty, especially from the air, with its red roofs and clusters of palm trees. There's a post office, and Kevin's Guest House has air-conditioned rooms and a dining room. Some small, good grocery stores stock fresh produce and bread.

A draft of 7 feet can be carried into the anchorage south of **Joulters Cays,** but a half flood is needed to get over the bar at the entrance. The channel has several isolated heads and bars, and the best anchorage is at the southwest end off the point. Much of the surrounding flats dries at low water. East of the Joulters there is no continuous reef, but there are many dangerous detached rocks.

From **Morgan's Bluff south to Fresh Creek** you can proceed either inside the reef or outside in deep water, entering again through any of the appropriate channels. The reef commences about 1.5 miles south of Morgan's Bluff and a short distance north of the white sand beach that runs to Nicholl's Town. If you make your passage inside the reef, keep about 100 yards offshore except off the second hill south of the northernmost point of Morgan's Bluff. Here you must hug the shore to within 50 yards to avoid a shoal patch to port known as Hens and Chickens. Good light is necessary.

In calm weather you might anchor off Nicholl's Town in 7-12 feet over one of the grassy patches, but holding is poor. The anchorage is also exposed to any onshore winds and the off-lying reefs offer little protection, so don't expect dead quiet with any wind at all. The Andros Beach Hotel remains closed and its dock is not recommended.

Nicholl's Town, a settlement of some 600 people, is the seat of local government for this area. The town is spread out, so hiring a taxi might be necessary to find some of the stores that sell hardware and such, built in what seems like the middle of the woods. There's a guest house, vacation villas, a

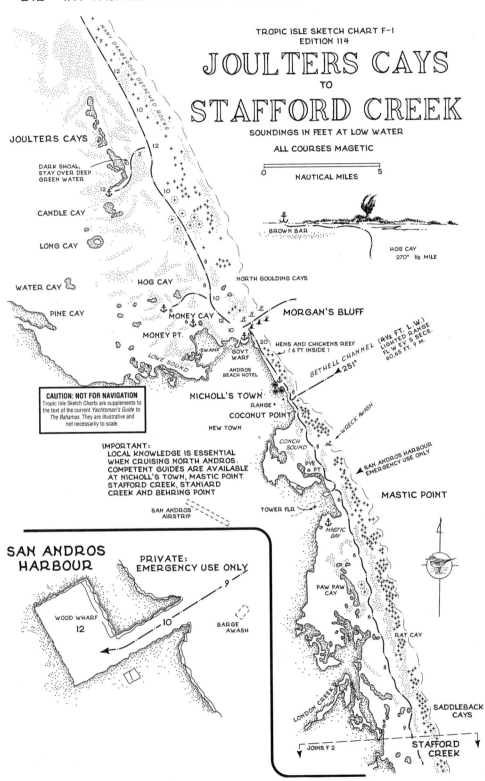

TROPIC ISLE SKETCH CHART F-1
EDITION 114

JOULTERS CAYS
TO
STAFFORD CREEK

SOUNDINGS IN FEET AT LOW WATER

ALL COURSES MAGETIC

0   NAUTICAL MILES   5

BROWN BAR

HOG CAY
270° ½ MILE

JOULTERS CAYS

DARK SHOAL,
STAY OVER DEEP
GREEN WATER

CANDLE CAY

LONG CAY

WATER CAY

HOG CAY

PINE CAY

MONEY CAY

MONEY PT.

NORTH GOULDING CAYS

MORGAN'S BLUFF

SWAMP

GOVT.
WARF

LOWE SOUND

ANDROS
BEACH HOTEL

HENS AND CHICKENS REEF
(6 FT INSIDE)

BETHELL CHANNEL (4½ FT. L.W.)
LIGHTED RANGE
FL W EV 5 SECS.
60,65 FT. 9 M.

◄—251°

CAUTION: NOT FOR NAVIGATION
Tropic Isle Sketch Charts are supplements to
the text of the current *Yachtsman's Guide to
The Bahamas*. They are illustrative and
not necessarily to scale.

NICHOLL'S TOWN

RANGE •

COCONUT POINT

NEW TOWN

CONCH
SOUND

PYE
PT.

WRECK AWASH

SAN ANDROS HARBOUR
EMERGENCY USE ONLY

IMPORTANT:
LOCAL KNOWLEDGE IS ESSENTIAL
WHEN CRUISING NORTH ANDROS.
COMPETENT GUIDES ARE AVAILABLE
AT NICHOLL'S TOWN, MASTIC POINT
STAFFORD CREEK, STANIARD
CREEK AND BEHRING POINT

MASTIC POINT

SAN ANDROS
AIRSTRIP

TOWER FLR

MASTIC
BAY

SAN ANDROS
HARBOUR

PRIVATE:
EMERGENCY USE ONLY

9

PAW PAW
CAY

WOOD WHARF
12

10

BARGE
AWASH

RAT CAY

LONDON CREEK

SADDLEBACK
CAYS

JOINS F 2

STAFFORD
CREEK

public clinic with doctor, and a telephone station. A mailboat travels weekly to Nassau and several small stores sell groceries, bread, and vegetables. Rolle's Takeaway has great Bahamian food to go. Eva's Picaroon Restaurant is a good place to eat and we're told you can find the best buy on beer in the islands at Tricoll's Bar. Between Nicholl's Town and San Andros, Rumours serves dinner, with music and dancing weekend nights.

Again, when proceeding south from Nicholl's Town inside the reef, local knowledge is advised. The point of Nicholl's Town should be rounded about 100 yards off. Then it is necessary to close the land to 50-75 yards to clear the reefs bordering the Bethell Channel entrance and the reef south of it. In rounding Coconut Point, keep at least 75 yards offshore to avoid a patch of shallow water that runs out from it.

The Bethell Channel is not a particularly good entrance to the inside passage. Use it in calm weather only, and in good light. It runs through a narrow break in the reef that carries about 4.5 feet at low water (see sketch chart F-1, Joulters Cays to Stafford Creek). Enter it between two white sandbars with the range bearing 251°. Approach the shore to within 75 yards to avoid the reefs on either side of the channel. From here a vessel drawing no more than 4 feet can work down the coast in the lee of the reef, past Conch Sound, where a world-record cave dive has been made. Farther on are many shoals and heads. In some of these areas high tide will be necessary to take even 4 feet through.

San Andros Harbour is of no interest to yachtsmen except in an emergency. It is clogged with sunken boats, and the entrance is shoaling. There are no facilities here. A sunken barge lies awash near the approach.

Continuing south past Paw Paw Cay and Rat Cay to Stafford Creek, pass well east of Calabash Cay and carry on in a southerly direction until the white stone schoolhouse at Blanket Sound bears 290°. The schoolhouse is largely obscured by

SCHOOL HOUSE, BLANKET SOUND

FROM N. END PIDGEON CAY

If you carry less than 4 feet and want to gain the creek itself, steer in on the 290° heading until you sight a stake inshore to starboard. Alter to pass just northeast of this and stay in good water, between shoals that lie south of the stake and others just north of it. Once clear, alter again to starboard, running parallel to the shore about 200 yards distant. You will pass on your port side a sunken rock that appears reddish. After a short distance, the mouth of Stafford Creek will open up. The deepest water lies on the north side.

The jetty hole noted on the sketch chart of Stafford Creek is a semi-whirlpool that can be extremely dangerous on the strength of the ebb tide. The eddies can carry a vessel against the low, rocky cliffs here with considerable violence. The settlement of **Stafford Creek** straggles along the shore north of the inlet. It is small and primitive, with no facilities.

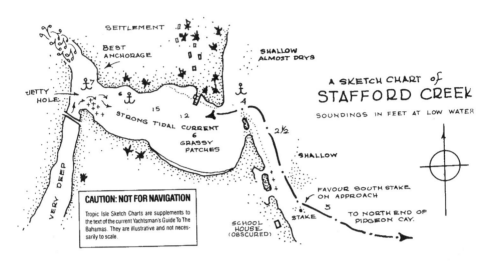

A SKETCH CHART of
STAFFORD CREEK
SOUNDINGS IN FEET AT LOW WATER

CAUTION: NOT FOR NAVIGATION
Tropic Isle Sketch Charts are supplements to
the text of the current Yachtsman's Guide To The
Bahamas. They are illustrative and not necessarily to scale.

Because the causeway blocks the deep inner creek at the jetty hole, exploration farther inland can be made only by dinghy. Ten miles of connecting creeks and lakes permit the more adventurous access to the site of the old Bahama Lumber Company far inland. There are some markers, and the red rocky bars are easily seen. It is all somewhat reminiscent of Albemarle and Pamlico Sounds in North Carolina. The tidal range is about 12 inches.

DOCK & HARBOR 'FACILITIES', STAFFORD CK.

As you continue south, Pigeon Cay has a beach on both the east and west sides. Off the beach on the western side is an overnight anchorage in 4-5 feet.

Staniard Rock Passage is a straightforward entrance through the reef which, like most, can be dangerous in strong onshore winds. Coming in, steer to pass a little over one-quarter mile north of Staniard Rock to clear a rocky shoal that lies north of it. Once inside the reef, if bound for Stafford Creek, you may steer direct for Pigeon Cay. When heading for Staniard Creek keep a lookout for isolated heads that lie one mile south-southeast.

Staniard Creek: Extensive work continues on Kamalame Cay Marina, a planned 10-berth facility on the south end of Long Bay Cay, a short distance in from the point. We are told that at our deadline for this edition there are three

Staniard Creek and Kamalame Cay area. (Tropic Isle photo)

berths available, which can accommodate boats up to 40 feet. At this writing the approach channel is good for a 3 foot draft at LW. This marina is part of Kamalame Cay, a new cottage-type resort being developed here. Rental units are available; we've seen them, and they're first-class by any standard. There's also a nice dining room and a beautiful beach. Call the resort/marina (242 368-6281) to confirm whether facilities and/or fuel you might need will be available when you arrive. They monitor VHF 16 and 68.

Note: Because Kamalame Cay Marina is still work in progress, we continue to provide information on this area as it was before development began. Staniard Creek has an excellent anchorage if you can get into it, but it has a shallow bar. From Staniard Rock steer about west-southwest for the rocky point at the end of the long white beach. The point is unmistakable with two small beaches and casuarinas. This is the southern point of the creek which marks the inlet. Approaching closely, you'll see a sandbank extending north from the point.

On approaching this bank, you will see a series of very dark patches on its edge. The channel, which appears green against the yellow sand, now report-

Kamalame Cay beach. (Tropic Isle photo)

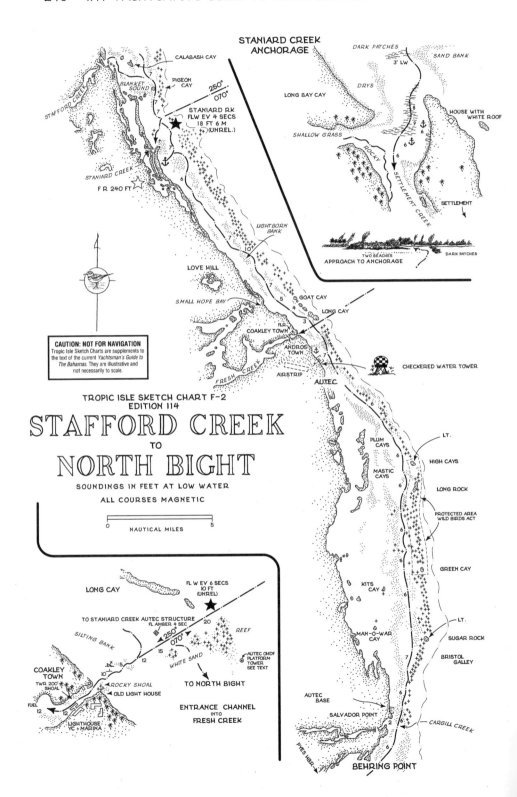

STANIARD CREEK
ANCHORAGE

DARK PATCHES
SAND BANK
3' LW

LONG BAY CAY
DRYS

HOUSE WITH
WHITE ROOF

SHALLOW GRASS

ROCKY

SETTLEMENT CREEK

SETTLEMENT

TWO BEACHES
APPROACH TO ANCHORAGE
DARK PATCHES

CALABASH CAY
BLANKET
SOUND
PIGEON
CAY
250°
070°
STAFFORD CREEK
STANIARD RK
FLW EV 4 SECS
18 FT 6 M
(UNREL.)

STANIARD CREEK

F R 240 FT

LIGHTBORN
BANK

LOVE HILL

SMALL HOPE BAY

GOAT CAY
LONG CAY

COAKLEY TOWN
ANDROS
TOWN
AIRSTRIP
AUTEC

FRESH CREEK

CHECKERED WATER TOWER

CAUTION: NOT FOR NAVIGATION
Tropic Isle Sketch Charts are supplements to
the text of the current *Yachtsman's Guide to
The Bahamas*. They are illustrative and
not necessarily to scale.

TROPIC ISLE SKETCH CHART F-2
EDITION 114

STAFFORD CREEK
TO
NORTH BIGHT

SOUNDINGS IN FEET AT LOW WATER

ALL COURSES MAGNETIC

0   NAUTICAL MILES   5

PLUM
CAYS

LT.

HIGH CAYS

MASTIC
CAYS

LONG ROCK

PROTECTED AREA
WILD BIRDS ACT

GREEN CAY

KITS
CAY

LT.

MAN-O-WAR
CAY

SUGAR ROCK

BRISTOL
GALLEY

LONG CAY

FL W EV 6 SECS
10 FT
(UNREL)

TO STANIARD CREEK AUTEC STRUCTURE
FL AMBER 4 SEC
250°
070°
REEF

SILTING BANK

WHITE SAND
20
15
12
AUTEC OMDF
PLATFORM
TOWER
SEE TEXT

COAKLEY
TOWN
TWR 200'
SHOAL
ROCKY SHOAL
OLD LIGHT HOUSE
TO NORTH BIGHT

FUEL
12
LIGHTHOUSE
YC + MARINA

ENTRANCE CHANNEL
INTO
FRESH CREEK

AUTEC
BASE
SALVADOR POINT

CARGILL CREEK

PYES HBR.

BEHRING POINT

Fresh Creek entrance, showing outer mark and AUTEC structure. (Tropic Isle photo)

edly carries only 3 feet or less at low water, so you'll have to feel your way in and play the tide. Following the green channel in, you will see a strip of dark water ahead. Steer into this and you will carry 6-8 feet into the anchorage. The land to the east is not high enough to shut out the prevailing winds, so the anchorage here is delightful, cool, and reasonably free from insects. A white beach runs along the southern side and dry sandbanks lie to the north.

From the anchorage the creek branches into three arms. The southernmost runs behind the settlement and carries comparatively deep water. The central arm becomes an extensive but shallow swamp, while the north arm provides the channel by which dinghies can reach Blanket Sound on the tide.

At about the center of the long crescent beach, about one mile south of the creek, there is a long dock off which you can anchor in 3 feet at low water. This is convenient for awaiting the tide to enter the creek. Sheltered under coconut palms, the attractive settlement at Staniard Creek stretches almost 2 miles along a lovely white sand beach. A wide paved street runs the length of the village. On either side, set well back from the road, each small, neat house stands in its own garden. This is a settlement worth visiting, but do not expect any facilities.

The inside passage between Staniard Creek and Fresh Creek isn't difficult, but it pays to keep closer to the reef than to the shore. There are a number of shallow patches and isolated heads, particularly when nearing the five small cays just north of Fresh Creek. Inside these cays there is just about 3-4 feet at low water, so you'll have to play the tide to work through here.

Just north of Coakley Town lies Small Hope Bay Lodge, a popular dive resort. Scuba equipment is provided for daily reef tours. The jewel-toned batiked clothing worn by many of the guests and employees is the product of Rosi Birch's extensive cottage industry, Androsia. The nearby factory is interesting to visit, and an extensive selection of the clothing is for sale at the resort's store.

Fresh Creek lies about 9 miles south of Staniard Creek and is one of the best harbors on Andros Island. Entering from the Tongue of the Ocean, pass close enough south of the light structure (a steel shaft south of the five small cays) to stay in the deep water between the structure and the plainly visible reef that lies just south of the channel. Continuing, pass approximately 100 feet south of the amber-lighted

Papa Gay's Chickcharnie Hotel. (Tropic Isle photo)

Lighthouse Yacht Club and Marina. (Tropic Isle photo)

AUTEC platform tower nearly halfway to the Fresh Creek entrance from the outer mark. A sandbar about 500 feet east of the mouth of Fresh Creek carries about 5 feet at low water. We have a recent report that the deepest approach over this is straight in on the centerline of the creek. Having crossed this sandbar, when gaining entrance to the creek, round the rocky bar that makes out from the south point and favor the north side on entering until across the bar. On the north side of the creek, holding is reportedly poor and scoured out. Also, you must allow passage for freight boats that arrive several times a week.

Coakley Town borders the north shore of Fresh Creek, **Andros Town** the south. Papa Gay's Chickcharnie Hotel, in Coakley Town, on your starboard as you enter, has a small concrete wharf that will carry 5 feet at low water. If you tie up, fender adequately for the strong tidal flow sluicing through. In pigeon-hunting season, the dock can resemble the aftermath of a pillow-factory explosion. The hotel, run by Papa Gay's son Charlie, has pleasant rooms available. The waterfront dining room is a scenic place to eat good Bahamian food, and the store sells food, notions, drugs, fishing gear, and hardware.

Coakley Town has a grocery store and laundromat. Across from the telephone station is Skinney's Landmark Restaurant and Satellite Lounge, another place with good Bahamian food and a nice bar. It also has a hot pepper sauce that you can buy, made by Carmetta, Skinney's wife. Try it; it will get your attention when you eat it and keep reminding you for some time thereafter.

On the south side of the creek in Andros Town, the Lighthouse Yacht Club and Marina offers 17 slips, water, electricity, and marine fuels. The hotel has a pretty dining room, and rooms are air-conditioned and spacious. Slips are limited, so reserve space before you arrive; there is little room in Fresh Creek to anchor. Strong tidal current running through can make docking here an adventure — call the dockmaster for advice and help. Also be prepared to do it yourself, because there may be nobody there. Most anchoring space could be occupied and whatever may seem available is probably pretty well scoured out. The four moorings along the edge of the channel on the Andros Town side are not maintained, and we recommend against them. If you should decide to use one, it would be best to examine it carefully above and below water. There is some talk of either prohibiting anchoring or improving the moorings and charging for their use. Maybe one of these things will happen, maybe not. The hotel can arrange dive excursions or bonefishing. Henry Ferguson is marina manager.

Fresh Creek. (Tropic Isle photo)

Hank Roberts and his wife Eva have a restaurant called Hank's Place, a block east of the generating plant. Excellent Bahamian food (including outstanding conch fritters) is served at reasonable prices, and frequent special events attract a spirited local crowd. Hank plans to begin building a small marina in the little bight just west of the Chickcharnie Hotel. His restaurant will be moved there by late 1999, when the marina should be partially completed.

If you need a rental car in Fresh Creek, call Mr. Evans at 368-2454.

About a block west of the roundabout is a government clinic.

Fresh Creek to North Bight. The passage inside the reef to North Bight will carry a draft of 4-5 feet at any state of tide, but good light is essential to negotiate the many rocky shoals and isolated heads. We stress the importance of good light conditions when under way, especially in areas like this where dangers lurk just beneath the surface. Occasionally, especially over a grassy bottom, a rocky head may not be visible until it is very close. In poor light it may not show up at all. Rocky shoals show up light brown or red, rocky bars and grass show up dark, and shallow bars and sands show up almost white. The best thing to do is avoid any suspicious water.

On leaving Fresh Creek, run out to where the bottom is clear white sand before turning south. About 1.5 miles south of Fresh Creek is the site of the U.S.-Bahamas collaborative venture known as AUTEC (Atlantic Undersea Test and Evaluation Center). The area is *strictly off limits* to yachtsman except under real

Ocean Haul Down Facility platform. (Tropic Isle photo)

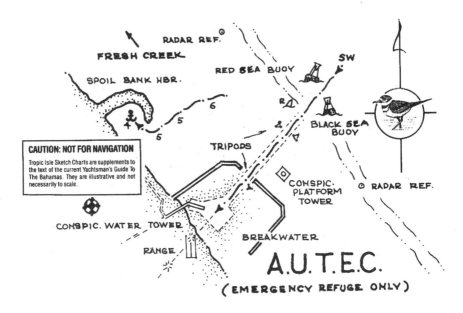

emergency conditions. Darkness, fuel shortage, inability to find another anchorage, etc., do not qualify as emergencies. The boats you might see inside AUTEC's harbor belongs to AUTEC personnel, and are on heavy permanent moorings. The bottom is scoured out, and the anchors carried aboard yachts won't hold here. What it boils down to is: You're not allowed in; if you go in you won't find any holding bottom; even if you did, you'd be ordered to leave in anything short of a real emergency. The sketch chart of the harbor layout is for emergency purposes only. AUTEC answers to *Snapper Base* on VHF 16.

Just south of the reef that lies on the south side of the entrance channel to Fresh Creek from the Tongue of the Ocean is an AUTEC platform known as an OHDF (Ocean Haul Down Facility). Give this 2 miles' clearance to seaward to avoid a cable that AUTEC runs out on the surface for that distance from the OHDF.

Between AUTEC and High Cay are a number of rocky shoals that can be easily avoided. There is reported good holding behind Long Rock just south of High Cay in 10 feet over a sandy bottom. Further south, temporary anchorage can be found close under the lee of Green Cay in 6 feet.

Salvador Point is easy to identify by the conspicuous AUTEC station that

Cargill Creek. (Tropic Isle photo)

stands on it. The small settlement of Cargill's Creek just south of it is clustered around a small beach shaded by a dense growth of coconut palms, where a number of fishing boats are usually drawn up.

Behring Point/Cargill Creek. Anchorage off Behring Point is exposed from the northeast through east to southeast, and is uncomfortable despite protection by the outer reef. A better anchorage is in Pye's Harbour, about 2.5 miles west. Here you'll be protected anchored in 7-8 feet at low water, except possibly in winds from the southeast quadrant. (We have a recent letter that tells of finding only very shallow water here.) Rupert Leadon's Andros Island Bonefish Club or Stanley Bain's Cargill Creek Lodge are two first-rate bonefishing clubs next to each other in Cargill Creek. If you were stranded for need of gasoline, either of these could help. Both can take care of all your bonefishing needs and provide good dinners (reserve before 5 p.m.; Bain's stands by on VHF 16, but you must get a message by other means to Leadon's.) Both have bars. Dig Dig's is another good place to eat.

Yachts of shallow draft (3-4 feet) can begin their explorations of North

Andros Island Bonefish Lodge. (Tropic Isle photo)

Bight from Behring Point. We recommend that you pick up a guide, as all the cays in the area look alike. There are plenty of good guides around, including Stanley or Rupert, or they can put you in touch with someone else.

Local knowledge is also advised for the extremely intricate passage from Behring Point to Middle Bight. Even local yachtsmen often prefer to make this transit in deep water outside the reef. It is possible for boats drawing not more than 3.5 feet to cruise inside from Pot Cay south under Big Wood Cay, into Middle Bight if the prevailing weather is too rough for the passage inside the reef.

Continuing south on leaving the anchorage at Behring Point, steer 165° for the small isolated clump of trees west of the thickly wooded point on the north coast of Big Wood Cay. This carries you clear (west) of the sunken rocks about 1.75 miles south of Behring Point.

On approaching the north point of Big Wood Cay, you'll see an area of very white water ahead. Skirt the eastern edge of this, steering about southeast, and keep a good lookout for the rocky patch that will appear light brown to your northeast. After passing between these shoals you'll see dark streaks on a white sand bottom. These streaks are rocks and coral. There appears to be fairly good water of about 6 feet over most of them (although one writer tells of finding considerably less water here). Steer around the plainly visible shallow white bar that extends northeast from the north point of Big Wood Cay.

The east coast of Big Wood Cay is low with a long, white beach that continues for some miles. At its back, like a picket fence, are neatly spaced coconut palms and casuarinas. Along the coast the best water is about midway between the shore and the reef. Again, keep a sharp lookout for the numerous coral heads. Some break the surface.

Umbrella Cay is a long, low, barren rock, devoid of vegetation. On it are three or four small palmetto shelters.

On approaching the southern corner of Big Wood Cay you will see an extensive area of bad water off the point. If you have been steering down about

---

Note Regarding AUTEC Bases and Facilities

AUTEC bases usually have well-marked entrance channels. This is not an invitation to use these facilities. They are off-limits to yachtsmen except under real emergency conditions. Darkness, fuel shortage, inability to find another anchorage, etc., do not quality as emergencies. Lighted AUTEC marks show amber lights. In the event of a storm, AUTEC will use its facilities to safeguard its boats and equipment.

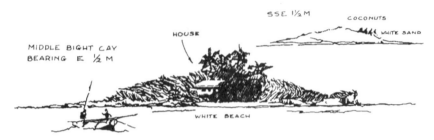

SSE. 1½ M

COCONUTS

HOUSE

WHITE SAND

MIDDLE BIGHT CAY
BEARING E ½ M

WHITE BEACH

south-southeast for **Middle Bight Cay,** you will see another large area of brown rocky shoal ahead. Alter course to port and leave the whole area to starboard. In this way you gain the deep channel that runs into the **Middle Bight** north of **Gibson Cay** (see sketch chart F-3, The Bights of Andros). Gibson Cay from the north end is long and low with a white sand beach near its center. Vegetation consists of bushes, small stunted trees, and a few casuarinas. On the southeast point of Big Wood Cay is a conspicuous AUTEC station with a number of high platform structures and a prominent white radar dome. Beyond the outer reef the installation has moored a red #2 sea buoy to mark the entrance to both Middle Bight and AUTEC's own inner harbor. Five tripod channel markers lead from the sea buoy in a west-northwesterly direction into the harbor itself. AUTEC has moored a number of unlighted buoys in shoal water between Gibson

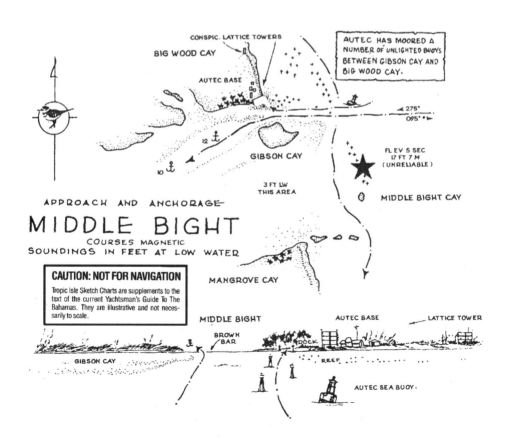

CONSPIC. LATTICE TOWERS

BIG WOOD CAY

AUTEC HAS MOORED A
NUMBER OF UNLIGHTED BUOYS
BETWEEN GIBSON CAY AND
BIG WOOD CAY.

AUTEC BASE

275°
095°

12

GIBSON CAY

10

FL EV 5 SEC
17 FT 7 M
(UNRELIABLE)

3 FT LW
THIS AREA

MIDDLE BIGHT CAY

APPROACH AND ANCHORAGE

MIDDLE BIGHT
COURSES MAGNETIC
SOUNDINGS IN FEET AT LOW WATER

CAUTION: NOT FOR NAVIGATION

Tropic Isle Sketch Charts are supplements to the
text of the current Yachtsman's Guide To The
Bahamas. They are illustrative and not necessarily to scale.

MANGROVE CAY

MIDDLE BIGHT

AUTEC BASE

LATTICE TOWER

BROWN
BAR

DOCK

GIBSON CAY

REEF

AUTEC SEA BUOY

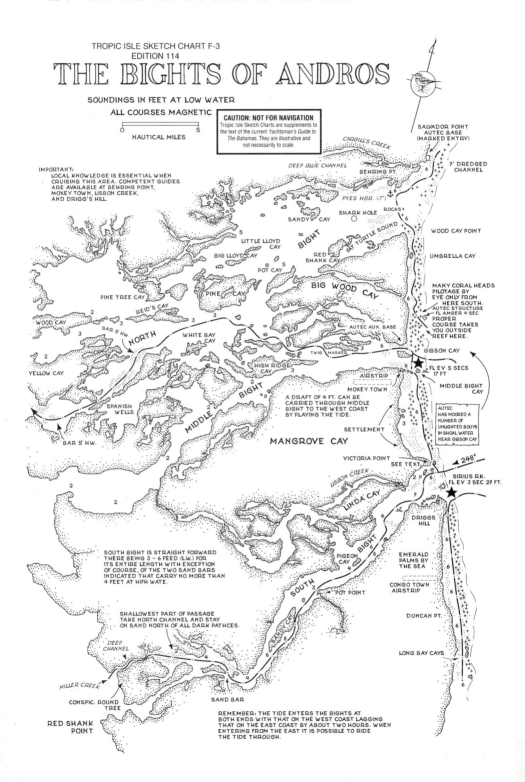

TROPIC ISLE SKETCH CHART F-3
EDITION 114

THE BIGHTS OF ANDROS

SOUNDINGS IN FEET AT LOW WATER

ALL COURSES MAGNETIC

NAUTICAL MILES

CAUTION: NOT FOR NAVIGATION
Tropic Isle Sketch Charts are supplements to
the text of the current *Yachtsman's Guide to
The Bahamas.* They are illustrative and
not necessarily to scale.

IMPORTANT:
LOCAL KNOWLEDGE IS ESSENTIAL WHEN
CRUISING THIS AREA. COMPETENT GUIDES
ARE AVAILABLE AT BEHRING POINT,
MOXEY TOWN, LISBON CREEK,
AND DRIGG'S HILL.

CARGILL'S CREEK

DEEP BLUE CHANNEL

BEHRING PT.

SALVADOR POINT
AUTEC BASE
(MARKED ENTRY)

9' DREDGED
CHANNEL

PYES HBR. (7')

ROCKS

SHARK HOLE

SANDY CAY

WOOD CAY POINT

FAT TURTLE SOUND

BIGHT

UMBRELLA CAY

LITTLE LLOYD
CAY

BIG LLOYD CAY

POT CAY

RED
SHANK CAY

BIG WOOD CAY

MANY CORAL HEADS
PILOTAGE BY
EYE ONLY FROM
HERE SOUTH.
AUTEC STRUCTURE
FL AMBER 4 SEC
PROPER
COURSE TAKES
YOU OUTSIDE
REEF HERE.

PINE TREE CAY

PINE CAY

REID'S CAY

AUTEC AUX. BASE

WOOD CAY

BAR 5' HW

NORTH

WHITE BAY
CAY

TWIG MARKER

GIBSON CAY

YELLOW CAY

HIGH RIDGE
CAY

FL EV 5 SECS
17 FT

MIDDLE BIGHT
CAY

AIRSTRIP

BIGHT

MOXEY TOWN

SPANISH
WELLS

MIDDLE

A DRAFT OF 4 FT. CAN BE
CARRIED THROUGH MIDDLE
BIGHT TO THE WEST COAST
BY PLAYING THE TIDE.

AUTEC
HAS MOORED A
NUMBER OF
UNLIGHTED BUOYS
IN SHOAL WATER
NEAR GIBSON CAY

BAR 5' HW.

SETTLEMENT

MANGROVE CAY

VICTORIA POINT

248°

SEE TEXT.

SIRIUS RK.
FL EV 3 SEC 29 FT.

LISBON CREEK

LINDA CAY

DRIGGS
HILL

SOUTH BIGHT IS STRAIGHT FORWARD
THERE BEING 3 – 6 FEED (L.W.) FOR
ITS ENTIRE LENGTH WITH EXCEPTION
OF COURSE, OF THE TWO SAND BARS
INDICATED THAT CARRY NO MORE THAN
4 FEET AT HIFH WATE.

PIGEON
CAY

BIGHT

EMERALD
PALMS BY
THE SEA

POT POINT

CONGO TOWN
AIRSTRIP

SOUTH

DUNCAN PT.

SHALLOWEST PART OF PASSAGE
TAKE NORTH CHANNEL AND STAY
ON SAND NORTH OF ALL DARK PATCHES.

DEEP
CHANNEL

LONG BAY CAYS

MILLER CREEK

CONSPIC. ROUND
TREE

SAND BAR

RED SHANK
POINT

REMEMBER: THE TIDE ENTERS THE BIGHTS AT
BOTH ENDS WITH THAT ON THE WEST COAST LAGGING
THAT ON THE EAST COAST BY ABOUT TWO HOURS. WHEN
ENTERING FROM THE EAST IT IS POSSIBLE TO RIDE
THE TIDE THROUGH.

Cay and Big Wood Cay.

To gain the Bight, proceed in, heading about 275°, from a point 300 yards south of the red sea buoy, taking care to pass south of the shallow rocky bar that extends south from the AUTEC base. Then follow the deeper blue channel that meanders southwest, keeping watch for several coral patches on your way to the anchorage. We have a recent letter telling that this channel is now marked by "huge" white and yellow buoys that mark the deep blue channel into the anchorage area. (If these buoys should be missing, this channel should be negotiated only in good light so hazards can be seen easily.) The anchorage will be found over grass in 8 feet of water far down the channel. About one mile westward is a creek with 7-9 ft. of water. The approach is shoal but it is possible to take in 5 feet at high water. The creek is broad and provides perfect protection. The same writer tells us this is called Fish Creek, and he describes it as a "great anchorage, but between the green flies, no-see-ums and the mosquitoes, you need screens here!!!!!" As illustrated in sketch chart F-3 (The Bights of Andros), Middle Bight connects with North Bight, opening up an entire archipelago for shallow water exploration.

Middle Bight to South Bight passage is far less intricate than the passage to Middle Bight. Rocky shoals exist off the north and east points of Gibson Cay, but if you stay in the deep channel until the white sandy bottom to the south is abeam you will clear them. From this point onward the scenery and surroundings improve considerably. The northern point of **Mangrove Cay** is picturesque in its setting of white sand and coconut palms. **Middle Bight Cay** is also pretty, high with a lovely beach on its western side.

The passage south, inside, is chiefly over a white sand bottom with small areas of grass here and there. It has been used by the mailboat, which draws 6 feet, but there are the usual coral heads. The shore of Mangrove Cay provides more interesting scenery, with the high rolling hills backing the low coastal belt.

Moxey Town, known locally as Little Harbour, is the northernmost settlement on Mangrove Cay and the site of the island's airstrip. Gasoline and diesel fuels can be delivered by drum to the government dock at the northeast point of the settlement by contacting Hubert King through his home number (369-0478). Leonard and Pearl Moxey operate Moxey's Guest House & Bonefishing Lodge in the center of town, where Pearl can prepare delicious conch soup or bonefish with coconut on reasonable notice. Another place to eat is the Traveler's Rest. There's a hardware store and laundromat. Ralph or Carl Moxey are good fishing guides.

Mangrove Cay's settlements border the beach for the length of the island and on around to Lisbon Creek. From north to south they are Moxey Town (Little Harbour), Burnt Rock, Pinders, Swains, Dorsett, Peats, Grants, Victoria Point, and Lisbon Creek. There are two conspicuous docks: the government dock in

MANGROVE CAY SETTLEMENT & DOCK
BEARING S.W 1 MILE

Lisbon Creek. (Tropic Isle photo)

Moxey Town and the government dock in Lisbon Creek. There is a telephone station and post office. Moxey Town is the site of the colorful 3-day August Monday Regatta where Bahamian skippers gather to test their sailing skills.

Approaching Victoria Point, just north of the entrance to South Bight, your course lies close east of White Bay Rock and west of Flat Rock. A shoal with barely any water on it will lie close to your starboard. Proceed steering to pass close east of Channel Rock. When these have been rounded you will be in the deep-water channel. The entrance from seaward is simple and straightforward. (See inset, sketch chart F-4, South Bight to Hawksbill Creek.)

Reasonable anchorage will be found close southeast of the southern **Victoria Point Cay** in 6 feet at low water, or on the south shore west of Forsyth Point in 5-9 feet at low water.

For much of the following information about **Lisbon Creek** and its new channel, we are indebted to two knowledgeable contributors, one of whom lives and works nearby. The other has for many years used a route to the Exumas via Andros, stopping at Lisbon Creek, then across to the central Exumas. The new

Leroi and Sylvia Bannister at the Aqua-Marine Club. (Tropic Isle photo)

dredged channel into Lisbon Creek will carry 6-7 feet at low water. The outer end of the dredged channel is quite visible and begins at a floating mark about 800 yards south of Victoria Point Cays (Point Cays on some charts) and about three quarters of a mile from just south of Channel Rock on a bearing of about 230°. Approaching this point, you must sail a course that keeps you in deep water and safely north of Channel Shoal. From its outer mark on into Lisbon Creek, the dredged channel is another three fourths of a mile long on a course straight to the mouth of the creek. Most of the dredge spoil was placed to the northwest of the channel and, until it subsides, it dries at low water. We visited Lisbon Creek recently and the spoil remains visible.

Inside the creek are new concrete government wharves to the east of Leroi Bannister's Aqua-Marine Club. These have a dredged depth alongside of 18 feet or so, and are used by commercial fishing boats and the mailboat. There is water here, a phone booth, and delivery of fuel by truck. To directly quote a contributor, "Lisbon Creek is a delightful community, so warm and friendly and beautiful to behold." Comfortable accommodations overlook the harbor at either Longley House or Bannister House, where Sylvia Bannister turns out some of the best Bahamian cooking imaginable. Leroi's Aqua-Marine Club is the main meeting spot, where everyone of consequence appears when visitors are in town.

Driggs Hill lies immediately south of the conspicuous AUTEC auxiliary base on **Golding Cay.** A new harbor has been dredged here with plans to accommodate cruise ships in the future, but at this writing there are no facilities or dockmaster. You may tie up alongside, but realize that this is designed for ships more than for yachts, so you'll need fenders and plenty of line. The channel leading in, which begins southeast of Sirius Rock, reportedly carries 12 feet and is well marked. The entrance can be dangerously exposed in northeasterly conditions. The harbor inside is reportedly dredged to 12-17 feet throughout.

South Bight is deeper than the others and, like them, runs clear across the island to the west coast. We have a recent letter telling that it is possible, by carefully playing the tide, to carry a draft of 4 feet through at high water, but be aware that the shallowest points are on sand bars that could fill in. Along the way are 20 to 30 spectacular blue holes and lush marine growth. Fishing is great and the colors better than any to be found in the northern part of the island. From South Bight a course of 095° will take you across the Tongue of the Ocean, onto and across the banks and straight toward Pipe Cay in the Exumas just a few miles north of Sampson Cay and Staniel Cay. As you come onto the bank you will see one of the old Decca towers, and then two more at approximately 8-mile intervals after the first along this course. According to DMA 26300, nine feet can be carried over this route.

Ezrina's Eatery serves excellent breakfast, lunch, and dinner, or try Dina's

Entry to dredged harbor at Driggs Hill (range markers in background). (Tropic Isle photo)

Golding Cay AUTEC, with Driggs Hill harbor in background. (Tropic Isle photo)

Restaurant a bit south in Long Bay. About 2 miles south of Driggs Hill, bordering the shore, is Emerald Palms By-the-Sea. The hotel, upgraded by The Bahamas Hotel Corporation, has air-conditioned rooms and a gourmet restaurant. They monitor VHF 16; call *Emerald Palms.* If you tie up at the harbor at Driggs Hill, you can walk over to the Batelco station to telephone Emerald Palms (329-4661) and they will send transportation to fetch you for dinner (reservations are required). About a mile further south, the Congo Beach Club is a nice guest house/restaurant right on the beach. Across the street is the excellent Congo Town Supermarket. Although there's no laundromat around Driggs Hill, you can ask around and find someone who will do laundry.

For much of the following information on South Andros, we are indebted to another contributor, who spent a couple months in this area in spring 1993. The passage south from Driggs Hill and Congo Town inside the reef parallels miles of beaches, coconut groves and friendly settlements. Since there are few places with all-around shelter, it is advisable to cruise this area during the most settled season. (We were there quite recently and it was fine.) A five-foot draft

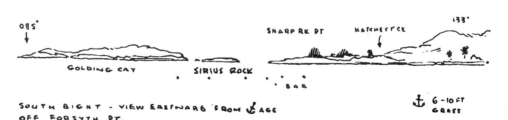

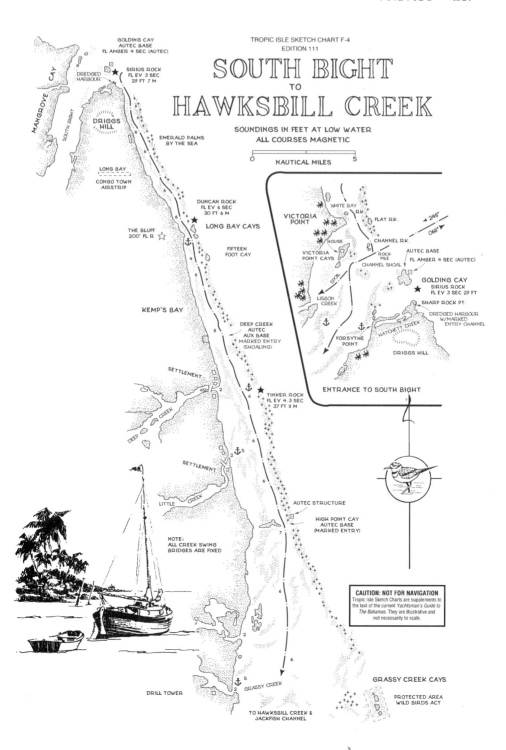

TROPIC ISLE SKETCH CHART F-4
EDITION 111

SOUTH BIGHT
TO
HAWKSBILL CREEK

SOUNDINGS IN FEET AT LOW WATER
ALL COURSES MAGNETIC

0 ———————————— 5
NAUTICAL MILES

GOLDING CAY
AUTEC BASE
FL AMBER 4 SEC (AUTEC)

SIRIUS ROCK
FL EV 3 SEC
29 FT 7 M

DREDGED
HARBOUR

MANGROVE CAY

SOUTH BIGHT

DRIGGS
HILL

EMERALD PALMS
BY THE SEA

LONG BAY

CONGO TOWN
AIRSTRIP

THE BLUFF
200' FL R

DUNCAN ROCK
FL EV 6 SEC
30 FT 6 M

LONG BAY CAYS

FIFTEEN
FOOT CAY

KEMP'S BAY

DEEP CREEK
AUTEC
AUX BASE
MARKED ENTRY
(SHOALING)

SETTLEMENT

DEEP CREEK

SETTLEMENT

LITTLE CREEK

TINKER ROCK
FL EV 4.3 SEC
37 FT 8 M

AUTEC STRUCTURE

HIGH POINT CAY
AUTEC BASE
(MARKED ENTRY)

NOTE:
ALL CREEK SWING
BRIDGES ARE FIXED

DRILL TOWER

GRASSY CREEK

TO HAWKSBILL CREEK &
JACKFISH CHANNEL

WHITE BAY
RK

VICTORIA
POINT

FLAT RK.

248°
068°

HOUSE

CHANNEL RK.

VICTORIA
POINT CAYS

ROCK
PILE

AUTEC BASE
FL AMBER 4 SEC (AUTEC)

CHANNEL SHOAL

GOLDING CAY
SIRIUS ROCK
FL EV 3 SEC 29 FT

SHARP ROCK PT.

DREDGED HARBOUR
W/MARKED
ENTRY CHANNEL

LISBON
CREEK

HATCHETT CREEK

FORSYTHE
POINT

DRIGGS HILL

ENTRANCE TO SOUTH BIGHT

GRASSY CREEK CAYS

PROTECTED AREA
WILD BIRDS ACT

CAUTION: NOT FOR NAVIGATION
Tropic Isle Sketch Charts are supplements to
the text of the current *Yachtsman's Guide to
The Bahamas*. They are illustrative and
not necessarily to scale.

Mailboat at Kemp's Cay. (Tropic Isle photo)

can be carried except for a 3.5-foot bar inside Fifteen Foot Cay. Marked AUTEC channels provide access through the reef.

South of Driggs Hill, the next anchorage is in the lee of the Long Bay Cays. On the mainland here is The Bluff, a fishing community on a bluff above a wide beach. There are several restaurants and a straw market here. Just south is the government complex for South Andros, with a Batelco office, post office, clinic and library. Try Silvia's restaurant for lunch.

Farther on is an abandoned AUTEC base at **Kemp's Bay,** where a well-marked, dredged channel leads into a sheltered concrete dock where you can tie up with the mailboat and local fishing boats. You may have to raft off the mailboat. Fuel (diesel and gas), water, and ice can be trucked here if your needs are great enough, or you can haul jerry cans. If you need a truck delivery, you may have to wait for the mailboat to leave to get the spot where the truck can reach you. Just a step away from the dock is the Royal Palm Beach Lodge, with air-conditioned rooms, and the Royal Palm Restaurant, which serves inexpensive local fare and dinner by reservation (as early as possible). Nearby is Rahming Marine, builders of fine fiberglass skiffs and fishing boats. They carry some parts and have an outboard mechanic. The Rahming family has a hardware store, grocery, laundromat, and rental cars. There's also a part-time bank. Dudley's Pink Pussy Cat Club has a rake 'n' scrape band. Nearby you can explore Deep Creek, the settlement at the bridge, or Black Point upstream.

The entrances to Deep Creek and Little Creek have causeways that preclude bringing in boats of any size, but the creeks are fun explore by dinghy. The unnamed creek north of Grassy Creek is too shallow to enter at all.

Continuing south, there are several large homes on the beach, and also Pure Gold Watersports, owned by Stan Clark. You can call him on VHF for local information. Little Creek settlement is home of Felix Smith, dean of the local bonefishing guides. After the prominent abandoned AUTEC site on High Point Cay, the last settlement on the road is pretty Mars Bay, whose harbor is actually a large blue hole surrounded by shallows.

Further south is Grassy Creek, where a 5-foot draft boat can work in following the south shore to several anchorages, including a concrete dock at an old oil-rig site. Along the Tongue of the Ocean, the Grassy Creek Cays provide a lee anchorage with a deep-water channel through the barrier reef just south of North Key. Snorkeling and fishing here is excellent. Finally you'll come to Hawksbill Creek, which offers no anchorage, as its entrance is obstructed by a 2-foot bar. At the very south tip of Andros is Jack Fish Channel, much like a river delta surrounded by miles of sand flats and islands. Here you are on your own, out of VHF range. Most of the west coast of Andros is very shallow, but there is tarpon fishing in the creek mouths. There are no settlements on the west coast.

Most of the west coast of Andros Island is very shallow but there is good tarpon fishing in the creek mouths. There are no settlements on the west coast.

Green Cay lies 17 miles, 84° from Tinker Rock and 26 miles 120° from Sirius Rock. Situated on the eastern side of the Tongue of the Ocean, this mile-square cay is a good reference point for the local fishing smacks working the banks between the Tongue and the Exuma Cays. Lee protection is all that is available here, the best being the open, reef-protected cove carrying 6-7 feet at low water on the southeast corner of the island. The narrow reef entrance at the south end of the cove carries no more than 4 feet at low water and should not be attempted except in good light. The south and east sides of the cay are reefbound and the fishing hereabouts is exceptional. We have a letter from a reader telling that the western harbor is good in prevailing winds. It is easy to enter, and holding is good. Favor the middle. Crumbling stone fences and salt ponds are evidence of past times when Green Cay was farmed. Fifteen miles east-northeast of Green Cay lie the bush-covered Scrub Cays.

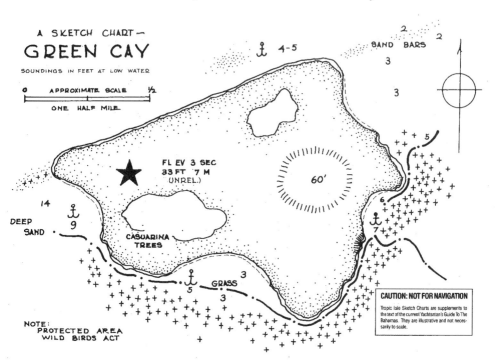

A SKETCH CHART —

GREEN CAY

SOUNDINGS IN FEET AT LOW WATER

APPROXIMATE SCALE
ONE HALF MILE.

FL EV 3 SEC
33 FT 7 M
(UNREL.)

CASUARINA TREES

DEEP SAND

GRASS

SAND BARS

60'

CAUTION: NOT FOR NAVIGATION
Tropic Isle Sketch Charts are supplements to the text of the current Yachtsman's Guide To The Bahamas. They are illustrative and not necessarily to scale.

NOTE:
PROTECTED AREA
WILD BIRDS ACT

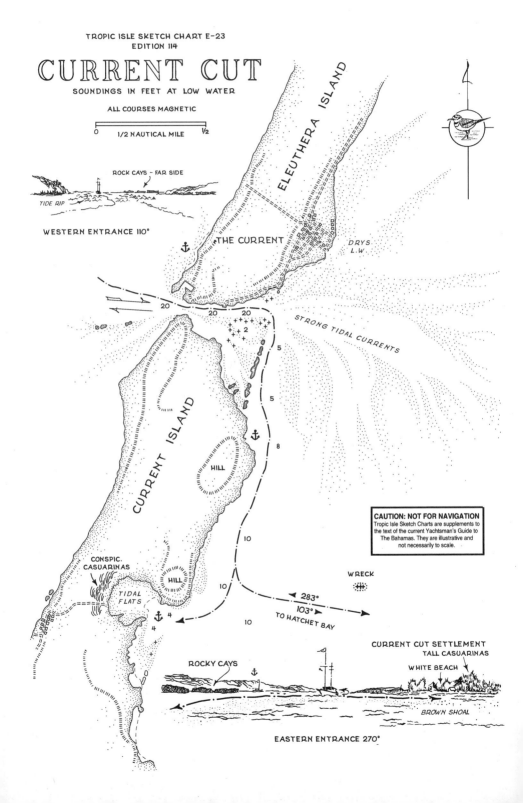

TROPIC ISLE SKETCH CHART E-23
EDITION 114

CURRENT CUT

SOUNDINGS IN FEET AT LOW WATER

ALL COURSES MAGNETIC

0   1/2 NAUTICAL MILE   ½

ELEUTHERA ISLAND

ROCK CAYS - FAR SIDE

TIDE RIP

WESTERN ENTRANCE 110°

THE CURRENT

DRYS L.W.

STRONG TIDAL CURRENTS

20   20   20
2
5

5

CURRENT ISLAND

8

HILL

CAUTION: NOT FOR NAVIGATION
Tropic Isle Sketch Charts are supplements to
the text of the current Yachtsman's Guide to
The Bahamas. They are illustrative and
not necessarily to scale.

10

WRECK

CONSPIC.
CASUARINAS

HILL

10

283°
103°
TO HATCHET BAY

TIDAL
FLATS

4
4

10

CURRENT CUT SETTLEMENT
TALL CASUARINAS

WHITE BEACH

ROCKY CAYS

BROWN SHOAL

EASTERN ENTRANCE 270°

THE CAYS TO ELEUTHERA

D.M.A. Charts: 26300, 26305, 26306, 26307. N.O.S. Chart: 11013. Tropic Isle Sketch Charts: E-14, 15, 16, 17, 20, 21, 23, 24.

Cruising eastward from Nassau toward Eleuthera, you have the choice of two routes, depending on the direction of the wind. In east or southeast weather it is better to run down north of the cays that extend between New Providence and Current Island. In winds from west to north the inside route over the bank offers the smoothest water. With the exceptions of Rose Island, Sandy Cay, and Green Cay, most of the cays in this chain are small and barren, some awash and others submerged at high tide. You must allow for the tidal current that sets strongly between them.

There are four principal channels between these cays leading from the ocean to the bank. These are: the **Douglas Channel** at the eastern end of Rose Island; the **Fleeming Channel,** southwest of Six Shillings Cays; a narrow passage close to the southwest tip of Current Island (see cut of Current Island Anchorage); and **Current Cut,** which separates Current Island and North Eleuthera.

If you choose the Current Island passage, lay a course approximately northeast (approaching from the ocean), close past the south side of **Little Pimlico** until abeam of the highest point of the island. Then turn to starboard and steer due east for the tip of **Current Island.** The channel lies close under the western shore of Current Island and may be followed to the anchorage off the white sand beach in 12-18 feet. North of the anchorage the channel shallows to a controlling depth of about 4-5 feet at low water, zigzags, and is difficult to pick out by eye. Add to this strong currents, and you can easily put yourself on ground, especially on a falling tide. There is a strong tidal current in the anchorage itself, especially at springs. On entering take care to avoid the shallow sandbar that extends in a southeasterly direction from a short distance off Little Pimlico, and allow for the strong tidal set. Off the extreme southwest tip of Little Pimlico Island there is a small rock and submerged reef. The bank can be gained from Current Island anchorage by returning to the point of Current Island and steering a course south-southeast for 1.5 miles, clearing the sandbar that extends southeast from that point. Also, from here, a draft of 9-12 feet can be carried to the east side of Current Cut by doubling the south point of Current Island close-to, rounding inside the bars, and then following the east shore of Current Island northeastward to Current Cut.

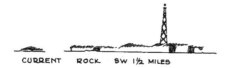

CURRENT ROCK SW 1½ MILES

LOBSTER CAY NE 2 MILES

Current Cut (Tropic Isle Sketch Charts: E-14, 23). Approaching the cut from the south, run up close-in to Current Island's east shore. Nearing the eastern entrance to the cut, you will see a line of six small, rocky cays extending out north-northeast from the Current Island shore. Off the end of these cays is a submerged rock with little water over it, and immediately beyond is the deep water of the cut itself. Don't allow yourself to slip too far east of these cays, because the water gets very shallow. Leave the submerged rock to port and, once in the channel, turn to port and run through, favoring the Eleuthera shore. This route is good for 5-6 feet at low water. We recommend that you wait for slack tide, as the water pours through here at 4-6 knots and, with tide running against a strong breeze, a nasty chop is raised at the entrance. The tide here usually follows Nassau by about 2-2.5 hours and is sometimes affected by the wind.

Within a short distance of the northeast end of Current Island there are two snug coves for shelter while awaiting the tide. They are protected in winds from southeast to west to almost northeast.

The best indication of the position of the cut is the conspicuous clump of casuarinas around Current settlement. Approaching the cut from the west, the location of the cut is clearly defined by continuous casuarinas on Eleuthera, while there are none on Current Island. Toward the eastern end of the cut is a commercial dock where the mailboat *Current Pride* unloads. This is not a good place for yachts to land, because space must be kept open for the mailboat and the dock itself is rough concrete and exposed to strong current. The narrow channel at the east end of the cut, which leads up to town, is now shoaled to 2.5 feet or less where it leaves the cut, so it's mainly a small boat channel.

The Current is perhaps the oldest settlement on Eleuthera. Some of its

Current Cut, looking west. (Tropic Isle photo)

CAYS TO ELEUTHERA

SOUNDINGS IN FEET AT LOW WATER
ALL COURSES MAGNETIC

Tropic Isle Sketch Chart E-24
Edition 113

NAUTICAL MILES

0   5

CAUTION: NOT FOR NAVIGATION
Tropic Isle Sketch Charts are supplements to
the text of the current *Yachtsman's Guide to
The Bahamas*. They are illustrative and
not necessarily to scale.

CAUTION:
WRECK AWASH
VISIBLE PORTION
SUBSIDING.
UNDERWATER
PORTION IS HAZARD.
SEE DMA 26307

EGG ISLAND ISLAND
LITTLE EGG ISLAND
FL EV 3 SEC 12 M
(UNREL.)
14

TO SPANISH WELLS

WRECK AWASH

SOUTHWEST REEF

228°
048°

TO CHUB ROCK

TO CHUB ROCK

EGG ISLAND TO CHUB ROCK 30 MILES
SEE CHART ROSE ISLAND D-4

234°
054°

215°
035°

24   18

FL EV 8 SEC 7 M
(UNREL.)

CURRENT ROCK

TO SPANISH WELLS

ELEUTHERA

CURRENT CUT

THE CURRENT

TO HATCHET BAY

WRECK AWASH

CURRENT ISLAND

LITTLE BAY

9

8

12

6

5

4-5

PIMLICO ISLAND

LITTLE PIMLICO

PERRY ROCK

4

12

18

SIX SHILLINGS CAYS

STAKE
BN

QUINTOS ROCKS

SHIP
30

FLEEMING CHANNEL

35

15

FL R EV 4 SEC
(UNREL.)

227°
047°

SHIP

BEARS 320°

UPPER SAMPHIRE CAY

20

18

LOWER SAMPHIRE CAY

243°
063°

BOOBY CAY

BOOBY ROCKS

SHIPS

12

DOUGLAS CHANNEL

15   12   15

DOUGLAS RKS.
BN

ROSE ISLAND

18

18

PIMLICO
ISLAND

LITTLE
PIMLICO

CURRENT ISLAND

CURRENT
ANCHORAGE

WHITE SAND BANK

SANDY SHOAL

12   18   4

12   15

9

18

12

12

1.5 MILES

SAND BANK

STRONG

244°
064°

TO CHUB ROCK

townspeople are claimed to be descendents of North American Indians exiled here after a massacre on Cape Cod. Local grocery stores sell Eleuthera-grown produce in season. At the L & M Take Away, a short walk from the waterfront, you can get excellent conch fritters and other seafood dishes, coconut pie, and ice cream, as well as burgers, hot dogs, and fries.

The **Egg Islands,** off the southwest tip of Royal Island, have no great attraction for yachtsmen except for some good fishing. The light at Great Egg Island, like many others, is unreliable. Also, there is a privately maintained light at the entrance to the harbor at Royal Island, which is recently reported flashing white every 6-8 seconds (estimated); you shouldn't be under way at night but, if you have to be, don't let this light confuse you.

In making the bank from the west, it is possible to pass south of Little Egg in good water, but beware that D.M.A. Chart 23607 does show an obstruction about 500 yards south of Little Egg Island. And if a swell is running, take care to avoid Barracouta Patch (10 feet at low water) another 500-600 yards further south by favoring the south side of the pass, taking what used to be a stranded freighter (a triangular piece of rust-colored metal is all that shows above water here) 200 yards to port. *Caution: Most of this wreck is just under the surface, so don't approach closely. Use D.M.A. Chart 26307, because when the last visible piece of this wreck disappears, the underwater remains will be a real hazard unless someone marks it.*

The intriguing history of this wreck is detailed in an article by Frank Slifka and Doug Perrine in the July/August 1988 *Sea Frontiers* magazine. The 260-foot *Arimora* caught fire in the Northeast Providence Channel in 1970, and ran aground in 15 feet of water as it approached Egg Island. The crew abandoned the burning ship and the freighter's full load of South American guano-based fertilizer escaped into the water. Although the fertilizer's high phosphate content initially destroyed most surrounding sea life, recent regrowth of an unusually dense population of fish, coral, mollusks, and sea slugs around the freighter has proven something of a mystery to marine biologists.

Opposite the cut between Great Egg Island and Royal Island is a grassy patch that carries only 6 feet at low water. Through this cut there is a deep but intricate channel. Off Rat Cay, which guards the eastern entrance to the cut, there is a profusion of coral heads around which the fishing is good. There are pretty beaches with coconut groves on the north side of the cut. Royal Island can be approached over the bank from the south if you take care to avoid the rocky patch about one mile south of the harbor entrance.

Royal Island has a beautiful, almost landlocked harbor that offers protection in almost any weather. The entrance lies a short distance east of the twin hills. A large stone house is now mostly obscured by trees. Enter only on the western side of the rocky cay in the center of the opening into the harbor. (It's reported that someone has put a small red mark on a stake on the submerged rock on the east side of the rocky cay. Do not let this confuse you into thinking

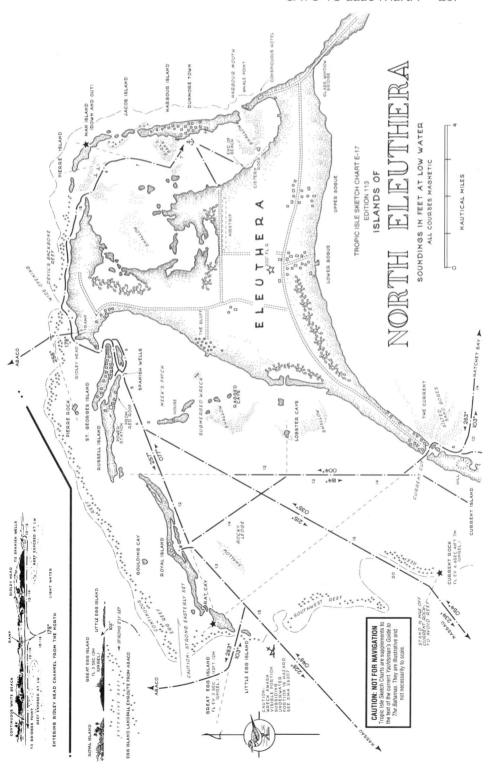

TROPIC ISLE SKETCH CHART E-17
EDITION 113

ISLANDS OF

NORTH ELEUTHERA

SOUNDINGS IN FEET AT LOW WATER
ALL COURSES MAGNETIC

NAUTICAL MILES

CAUTION: NOT FOR NAVIGATION
Tropic Isle Sketch Charts are supplements to
the text of the current *Yachtsman's Guide to
The Bahamas.* They are illustrative and
not necessarily to scale.

Royal Island Harbour, looking southeast. (Tropic Isle photo)

you should enter on that side.) There are obstructions and rocks awash east of the little cay (see landfall sketch). At the far east end of the harbor is a false entrance, usable only by small boats. The harbor and its entrance will carry about 9 feet. A few years ago there was something here called the Royal Island Yacht Club. Some of their old rental moorings are still here, but they are neglected and we advise against using them. There is plenty of space to anchor, and holding is good if you find one of the sandy spots. The rest, mostly grass, is poor holding. The best anchorage is off the dock or toward the western end of the harbor, but don't anchor among the moorings. Boats on their own anchors swing differently than boats on fixed moorings, and the two don't mix. There are no garbage facilities.

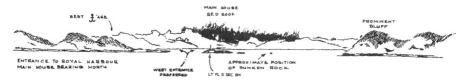

Spanish Wells (Tropic Isle Sketch Charts: E-17, 20) is a remarkably orderly community on **St. George's Cay.** Its name is said to have originated three centuries ago, when Spanish explorers declared the local well water the sweetest in The Bahamas. Nowadays water is piped in from the community wells on Eleuthera, 2 miles away. Some Spanish Wellsians claim direct descent from the original Eleutherian Adventurers who shipwrecked on the treacherous nearby reefs in 1648. Others are descendants of Loyalists who sought refuge here at the end of the U.S. War of Independence. The town has a history of self-sufficiency; even the power system is locally owned and run. Most residents grow up, marry, and remain here. Among them are some of the best fishermen, divers, and seafarers in The Bahamas. Prosperity is reflected in large, well-maintained cement-block homes and a profusion of satellite dishes.

There are two entrances to Spanish Wells, both well marked. In both these channels, the types and numbers of marks may change from time to time, and colors may become unrecognizable, but the scheme usually remains the same. The favored route is between Charles Island and Russell Island, where a dredged, well-marked channel carries 6.5 feet at low water. Approaching from the

HARBOUR ISLAND, BAHAMAS

Romora Bay
Club

We focus on luxury with the
finest in accommodations,
cuisine, activities and service.

Accommodations:
· Thirty-three rooms, villas, and
  bungalows
· Private Patio
· Air-conditioning
· Telephone
· VCR and CD player
· Room Service.

Cuisine:
· World-class restaurant under the
  direction of chef Ludocic Jarlands.
  offering the finest cuisine and wine.

Entertainment:
· Live music and disco
· Happy Hour
· Movie and music library
· Books and parlour games

Activities:
· Natural 3,000 sq. ft. swimming area
· Jeff Fox's full SCUBA Dive program
· Deep-sea fishing and bonefishing
· Snorkeling
· Sailing
· Windsurfing
· Kayaking
· Boogie boarding,
· Water skiing
· Horseback riding
· Fitness
· Tennis

*Romora Bay Club is located on the
sunny, protected bay side of Harbour
Island, halfway between Valentine's
and Harbour Island Marina.
The island's spectacular 3-mile-long
pink-sand beach waits for you just
150 yards from our property.*

Romora Bay Club
Harbour Island, Bahamas
France: 33.1 45 67 10 30 England: WSM 44 1494 874 106
Bahamas: Phone 1 (242) 333-2325, Fax 1 (242) 333-2500
e-mail: romora@batelnet.bs · Visit Our Website at http:www.romorabay.com

HARBOUR ISLAND • ELEUTHERA

FOLLOW YOUR HEART...

Valentine's...a wonderfully low-key quaint and exciting out island adventure that indelibly emblazons its memories not only on the minds, but in the hearts of all who experience.

Only sixty miles northeast of Nassau on beautiful Harbour Island, Valentine's Resort and Marina will fulfill your every need:

- 39 slip marina, yachts up to 160'/12' draft.
- Full dockside electric (30, 50, 100 amps)

- Unlimited fresh water
- Cable hook-up
- State-of-the-art fueling
- World-class dive center
- 2 restaurants and dockside bar
- 21 attractive rooms with pool and tennis courts
- Explore and shop in historic Dunmore Town
- Shimmering pink powder beaches
- Great for meetings, weddings, tournaments
  Visit our website www.ValentinesResort.com for
tips on local navigation.

Dive Center reservations:
1-800-383-6480 or e-mail
vdc@batelnet.bs.

VALENTINE'S
RESORT & MARINA

Resort and Marina reservations:
1-242-333-2142 or e-mail
info@valentinesresort.com.

TROPIC ISLE SKETCH CHART E-20
EDITION 114

SPANISH WELLS
AND RIDLEY HEAD CHANNEL

SOUNDINGS IN FEET AT LOW WATER
COURSES MAGNETIC

NAUTICAL MILE

0   ½   ½

EASTERN APPROACH TO SPANISH WELLS HARBOUR

NOTE: THROUGHOUT THE AREA IMMEDIATELY AROUND SPANISH WELLS TYPES AND NUMBERS OF MARKS MAY VARY AND BECOME UNRECOGNIZABLE BUT THE SCHEME REMAINS THE SAME.

ELEUTHERA ISLAND
(NORTH END)

REEF

REEF BREAKS

BRIDGES PT.

20

REEF PASSAGE VIA DEVILS BACKBONE TO HARBOUR ISLAND.

RIDLEY HEAD CHANNEL

RAMP

39

12

RIDLEY HEAD MARK

12

SETTLED WEATHER RENDEZVOUS FOR PILOT. STAND-BY OVER PATCH OF LIGHT WATER

PIERRE ROCK BEARS 258°

CONTINUOUS REEF

12

BEACH

12

(PRIVATE)

FERRY LANDING

GRASS

GRASS

GRASSY RIDGE

QK FL

FL 3 SEC

1 - 2

1 - 2

SHALLOW

GRASS

1 - 2

GUN POINT

12

18

SHALLOW

15

SHALLOW

SHOAL

15

12

8

10

7

12

VIEW "B"

ROUND GUN POINT 25 YDS OFF

6

Shallow WHITE BAR

SHALLOW

BEACH

PIERRE ROCK

SHALLOW

SPANISH WELLS

GOVT BLDGS. SCHOOL

HARBOUR

14

16

CHARLES ISLAND

7

R

G

R

GRASS

SHALLOW GRASS

WATER TOWER
FL.R.LT.

FL.R.LT.

WATER TOWER
FR

CONT. WHARF

WATER TOWER

SR WELLS MARINE

R&B BOATYARD

MARINE

POLE

POLE

5-6

6½

5-6

5

5

DRYS

DRYS

SPOIL BANK

DRYS

DRYS

SR WELLS YACHT HAVEN

6

7

7

8

CONTINUOUS BEACH 10-12 FT

DREDGED CHANNEL 10-12 FT

ST. GEORGE'S CAY

33

BRIDGE

MUDDY HOLE
HURRICANE HOLE
BOAT STORAGE

PROMINENT POWER STA.

3

2

3

4

RUSSELL ISLAND

257° TO ROYAL ISLAND

8

6

CAUTION: NOT FOR NAVIGATION
Tropic Isle Sketch Charts are supplements to the text of the current Yachtsman's Guide to The Bahamas. They are illustrative and not necessarily to scale.

TO AVOID SHOAL AT CHANNEL ENTRANCE PARALLEL STAKE MARKERS TO STBD.

southwest, enter between the green-tipped H-beam on your port and the red-tipped H-beam on your starboard (red-right-returning). A bit farther in, another red-tipped H-beam should also be kept to starboard. Be sure not to stray out of this channel or you'll be aground. We have a recent letter telling of a grounding on the west side of this channel due to the channel's being stirred up and impossible to read. Because of a falling tide, this became a 5-hour ordeal.

The second, older entrance, northeast of Charles Island and marked with stakes, is straight, wide, and deep, carrying 10 feet or better at low water. Just inside, the dredged anchorage offers 9-17 feet. There are now rental moorings here that are convenient, but they make it difficult to find a place where you can set your own tackle. Two anchors are advised here because of the strong tidal current. The concrete wharf that borders the town is not available for visiting pleasure craft.

Opposite the western tip of Charles Island is Spanish Wells Marine and Hardware, with water, gas, diesel fuel, ice, electricity, and hauling facilities for boats up to 30 feet. Engine (Mercury and Mariner) repairs can be made. The fully stocked marine store sometimes has fresh lobster or fish for sale at the counter. Four air-conditioned efficiency apartments are above the store. Further east on the harbor road, Ronald's Servicenter has a variety of marine supplies and fresh fish and ice for sale.

R & B Boat Yard is the blue building with a not very prominent sign a bit east of Spanish Wells Maine and Hardware. Their marine railway, which can haul boats up to 120 tons, extends out more than halfway across the harbor and

Be sure to stop at the newest, most modern Marina in the Bahamas.

SPANISH WELLS YACHT HAVEN

P.O. BOX EL 27427 • SPANISH WELLS • BAHAMAS

Phone (242) 333-4255 • FAX (242) 333-4649

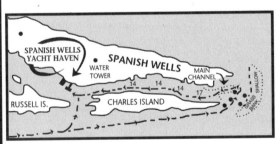

- 40 SLIPS
- COVERED STORAGE
- MODERN LAUNDROMAT
- AIR-CONDITIONED ROOMS, APARTMENTS
- SHOWER FACILITIES
- SWIMMING POOL
- ELECTRICITY 220 & 110
- MONITOR VHF CH. 16
- REVERSE OSMOSIS WATER
- SATELLITE TV IN ROOMS
- BAR & RESTAURANT, ICE

CALL US FOR PILOT

We honor:

- MASTERCARD ■ VISA ■ AMERICAN EXPRESS
- ESSO CREDIT CARDS

MARINE FUELS and LUBRICANTS

South entrance to Spanish Wells. (Tropic Isle photo)

is a hazard you must avoid. Conveniently located next door is Pinder's Supermarket.

The well-marked channel that runs westward from the inner end of the new entrance channel will carry 5 feet at low water. As you enter, leave to your starboard the post topped with a sign directing you to Yacht Haven. Boats drawing 7 feet and perhaps more can run as far as Spanish Wells Yacht Haven on the tide. The marina's relatively new docks, rebuilt after Hurricane Andrew, can accommodate boats of up to 8.5-foot draft. All petroleum products, electrical service, satellite TV hookups, a laundromat (only for guests or boats docked at the marina) and good water are available. Inquire about long-term storage rates. There's a bar with a pool table, and the Harbour View Restaurant serves excellent fresh seafood. Some rooms and efficiencies are available. Water sports can be arranged and bikes can be rented. The marina manager is Leroy Kelly.

Spanish Wells
Pilot Service

Most Experienced Guides in Spanish Wells

BRADLEY NEWBOLD & EDSEL ROBERTS

For information call **"Cinnabar"** or **"Dolphin"** on VHF Channel 16 from 7a.m. to 8p.m. or phone (242)333-4079 or 333-4209

Call us for moorings at Spanish Wells.

Spanish Wells Yacht Haven. (Tropic Isle photo)

The channel continues down the creek between St. George's Cay and Russell Island. It has been dredged to carry 5-6 feet at low water, over a mud bottom, as far as **Muddy Hole,** the local hurricane shelter. Wet storage is available in Muddy Hole to yachts drawing up to 5 feet. Inside there is 2-3 feet or less toward the center; depths of up to 5 feet are found around the periphery.

It should be noted that there seems to be no speed limit or wake restriction within Spanish Wells harbor. As a precaution, tie off to the adjoining slip or dock to avoid damage to your topsides.

Spanish Wells is uniquely intriguing, an island unto itself in The Bahamas. In the fall and winter, many of the men are away for weeks at a time one of the impressive modern fishing boats you might see in the harbor, returning with freezer compartments loaded with crawfish. In the interim, things can be eerily quiet — it's possible to walk through town at lunch time and not encounter a soul, with perhaps the muffled sounds of silverware being laid out and television static escaping from closed shutters. On Sundays, almost everybody stays at home, and on Wednesday afternoons stores are closed. The curious dearth of shade trees leaves the town in stark relief at midday, but some of the houses have beautiful abundant gardens, and virtually all of them are meticulously groomed. In the morning or late afternoon, you'll probably see matrons young and old sweeping porches or washing down driveways, towheaded children on tricycles, and tribes of whooping teenagers on motorbikes. Over the hill on the north shore is a beach with glasslike shallow water extending out for a considerable distance.

A bit out of town to the west is the sizable Spanish Wells Food Fair. Locals are proud to point out that, like the power company, the store is locally owned and run. Across from it, Kathy's Bakery sells good hot Bahamian bread. About two blocks below the Food Fair is the new Spanish Wells Canvas Shop, run by Johnny and Nancy Underwood. They make canvas repairs, bimini tops, and frames. There's also a pharmacy, and in town are a number of small grocery shops. Pinder's Tune-Up, halfway to the Food Fair, sells propane and might be able to help out with small engine repairs. Across the street is Manuel's Dive Station, a combined dive shop and plant nursery (as someone told us, "you can't be too versatile in the Islands.") The Spanish Wells Museum celebrates this area's

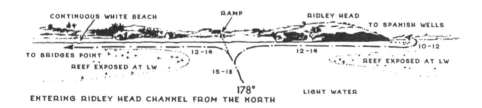

ENTERING RIDLEY HEAD CHANNEL FROM THE NORTH

rich history and culture from the Lucayans through the 20th century. Across the street is a tiny quilt shop run by Cecile Dunnam, where local women gather to make colorful quilts. Nearby are Lynette's Dry Goods store and the Islander Shop, for T-shirts, souvenirs, and such. Jack's Outback (formerly Carol's Place), on the harbor road, serves hamburgers and sandwiches. Captain's Diner serves seafood, steak, and chicken (in the same building is a small grocery with the somewhat misleading name of C. W. Hardware). At the back of Captain's Diner is a coin laundromat. The new Anchor Snack Bar serves light fare. The area's only liquor store is across the outer harbor on Eleuthera, by the water-taxi dock.

Dr. Steve Bailey has opened a clinic and keeps office hours Monday, Tuesday, Thursday, and Friday from 8 a.m. to 12 p.m. and 1 p.m. to 4 p.m. Call

Little Woody

SPANISH WELLS
YACHT PILOT & FISHING GUIDE

Deep Sea Fishing w/Live Bait
Reef Fishing, Bone Fishing
Reef Snorkeling & Beach Fun

"Come & Sea"

Monday - Saturday Anytime
Sunday 12:15 - 3:00P.M.
WOODY PERRY
P.O. Box EL27470
Spanish Wells, BAH.
Ph. 242-333-4433/VHF. Ch 16

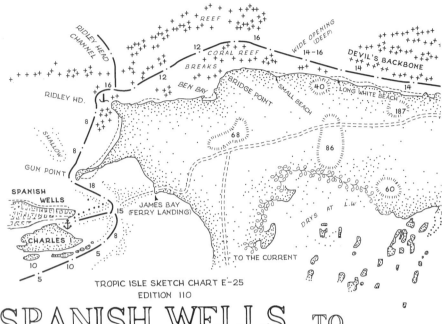

TROPIC ISLE SKETCH CHART E-25
EDITION 110

SPANISH WELLS TO HARBOUR ISLAND

him at 242-333-4869. He is on call outside of office hours for an extra charge.

You are strongly advised to hire a local pilot to negotiate Ridley Head Channel or the Devil's Backbone passage to Harbour Island. Most of them can also take you to fishing spots off some of the most beautiful reefs in the world, bordering the north side of Russell and Royal Islands. Call one of the pilots advertised herein, or try *Pilot* on VHF 16.

Ridley Head Channel. There used to be a lateral mark in the opening in the outer reef in this channel marking the reefs on the east side of the channel, but it has been missing for several years. Reefs to the west of the channel are also unmarked. *In order to be able to see these reefs and coral heads, attempt this channel only in good light conditions. You should have a pilot to guide you, at least for the first time.* Vessels arriving from Abaco usually pick up their pilot at the "fix" off Ridley Head Channel, as indicated on sketch charts E-17 (Islands of North Eleuthera) and E-20 (Spanish Wells). This entrance is recommended

> *Marks between Spanish Wells and the Ridley Head Channel, in the Ridley Head Channel, and along the route from Spanish Wells to Harbour Island are privately placed and maintained. They can be changed, missing, or altered at any time.* **Local knowledge is essential throughout these areas, and hiring one of the local pilots is highly recommended.**

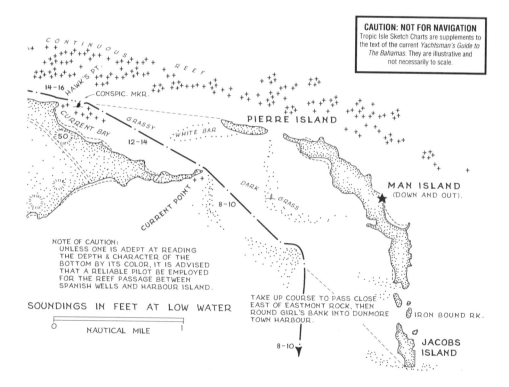

CAUTION: NOT FOR NAVIGATION
Tropic Isle Sketch Charts are supplements to
the text of the current *Yachtsman's Guide to
The Bahamas*. They are illustrative and
not necessarily to scale.

only in fair weather. Make arrangements with any of the guides via Nassau Marine or VHF Channel 16. Although treacherous, Ridley Head is convenient for yachts wishing to gain deeper water by the quickest method, especially if bound for Abaco, as it eliminates the detour by way of the Egg Islands.

To reach Ridley Head Channel from Spanish Wells, turn to port after leaving either harbor entrance and follow the Harbour Island channel around Gun Point to Ridley Head. Leaving to starboard the prominent H-beam that marks extensive reefs off Ridley Head, round Ridley Head until the small ramp above the west end of the white sand beach just east of Ridley Head bears 178°, then turn north to sea on a 358° heading. Proceed carefully in good light to be sure this takes you between the two submerged but shallow reefs, marked as

SPANISH WELLS PILOT SERVICE
CALL **A-1 BROADSHAD**
FISHING & SNORKELING
TELEPHONE: 242-333-4427
FAX: 242-333-4526   VHF 16

described above, into deep water. The only other danger on this course is a shallow, rocky bar that should be left some distance to starboard. Once clear of this, you may lay your course direct for Hole in the Wall or Little Harbour.

Spanish Wells to Harbour Island. There are two routes from Spanish Wells to Dunmore Town, *both requiring the aid of a local pilot unless you are well experienced with these waters and extremely proficient in reading reefs.* The first lies outside the Egg Islands and North Eleuthera, and is open ocean all the way, provided the off-lying reefs are given a wide berth. In fresh onshore winds, this passage can be very heavy going indeed. Sail down the east coast of Harbour Island, and enter the sound through the channel at the south end of the island, known as Harbour Mouth. Local sportfishing boats with 4 feet draft use this channel regularly, but we feel that for the first time at least, a local pilot is necessary; there is always a strong tidal rip in this cut, even in calm weather, and the sandbanks inside are constantly shifting and extremely shallow in places. Because of these constantly changing conditions, we have found Harbour Mouth impossible to accurately depict, and we again recommend to the inexperienced the aid of someone familiar with the day-to-day conditions here.

The second route, inside the reefs, for vessels of lesser draft (see sketch chart E-25, Spanish Wells to Harbour Island) is both narrow and intricate, but because of its shorter 11-mile length, is preferred. *The passage must be attempted in good light, when the reefs are visible, and under favorable weather conditions. The services of a pilot are highly recommended, and are essential for first-timers. Marks along this route are frequently reported missing or changed.* Even when the light is good, a momentary cloud passing over the sun can obscure visibility and you can put yourself aground in a second, perhaps on something hard. In northerly conditions the Devil's Backbone is impassable.

The route from Spanish Wells Harbour to Gun Point is straightforward as indicated on sketch chart E-20. From Gun Point, a course may be laid for a point about 150 yards off Ridley Head so as to clear the extensive reef that extends north of it, which is marked by an H-beam. Between Ridley Head and Bridge Point there are a number of heads. The first, which lies north of the beach just east of Ridley Head, should be left to port. The second, farther east, should be left to starboard. The breaking reef short of Bridge Point is also left to starboard. Round Bridge Point well off, staying in the lighter water. You must avoid the extensive reef, no longer marked, that works out from the shore here. For the next three-quarters of a mile there is a break in the outer reef and the coast is exposed to the full force of any onshore sea and swell. This is known as "Wide Opening." Having rounded Bridge Point, steer for the conspicuous expanse of white sand beach at the far end of Wide Opening (about three-quarters of a mile) and gradually close with the shore. The course now lies close in to the beach, about 30 yards off in order to clear the reef known as the **Devil's Backbone,** which should be plainly visible.

When a considerable sea is running, it is necessary to pass closer to the Devil's Backbone than to the beach, as the channel here is so narrow that the force of the sea might set the vessel ashore were she in mid-channel or south of it. East of Hawk's Point, marking the end of a shallow rocky bar, stands another pipe beacon. It is mounted on a concrete platform and from a distance looks like a man standing in a boat. Pass north of it and steer for Current Point, as the worst is over. Once past Current Point, leave the H-beam marking a grassy area to port, staying about 50 feet south of the marker. When about one-half mile southeast of the marker, having rounded the bank southwest of the channel, take up a course to pass close east of Eastmost Rock. Once abeam of Eastmost Rock, give **Girls Bank** a wide berth until south of it, when you can round up into the anchorage off Dunmore Town. A draft of 5 feet can be carried across here at low water. It must be emphasized that this passage should not be made in other than good conditions of light and weather, when the many dangers can be seen. (Note: Locally, Hawk's Point is sometimes referred to as Current Point, and what is identified on charts as Current Point is sometimes referred to as Long Point.)

A trip to **Harbour Island** is well worth making. The anchorage off **Dunmore Town** offers 12 feet and is well protected from the prevailing easterly winds. In strong winds from south to southwest, which are uncommon, the

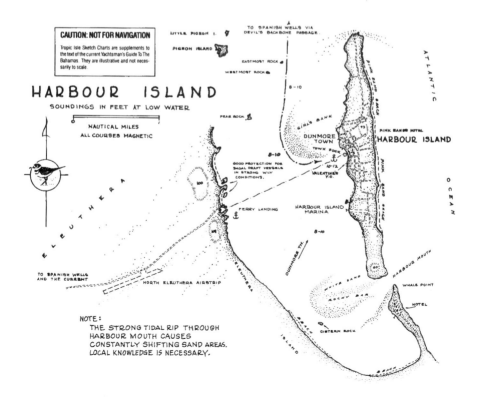

CAUTION: NOT FOR NAVIGATION

Tropic Isle Sketch Charts are supplements to the text of the current Yachtsman's Guide To The Bahamas. They are illustrative and not necessarily to scale.

HARBOUR   ISLAND

SOUNDINGS IN FEET AT LOW WATER

NAUTICAL MILES
ALL COURSES MAGNETIC

NOTE:
THE STRONG TIDAL RIP THROUGH HARBOUR MOUTH CAUSES CONSTANTLY SHIFTING SAND AREAS. LOCAL KNOWLEDGE IS NECESSARY.

PINK CUSTOMS HOUSE

GOVERNMENT PIER

GIRLS BANK   10   DUNMORE TOWN EAST 1/2 MILE

anchorage is somewhat exposed because of the size of the Sound. You can find good cover in westerly conditions east of the ferry landing on Eleuthera.

One of the oldest established settlements in The Bahamas, Dunmore Town is a pretty little town of brightly painted homes, graceful picket fences wound with wildflowers, and narrow streets bordered by stone walls. The town is named after Governor Lord Dunmore, whose summer home in the 18th century commanded a view from the highest point of town, now the site of the Harbour Island commissioner's handsome old wood-frame residence. The Loyalist Cottage on Bay Street dates back to the 1790s, and many of the town's beautifully renovated houses and inns were built in the 1800s, when Dunmore Town was a prosperous harbor and shipbuilding center. The style of the village is somewhat reminiscent of the vacation spas along the Carolina shores. In late afternoon children play or ride their bikes on the back streets while adults congregate outside to socialize. Native islanders, or Brilanders, are for the most part seafarers or farmers who work the mainland of Eleuthera, across the Sound.

Dunmore Town has long been one of the leading winter getaways in The Bahamas. Most of the resorts offer guests quiet privacy and an atmosphere of gentility, and there are many fine restaurants. The wide 3-mile-long beach is tinted pink with particles of coral. Unusual dive excursions can be arranged, including a visit to a sunken train on the Devil's Backbone or a speedy underwater ride through Current Cut on the tide. In town are several lively nightclubs and taverns, ice cream parlors, good lunch spots, and shops.

Although seldom used as such by boats, Dunmore Town is a port of entry. The large pink customs house sits prominently at the end of the town dock. Fuel can be delivered to the dock.

Just 200 yards south of the government dock lies Valentine's Resort and Marina. The docks can accommodate 39 boats. This is a popular stop and you should call ahead on VHF 16 to check on space availability. Fuel will be available at your slip, and showers are available with dockage. There are two good restaurants and a dockside bar. Valentine's Dive Center offers specialty and advanced certification as well as basic instruction and dive tours.

The Romora Bay Club, once an elegant private home, is located just south of town. The beautifully landscaped hills leading down to the sea are dotted with secluded comfortable villas, and there's a panoramic view from the open-air bar, where we were mesmerized one evening by the splendor of a thunderstorm on the horizon. The food at the restaurant is excellent, served on the trellised stone patio up the hill at the main house. Inside is a nice bar, a baby grand piano, and comfortable chairs and sofas for lounging or playing a game of backgammon.

Harbour Island Marina. (Tropic Isle photo)

New management has nicely refurbished all accommodations, which include rooms, villas, and bungalows. The PADI-trained staff at Pro Dive Services at Romora Bay emphasizes instruction and tours individualized to your preference and schedule. The small service dock offers no facilities for yachts.

South of Romora Bay, the Harbour Island Club and Marina has 32 slips, with those on the outside accommodating boats of up to 10-foot draft and the inner slips good for 6-8 feet. Diesel, gas, electricity, good drinking water, laundry services, and showers are available. Lunch is served at the restaurant, and a pretty cocktail lounge overlooks the water. New Zealander J. Roger Ironside is the man in charge; his call sign is *Jolly Roger.*

On the main street near the head of the dock is a huge tree decked out in Christmas bulbs, with a community bulletin board attached below. On the benches in its shade are usually a number of Brilanders passing the time (we were

The
Harbour Island
Club & Marina

A BOATING & SPORTSMAN'S PARADISE
Shower and Restrooms • 120/208 VAC 30/50 AMP power hook-up
Fuel Clean Filtered SHELL Gas and Diesel • Laundry Services
Full Dining Facilities within easy walking distance • Cocktail Lounge
32 Slips • Accommodates the Largest of Yachts
For additional information, please call Dockmaster

THE HARBOUR ISLAND CLUB & MARINA
P.O. BOX EL27183 • HARBOUR ISLAND, BAHAMAS
TEL./FAX: 242-333-2427

told this spot is called the House of Assembly).

There are several excellent restaurants on Harbour Island. Dick Malcolm, former owner of the Rock House, has opened Picaroon's Landing in Lady Solomon's house near the foot of the government dock. The Dunmore Beach Club is known for outstanding cuisine and ambience — dinner reservations are a must and best made by midday; the club monitors VHF 16 as a convenience for boaters. The Ocean View is another nice place (the Ocean View's owner, Pip, also has a tearoom in Temperance Square called Miss Mae's). Runaway Hill is a pretty 10-room country-inn kind of place on the beach, with a good restaurant. Coral Sands was recommended by a reader as a lovely setting for dinner. (Dinner reservations at most of these restaurants are required, and are a good idea in any case, especially in winter. Some places require jackets and ties, so you might want to inquire while making reservations to avoid a hike back to your boat.)

For more casual eating, Angela's Starfish Restaurant serves good food including tasty lobster salad. The vividly hued interior is decorated with green tinsel, mirrors, and starfish, and a sign prohibits profane language and bare backs. The menu is written on the blackboard up front — write down your order and have a seat. We enjoyed listening in on the good-natured bantering from the kitchen. Sometimes starfish-shaped cookies are for sale. C&G Restaurant serves lunch and dinner, with good subs, sandwiches, and fish'n'chips. The Harbour Lounge serves lunch and dinner, and you can get snacks at The Shack, at the foot of the government dock.

You can buy groceries at the Pigly-Wigly, Tip Top, Johnson's, or Sawyer's. Next to the Pigly-Wigly, a shop sells Androsia batiked clothing. Frank's Art Gallery, near Valentine's, has island crafts, town maps, sequined hats, and souvenirs for sale. Sanya's "De Islun' Music Mart & Musicational Centre," owned by schoolteacher Donald Sawyer ("The Music Giant") sells music tapes and also instruments and music lessons in case you might want to emulate Jimmy Buffett in your travels.

The nightclub where everybody goes is Sea Grapes on Colebrook Street, owned by the reggae-rock band, the Funk Gang. Also popular are JJ's Tavern, Vick-Um's, a local hangout, or Willie's or Gustey's Tavern (with a sand floor) for shooting pool and drinking beer. Local entertainers make the rounds to various spots around town weekly.

Pink sand beach, Harbour Island. (Tropic Isle photo)

The Glass Window bridge, with the Bight in the foreground. (Tropic Isle photo)

ELEUTHERA

D.M.A. Charts: 26299, 26300, 26305, 26306, 26307, 26279, 26280. N.O.S. Chart: 11013. Tropic Isle Sketch Charts: E-14, 15, 16, 17, 18, 19, 20, 21, 22, 23.

Eleuthera, which lies at its nearest point some 30 miles northeast of Nassau, is undoubtedly one of the most beautiful islands in The Bahamas. From north to south it is approximately 90 miles long and, in most places, little more than 2 or 3 miles wide except at the extreme northern and southern ends. For the most part the countryside consists of rolling hills and valleys studded with tranquil lakes and woodlands, in places strongly reminiscent of Scotland or, at any rate, a more northern clime. The coasts alternate between high steep cliffs and stunning beaches. There are a several settlements on the island and at least three good harbors.

Eleuthera was first settled in 1649 when a band of 100 persons and two clergymen arrived from England and Bermuda. Under the Governorship of Captain William Sayle, this party, known as the Eleutherian Adventurers, set up what was probably the first true democracy of the Western world. The life led by the Adventurers was by no means easy. They had to contend with the depredations of the Spaniards and the attentions of pirates in addition to the trials of establishing themselves in a virgin country.

Eleuthera has always been largely agricultural and was once a pineapple growing center, shipping thousands of tons annually to America and England. The pineapple business has declined, but large crops of pineapples, tomatoes,

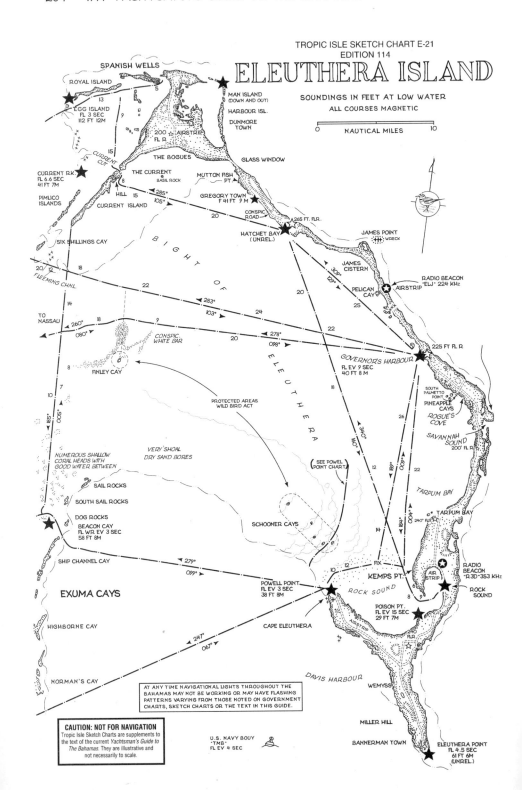

TROPIC ISLE SKETCH CHART E-21
EDITION 114

ELEUTHERA ISLAND

SOUNDINGS IN FEET AT LOW WATER
ALL COURSES MAGNETIC

NAUTICAL MILES
0   10

CAUTION: NOT FOR NAVIGATION
Tropic Isle Sketch Charts are supplements to
the text of the current *Yachtsman's Guide to
The Bahamas.* They are illustrative and
not necessarily to scale.

AT ANY TIME NAVIGATIONAL LIGHTS THROUGHOUT THE
BAHAMAS MAY NOT BE WORKING OR MAY HAVE FLASHING
PATTERNS VARYING FROM THOSE NOTED ON GOVERNMENT
CHARTS, SKETCH CHARTS OR THE TEXT IN THIS GUIDE.

U.S. NAVY BUOY
"TMB"
FL EV 4 SEC

> **PLEASE NOTE:** *For a description of* **Batelco towers in all areas and their light characteristics,** *please check page 39 of this Guide.*

citrus, and corn are still shipped to the Nassau market. At one time, Hatchet Bay was the location of the largest dairy and stock-raising enterprise in the islands.

Roads are excellent and taxi service throughout Eleuthera efficient indeed, with drivers are equipped with radios, business cards and memorable monikers.

The coast of Eleuthera is described here according to the usual course taken by yachts visiting the island from Nassau: starting at the southern end of Current Island and working eastward along the Bight. There is very little shelter available along the Eleuthera coast between Hatchet Bay and Governor's Harbour from any except prevailing winds.

Current Island itself is low, undulating, and covered with thick scrub and palmetto. There are one or two primitive settlements on the island. There is 9-12 feet of water close in along its eastern shore for its entire length to Current Cut. The Cut from the east is easy to discern as the settlement of **The Current** itself may be distinguished by a conspicuous stand of casuarinas. (Please refer to the chapter in this *Guide* on "Cays to Eleuthera" for more detailed information on The Current.)

There are some interesting settlements on the northern part of Eleuthera where the land spreads out in a triangular shape above the Glass Window. On the road leading into **The Bluff**, a sign reads "Town of Smiling People." It's an affably sleepy place where young girls with colorfully beaded hair play together in the shade of front porches. Some of the houses have incredible gardens decorated with statuary, conch shells, Christmas lights, bird baths and flamingos. There is a dry goods and hardware store, and the local gathering spot is Kemb's Club. The settlements of **Lower and Upper Bogue** are small, with the coastline offering no protection in the prevailing winds. The name "Bogue" apparently is a derivative of "bog." The area was established after emancipation of the slaves, who took advantage of the large amount of common land available here at the time. Lower Bogue is the larger of the two towns, with several hundred people and lots of sociable roadside activity going on. Lady B's Life-Saver Restaurant serves good cracked conch, and the Seven Seas Restaurant advertises a happy hour every Sunday and nightly disco.

About 2 miles east of Upper Bogue is a striking rock formation known as the **Glass Window.** Here the land, high on either side, falls away abruptly to nearly sea level, for all practical purposes dividing the island in two. The Glass

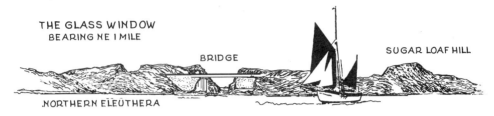

THE GLASS WINDOW
BEARING NE 1 MILE

BRIDGE

SUGAR LOAF HILL

NORTHERN ELEUTHERA

Window is framed by a bridge that connects northern and southern Eleuthera by hard road. The view from the bridge is unique and quite striking, with the restless dark Atlantic Ocean immediately to the east and the serene emerald water of the Bight to the west.

As a spectacular reminder that rage conditions can occur without any wind because they're often caused by storms hundreds of miles away in the Atlantic, on Halloween Day of 1991 a huge rogue wave knocked the Glass Window bridge askew by 7 feet. This was the same rage that knocked a hole in the jetty at the west end of Paradise Island, and which also did huge amounts of damage from Florida to New England. In most of the these places, the weather was beautiful and calm while the beach areas were being pounded to pieces.

Southeast of Mutton Fish Point, the coastline becomes high with sheer cliffs rising to 60 feet.

Gregory Town is a small, picturesque village at the head of a narrow, deep cleft in the cliffs. But for the palms, the winding roads and abrupt hills make it a bit reminiscent of a Cornish village. Gregory Town is well worth a visit, but the ever-present surge and poor holding (thin, soft sand and mud over smooth rock) make anchoring in the cove overnight unsafe. However, it's just a short taxi ride from Hatchet Bay or excursion from Harbour Island. Several guest houses and small resorts in the area, some on the beach, can provide overnight accommodations. The town is favored by Europeans and surfers. Gregory Town's famous pineapple crop has declined over the years, but you'll still find fragrant stacks of the fruit for sale on front porches, and local pineapple rum can be purchased. Across the street from Thompson Bros. Supermarket is Jay's Laundromat. Monica and Daisy Thompson at Thompson's Bakery, at the top of the hill, make locally famous fresh bread, pies, tarts, and cakes using exotic homegrown fruits (they also serve hamburgers, sandwiches, and pizza). Gregory and Pamela Thompson's Island Made Gift Shop has a fascinating variety of Bahamian arts and crafts, shells, jewelry, dolls, T-shirts, miscellaneous found objects, and Pamela's hand-painted driftwood and clothing. Elvina's Restaurant

Gregory Town. (Tropic Isle photo)

Entrance to Hatchet Bay. (Tropic Isle photo)

and Bar (popular with surfers) has a pool table, satellite TV, car rentals, and the New Gems Washerteria. The restaurant at Cambridge Villas features good island cooking and weekend disco nights. On the road to Hatchet Bay, Cush's Place serves breakfast, lunch, and dinner and features entertainment by owner and calypso artist Dr. Seabreeze.

Between Gregory Town and Hatchet Bay, 5 miles south, the coast continues high and precipitous with many weird formations eroded into the limestone cliffs. Inland the countryside is rolling pasture with a number of new houses and several prominent stone silos (once used for feed for a large plantation that raised Angus cattle, now abandoned). These, coupled with the land scars just to their north, make excellent landmarks when steering for Hatchet Bay from Nassau. There is a noticeable absence of shoreside buildings along the 2-mile coast immediately north of Hatchet Bay.

Hatchet Bay offers protection in almost any weather. The entrance is not always easy to pick up from offshore. The white silos mentioned above make a good reference, as the entrance lies several miles eastward of the easternmost pair. A conspicuous hill lies behind the entrance, and around it is a dense stand of casuarinas. A light tower with a weak light stands on the west side of the cut, but the 265-foot Batelco tower in town is now a more prominent landmark. A course of 050° on this tower will lead you just about right to the entrance.

Hatchet Bay's entrance, artificially cut through the sheer cliffs, is 90 feet wide but looks less. Inside, two rough stone breakwaters extend for a short distance, terminating in black wooden piles that show little above high water. All the anchorages here are grassy and poor holding. If staying overnight, especially if sheltering from bad weather, set your anchor with special care or pick up one of the Marine Service of Eleuthera's moorings (check availability of moorings or dock space by calling *Marine Services of Eleuthera* or *Hatchet Bay* on VHF 16). Do not anchor off **Alice Town**, where you would be in the channel for the Nassau freight boats that come and go at all hours, day and night. They dock at the finger that juts out on the east side of Marine Service of Eleuthera's docks.

CLIFFS   OLD LIGHT TOWER (UNREL.)   265 FT FL R

ROCKS   ROCKS
ENTRANCE 020° ⅓ MILE

ENTRANCE TO HATCHET BAY

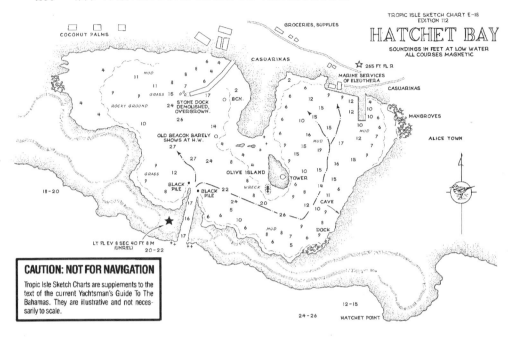

Marine Service of Eleuthera operates Eleuthera Bahamas Charters' fleet of power and sailing vessels as well as Charter Cats of the Bahamas. Fuel, water, electric hookups and miscellaneous supplies are available, and parts can be flown in duty-free. A 50-ton crane can lift boats up to about 45 feet. Red Rolle's Harbour View restaurant here serves breakfast and dinner by reservation as well as lunch (no reservation required), specializing in seafood and other Bahamian specialties. On weekend nights it can be noisy, which must mean it's a happening kind of a place. Across the street is Evan Sawyer's grocery and hardware store, next to a liquor store, and Lutra Water can provide ice and water. The people at Marine Service of Eleuthera can make suggestions and help you arrange car rental or other transportation to restaurants and night spots in Gregory Town or elsewhere. The August Monday Hatchet Bay Fest features informal sailboat

Hatchet Bay. (Tropic Isle photo)

and dinghy races, food, music, and beer.

In Alice Town are some small grocery stores, a liquor store, a laundromat, and a telephone exchange. Josephine Johnson bakes tasty bread. Seasonal fruit and produce are sold by the case at a nearby packing plant. On some mornings, local trucks bring fresh fish or produce down to the dock; listen to VHF 16 for announcements. The Forget Me Not often has weekend fish fries and sells gasoline. Marilyn's Take Out sells food to go, and Miss Adderley's Ice Cream Parlor also has good hamburgers. If you like caves, there are two north of town worth a visit. They shelter thousands of bats, prolific producers of guano, so watch your step. There is also a beach, internationally famous among surfers, on the Atlantic side about 3 miles north of Hatchet Bay.

Two and a half miles south of Hatchet Bay, the Rainbow Inn's excellent restaurant has a lovely view of the sea and a bar with frequent entertainment. Comfortable efficiencies are available in octagonal bungalows (now one-story instead of two, courtesy of Hurricane Andrew). A few miles south, Bernard Bethel's Big Rock General Store has everything from groceries and homegrown vegetables to bicycles and washer/driers. Delivery is available to yachtsmen, with a certain minimum order.

Between Hatchet Bay and Governor's Harbour, 16 miles to the southeast, deep water runs close inshore. There are several attractive bays and beaches sheltered by high land. The little settlement of **James Cistern** has no facilities for yachtsmen, but is worth visiting by land if you have the time. The ladies barbecuing chicken on the beach might offer some for sale to passersby, and bread is baked in old Dutch ovens behind the houses up the hill. Just north of town is a general store. When we passed through town, twenty or so young children equipped with cutlasses were poking up trash along the road, part of Eleuthera's remarkable cleanup campaign.

In strong westerly conditions, boats can find protection under **Pelican Cay.** The mainland behind Pelican Cay is the former site of a U.S. missile tracking system, now maintained by the Bahamian government.

GOVERNORS HARBOUR · VIEW OF APPROACH FROM THE N.W.

Governor's Harbour, with its houses straggling from the hilltop to the water's edge, can be seen from a considerable distance. As you approach, **Cupid's Cay** will become visible. It is said that the original headquarters of the Eleutherian Adventurers were built on the cay, now joined to the mainland by a narrow causeway. Some examples of early Colonial architecture still exist, now in a state of disrepair.

Governor's Harbour is easy of access. The western end of Cupid's Cay may be passed close-to, as deep water runs right up to the rocks. On the north side of Cupid's Cay are cruise-ship docks, although so far mostly freight boats use

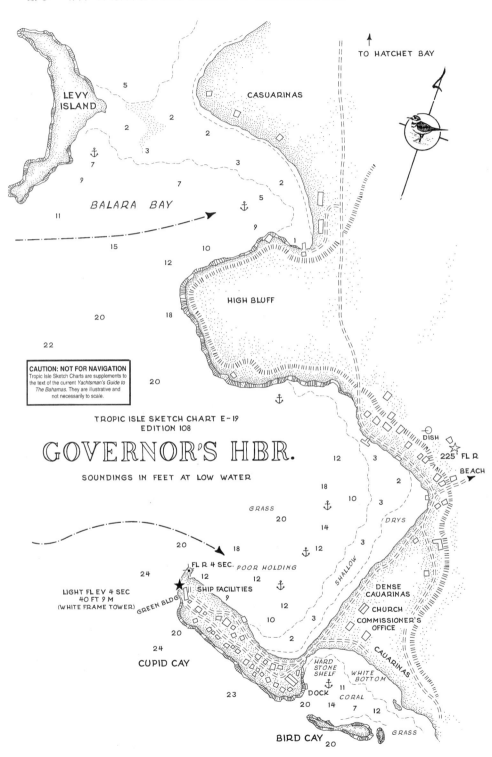

TO HATCHET BAY

LEVY ISLAND

CASUARINAS

5

2

2

3

2

7

9

7

BALARA BAY

5

11

9

15

10

12

1

20

18

HIGH BLUFF

22

CAUTION: NOT FOR NAVIGATION
Tropic Isle Sketch Charts are supplements to
the text of the current *Yachtsman's Guide to
The Bahamas*. They are illustrative and
not necessarily to scale.

20

TROPIC ISLE SKETCH CHART E-19
EDITION 108

GOVERNOR'S HBR.

SOUNDINGS IN FEET AT LOW WATER

DISH

225 FL R

BEACH

12   3

2

18

10   3

GRASS

20

DRYS

14

SHALLOW

12   3

20

18

FL R 4 SEC. POOR HOLDING

24

12

12

DENSE
CASUARINAS

LIGHT FL EV 4 SEC
40 FT 9 M
(WHITE FRAME TOWER)

SHIP FACILITIES

9

CHURCH

GREEN BLDG

COMMISSIONER'S
OFFICE

10   3

20

2

CASUARINAS

24

CUPID CAY

HARD
STONE
SHELF

WHITE
BOTTOM

23

DOCK

11

20   14   7   12

CORAL

GRASS

BIRD CAY   20

Cupid's Cay. (Tropic Isle photo)

them. Anchorage may be found anywhere in the dark water (grassy bottom) in 12-18 feet. Toward the causeway and the church, the bottom gives way to white shallows. Unfortunately this anchorage, delightful under prevailing conditions, is exposed to the west and northwest, and the holding is poor — shallow sand over rock. A few years ago a number of moorings were set here and in the anchorage east of Cupid's Cay. There may be one or two of these left, but we have a number of letters warning that they have deteriorated to the point that they are hazardous, and boats have broken loose from them and gone ashore with severe damage. We strongly advise against using any of these moorings that might remain in either harbor. Another problem here that we've had letters about is the Club Med ski boats that "drive you crazy as they incessantly buzz the moored boats," to quote one of the letters.

Because of the exposure of this anchorage, you might want to shift to the anchorage under Levy Island, 7 feet over sand, when frontal (westerly) winter weather approaches. The anchorage east of Cupid's Cay is reported rocky and poor holding, but it offers the most protection in north to northwest winds between Rock Sound and Hatchet Bay. (Do not venture into the white water, which is shallow, or too far southeast, where the bottom becomes foul with coral.) In this anchorage there are still a few of the old moorings described in the previous paragraph. We repeat that these have deteriorated to the point that they are hazardous, and we advise against using them. A mild surge usually persists in all of these anchorages. In strong westerly conditions, some yachtsmen prefer to anchor under Pelican Cay, previously mentioned.

In Governor's Harbour you'll find groceries, frozen foods, dairy products

Governor's Harbour. (Tropic Isle photo)

and liquors for sale, a post office, bank, a clinic with resident doctor and dentist, and a telephone station up the hill. Near the traffic light, Eleuthera Supply has groceries, and hamburgers are sold out of Winkie's Wagon. Norma's Gift Shop, next to the police station, sells T-shirts, handmade clothing, jewelry and souvenirs. The Gift Place, on the corner of Queen's Highway and Haynes Avenue, has fine T-shirts, prints, paintings, and books on The Bahamas for sale in its tiny gallery-like shop (also film, postcards, and suntan lotion). At the movie theatre, a short walk east of town, you can watch two movies any night and eat popcorn, ice cream, or even conch salad. Two car rentals, Highway George and Johnson's Service Station, are up the hill just before the movie theatre. The Harbour Inn on Cupid's Cay sells drinks and food, not fancy but with a lot of local flavor. Down the hill from the Batelco station, you can order Italian cuisine at the Picchio restaurant. The Sunset Inn advertises breakfast, lunch, and dinner daily, a Bahamian menu (Saturday souse/Sunday stewfish), a variety of beers, and a pool table. About three miles north of town, the Kohinoor specializes in good Bahamian and international dishes.

Across the island on the town's ocean shore is a beautiful beach protected from swells by the outlying reef, a near-perfect site for the Club Med located there. Visitors can book a room for the night on a space-available basis. For the price of lunch, you can spend the afternoon and participate in all water sports offered at the Club Med marina on the Governor's Harbour side of town. The dinner price includes a show put on by the staff and disco. It is necessary to make arrangements for any of this ahead if time.

Between Governor's Harbour and the rocks off Tarpum Bay, deep water runs close to shore and there are no dangerous reefs or shoals. Some protection can be gained by anchoring in the lee of the Pineapple Cays (over a rocky bottom). Nearby, **Rogue's Cove** is a tiny harbor (8-10 feet LW), too small for anchoring and really only good for dinghies. Some rough concrete docks here look like they should be avoided. A short walk from **Palmetto Point**'s long pier

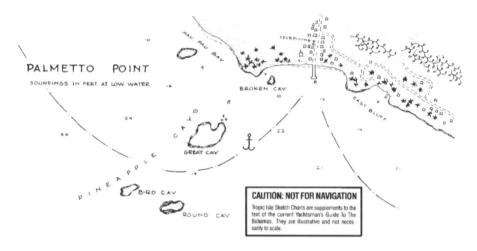

CAUTION: NOT FOR NAVIGATION
Tropic Isle Sketch Charts are supplements to the
text of the current Yachtsman's Guide To The
Bahamas. They are illustrative and not necessarily to scale.

(8 feet at low water) are grocery and dry-good shops, with a coin laundry a couple miles west of the dock. Mate and Jenny's Pizza Shack, famous for conch pizza, has a pool table. At North Palmetto Point, the Unique Village Restaurant & Lounge is open daily for lunch and dinner, with a Sunday brunch. Apartments and villas are available on the beach.

On approaching the settlement of **Tarpum Bay,** there is a long line of off-lying rocks to the northeast, a little less than half a mile from the shore. Some of these are awash at high water. Tarpum Bay settlement itself, shaded by casuarinas, is a pretty, sleepy little village. Years ago it was the prosperous center of the pineapple trade, but today the pleasant, old-world houses drowse in the sun while occasional tourists snap pictures of the quaintly weathered ginger-bread. A quiet anchorage (rock and sand, difficult to get a good hold) may be found in prevailing conditions off the dock at Tarpum Bay. The dock itself looks inviting but only has about 3 feet alongside. Ashore are some restaurants, bars,

Palmetto Point. (Tropic Isle photo)

Tarpum Bay waterfront. (Tropic Isle photo)

and rooming houses, and there's a well-stocked grocery store and a hardware store within walking distance a bit inland east of the dock. If you don't have a lot of time but want to explore and pick up some provisions, local taxi drivers can guide you. In the evenings, fishermen sell their fresh catch at the dock.

The village has attracted artists and craftsmen, including Lord Gordon McMillan Hughes, artist and Bahamian history authority. His studio is across from Hilton's Haven, a small, nicely run guest house. About a block off the main street, near the water tanks, is the studio of American artist Mal Flanders. Near town is a new beachside resort, Club Eleuthera, with over 100 rooms and a restaurant/grill.

Tarpum Bay to Rock Sound: For a distance of 9 miles, vessels drawing 5 feet or more are advised to parallel the coast, standing at least one mile off all the way. There are many coral patches along this route, especially west and south of Kemp's Point (the westernmost point of shore) so good light and a sharp lookout are essential. At the fix where **Poison Point** bears 155°, take up that heading as indicated on sketch chart E-22 (Powell Point to Rock Sound), keeping a careful lookout. Off Sound Point a shallow bar extends a short distance southeast. On entering pass a little south of midway between the points for the best water, about 12 feet. After passing Starve Creek you may bear up for the government pier near the south end of Rock Sound settlement. Although 8 feet can be carried up to the anchorage off the settlement proper, yachts drawing 7 feet or over will probably prefer to lie in the southern part of the sound in 10-12 feet of water.

Two hundred yards off the settlement lies a shallow bank distinguishable in good light by pale grassy patches. It carries only 4-6 feet at low water. Better anchorage will be found in 8 feet marl between this bank and the settlement, or north of the government's concrete wharf. North of this point the water shallows progressively.

Rock Sound is one of the best places to stock up in this part of The Bahamas, with provisioning and hardware facilities as well as mechanical repair and welding services. The most convenient place to anchor is in 5 feet of water off the beach in back of Edwina Burrows' restaurant and cottages, a little north of the government dock. You can get water at the government dock but you'll need a 100-foot hose. Right off the dock, Ron's Marine and Auto Parts can do engine repairs, and Ron also sells sodas, fresh fruit, fresh conch salad, and perhaps some of the fine BBQ chicken he prepares for supply-boat workers. Connected to Ron's shop is an excellent new laundromat with reasonable prices. Around the corner from Edwina's is a shopping center, bank, and fuel pumps. Towards town, fresh fruit and vegetables are sold at Nat's produce stand (all grown on Nat's farm). The bakery in town sells great coconut tarts. A contributor wrote us to recommend The Almond Tree gift shop, which sells on consignment local handicrafts of excellent quality. The same contributor also was impressed by a New York-trained tailor in town who did a great patching job on her husband's well-worn jeans. Several ladies in town serve macaroni and cheese, chicken, peas 'n' rice, and cole slaw out of lunch vans. The Harbourview Restaurant and Lounge on the waterfront serves Bahamian food as well as burgers and snacks. Sammy's Place is popular for its homey atmosphere and inexpensive food, prepared by excellent cook and proprietress Kathleen Culmer, Sammy's wife. It's a short walk out of town, with signs to mark the way. Comfortable air-conditioned rooms are available, and Sammy's daughter Margaritta runs the boutique next door. The abandoned fuel dock about a mile north of town is a short walk from the Rock Sound Air Terminal.

The Cotton Bay Club (closed at this writing with indefinite plans to reopen), a 10-mile drive south of Rock Sound, has an 18-hole championship course designed by Robert Trent Jones. The club is a short drive north of Davis Harbour. Around June, watch hereabouts for the large dark moths locally called "money bats" — legend has it that if one lands on you, wealth awaits.

Approximately one mile east of Rock Sound is the famous "ocean hole." Any taxi driver knows the way. Although a considerable distance from either coast, this completely landlocked tidal lake is rumored to be bottomless. Fish find their way into it through subterranean tunnels from the sea.

Rock Sound to Powell Point: Unless you are experienced in picking your way through the numerous coral heads that litter the direct course between the mouth of Rock Sound and Powell Point, we recommend that you return to the fix off Kemp's Point and follow the courses outlined on sketch chart E-22 (Powell Point to Rock Sound). Remember, when you are at the fix, Sandy Cay and Powell Point are plainly open.

Immediately south of Powell Point lies Cape Eleuthera Marina. Diesel,

Cape Eleuthera Marina. (Tropic Isle photo)

TROPIC ISLE SKETCH CHART E-22
EDITION 114

POWELL POINT
TO
ROCK SOUND

SOUNDINGS IN FEET AT LOW WATER

ALL COURSES MAGNETIC

NAUTICAL MILES

CAUTION: NOT FOR NAVIGATION
Tropic Isle Sketch Charts are supplements to the text of the current Yachtsman's Guide to The Bahamas. They are illustrative and not necessarily to scale.

ROCK SOUND

ROCK SOUND

AIRSTRIP

ABANDONED FUEL DOCK

KEMP'S PT.

SOUND POINT

STARVE CREEK

POISON PT. FL EV 15 SEC 29 FT 7 M

PROMINENT HEADLAND

CORAL HEADS

HEADS WITH LESS THAN 2' AT L.W.

DISTANT BATELCO TOWER

NUMEROUS HEADS

BEARS 142°

BEARS 163°

TO GOVERNOR'S HARBOUR

TARPUM HEAD BEARS 047°

FIX

NOTE: APPROX. 4.2 MILES BETWEEN FIXES IN SHIP CHANNEL.

SOUTHERNMOST SCHOONER CAY BEARS 287°

A STRONG EBB TIDE WILL SET SLOW VESSELS ONTO N. BANK OF CHANNEL. COMPENSATE.

SHIP CHANNEL

SHIFTING SAND

CUL - DE - SAC 1 - 2

DRYS

DRYS

DRYS

22' MKR.

SANDY C.

KEEPING A SHARP LOOKOUT FOR HEADS IN GOOD LIGHT, 5 FT. CAN BE CARRIED ACROSS THIS BANK AT LOW WATER.

ROCKY SHOAL

GRASSY PATCHES

POWELL POINT FL EV 3 SEC 38 FT 8 M

AIRSTRIP (ABANDONED)

TO ROCK SOUND

CAPE ELEUTHERA

CHUB RK.

IN GOOD LT. 8' CAN BE CARRIED THROUGH TO THE BANKS BY FOLLOWING THE L. SIDE OF THE CH. UNTIL IT BECOMES INDISTINCT. THEN FOLLOW R. BANK UNTIL IN OPEN WATER. FROM THERE HATCHET B. BEARS 344°, GOVERNOR'S HBR, 034°.

PROTECTED AREA WILD BIRDS ACT

FOLLOW LEFT BANK GOING NORTH

THIRD SCHOONER CAY, ONE MILE

SCHOONER CAYS

TREES

DEEP CHANNEL

BEARS 336°

BEARS 197°

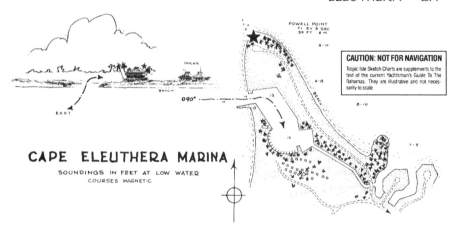

CAPE ELEUTHERA MARINA
SOUNDINGS IN FEET AT LOW WATER
COURSES MAGNETIC.

CAUTION: NOT FOR NAVIGATION
Tropic Isle Sketch Charts are supplements to the text of the current Yachtsman's Guide To The Bahamas. They are illustrative and not necessarily to scale

gasoline, and water are available, and electricity at some slips. There is a fee for tying up at the dock.

Continuing from Cape Eleuthera and proceeding south for less than a mile will bring you to an unnamed harbor that could provide shelter if necessary. It is part of Cape Eleuthera's property, and the management collects a fee for anchoring here. There can be, at times, a good number of bugs. Continuing, the coast south to Eleuthera Point is comprised mainly of low cliffs and long beaches.

Exuma Sound (north): Having completed their Eleuthera cruise at Cape Eleuthera, many yachtsmen return to Nassau by way of Exuma Sound, eliminating the necessity of retracing their course. From Cape Eleuthera a direct course may be steered for the north end of Ship Channel Cay. Before entering Ship Channel, work a bit north so the light on Beacon Cay can be kept on a 303° bearing (or in the red sector of the light at night) to pass safely between a 3-foot area south of the dog rocks and 5-foot area north of Bluff Cay. (We caution you not to do this at night and to use appropriate government charts for clarification.) When these shallow areas are no longer a factor, adjust your course to remain in the deep water north of Beacon Cay, or if proceeding south to Allan's Cay, pass east of the Bush Cays and South Rock (avoiding the very shallow sandbank that lies west of the north end of Ship Channel Cay), after which the best water will be found with the two Bush Cays in transit.

Cape Eleuthera
VHF Channel 16
DIESEL - GASOLINE - WATER - ICE
METERED ELECTRICITY
TEL: (242) 334-6327/ TEL & FAX: (242) 334-6326

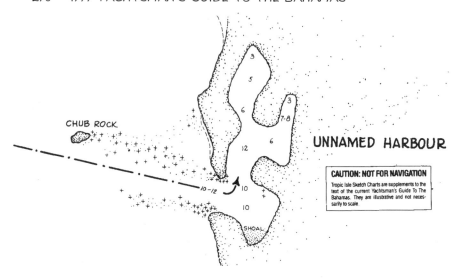

CHUB ROCK

UNNAMED HARBOUR

CAUTION: NOT FOR NAVIGATION
Tropic Isle Sketch Charts are supplements to the text of the current Yachtsman's Guide To The Bahamas. They are illustrative and not necessarily to scale.

SHOAL

A U.S. Navy buoy (Fl. ev. 4 secs. vis. 5 m) is stationed about 15 miles southwest of Cape Eleuthera. It has been reported to have shifted locations from time to time; if these reports are true, it is not of much use as a reference point when crossing Exuma Sound. Monitor VHF 16 when cruising here to be aware of U.S. Navy activities. If there are restrictions you haven't heard, you may be called and directed to make a course change.

Davis Harbour lies midway between Weymss Bight and a low sandpile one mile to the north. It is also marked by the highest stand of casuarinas in the area. Even with these directions it's hard to find because the coast in this area is rather featureless. It should help if you do some chart work to help locate the outer marker by means of distance made good from a known point. If approaching from the Exumas, whether using GPS or not, factoring in an offset might be a good idea. When approaching from Powell Point, the Exumas, or Eleuthera Point, be sure to enter the channel at the outer marker, which most recently is a radar reflector buoy about a mile offshore. Pass this to your starboard

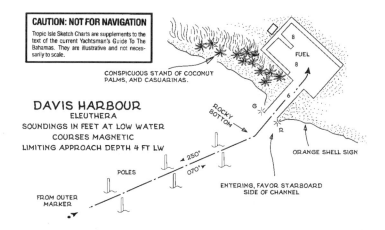

CAUTION: NOT FOR NAVIGATION
Tropic Isle Sketch Charts are supplements to the text of the current Yachtsman's Guide To The Bahamas. They are illustrative and not necessarily to scale.

FUEL

CONSPICUOUS STAND OF COCONUT PALMS, AND CASUARINAS.

DAVIS HARBOUR
ELEUTHERA
SOUNDINGS IN FEET AT LOW WATER
COURSES MAGNETIC
LIMITING APPROACH DEPTH 4 FT LW

ROCKY BOTTOM

POLES

250°
070°

ORANGE SHELL SIGN

ENTERING, FAVOR STARBOARD SIDE OF CHANNEL

FROM OUTER MARKER

Davis Harbour Marina
South Eleuthera

Davis Harbour has been a well-known boating facility for over 30 years. Located on the southern tip of Eleuthera, Davis Harbour is close to popular bone fishing and deep sea fishing areas. Private scenic view bar, barbeque and lounge deck. Walking distance to local bakery, restaurants, fast food carry out and craft shops. Easy cab ride to Rock Sound.

Recent expansions and refurbishing of Davis Harbour Marina ensures its standing as a first class facility.

PRIVATE
HOBO
YACHT CLUB
DAVIS HARBOUR, ELEUTHERA
PRIVATELY OWNED

- New Bar, lounge and TV deck
- Newly constructed dock
- Reinforced pilings
- Electrical meters and outlets
- Upgraded lighting
- Fresh water reverse osmosis system
- Fuel supplied by Shell Oil Company
- 1998 dredging provides 7' MLT deep entrance channel
- Marker buoy for entrance - GPS - Lat/Lon 24 43.78 76° 13.99

Dockmaster - Delroy Richards
Davis Harbour Marina • P.O. Box 28 • Rock Sound, Eleuthera, Bahamas
Phone 242 334-6303 / FAX 242 334-6396 / E-Mail 242 334-6397

Davis Harbour. (Tropic Isle photo)

and proceed toward the entrance jetties on about a 70° heading; a Shell sign above the casuarinas may be your best landmark. Just outside the jetties are several stakes marking the channel to the entrance. This approach has been dredged, but there is a spot toward the outer marker that still has only about 5 feet at low water, so this is the controlling depth. Once inside you have 8 feet in a well-protected marina, with fuels, water, ice and electricity. Recent improvements include a new dockmaster's office and desalinization plant, showers, a laundromat, and 24-hour security. The marina monitors VHF 16; Delroy Richards is the dockmaster.

Between Powell Point and Eleuthera Point, anchorage may be found in a number of places along the coast in prevailing winds, but caution is advised in approaching the land as rocky shelves extend some distance offshore. Off Eleuthera Point are several conspicuous rocks, and shoals extend for a consid-

"It's not a lobster, Harry! Just get the damn Guide and find out if it's dinner or if we are!"

YACHTSMAN'S
Guide to the **Virgin Islands**
Over 300 pages of indispensable information including 16 pages of full color aerial photos.

Call (305) 893-4277
Or write to: Tropic Isle Publishers
P.O. Box 610938, North Miami, FL 33261-0938

erable distance to the south and southeast of it. A minimum berth of 2 miles is advised while rounding this point.

There are several small settlements in this area, convenient to both Cape Eleuthera and Davis Harbour. **Green Castle,** the largest, has grocery stores, a drug store, a liquor store, and various restaurants and clubs. In **Deep Creek**, between Davis Harbour and Cape Eleuthera, you can get excellent Bahamian cooking at Sheryl's Inn. Her cracked conch and peas 'n' rice are especially well-prepared, and the place is neat and inviting, with crisp white tablecloths and a sign over the bar: "Absolutely no hustling or swearing." You can buy beer or other beverages at the store across the street. Another place to eat nearby is Bertha's Go Go Ribs. Shops sell groceries and notions. Other towns include **Freetown** and **Weymss Bight** (pronounced *Wims' es*), where there's a gas station and an air-conditioned restaurant called Mary's Place, serving Bahamian food, wine, and beer. At **Bannerman Town,** there are a few houses, some makeshift basketball hoops and, where the power line ends, the majestic remains of a church. A cruise ship now stops at Bannerman Town, and the red roofs of its shoreside facilities are something of a landmark. In the area surrounding these villages are several creeks with good bonefishing.

You can visit remote Eleuthera Point by way of a rocky unpaved road of several miles. There is an old uninhabited lighthouse, renovated by the Raleigh Expedition in 1968, and the ruins of a cookhouse. Spectacular cliffs and beaches surround the point, with natural gardens of palms and shrubs growing at the base of beautiful wind-sculptured rock formations. At sea level there are some shallow caves. From the cliff tops you can see Little San Salvador and perhaps Cat Island. Be careful to avoid the crumbling edges of the rocks; the drop-off is 60 or 70 feet.

Bannerman Town cruise-ship facilities. (Tropic Isle photo)

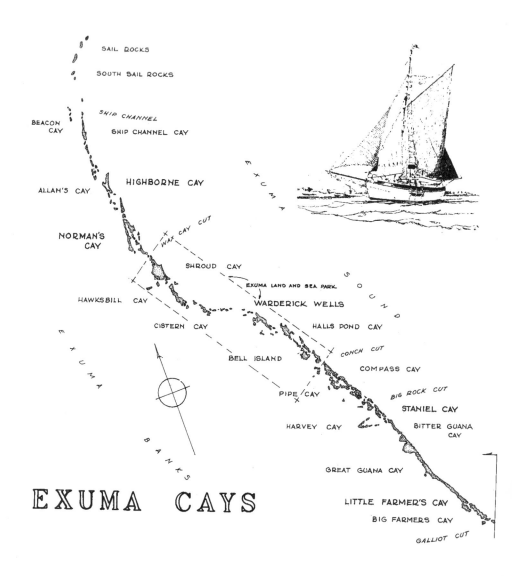

EXUMA CAYS

D.M.A. Charts: 26253, 26257, 26286, 26303, 26305. N.O.S. Chart: 11013.
Tropic Isle Sketch Charts: J-35, 36, 37, 38, 39, 40, 41, 42, 43, 44, 45, 46.

The Exuma Cays sweep in an almost unbroken chain from Beacon Cay in the north to the islands of Great and Little Exuma in the south, a distance of over 90 miles. They form possibly the most exquisite cruising ground in the western hemisphere. Local lore has it that there are 365 cays in the Exuma group, with some of the most beautiful anchorages and harbors possible to find anywhere. Settlements are few and far between. Most are small, picturesque, and rather primitive, and the people are friendly and courteous.

The cays themselves vary in size. Some are low and barren; others, like Highborne Cay, have rolling hills covered with dense vegetation and small trees. Almost all have beautiful beaches and snug anchorages. The water is crystal-clear and the vivid colors, on a normal bright day with a moderate trade wind ruffling the surface, cannot be adequately described. You must see for yourself.

Beneath the surface are exquisite coral formations alive with brilliant, darting schools of fish. A mask and snorkel will allow you to spend hours watching the exotic other world that lies a fathom or two under your keel.

Fishing of all kinds is excellent. A hand line and a piece of conch or a trolling line with a feather lure will get you all the fish you need. There are usually plenty of crawfish under ledges and around coral heads.

The Exuma Cays Land and Sea Park, founded and administered by The Bahamas National Trust, extends from the center of Wax Cay Cut in the north to the center of Conch Cut in the south where it includes the Rocky Dundas — an area some 22 miles long by 8 miles wide. The side borders are generally 3-5 miles offshore. The park has been set aside as a replenishment, restoration, and nursery area. There is no taking by any means of marine, plant, or animal life, whether living, dead, or fossilized (beachcombing for shells, etc., is prohibited).

Ray Darville, Exuma Cays Land and Sea Park warden, offers assistance and information to park visitors, enforces Bahamas National Trust regulations and wildlife laws, patrols the park, and inspects facilities. He monitors VHF 16 from park headquarters at Warderick Wells and asks that you contact him by radio before entering North Warderick Wells anchorage. Anchoring is not permitted at the North Warderick Wells anchorage. It is permitted at the Hog

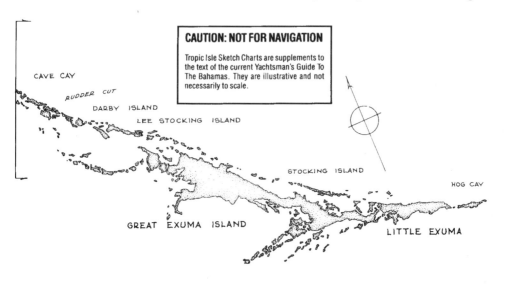

Cay anchorage at the south end of Warderick Wells. There is daily user fee of $5 (per day) to anchor in the Park. Mooring fees are $15 per day for boats up to 45 feet LOA, $20 per day for boats from 45-55 feet LOA, $30 per day for boats 55-70 feet LOA, $50 per day for boats 70-90 feet LOA, and $100 a day for boats over 90 feet LOA. Moorings are rated for 30 m.p.h. winds; moor at your own risk. If you damage a mooring, please report it to park management.

Birds thrive on all but the smallest cays. The Bahamas mockingbird, the Bahama bananaquit, and seabirds, particularly terns and waders, are most common. Even the elegant, long-tailed tropicbird nests on most of the cays with

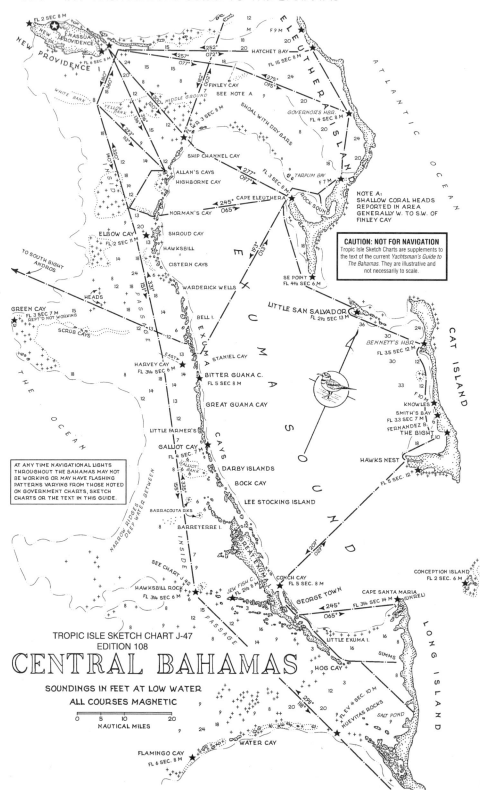

NOTE A:
SHALLOW CORAL HEADS
REPORTED IN AREA
GENERALLY W. TO S.W. OF
FINLEY CAY

CAUTION: NOT FOR NAVIGATION
Tropic Isle Sketch Charts are supplements to
the text of the current *Yachtsman's Guide to
The Bahamas*. They are illustrative and
not necessarily to scale.

AT ANY TIME NAVIGATIONAL LIGHTS
THROUGHOUT THE BAHAMAS MAY NOT
BE WORKING OR MAY HAVE FLASHING
PATTERNS VARYING FROM THOSE NOTED
ON GOVERNMENT CHARTS, SKETCH
CHARTS OR THE TEXT IN THIS GUIDE.

TROPIC ISLE SKETCH CHART J-47
EDITION 108

CENTRAL BAHAMAS

SOUNDINGS IN FEET AT LOW WATER
ALL COURSES MAGNETIC

0   5   10   20
NAUTICAL MILES

high bluffs on the ocean side. Large lizards you might spot are the curly tails (Leiouphalus), the blue-tailed ameivas, and several species of anoles. A few iguanas also now live on Warderick Wells (all iguanas in The Bahamas are protected by law and may not be captured, killed, or exported). Underwater, the abundance of hard and soft coral reefs provide food and shelter for countless reef fish, including wrasse, grunts, snappers, demoiselles, parrotfish, grouper, basslets, angelfish, butterflyfish, triggerfish, gobies, trumpetfish, and goatfish.

On several cays are mailboxes containing Natural Trust information and membership application forms. Please take this literature and join the National Trust, contributing to their continuing effort to make this cruising area so special.

Routes to the Exuma Cays: There are two most commonly used routes to the Exuma Cays. Whichever you choose, we strongly recommend taking your departure from the starting point where Porgee Rock bears 280°, and is distant 2 miles. Familiarize yourself with DMA Chart 26306, which shows the series of heads that lie eastward of New Providence. The purpose of beginning at the above described starting point where Porgee Rock bears 280°, distant 2 miles, is to take you clear of this bad area. Returning from the Exumas, again look at DMA chart 26306, and make sure you stay clear of the foul area.

Route 1: From the above described starting point, most yachts proceed to the Exuma Cays across the Yellow Bank, an area besprinkled with coral heads, some of which have only 3 feet of water over them. However, there is usually from 9-12 feet of water between heads, allowing ample space to steer around them. We recommend that you plan to leave Nassau so that you arrive on the Yellow Bank no earlier than 11:00 a.m.; before that, the sun will be low and ahead of you, and heads will be invisible until you are almost on them. Keep in mind that coral heads might be found in many places on the banks, even if they're not shown on charts, sketch charts, or in this *Guide.* It would be very dangerous to assume you can pass over coral heads, even if you might have found, at one time or another, that you can pass over some of them.

Caution: We've spoken to someone who told us of having hit a coral head in the area generally west to southwest of Finley Cay while en route from Beacon Cay to the south tip of Current Island. He was in a sailboat drawing 5 feet. Another described a close encounter, in the same general area, although not actual contact with "one enormous patch which appeared to be just below the surface." More recently a writer told us of having run aground on the 4-foot spot, shown on DMA chart 26306, which lies about 73°, 1.2 miles off East End Point, New Providence, and about the same distance south-southeast of Porgee Rock. Keep a watch and use government charts to check all your courses for hazards.

Taking the direct course, a vessel up to 6 feet in draft and with sufficient power to make the 34-mile run from Nassau to Allan's Cay in 5-6 hours could

Notice to Yachtsmen: *While enjoying the privilege of cruising Bahamian waters, please be aware of your responsibility in keeping these islands clean for future visits. Do not dispose of garbage over the shallow Bahama Banks or on the uninhabited islands and cays. Many marinas or settlements maintain disposal sites. Use them!*

Bahamas National Trust
Rules of the Exuma Cays Land and Sea Park

Bylaws made by the Trust under the Bahamas National Trust Act (Section 24) are summarized as follows:

1. The bylaws operate in conjunction with all other laws of The Bahamas (such as the Wild Birds Protection Act).

2. The Park has been designated as a marine replenishment area and nursery for the entire Bahamas, therefore the capture and/or removal of any fish, turtle, crawfish, conch, or whelk from the Park is prohibited.

3. The destruction, injury, or removal of any living or dead plant life, beach sand, corals, sea fans, or gorgonians from the Park is prohibited.

4. The molestation, injury, or destruction of any land animal or bird life, or the eggs of any animal or bird is prohibited, as is the use of nets or snares for the taking or destruction of any animal or bird life in the Park.

5. Permission may be granted in individual instances for the capture and/or removal of a designated number of land or sea animals and/or plants required for valid scientific research. In each instance the scientific institution concerned must obtain a permit from the Trust prior to capture or removal of the specimens.

6. Dumping of any wastes, oil, or rubbish, either on land or in the sea is prohibited. See section of this Guide on What the Skipper Should Know, Garbage disposal. See also the Bahamas National Trust garbage disposal brochure (available in Park mailboxes and at customs offices.).

7. No person shall injure, deface, or remove any building, structure, sign, ruins, or other artifacts within the Park.

8. The posting of any sign, placard, advertisement, or notice within the Park is prohibited, as is the erection of any building, shed, tent, or other structure.

9. No person shall display, use, fire or discharge any explosives, firearm, harpoon gun, spear or other fishing apparatus within the Park.

10. These bylaws do not affect the rights of any person acting legally by virtue of some estate, right or interest in, over or affecting the lands and submarine areas of the Park (i.e. privately owned cays.).

11. Willful obstruction, disturbance or annoyance of anyone in the proper use of the lands and submarine areas, or of any officer of the Bahamas National Trust in the exercise of his or her duties is prohibited.

12. Anyone charged with an offence against any of these bylaws shall be liable on summary conviction to a penalty not exceeding $500 and to the confiscation of any boat, vessel, or aircraft and all equipment, stores, provisions, or other effects used for the purpose of committing the offence.

13. The Park is bounded by lines joining: (1) lat 24° 30' 37"N, lon 76° 52' 37"W; (2) lat 24° 35' 30"N, lon 76° 45' 50"W; (3) lat 24° 18' 37"N, lon 76° 28' 47"W; (4) lat 24° 14' 25"N, lon 76° 36' 01"W respectively.

BAHAMAS NATIONAL TRUST...

•Is the only national non-governmental organization in the Bahamas for resource conservation and preservation.

•Plays a leading role in advising government on environmental and development issues.

• Manages the entire national park system of the country

• Is a leader in historic preservation and restoration initiatives

• Promotes educational programmes that bring greater environmmental awareness to all Bahamians

The Bahamas National Trust is fighting to protect the natural and historic resources of the Bahamas

❑ I enclose a donation of $ _____ to further the work of **THE BAHAMAS NATIONAL TRUST**.

❑ I wish to become a member of **THE BAHAMAS NATIONAL TRUST**. Please send me membership forms.

❑ Please send me further details on the work of **THE BAHAMAS NATIONAL TRUST**.

Name _____

Address _____

_____

FOR U.S. TAX PURPOSES MAKE CHECK PAYABLE TO:
ENVIRONMENTAL SYSTEMS PROTECTION FUND

The Bahamas National Trust, P.O. Box N-4105, Nassau, Bahamas

CENTER FOR WHALE RESEARCH, INC.

ATTENTION YACHTSMEN

The **Bahamas Marine Mammal Survey Team** needs you! Please report ANY sightings of dolphins, whales, manatees or even seals seen in the Bahamas or adjacent waters. Preliminary survey work done in 1991 provided important information on the distribution and abundance of these magnificent mammals, including sightings of rare whales and dolphins. The extensive area covered by yachtsmen offers the survey greater sighting success, so keep a keen eye out for the tell-tale signs of these leviathans (dorsal fins, flukes, distant blows). When crossing deep channels, one can expect to see pilot whales, beaked whales, sperm whales and other toothed whales, as well as humpback whales during their migration north or south each spring and fall. When on the shallow banks, bottlenose and spotted dolphins are abundant and often interact with vessels. When an animal is sighted, be very observant (take photographs if possible), and complete the attached sighting form. Please mail it to: Marine Mammal Survey, The Bahamas National Trust (BNT), P.O. Box 4105, Nassau, Bahamas. (Contact BNT for information on radio net reporting.) Thank you for your help... Together we can learn more about the fellow inhabitants of these waters.

— — — — — — — — — — Detach and mail — — — — — — — — — — —

IT IS IMPORTANT TO NOTE THE FOLLOWING:

Location:	**Time:**
Date:	**Number of animals:**
Species:	**Colour(s):**
Size (in feet):	**Striped?:**
Comments:	**Spotted?:**

Pilot Whale
12-20 feet
Black

Beaked Whale
16-25 feet
Brown/grey

Sperm Whale
40-60 feet
Brown

Dolphin
7-14 feet
Grey

Humpback Whale
25-45 feet
Black

Submitted by:
Name:_____
Street:_____
City:_____
State:_____Country:_____
☐ Please send more information on the
marine mammals of the Bahamas.

leave Nassau about 9:00 a.m., cross the Yellow Bank shortly after midday, and arrive at Allan's Cay in late afternoon.

Route 2: Sailboats and auxiliaries should begin at the above described starting point and, to avoid the foul water east of New Providence, work around east of it to a position 2 miles south-southeast of Porgee Rock. From here, they can steer 180° for 11 miles to a junction of the **White and Yellow Banks,** thence 113° for 21 miles to Allan's Cay. Although there don't seem to be any coral heads that appear too shallow on this route, an alert watch is, as always, necessary. Returning from the Exumas by this route, have DMA 26306 at hand, and reverse the process to avoid the foul ground east of New Providence. Do not steer straight for Porgee Rock.

For those who want a protected banks passage southeast, bypassing the Exuma Cays en route to the south end of Long Island and the Crooked Island group, sketch chart J-47 (Central Bahamas) indicates the course most used by the Nassau mailboats that service those islands.

Pilotage in the Exuma Cays: As you cruise here you'll notice this is an area that's been discovered. New houses, air strips, and towers are cropping up with some frequency. What we describe as prominent will be rendered less so by new additions nearby. It's best to try to confirm your location by natural features that never change, such as the shape of islands, heights of land, gaps between islands, etc. Man-made things can appear and disappear so fast and in such quantity that we can't chart them all, and we do not attempt to do so.

As is generally the case throughout Bahamas, pilotage among the Exuma Cays is almost entirely by eye, judging water depth by color and avoiding patches that appear light or doubtful. Sunglasses with Polaroid lenses will help. (Also see the chapter in this *Guide* on What the Skipper Should Know.)

As you cruise south inside the cays (that is, on the bank), the sun will be ahead of you until about 1:00 p.m., and banks or heads will be difficult to see until you are almost on them. With a yacht drawing over 4.5 feet, leave your anchorage in the morning when the sun, in the east, is behind you, and stand to the westward until you are in deep water where you cannot get into mischief. By the time you reach the approach channel to your next anchorage the sun will be westering and you will have good light to pick your way among the banks again. Most approach channels are wide, deep, and clearly defined. A yacht drawing 8 feet or more can make a long cruise among the cays without difficulty.

Both ebb and flood tidal currents run with considerable velocity through the numerous cuts, so mooring with two anchors is advised. If any doubt exists as to where an entrance channel may lie, anchor and explore first by dinghy.

Sail Rocks and Dog Rocks are barren detached rocks at the northernmost end of the Exuma Cays, about 1.5 miles east of Beacon Cay. **Beacon Cay,** with

Beacon Cay. (Tropic Isle photo)

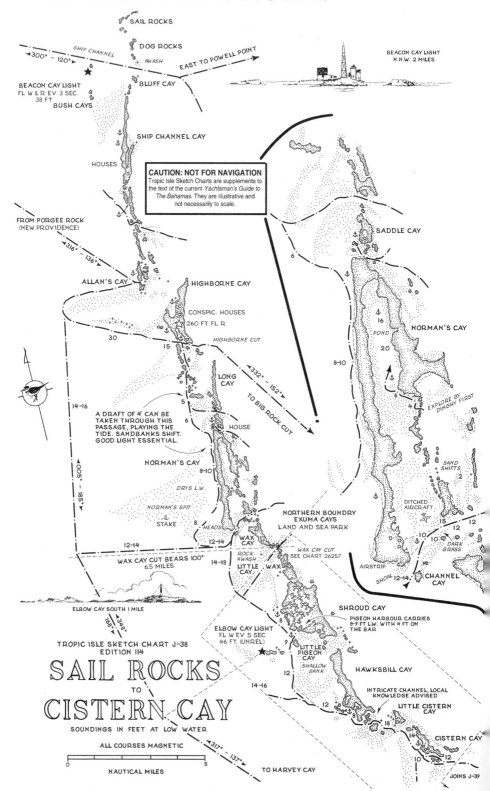

SAIL ROCKS

DOG ROCKS
AWASH

SHIP CHANNEL
←300° - 120°→

EAST TO POWELL POINT

BEACON CAY LIGHT
N.N.W. 2 MILES

BLUFF CAY

BEACON CAY LIGHT
FL W & R EV 3 SEC
38 FT
BUSH CAYS

SHIP CHANNEL CAY

HOUSES

CAUTION: NOT FOR NAVIGATION
Tropic Isle Sketch Charts are supplements to
the text of the current *Yachtsman's Guide to
The Bahamas*. They are illustrative and
not necessarily to scale.

SADDLE CAY

FROM PORGEE ROCK
(NEW PROVIDENCE)

←316° - 136°→

ALLAN'S CAY

HIGHBORNE CAY

CONSPIC. HOUSES
260 FT FL R

NORMAN'S CAY
POND
16

30

15

HIGHBORNE CUT

8-10

20

←332° - 152°→

TO BIG ROCK CUT

LONG
CAY

6

EXPLORE BY
DINGHY FIRST

4

SAND
SHIFTS
2

14-16

5

A DRAFT OF 4' CAN BE
TAKEN THROUGH THIS
PASSAGE, PLAYING THE
TIDE. SANDBANKS SHIFT.
GOOD LIGHT ESSENTIAL.

6

HOUSE

←005° - 185°→

NORMAN'S CAY

8-10

DRYS L.W.

NORMAN'S SPIT

STAKE

8   HEADS

DITCHED
AIRCRAFT
15   12

12
10   10. DARK
GRASS

NORTHERN BOUNDRY
EXUMA CAYS
LAND AND SEA PARK

WAX
CAY

12-14

12-14

WAX CAY CUT
SEE CHART 26257

14-18

ROCK
AWASH
LITTLE
CAY   WAX

AIRSTRIP

SHOAL 12-14

CHANNEL
CAY

WAX CAY CUT BEARS 100°
6.5 MILES

ELBOW CAY SOUTH 1 MILE

SHROUD CAY

PIGEON HARBOUR CARRIES
8-9 FT LW. WITH 4 FT ON
THE BAR

←168° - 348°→

ELBOW CAY LIGHT
FL W EV 5 SEC
46 FT (UNREL)

9

LITTLE
PIGEON
CAY

SHALLOW
BANK

HAWKSBILL CAY

TROPIC ISLE SKETCH CHART J-38
EDITION 114

SAIL ROCKS
TO
CISTERN CAY

SOUNDINGS IN FEET AT LOW WATER

ALL COURSES MAGNETIC

12

14-16

12

INTRICATE CHANNEL, LOCAL
KNOWLEDGE ADVISED

LITTLE CISTERN
CAY

18

14   CISTERN CAY

10   12

0   5

NAUTICAL MILES

←317° - 137°→

TO HARVEY CAY

JOINS J-39

its light tower and ruined house, stands 2 miles from the edge of the Bank and marks Ship Channel, which leads to or from Exuma Sound. Beacon Cay has a red light sector that is visible toward Exuma Sound. Once in the good water just east of Beacon Cay, a 303°-123° heading to or from Beacon Cay will keep you in the red sector and on a course to pass between a 3-foot area south of the dog rocks and a 5-foot area north of Bluff Cay. (We caution you not to do this at night and to use appropriate government charts for clarification.)

About one mile south-southwest of Beacon Cay are two small, rocky, scrub-covered cays known as the Bush Cays. In westerly weather you can anchor under their lee in about 18 feet. Be aware, though, that the strong tidal current is likely to make this anchorage uncomfortable. A better anchorage, if you have good light, is in 12-20 feet between the small cays that lie north of the north end of Ship Channel Cay and the very shallow sandbank that lies just to the west.

Ship Channel Cay is a long, low island rising to a hump at its southern end. If approaching the Exuma Cays on a direct course from Nassau, the bluff on Ship Channel Cay is usually your first landfall, followed shortly by the high land of Highborne Cay.

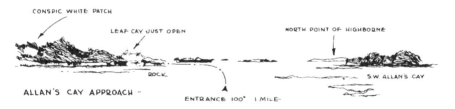

The **Allan's Cay group** (Tropic Isle Sketch Charts: J-35, 36, 38) is easily distinguished from a distance of 2-3 miles by the conspicuous undulations on **Southwest Allan's Cay**. The safe approach to the harbor is on a 100° course whereby the north point of Highborne Cay is just visible through the entrance. A coral head with 6-7 feet over it lies a short distance west of the northern point of the entrance. A draft of 9-10 feet can be taken in safely.

Inside, the best anchorage is opposite the white beach on Leaf Cay in about

Allan's Cay Harbour. (Tropic Isle photo)

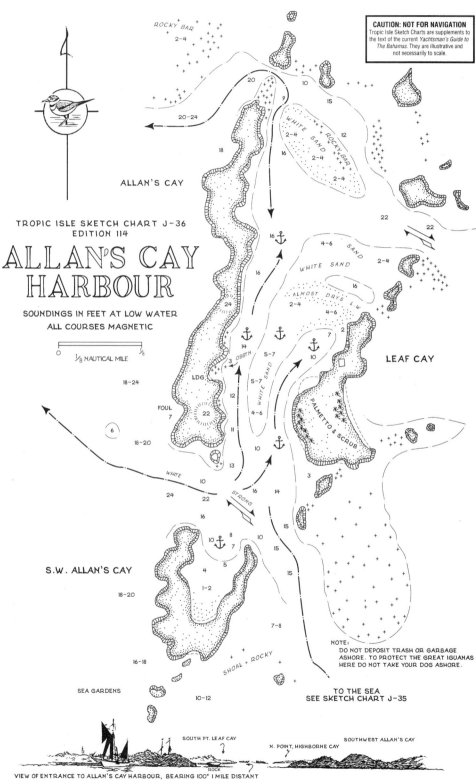

CAUTION: NOT FOR NAVIGATION
Tropic Isle Sketch Charts are supplements to the text of the current *Yachtsman's Guide to The Bahamas*. They are illustrative and not necessarily to scale.

ROCKY BAR
2-4

ALLAN'S CAY

WHITE SAND
2-4
2-4
2-4

ROCKY BAR

20-24

20

18

16

22

22

TROPIC ISLE SKETCH CHART J-36
EDITION 114

ALLAN'S CAY HARBOUR

SOUNDINGS IN FEET AT LOW WATER
ALL COURSES MAGNETIC

0   ⅛ NAUTICAL MILE   ⅛

18-24

18-20

6

LDG

FOUL
7   22

WHITE
24   22

16

OBST'N
3

12

11

13

10

16   14

4-6   SAND
WHITE SAND
16
ALMOST DRYS L.W.
2-4
4-6

2-4

14
5-7
5-7
WHITE SAND
4-6
10

7   2
10

LEAF CAY

PALMETTO & SCRUB

3

15

S.W. ALLAN'S CAY

18-20

16-18

SEA GARDENS

10   8
7
5
4
1-2

STRONG
16   14

15

15

15

15

7-8

SHOAL + ROCKY

10-12

NOTE:
DO NOT DEPOSIT TRASH OR GARBAGE ASHORE. TO PROTECT THE GREAT IGUANAS HERE DO NOT TAKE YOUR DOG ASHORE.

TO THE SEA
SEE SKETCH CHART J-35

SOUTH PT. LEAF CAY
ROCK
N. POINT, HIGHBORNE CAY
SOUTHWEST ALLAN'S CAY

VIEW OF ENTRANCE TO ALLAN'S CAY HARBOUR, BEARING 100° 1 MILE DISTANT

15 feet over sand or grass, but be careful not to proceed too far past the beach as the water shoals and a sandbar closes the channel. An equally good anchorage can also be found in 12-18 feet on the western side of the harbor. Shoal-draft vessels can anchor on the central bank in 6 feet, leaving the deeper water for deep-draft vessels. A strong tidal current runs through the harbor, so in all cases two anchors are advised. Allan's Cay Harbour gives good protection in most weather, but can be exceedingly rough in a norther. It is popular with yachtsmen and also local fishermen. The bay on S.W. Allan's Cay is for the most part shallow, but 6 feet can be found over a grassy bottom.

Leaf Cay is by far the prettiest and most accessible in the group but, unfortunately, thoughtless cruising visitors have used it for a garbage dump. Periodically members of The Bahamas National Trust make a pilgrimage here to clean up this disgrace, but it persists. Please do not deposit your garbage here.

The Allan's Cay group is one of the remaining habitats of iguanas in The Bahamas. A dinghy ride to the beach at either Leaf Cay or Southwest Allan's Cay is a must. Stand quietly on the shore and watch as first one, then another, then another, iguana comes to see what you'll do. In several minutes, the beach will contain 20 to 30 motionless iguanas of widely varying sizes, poised silently in watchfulness. It's best not to feed these creatures; they have a sharp bite and their eyes cannot distinguish between your hand and a tasty morsel.

Please note that all iguanas in The Bahamas are protected by law and may not be captured, killed, or exported. Please don't take your dog ashore here.

Highborne Cay, a favorite outpost of seasoned yachtsmen, is 2 miles

HIGHBORNE CAY Marina

For Information
or Reservations:

Mailing Address:
Box 6342 Nassau, Bahamas
Phone: (242) 355-1008
Fax: (242) 355-1003

SAIL WELL - GO SHELL!

- The Bahamas' Best Kept Secret
- Gateway to the Exumas
- Easy access: just 35 miles S.E. of Nassau
- Unique combination of modern facilities in a pristine island environment.
- Dockage for yachts to 150'
- Shore power up to 200 amp 3 phase service
- Well stocked grocery & liquor store
- Excellent deep sea fishing & snorkeling
- Four secluded rental houses

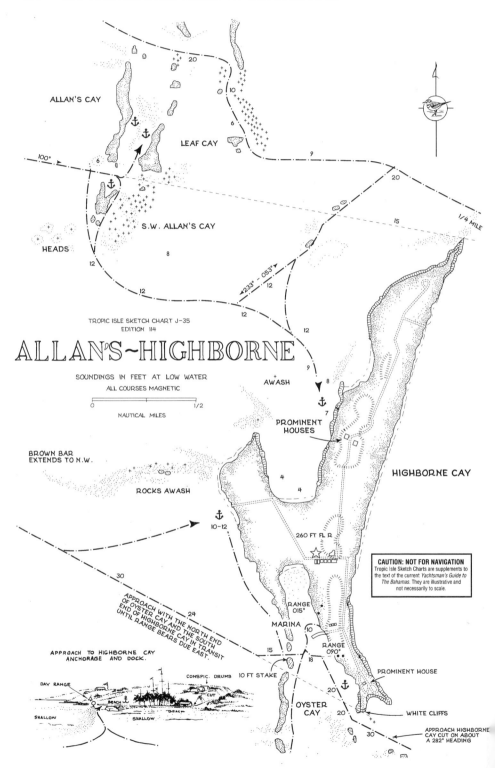

ALLAN'S CAY

LEAF CAY

100°

S.W. ALLAN'S CAY

HEADS

TROPIC ISLE SKETCH CHART J-35
EDITION 114

ALLAN'S~HIGHBORNE

SOUNDINGS IN FEET AT LOW WATER
ALL COURSES MAGNETIC

0   1/2

NAUTICAL MILES

BROWN BAR
EXTENDS TO N.W.

ROCKS AWASH

AWASH

PROMINENT
HOUSES

HIGHBORNE CAY

260 FT FL R

CAUTION: NOT FOR NAVIGATION
Tropic Isle Sketch Charts are supplements to
the text of the current *Yachtsman's Guide to
The Bahamas.* They are illustrative and
not necessarily to scale.

RANGE
015°

MARINA

RANGE
090°

APPROACH WITH THE NORTH END
OF OYSTER CAY AND THE SOUTH
END OF HIGHBORNE CAY IN TRANSIT
UNTIL RANGE BEARS DUE EAST.

APPROACH TO HIGHBORNE CAY
ANCHORAGE AND DOCK.

DAY RANGE

CONSPIC. DRUMS   10 FT STAKE

PROMINENT HOUSE

CUT

BEACH

BEACH

SHALLOW

SHALLOW

OYSTER
CAY

WHITE CLIFFS

APPROACH HIGHBORNE
CAY CUT ON ABOUT
A 282° HEADING

233° - 053°

Highborne Cay. (Tropic Isle photo)

long and comparatively high with several undulations and three conspicuously high humps. It is easily identified from several miles by the 260-ft. Batelco tower at the southern end of the island, topped with a fixed and flashing red light. Closer in, you'll see a long, white, sandy beach with telephone poles at its south end. The approach controlling approach is 9 feet. The marina offers 30 berths with 10 feet alongside, fuel, power, potable water, and public telephones. A few rental houses are available and the upgraded commissary sells fresh meats, groceries, produce, and spirits. Contact island managers Ian MacBeth and Barbara Thrall on VHF 16 for assistance or information. Janet's Catering offers fresh bread as well as catering service. Transportation to the store is provided from the marina, and the marina area and dock beach are open for use by boats at anchor. BASRA's automatic VHF repeater station on the telephone tower picks up emergency traffic on U.S. Channel 22A and relays it to a 24-hour listening station in Nassau and on to the BASRA duty officer. The range is about 50 miles.

There is an anchorage inside the southeast point of the island that is good for 10 feet or more. However, a strong tidal current runs through the cut and this anchorage will be surgy in southeasterly winds. The approach is on a 090° heading (see sketch chart J-35). Due to the popularity of the marina, calling ahead for reservations is recommended.

While here, we saw a family of stingrays (mother, father, and baby) circle the harbor in silent grace. There was also a magnificent birdlike spotted eagle ray. On the eastern shore is one of the loveliest beaches in The Bahamas.

Saddle Cay. (Tropic Isle photo)

Norman's Cay, seen from the south. (Tropic Isle photo)

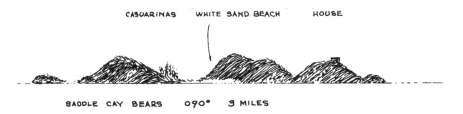

CASUARINAS   WHITE SAND BEACH   HOUSE

SADDLE CAY BEARS   090°   3 MILES

Saddle Cay lies close south of Long Cay, and has a conspicuous white house high on the hilltop. There is a good anchorage in the sand cove at the south end of the island. It is best approached by going outside between Long Cay and Saddle Cay and entering from the southeast. The island is private.

Norman's Cay (Tropic Isle Sketch Chart: J-38), about 4 miles long, is easily identified by the long sandy beach on its western side. It is higher at its north end than at the south, with its highest elevation about center. The south end is marked by dense trees and some prominent white buildings on the beach. The island with its adjacent cays forms a large, shallow lagoon with good bonefishing.

When making the passage from Highborne or Saddle Cays to Norman's Cay, it is advisable to stand out west for 4.5 miles before shaping southward to avoid **Norman's Spit,** marked toward its west end with a stake. If you stay further offshore as shown on sketch chart J-38 (Sail Rocks to Cistern Cay), you won't have to worry about the stake, which is very hard to find. There is a channel

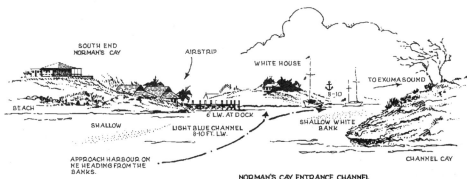

SOUTH END
NORMAN'S CAY   AIRSTRIP   WHITE HOUSE   TO EXUMA SOUND

8-10

BEACH

SHALLOW   6' L.W. AT DOCK   SHALLOW WHITE BANK

LIGHT BLUE CHANNEL
8-10 FT. L.W.

APPROACH HARBOUR ON   CHANNEL CAY
NE HEADING FROM THE
BANKS.

NORMAN'S CAY ENTRANCE CHANNEL
VIEW "A;" CHART: SAIL ROCKS TO CISTERN CAY (INSET)

WAX   CAY   W.S.W. 8   MILES

(FIRST EXUMA LANDFALL ENROUTE FROM POWELL POINT)

for vessels drawing under 6 feet close inshore; however, boats taking this route must negotiate a cluster of coral heads and shoals at the south end of the cay.

Having passed the end of Norman's Spit, hold to the 185° course as shown on the sketch chart until Wax Cay Cut bears about 100°; then steer for it. As you approach, the aforementioned shoal that extends southwest from the end of Norman's Cay will be apparent and the blue, deep-water channel can be seen trending away in a northeasterly direction close to the shore of Channel Cay. Another shoal extends roughly north from Channel Cay, but is easily seen and left to starboard.

The anchorage is about 100 yards east of the bluff and off the dock immediately inside. Don't go too far north. There's good holding in 8-10 feet over grass, and protection except from southwest or east winds. The bight extending north of the anchorage is very shallow but great for dinghy explorers.

To enter Norman's Cay anchorage from Exuma Sound, steer for the light gray roof that lies well north of the radio tower on a heading of 265°, keeping squarely in the center of the blue-water channel. When the last rock to port closes the west point of Wax Cay Cut, steer for the building high on Norman's Bluff.

Ashore, you can sometimes get water from the cistern at the old clubhouse. MacDuff's of Norman's Cay has cottages available on the west side of the airstrip, right on the beach. Their store stocks bare essentials, water, ice, and some beverages. Most of the island north of the airstrip belongs to vacation-home owners, there at various times of the year. Because of recent vandalism, their Homeowner's Association requests that access to that part of the island be by invitation only.

PROMINENT SCAR

W WHITE CLIFFS   BEACH   WHITE CLIFFS   BEACH   MARLE SHORE   WHITE

WAX CAY S.W. I MILE

Wax Cay, which marks the north end of the Exuma Cays Land and Sea Park, has two conspicuous hills, the highest rising to 93 feet. This cay lies a short distance east-southeast of Norman's Cay anchorage. It is about a mile long, with some fine beaches. **Little Wax Cay** is one of the few homes of The Bahamas' only endemic land mammal, the hutia, a rabbit-sized, nocturnal creature. This endangered species is fully protected by law. Do not take your dog ashore here.

Shroud Cay is an archipelago of small cays divided by creeks. A direct course can be laid from a position one mile southwest of the entrance to Norman's Cay to a position halfway between Elbow Cay and the west side of Shroud Cay in 9-12 feet of water. Deep-draft yachts should do this only on a

Shroud Cay. (Tropic Isle photo)

rising tide as this course passes over a white sandbank. The detour around the edge of the bank in 18 feet adds little to the distance. A pleasant anchorage will be found off the small sandy cove at the northwest corner of the island. To reach Pigeon Harbour, follow the coast of Shroud Cay fairly close. At low tide the water shoals gradually from 12 to 6 feet off the entrance to the creek. This harbor does not have much to recommend it except as a refuge in a norther. There are 3 feet on the bar at low water and a little over 4 feet inside between the flats. The channel is so narrow that a vessel of 40 feet would have difficulty turning around. Sand flies and mosquitoes are not unknown inside. We have a letter from a reader describing walking trails ashore with interesting birds and wildlife, and a dinghy trip across the island through the northern bight to a superb ocean beach.

Little Pigeon Cay is private property. Deeper-draft vessels should give the west end of **Elbow Cay** 1-2 miles berth to avoid the coral shoal that runs out in a northwesterly direction. If bound south from Shroud Cay, you can pass Elbow Cay to starboard, leaving Little Pigeon Cay to the northeast.

Hawksbill Cay is one of the most attractive cays in the Exuma Cays Land and Sea Park. It is uninhabited and has several beautiful beaches on its western side. The approach is on a southeasterly bearing for the south end of the island (see sketch chart J-38, Sail Rocks to Cistern Cay). When about 2 miles off, you will see a number of detached rocks. Leave these to port. To the southwest of your course there is a coral head, plus a number of others between the rocks and the point of the island. The best anchorage, in 6-9 feet over grass, lies southeast of the rocks off the mouth of the creek. There is a stone monument on the crest of the hill southeast of the creek mouth. Ashore, park wardens have cleared trails leading to the extensive ruins of a Loyalist plantation. The trails start from the small beach just north of the middle beach on the west side of the island.

Hawksbill Cay to Little Cistern Cay is a short but intricate passage, for which we recommend local knowledge. Under surge conditions it could be dangerous. Little Cistern Cay has a day anchorage off its northwestern beach. **Cistern Cay** has good anchorages, but the island is private property and visits

Cruise the Unbelievably Coloured Waters of the Exumas to

EXUMA DOCKING SERVICES

In Beautiful Elizabeth Harbour

Service is our thing!

**The Only Marina in George Town
Eight-Foot Draft at Low Tide**

*Fresh Water • Electricity • 110/220 Volts
Gasoline • Diesel Fuel • Oils
Laundry • Showers • Ice •
Rental Cars
Restaurant Open 7:00am to 9:30pm
Marine and Automotive Accessories
A Well-Stocked Liquor Store*

Exxon, MasterCard & Visa Cards Honored
P.O. Box EX.29019, George Town, Exuma
Dial Direct 242-336-2578/2101
Fax: 242-336-2023
Radio Call "Sugar One" VHF Channel 16
Hours: Mon. through Sat. 7am-6pm Sun. 8am-1pm

Yachtsman's Guide to the Virgin Islands

Over 300 pages of indispensable information including
16 pages of full color aerial photos.

Yachtsman's Guide to the Bahamas

Over 450 pages of indispensable information

- The most complete guides available for cruising
  the Bahamas and Virgin Islands.
- Profusely illustrated with our beautiful hand-drawn
  sketch charts, landfall sketches and photographs.
- Detailed island by island profiles and things to
  do ashore.

Sketch Charts also available
separately in 11"x17" format.
Call or use order form in
the Guide.

Call (305) 893-4277

Or write to:
Tropic Isle Publishers
P.O. Box 610938
North Miami, FL 33261-0938

*"Someday, Father, I shall write great guides for yachtsmen.
Sailors like us will never wander aimlessly again. That is...
if we ever get back. Sir, will we soon see land?"*

Warderick Wells. (Tropic Isle photo)

MEMBERSHIP APPLICATION

We need and welcome Associate or
Supporting Members.
You are not required to take an active part
in BASRA.

TO BAHAMAS AIR-SEA RESCUE ASSOCIATION
P.O. BOX SS-6247, NASSAU, BAHAMAS
TEL. (242) 325-8864 / FAX (242) 325-2737

I hereby apply for membership in BASRA. ☐ I enclose $30 for one
year's subscription. ☐ I enclose $500 for Life membership. I wish to
take an active part in BASRA. ☐ Yes. ☐ No.
Additional enclosed $_____ for flag(s) at $10 each.
(Please include $5 for postage.)

NAME_____DATE_____

ADDRESS_____

SIGNATURE_____

Please make checks payable to Bahamas Air-Sea Rescue Association

WARDERICK WELLS CAY (NORTH END) S.W. 2 MILES

ashore are by invitation only.

Between Cistern Cay and Warderick Wells Cay are several sandbanks and a brown bar with less than 3 feet at low water that must be avoided. While a channel for shoal-draft vessels is indicated on sketch chart J-39 (Cistern Cay to Bitter Guana Cay), it is a dangerous passage under surge conditions or in poor light. We recommend that the inside, or banks, passage be used even though you will have to detour seemingly far to westward.

Because the banks shift in this area, the following directions for approaching **Warderick Wells Cay** should be used with caution. From a position with the high point of Cistern Cay bearing 340° and the north tip of Warderick Wells bearing 060°, steer approximately 070° along the edge of the bank for a distance of about 2 miles. Then change course to about 040°, keeping clear of the shallow water to port, and head for the pale cliff on Warderick Wells, which from a distance looks like houses. When the north tip of Warderick Wells bears 045°, alter course to that heading. Nearing Warderick Wells Cay, you will pass three detached cays to starboard and a number of small rocks to port. Steer for the small beach at the extreme north end of Warderick Wells until the entrance to

Why should you give $30 towards a service you hope you'll never need?

An unexpected event at sea or in the air — a failed engine - a broken stay — bad weather — and suddenly you're in serious trouble. You've got more than you can handle. You need help fast — you need BASRA ... BAHAMAS AIR-SEA RESCUE ASSOCIATION..

True enough, you may never need us — your friends or relatives may never need us — but you'll feel good to know that just for that $30 a year membership, BASRA is ready and equipped. Join today ... fill out the coupon on the reverse side and mail it today.

BAHAMAS AIR-SEA RESCUE ASSOCIATION

When you join BASRA, you get a membership card and decal. BASRA flags are available at $10 each.

We also offer to members "File-A-Float": Send us your float plan (mail, fax, or phone) and, should you need to be contacted, we will be able to locate you in our islands quickly and efficiently.

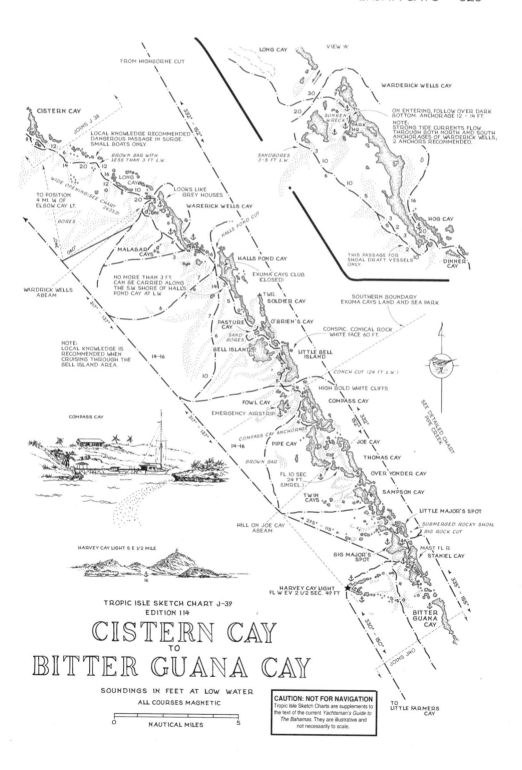

LONG CAY

VIEW 'A'

FROM HIGHBORNE CUT

WARDERICK WELLS CAY

CISTERN CAY

JOINS J 38

LOCAL KNOWLEDGE RECOMMENDED.
DANGEROUS PASSAGE IN SURGE.
SMALL BOATS ONLY.

ON ENTERING, FOLLOW OVER DARK
BOTTOM. ANCHORAGE 12 - 14 FT.
NOTE:
STRONG TIDE CURRENTS FLOW
THROUGH BOTH NORTH AND SOUTH
ANCHORAGES OF WARDERICK WELLS,
2 ANCHORS RECOMMENDED.

BROWN BAR WITH
LESS THAN 3 FT LW.

SANDBORES
3-5 FT LW.

SUNKEN
WRECK

PARK
HQ

WIDE OPENING (SEE CHART
24, 25, 31)

LONG
CAY

LOOKS LIKE
GREY HOUSES

TO POSITION
4 MI. W OF
ELBOW CAY LT.

WARERICK WELLS CAY

HOG CAY

BORES

HALLS POND CUT

MALABAR
CAYS

THIS PASSAGE FOR
SHOAL DRAFT VESSELS
ONLY.

DINNER
CAY

WARDRICK WELLS
ABEAM

HALLS POND CAY

EXUMA CAYS CLUB
(CLOSED)

NO MORE THAN 3 FT.
CAN BE CARRIED ALONG
THE S.W. SHORE OF HALLS
POND CAY AT LW.

TWR.
SOLDIER CAY

SOUTHERN BOUNDARY
EXUMA CAYS LAND AND SEA PARK

PASTURE
CAY

O'BRIEN'S CAY

CONSPIC. CONICAL ROCK
WHITE FACE 60 FT.

NOTE:
LOCAL KNOWLEDGE IS
RECOMMENDED WHEN
CRUISING THROUGH THE
BELL ISLAND AREA.

SAND
BORES

BELL ISLAND

LITTLE BELL
ISLAND

CONCH CUT (24 FT L.W.)

HIGH BOLD WHITE CLIFFS

FOWL CAY

COMPASS CAY

COMPASS CAY

EMERGENCY AIRSTRIP

SEE DETAILED CHART
PIPE CREEK

COMPASS CAY ANCHORAGE

PIPE CAY

JOE CAY

BROWN BAR

THOMAS CAY

FL 10 SEC
24 FT
(UNREL)

OVER YONDER CAY

TWIN
CAYS

SAMPSON CAY

LITTLE MAJOR'S SPOT

HILL ON JOE CAY
ABEAM

SUBMERGED ROCKY SHOAL
BIG ROCK CUT

HARVEY CAY LIGHT S E 1/2 MILE

BIG MAJOR'S
SPOT

MAST FL R
STANIEL CAY

HARVEY CAY LIGHT
FL W EV 2 1/2 SEC. 49 FT

BITTER
GUANA
CAY

CAUTION: NOT FOR NAVIGATION
Tropic Isle Sketch Charts are supplements to
the text of the current *Yachtsman's Guide to
The Bahamas*. They are illustrative and
not necessarily to scale.

JOINS J40

TO
LITTLE FARMERS
CAY

TROPIC ISLE SKETCH CHART J-39
EDITION 114

CISTERN CAY
TO
BITTER GUANA CAY

SOUNDINGS IN FEET AT LOW WATER

ALL COURSES MAGNETIC

0   NAUTICAL MILES   5

the anchorage opens up. Do not stand over too far toward the eastern side as there are a number of rocky heads and ledges. Once in the center of the entrance, swing easily to starboard and a line of dark water (grassy bottom) will appear. Stay over this and it will lead you around the point of a very shallow sandbank in the center of the harbor and to the mooring area. Anchoring is no longer permitted in the North Warderick Wells anchorage, but is permitted in the Hog Cay anchorage at the south end of Warderick Wells. Moorings are available both places for whatever fee applies to your vessel. These are rated for 30 m.p.h. winds; moor at your own risk. If you damage a mooring, please report it to park management. Also available is a "Support Fleet Membership" for double your boat's particular mooring fee plus $20. The National Trust's warden headquarters on the south point of the north harbor is a prominent landmark.

The Hog Cay mooring area in the excellent harbor at the cay's southern end can be reached either from Exuma Sound or by going west around the banks and approaching from south of Dinner Cay and Hog Cay. The latter entry is intricate, but easy in moderate weather. There is 12-18 feet on the bar here, and more inside.

Warderick Wells remains the most popular cay in the Exuma Cays Land and Sea Park. Park Warden Ray Darville is stationed at the park headquarters and is happy to provide information and answer questions. He monitors VHF 16 from the park headquarters at Warderick Wells and asks that you contact him by radio before entering North Warderick Wells anchorage. At the headquarters, trail maps are available and a resource library displays coral, wildlife, and plant specimens. According to the Bahamas National Trust newsletter, in April 1996, at the BNT's request, Royal Bahamas Defense Force officers were stationed at the Exuma Cays Land and Sea Park headquarters on a permanent rotational basis to help Park Warden Ray Darville with the enforcement of bylaws. Their presence was requested because of continued poaching and the need to protect the warden and park volunteers. A new building is planned, which will house the Defense Force officers, provide living space for the warden, and accommodate visiting scientists.

Over 4 miles of trails on Warderick Wells lead to rare plants, caves, wells, and the ruins of a small Loyalist plantation. (A land grant was given to a family named Davis around 1785, so the plantation was probably built soon thereafter.) Local legend has it that a shipload of missionaries once wrecked and eventually perished on the island; now, on moonlit nights, a ghostly congregation might be heard singing hymns, followed by voices talking and calling to one another.

Remember that fishing or the taking of any wildlife within park limits is prohibited. There are now a few iguanas and some hutia living on Warderick Wells, so please don't take your dog ashore without a leash.

Hall's Pond Cay is a long, narrow island with shoal banks on its southwestern side. The Exuma Cays Club building (at this writing privately owned) stands atop its westernmost promontory with a spectacular view of Warderick Wells and its surrounding banks. When making entrance to Hall's Pond Cay from the west, a bearing of 051° on the clubhouse will bring you to a sandbar extending out in an inverted U-shape. Good light is essential to spot this. Enter over the tip of the bar in 4-5 feet at low water. The crumbling docks

Hall's Pond Cay. (Tropic Isle photo)

of the closed club lie adjacent to the deep-water channel of Hall's Pond Cut, where the strong surge from Exuma Sound usually works in; in southerly conditions the sharp chop of the banks makes these docks untenable. Two National Trust moorings are available. These are rated for 30 m.p.h. winds; moor at your own risk. If you damage a mooring, please report it to park management. Visitors are welcome. When we flew over the island recently, we observed that it is absolutely covered with roads that seem to go nowhere in particular, as though a hyperkinetic bulldozer operator had been wound up and released here.

Bell Island is a high, rather forbidding-looking island. The approach lies between a series of sandbanks that extend 2 miles to the southwest. Two reefs in the vicinity of Bell Island and Soldier Cay have been set aside as natural seaquarium sites for snorkeling. Bell Island is private property and visits ashore are by invitation only. On the west side of the island, there's construction under way that looks big enough to be a hotel, but we're told it's a private residence.

CONSPICUOUS WHITE CLIFFS AT LITTLE BELL I. S.W. 2 MILES

Little Bell Island (Cambridge Cay on some charts) lies just southeast of Bell Island. Its northwest side forms a little inverted hook enclosing a shallow,

Range, northern entrance to Little Bell Island. (Tropic Isle photo)

Little Bell Island anchorage. (Tropic Isle photo)

south-facing bight just south of which is a good, sheltered anchorage. In addition to being accessible from Conch Cut, this anchorage can be reached from Exuma Sound by working your way in to a point southeast of the southern end of O'Brien's Cay. Avoid the rocks and reefs that extend north from Little Bell and then follow the good water southward to the west of them. Good light is essential. Then the reefs that even extend north and northwest of the rocks can be seen as a brown bar. Once safely inside the reefs, move in obliquely toward the beach on the northwest side of Little Bell. (Someone has placed a range near the south end of this beach to guide you in, but we cannot be sure it will be maintained.) Follow good water parallel to the shore southward until the anchorage opens up. Little Bell Island is private property and visits ashore are by invitation only.

From the **Rocky Dundas** in Conch Cut a draft of 5 feet can be taken into the south entrance to Little Bell Island at low water, providing light is sufficient to see the shallow bars inside. Upon entering pass through the few coral heads immediately northeast of the brown bar (see sketch chart of Conch Cut). Proceed northeast, then take the small rock to starboard and continue north toward the Bell Island anchorage. Good light and the ability to read water are essential or you'll be aground. Beware of the current that runs strong over the bars.

Paradise Bay, at the south end of Little Bell Island, is comfortable in settled weather and provides excellent snorkeling among the nearby coral.

Conch Cut, which marks the southern end of the Exuma Cays Land and Sea Park, is one of the best passes into and out of Exuma Sound. There is a rock awash in the center of the cut: be careful to pass it only on the north side. The southern half of Conch Cut is foul and should be avoided. From the bank, the north end of Compass Cay, which forms the south side of Conch Cut, is easily recognized by a high, white cliff.

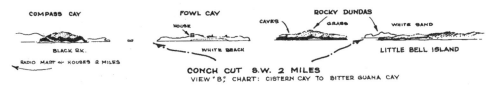

CONCH CUT S.W. 2 MILES
VIEW "B" CHART: CISTERN CAY TO BITTER GUANA CAY

The **Rocky Dundas** are the two large, scrub-covered rocks southwest of Conch Cut. The caves in the southern rock have impressive stalagmite and

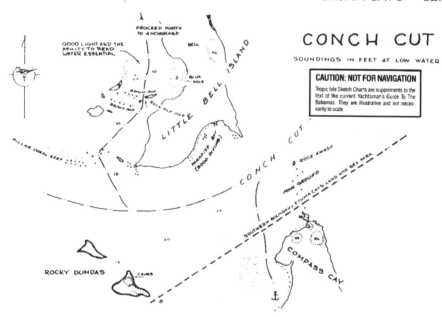

CONCH CUT

SOUNDINGS IN FEET AT LOW WATER

CAUTION: NOT FOR NAVIGATION
Tropic Isle Sketch Charts are supplements to the text of the current Yachtsman's Guide To The Bahamas. They are illustrative and not necessarily to scale.

stalactite formations. Off the caves is a free National Trust dinghy mooring. An excursion to the Rocky Dundas should be made only in settled weather.

Fowl Cay is apt to blend into Compass Cay when viewed from the west, but it can be recognized from a distance by a small white house close to its top. There is good water all around Fowl Cay once you get into it. Proceed from the banks as if you were going out Conch Cut, but then round the Rocky Dundas and approach Fowl Cay from the east as indicated on sketch chart J-43 (Pipe Creek). Fowl Cay is private property. The airstrip is for emergency landing only.

Compass Cay (Tropic Isle Sketch Charts: J-39, 43) is actually two high, rolling cays lying parallel to each other and divided only by shallow mangroves. This central area has several deep holes into which shoal-draft vessels could be taken in an emergency. The cay is bounded on the northeast shore by bold white cliffs with a sweeping beach at the south end. A prominent white roof can be seen on its southern hill, both from far at sea and on the banks. A strong tidal current

=COMPASS CAY MARINA Ltd.=
COMPASS CAY • EXUMA • BAHAMAS
- *Long Term Boat Storage from 30¢ a Foot per Day* •
- *Daily Dockage at a Competitive Rate of 70¢ a Foot* •
- *Marked Channels into Marina* •
- *Natural Hurricane Hole and Well-Protected Harbour* •
- *Magnificent Crescent Ocean Beach* •
- *Explore the Island's Natural Beauty on miles of Marked Trails* •

COMPASS CAY MARINA Ltd. • STANIEL CAY POST OFFICE • EXUMA • BAHAMAS

TEL/FAX +1 (242) 355 - 2064

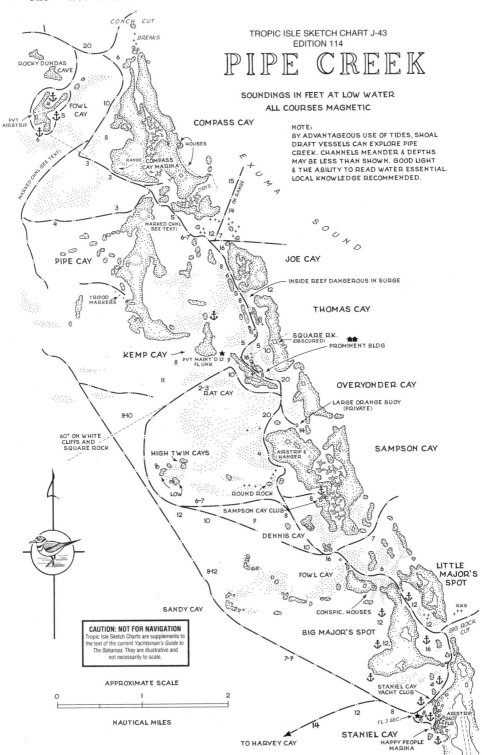

TROPIC ISLE SKETCH CHART J-43
EDITION 114

PIPE CREEK

SOUNDINGS IN FEET AT LOW WATER
ALL COURSES MAGNETIC

NOTE:
BY ADVANTAGEOUS USE OF TIDES, SHOAL
DRAFT VESSELS CAN EXPLORE PIPE
CREEK. CHANNELS MEANDER & DEPTHS
MAY BE LESS THAN SHOWN. GOOD LIGHT
& THE ABILITY TO READ WATER ESSENTIAL.
LOCAL KNOWLEDGE RECOMMENDED.

CONCH CUT
BREAKS
ROCKY DUNDAS CAVE
FOWL CAY
PVT AIRSTRIP
COMPASS CAY
HOUSES
RANGE: COMPASS CAY MARINA
DRYS
MARKED CHNL (SEE TEXT)
EXUMA SOUND
ON RANGE
PIPE CAY
JOE CAY
INSIDE REEF DANGEROUS IN SURGE
THOMAS CAY
TRIPOD MARKERS
SQUARE RK. (OBSCURED)
PROMINENT BLDG
KEMP CAY
PVT MAINT'D LT FL UNK
OVERYONDER CAY
RAT CAY
LARGE ORANGE BUOY (PRIVATE)
60° ON WHITE CLIFFS AND SQUARE ROCK
HIGH TWIN CAYS
AIRSTRIP & HANGER
SAMPSON CAY
LOW
ROUND ROCK
SAMPSON CAY CLUB
DENNIS CAY
LITTLE MAJOR'S SPOT
FOWL CAY
RKS
BIG ROCK CUT
SANDY CAY
CONSPIC. HOUSES
BIG MAJOR'S SPOT
STANIEL CAY YACHT CLUB
AIRSTRIP
FL FL
TO HARVEY CAY
STANIEL CAY
HAPPY PEOPLE MARINA
FL 3 SEC

CAUTION: NOT FOR NAVIGATION
Tropic Isle Sketch Charts are supplements to
the text of the current *Yachtsman's Guide to
The Bahamas*. They are illustrative and
not necessarily to scale.

APPROXIMATE SCALE

0   1   2

NAUTICAL MILES

Compass Cay. (Tropic Isle photo)

flows through the center of the harbor, which has a rock bottom and offers poor holding.

The approaches to Compass Cay are shown on sketch chart J-43 (Pipe Creek). There are now marked approaches from just inside the Joe Cay/ Compass Cay Cut to Compass Cay Marina and from the west side of the sandbank west of the north end of Pipe Cay up northeast around the bank and then southeast along the shore of Compass Cay and on into the marina. The first of these approaches is good for about 5 feet at low water, and the latter for about 3 - 3.5 feet at low water. Call Tucker Rolle *(Budget*)or *Compass Cay* on VHF 16 for information, availability, depths, or other help getting in.

Compass Cay Marina has 11 slips with electricity and water available. A small store selling basic food items and sundries is planned for late 1998. There is a dockside aquarium with hundreds of fish for snorkeling or viewing from the dock. Three air-conditioned 3-bedroom houses are available for rent, with marina or ocean views. The island has miles of marked hiking trails and many beaches to explore, and the creek next to the marina is good for bonefishing. Tucker Rolle is the man in charge.

Both **Overyonder Cay** and **Rat Cay** are privately owned. Visits ashore are by invitation only.

Pipe Creek comprises an archipelago of comparatively small cays, a

Pipe Creek. (Fields photo)

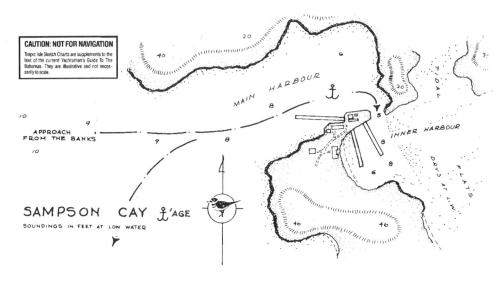

CAUTION: NOT FOR NAVIGATION

Tropic Isle Sketch Charts are supplements to the text of the current Yachtsman's Guide To The Bahamas. They are illustrative and not necessarily to scale.

MAIN HARBOUR

INNER HARBOUR

TIDAL

DRYS AT LOW

FLATS

APPROACH FROM THE BANKS

SAMPSON CAY ⚓'AGE

SOUNDINGS IN FEET AT LOW WATER

wonderful area for *shoal-draft* boats to explore. If you've not been here before, at least seek local knowledge; better yet, use a guide your first time through. There are about 17 of these cays in the 7 miles that separate Compass Cay from Staniel Cay. Sketch chart J-43 (Pipe Creek) will give you an idea of what's possible here, *but it must be remembered that these channels continually meander and often shallow out, so you must know how to read the water and feel your way through in good light, using the tide and your depth sounder or a lead line. Throughout, but especially north of Sampson, much of what you can run onto is reefs and rocky bars.* The cut between Joe and Compass Cays has many coral heads and rock or coral bars. It is difficult at best, and impossible in a breaking sea.

The approach to **Sampson Cay** main harbor is straightforward with a

Sampson Cay. (Tropic Isle photo)

SAMPSON CAY
CLUB & MARINA
NAUTICAL RESTAURANT & BAR

Still Unspoiled

- Dockage/220 Electric Service
- Gasoline • Fuel/Oil • Ice • Water
- Groceries • Liquor
- Protected Long Term Storage
- Air-conditioned Cottages • Air Fills
- Marine Repairs • Moorings •
- Towing/Salvage/Rescue •

CLOSED SUNDAYS

VHF Channel 16

242-355-2034

P.O. Box N 4021, Nassau, Bahamas

Home Port for

OVERSEAS SALVAGE

Agents for: Wholesale Wine & Spirits Ltd.
Agents for: Asa H. Pritchard,
Wholesale Food Distributors

SAIL WELL - GO SHELL

least depth of 7-8 feet at low water. The small but intimate Sampson Cay Club, operated by Marcus and Rosemary Mitchell, is beside the lovely anchorage. Fuel, electricity, water, ice, and other shoreside services are available at the dock, which can accommodate drafts up to 7 feet at the outer dock, which can accommodate drafts up to 7 feet at the outer portion and 6 feet closer in at low water. Moorings are also available. An ample selection of frozen meats and seafood, as well as fresh vegetables, canned foods, and spirits are sold in the commissary. On Sundays, the fuel docks and commissary are closed, but you are welcome to tie up and plug in. There is a protected inner harbor here with slips for 24 boats, a good place to leave your boat for any length of time, if you must. Check with the dockmaster, however, before entering the back harbor. Garbage has become a problem here, as it has everywhere, and will now be accepted from registered guests only.

With its handsome stone architecture, excellent food and friendly bar, Sampson Cay Club is an attractive port of call. Nice air-conditioned cottages are available on the beach, with potable water. At the dinner table you might meet an interesting assortment of adventurers from all over the world. Reservations are required for all dining; call on VHF 16 (the dining room is closed on Sunday unless there are cottage guests).

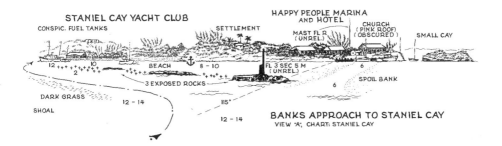

BANKS APPROACH TO STANIEL CAY
VIEW "A", CHART: STANIEL CAY

Staniel Cay (Tropic Isle Sketch Charts: J-37, 39, 43). The channel leading into Staniel Cay from the banks, carrying 6 feet at low water, runs on a bearing of 115° on the light (unreliable) on the southernmost of the three exposed rocks that lie east of the village between the Happy People Marina and

STANIEL CAY YACHT CLUB

Exumas   SC ▷   Bahamas

• Fully renovated and remodeled • Full service marina • Deep-water dockage
• Beautiful waterfront cottages (air-conditioned) • Boats for rent; guides available upon request
• Renowned Bahamian-American cuisine • Friendly, casual atmosphere

For reservations, information and rates: Phone (242) 355-2024 Fax (242) 355-2044 VHF Ch.16
U.S. Phone (954) 467-8920 Fax (954) 522-3248 • Visit our web site at http://www.stanielcay.com

STANIEL CAY

TROPIC ISLE SKETCH CHART J-37
EDITION 113

SOUNDINGS IN FEET AT LOW WATER
ALL COURSES MAGNETIC

FUEL TANKS

STANIEL CAY YACHT CLUB

MAST F R
CHURCH

CREEK

16

14

10

12

6-8

HAPPY PEOPLE MARINA

SMALL CAY

ROCKY SHOAL

STRONG TIDAL CURRENT

10-12

14

3 EXPOSED ROCKS

DEEP BLUE CHANNEL

SPOIL BANK

6

8

FL 3 SEC

10-12

DARK GRASS

VIEW "A"

115°

LITTLE MAJOR'S SPOT

SANDY CAY

BIG MAJOR'S SPOT

SUBMERGED ROCKS 6 FT.

BIG ROCK CUT FAVOR NORTH SIDE WHEN ENTERING

VIEW "B"

SEA BREAKS

CROWN OF THORNS ROCK

STANIEL CAY

CLUB THUNDERBALL

MOORINGS

ROCK SEPARATES BEACHES

STANIEL CAY YACHT CLUB

AIRSTRIP

10-12

TREE

10-12

PROTECTED AREA

MOORINGS

FLD

CHURCH

HAPPY PEOPLE MARINA

8

10

12

LESS THAN 5 FEET AT

295°

115°

DAY RANGE:
LINE UP S. MOST ROCK
(LIGHT) WITH PINK
ROOF CHURCH (OBSC.)

HARVEY CAY

CONSPIC. PINK HOUSE

FL EV 2½ SEC
49 FT 6 M

BANKS APPROACH TO STANIEL CAY
VIEW "K", CHART: STANIEL CAY

SMALL CAY

HAPPY PEOPLE MARINA AND HOT DOG

MAST & D (PINK ROOF OBSCURED)

CHURCH (PINK ROOF) OBSCURED

SPOIL BANK

FL 1 SEC 5 M

SETTLEMENT

8 - 10

12 - 14

STANIEL CAY YACHT CLUB

CONSPIC. FUEL TANKS

BEACH

3 EXPOSED ROCKS

DARK GRASS

SHOAL

12 - 14

CAUTION: NOT FOR NAVIGATION
Tropic Isle Sketch Charts are supplements to
the text of the current *Yachtsman's Guide to
The Bahamas.* They are illustrative and
not necessarily to scale.

Staniel Cay. (Tropic Isle photo)

the Staniel Cay Yacht Club. Boats with a 6-foot draft or more should proceed carefully in this approach at low water, because the banks shift, and the mailboat sometimes grounds here. When about 100 yards short of the light on the rock, you will see the deep blue channel trending away in a northerly direction. This leads to the Staniel Cay Yacht Club. The dredged channel immediately south of the light leads into the Happy People Marina.

The recently renovated Staniel Cay Yacht Club includes a new dock with electricity, water, ice, and a convenient telephone booth. The dock carries 7.5 feet at low water; the dockmaster is Kuenson Rolle and club manager is Nicole Ferguson. On Sundays, the dock is open for an hour from 9 a.m. to 10 a.m. In a fresh nor'wester the docks are untenable and boats must find mooring elsewhere. There are five waterfront cottages and a large cottage available for families or groups. The restaurant serves breakfast, lunch (daily except Sunday), and dinner (including Sunday, when it reopens at 5 p.m.), and also prepares box lunches. Specialties are seafood and fresh-baked bread, desserts and, with notice, birthday cakes. Reservations are welcome. The Club also can, with reasonable notice, arrange banquets or parties, including pig roasts. In the clubhouse is a gift shop.

Conveniently out of the tide, Kenneth Rolle's Happy People Marina and

Hosts:
Bill & Leslie Cunningham
Curtis & Patti Clark

Phone: (242) 342-7050
Fax: (242) 342-7051
VHF 16

hawk's nest
Resort & Marina
Cat Island, Bahamas

FISHING · SNORKELING · DIVING · 4600' RUNWAY

email: hawknest@batelnet.bs

Club Thunderball and moorings. (Tropic Isle photo)

Hotel will accommodate 6-8 yachts in 6 feet low water with ice, water, electricity, and a convenient phone booth. Pleasant rooms overlook the harbor as does the nice new rental apartment called the Happy Suite, with two bedrooms, a kitchen, and living room. The Royal Entertainers Lounge, a few steps away, serves breakfast, lunch, and dinner. A lunch treat is a Theazielburger made by Kenneth's wife, Theaziel. Her dinner menu includes grouper, cracked conch, chicken, pork chops, and crawfish. For dinner, she would like reservations by 4 p.m. but she may be able to accommodate you later (for lunch, just call in). Next door to the marina is Lindsay's Boutique.

Two small groceries, Burke Smith's Blue Store and Hugh Smith's Pink Store, are easy to spot. The post office is the green building next to the Blue Store. On the creek south of town, Berkie Rolle's Isles General Store sells basic marine supplies (according to Berkie's wife Vivian, "We keep everyone afloat 'til they get where they're going"), LP gas, dive equipment, and basic food supplies. Boat parts or marine supplies not in stock can be special-ordered. Small boats are available for rent, and you can book a flight with one of Staniel's various air charter services through the store. Berkie's wife Vivian runs the store, where she also sells her delicious fresh-baked bread. The store is accessible by dinghy at all tides, convenient when you must bring your propane tank in for filling. Many local women bake bread to order or do laundry. There is a telephone station (and some booths around town for credit-card calls), a straw market, and a tennis court. A lending library occupies one of the oldest buildings on the cay, restored and decorated in island colors. Residents request that boaters deposit garbage at marina disposal facilities.

Big Major's and Little Major's Spot. (Fields photo)

With an annual bonefishing tournament, beach picnics featuring Bahamian cooking to which yachtsmen are cordially invited, as well as the conviviality at both the Yacht Club and Happy People, Staniel Cay is an ideal out-island community. At the popular New Year's Day Regatta, everyone wins a prize. The natural-born seamen of the island have the distinction of building and owning *Tida Wave, Sea Hound,* and *Lady Muriel*, all champions at Out Islands Regattas. The tiller of the *Lady Muriel,* aboard which H.R.H. Prince Philip was once a guest, decorates the bar at the Royal Entertainer's Lounge.

Opposite Crown of Thorns Rock, just south of Big Rock Cut and east of Thunderball Cave is Club Thunderball, a pink building atop a promontory with panoramic views on all sides. It's open daily, with good food, music and dancing, satellite TV, a pool table, frequent dinner specials and beach parties. There are 12 rental moorings along the shore just south of Club Thunderball's dock; call ahead to reserve them.

Bonefishing and reef and deep-sea fishing hereabouts are excellent. Reliable guides include Hugh, Burke, or Sandy Gray, Tony Gray, and Wade Nixon. Any of them would be glad to point out or guide you to Thunderball Cave, site of a number of underwater scenes from two James Bond films, *Thunderball* and *Never Say Never Again,* as well as the Disney movie, *Splash. Note: The cave is protected and nothing may be taken from it. The current is reported dangerously strong for inexperienced swimmers except at slack tide.*

If caught in a norther at Staniel Cay, you can find shelter in winds from west through east in the anchorages in the mouth of Pipe Creek, between **Little and Big Major's Spot** in 9-12 feet. If the south anchorage develops a surge, you can try the anchorage further north between the two cays, favoring the west side. But don't go too far north here as there is a reef and scoured-out area with less than 5 feet at low water. This looks like sand but isn't. So be careful where you anchor, and check your swinging area. Both these anchorages become surgy and at times untenable in strong easterly winds, when seas work in through the cuts and rebound throughout the area. Also be aware that currents here can be swift. Be sure your anchors are set in sand, because although there are areas of good holding, much of the bottom is scoured out. As winds work into the east, it may be best to move to the west of Big Major's Spot or west of Staniel itself once that anchorage is in a lee. The northern half of Little Major's Spot is privately owned.

BIG ROCK CUT S.W. 1 MILE
VIEW "B"   CHART: STANIEL CAY

WEAK LANDFALL; THE SHORE ADJACENT TO BIG ROCK CUT MERGES TO APPEAR THE SAME FROM OVER ONE MILE OFF.

Big Rock Cut (perhaps most easily identifiable from seaward by looking northward of the Batelco tower on Staniel Cay) leads out into Exuma Sound between Little Major's Spot and Staniel Cay. Although not so deep as many of the cuts, it carries at least 9 feet at low water. Proceeding south toward the yacht

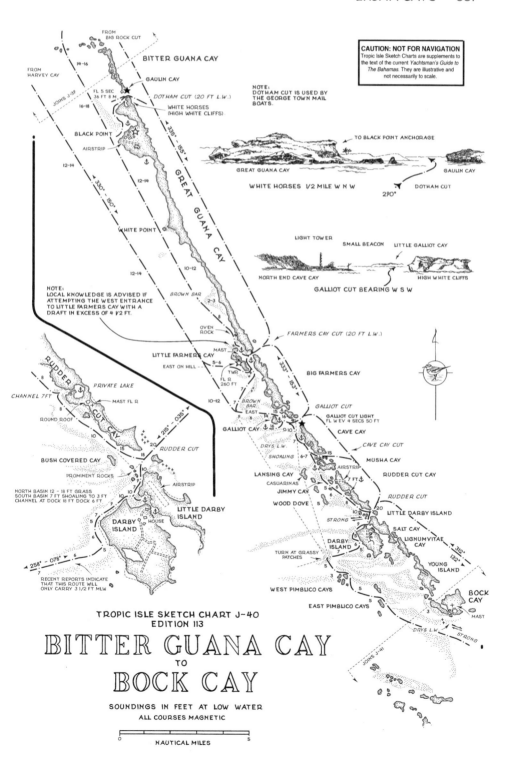

CAUTION: NOT FOR NAVIGATION
Tropic Isle Sketch Charts are supplements to
the text of the current *Yachtsman's Guide to
The Bahamas*. They are illustrative and
not necessarily to scale.

FROM
BIG ROCK CUT

BITTER GUANA CAY

FROM
HARVEY CAY

14-16

GAULIN CAY

JOINS J-39

FL 5 SEC
36 FT 8 M

DOTHAM CUT (20 FT L.W.)

16-18

WHITE HORSES
(HIGH WHITE CLIFFS)

BLACK POINT

AIRSTRIP

12-14

335° - 155°

330° - 150°

12-14

GREAT GUANA CAY

WHITE POINT

12-14

10-12

BROWN BAR

NOTE:
LOCAL KNOWLEDGE IS ADVISED IF
ATTEMPTING THE WEST ENTRANCE
TO LITTLE FARMERS CAY WITH A
DRAFT IN EXCESS OF 4 1/2 FT.

OVEN
ROCK

MAST

LITTLE FARMERS CAY

EAST ON HILL

TWR
FL R
260 FT

RUDDER

PRIVATE LAKE

CHANNEL 7FT

8

MAST FL R

ROUND ROOF

10-12

7

BROWN
BAR
EAST

CUT CAY

10

15

BUSH COVERED CAY

PROMINENT ROCKS

18

20

RUDDER CUT

285° - 035°

NORTH BASIN 12 - 18 FT GRASS
SOUTH BASIN 7 FT SHOALING TO 3 FT
CHANNEL AT DOCK 18 FT DOCK 6 FT

10

AIRSTRIP

10

7

5

6

DARBY
ISLAND

LITTLE DARBY
ISLAND

HOUSE

6

5

258° - 078°

7

6

RECENT REPORTS INDICATE
THAT THIS ROUTE WILL
ONLY CARRY 3 1/2 FT MLW

NOTE:
DOTHAM CUT IS USED BY
THE GEORGE TOWN MAIL
BOATS.

TO BLACK POINT ANCHORAGE

GREAT GUANA CAY

GAULIN CAY

WHITE HORSES 1/2 MILE W N W

290°

DOTHAM CUT

LIGHT TOWER

SMALL BEACON

LITTLE GALLIOT CAY

NORTH END CAVE CAY

HIGH WHITE CLIFFS

GALLIOT CUT BEARING W S W

FARMERS CAY CUT (20 FT L.W.)

333° - 153°

BIG FARMERS CAY

GALLIOT CUT

15

16

GALLIOT CUT LIGHT
FL W EV 4 SECS 50 FT

GALLIOT CAY

15

9 10

CAVE CAY

DRYS L.W.

SHOALING

6-7

15

CAVE CAY CUT

LANSING CAY

CASUARINAS

AIRSTRIP

7 FT

MUSHA CAY

RUDDER CUT CAY

JIMMY CAY

5

8

RUDDER CUT

WOOD DOVE

5

10

20

LITTLE DARBY ISLAND

STRONG

9

SALT CAY

312°

132°

DARBY
ISLAND

LIGNUMVITAE
CAY

TURN AT GRASSY
PATCHES

7

5

YOUNG
ISLAND

3

5

BOCK
CAY

WEST PIMBLICO CAYS

4

5

MAST

EAST PIMBLICO CAYS

3

DRYS L.W.

STRONG

JOINS J-41

TROPIC ISLE SKETCH CHART J-40
EDITION 113

BITTER GUANA CAY
TO
BOCK CAY

SOUNDINGS IN FEET AT LOW WATER
ALL COURSES MAGNETIC

0   NAUTICAL MILES   5

club docks, you will see two rocks off the tip of Big Major's Spot, one directly off the tip and the other, called Crown of Thorns Rock, in the middle of the passage. Crown of Thorns Rock sometimes has a mark on it, but often not. It is a hazard, submerged at extremely high tides. Leave both rocks to starboard when you are southbound approaching the yacht club.

Harvey Cay has deep water on both sides. A number of small cays and rocks enclose a very shallow sandbank in the center. A deep cove on its northwest end, close under the light, provides a temporary day anchorage close to shore with 21 feet of water. There is no appreciable tidal current. Deep water runs close around the end of the island. There is another anchorage on the south side of Harvey Cay, which gives good protection in northeast winds, as shown on sketch chart J-37 (Staniel Cay).

When proceeding from Harvey Cay to Black Point, it is advisable to lay a course to a position one mile southwest of Black Point, as a sandbank with only 7 feet lies in the entrance of the bay.

Bitter Guana Cay, next southeast of Staniel Cay, is easily recognized by the peculiar shape of its white cliff. Between Gaulin Cay (where iguanas are said to roam) and the northwest end of Great Guana Cay is Dotham Cut, good for 9 feet at low water. Unless the wind is blowing too hard outside with a heavy surge funneling in, this passage is straightforward into the sound.

Great Guana Cay. In the prevailing winds, from north to east to almost southwest, the anchorage in Black Point Bay is pleasant. However, in strong southerly winds some surge will work in around Black Point. Proceeding in, keep about 25-30 yards from the shore in about 12-18 feet. An anchorage in this depth may be found off the wooden dock in the first cove. You can also anchor in about 10 feet about one-third mile farther northeast, or you can bring up in about the same depth just short of the white sand flats at the head of the bay. On the northwest shore the water is deeper still.

Black Point settlement is the largest in the Exuma Cays (except those on Great Exuma), with about 300 people. There's a telephone station, a post office at the head of the dock, a clinic, laundry service, several small stores, a new airport, good restaurants, and friendly bars. The Scorpio Inn has a good Bahamian menu, and locals and visitors gather at its popular bar for dominoes, pool, and dancing. Lorene's Cafe (whose proprietor told us her name is actually Lorraine, despite the sign) offers excellent, inexpensive Bahamian food with satellite TV. Lorraine is also opening a bakery. Her husband, Uriah Rolle, builds houses and boats. Diane and Simon Smith's 3-room J & D Apartments have air-conditioning, private baths, upstairs balconies, and TV. Downstairs is Deshamon's Restaurant (call *Deshamon's* on VHF 16). They also rent 25 hp Whalers. Diane

Black Point town dock. (Tropic Isle photo)

has a straw market on sight. The town's Constable is Kevin Rolle, whose wife Esther has a beauty salon and barber shop. Leander Pinder is opening a food store with fresh vegetables. Lots of straw work is done in town by ladies who sit under trees plaiting while tending their babies and young children. August Monday (Emancipation Day) attracts local boats to compete for prizes here. Festivities include shoreside games and a town picnic. Walter Robinson is a reliable guide for the central Exumas. Willie Rolle can also help with local knowledge. Good fishing guides are Simon Smith and Wentzel Rolle.

LITTLE FARMER'S CAY
SETTLEMENT PIER SOUTH 100 YARDS
VIEW "B" CHART: J46

One mile north of **Little Farmer's Cay** is a conspicuous large rock, conical in shape, which looks just like a Bahamian stone oven. There are at least four channels by which the attractive harbor at Little Farmer's Cay may be gained (if you need assistance, call at *Ocean Cabin* on VHF 16 and Terry Bain will help guide you in). Aside from Farmer's Cay Cut, we consider the channel that approaches the southeast end of the Cay on a 022° bearing, with Farmer's Cay Cut just open, the best. This leads in from the deep channel that skirts the Farmer's Cay Bank, across an area of uniform 5 feet depth at low water, and clear of the coral and grass patches that lie off the Little Farmer's Cay shore (see sketch chart J-46, Farmer's Cay and Galliot Cut).

Approaching the east point of Little Farmer's Cay, avoid the visible white shoal by altering course and steering for the western corner of the white beach on Big Farmer's Cay. Take care to also avoid a shallow grassy bar on your starboard side. From here the deep channel in the harbor is clearly visible.

A second approach lies close along the southeastern shore of Little Farmer's Cay. This channel is slightly deeper than the first but it is more intricate. The approach from the bank is on an easterly heading as indicated on sketch chart J-46 (Farmer's Cay and Galliot Cut). There is 5-6 feet at low water on this heading until well under the shore of Little Farmer's Cay, where the water deepens to 7 feet. This channel lies 75-100 feet off the rocky shore all the way and joins the south channel at the dark patches.

The north entrance is good for 5-6 feet at low water, and as with all low-water figures, certain wind and lunar conditions could result in less water here. The channel runs from a point about 100 yards off Oven Rock straight for the end of the airstrip on the northwest point of Little Farmer's Cay. When about 200 yards off this point, turn to pass just off the dock at the Farmer's Cay Yacht Club and Marina. The brown and white bank that works out from Great Guana Cay and the light blue water channels are unmistakable. This channel reportedly has been privately marked. Call FCYC for help sorting it out.

Farmer's Cay Yacht Club and Marina, on the east side of the north end of

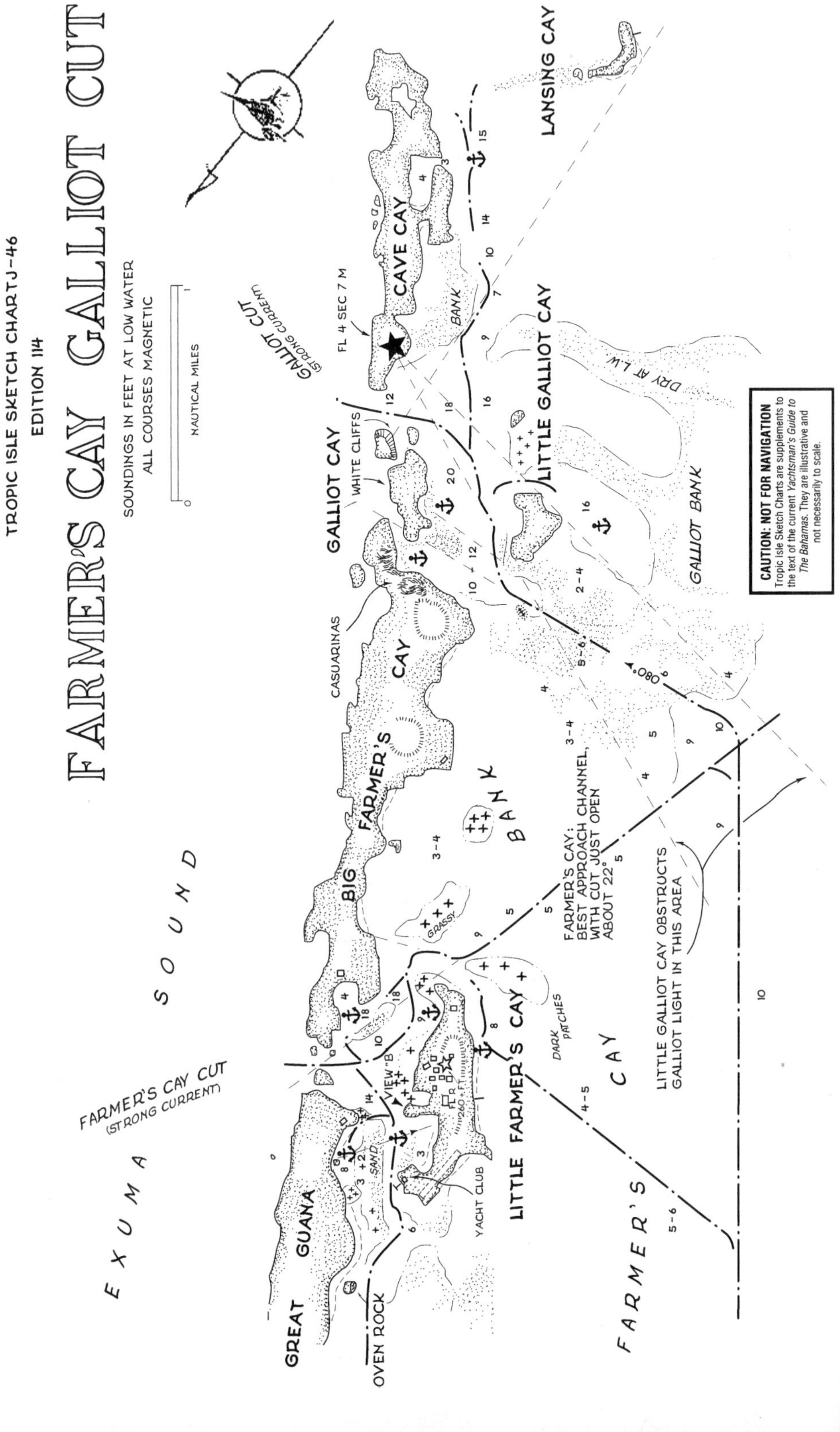

FARMER'S CAY GALLIOT CUT

TROPIC ISLE SKETCH CHART J-46
EDITION 114

SOUNDINGS IN FEET AT LOW WATER
ALL COURSES MAGNETIC

NAUTICAL MILES

CAUTION: NOT FOR NAVIGATION
Tropic Isle Sketch Charts are supplements to the text of the current *Yachtsman's Guide to The Bahamas*. They are illustrative and not necessarily to scale.

LANSING CAY

CAVE CAY

FL 4 SEC 7 M

BANK

GALLIOT CUT
(STRONG CURRENT)

GALLIOT CAY

WHITE CLIFFS

LITTLE GALLIOT CAY

DRY AT L.W.

GALLIOT BANK

CASUARINAS

FARMER'S
CAY

BIG

BANK

EXUMA   SOUND

GRASSY

DARK
PATCHES

FARMER'S CAY:
BEST APPROACH CHANNEL,
WITH CUT JUST OPEN
ABOUT 22°

LITTLE GALLIOT CAY OBSTRUCTS
GALLIOT LIGHT IN THIS AREA

FARMER'S CAY CUT
(STRONG CURRENT)

VIEW B

SAND

LITTLE FARMER'S CAY

GREAT GUANA

OVEN ROCK

YACHT CLUB

FARMER'S   CAY

Farmer's Cay Yacht Club. (Tropic Isle photo)

Little Farmer's Cay, has docking facilities with 7.5-8 feet at the outer dock (there's also a dinghy dock). A strong current runs here, so you might want assistance docking, and you'll probably need your fenders. The marina offers marine fuels, water, ice, some food supplies, a telephone, electricity, rooms, and a bar/restaurant serving good Bahamian fare for breakfast, lunch, and dinner (reservations are requested for dinner). Roosevelt Nixon, owner/manager of the yacht club, has built a bridge over the creek behind the club building to shorten the walk into town. Shirley Boleyn Nixon, Roosevelt's wife, is nurse at the clinic.

There are several pleasant anchorages around the harbor. Ocean Cabin has two moorings in the Guana Cay anchorage, and one in the harbor just off the Farmer's Cay channel (between L. Farmer's and Guana Cay). These are for rent for $10 per night (call *Ocean Cabin* on VHF 16).

If you arrive via the town dock in Little Harbour, you will first see a "Welcome to Farmer's Cay" sign, followed by what used to be the telecommunications building (now a warehouse and government office). Next to the main dock is a new dinghy dock. To get to the Batelco office, follow the road along the bay up the hill road (look for a red-roofed church). A telephone booth is at the corner going up the hill toward the church. Duke and Eugenia Percentie's well-stocked grocery, just up from the dock, has liquor for sale. The post office is at the corner of Little Harbour next to Hallan Rolle's green and white house.

Terry Bain runs Ocean Cabin restaurant with his wife Earnestine, who bakes bread and cakes to order (orders for baked goods or reservations for dinner should be made early in the morning; call *Ocean Cabin* on VHF 16). Wholesale liquor, wines, beer and limited block ice are available, and air or boat charters

Little Farmer's Cay and Farmer's Cay Cut. (Tropic Isle photo)

and hiking excursions can be arranged. Terry also runs a local rescue and towing team, the OCaFaCA RATS. During the season weekly events include pre-dinner crab races on Wednesday and chicken runs on Saturday. Terry also organizes the annual Farmer's Cay Festival, held on the first Friday and Saturday of February, with contests, an "international" hermit crab race, children's events, food all day, and disco all night. The annual full-moon Beer Festival is in July.

Hallan Rolle is an experienced pilot as well as a snorkeling, diving, or sight-seeing guide. A tour might include an 80-foot descent into a land cave on Great Guana Cay. Hallan's son Stanley is a cave and fishing guide. Hallan also supplies propane, and his wife, Mavis, runs the post office. The famous Bahamian racing craft, *Brothers,* was built on Little Farmer's Cay by Mavis's father, J. L. Maycock. Fresh grouper, crawfish, and conch are available through Hallan (call *Little Jeff* on VHF16) or Cecil Smith (*call Lamond*). Fleether Tinker, Jr., a wood carver, has a shop in his home on the corner of the road past the schoolteacher's house. On the northwest side of the island is a 2700' airstrip.

Farmer's Cay Cut is an excellent exit into Exuma Sound, being deep, short, and free from dangers. **Big Farmer's Cay** has some good beaches and coconut plantations on the western side but unfortunately the water off this coast is shallow. It is a large cay with undulating, brush-covered hills.

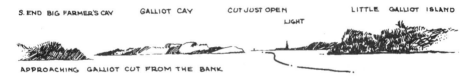

S. END BIG FARMER'S CAY   GALLIOT CAY   CUT JUST OPEN   LITTLE GALLIOT ISLAND
                                                   LIGHT

APPROACHING GALLIOT CUT FROM THE BANK

Galliot Cut: The channel that leads from the banks to Little Galliot Cay lies in an easterly direction. The edges of the banks on either side are not clearly defined, and seem to be gradually shoaling so that the controlling depth in the channel is only 6 feet. When Little Galliot Cay is reached, the water deepens considerably and is free from dangers. The cut itself is south of the rocks and cays just south of Galliot Cay. It is 12-15 feet deep and straightforward. A very strong tidal current, both ebb and flood, runs through Galliot Cut. When the ebb runs out against a strong east-northeast wind, a sea builds that will be dangerous to small craft. Because of the aforementioned shoaling, the George Town mailboats no longer use Galliot Cut. Instead they enter and depart the banks via Dotham Cut, north of Black Point.

Proceeding south inside, you must round the shallow bank that extends southwest from the north end of Cave Cay. Also round the point of a white sandbank that runs southeast from the banks south of Little Galliot Cay. The channel between these two banks, which overlap slightly, is fairly wide and carries a least depth of 9 feet. A sure way of crossing, if running in poor light but with a favorable tide, is to run on a line between the white cliffs at Galliot Cut and the west shore of Lansing Cay (see sketch chart J-46, Farmer's Cay and Galliot Cut). While this is not the deepest water (the 9-feet depth lies a few yards west), it guarantees you 7 feet least depth at low water.

Cave Cay is a beautiful island with high cliffs and hills. The ruins of an old stone house still remain and thick stone walls enclose land that once was pasture.

There are several caves on the island and a landlocked harbor dredged to accommodate boats of 4 feet draft entering at low water. The island is private property and the owner asks that visitors using the anchorage do not litter. Visits ashore are by invitation only.

Cave Cay Cut is deep and straightforward. The channel favors the southern end of Cave Cay. Leave the small rocks that lie close north of Musha Cay to the south. We have a letter from a reader warning that the bank between Musha Cay and Cave Cay is shoaling to the point that it is doubtful that 6 feet can be taken through.

We do not advise yachts drawing over 5 feet to proceed farther south inside the cays, as the bank south and west of Musha Cay and the north end of Rudder Cut Cay carries only about 3-3.5 feet at low water and is not clearly defined.

Musha Cay can be identified by its central hill. The sound between the cay and Rudder Cut Cay almost dries at low water. Musha Cay is privately owned and visits ashore are by invitation only.

Lansing Cay, which lies three-quarters of a mile southwest of Musha Cay, is low and has several casuarina groves on it. This cay also has some good beaches, but the approach is in 3-4 feet at low water.

Past Jimmy Cay the water again shallows to about 8 feet at high water, but it deepens considerably as you approach the prominent headland on Rudder Cut Cay. About 150 yards off the western beach is an anchorage in 12-14 feet over sand, grass, and coral. From here to Rudder Cut the best water, 14-18 feet, lies close along the shore.

N. END, DARBY IS.   CONSPIC. CONICAL RK.   RUDDER CUT CAY

RUDDER CUT BEARING ABOUT S.W.

Rudder Cut Cay has two interesting caves between the beaches on the headland. The dredged lake in the center of the cay has an anchorage on its north side in 8 feet over thin mud, reportedly with some construction debris on the bottom. Rudder Cut Cay is private property, and the lake has at times been barred from visitors with a chain across the entrance.

Rudder Cut is another good pass into Exuma Sound. It is deep and the entrance is partially protected by a small cay in the center of the cut. While there are channels on either side of this cay, the westernmost (lying close under the Rudder Cut Cay shore) is preferred as it guarantees 20 feet throughout.

If proceeding southeast along the bank side of Rudder Cut Cay toward the cut, keep close to the shore until past the low, bush-covered cay to starboard,

Cave Cay harbor entrance. (Tropic Isle photo)

keeping the prominent rocks to starboard. When the cut bears northeast you may proceed out on that course, still favoring the Rudder Cut Cay shore. A half-tide rock exists a short distance off the eastern point of Rudder Cut Cay. A very strong tidal current, both ebb and flood, runs through this cut. Entering from seaward, approach on a southwesterly course toward the three prominent rocks. When inside, turn to starboard, hugging the Rudder Cut Cay shore.

If bound from Rudder Cut Cay to **Darby Island,** proceed as for the cut, but leave the prominent rocks to starboard. Although deep water runs close to the rocks, the flood tide sets strongly between them, so maintain a safe berth. Once past the rocks, steer midway between the eastmost of them and the shore of **Little Darby Island.** The channel into the harbor is narrow but carries 6 feet at low water, so stay close (50-75 feet) off the Little Darby shore going in. Inside, the channel is marked by a stake. The anchorage is obvious. Both of the Darby Islands are private property with visits ashore permitted only by invitation. The large green structure on the hill was built in 1939, at which time 20,000 coconut palms were planted and herds of sheep, cattle, and goats roamed these cays.

Salt Cay, Betty Cay, Goat Cay, and Guana Cay have been registered as a bird sanctuary. Birds of many types migrate via these cays and it is hoped that this effort might help preserve such migratory fowl as duck and pigeon.

From Darby Island via the banks the best channel lies as indicated on sketch charts J-40 (Bitter Guana Cay to Bock Cay) and J-41 (Bock Cay to Channel Cay): working around the **West Pimblico Cays,** then east-southeast between the **East Pimblico Cays** to the northwest end of **Norman's Pond Cay.** Then pass close to the western point of **Leaf Cay,** around the western end of **Lee Stocking Island and Williams Cay,** and then into 5 feet of water to Children's Bay Cay, where the channel deepens to 12-14 feet. Lee Stocking Island is the site of the Caribbean Marine Research Center field laboratory, where permanent as well as visiting scientists study the various problems of national resources and marine food production in the Caribbean. You can inquire about tours of the facility, which are sometimes conducted for visitors. CMRC is a branch of the National Undersea Research Program of NOAA.

CONSPIC WHITE PATCHES.
BEACH

LEE STOCKING ISLAND: W.S.W. 2 MILES.

The anchorage in Children's Bay is just beyond the dock in 7 feet over grass and sand. Protection is good from all except west winds. **Children's Bay Cay** is a well-developed private island with palm-fringed beaches, graceful wall-lined paths, and a variety of attractive buildings. Visits ashore are by invitation only.

Between Rat Cay and Pigeon Cay the channel is narrow. It is also narrow between Square Cay and Square Rock, the latter being unmistakable from its name. **Square Rock Cut** is a good but narrow passage into Exuma Sound, carrying 14 feet at low water. The shallowest part of this portion of the inside passage is on the banks between Sugar Cay and Glass Cay, where several sandbars carry little more than 4 feet at low water.

Barraterre can be reached via the east-west channel of 8 feet that lies in line with the north point of Barraterre and Square Rock Cut. After rounding the yellow bank one-half mile east of the point, steer in close to the shore. At low water you have 4 feet to the anchorage and 6 feet over sand just off the dock. You can also anchor north of the Fisherman's Inn, which is on the headland just north of the pier, in 6 feet. Norman Lloyd's Fisherman's Inn serves breakfast, lunch, and dinner, specializing in fresh seafood (dinner reservations are recommended). Norman can taxi passengers to George Town, useful if you need to get people to or from the airport and don't want to take your boat all the way down to George Town. If you wander around Barraterre you'll see where, in the shade of a grove of trees, Hughrie Lloyd builds beautiful little sailboats that have done well in the regattas. McKenzie's sells food, liquor, straw work, and shells. Ray Ann's Variety Store has produce and sundries. Onions, tomatoes, cabbages, sweet peppers, bananas, mangoes, grapefruits, and avocados are grown near town using the pothole-farming technique. When we asked an Exuma native about the origin of the name "Barraterre," we were told there was a lazy guy named Barry who was always tarrying there (at the very least this is a clue to Barraterre's pronunciation). Jeff Thompson, in his *Historical/Pictorial Guide to Exuma,* provides another explanation: sponge fishermen once used Barraterre as a "bar" to tarry on before returning home.)

Proceeding outside from Galliot or Rudder Cut toward George Town, there are no off-lying dangers. A vessel may keep within a short distance of the small cays lining the coast. Good landmarks on this route are the large green house on Darby Island; Norman's Pond Rocks; the beacon on Adderley Cay; the hills of Lee Stocking Island; and the white roofs on Children's Bay Cay; Square Rock; **Three Sisters Rocks,** which can be seen from 6 miles (see note below); and the stone beacon on the north end of Soldier Cay. Stocking Island, which forms the north side of Elizabeth Harbour, can be seen from 15 miles.

Note Regarding Three Sisters Rocks

In this Guide we use the term "Three Sisters Rocks" only to refer to the rocks northeast of Barraterre, as designated on D.M.A Chart 26301 and on our sketch chart J-41. Be aware that locally many people refer to the "conspicuous rocks" off Mt. Thompson (see sketch chart J-41) as the Three Sisters Rocks. **Do not confuse the two designations when navigating.** If designating a location as near either of these becomes critical, be sure to explain which "Three Sisters Rocks" you refer to. For example, the northern ones could be described as "the Three Sisters Rocks off Barraterre," and the southern ones as "the Three Sisters Rocks off Mt. Thompson."

WEST PIMBLICO CAYS

FROM RUDDER CUT

YOUNG ISLAND

EAST PIMBLICO CAYS

BOCK CAY
MAST

NORMAN POND ROCKS   SOUTH 1 MILE

JOINS J-40

THIS SAND BAR PARTLY DRY AT L.W.

LEAF CAY

ADDERLY CAY

ADDERLY CUT 12 FT L.W.

AIRSTRIP

NORMAN'S POND CAY

RUINS

BOCK CAT CAY

ADDERLY BEACON S.W. 1 MILE

312° - 132°

WILLIAMS CAY

LEE STOCKING ISLAND

ALLEN CAY

MAST

CHILDREN'S BAY CAY

BRIGANTINE CAYS

CHILDREN'S BAY CUT IS NARROW (00 FT) ENTER IN SETTLED WEATHER ONLY.

RAT CAY

PUDDING CUT

PIGEON CAY

SQUARE ROCK

SQUARE CAY CUT 16 FT L.W. 12 FT L.W. INSIDE

CUT CAY

CLOVE CAY
MAST FL R

JIMMY CAY

150 FL R

THREE SISTERS ROCKS

BARRA TERRE

HOG ISLAND

GLASS CAY

MAIL BOAT CHANNEL 10 FT L.W.

CAUTION: NOT FOR NAVIGATION
Tropic Isle Sketch Charts are supplements to the text of the current *Yachtsman's Guide to The Bahamas*. They are illustrative and not necessarily to scale.

SUGAR CAY
RED ROOF

BLACK CAY

EXUMA POINT

WHITE BAY CAY

SOLDIER CAY BEACON S.W.

ALEXANDER

FL R 260 FT

GOVT. DOCK

BOTH NORTH AND SOUTH SOLDIER CUTS ARE BORDERED BY BROWN CORAL REEFS ON THEIR NORTHERN SIDES.

ROLLEVILLE

NOTE A: SEE NOTE IN TEST REGARDING THREE SISTERS ROCKS.

STEVENTON

GOVT. DOCK

CONSPIC. YELLOW BUILDING ON POINT.

ROCKY POINT

ROKER'S POINT

RICHMOND HILL

CONSPIC. DISH ANTENNAE

THE FOREST

BIRD CAY

FARMER'S HILL

NOTE A:
THE TIDES ON THE BANKS LAG THOSE OF THE SOUND BY 5-6 HOURS.

CONSPIC. ROCKS (SEE NOTE A)

318° - 138°

STEER FOR STOCKING ISLAND MARKER BEACON

MT. THOMPSON

RAMSEY

DUCK CAY

TROPIC ISLE SKETCH CHART J-41
EDITION 108

AIRSTRIP

FLAT CAY

288° - 108°

CHANNEL CAY

BOCK CAY
TO
CHANNEL CAY

JOINS J-42

SOUNDINGS IN FEET AT LOW WATER

ALL COURSES MAGNETIC

0   NAUTICAL MILES   5

GREAT EXUMA ISLAND

YELLOW BANK

GREAT EXUMA ISLAND

D.M.A. Charts: 26279, 26280, 26286, 27040. N.O.S. Chart: 11013. Tropic Isle Sketch Charts: J-41, 42, 44.

Historically, Great Exuma is one of the most interesting islands in The Bahamas. It also has some first-rate scenery. Thanks to George Town and Elizabeth Harbour, into which a draft of 16 feet can be taken by the eastern entrance, the island has been in turn a pirate rendezvous, a refitting base for British man-of-wars, and a World War II U.S. Naval Base. Before slavery was abolished, the fertile countryside prospered with plantations established by American Loyalists. Their ruins are still to be seen.

BEACH   BEACH & LANDING   LOW CLIFFS   LONG BEACH
ROLLEVILLE, GT EXUMA, BEARING SOUTH FROM ANCHORAGE

On the approach to Great Exuma from the northwest, the first settlement and anchorage is at **Rolleville,** where the best anchorage is in the lee of Black Cay, about a mile from the settlement. The entrance channel used by the freight boat is between the small unnamed cay west of Black Cay and Glass Cay, as indicated on sketch chart J-41, (Bock Cay to Channel Cay.) *Caution: Never attempt this passage in a heavy ground swell.* Glass Cay lies one-half mile south of Three Sisters Rocks (northeast of Barraterre) and can be identified by the two small beaches on its eastern side. Inside, the channel to the settlement lies over a dark grassy bottom.

The stone beacon on the north side of **Soldier Cay** marks the channel (10 feet at low water). When entering, favor the south side to avoid the shallow brown bar that works into it from the north. The somewhat wider channel on the south side of Soldier Cay carries 8-10 feet at low water. Take care to avoid the shallow brown bar that extends into it from Soldier Cay's southern shore.

It can be a hot climb up through Rolleville to Kermit's Hilltop Restaurant and Tavern, but a seat at a rooftop table with an ice-cold beer and friendly companions makes it worthwhile. Lunches or full-course dinners can be arranged with notice. There's an open-air dance floor and live music on weekends.

Between Rolleville and **Steventon,** the next settlement to the southeast, all but shoal-draft vessels must return outside, as the water between the cays and the mainland is shallow. The anchorage off Steventon is fairly well-protected from most winds, but it should never be attempted in strong weather from the north or northeast or in a heavy ground swell. The bottom in Steventon Bay is white sand with distinct coral patches. There is 7-10 feet in the bay and the best anchorage is about 150 yards off the dock. Steventon, with thick groves of coconut palms, resembles a South Sea island scene. There is a medical clinic,

From Steventon you are within easy reach of Elizabeth Harbour. Approaching from the northwest, the first landmark you will sight is the high, wedge-shaped mass of Stocking Island with a white stone beacon at its summit.

Elizabeth Harbour (Tropic Isle Sketch Charts: J-42, 44). The approach described here is a dangerous entrance in anything but adequate light conditions, when hazards can be seen distinctly.

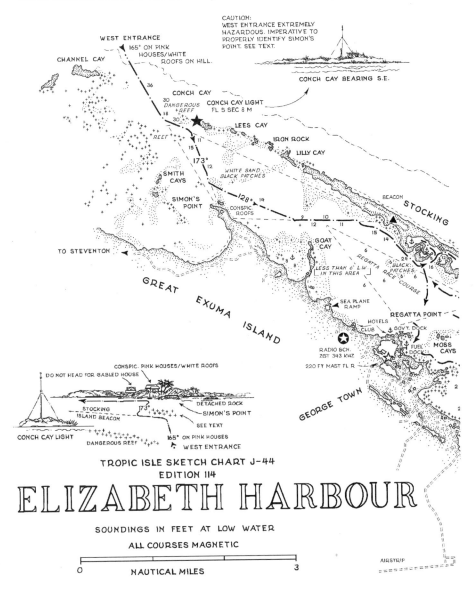

TROPIC ISLE SKETCH CHART J-44
EDITION 114

ELIZABETH HARBOUR

SOUNDINGS IN FEET AT LOW WATER

ALL COURSES MAGNETIC

0   NAUTICAL MILES   3

Caution #1: *Unfortunately, as new construction takes place, approach landmarks have become less distinctive. The approach to the western entrance of Elizabeth Harbour is on a course of 165° on* **Simon's Point,** *which can be identified by a pair of large pink houses together with a grove of palm trees, all silhouetted against the sky. (Be aware that a coat of paint could change the color of these houses in a day.) Just southeast (to the left as you enter) of the pink houses there is a prominent two-story, gabled house. Do* **not** *head for this; it is mentioned here only to help you locate your target on Simon's Point. If you mistakenly take your bearing on a house east of*

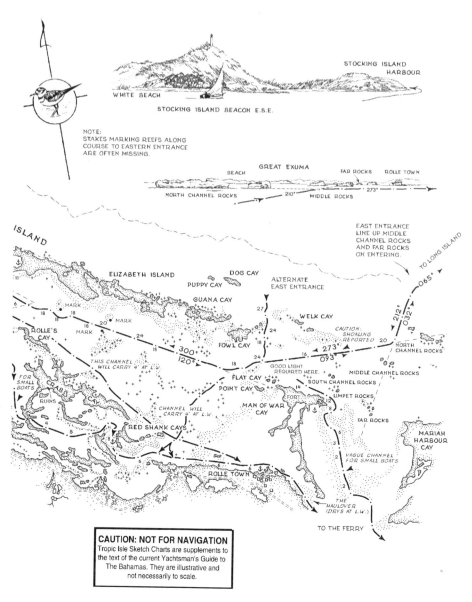

CAUTION: NOT FOR NAVIGATION
Tropic Isle Sketch Charts are supplements to
the text of the current Yachtsman's Guide to
The Bahamas. They are illustrative and
not necessarily to scale.

> **PLEASE NOTE:** For a description of **Batelco towers in all areas and their light characteristics**, please check page 39 of this Guide.

Simon's Point, the 165° course will take you onto the reef. Be right, and do not "just give it a try." If in doubt, there are local guides who will come out and take you in for a fee. Call them on VHF 16: Wendell Cooper (Interlude) and Wendell McGregor (Little Toot).

Caution #2: In a heavy ground swell, particularly during the ebb, the seas tend to break for much of the distance between Channel Cay and Conch Cay, and the cut can be impassable. Calm weather is equally dangerous because without breaking seas, the shallow reef off Conch Cay is difficult, if not impossible, to see. It's there, and boats are frequently lost on it. Four sailboats between 38 and 42 feet were total losses between March 1986 and August 1995. Others have been grounded, but freed with assistance.

Caution #3: This passage has been marked one way or another, usually by private interests, many times. Usually the marks do not last long. Marks may or may not be replaced; if they are, the type mark and the marking scheme that will be used are unknown to us at our publication deadline. Additionally, since this passage is often an extremely rough place, we caution that even if marks are placed, there is always the possibility that they might at any time be off station or missing. For these reasons we continue to give guidance as to how to enter here based as much as possible on permanent landmarks rather than on marks which have over the years proven unreliable.

Proceed on 165° until past the reef off Conch Cay, at which point Conch Cay Light should bear due east. Alter course and steer for the Stocking Island Beacon (about 130°). On this leg, you must pass between the southwest side of the reef off Conch Cay and a rocky bar, usually known as Etheridge Shoal, which lies about parallel to it approximately a quarter mile to the west-southwest. In good light this can be seen quite distinctly. Etheridge Shoal is often marked in some way, and often not. When we were working on this edition there was a red and white horizontally striped buoy near its southeast end, and this was the only mark in this entire approach.

Once clear of the rocky bar, when Simon's Point bears about 173° and Conch Cay Light is about 350 yards northeast, steer directly for Simon's Point on the 173° course until you are over the black patches or within 200 yards of the point, at the same time keeping a lookout for rocky patches you will pass on

Conch Cay (looking out). (Tropic Isle photo)

Anchorage under Stocking Island beach. (Tropic Isle photo)

your starboard hand. From this point steer 128° until on a line between the pink houses of Simon's Point and the beacon on Stocking Island. Then alter course to the beacon, thus avoiding the shallow sandbank that extends southwest from the vicinity of Lily Cay.

Once past the shallow sandbank extending southwest from the vicinity of Lily Cay, the deep channel follows the Stocking Island shore and is unmistakable. When the entrance of Stocking Island Harbour is brought abeam, you may alter course and head for the George Town dock, one mile to the southwest.

Caution: Boats that anchor southwest of the Stocking Island Beacon should remember that mail and freight boats ply the channel here at all hours, day and night. Stay clear of it by anchoring northeast of a line drawn between the point of land at the entrance to the Stocking Island lagoons and

GEORGE TOWN, EXUMA, BAHAMAS

CLUB peace & plenty HOTEL

Home of the Cruisers Regatta in March and the Out Island Regatta in April. Boaters have 360° protection in bad weather at Hurricane Hole.

Enjoy unspoiled charm at the famous 35-room Club Peace & Plenty, George Town, Exuma, on Elizabeth Harbour. Informal luxury is the order of the day, featuring air-conditioned rooms with tile floors and seaview balconies, cozy bar and dinghy dock. You will love our private Stocking Island, only one mile away with a beach club, bar and restaurant service.

The 16-room Peace & Plenty Beach Inn with white sandy beach and popular sponge bar on our dinghy dock is located one mile west of George Town.

Both hotels monitor Channel 16 VHF for your convenience and safety. All watersports plus excellent Bahamian and American cuisine, with our unique 3 resort dine-around plan. Enjoy Saturday Night barbecue and dances on the pool patio. All boaters and pilots are most welcome.

For reservations:
U.S.A. call toll-free 1-800-525-2210,
or direct 242-336-2551/2. Fax 242-336-2093.
In Fort Lauderdale call 954-359-9899, or write P&P Management Company, 1170 Lee Wagener Blvd., 111, Fort Lauderdale, FL 33315.
E-Mail: ssbpeace aol.com
www address: http://www.peaceandplenty.com

TROPIC ISLE SKETCH CHART J-42
EDITION 114

ELIZABETH HARBOUR

TO

HOG CAY

SOUNDINGS IN FEET AT LOW WATER

ALL COURSES MAGNETIC

0   NAUTICAL MILES   5

CAUTION: NOT FOR NAVIGATION
Tropic Isle Sketch Charts are supplements to
the text of the current *Yachtsman's Guide to
The Bahamas.* They are illustrative and
not necessarily to scale.

AT ANY TIME NAVIGATIONAL LIGHTS
THROUGHOUT THE BAHAMAS MAY
NOT BE WORKING OR MAY HAVE
FLASHING PATTERNS VARYING FROM
THOSE NOTED ON GOVERNMENT
CHARTS, SKETCH CHARTS OR THE
TEXT IN THIS GUIDE.

SOUTH TO PEAR CAY CHANNEL
SEE N.O. CHART 26240

Stocking Island. (Tropic Isle photo)

the northwest end of the long sand beach northwest of the beacon. If you anchor in the channel or even swing into it, you can cause heavy commercial boats to go aground as they try to avoid you, or worse, you may be hit if they don't see you. In this, as in all anchorages, be sure to show an anchor light at night.

There are many nice anchorages in the harbor, although the best are at **Stocking Island.** (Unfortunately, however, these anchorages are often crowded with boats that seem to have become permanent fixtures. If you listen to the chatter on the VHF, all they seem to do is make arrangements for cocktail parties and tell why it is impossible for them do anything except stay anchored where they are. They all always seem to have a broken something-or-other that prevents them from ever going anywhere. So don't have high expectations of finding a place to anchor here.) The main anchorage here has a depth of 12-18 feet over a grassy bottom. It is almost landlocked and gives protection in all weather. To the west of the main anchorage is a 6-feet-at-high-water channel to the left of the small white marker that leads to a landlocked lagoon. Across Basin 2, as this lagoon is called, is the entrance to still another lagoon, Basin 3, where 6 feet can be carried at high water by staying close to the left on entering. Inside is plenty of water surrounded by high land. On the northeast shore is a private home.

From the main anchorage to the east, there is yet another protected anchorage that can be reached via a dredged channel. The channel is marked and carries 6 feet at high water. This basin has good water and is enclosed. The

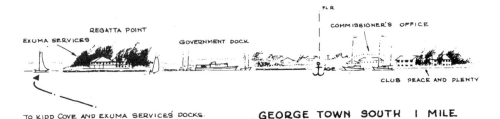

TO KIDD COVE AND EXUMA SERVICES DOCKS.   **GEORGE TOWN SOUTH 1 MILE**

pink buildings on the south shore are private homes.

Among the attractions of Stocking Island is a coastline almost surrounded by exquisite beaches and lush coconut groves. The ocean beach, one of the most beautiful in The Bahamas, is over a mile long. Shell collectors might find murex, butterfly, hawk's wing, and olive shells.

George Town, a delightfully picturesque community of about 900 people, serves as the southernmost cruising headquarters for visiting yachtsmen exploring The Bahamas. The town is ideally suited for this role, not only because of its excellent anchorages, but also because local businesses carry the most complete stock of supplies in the Exumas and the local airport has frequent air connections to Nassau and South Florida.

Anchorage may be found 100 yards in front of the Peace and Plenty Hotel, a large pink structure that, with the pink government administration building to its left, dominates the George Town side of Elizabeth Harbour. You will find 6-7 feet at low water in a large area off Peace and Plenty. Anchor carefully as there is a persistent surge. Legend has it that the hotel was originally built as a slave market, after which it became a sponge warehouse and eventually a hostelry. Owned for many years by Stanley and Jeanne Benjamin, Club Peace and Plenty serves a delicious Bahamian menu (call for reservations on VHF 16), and there's an intimate, friendly bar. On dance nights there's live music on the terrace overlooking the harbor. The large dinghy dock is convenient for trips into town. Nearby is the P&P Beach Inn (they've also opened a Bonefish Lodge 10 miles east near the ferry bridge). Across the harbor, hamburgers, hot dogs, and such are served at the P&P Stocking Island Beach Club. East of Peace and Plenty is the government dock, where you will find about 8.5 feet at low water.

George Town. (Tropic Isle photo)

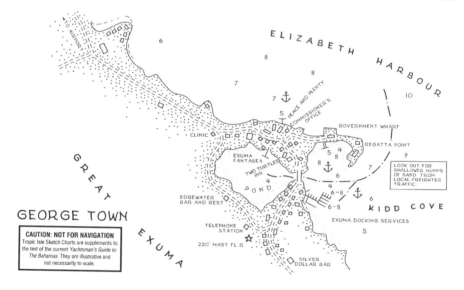

GEORGE TOWN

CAUTION: NOT FOR NAVIGATION
Tropic Isle Sketch Charts are supplements to
the text of the current *Yachtsman's Guide to
The Bahamas*. They are illustrative and
not necessarily to scale.

You can also anchor in Kidd Cove (said to be a favorite anchorage of Captain Kidd) under Regatta Point, where depth ranges from 5-8 feet and less near the shore. Stay clear of the channel into Exuma Docking Services. In this anchorage, you may find some shallower humps of sand plowed up by freighter

EXUMA MARKETS

Complete Grocery Supplies
Fresh Produce • Fresh Meats
Non-Prescription Drugs

We hold your mail and fax messages.

P.O. Box EX 29031
George Town,
Exuma, Bahamas

Phone: (242) 336-2033
Fax: (242) 336-2645

Exuma Docking Services. (Tropic Isle photo)

and tanker traffic, usually because someone blocked the channel, forcing the commercial boats out of it. There is good protection from all winds except southeast. To reach Kidd Cove, pass about 75-100 yards east and south of Regatta Point to avoid the rocky bar there. (Note: George Town is reported to be considering requiring holding tank pump-outs, so be prepared to be prepared. Considering the number of boats that become practically permanent residents here, and that this is pretty much a landlocked harbor, this seems to make sense.)

Petroleum products, ice, water, electricity, and telephone, as well as a chandlery, a laundromat, car rental, and a liquor store are among the facilities at Exuma Docking Services, where 5-8 feet is available at low water at the dock. The entrance channel is good for 6 feet at low water. (There have been, from time to time, plans to mark this channel.) When a chop works in from the east, you may need fenders. Sam's Place serves very good breakfasts, lunches and dinners. Exuma Docking Services monitors VHF 16 and answers to *Sugar One*. Call first to check availability of space along the fuel dock. Across the street is Denzella Rolle's N & D Fruits and Vegetables. Besides her superfresh produce,

Denzella Rolle's N & D Fruit and Veggie shop. (Tropic Isle photo)

Club Peace and Plenty. (Tropic Isle photo)

she has ice cream, conch salad, coffee, hot dogs, ice, r/o water, same-day laundry service, and scooters, bikes, cars, and apartments for rent. Don't leave without meeting Denzella, observer of the human condition, philosopher, and humorist. Just a few steps south of N & D is Fishin Good Seafood's market.

On The Pond, Minn's Watersports is back, a small-boat marina and Boston Whaler dealer with boat rental, dry storage, and OMC sales and service. Basil Minns' son-in-law Kent Polley is manager. Basil's daughter and Kent's wife, Diane, runs The Sandpiper, an exceptional Bahamian-crafts gift shop where you can purchase her own striking serigraph prints of Bahamian scenes. There's also a selection of paperbacks, Caribbean postcards, ceramics, and fine straw bags. *Yachtsman's Guides* and Tropic Isle sketch charts are also available. In the back of the shop, Diane and her sister, Lorraine Lee, have a silk screen factory called Island T's, where they design and print T-shirts and other silkscreened items for sale in the shop or wholesale to other outlets. The children's T-shirts are designed by Diane's and Lorraine's children, who earn $1.25 on each shirt sold. Diane's father, Basil Minns, is the George Town correspondent for this *Guide*. Across The Pond, Andrea and Victor "Rap" Brown are your hosts at Eddie's Edgewater, serving breakfast, lunch and dinner daily (excellent fresh fish, conch, and chicken cooked Bahamian-style). It's popular, so call for reservations. On Monday and Thursday evenings, hors d'oeuvres are free and a local rake 'n' scrape band plays. As Rap says, you can "dance the night away."

The Exuma Dive Centre, run by John and Connie Dey, offers scuba instruction and equipment rental, scooter rentals, boat rentals, and arrangements for bonefishing and deep sea fishing. The Dive Centre is also agent for Fandango Air, which flies passengers twice weekly to and from Fort Lauderdale and can also haul freight. You can order parts to be delivered to Combs Air Service in Fort Lauderdale and meet your stuff at the George Town airport and shepherd it through customs.

The island administrator for Exuma is stationed in George Town, which is

LOOK FOR US AT YACHTSMANSGUIDE.COM

Denzella points the way. (Tropic Isle photo)

a port of entry. His office is in the Government Building west of the town park, along with the post office. There are pay telephones at Exuma Docking Services, Two Turtles, and Peace and Plenty. The town telephone station, a short walk south of Exuma Docking Services, is open daily.

There are several ice machines around town, and water is available at the government dock (pay for it at the island administrator's office, upstairs in the pink building next to the Peace and Plenty). Exuma Markets, owned and operated by Sandy and Michael Minns, carries a large stock of groceries and fresh produce, dairy products, and meat. They will also hold mail for you (have your mail addressed to you c/o Exuma Markets), and will send or receive faxes. Exuma Markets is just over the bridge, with a convenient dinghy dock behind it on The Pond. In the John Marshall complex, the Town Cafe restaurant and bakery serves breakfast and lunch Monday through Saturday, including deli sandwiches, grill specials, and Bahamian dishes. The bakery prepares fresh bread and pastry and bakes cakes to order. Next to the Cafe is John Marshall's gas station and the John Marshall Liquor Store. A Shop Rite has opened where John Marshall had his store. For hardware, try Clark's Hardware or, north of town, Darville's fully stocked store. Near the bridge, a small marine hardware/ tackle store called Top and Bottom carries some supplies. There are laundromats at Exuma Docking Services or the Harbour View on the Pond.

Just up the hill from Peace and Plenty is a pink clinic where a doctor, nurse, and dentist keep regular hours. You can get a haircut by Janet at My T Fine, upstairs by the big tree near Batelco. At the town library is an extensive book swap, free to those whose join the Library Association for a $2 membership fee.

The National Family Island Regatta, held each year in April, is a festive event attracting yachtsmen from all over, as well as residents and visitors from all the islands. The regatta is a spectacular four-day sailing series held in Elizabeth Harbour where, on a bright, windy day, the beautiful Bahamian boats are a sight to behold. During the races spectators are permitted to move about the race course in their dinghies or big boats. Elizabeth Harbour is also the site of the Annual George Town Cruising Regatta in mid-March, which includes racing events for cruising yachtsmen, windsurfing, dinghy and sunfish competitions, and a variety of activities ranging from a talent show to a castle-building contest.

A popular happy-hour meeting place is the Two Turtles Inn, with casual dining inside and out, a bar, Friday night barbecues, Tuesday fish fries, satellite TV, and nice clean air-conditioned rooms with baths (three of the rooms have kitchenettes). On the premises is the Art and Nature boutique. Under the tree across the street from Sam Gray, Jr.'s liquor store, Freda Hall serves lunch and fresh bread every afternoon except Sunday. She will also serve small groups dinner in her home by prior arrangement. The Flamingo Bay Restaurant was praised by a contributor for excellent food (lunch and dinner, seafood a specialty), a nice bar, playable tennis courts (where they met other tennis players from other boats) and volleyball on the beach. They have a dinghy dock. For a sophisticated (and not inexpensive) meal, another contributor recommends the *prix fixe* dinner at Higgins Landing on Stocking Island. If you're arriving or leaving George Town by air, Kermit's bar and restaurant at the airport is open from 7:30 a.m. until 8:00 p.m. (hours are subject to change, however, so check ahead if you're depending on a meal). Regatta Point offers one- and two-bedroom spacious and airy efficiencies with full kitchens and a spectacular harbor view. The Gray family of Exuma Docking Services has opened the Mount Pleasant Suites Hotel, about three miles west of George Town, near Hooper's Bay beach. Accommodations include a two-bedroom townhouse suite and 23 one-bedroom suites, all with kitchens, air-conditioning and satellite TV.

Roads run the length of the island north to Rolleville and south to Little Exuma. Both routes make worthwhile excursions, with stops at such interesting places as Moss Town, The Forest, or Roker's Point. Along the route you'll see remains of old plantations. Several of the taxi and minibus drivers based in George Town offer tours with creative local history lessons thrown in.

Toward the east end of Elizabeth Harbour there is a mark on the southern point of a shoal northeast of Rolle's Cay. A little more than one-half mile east-southeast of this, two marks about 75 yards apart mark dangerous reefs on both sides of the channel; pass between them. All these marks are privately placed, are difficult to see in some light conditions, and could be missing. They could at various times be buoys, little floats, stakes or other types of marks.

To make your way in or out of the eastern entrance of Elizabeth Harbour (see sketch charts J-42, Elizabeth Harbour to Hog Cay, and J-44, Elizabeth Harbour) you must have good light so you can negotiate this channel by eye. Marks are few and often missing, and there are reefy and shoal areas that must be negotiated. Listening in on your radio, you'll frequently hear people tell of having hit a reef or bottom in various spots along the way here. We have a recent letter from a reader that tells of having "hit the ground several times with a draft of 8 feet at high water" near the area west of North Channel Rock where the sketch chart shows shoaling reported.

Those who like more peace and quiet can anchor in Master Harbour, west of the **Red Shank Cays** in 9-12 feet. Here, George Town Marina offers repairs

George Town Marina. (Tropic Isle photo)

and boat storage, with a 50-ton travelift for boats up to 50 feet. Mark Turnquest is the man in change. **Man Of War Cay,** lying at the south side of the eastern entrance to Elizabeth Harbour, has an old fortification erected by the Royal Navy in the days of the buccaneers. **Mariah Harbour Cay** is surrounded by beaches and coves. The shelling here is excellent.

Rolle Town lies a few miles east of George Town and is reachable by road. A draft of 6 feet can be carried down the east side of Crab Cay on the tide and into the anchorage off the Rolle Town dock. This interesting hilltop settlement, birthplace of television actress Esther Rolle, is laid out in true plantation style around a large rectangular village green and overlooking the harbor to the north. Near the town, the tombs of the McKay family from Scotland bear inscriptions that attest poignantly to the hardships of plantation life in the late 1700s.

A narrow and intricate shallow water cut divides the islands of Great and Little Exuma, and a single-lane fixed bridge now spans the cut where a hand-drawn ferry formerly operated. The bridge offers 8 feet clearance to small craft at low water.

Little Exuma (Tropic Isle Sketch Chart: J-42) is about 12 miles long and just over a mile wide. There are three settlements: **The Ferry, Forbes Hill,** and **William's Town.** The Ferry is a quaint and industrious community from which many residents commute daily to George Town. Of interest is the private chapel of the Fitzgerald family, who migrated here from Ireland many generations ago.

At Williams Town you'll find an orderly little community bordered on the south by an abandoned salt pond and on the east by Cotton House, the oldest residence in the Exumas, dating back to the earliest plantation days. Williams Town is worth a visit, but be aware that the anchorage off the settlement is an uneasy one. The white stone column shown on the sketch chart just northwest of town is an interesting navigation mark. According to local sources, it was placed to guide salt schooners to the anchorage where they could receive cargo by lighter. In the land of broomstick navigation marks, suddenly here's a column that looks as though it were imported from a Greek or Roman ruin.

The narrow cut that separates Little Exuma from Hog Cay, known as **Hog Cay Cut** (see sketch chart J-45, Hog Cay Cut) carries barely 3 feet at low water. It provides a shortcut for those bound for the Jumentos Cays, Ragged Island, or the south end of Long Island. A strong tidal current flows through the cut and works across the narrow channel at the south side. We recommend that you await slack tide before proceeding through this cut. You should negotiate this cut in good light, because the sketch chart can only give an approximation of the channel's location. Plan carefully, because if you go aground it will most likely be on a hard bottom, and if you go on at high slack, you'll shortly be losing water. There isn't much help available hereabouts.

Hog Cay is private property and extensively cultivated. The farmer-manager lives in the conspicuous house in the center of the island and is friendly to visitors. A short distance from the house stand the remains of a lookout tower with an ancient 5-foot cannon at its base, undoubtedly an outpost for Elizabeth Harbour in the old days. Beware of the fierce turkey that roams Hog Cay.

White Cay, easternmost of the Exumas, has long, sandy beaches and prominent dunes. Iguanas, an endangered species, live here, so please do not take your dog ashore. If bound for Long Island, round the conspicuous white sandbank that now extends about a mile, perhaps more, north of the cay and lay your course for Simms settlement. You will have 8-10 feet all the way.

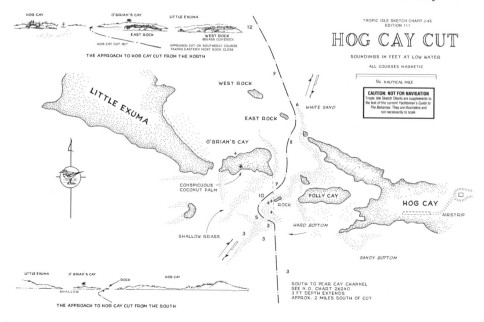

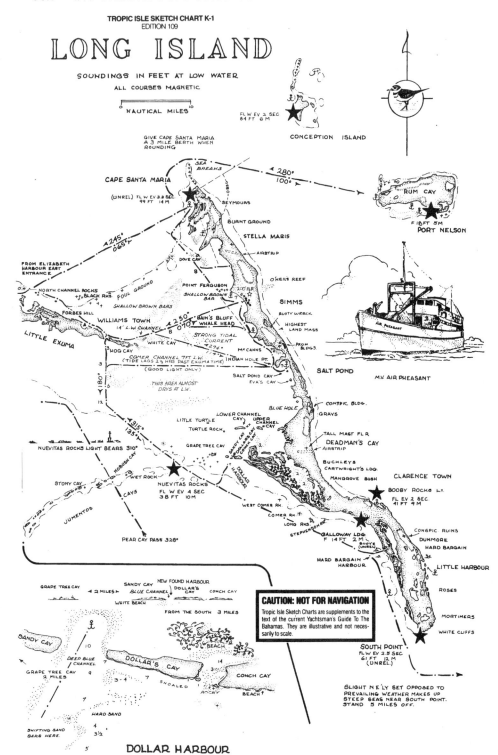

TROPIC ISLE SKETCH CHART K-1
EDITION 109

LONG ISLAND

SOUNDINGS IN FEET AT LOW WATER

ALL COURSES MAGNETIC

NAUTICAL MILES

CONCEPTION ISLAND

FL W EV 2 SEC
84 FT 6 M

GIVE CAPE SANTA MARIA
A 3 MILE BERTH WHEN
ROUNDING

SEA BREAKS

CAPE SANTA MARIA

(UNREL) FL W EV 3.3 SEC
99 FT 14 M

SEYMOURS

BURNT GROUND

STELLA MARIS

AIRSTRIP

RUM CAY

PORT NELSON
F 18FT 5M

DOVE CAY

FROM ELIZABETH
HARBOUR EAST
ENTRANCE

FOUL GROUND

NORTH CHANNEL ROCKS
BLACK RKS.

POINT FERGUSON
SHALLOW BROWN BAR

O'NEILS REEF

SIMMS

SHALLOW BROWN BARS

FORBES HILL

WILLIAMS TOWN
14' L.W. CHANNEL

BAIN'S BLUFF
WHALE HEAD

RUSTY WRECK

HIGHEST
LAND MASS

LITTLE EXUMA

WHITE CAY

STRONG TIDAL
CURRENT

McCANNS

PROM.
BLDGS.

HOG CAY

COMER CHANNEL 7FT L.W.
(TIDE LAGS 2½ HRS PAST EXUMA TIME)
(GOOD LIGHT ONLY)

INDIAN HOLE PT.

SALT POND CAY
EVA'S CAY

SALT POND

M.V. AIR PHEASANT

THIS AREA ALMOST
DRYS AT L.W.

BLUE HOLE

CONSPIC. BLDG.

GRAYS

LOWER CHANNEL
CAY

UPPER
CHANNEL
CAY

LITTLE TURTLE
CAY

TALL MAST FL R

DEADMAN'S CAY
AIRSTRIP

TURTLE ROCK

GRAPE TREE CAY

BUCKLEYS
CARTWRIGHT'S LDG.

NUEVITAS ROCKS LIGHT BEARS 310°

MANGROVE BUSH

CLARENCE TOWN

STONY CAY

WET ROCK

NUEVITAS ROCKS
FL W EV 4 SEC
38 FT 10M

BOOBY ROCKS LT.
FL EV 2 SEC.
41 FT 9 M

CAYS

JUMENTOS

WEST COMER RK.

COMER RK.

LONG RKS.

STEPHENSON RK.

GALLOWAY LDG.
F 14FT 2M

CONSPIC. RUINS

DUNMORE
HARD BARGAIN

PEAR CAY PASS 328°

BUOYS
(UNREL)

HARD BARGAIN
HARBOUR

LITTLE HARBOUR

ROSES

GRAPE TREE CAY

SANDY CAY

NEW FOUND HARBOUR

BLUE CHANNEL

2 MILES

DOLLAR'S
CAY

CONCH CAY

MORTIMERS

WHITE CLIFFS

WHITE BEACH

FROM THE SOUTH 3 MILES

CAUTION: NOT FOR NAVIGATION
Tropic Isle Sketch Charts are supplements to the
text of the current Yachtsman's Guide To The
Bahamas. They are illustrative and not necessarily to scale.

SOUTH POINT
FL W EV 2.5 SEC
61 FT 12 M
(UNREL.)

SANDY CAY

DEEP BLUE
CHANNEL

DOLLAR'S CAY

BEACH

GRAPE TREE CAY
2 MILES

SHOALED

CONCH CAY

BEACH

SLIGHT N E'LY SET OPPOSED TO
PREVAILING WEATHER MAKES UP
STEEP SEAS NEAR SOUTH POINT.
STAND 5 MILES OFF.

ROCKY

HARD SAND

SHIFTING SAND
BARE HERE.

DOLLAR HARBOUR

Long Island

D.M.A. Charts: 26240, 26253, 26279, 26280. N.O.S. Chart: 11013. Tropic Isle Sketch Charts: K-1, 2,3.

Long Island's northernmost point, Cape Santa Maria, lies 27 miles east-northeast of George Town, Great Exuma, and about the same distance south-southeast of Devil's Point, Cat Island. It extends 75 miles from Cape Santa Maria to South Point and nowhere is more than 4 miles wide. This is perhaps one of the most dramatic islands of The Bahamas in natural beauty. Its bold headlands, towering cliffs, and rolling hills are in direct contrast with the South Sea flavor found elsewhere in The Bahamas.

Originally named Yuma, Long Island was rechristened Fernandina by Columbus on his first visit in 1492. Evidence of Arawak Indian occupation at that time has been substantiated by the discovery of an Indian village in the vicinity of Glenton. Long Island once enjoyed a period of great prosperity, more so perhaps than any other island of the group, as the soil is fertile and well suited for the growing of cotton, corn, fruit, and other crops. When first resettled by American Loyalists in 1790, more than 4000 acres were put under cotton alone, while stock raising and farming flourished. With the abolition of slavery, however, the plantations were abandoned.

Long Island's settlements are widely strung along its length, leaving many hard of access by boat alone.

Today Long Island, with a population of over 5000, is first in The Bahamas in stock raising, while its industrious farmers also raise corn, peas, bananas, pineapple and other fruits. The "pothole" farming method is used throughout the island, involving either blasting fertile potholes out of the rocky soil or raising bananas and corn in natural holes. Deadman's Cay, where today one can see hundreds of banana stands, developed this method.

Cape Santa Maria is a bold and conspicuous headland off which shoals extend for 3 miles to the north. In strong weather these break heavily, but in calm weather they are difficult to detect. We advise rounding Cape Santa Maria at a least distance of 3 miles. There are reefs about 1.25 miles west of the light as shown on D.M.A. Chart 26301.

A course of 065° will take you from the eastern entrance of Elizabeth Harbour to a point off the Calabash Reef or to the anchorage south of Cape Santa Maria light. The reef entrance into Calabash Bay is on a 090° bearing on the prominent house on **Galliot Cay** that stands alone well south of the buildings

Cape Santa Maria and light. (Tropic Isle photo)

TROPIC ISLE SKETCH CHART
EDITION 108

LONG ISLAND NORTH END

SOUNDINGS IN FEET AT LOW WATER

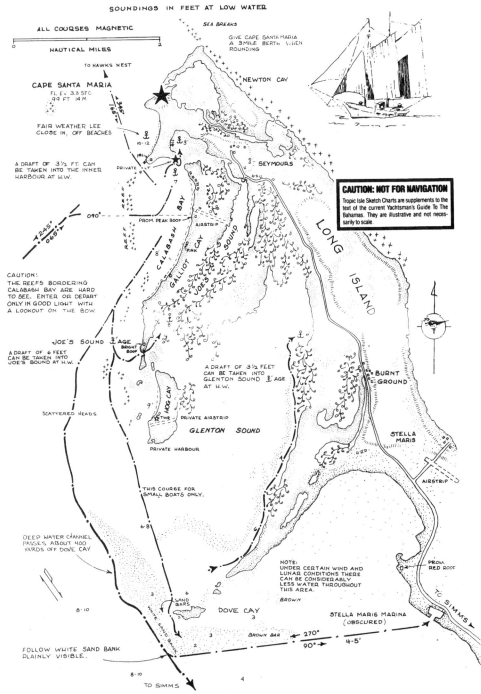

ALL COURSES MAGNETIC

NAUTICAL MILES

0   2

TO HAWKS NEST

CAPE SANTA MARIA
FL. EV. 3.3 SEC.
99 FT. 14 M.

FAIR WEATHER LEE
CLOSE IN, OFF BEACHES

A DRAFT OF 3½ FT. CAN
BE TAKEN INTO THE INNER
HARBOUR AT H.W.

SEA BREAKS

GIVE CAPE SANTA MARIA
A 3 MILE BERTH WHEN
ROUNDING

NEWTON CAY

SEYMOURS

345°
165°

PRIVATE FLT.

10-12

3'

7

REEF

REEF

245°
065°

090°

PROM. PEAK ROOF

AIRSTRIP

CALABASH   BAY

PINK CAY

GALLIOT CAY

JOE'S SOUND

LONG   ISLAND

CAUTION: NOT FOR NAVIGATION
Tropic Isle Sketch Charts are supplements to the
text of the current Yachtsman's Guide To The
Bahamas. They are illustrative and not necessarily to scale.

CAUTION:
THE REEFS BORDERING
CALABASH BAY ARE HARD
TO SEE. ENTER OR DEPART
ONLY IN GOOD LIGHT WITH
A LOOKOUT ON THE BOW.

JOE'S SOUND ⚓ AGE
A DRAFT OF 6 FEET
CAN BE TAKEN INTO
JOE'S SOUND AT H.W.

BRIGHT ROOF

SCATTERED HEADS

HOG CAY

9'

TWR

PRIVATE HARBOUR

THIS COURSE FOR
SMALL BOATS ONLY.

6-8

A DRAFT OF 3½ FEET
CAN BE TAKEN INTO
GLENTON SOUND ⚓ AGE
AT H.W.

PRIVATE AIRSTRIP

GLENTON   SOUND

BURNT
GROUND

STELLA
MARIS

AIRSTRIP

DEEP WATER CHANNEL
PASSES ABOUT 400
YARDS OFF DOVE CAY.

8-10

3

SAND
BARS

6

WHITE SAND BANK

DOVE CAY
3

NOTE:
UNDER CERTAIN WIND AND
LUNAR CONDITIONS THERE
CAN BE CONSIDERABLY
LESS WATER THROUGHOUT
THIS AREA.

BROWN

PROM.
RED ROOF

TO SIMMS

STELLA MARIS MARINA
(OBSCURED)

FOLLOW WHITE SAND BANK
PLAINLY VISIBLE.

8-10

TO SIMMS

3

2

BROWN BAR   270°

90°   4-5'

4

Cape Santa Maria Beach Resort. (Tropic Isle photo)

of the Cape Santa Maria Beach Resort at the north end of the beach. Stay in good water, leaving a brown bar close to port. Inside, about 300 yards south of the resort buildings, there is 7-9 feet over clear white sand about 100 yards off the beach. The Canadian-owned Cape Santa Maria Beach Club caters to bonefishing enthusiasts, with air-conditioned cottages, a bar and restaurant, and a beautiful beach. There are no boating facilities. Yachtsmen are welcome, but meal reservations require 24 hours' notice.

The bay immediately south of Cape Santa Maria Light offers a comfortable, fair-weather lee and a good-holding, sand bottom. Using this anchorage would avoid having to negotiate the reef entrance in poor light. Each of these harbors has a strong surge.

Seymours, the northernmost settlement, is connected with the rest of Long Island by road. It is an attractive community of 150 people with neatly kept homes perched on high ground with a splendid view of the north end of the island as well as Conception Island and Hog Cay, Exuma, on clear days. Like most Long Islanders, the people of Seymours are friendly and industrious. On the high slopes of Santa Maria Sound they raise fruit and vegetables, available in season.

Long Island, West Coast: Continuing south from Cape Santa Maria down the west coast of Long Island is an interesting cruise. It is possible to carry 5 feet at low water past **Hog Cay** and **Dove Cay** and then on to an anchorage one-half mile west of the Simms settlement dock. Once clear of the Dove Cay

---

PLEASE NOTE: *For a description of* **Batelco towers in all areas and their light characteristics**, *please check page 39 of this Guide.*

bank and the brown bar south and east of Dove Cay, approach to the Stella Maris Marina has a limiting mean low water depth of about 4.5 feet over a soft sand/silt bottom. At lower lows and in certain winds, or a combination of these, there will be considerably less water. Under some circumstances, many boats (especially those with a draft of 4.5 feet or more) may have to wait for the higher high tides. From a point in the good water just south of Dove Cay, the marina is in the south end of a large clump of casuarinas, which bears about 90°. Approaching, there are usually stakes — very spindly when we were last there — that mark the deepest channel; pass just south of them. The south side of the marina entrance is marked with a vertical orange-painted (but badly faded on our recent visit) 4x8-foot sheet of plywood and white-over-red lights. Where water is thin and marks are privately placed, it's wise to call for guidance and an update about the marking scheme. (Do not allow the Batelco tower in Simms about 5 miles southeast to confuse you.)

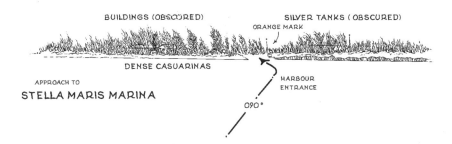

Stella Maris is primarily a plantation-style resort complex and real estate development, with a nice hotel, marina, and airport. It is also a port of entry, with customs and immigration offices at the airport. The small harbor offers all petroleum products plus a workshop and a marine railway capable of hauling boats up to 80 feet long with up to 5.5 feet draft. Dockage space for visitors is

Stella Maris Marina. (Tropic Isle photo)

StellaMaris Marina

...the only full-service marina in the Southern Bahamas... conveniently and leeside-safely situated along the area's major travel routes: 30 miles from Georgetown/Exuma · 35 miles from Cat Island/Southend · 25 miles from Conception Island · 40 miles from Rum Cay · 75 miles from San Salvador

OFFERING:
Boat rail/ramp for up to 6' draft/100 length; 12 boat slips for up to 18-20' beam; two 70-100' docks; 120V/30amps+240V/50amps dockside electricity; dockside water; fully qualified services/facilities for diesel engines, marine clutches. ARC-Gas-TIG welding; machine shop; generator plants; hydraulic, electrical, air-conditiong, refrigeration systems. Short & long term wet & dry storage. Basic marine hardware, material, paint stock on site. Short term Nassau & Florida imports a matter of routine! Esso fuels & lubricants.

MARINE CLIENTS ENJOY:
Radio advice, travel guidance, message services (VHF 16 - then working channels) during hotel operating hours · Marina approach guidance on demand from about 3 miles distance · Marina shower room privileges · Hotel beach & swimming pool privileges

RESORT CLUB:
Great accommodations...up to 4 bedrooms with pool villas · superb snorkeling/ diving/fishing · bikes/rental cars-own airport with Florida and Nassau airline service, plus Club's own commuter service-even single engine self-fly aircraft! Excellent cuisine, pleasant island entertainment! Stella Maris can be your BOATING-FLYING-SUN & SEA Bahamas Vacation Headquarters!

LONG ISLAND...UNSPOILED, VERY NATURAL, QUIET & FRIENDLY
Contact 'Stella Maris' at USA 954-359-8236 / 800-426-0466 Fax 954-359-8238
Bahamas 242-338-2051/2050/2053 Fax 242-338-2052
P.O. Box LI 30.105, Stella Maris, Long Island, Bahamas
www.stellamarisresort.com · E-mail smrc@stellamarisresort.com   **Esso**
"Happy Cruising"

Stella Maris Marina. (Tropic Isle photo)

limited to about 12 slips with 8 feet at low water. Availability may be limited, so call ahead. A coin laundry is right opposite the marina, and within a couple miles are a shopping complex, post office, and bank. Potcakes' Bar, about 100 yards south of the marina on the main road, offers drinks, snacks, music, a pool table, satellite TV, and weekly dances with live music. At the Stella Maris Inn, overlooking Long Island's spectacular rocky east coast, ice, laundry facilities, car and bicycle rentals, and a restaurant and evening lounge are among the services. The hotel offers a variety of watersports daily including SCUBA, snorkeling, bonefishing, game fishing, and reef fishing. The management here knows how to put together a good time — when we were there, the Cave Party (a weekly event; check ahead for which night) was great fun, with good food, a local band playing country music with a Bahamian beat, and interesting guests of a variety of nationalities dancing and enjoying themselves.

PART OF SIMMS SETTLEMENT FROM ANCHORAGE: CONCRETE DOCK   GOV'T DOCK
APPROX. 3/4 MILE ➤

One of the oldest settlements on Long Island, **Simms** has streets lined with neat stone walls and casuarina-shaded homes. You might meet Constable Braynon, a gracious host who will show you his town and tell you quite a bit of Long Island history in the process. Simms is a farming and stock-raising community. One of the loveliest settings you'll see on the island is the ancient, mimosa-shaded cemetery at the Episcopal Church. There's a telephone station, a clinic with resident nurse, barber shop, small stores, and the Blue Chip restaurant. Fresh bread can be ordered in town. The mailboat stops weekly.

Six feet may be carried south around Bains Bluff and Indian Hole Point to Salt Pond, where the anchorage is protected. Sailing here directly from George Town, continue easterly along the north shore of Hog Cay, Exuma, leaving the north shore of White Cay at least a mile to starboard. When abeam of White Cay's east end, take up 114°, which will carry you clear of the White Cay bank

LOOK FOR US AT YACHTSMANSGUIDE.COM

Simms. (Tropic Isle photo)

and offers a least depth of 7 feet to Indian Hole Point. The **Salt Pond** anchorage provides the only shelter on this coast from southwest-west winds. Under such conditions local boats move under the lee of Salt Pond Cay, which lies a short distance from shore, or to the south end of the bay in the lee of **Eva's Cay.**

Inasmuch as Salt Pond has the most sheltered anchorage on the west coast, it's possible to make this a cruising headquarters. Harding's Supply Center, on the road between the main dock and the regatta dock, is well stocked with groceries, meat, housewares, drugs, marine and fishing supplies, and building supplies. Owner Willis Harding also provides parts and service for Evinrude and Johnson outboards, has a lumber store behind the Supply Center, and runs a real estate agency. At his dock there's 5 feet at low water. There are more stores up or down the road. Roy Harding's L.I. Petroleum Distributors maintains the fuel dock. Roy also has oceanfront rooms for rent at Windtryst.).

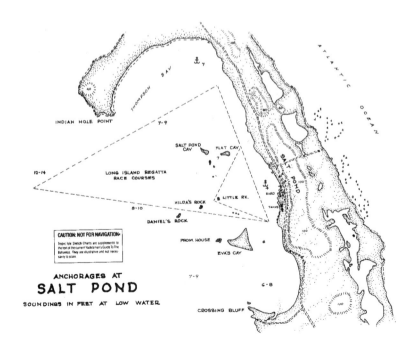

ANCHORAGES AT
SALT POND
SOUNDINGS IN FEET AT LOW WATER

NW ½ MILE

INDIAN HOLE POINT FORMS NORTHERN ARM OF SALT POND ANCHORAGE

Salt Pond is the site of the annual Long Island Regatta, sponsored by the Long Island Sailing Club on the brilliant blue bight off the settlement. This sailor's carnival, scheduled in May, has attracted upwards of 50 boats from as far away as Abaco. Inspired by the George Town Regatta, this event echoes the same principle of maintaining and improving the standards of The Bahamas workboat fleet through competition. Anyone seeking information or wishing to contribute to this worthy enterprise should contact Sailing Club Commodore Roy Harding or Secretary John McKie, both at Salt Pond, Long Island, Bahamas. About three miles south of the Regatta site, the Midway Inn Restaurant Bar & Lounge serves Bahamian food, with a TV, pool table, table tennis, and dancing for entertainment.

Long Island's BASRA representative John McKie lives in the house atop the high hill to the north of Salt Pond. His concrete dock and guest house on the harbor, if not occupied, welcome the cruising visitor. Check with John before docking; his call sign is *Sun Seeker*. John has sailed his ketch about the Long Island banks for years and is an inexhaustible source of information.

The yellow Thompson Bay Inn, a short walk up the road, has small, comfortable rooms, a restaurant serving Bahamian fare (breakfast, lunch, and dinner), and car rental weekly or monthly. Alphonso Bowe, a former mailboat captain of imposing breadth and basso voice, is the proprietor. The bar is a good place to share a beer and a game of pool with friendly Long Islanders. On some nights there's dancing and live music in the inn's dance hall.

Several communities worth visiting lie a short distance south of Salt Pond and can be reached easily by car. A couple miles north in McCanns, Dorothy Miller, renowned for her cracked conch and other Bahamian specialties, has opened her own takeaway. At Deadman's Cay, Carroll's Store stocks canned, fresh, and frozen foods, drugs, and dry goods, and has a spotless snack bar where sandwiches and ice cream are special treats. Long Island's main airstrip, a mile east of Deadman's Cay, is serviced by Nassau flights on a regular schedule.

Buckleys, Cartwright's Landing, and **Mangrove Bush** are picturesque communities where pothole farming can be observed and pineapples, tomatoes, mangoes, cabbage, and limes are available in season. DeWitt Hunt of Buckleys is one of the island's leading pineapple growers and will be happy to show you some of his plants. In Mangrove Bush, Mack Knowles is following in the footsteps of his father Rupert, who was one of The Bahamas' leading boatbuilders until his death in 1988. Their boatyard is worth a visit.

Again, 6 feet can be taken as far south as Duncanson Point, after which the water becomes extremely shallow. The large settlement of Deadman's Cay can be reached only by vessels under 4 feet draft on the tide and with local knowledge. Those wishing to continue down the lee of Long Island to its southern tip must use the **Comer Channel.**

Silted-in Hard Bargain Harbour. (Tropic Isle photo)

New Found Harbour has shoaled to the point that readers are advising us that it is of no use. The anchorage in the deep blue channel of Dollar Harbour between Dollar's Cay and Sandy Cay (8-10 feet over deep sand) is reported good, although more open. During the summer when the sharks are rearing their young, they pass by in a continuous parade. A letter from a reader advises us that much of this area is filling with sand and changing to the point that there are now "fair-sized shrubs" growing between Grape Tree Cay and Sandy Cay.

Galloway Landing holds little for the yachtsman other than its reference light and a lee in a northeaster.

Hard Bargain Harbour, formerly only useful as a harbor of refuge, is now silted in and no longer of any use at all.

Long Island, East Coast: The east coast of Long Island is high, rugged, and inhospitable with spectacular white cliffs alternating with sandy beaches along its length. Many rocky heads exist close offshore, so give this coast a berth of at least 1.5 miles. The current appears to set in a northwesterly direction. Long Island's east coast has two principal harbors, Clarence Town and Little Harbour.

Clarence Town: (D.M.A. Charts: 26253, 26280. Tropic Isle Sketch Charts: K-1, 3). As indicated on sketch chart K-3 (East Coast Harbours), the approach to Clarence Town Harbour is on a course of 155° on the westernmost point of **Strachan Cay.** When Old Clarence Light bears 200°, turn in on that heading for the short distance indicated, then take up the 155° heading until past the line of Sandy Point and Clarence Town wharf. This will keep you well off the point of reef that extends east. Here you can anchor in 10 feet over conch grass and sand that shoals gently to the beach. The Clarence Town dock will accommodate boats with 10-12 feet draft alongside. Fuel can be brought in by truck. Ask for Henry Major, the dockmaster.

Clarence Town Harbour is uncomfortable under strong prevailing conditions. If caught in strong northerly or northwesterly winds, only slightly better protection will be found off Sandy Point under Strachan Cay. The exposed cable shown in this area is about 1.5 inches in diameter, black in color, and easy to see from the surface. Anchor well away from it.

Clarence Town is indeed one of the prettiest settlements in The Bahamas. Its well-kept roads wind gently from the dock up through a friendly community to the two largest churches to be seen outside of Nassau. These twin-spired churches were designed and built by the late Father Jerome, an architect and religious figure well-known throughout The Bahamas. The older structure is St. Paul's Anglican Church, east of town. The newer is St. Peter's Catholic Church, built when Father Jerome returned after his conversion to Catholicism. With

TROPIC ISLE SKETCH CHART K-3
EDITION 112

EAST COAST HARBOURS

SOUNDINGS IN FEET AT LOW WATER
ALL COURSES MAGNETIC

½ NAUTICAL MILE

CAUTION: NOT FOR NAVIGATION
Tropic Isle Sketch Charts are supplements to
the text of the current *Yachtsman's Guide to
The Bahamas*. They are illustrative and
not necessarily to scale.

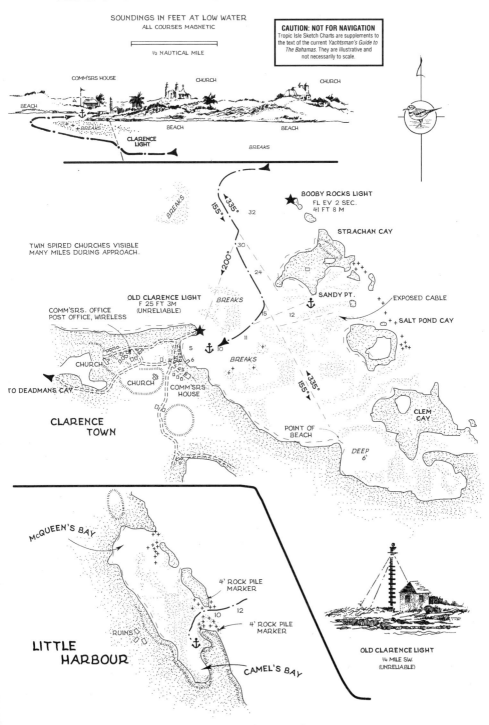

COMM'SRS HOUSE
CHURCH
CHURCH
BEACH
BREAKS
BEACH
BEACH
CLARENCE
LIGHT
BREAKS

BREAKS

155°
335°
200°
32

BOOBY ROCKS LIGHT
FL EV 2 SEC.
41 FT 8 M

STRACHAN CAY

TWIN SPIRED CHURCHES VISIBLE
MANY MILES DURING APPROACH.

30
24
SANDY PT.
EXPOSED CABLE

OLD CLARENCE LIGHT
F 25 FT 3M
(UNRELIABLE)
BREAKS
SALT POND CAY

COMM'SRS. OFFICE
POST OFFICE, WIRELESS
15   12

CHURCH
5   6   BREAKS
10
11

TO DEADMANS CAY
CHURCH   COMM'SRS
HOUSE

CLARENCE
TOWN

335°
155°

CLEM
CAY

POINT OF
BEACH

DEEP
6'

McQUEEN'S BAY

4' ROCK PILE
MARKER

10   12

4' ROCK PILE
MARKER

RUINS

LITTLE
HARBOUR

CAMEL'S BAY

OLD CLARENCE LIGHT
¼ MILE S.W.
(UNRELIABLE)

Clarence Town, St. Peter's Catholic Church. (Tropic Isle photo)

permission, it's possible to climb the narrow passage up into the southeast tower for a panoramic view of the area. Proceed at your own risk, however; depending on your diameter, you may find yourself in a predicament.

With a population of about 125, Clarence Town can supply groceries, fresh meats, and vegetables in season. Harbour Grocery has a telephone and will deliver purchases to the dock, including beer. The friendly Harbour Rest, at the dock, serves breakfast, lunch, and dinner (good Bahamian cooking), and there's a bar. Fresh-baked pastries, bread, and pizza are available at Oasis Bakery, Restaurant, and Bar, as well as Bahamian/American/Oriental cuisine. Local fishermen can supply fresh fish. About a mile's walk north of town, past the new Community Center and old salt ponds, the Oasis Bakery prepares good, reasonably priced bread, buns and pies. The mailboat calls weekly with produce from Nassau, and there's a clinic with a resident nurse. The commissioner's modern office is located next to the telephone station just above the dock.

There is a network of caves about 6 miles north of town worth exploring, with gigantic stalactites and stalagmites, places where Indians carved out stone bowls centuries ago, and a population of small fruit bats. The caves are intricate so you'll need a guide — call *Cave Man* on VHF 16 to contact Leonard Cartwright, who can take you there and give you a knowledgeable tour.

Continuing down the east coast of Long Island are many colonial ruins, unfortunately mostly not visible from the sea, but interesting to see by car. One of the largest we've noted is between Clarence Town and **Dunmore,** 7 miles south. This large castle-like building stands well back from the road on a high bluff overlooking the ocean and is said to have been the summer home of one of The Bahamas' first governors. Continuing south, you will pass **Hard Bargain, Roses,** and **Mortimers.**

Little Harbour lies 10 miles south of Clarence Town and provides good shelter. The south opening is the main entrance, where 10-12 feet can be found on the bar at low water. We recommend that you favor the north side of the channel on entering, then, when just inside, take up 215° to the anchorage. This harbor should never be entered in darkness. In Little Harbour, Allan Dean is helpful to visiting yachtsmen.

There are some other small harbors on the southeast coast of Long Island, but they should be attempted only with local knowledge. Shelter from prevailing winds can be found along the southwest coast after rounding South Point.

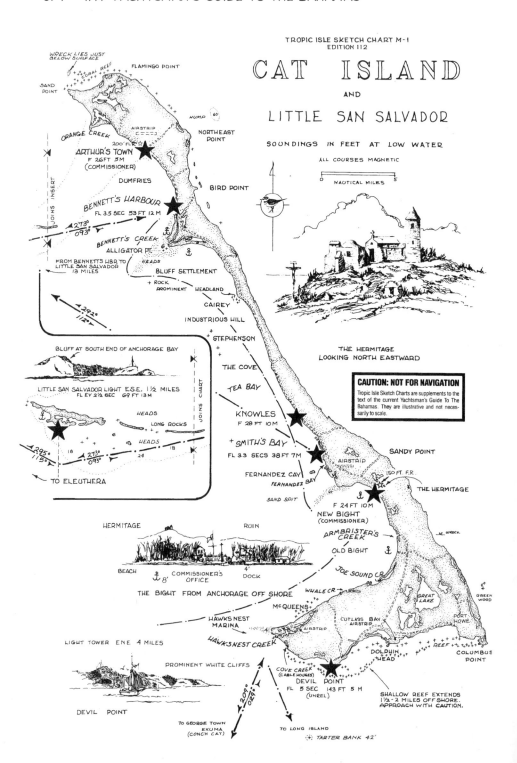

TROPIC ISLE SKETCH CHART M-1
EDITION 112

CAT ISLAND

AND

LITTLE SAN SALVADOR

SOUNDINGS IN FEET AT LOW WATER

ALL COURSES MAGNETIC

0   NAUTICAL MILES   5

WRECK LIES JUST BELOW SURFACE
FLAMINGO POINT
CORAL REEF
SAND POINT
HUMP   60'
NORTHEAST POINT
AIRSTRIP
200' FL
ARTHUR'S TOWN
F 26FT 5M
(COMMISSIONER)
DUMFRIES
BIRD POINT
JOINS INSERT
BENNETT'S HARBOUR
FL 3.5 SEC 53FT 12M
273°
093°
BENNETT'S CREEK
ALLIGATOR PT.
FROM BENNETT'S HBR TO
LITTLE SAN SALVADOR
13 MILES
HEADS
BLUFF SETTLEMENT
ROCK PROMINENT   HEADLAND
CAIREY
INDUSTRIOUS HILL
292°
112°
STEPHENSON

THE HERMITAGE
LOOKING NORTH EASTWARD

BLUFF AT SOUTH END OF ANCHORAGE BAY
LITTLE SAN SALVADOR LIGHT E.S.E. 1½ MILES
FL EV 2½ SEC   69 FT 13M
THE COVE
TEA BAY
JOINS CHART
HEADS
LONG ROCKS
HEADS
295°
115°
273°
093°
18   6   24   18
TO ELEUTHERA
KNOWLES
F 28 FT 10M
SMITH'S BAY
FL 3.3 SECS 38FT 7M
FERNANDEZ CAY
FERNANDEZ BAY
SAND SPIT
AIRSTRIP
150 FT. F.R.
SANDY POINT
THE HERMITAGE
F 24 FT 10M
NEW BIGHT
(COMMISSIONER)

CAUTION: NOT FOR NAVIGATION
Tropic Isle Sketch Charts are supplements to the
text of the current Yachtsman's Guide To The
Bahamas. They are illustrative and not necessarily to scale.

HERMITAGE   RUIN
BEACH   COMMISSIONER'S OFFICE   DOCK
8'   4'
THE BIGHT FROM ANCHORAGE OFF SHORE
ARMBRISTER'S CREEK
OLD BIGHT
JOE SOUND CR.
WHALE CR.   GREAT LAKE   GREEN WOOD
WRECK
McQUEENS
HAWKS NEST MARINA
AIRSTRIP   CUTLASS BAY AIRSTRIP   PORT HOWE
HAWKSNEST CREEK
LIGHT TOWER ENE 4 MILES
DOLPHIN HEAD   REEF   COLUMBUS POINT
PROMINENT WHITE CLIFFS
COVE CREEK
(CABLE HOUSES)
DEVIL POINT
FL 5 SEC 143 FT 5 M
(UNREL)
209°
029°
DEVIL   POINT
SHALLOW REEF EXTENDS
1½ - 2 MILES OFF SHORE.
APPROACH WITH CAUTION.
TO GEORGE TOWN
EXUMA
(CONCH CAT)
TO LONG ISLAND
TARTER BANK 42'

Cat Island

D.M.A. Charts: 26279, 26280, 26284. N.O.S. Chart: 11013. Tropic Isle Sketch Charts: M-1, 2, 3.

Cat Island, 48 miles long and averaging 1 to 4 miles in width, is one of the highest islands in The Bahamas, reaching 200 feet in several places. It offers some of the finest scenery and untrod beaches to be found in The Bahamas. In settled weather an anchorage may be found almost anywhere along its western coast, either off deserted beaches or at any of the numerous settlements.

Inside the Bight of Cat Island is the only recommended cruising ground, the south coast being reefbound and the north and east coasts steep-to and for the most part inhospitable. Inside the barrier reef, however, are a number of pink beaches well worth combing.

Many years ago there were several large plantations on the island and the ruins of some of these imposing houses can still be found. At that time cattle were raised in great numbers as the pasturage was excellent, and later the red soil necessary for the growth of pineapples produced them in abundance. Today farming is still the mainstay of the economy with tomatoes and pineapples the principal crops. Peas, bananas, and watermelon are also shipped to the Nassau market. It is notable that in 1962, the first year of women's eligibility to vote in The Bahamas, 97 percent of Cat Island women took advantage of that privilege.

There are some deep creeks the length of Cat Island that have no more than a foot or two in their entrances at low water, but with small basins with 5-6 feet at low water just inside. Most of their entrances are silted sand that would pose no problem to dredge, while inland each offers excellent bonefishing among the mangroves. One of the best of these is **Orange Creek** near Arthur's Town, where 4 feet can be taken in at high water. The sandbar at the entrance

Bennett's Creek and Alligator Point. (Tropic Isle photo)

to **Bennett's Creek** is reported to have shoaled to a depth of 3 feet or less at low water, but the creek is worth exploring by dinghy.

When approaching or leaving Bennett's Harbour watch out for extensive shoaling reported north of Alligator Point. Good cover is scarce in the Bight so the best of a bad situation in northerly weather might be to shelter in the anchorage along the conspicuous white beach on the south side of Alligator Point. In case of a 25-knot southeaster, frequent in winter, the best bet would be to anchor in the small sand beach cove about one-quarter mile north of the entrance. We found 9 feet at low water very close in. There is a sand bottom that should be good holding.

In the Bight, inside the edge of soundings, a contour line that runs roughly parallel to the coast and about 9 miles from it, are many rocky heads and patches. So far as we could find these have ample water over them. The least depth we found was 18 feet, usually more. This doesn't mean that shallow heads do not exist and, on principle, they should be avoided. Close inshore, however, you will find occasional heads with less than 6 feet of water over them. Also, off several of the points, rocky bars extend perhaps one-quarter mile offshore.

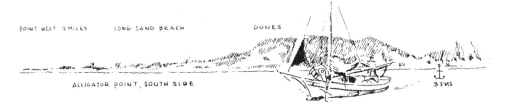

If yours is a sailboat we recommend cruising Cat Island from south to north, possibly on your return north following the spring regattas in George Town or Salt Pond. With the prevailing wind on your quarter, coasting down the length of Cat Island's lee is an unforgettable experience. There is good water close to shore and only three sand spits to be avoided. They are plotted on sketch chart M-1 (Cat Island). This cruise can wind up taking in Little San Salvador and Eleuthera Island or running straight across Exuma Sound after rounding Eleuthera Point to Ship Channel and Nassau. Taking this suggestion, your first landfall on a course of 029° from George Town (Conch Cay) will be Hawksnest Hill near Southwest Point, easily identified. There has been an AUTEC buoy 20 miles out from Conch Cay on this course.

Hawksnest Creek provides good shelter, and the marina can accommodate boats of 6-7 foot draft at low water. The approach channel just north of the rock at the entry point will carry about 5 feet at mean low water, although this could be less depending on moon phase and the height of low water, and wind, so you may have to play the tide. As you maneuver in or out of the marina or gas dock, remember to take the current into consideration. There's room to anchor about 200 yards farther up the creek past the marina entrance in about 5-6 feet of water. The Hawk's Nest Resort and Marina has 8 slips, gas, diesel, well water, ice, electricity, showers, a restaurant and bar, and rooms available. Restaurant reservations are suggested by 3 p.m. There is a 4600-foot runway

"Just head east, Mavis, he sez to me. There's a place on the beach where they serve wonderful conch fritters. You can't miss it, he sez. This is the last time I take to the water without me Guide!"

Yachtsman's Guide
to the
Virgin Islands

Over 300 pages of indispensable information including 16 pages of full color aerial photos.

Yachtsman's Guide to the Bahamas
Over 450 pages of indispensable information

- The most complete guides available for cruising these waters.
- Profusely illustrated with our beautiful hand-drawn sketch charts, landfall sketches and photographs.
- Detailed island by island profiles and things to do ashore.

Call (305) 893-4277
Or write to: Tropic Isle Publishers
P.O. Box 610938, North Miami, FL 33261-0938

CRUISING GUIDE
TO THE
Florida Keys

- PLACES TO GO
- THINGS TO SEE
- DETAILED CHARTS
- WEATHER INFO
- AERIAL SATELLITE PHOTOS
- UNDERWATER ACTIVITIES

Send $19.95 to:
Tropic Isle Publishers
P.O. Box 610938
North Miami, FL 33261-0938

Add $3 Postage & Handling for orders inside the U.S., $5 for orders outside the U.S.
Florida residents add applicable Sales Tax.

$19.95
Cruising Guide to the Florida Keys
New 10th Edition!

With Florida West Coast Supplement
CONTENTS: PLACES TO GO, THINGS TO SEE, AERIAL SATELLITE PHOTOS, MARINAS, 42 DETAILED CHARTS, WEATHERS & TIDE INFORMATION

Hawksnest Creek entrance and Hawk's Nest Marina. (Tropic Isle photo)

at the resort. It would be wise to confirm ahead of time that any facilities you might need are available (call 242-342-7050). The club monitors VHF 16.

Cove Creek, a short distance to the southeast and close by two small, white cable houses, is not an attractive anchorage, as it lies inside a dangerous stretch of reef. Devil's Point, with its settlement and light tower, is high and spectacular. A dozen varieties of game fish were taken on one outing on **Tarter Bank,** 4 miles south of Devil's Point.

Nestled comfortably under Dolphin Head is the Cutlass Bay Club, a quiet clothing-optional resort. Bordering on its own inner harbor, the unmarked entrance channel should not be attempted without local knowledge. Still farther east, off **Port Howe,** is a reefbound harbor, which also should not be attempted without local knowledge. With the deeps just beyond the reef here, it is our guess that under most conditions a generous surge might be felt.

Proceeding north to the Bight from Hawksnest Creek, you must round a very shallow white sandbank extending west from the point for about 1.5 miles.

Old Bight, 7 miles northeast, is bordered by one of the prettiest 3-mile strands of beach you'll ever see, and the mile's walk into the village from the town dock might yield some tasty sugarloaf pineapples when in season. A clinic with resident nurse is located there. **New Bight,** 4 miles to the north, has grocery stores and a telephone service. Home-baked bread is available and ship's laundry can be washed. The commissioner for South Cat Island is stationed here.

Father Jerome's Hermitage is a 15-minute hike to the top of Comer Hill, at 204 feet the highest point of The Bahamas. The summit offers a breathtaking

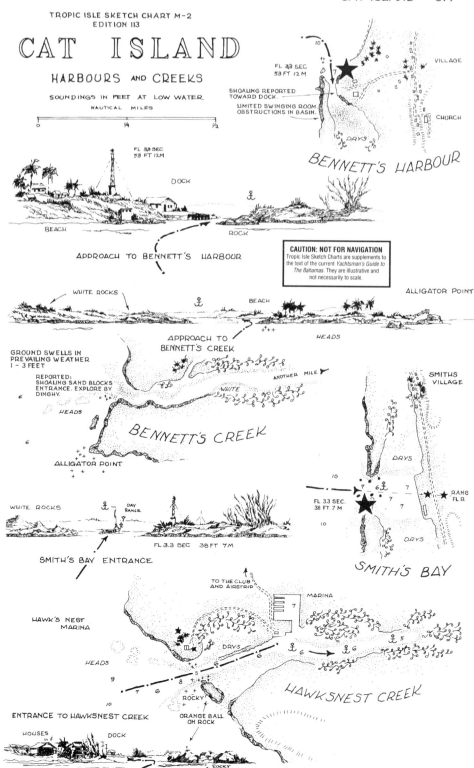

TROPIC ISLE SKETCH CHART M-2
EDITION 113

CAT ISLAND

HARBOURS AND CREEKS

SOUNDINGS IN FEET AT LOW WATER

NAUTICAL MILES

0   ¼   ½

FL 3.3 SEC
53 FT 12 M

SHOALING REPORTED TOWARD DOCK.

LIMITED SWINGING ROOM. OBSTRUCTIONS IN BASIN.

VILLAGE

CHURCH

DRYS

BENNETT'S HARBOUR

FL 3.3 SEC
58 FT 12 M

DOCK

BEACH

ROCK

APPROACH TO BENNETT'S HARBOUR

CAUTION: NOT FOR NAVIGATION
Tropic Isle Sketch Charts are supplements to the text of the current *Yachtsman's Guide to The Bahamas*. They are illustrative and not necessarily to scale.

WHITE ROCKS

BEACH

ALLIGATOR POINT

APPROACH TO BENNETT'S CREEK

HEADS

GROUND SWELLS IN PREVAILING WEATHER 1 - 3 FEET

REPORTED: SHOALING SAND BLOCKS ENTRANCE. EXPLORE BY DINGHY.

6

HEADS

6

WHITE

ANOTHER MILE

BENNETT'S CREEK

ALLIGATOR POINT

SMITHS VILLAGE

DRYS

10

FL 33 SEC
38 FT 7 M

7   6   7

7   7

RANG FL R

10

DRYS

SMITH'S BAY

WHITE ROCKS

DAY RANGE

FL 3.3 SEC   38 FT 7M

SMITH'S BAY ENTRANCE

TO THE CLUB AND AIRSTRIP

MARINA

7

HAWK'S NEST MARINA

DRYS

7

6   6   5

HEADS

9

7   6   8   5

10

ROCKY

ENTRANCE TO HAWKSNEST CREEK

ORANGE BALL ON ROCK

HAWKSNEST CREEK

HOUSES

DOCK

ROCKY

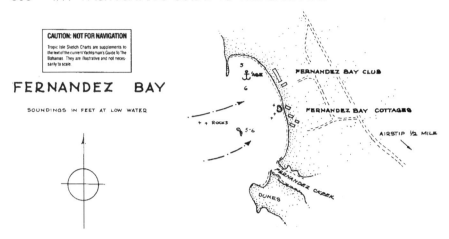

CAUTION: NOT FOR NAVIGATION

Tropic Isle Sketch Charts are supplements to the text of the current Yachtsman's Guide To The Bahamas. They are illustrative and not necessarily to scale.

FERNANDEZ   BAY

SOUNDINGS IN FEET AT LOW WATER

FERNANDEZ BAY CLUB

FERNANDEZ BAY COTTAGES

AIRSTIP ½ MILE

+ + ROCKS

FERNANDEZ CREEK

DUNES

360° view and a glimpse into the life of Father Jerome, builder and occupant of the Hermitage until his death at age 80 in the late 1950s. An architect as a young man, he became an Anglican missionary and then converted to Catholicism. After the hurricane of 1908 he came to The Bahamas to rebuild churches with mortar and stone that would withstand tropical weather. At age 62 he built the Hermitage as his home and eventually his final resting place. The steep stone steps climbing past the grim Stations of the Cross indicate that the Father either had tiny feet or was exceptionally adroit. The chapel, bell tower, and personal quarters are scaled-down replicas of hermitages in Europe.

Between the Bight and Fernandez Cay a shallow, white sand spit extends 2.5 miles south, with less than 4 feet over it at low water. Fernandez Cay, off **Smith Town,** is a tiny, scrub-covered islet behind which one might find limited emergency shelter if caught here in westerly weather. There is about 12 feet close under its eastern side.

In prevailing weather **Fernandez Bay** offers enchanting surroundings with a brilliant crescent beach, high rocks, and creeks to explore. At Fernandez Bay Village, the Armbrister family has ten attractive beachfront villas or cottages available, most with fully-equipped kitchens. There's a handy grocery/liquor store, and excellent dinners can be arranged given prior notice. If you want to dispose of garbage, please bring it ashore, where the resort will provide trash receptacles. The Nassau freight boat calls weekly at **Smith's Bay,** returning to New Providence with produce grown on the island. Fuel can reportedly be delivered here by pickup truck by calling "service station" on VHF 16. Negotiate prices and extra charges before agreeing to take delivery.

Continuing north past **Knowles,** where a government packing house sells produce, you pass coconut-studded **Tea Bay, The Cove,** and **Stephenson** (where there are interesting caves). Further on is the expanse of virgin beach east of **Alligator Point.** Here there is a comfortable anchorage in 12-18 feet over sand, but only in northerly weather. At the tip of Alligator Point is the entrance to Bennett's Creek, reportedly blocked by a sandbar of 3 feet or less. However, the creek, surrounded by virgin land, is a recommended adventure by dinghy.

Bennett's Harbour is a comfortable but very small anchorage where one would be safe in anything short of a hurricane. If you have a sailboat, you may

Bennett's Harbour. (Tropic Isle photo)

want to avoid entering the harbor during the last half of flood tide, when an extremely strong current has been reported to flow through. Be careful to avoid the two sunken vessels in the harbor. The sandbar inside the harbor is reported to be encroaching on the dock area to depths of 4 feet, so take care. Swinging room is severely limited. Ashore, delicious bread is baked on request, and your laundry will be washed in rainwater.

North of Bennett's Harbour lie **Dumfries, Arthur's Town** and **Orange Creek.** Arthur's Town, local government headquarters for the north end of Cat Island, has a telephone station, police station, and an airstrip immediately north of the settlement serviced three times a week by Bahamasair. Also here is the Cookie House, Pat Rolle's nice little restaurant serving Bahamian fare, with baked goods for sale. Between Arthur's Town and Orange Creek, situated right on the water's edge (you'll see how it got its name) is the Sea Spray Hotel with 16 rooms, a suite, and a restaurant and bar. At Orange Creek is a fair weather anchorage just off the beach. In town there is a nurse and clinic. The Orange Creek Inn has 16 rooms, with an excellent store, a walk-in freezer with ice, a laundromat, and telephone. Nick Cripps, formerly of the Marsh Harbour Marina, has plans that should begin to come together in 1998 for the new 60-slip North Cat Island Marina in the creek here. If, as time goes on, you need to learn what facilities are available, call Nick at 242-354-4004. Nick has also put together, with Cat Island historian/educator Eris Moncur, an excellent history/culture/travel guide, *Mystical Cat Island.*

Orange Creek. (Tropic Isle photo)

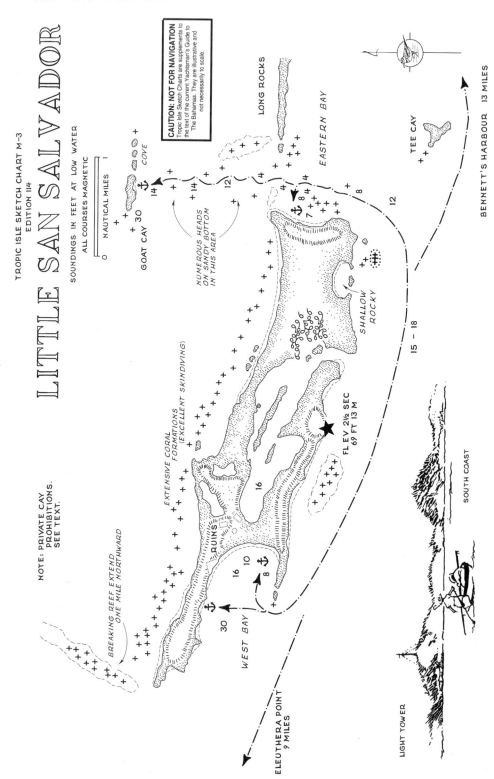

TROPIC ISLE SKETCH CHART M-3
EDITION 114

LITTLE SAN SALVADOR

SOUNDINGS IN FEET AT LOW WATER
ALL COURSES MAGNETIC

0 — NAUTICAL MILES — 1

NOTE: PRIVATE CAY
PROHIBITIONS.
SEE TEXT.

CAUTION: NOT FOR NAVIGATION
Tropic Isle Sketch Charts are supplements to
the text of the current Yachtsman's Guide to
The Bahamas. They are illustrative and
not necessarily to scale.

LONG ROCKS

EASTERN BAY

TEE CAY

BENNETT'S HARBOUR   13 MILES

COVE

GOAT CAY   30

NUMEROUS HEADS
ON SANDY BOTTOM
IN THIS AREA

SHALLOW
ROCKY

15 - 18

FL EV 2½ SEC
69 FT 13 M

EXTENSIVE CORAL
FORMATIONS
(EXCELLENT SKINDIVING)

BREAKING REEF EXTEND
ONE MILE NORTHWARD

RUINS

16

10

8

16

30

WEST BAY

ELEUTHERA POINT
9 MILES

SOUTH COAST

LIGHT TOWER

BLUFF AT SOUTH END OF ANCHORAGE BAY

LITTLE SAN SALVADOR: LIGHT TOWER ESE 1½ MILES:

LITTLE SAN SALVADOR

D.M.A. Charts: 26279, 26280. N.O.S. Chart: 11013. Tropic Isle Sketch Charts: M-1, 3.

Note: *We have sad news to report. Holland America Line-Westours, Inc. has purchased Little San Salvador, which it has renamed for its purposes Half Moon Cay (which they probably pronounce to rhyme with day). We are dismayed to inform you that the island is now private and is being used for the usual packaged-paradise cruise ship activities. HAL-W tells us that anchoring in any of the island's bays or anchorages and entry into the lagoon by yachtsmen are prohibited. If shelter is required in cases of emergency or inclement weather, the vessel should contact the island manager via VHF radio.*

This is a sad state of affairs. Little San Salvador was certainly among the beauty spots of the islands. Another pristine and ecologically delicate place bites the dust. $o much for ecotourism.

For emergency purposes, and to show you what's been lost, we describe Little San Salvador and its anchorages. Little San Salvador lies 9 miles east-southeast of Eleuthera Point and 13 miles west of Alligator Point, Cat Island. The island is 5 miles long and a little over a mile wide, with much of its interior an extensive lagoon. Passage into the lagoon is no longer allowed, because it is designated a marine sanctuary, and HAL-W has an "eco" walking trail around it. (As long as you have something "eco," you're one of the good guys.)

Little San Salvador is comparatively high. At its western end are high rocky ridges thickly covered with scrub, small trees, and sago palms. Along the shore are coconut groves. In the vicinity of the light tower, which stands about midway on the southern coast, are high, white cliffs. Immediately west of this light is a dangerous shallow rocky area, but apart from this most of the heads are easily seen and well below the surface.

West Bay anchorage provides good holding over a hard sand bottom, favoring either the south or north part of the bay according to the wind. HAL-W has a marina here for their own use with 8 feet of water in its entrance. In West Bay, any wind at all from west of south will bring in a surge, and a blow from the southwest to north-northwest will render the harbor untenable. In winds from these directions a reasonably comfortable (but also prohibited, we're told) anchorage will be found at the island's eastern end. The safest route to this

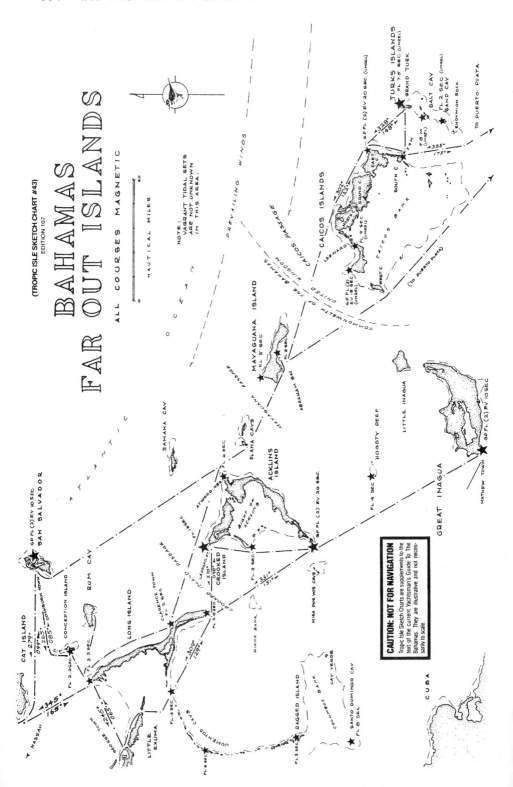

anchorage is the southern one, indicated on sketch chart M-3 (Little San Salvador), but be aware of the coral patches near the surface when passing east of Little San Salvador and north toward Goat Cay. The passage is reported to carry no more than 4-5 feet in some areas for some distance between Little San Salvador and Long Rocks.

Goat Cay, a naturalist's paradise, has an attractive sandy cove. Hundreds of sea birds make their home here during the nesting season. There are many exceptionally tame curly-tailed lizards, and doves can be heard cooing among the sea grapes. The island is densely vegetated and hikers will need protection against the prickly cactus that guards some of the more interesting areas.

To the east of Little San Salvador is a long narrow island and series of rocks, the whole chain known as **Long Rocks.** When leaving or approaching Little San Salvador from Cat Island, keep well south of Long Rocks.

The Bahamas Far Out Islands: What to Expect

To the east beyond Cat Island, Long Island, and the Crooked Island Passage lie The Bahamas Far Out Islands, where offshore skills determine the success of a cruise. In this remote part of the islands where distances are greater and yachting services somewhat scarce, the boatman's lot is one of self-reliance and resourcefulness. Here, south of the 22nd parallel, where the trades blow a steady 20-25 knots in the winter and 15 knots all summer, a strong and competent crew is essential. Vagrant currents have been reported as far east of Acklins Island as the Silver Banks. The captain of one of the tankers that ply the islands told us he occasionally experiences an especially strong northeasterly set after rounding Castle Island en route to Inagua. He also warned of another that he encounters sometimes in the passage between San Salvador on the east and Rum Cay and Conception Island to the west. This is a northwest set which, he says, increases as you approach the reef northeast of Conception Island. Unpredictable, these sets are usually prevalent during a waxing moon, and can be as strong as 2-3 knots in, usually, a southwest and northeasterly direction. Landfalls here can also be confusing as all islands east of Acklins are low and difficult to identify. A prudent navigator would seriously consider these factors.

Aptly dubbed the "thorny path" by offshore sailor Carleton Mitchell, two routes plotted on the accompanying chart offer a punch to windward of varying degree, depending on your destination in the Antilles. The longer more northerly routes that lie north of Long Island and Acklins, and face straight into the trades, are recommended for larger vessels bound for Puerto Plata in the Dominican Republic, Puerto Rico, and the Virgin Islands. The shorter southerly route via Great Inagua and Haiti provides a close reach to Hispaniola and the protection of that island's mountainous terrain for working east along its northern coast.

If, however, your destination does not lie in the Antilles and you are merely curious to visit the islands of Columbus' first landfall, there is adventure in store, but be prepared to work for it. The Bahamas Far Out Islands do not provide the tranquil waters of Abaco, New Providence, and the Exumas, but rather a taste of the Caribbean where the trade winds blow steady all year round.

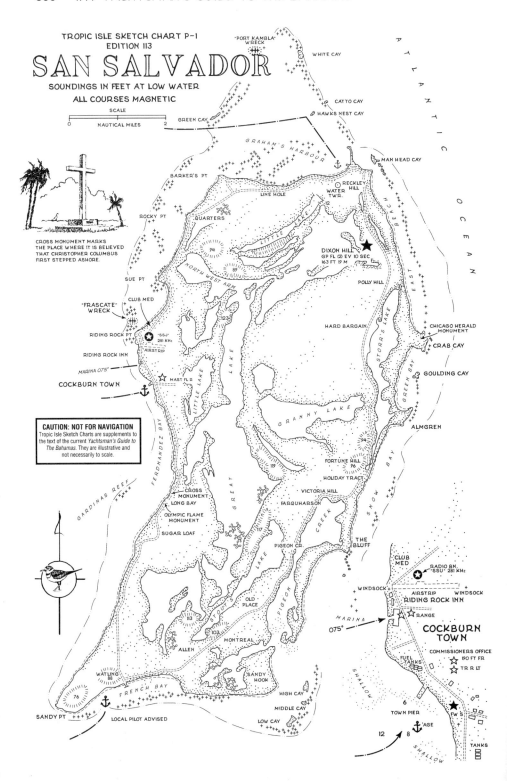

TROPIC ISLE SKETCH CHART P-1
EDITION 113

SAN SALVADOR

SOUNDINGS IN FEET AT LOW WATER

ALL COURSES MAGNETIC

SCALE

0   NAUTICAL MILES   2

CROSS MONUMENT MARKS
THE PLACE WHERE IT IS BELIEVED
THAT CHRISTOPHER COLUMBUS
FIRST STEPPED ASHORE.

"PORT KAMBLA"
WRECK

WHITE CAY

CATTO CAY

HAWKS NEST CAY

GREEN CAY

GRAHAM'S HARBOUR

MAN HEAD CAY

BARKER'S PT

LINE HOLE

RECKLEY
HILL

WATER
TWR.

ROCKY PT

QUARTERS

LITTLE LAKE

DIXON HILL
GP FL (2) EV 10 SEC
163 FT 19 M

NORTH WEST ARM

94

89

POLLY HILL

SUE PT

CLUB MED

"FRASCATE"
WRECK

RIDING ROCK PT

"SSJ"
281 KHz

AIRSTRIP

HARD BARGAIN

CHICAGO HERALD
MONUMENT

CRAB CAY

RIDING ROCK INN

GOULDING CAY

MARINA 075°

MAST FL R

COCKBURN TOWN

LITTLE LAKE

STORR'S LAKE

GREEN BAY

GRANNY LAKE

ALMGREN

CAUTION: NOT FOR NAVIGATION
Tropic Isle Sketch Charts are supplements to
the text of the current *Yachtsman's Guide to
The Bahamas.* They are illustrative and
not necessarily to scale.

FORTUNE HILL
96

119

HOLIDAY TRACT

FERDINANDEZ BAY

GARDINAS REEF

CROSS
MONUMENT

LONG BAY

OLYMPIC FLAME
MONUMENT

SUGAR LOAF

GREAT

LAKE

17

VICTORIA HILL

FARQUHARSON

PIGEON CR.

THE
BLUFF

SNOW BAY

CLUB
MED

RADIO BN.
"SSU" 281 KHz

WINDSOCK

AIRSTRIP   WINDSOCK

RIDING ROCK INN

OLD
PLACE

113

STOUT'S

102

MONTREAL

LAKE

PIGEON CREEK

MARINA

RANGE

075°

COCKBURN
TOWN

COMMISSIONERS OFFICE

190 FT FR

TR R LT

ALLEN

WATLING

76

FRENCH BAY

SANDY
HOOK

HIGH CAY

FUEL
TANKS

SHALLOW

SANDY PT

LOCAL PILOT ADVISED

MIDDLE CAY

LOW CAY

TOWN PIER

6

'AGE

FW 5

12   8

SHALLOW

TANKS

SAN SALVADOR

D.M.A. Charts: 26279, 26280, 26281. N.O.S. Chart: 11013. Tropic Isle Sketch Chart: P-1.

Historically San Salvador may be the most important of the Bahama Islands, for it was here Christopher Columbus allegedly first set foot in the New World in 1492. Columbus scholars differ as to whether Samana Cay or even Grand Turk was actually the site; convincing evidence of an event 500 years past can be hard to come by. Originally San Salvador was called Guanahani by natives and was rechristened San Salvador by Columbus. The island is 12 miles long, about 6 miles wide, and comparatively high by Bahamian standards, Mt. Kerr rising to 140 feet. Much of the interior of the island is made up of lakes.

San Salvador is a landmark and point of reference to large freighters and ships beginning their entrance to the Crooked Island passage. Yachtsmen should exercise caution, especially about 5 miles out on the west side, where there is heavy shipping traffic.

Cockburn Town, nestled around the big almond tree at harborside, is a port of entry and the center of activity on the island. The commissioner's office and residence are nearby. Quaintly staggered pink and yellow buildings are interspersed with flowering shrubs and trees, and the iridescent blue of the harbor is as vivid as any in The Bahamas. Cockburn Town has limited supplies. There are food stores, a telephone station, a clinic, and a resident doctor and

Cockburn Town light. (Tropic Isle photo)

Straw market, Cockburn Town. (Tropic Isle photo)

nurse. Gwen the straw lady has straw goods and shell jewelry for sale under the Lazy Tree, and nearby you can get ice cream at the Ocean View. The Three Ships and Halem Square are two restaurants serving Bahamian food in town (Halem Square has a pool table). At the tiny New World Museum are artifacts dating back to the Lucayan Indians. Just north of the airport is a Club Med resort.

The Riding Rock Marina and Inn has expanded the marina, and now has 7 slips with fuel, electricity, water, showers, laundry facilities, ice, a restaurant and accommodations. The controlling depth into the harbor is 6.5 feet at low water; inside there is 9-12 feet. Management reports the breakwater has been extended 100 feet or so to control the heavy surge that had been a serious problem here in winds from west through northwest, most frequently in winter. However, you should still have the ability to cope with a surge, as we continue to get letters describing this as a serious problem here. A range guides you in, and it's essential to line up on it far enough out so you pass safely through and don't land on the rocks outside the entrance. The channel has steep, abrupt sides; be on the range and stay in mid-channel. The marina monitors VHF Channel 6. Chris McLaughlin is the marina manager. Riding Rock is primarily a dive resort and offers tours and dive packages.

Along a sandy stretch of beach about 3 miles south of Cockburn Town is a simple white stone cross erected in 1956 to commemorate Columbus's landing in 1492. Another smaller cross monument is said to be half-hidden by trees north of the larger monument. Down the road is the imposing Olympic monument designed to convey the Olympic flame from Athens to all of the New World. Around the other side of the island is another commemorative Columbus

PLEASE NOTE: *For a description of* **Batelco towers in all areas and their light characteristics**, *please check page 39 of this Guide.*

monument, put up in 1891 by the *Chicago Herald*. Overlooking the reefbound east shore of the island from a high bluff, this spot seems to us an improbable place for the great navigator to have first waded ashore.

At Sandy Point, the most southwesterly point of the island, are the ruins known as Watling's Castle. Although legend has it that the house was built by freebooter John Watling in the 1600s, the ruins are probably of a later date. (San Salvador was known as Watling's Island for many years). Remains of the kitchen and slave quarters as well as the main house are evident. Long pants will protect your legs along the nearly overgrown path leading up to the ruins.

On Dixon Hill at the northeast point of the island, visitors can take a conducted tour of the lighthouse, built by the British many years ago.

There are no safe natural harbors on San Salvador, but in the prevailing trades the anchorage in the Bight off Cockburn Town is quite comfortable. Approaching from either north or south, stay well offshore at least one mile until you see lights or other defined landmarks of the town. A microwave tower stands next to the old radio mast south of town, with a distinctive dish on top. Don't attempt to come in at any other area. The range markers that used to aid approach from the south are down, but some fuel tanks are visible. The radio mast with a red light and the newer microwave tower topped with a conspicuous dish are good markers for approaching the government dock. Look out for shoaling at the end of the dock and to either side.

If caught at Cockburn Town by a norther, you should move at once to a good anchorage in **French Bay** at the south end of the island, where good shelter from winds from northwest to east will be found. This is a reef anchorage full of coral heads, and extreme caution should be taken on proceeding to a safe area. Keep watch at the bow at all times. Give Sandy Point a wide berth and proceed in toward shore approximately halfway between the shoreline and the breaking end of the reef. Deep-draft vessels can anchor here. Do not approach the wooden dock, which has shallow water.

An alternate anchorage is the open **Grahams Harbour** at the northeast corner, where a draft of 7 feet can be carried in. Columbus may have described this spacious harbor when he said: "It could hold all the ships in Christendom." The approach is directly from the west toward Green Cay, which is passed to the south approximately 100 yards, staying over the green strand that leads into the harbor. The heading is then directly toward a low cay (Hawksnest Cay) leaving it to port. Pass fairly close and turn southeast toward an abandoned dock directly in front of the small, pink house. A good marker is a red-and-white checkerboard water tower at the old U.S. naval base, but *do not* steer for it as there are shallow heads in that area. This is a good harbor for winds from east through south through west, though it always seems to carry a surge through it.

Pigeon Creek is a good safe anchorage, but only for shallow-draft vessels. Three feet can be taken well up into the harbor at high water, but the entrance is tricky and not to be attempted without a pilot. Contact the San Salvador Port Authorities at the commissioner's office for pilot service.

Rum Cay

D.M.A. Charts: 26279, 26280, 26284. N.O.S. Chart: 11013. Tropic Isle Sketch Chart: P-3.

Rum Cay could be named the "Sleeping Beauty of The Bahamas," with its historic ruins, rolling hills, and necklace of coral reef encircling its shores. Lying about 20 miles east of Cape Santa Maria and about 20 miles southwest of San Salvador, Rum Cay is 9 miles long and 5 miles at its widest point. While much of the countryside is low and flat, a few of the rolling hills rise to about 120 feet.

Originally named Santa María de la Concepción by Columbus, Rum Cay may have derived its present name from the wreck upon its shore of a West Indiaman laden with that commodity. Rum Cay once enjoyed prosperity through the export of salt to Nova Scotia, but hurricanes in 1908 and 1926 devastated the pans beyond repair. For some years thereafter pineapples were exported and cattle raised, but these endeavors also fell on hard times. Today only about 60 people live at Port Nelson, on the south coast. The virtual wilderness of the rest of the island provides excellent opportunities for nature exploration.

There are two approaches to the anchorage off Port Nelson; the first and perhaps the most straightforward is between the end of the reef off Sumner Point and the shoal that lies west of it. This approach is with the prominent white houses (recently reported somewhat obscured) on Cotton Field Point bearing 018° as indicated on sketch chart P-3 (Rum Cay). Keep a good lookout for coral heads in this area, particularly west of the 018° course. Short of the town pier is a shallow white sandbank now growing somewhat toward the west. By passing around the south end of it and avoiding one or two heads, a yacht drawing 5 feet could approach the pier more closely and anchor in clear white sand.

CONSPICUOUS HOUSE ON COTTONFIELD PT. 010°

ST. GEORGE'S BAY   LAND FALLS AWAY TO PORT NELSON

RUM CAY: APPROACHING REEF ENTRANCE   LONG BEACH

The second approach to Port Nelson is from the west and lies close under the south shore of the island with the houses on Cotton Field Point bearing 087°. Continue in on this heading and again follow the sketch chart. This course has the advantage of minimizing the sometimes strong westerly set that runs outside. Cotton Field Point is easily identified, apart from the houses, as the first high land west of the settlement.

A privately maintained light has been installed on Cotton Field Point. It flashes every 8 seconds and has white sectors, the centerlines of which are over

TROPIC ISLE SKETCH CHART P-3
EDITION 109

RUM CAY

SOUNDINGS IN FEET AT LOW WATER
ALL COURSES MAGNETIC

CAUTION: NOT FOR NAVIGATION
Tropic Isle Sketch Charts are supplements to
the text of the current Yachtsman's Guide to
The Bahamas. They are illustrative and
not necessarily to scale

NAUTICAL MILE

St. Georges Bay's western entry (87° on the light) and southern entry (018° on the light). The reefy, coral-studded area between these is under an amber sector. All other directions from which the light is visible are under a red sector. The light shows from 78 feet above sea level and should be visible for nearly 10 miles. As with all aids, especially those privately maintained, this light may be changed, inoperative, or discontinued at any time.

Just inside the tip of Sumner Point, at the east end of St. George's Bay, the new Sumner Point Marina offers dockage, moorings, fuel, electricity, ice, and an outstanding restaurant and bar. The approach, which can carry about 5 feet at mean low water (and maybe less at lower low water or under certain wind

Sumner Point Marina. (Tropic Isle photo)

ISE CASUARINAS + COCONUTS
LIGHT & DOCK
LAND RISES TOWARD S.E. PT.

PORT NELSON DOCK 075° FROM ⚓'AGE

and lunar conditions), is just inside the reef that extends westward from Sumner Point. It is privately marked by PVC stakes and/or buoys. As with all marks, privately placed or not, these may be missing or the scheme may be changed at any time. It's wise to call the marina to get help for this approach. Slips will accommodate boats up to 8-foot draft. Although the approaches to St. George's Bay are quite straightforward, marina management will provide guides for anyone wishing help. A large inner harbor is now open, where there is complete shelter in almost any weather. The marina is run by Bobby, Jeni, Bob, Fran, and Jon; their warm hospitality has greatly impressed us and a number of our contributors ("5-star chow," "deserves a stop," "an oasis in the Bahamas"). A new airstrip is being built on the island. Altogether, Rum Cay is now a convenient stopover for traffic bound one way or the other through this area as well as a cruising and fishing destination in its own right.

Port Nelson is a picturesque village in an extensive coconut grove, where the friendliness of the people makes up for their small numbers (perhaps 50 or 60 in all). The dock has been rebuilt, but reportedly has only about 4 feet (LW) on the west side and south end. Planned dredging of a channel to the dock has not taken place, so boats drawing 5 feet or more are advised to anchor out and dinghy in. The government employs a local resident to light a kerosene lantern each night and place it on the light tower near the dock. However, modern times are catching up with this little outpost, bringing electricity, telephone service, paved roads, and street lights. Ted Bain operates the Oceanview Bar, and Doloris Wilson and daughters Kay and Donna serve excellent Bahamian dinners at Kay's Restaurant and Bar. Enjoy an evening ashore and be sure to sign the guest book. Down the street from the schoolhouse is Toby's Bar, operated by Will Kelly and a good place "to enjoy a cool drink and meet new friends," according to a contributor. The Friday Happy Hour includes snacks. George Gaitor runs Two Sisters Take-A-Way, specializing in carry-out meals of delicious conch, fish, chicken, lobster and fresh bread (dockside delivery of lunch or dinner is available to Sumner Point Marina). We suggest you give any of the restaurants here a few hours' notice if you plan to eat there. The tiny telecommunications building, manned by Sam Maycock, is open during the day but not at lunchtime. Next to the Oceanview, Reuben and Hermie Bain's Variety Store sells fresh eggs and a few staples. Hermie, midwife on Rum Cay for over 20 years, has a guesthouse, and accommodations are also available from Constable Ted Bain.

Government Dock, Port Nelson. (Tropic Isle photo)

CONCEPTION ISLAND

D.M.A. Charts: 26279, 26280, 26284. N.O.S. Chart: 11013. Tropic Isle Sketch Chart: P-2.

This small island, 23 miles southeast of Cat Island and 14 miles northeast of Cape Santa Maria, is but 2.75 miles long and 2 miles across at its widest point. Rising to an altitude of 60 feet, it is surrounded on its north, east, and south sides by banks and dangerous reefs that extend some 5 miles to the north and over 2 miles to the east and southeast.

On its eastern side are several small cays and rocks, including Booby Cay, which is 79 feet high. An extensive shallow creek makes up most of the interior of the island, the entrance to which is shoal and passable only by dinghy.

Conception Island is a land park under the protection of The Bahamas National Trust. It provides a watering place and sanctuary for migratory birds. Its beaches are known laying sites for the green turtle and its reefs provide the best in virgin dive sites. This park has been set aside for yachting, beachcombing,

West Bay, Conception Island. (Tropic Isle photo)

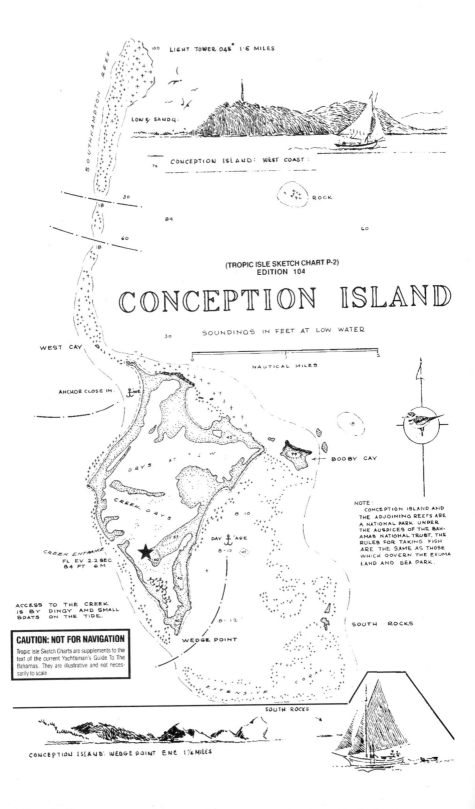

LIGHT TOWER 045° 1·5 MILES

100

SOUTHHAMPTON REEF

LOW & SANDY.

CONCEPTION ISLAND: WEST COAST.

74

ROCK

30

18

84

60

18

60

(TROPIC ISLE SKETCH CHART P-2)
EDITION 104

CONCEPTION ISLAND

SOUNDINGS IN FEET AT LOW WATER

30

NAUTICAL MILES

0   2

WEST CAY

ANCHOR CLOSE IN

DRYS AT LOW

CREEK DRYS

BOOBY CAY

8

8 10

ANCHORAGE

8-12

NOTE:
CONCEPTION ISLAND AND
THE ADJOINING REEFS ARE
A NATIONAL PARK UNDER
THE AUSPICES OF THE BAH-
AMAS NATIONAL TRUST. THE
RULES FOR TAKING FISH
ARE THE SAME AS THOSE
WHICH GOVERN THE EXUMA
LAND AND SEA PARK.

CREEK ENTRANCE
FL EV 2.2 SEC
84 FT 6 M

53

40

ACCESS TO THE CREEK
IS BY DINGY AND SMALL
BOATS ON THE TIDE.

8-12

SOUTH ROCKS

CAUTION: NOT FOR NAVIGATION

Tropic Isle Sketch Charts are supplements to the
text of the current Yachtsman's Guide To The
Bahamas. They are illustrative and not necessarily to scale.

WEDGE POINT

EXTENSIVE   CORAL

SOUTH ROCKS

CONCEPTION ISLAND: WEDGE POINT ENE 1¼ MILES

SOUTH ROCKS

CONCEPTION ISLAND : WEDGE POINT E.N.E.

skin-diving, and to preserve the natural beauty of the area for the enjoyment of all. Visitors are reminded that it is unlawful to remove any plant life, corals, sea fans or gorgonians, animals, or bird or turtle eggs. The dumping of all forms of litter or waste is of course also prohibited. These laws, enforceable with heavy penalties on conviction, have been written to insure the preservation of the park for Bahamians and visitors alike.

This island is uninhabited, but well worth a visit in settled easterly weather. The best anchorage is in the sandy bay about 1.5 miles north of the light tower, with West Cay bearing due north. This bay affords protection from south through north and the soundings vary from 30 to 60 feet over clear white sand, one-half mile offshore. The water shoals gradually toward the beach. A number of coral heads will be seen in the bay, but most are deep and there is plenty of room between them. In fresh southeasterly weather some surge will be experienced.

Wedge Point, at the southern extremity of Conception Island, is conspicuous. From here the reef trends away in a southeasterly direction for about 2 miles and should be given a wide berth. For the anchorage east of the light, the entrance course that runs south of Wedge Point passes through an area of deep coral heads that appear especially threatening due to the clarity of the water. Keep a good lookout and favor Wedge Point when entering.

RAGGED ISLAND
AND ADJACENT CAYS

D.M.A. Charts: 26255, 26256, 26257, 27040. Tropic Isle Sketch Chart: 0-1.
Ragged Island is at the southerly tip of the **Jumentos Cays**, a chain of cays that stretches for 90 miles in a great semicircle from the west point of Long Island and forms the southeast boundary of the Great Bahama Bank. In winter this can be a stormy area, but in good weather a wonderful cruising ground. You'll see very few other boats here — perhaps a cruising boat or so and a few native fishing boats. You're pretty much on your own, and you must be self-sufficient and able to navigate by eyeball.

Ragged Island itself is 4 miles long with an area of about 5 square miles. It is windswept and barren; what vegetation there is consists of stunted shrubs and bushes. **Duncan Town** is a remote settlement of about 75-100 people, most of whom eke out livings as fishermen. They'll help however they can when

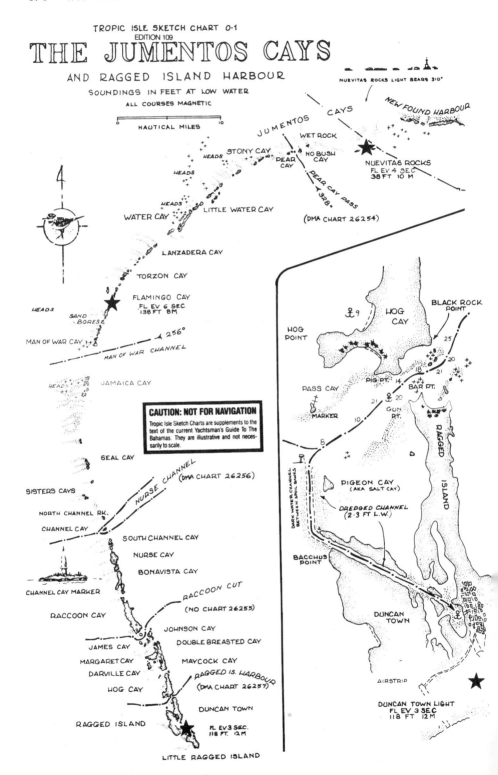

TROPIC ISLE SKETCH CHART O-1
EDITION 109

THE JUMENTOS CAYS

AND RAGGED ISLAND HARBOUR

SOUNDINGS IN FEET AT LOW WATER

ALL COURSES MAGNETIC

NEW FOUND HARBOUR

NUEVITAS ROCKS LIGHT BEARS 310°

JUMENTOS CAYS

NAUTICAL MILES

WET ROCK

STONY CAY

NO BUSH CAY

PEAR CAY

NUEVITAS ROCKS
FL EV 4 SEC
38 FT 10 M

HEADS

HEADS

PEAR CAY PASS

328°

LITTLE WATER CAY

(DMA CHART 26254)

WATER CAY

HEADS

LANZADERA CAY

TORZON CAY

FLAMINGO CAY
FL EV 6 SEC
138 FT 8M

HEADS

SAND BORES

MAN OF WAR CAY

256°

MAN OF WAR CHANNEL

BLACK ROCK POINT

HOG CAY

HOG POINT

25

20

PIG PT.

18

21

JAMAICA CAY

HEADS

PASS CAY

BAR PT.

21

20

GUN PT.

MARKER

10

CAUTION: NOT FOR NAVIGATION
Tropic Isle Sketch Charts are supplements to the
text of the current Yachtsman's Guide To The
Bahamas. They are illustrative and not necessarily to scale.

8

RAGGED ISLAND

SEAL CAY

NURSE CHANNEL

(DMA CHART 26256)

PIGEON CAY
(AKA SALT CAY)

SISTERS CAYS

DREDGED CHANNEL
(2-3 FT L.W.)

NORTH CHANNEL RK.

CHANNEL CAY

SOUTH CHANNEL CAY

NURSE CAY

BONAVISTA CAY

BACCHUS POINT

CHANNEL CAY MARKER

RACCOON CUT

(NO CHART 26255)

RACCOON CAY

JOHNSON CAY

DOUBLE BREASTED CAY

DUNCAN TOWN

JAMES CAY

MARGARET CAY

MAYCOCK CAY

DARVILLE CAY

RAGGED IS. HARBOUR

HOG CAY

(DMA CHART 26257)

AIRSTRIP

DUNCAN TOWN

DUNCAN TOWN LIGHT
FL EV 3 SEC
118 FT 12 M

RAGGED ISLAND

FL EV 3 SEC.
118 FT. 12 M

LITTLE RAGGED ISLAND

Ragged Island harbor. (Tropic Isle photo)

the need arises. Many people have moved away over the years, and many of the pretty little houses are boarded up. Some farming is done on nearby cays, and small quantities of salt are still raked at the salt pan on the east side of town. In town are Angie's Grocery, Maxine's Drugs and Notions, Sheila's Fisherman's Lounge, and Louise's Sweet Place (good bread and pies to order). About 2 miles out of town is an establishment that gets our award for the most original use of a crashed DC-3, Percy's Eagle Nest. Here you can shoot pool, drink a few beers, and get a meal, if ordered ahead. The DC-3 is raised up over the bar on concrete piers and appears, from the outside, to have crash-landed on the building. The gangway comes down into the bar so you may take your drink up into the plane's cabin and lounge around some tables there. At the time of our visit, a new police station was being built, while the red-roofed commissioner's office with its matching cisterns stood deserted because there's no such official here anymore. The commissioner from George Town calls here monthly to do his chores.

Batelco has relocated from just east of the government dock to the hill on the south end of town, last stop before the airport. Mrs. Leander Maycock, Batelco operator, stands by on VHF 16 and can help arrange for delivery of supplies from Nassau. For information about the area and surrounding waters, look up either of our friends Captain Lester Wallace or Miah Maycock, who showed us around the town, harbor, and approaches on our recent visit.

Lying between Ragged Island and Hog Cay, **Ragged Island Harbour**

Percy's Eagle Nest. (Tropic Isle photo)

can be approached from either east or west. The anchorage lies 200 yards south of Pig Point and the maximum draft for the east channel is 12 feet. A mailboat calls weekly and anchors here to lighter cargo and passengers ashore.

It is possible to gain the small inner harbor off the town dock at Duncan Town by the dredged channel that comes south from Pass Cay (stay over the dark water between the spoil bank), then through the mangroves to town. This channel is about 2 miles long and has a controlling depth of 3-3.5 feet at low water. It is only 30 feet wide, so plan your approach so as not to meet any other traffic. The turning basin off the Duncan Town dock is 135 feet by 150 feet with additional anchorage for boats drawing up to 4 feet.

Hog Cay lies across the harbor from Ragged Island. It is well-wooded, more fertile, and prettier. Between Hog Cay and Raccoon Cay, 5 miles north, there are a number of small cays: **Darvill, Maycock, Double Breasted, and Margaret Cays.** Among them are some attractive coves and beaches, but the tidal currents run strongly through them. **Raccoon Cay** is where vessels which drew too much water to enter Ragged Island Harbour used to lie to load salt, gaining shelter from Johnson's Cay. The ruins of some old buildings and salt pans can be seen. Between **Nairn Cay** and Raccoon Cay is a snug little anchorage in east and southeast winds. There are several deep coves on the western side of the island. **Bonavista Cay** is an attractive, uninhabited cay where there is 12 feet of water on the west side and a first-rate beach. Shelter from northerly winds can be found in a cove on the southeast corner. One writer describes the cay as a "veritable farm with horses, chickens, sheep, and goats." **Nurse Cay Channel** (18 feet at high water) is a good entrance to or from the bank. It is easily recognized by the beacon that stands on Channel Cay. The tide sets strongly through this cut. Between Nurse Cay Channel and Man of War Channel, a distance of 16 miles, there are many rocks, reefs, and cays, some with deep-water passages between them. Fishing in this area is excellent. **Flamingo Cay,** identified by its light tower (reported not working), is comparatively high, well-wooded, and has a number of good beaches, from which you might explore some ruins and burial sites, and a cave. The best anchorages are in the coves on the west shore, well out of the surge. **Water Cay** is easily identified by the white cliffs in the center of the cay, and its three prominent hills. The cay is long and undulating, some parts of it so low that in bad weather the sea washes across. Access to the anchorage (12 feet) midway off its west shore must be made via the eyeball method, first investigating the approach channels in the dinghy.

CROOKED ISLAND DISTRICT

D.M.A. Charts: 26240, 26253, 26260, 26263, 26268, 26279, 26280, 26288. N.O.S. Chart: 11013. Tropic Isle Sketch Charts: N-1, 2, 3.

Bahamas history relates that as Columbus sailed down the lee of the islands now known as **Crooked Island, Long Cay,** and **Acklins Island,** his aesthetic sense was aroused by the aroma of native herbs that wafted out to his ship, and in gratitude for the pleasant scent after his long sojourn at sea he dubbed this

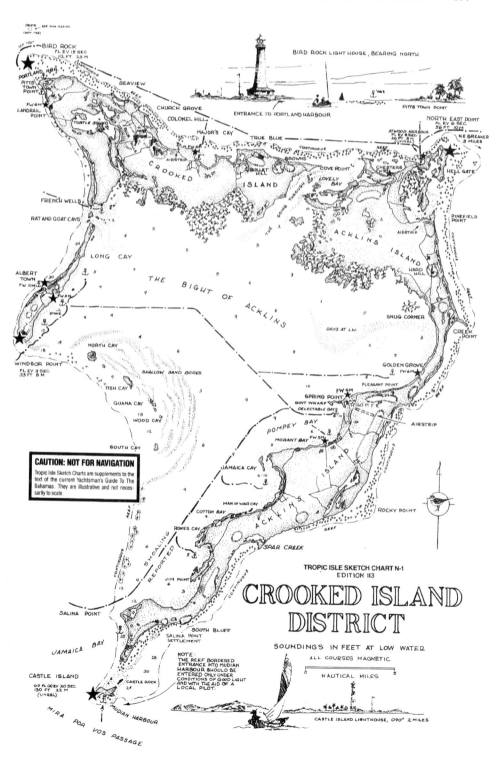

BIRD ROCK LIGHT HOUSE, BEARING NORTH

ENTRANCE TO PORTLAND HARBOUR

PITTS TOWN POINT

CAUTION: NOT FOR NAVIGATION
Tropic Isle Sketch Charts are supplements to the text of the current Yachtsman's Guide To The Bahamas. They are illustrative and not necessarily to scale.

TROPIC ISLE SKETCH CHART N-1
EDITION 113

CROOKED ISLAND DISTRICT

SOUNDINGS IN FEET AT LOW WATER
ALL COURSES MAGNETIC

NAUTICAL MILES

NOTE:
THE REEF BORDERED ENTRANCE INTO MUDIAN HARBOUR SHOULD BE ENTERED ONLY UNDER CONDITIONS OF GOOD LIGHT AND WITH THE AID OF A LOCAL PILOT.

CASTLE ISLAND LIGHTHOUSE, 090° 2 MILES

group "the fragrant islands." One of these herbs, cascarilla bark, is the islands' chief export today for use in making medicines and distaff-liqueur.

The Crooked Island District is a triangular archipelago forming the eastern border of the busy **Crooked Island Passage,** and measuring 45 miles from **Bird Rock** Light to Castle Island Light at the southernmost point. The north side of the triangle measures 30 miles from Bird Rock east to Hell Gate at the north end of Acklins.

As a fair-weather cruising area, the group offers several good harbors joining miles of deep, scenic creeks and tidal flats where record tarpon and bonefish abound. The **Bight of Acklins** offers protected cruising to vessels drawing no more than 4 feet, and yachts this size can reach many of the quaint, friendly settlements of the Crooked Island group. We have recent reports confirming that 7 feet can be carried across the Bight from just off the fishermen's dock and conch crawl on the Bight side of Albert Town on a magnetic course of 095° to a point at which you take up 154° (magnetic) to a position about 2 miles west of the anchorage south of the Spring Point government dock in Delectable Bay. Then eyeball into the anchorage or dock.

Crooked Island

Crooked Island forms the northwesternmost corner of the group and covers a considerable area. It is high, and the Blue Hills in particular are an excellent landmark. The north coast of Crooked Island has a dangerous off-lying reef and should be given a wide berth. There are several wide channels across the reef but good light and local knowledge are strongly advised.

Notice: Several years ago we had a report from a yachtsman who damaged his underwater gear on what he described as an "uncharted, detached reef about a mile north of Bird Rock Light." Whether this was actually part of the reef north of the light that shows on government charts and on our sketch chart, or the obstruction shown on D.M.A Chart 26240 as "Obstr (rep 1928)," or something else, we cannot say — nor can we be more specific as to location, because we don't know how precisely he was able to measure his location at the time he hit the obstruction. Proceed with caution, and realize that your depth sounder will give practically no warning of hazards that rise abruptly from the depths.

South of Bird Rock lies **Portland Harbour,** which Columbus is reported to have found greatly to his liking. Why, we'll never know, as there is always an unforgivable surge running through it. The entrance lies about 300 yards south of Bird Rock in about 20 feet over rock and sand. Under prevailing conditions the best anchorage lies three-quarters mile south of the hotel about 100 yards off the two northernmost houses.

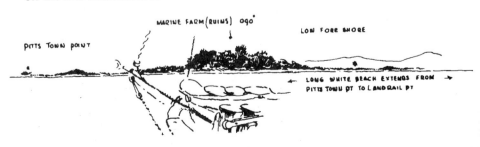

LOOK FOR US AT YACHTSMANSGUIDE.COM

At **Pittstown Point** are the ruins of the first post office in The Bahamas, which now forms the nucleus of one of The Bahamas' farthest Out Island hotels, Pittstown Point Landings. Twelve rooms are available, with a bar and restaurant specializing in local catch including lobster, grouper, and conch. Overlooking Portland Harbour and Bird Rock Lighthouse, this is a beautiful place with wonderful diving and fishing possibilities. There is a 2000-foot paved airstrip and air charter services are available through the hotel. Management is discussing plans to relight the lighthouse. By the way, Pittstown Point Landings is the only establishment around here that accepts anything but cash.

You can make arrangements to photograph Bird Rock Lighthouse or visit the nearby caves, among the largest in The Bahamas. They are not easy to find, so get a guide. In their huge, cathedral-like rooms are stalactites so translucent that they appear carved from white jade. The ancient British fortifications at Marine Farm are named for the regiment that guarded the northern end of the Crooked Island Passage here at the height of the Spanish Main activities. There remain six four-ton cannons in excellent repair, some with the crown still visible.

The best landing, if you wish to visit **Landrail Point**, is at the public wharf where the Nassau mailboat calls weekly. Anchor off the beach and call BASRA (Andy Gibson) in Landrail Point if you need assistance or local knowledge. Here,

CRUISING GUIDE

TO THE

Florida Keys

$19.95

Cruising Guide to the Florida Keys

New 10th Edition!

- PLACES TO GO
- THINGS TO SEE
- DETAILED CHARTS
- WEATHER INFO
- AERIAL SATELLITE PHOTOS
- UNDERWATER ACTIVITIES

Send $19.95 to:
Tropic Isle Publishers
P.O. Box 610938
North Miami, FL 33261-0938

Add $3 Postage & Handling for orders inside the U.S., $5 for orders outside the U.S. Florida residents add applicable Sales Tax.

With Florida West Coast Supplement

CONTENTS: PLACES TO GO, THINGS TO SEE, AERIAL SATELLITE PHOTOS, MARINAS, 42 DETAILED CHARTS, WEATHERS & TIDE INFORMATION

Little dug harbor at Landrail Point. (Tropic Isle photo)

7 feet of water is available at the concrete wharf, where metered fuels can at times be obtained through Daisy Scavella, operator of Scavella's Grocery. Landrail Point also has good well water, which can be delivered by drum if necessary. The ever-present surge here can be dangerous and could damage your vessel if you are not bumpered properly, so approach the wharf with care. One reader recommends Med-style mooring and an anchor watch here because of the surge. Whatever you do, do it in good light, as there are many rocky heads hereabouts. There is a tiny artificial harbor here, cut from the rocks, where you can land a dinghy. Be careful not to block the fishermen's boats.

Landrail Point is a pretty settlement planted profusely with citrus. The inhabitants, Seventh Day Adventists, are most hospitable. Seafood and seasonal produce are available, but no tobacco or alcohol is sold or served. Keep in mind that Seventh Day Adventists do not work from sundown Friday until sundown

Willie at Gibson's Lunch Room, Landrail Point. (Tropic Isle photo)

French Wells harbor. (Tropic Isle photo)

Saturday. Marina Gibson has a guest house and bright yellow restaurant that she's operated for close to 40 years. Assisted by her daughter Wilhemina ("Willie"). Marina is an outstanding cook who bakes the best bread and corn bread around. She sells frozen meat, chicken, and ice cream, and a freshwater shower is available. Marina's son Andy is the local BASRA represetative and monitors VHF 16. Marina will hold any mail or packages for your arrival (address: c/o Gibson Store, Landrail Point, Crooked Island, Bahamas).

A pleasant walk south from the settlement will bring the visitor to the ancient ruin of Hope House, a 17th-century colonial mansion.

Seven miles south of Landrail Point is **French Wells,** where again you may anchor off the beach in 12 feet. Much of the ground is foul, however, so proceed with good light and use your lead line. We have a letter from a reader telling of sighting a flock of over 60 flamingos here.

In the cut between the south end of Crooked Island and the north end of Long Cay are **Rat and Goat Cays.** In the entrance channel on sketch chart N-3 (French Wells), we show 3-4 feet depth at low water, but recent reports indicate that the channel, which can be found bearing about 090° between dark grass to the south and a sand bore to the north, permits a draft of 6-7 feet to enter the anchorage south of Gun Point. Proceed with caution, using your lead line or depth sounder, because in this type of situation depths can decrease and channels will meander.

French Wells Harbour is protected from the east by a very shallow bank and is good for 10 feet inside. The holding ground, sand, is good. Deep, narrow French Wells Creek is accessible only to skiffs, there being a mere 6 inches on the bar at low water. A tranquil spot, the creek's deep pools abound with tarpon.

The channel leading into **Turtle Sound** begins at the line of tree markers at the east end of the harbor. Keeping the markers close to starboard, small craft with draft less than 3 feet, playing the tide, can be taken all the way inland to fish the meandering creeks. Protected by high bluffs, this sheltered inland cruising ground offers much pleasure to the small cruiser who could roam the sound for days, bringing up in a different anchorage each night.

Church Grove and **Colonel Hill** are well worth the visit if transportation can be arranged. There is a dinghy dock at Church Grove Landing, a scenic 2-

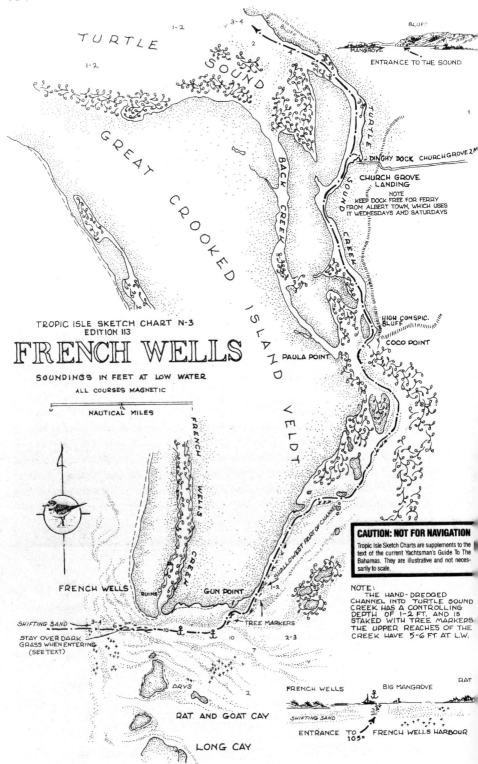

TURTLE SOUND

1-2   3-4

BLUFF

BLUFF

MANGROVE

ENTRANCE TO THE SOUND

1-2

GREAT

DINGHY DOCK   CHURCH GROVE 2 M

CHURCH GROVE LANDING

NOTE
KEEP DOCK FREE FOR FERRY
FROM ALBERT TOWN, WHICH USES
IT WEDNESDAYS AND SATURDAYS

CROOKED

BACK CREEK BLUFF

TURTLE SOUND CREEK

8-9½

HIGH CONSPIC. BLUFF

COCO POINT

TROPIC ISLE SKETCH CHART N-3
EDITION 113

ISLAND

PAULA POINT

FRENCH WELLS

SOUNDINGS IN FEET AT LOW WATER

ALL COURSES MAGNETIC

VELDT

NAUTICAL MILES

FRENCH WELLS CREEK

CAUTION: NOT FOR NAVIGATION

Tropic Isle Sketch Charts are supplements to the
text of the current Yachtsman's Guide To The
Bahamas. They are illustrative and not necessarily to scale.

SHALLOWEST PART OF CHANNEL

NOTE:
THE HAND-DREDGED
CHANNEL INTO TURTLE SOUND
CREEK HAS A CONTROLLING
DEPTH OF 1-2 FT. AND IS
STAKED WITH TREE MARKERS
THE UPPER REACHES OF THE
CREEK HAVE 5-6 FT. AT L.W.

FRENCH WELLS   RUINS   GUN POINT   1-2

SHIFTING SAND   3-4   6   10   TREE MARKERS

10   2-3   7

STAY OVER DARK
GRASS WHEN ENTERING
(SEE TEXT)

DRYS   2

FRENCH WELLS   BIG MANGROVE   RAT

SHIFTING SAND

RAT AND GOAT CAY

ENTRANCE TO   FRENCH WELLS HARBOUR
105°

LONG CAY

mile hike from Church Grove. A ferry from Windsor (also called Albert Town) ties up here on Wednesdays and Saturdays, so don't block the dock at these times. Within walking distance is a public well. In Church Grove are two taverns, the Midway Lounge and Bloom of the Valley Bar. The Batelco station is manned by Ernest Mars, whose family makes up the population of nearby Bullet Hill. A near-complete line of staples and drugs is carried at Eunice Deleveaux's hilltop store, restaurant, and guest house. Colonel Hill has an airstrip with weekly flights to Nassau, as well as telephone service.

The anchorage under the small cays in Major's Cay Harbour is comfortable in settled weather, with 7-8 feet over a thin sand bottom. Proceed through the break in the reef on a course of 182°, steering for the prominent stand of casuarinas slightly west of and beyond the cays, as indicated on sketch chart N-2 (Crooked-Acklins Islands). Do not use the reef opening that bears 175° on the casuarinas as it leads into shallow coral.

Farther to the east, True Blue offers another settled-weather lee off the village in 8-10 feet over sand. Steer for the coconuts east of the village. The population here has dwindled to a very few elderly residents.

The wide channel to **Browns** is entered by steering 190° on the coconut trees east of the bare, hillside settlement (which we are told is now deserted). The anchorage is off the town in 8-10 feet over sand.

Cove Landing, where local dinghies are anchored, is used by the people of Lovely Bay and Chesters when they visit Crooked Island. The eastern end of the Crooked Island road, which began at Landrail Point, ends here at Cove Landing.

Long Cay

The anchorage off **Albert Town** (also called Windsor) is not a good one. It is uncomfortable in all except southeast winds and full of breaking coral heads. We have a letter telling of a better anchorage about a quarter mile north of the wharf "in the last big sandy area." The writer continues: "… take a few compass bearings and sleep easy, knowing you could get out of here in a hurry if you had too." The wharf here, like the one at Landrail Point, will do damage if you do not fender properly. Up the road from the dinghy dock is a freshwater well.

The attractive settlement of Albert Town fell on hard times with the failing of the sponge and salt industries. A testimony to more prosperous times is the Anglican Church, the largest built in The Bahamas south of Nassau. Today

WINDSOR POINT

FORTUNE HILL BEARING N.5 M.DIST.

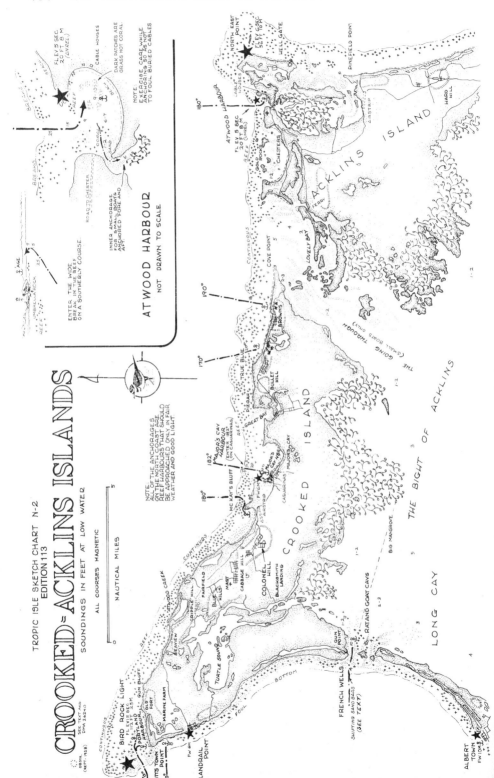

perhaps 30 people remain (including nine schoolchildren and one teacher). Most of the men are fishermen. Former mailboat captain Stephen Rose operates the Ready Money store, where beer, juice, and limited canned goods and supplies are for sale. Mr. Rose also owns most of Long Cay's 2,000 goats. He's an excellent guide for the area and knows the fishing waters south of Long Cay well. A lady who bakes bread here answers to *Windsor* on VHF 16. Fortune Hill, 2 miles south of Albert Town, is a good landmark, especially when approaching from the south, as it can be seen from a distance of about 12 miles.

South of Albert Town, on the west coast of Long Cay, there is no anchorage until you reach Windsor Point. Here a vessel drawing 6-7 feet may find protection in winds from southwest to north in 9-12 feet over clear sand. To the east shallow banks discourage any sea making up from that direction.

Between Windsor Point and the south point of Acklins Island, the edge of the bank curves away to the southeast. For much of its length it is studded with coral heads and should not be approached closely, especially at night. Here, North Cay is surrounded with banks and heads, but with care the cays extending southward may be approached fairly closely. Some of the finest game fishing in The Bahamas has been enjoyed along these cays, a favorite fishing ground of President Franklin D. Roosevelt.

These cays are inhabited by the Bahama iguana, an endangered species. Please do not take your dog ashore.

Acklins Island

This island, which is long, narrow, and hilly, forms the eastern side of the Crooked Island District triangle. Unfortunately the Bight of Acklins is shallow and a bad place to be caught in a norther. However, there are many pleasant coves and bays along the Acklins shore. Names such as **Delectable Bay, Lovely Bay, Binnacle Hill** and **Snug Corner** are tempting and with the right draft one can enjoy this virgin cruising ground. Like the people of Crooked Island, Acklins Islanders are mainly hard-working, cheerful farmers whose generosity is extended to strangers when the fruits of their labor are in season. Few supplies can be picked up at the various settlements. Fuel is available at **Spring Point** by contacting Felix at the Batelco station on VHF 16, or at his home, where he answers to *Central*. A road connects all of the settlements of Acklins from Lovely Bay all the way south to Salina Point. There are medical clinics at both Spring Point and Chesters. A good man to know at Spring Point is Curtis Hanna, who runs the local Airport Inn & Restaurant and answers to *Red Devil* on VHF. The highest point on Acklins is **Hard Hill.**

We have word from a group of readers that while anchored in Jamaica Bay at the south end of Acklins Island, they discovered the nearby community of Salina Point, which, they relate, can supply fresh-baked bread and grocery items. There is also a restaurant and lounge here as well as a telephone station. They tell of friendly hospitality. There are signs placed on shore in Jamaica Bay to notify yachts needing provisioning or assistance whom to contact via VHF 16. People from the village will provide transportation into the community.

Off the southern end of Acklins lies **Castle Island,** southeast bastion of the Crooked Island Passage, with its lighthouse. The island itself is low and sandy,

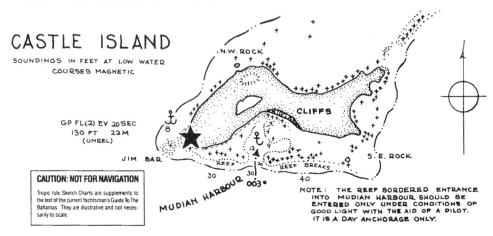

CASTLE ISLAND

SOUNDINGS IN FEET AT LOW WATER
COURSES MAGNETIC

GP FL(2) EV 20 SEC
130 FT   22 M
(UNREL)

JIM BAR

CAUTION: NOT FOR NAVIGATION

Tropic Isle Sketch Charts are supplements to the text of the current Yachtsman's Guide To The Bahamas. They are illustrative and not necessarily to scale.

N.W. ROCK

CLIFFS

S. E. ROCK

REEF   REEF BREAKS

30   30
40
MUDIAN HARBOUR   003●

NOTE: THE REEF BORDERED ENTRANCE INTO MUDIAN HARBOUR SHOULD BE ENTERED ONLY UNDER CONDITIONS OF GOOD LIGHT WITH THE AID OF A PILOT. IT IS A DAY ANCHORAGE ONLY.

except at its northern end where it becomes fairly high and rugged. Depending on the direction of the wind, anchorage can be found on the bank on either side of Castle Island or in **Mudian Harbour,** capable of accommodating a draft of 12 feet. *Approach this harbor with caution only in good light and with local knowledge if possible.*

The currents in the vicinity of Castle Island are strong and unpredictable. A west or southwesterly current normally sets across the mouth of the Crooked Island Passage toward the Mira Por Vos Shoals. On a cruise here, however, we were once becalmed a mile south of the lighthouse. On that occasion we experienced such strong northeasterly set that to gain an offing became imperative. Several powered vessels have stranded on Castle Island. Although the passage is wide and straightforward, care must be exercised in making it.

The east coast of Acklins is high and rugged. Dangerous reefs extend its entire length and there are no harbors. There are, however, spectacular beaches. If you're cruising the Bight, any of the local inhabitants could show you across the island.

Off Northeast Point, or Hell Gate, Northeast Breaker presents a hazard as it lies 3 miles offshore and is unmarked. However, as it always breaks, even in the calmest weather, it is plainly visible. Best to give the point a 6-mile offing when rounding Hell Gate to the south.

On the north coast of Acklins and 2 miles southwest of Northeast Point, **Atwood Harbour** may be reached through a wide pass in the reef. This harbor is the best in the Crooked Island District, affording ample protection in anything other than northwesterly weather, to vessels carrying up to 8 feet draft. Approach Atwood Harbour *in good light only.* Cross the reef on a southerly course (see sketch chart N-2, Crooked-Acklins Islands) and bring up in the

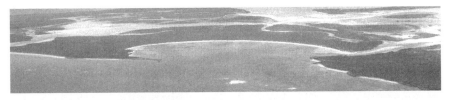

Atwood Harbour. (Tropic Isle photo)

northeast corner of the harbor in 9-10 feet over sand at low water, taking care not to foul the marine cables when anchoring. There are some heads you can hit as you make your turn to port and approach the anchorage, so proceed with caution and don't make the turn too tight. Under no circumstances should you enter this harbor at night. In the anchorage, the dark patches are grass. A narrow creek meanders south from the western end of the harbor, where there is a pond with 5-6 feet over soft sand at low water.

A road leads from the western end of the harbor 2 miles to Chesters, where gasoline, limited supplies, and telephones are available. Further on, the settlement of Lovely Bay is one of the prettier in the district, but there is no harbor of consequence. It can be reached by road from Chesters or via dinghy (it's a long ride, however). Fish are sold at the dock in the afternoon.

Samana Cay lies 20 miles north-northeast of the northeast point of Acklins. Just 9 miles long and 100 feet at its highest point, the cay is completely surrounded by coral reefs, and venturing ashore without local knowledge can be treacherous. We advise against including Samana as a port-of-call. A good landmark is the stranded freighter on the northeast side of Samana's east reef, its rusting hulk a dangerous booby trap; do not venture aboard it.

Sailing correspondent Kurt Stimens visited the cay in April 1984, and worked his 41-foot Morgan through a narrow reef-studded entrance to an anchorage on Samana's south coast between Samana itself and the small cay south of it called variously Prickly Pear, Propeller, or Pimlico, depending upon whom you ask. Since then, we've had a number of reports on this anchorage, all indicating that local knowledge and the ability to find your own way in are necessary here. The reefs hereabouts have claimed many vessels, although none of the wrecks right in this vicinity are any longer visible. In the village, now mostly in ruins, a few people from Acklins occasionally camp in some remaining houses while here to chip cascarilla bark or fish and conch. There are no provisions here — not even fresh water, as the well in the old village now is salty.

On a line and almost midway between Northeast Point on Acklins and the northwesternmost point of Mayaguana Island, lie the **Plana or French Cays.** These two cays, stretching 9 miles in an east-west direction, offer excellent beachcombing on their southern beaches and a comfortable lee anchorage in 20 feet over sand midway off the western cay. If you go too far north, the water shallows, and there are heads.

East Plana Cay was in the past marked at its eastern end by a prominent mast, which has now fallen and lies horizontal on the hill. This cay is the home of The Bahamas' only endemic mammal. The hutia, a rabbit-sized rodent, is nocturnal. To protect this endangered species, don't take your dog ashore.

Mira Por Vos Passage and Islets

D.M.A. Charts: 26240, 26253, 26288.

The Spaniards who so aptly named the Mira Por Vos Shoals obviously knew what they were talking about. This area of reefs, banks, and small cays lies on the southeast side of the Crooked Island Passage and covers some 40 square miles. Unlighted and unmarked, it forms a trap for the unwary, although the lighthouse on Castle Island, 7 miles to the east, with its 17-mile range, is a reliable guide. It is prudent to favor that side of the channel, especially at night.

The Mira Por Vos Shoals consist of a shallow bank where soundings are seldom over 60 feet. In many places on this bank there are dangerous heads. South Cay, a sandy islet that stands some 8-10 feet above high water, is the largest, and under its lee an anchorage can be found if necessary. The bar that extends from South Cay to Northeast Rocks is very shallow indeed. North Rock lies a little over 2 miles northwest of Northeast Rocks and, as the highest, serves as a rookery for brown boobies. Fishing in this vicinity is good.

The tidal currents set across the Mira Por Vos Shoals in a southwest-westerly direction, but vary at times.

HOGSTY REEF

D.M.A. Charts: 26240, 26263.

This reef lies 37 miles southeast of Castle Island about halfway to Great Inagua, but a little to the east of the direct course. Over centuries it has proved a graveyard for ships. Today the Hogsty is seldom visited except by fishermen.

Hogsty Reef is composed of a roughly horseshoe-shaped outer reef that dries in places at low water, enclosing a lagoon where depths of 20-30 feet may be found. The western end of the lagoon is open and vessels may, with care, find anchorage among the heads inside. Northwest Cay, on which the light stands, rises to some 8 feet above high water. Southeast Cay is but 2 feet in height.

Fishing is reported to be excellent here, but we suggest that it be visited only in settled weather. The tidal currents in the vicinity set normally to the west and southwest, but a reverse stream is occasionally experienced. The most conspicuous landmark, visible farther than the light tower, is a large, stranded freighter awash on the north central part of the reef. From a distance of 5-8 miles it might be mistaken for a ship under way. Its rusting hulk is a booby trap for explorers. We also have a recent letter advising that there is a second wreck here, but we do not have a location for it.

MAYAGUANA

D.M.A. Charts: 26252, 26260, 26263, 26268.

This island, though somewhat off the beaten track for yachts cruising The Bahamas, is a useful port of call for those bound to and from the Caribbean, as it lies 50 miles east of Acklins Island and on the direct route. Mayaguana is 24 miles long and 6 miles across at its widest point. As in many of the more "remote" islands of The Bahamas, modern times have begun to arrive here, with electricity and full telephone service expected by the end of 1996.

Abraham's Bay. (Tropic Isle photo)

Around the coasts are a few anchorages and two good harbors. Of these, **Abraham's Bay** on the south coast is best. There are two entrances through the reef that forms the southern side of the harbor. The easiest is at the southwest corner of the reef, close southeast of Start Point. This is good for a 12-foot draft. Once inside, a boat drawing 6 feet can work itself up through the bay to the settlement. The second entrance is one-half mile west of Guano Point, carries 7 feet at low water, and is more intricate. It lies very close to the reef and should not be attempted in southeasterly conditions or strong onshore conditions. Enter only in good light when there is no swell. Abraham's Bay is not a port of entry.

For security reasons, we don't recommend anchorage in Horse Pond Bay.

Abraham's Bay is the largest settlement on Mayaguana, with the commissioner's office and telephone station located there. The Bahamas police force monitors VHF 16 with a working range of 50 miles. The inhabitants, who see few visitors, are especially friendly and helpful. Several small stores carry eggs and fresh vegetables in season. Donald and Irene Charlton sell their own farm-grown, reasonably priced fresh fruit and vegetables. Doris and Cap Brown serve very tasty Bahamian dinners at their restaurant and guest house. Reggie's 6-room guest house also has a good restaurant, and Reggie can provide water as well as helpful information about the island. Next door, the Latitude 22+° bar/restaurant serves breakfast, lunch and dinner (Bahamian fare). Call them on VHF 16 if you land by dinghy and need a pickup to get there. Paradise Villas has some accommodations available and a restaurant/bar serving out of their house. Rooms and meals are also offered at Camelot House (call *Camelot* on VHF 16).

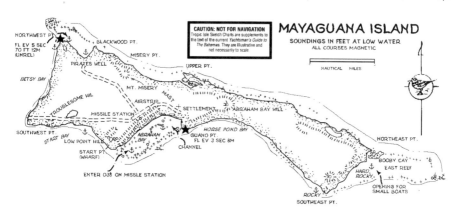

For a water taxi service, contact *Papa Charlie* or *Thunderstorm* on VHF 16 (*Thunderstorm* is Bosie Brooks, who can also haul diesel out to your boat). Emergency fuels and water are supplied in jerry cans and transported to the public wharf, which carries only inches of water at high tide. For propane, call *Gulf Gas* on VHF 16. A good temporary anchorage can be found in Start Bay about 2.5 miles northwest of the wharf and tanks at Start Point.

On the west coast, anchorage may be found off the settlement in Betsy Bay in east to southeast winds. We have varying reports of the holding ranging from poor to good in 35-40 feet over large sand holes in front of the village, where there is a short microwave tower with dish antenna. If you try it, be careful to avoid fouling your anchor in coral. In winds from northeast and southeast there is a good overnight anchorage close under the light tower on Northwest Point. If you wish to remain longer it pays to round Northwest Point through a narrow break in the reef and run down to **Pirate's Well,** anchoring off the settlement. The entrance through the reef lies close under the point, where a draft of about 7 feet can be taken in, but the water shoals gradually and if you draw over 5 feet you may touch occasionally before reaching the settlement. This is a pleasant anchorage, although in strong onshore winds it may be choppy. Yachts are rare here and you'll find the population eager to make your stay pleasant. There is a tiny store, and a 15-room motel is under construction at this writing.

The reef harbor at the eastern end of the island, popular with local fishing boats, is entered through a narrow break in the reef south of Booby Cay.

GREAT INAGUA

D.M.A. Charts: 26267, 26260, 26268.

The island of Great Inagua is one of the largest of the Bahama group, measuring 40 miles from east to west and about 20 miles wide. For the most part the island is low and flat, with the exception of 90-foot James Hill on the north coast, 132-foot East Hill, and 102-foot Salt Pond Hill on the south coast.

The anchorage off Matthew Town is an open roadstead, and untenable in winds of any strength from north to west to almost south-southeast. In prevailing winds you may anchor about 150 yards offshore in 18-24 feet over sand with the town dock and commissioner's office bearing about 090°. Do not attempt to tie up at the town pier. A perpetual surge makes this anchorage uneasy, so we suggest using a stern anchor to hold the bow into the swells. An easier anchorage, some say, is off the airstrip one mile to the north. The loom of the bright dockside lights

GREAT INAGUA : S.W. POINT LIGHTHOUSE : 195° ½ M

Dredged harbor north of Matthew Town. (Tropic Isle photo)

at the loading pier, 7 miles to the north, can be seen 10 miles away.

There are no natural harbors on Great Inagua, and much of the coast is fringed with reef. There is, however, a 200x200-foot dredged harbor immediately north of the town with a controlling depth of 5 feet at low water in the approach. This harbor is untenable in winds from SSW to N. There are three wrecks on the north side of the harbor which, according to local sources, all occurred in these adverse conditions. Local advice is to leave before a norther arrives, otherwise exit will be impossible. Where to go is another question, because anchoring out in the roadstead or trying to find shelter inside Molasses Reef both leave a lot to be desired. Approach to the harbor entrance is 126°M through the center of the entrance on a single leading mark at the southeast corner of the harbor. A rocky ledge extends seaward for some distance just south of the entry channel. Inside, the best water, about 12 feet, is along the concrete wall on the south side. Call 339-1300 for diesel fuel and water. Both are supplied

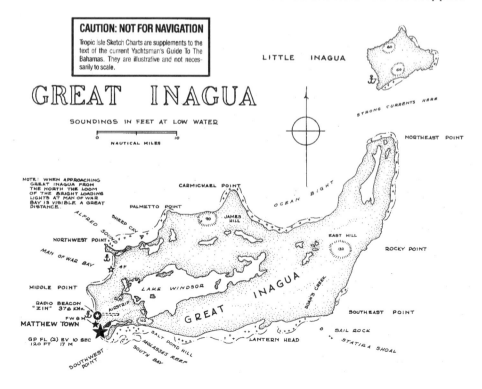

CAUTION: NOT FOR NAVIGATION

Tropic Isle Sketch Charts are supplements to the text of the current Yachtsman's Guide To The Bahamas. They are illustrative and not necessarily to scale.

LITTLE   INAGUA

GREAT   INAGUA

SOUNDINGS IN FEET AT LOW WATER

NAUTICAL MILES

STRONG CURRENTS HERE

NORTHEAST POINT

NOTE: WHEN APPROACHING GREAT INAGUA FROM THE NORTH THE LOOM OF THE BRIGHT LOADING LIGHTS AT MAN OF WAR BAY IS VISIBLE A GREAT DISTANCE.

CARMICHAEL POINT

OCEAN BIGHT

PALMETTO POINT

SHEEP CAY

JAMES HILL

ALFRED SOUND

NORTHWEST POINT

EAST HILL

ROCKY POINT

MAN OF WAR BAY

MIDDLE POINT

LAKE WINDSOR

INAGUA

BOAM'S CREEK

RADIO BEACON "ZIN" 376 KHz.

AIRSTRIP

GREAT

SOUTHEAST POINT

FW & M

MATTHEW TOWN

GP FL (2) EV 10 SEC 120 FT   17 M

SALT POND HILL

SAIL ROCK

LANTERN HEAD

STATIRA SHOAL

MOLASSES REEF

SOUTHWEST POINT

SOUTH BAY

from the small building at the southeast side of the harbor. There is a berthing charge (recently reported to be $2.00), and a reader advises that water costs 20 cents per gallon. Be sure that whoever you pay can give you a government receipt. Just north of the basin is a new Batelco station where you can make calls.

Matthew Town, a port of entry, has an airstrip, weekly flights to Nassau, a telephone station, a hospital with resident doctor, and a cinema. The Royal Bahamas Defence Force now has a Southern Satellite Base here, HMBS Matthew Town. Cleveland Palacious, who owns the Topps Restaurant and Bar (a fine spot), usually stands by on VHF 16 and can help if you need local information. The Nassau mailboat calls weekly.

Morton Salt Company now harvests one million tons per year from the extensive pans on Great Inagua. They also maintain modern machine shops where emergency repairs can be carried out. Well-stocked grocery and hardware stores are also available to the visitor. Please keep in mind when visiting Matthew Town that the entire community is devoted to the salt industry and the local economy is not tourism-oriented.

The Bahamas National Trust maintains the Inagua National Park, consisting of 287 square miles. The park is primarily a sanctuary for the largest breeding population of the West Indian flamingo in the world, which the Trust in cooperation with the National Audubon Society has brought from near extinction to a thriving population estimated at 50,000. Within the protection of the park in the Union Creek Reserve, an enclosed tidal creek where sea turtle research is conducted. Also inhabiting the park are Bahama parrots, West Indian tree ducks, hummingbirds, roseate spoonbills, pelicans, herons, egrets, wild donkeys, and boars. Wardens James and Henry Nixon can arrange jeep tours when their duties allow. The round trip takes an entire day and is rugged going.

Much of the south coast of Great Inagua has off-lying reefs, especially in the vicinity of Southeast Point, where they extend as much as 5 miles offshore. Under Lantern Head a good anchorage can be found, but local knowledge is essential.

The reefbound east coast of Inagua should be given a wide berth. Between the islands of Great and Little Inagua the current sets to westward.

On the north coast. Ocean Bight is a place to be avoided by small craft. No anchorage is available, as the shore is steep-to and forbidding.

Four miles southwest of Palmetto Point is Sheep Cay, which lies just within the reef. Vessels drawing no more than 5 feet may enter through a gap in the reef a short distance east of the cay and bring up in its lee. Once again local knowledge is advised. Between Sheep Cay and Northwest Point the reef lies a considerable distance offshore. Between it and land is Alfred Sound, not recommended as an anchorage. Except in winds from southwest to northwest we think the anchorage under the northern shore of Man of War Bay would be preferable. Here the land is moderately high and the Morton Salt Company has its loading docks. The southern shore of Man of War Bay is steep-to and offers no anchorage. From Middle Point to Matthew Town the coast is clear with no off-lying dangers.

Little Inagua is also largely fringed by off-lying reefs and lies northeast of Great Inagua. It is low, with an area of about 30 square miles, and uninhabited except by wild donkeys, goats, and birds. The only anchorage on Little Inagua is on the southwest coast, where a shallow bay carries 12-18 feet. This bay is reached through a break in the reef, so exercise caution.

Grand Turk. (Tropic Isle photo)

TURKS AND CAICOS ISLANDS

The Turks and Caicos Islands lie to the southeast of The Bahamas between latitudes 021° and 022° N and longitudes 071° and 73°30' W, about 100 miles north of Hispaniola. The Turks Islands lie to the east of the Turks Islands passage, and the Caicos Islands to the west. The Turks Islands consist of Grand Turk and Salt Cay, two inhabited islands, six uninhabited cays, and many rocks. The principal islands of the Caicos group are South Caicos, Middle (or Grand) Caicos, North Caicos, Providenciales, and West Caicos. Geographically the islands are part of The Bahamas chain and have the same flat terrain, with no land over 250 feet high. The total land area is estimated at 193 square miles, with some of the most beautiful beaches in the West Indies.

The Turks and Caicos Islands are a British Crown Colony. Yachts and aircraft must clear with authorities both on arrival and departure, and may enter at Grand Turk, North or South Caicos, or Providenciales. Vessels should be aware that approaches to the west coast of Grand Turk, the north shore of Providenciales, approaches into South Caicos and landfalls along the west coasts of West Caicos and Providenciales (Northwest Point) all lie within protected areas. Anchoring is strictly controlled in these area and information must be obtained from customs officials or from staff of the Department of Environment and Coastal Resources prior to anchoring. All firearms must be reported both on entering and leaving the country. You will probably be required to surrender firearms to the harbormaster for the duration of your stay, unless you are just passing through, in which case, at the discretion of the clearing official, this may not be required. Make arrangements for the return of surrendered items well ahead of your departure, because this can take half a day. Sportfishing without

CAUTION: NOT FOR NAVIGATION
Tropic Isle Sketch Charts are supplements to the text of the current Yachtsman's Guide to The Bahamas. They are illustrative and not necessarily to scale.

TROPIC ISLE SKETCH CHART L-1
EDITION 113

TURKS AND CAICOS ISLANDS

SOUNDINGS IN FEET AT LOW WATER
ALL COURSES MAGNETIC

NAUTICAL MILES

Important: National Park and Nature Reserve Rules, Designated Anchorage Sites, and Anchoring Regulations

The Protected Areas System of the Turks and Caicos Islands includes National Parks, Nature Reserves, Sanctuaries (entry prohibited without a permit), and Historical Sites. IA National Parks Service is being established in Providenciales to manage the Protected Area System. Interesting places to explore in the parks include underground caves and Arawak Indian sites on Middle Caicos, plantation ruins on North Caicos, and old salt industry sites on Salt Cay. Also, the marine protected areas of Grand Turk, South Caicos, Providenciales, and West Caicos are home to magnificent tropical flora and fauna. Within the National Parks and Nature Reserves, you may not: (1) Remove, damage, or destroy any land or sea animal, plant, or man-made artifact; (2) litter or dump on land or sea; (3) use spear guns, fish traps, pole spears, or seine nets; (4) use jet skis or hovercraft; (5) moor vessels on seabed other than clear sandy bottom; (6) moor vessels over 60 feet; (7) water-ski except in designated areas; or (8) drive boats within 100 yards of the shoreline.

Dive mooring buoys located in many Protected Areas are for use of vessels engaged in diving and not for temporary or extended mooring. They may not be used by vessels over 60 feet in length. Visiting vessels must clear these moorings after diving or at the request of commercial dive vessels who pay fees to operate within protected areas.

Anchorage rules have been established by the Department of Environment and Coastal Resources. Mariners should, without fail, upon entry into the Turks and Caicos, seek from Customs, Harbormasters, or the Department of Environment and Coastal Resources (offices in Provo, South Caicos and Grand Turk) the designated anchorage locations (or write to the Director, Dept. of Environment and Coastal Resources, South Base, Grand Turk, Turks and Caicos Islands.)

The Department of Environment and Coastal Resources and the National Parks Service have available Marine Information Packages that show the designated anchorages. It is important to obtain current information about required anchoring practice and the location of designated anchorages. There is enforcement and possible prosecution and penalties for violations.

Most of the designated anchorages are generally more or less rectangular or triangular, with sides ranging from about .2 to .5 miles long. Designated anchorages are off Cockburn Town and Governor's Beach (Grand Turk); in Cockburn Harbour, South Caicos, where there is a lobster and conch reserve; and in Provo where there are two marine National Parks. The Northwest Point National Park lies off the west coast of Provo and offers exceptional wall diving; there is a designated anchor zone. Princess Alexandra National Park includes much of the north shore of Provo and the small cays lying off Provo's northeast corner. For the many vessels that visit Provo there are four anchor zones: (1) in the vicinity of Turtle Cove for vessels bound for the marina but unable to gain access due to low tide or poor light (contact the marina for the location of this anchorage); (2) Stubbs Cut Anchorage Zone; (3) between the Ramada (Turquoise Reef) dock and toward a point outside the Le Deck swimming area; (4) the Ft. George Anchorage Zone.

When anchoring outside protected areas, vessels are still required not to damage coral.

Grand Turk Cable and Wireless tower on the waterfront. (Tropic Isle photo)

a permit is punishable by law, and all spear guns, pole spears, Hawaiian slings, and the use of scuba to take any marine product are illegal. There is a fine for not complying with the law, which is enforced by police and DECR marine patrols. It is illegal for visiting vessels to take either conch or lobster from the waters of the Turks and Caicos Islands.

Most aids to navigation in the Turks and Caicos Islands are unreliable. It should also be noted that VHF 68 has become the hailing channel for many marine interests on Provo, and they request that yachtsmen not use it as a working channel. If you can't raise someone on VHF 16, try 68.

American Airlines has daily flights from Miami to Providenciales. Turks & Caicos Airways, the national airlines, services all the inhabited cays of the Turks and Caicos, and a number of charter companies fly out of Provo and Grand Turk.

Turks Islands

D.M.A. Charts: 25720, 26261, 26262. British Admiralty Charts: 409, 1266, 1441. Tropic Isle Sketch Chart: L-1.

The Turks Islands lie on a bank some 37 miles long and 3-15 miles wide. There are three principal islands and many small islets, cays, and rocks. Much of the bank is a forest of rocky heads and reefs.

Grand Turk, the largest of the Turks Islands, is 6 miles long, 1.5 miles wide, and rises to about 70 feet on its eastern side. It is the seat of government and principal port, and the location of the government-owned Radio Turks and Caicos. The station broadcasts 24 hours a day on 98.5 FM in Grand Turk and 105.9 FM in Provo, with local news at 1:30 and 6:30 p.m.

From about northeast around to southwest, the coast of Grand Turk is fouled by off-lying reefs extending from a mile to 10 miles off. The reef extends one-half mile off on the northwest side and only about 600 yards off most of the western side of the island. The Navy facility, once a brightly lighted landmark, is now closed. Remember that the entire west coast of Grand Turk is a National Park and the Protected Area rules apply. There are designated anchorages off town and at Governor's Beach.

In the anchorage off town (where hopefully the designated anchorage area will soon be marked), you're likely to see sloops from Haiti and the Dominican Republic anchored off or unloading at the dock. Entry is through a break in the reef due west of the most southerly of the two small piers and is good for only about 6 feet. This southern pier is being gradually torn down, and is in such disrepair that it is unusable; the north pier is being rebuilt as a customs dock. Both piers are about 350-400 yards north of the very prominent Cable and Wireless tower and dishes right on the waterfront on Front Street in the center of town. There are usually marks off the town that look like channel markers, but they are not; they are placed by local dive operators to mark dive sites. The anchorage is unprotected in winds from south to southwest around to north, and is comfortable only in mild, settled prevailing weather.

A more comfortable anchorage (and again a designated anchorage hopefully soon to be marked) can be found at the southwest end of the island off the government pier where the ships dock. Approach is due west and anchorage is in clear sand just north of the dock. There is a recently completed commercial concrete pier here, with 10-12 feet at low water. Gas and diesel fuel can be delivered here by tank truck. Call *Texaco 1* to get in touch with Texaco refueling. This is a park area, and the governor's mansion is right by the beach. There can be a fee for using government piers, so ascertain costs from the harbormaster before committing yourself. Near the south dock anchorage is the Arawak Inn, a good restaurant and seaside bar, where horseback riding can be arranged if you like. If a cold front brings westerly winds, the Hawks Nest anchorage on the southeast end of the island can be entered via one of the three cuts through the reef shown on D.M.A. Chart 26262. These must be negotiated in good light to avoid the reefs. The anchorage here is off the ruins northwest of Talbot Shoal and is good in winds from west through east-northeast. Long, Pear, East, and Cotton Cays provide a mini-cruising area with nice picnic spots. Negotiate by eyeball navigation to locate reefs to avoid or dive on. Poaching has been a problem in this area, so we suggest you notify the harbormaster before you go exploring here. If you don't, you may be stopped by patrol boats and searched.

The salt lake named North Creek at the north end of the island has been opened up by dredging and should give protection in almost any weather short of a direct hit by some monster storm. (*It is essential that you get help before entering the first time. Call* Harbormaster *on VHF 16. We have a letter recommending against this entry for sailboats of any other boats with low*

Entrance, North Creek. (Tropic Isle photo)

Flamingo Cove's floating dock complex on North Creek. (Tropic Isle photo)

power propulsion in any but benign conditions.) Even though many of the coral heads that used to make this approach even more difficult have now been blasted and removed, good light is essential here, so you can work your way in to the entrance. From a point well outside of the reef, with the PVC mark off the end of the breakwater bearing about 155°-160°, head for it to find a starting point for working your way in here. When you show depths of 40-50 feet, head so as to leave the PVC stake to your port. Even with these directions and the presence of marks, you still have to thread your way among heads. Once through the approach, the actual entrance is narrow, tricky, and good for only 5 feet or a bit less at low water. It is between the conspicuous spoil bank breakwater on the west and a pile of rocks off the end to the east. The aforementioned white PVC stake just off the end of the breakwater marks the east side of the entrance channel. The tide sluices in and out of the lake strongly, so we recommend entering only a slack tide or against the current. Unfavorable conditions can produce seas that break right across the entrance and even farther out in the approach. As with any breaking inlet, there is danger of broaching or being carried onto one obstruction or another here. Inside, the creek shoals off toward the western side or if you go too far in. Elsewhere, there is lots of room to anchor in 10-12 feet and holding is good in sand and mud. A floating dock complex on the east side of the creek offers diesel fuel, water, electricity and taxi service. Contact *MPL* or *Flamingo Cove* on VHF 16. Farther in on the western shore, closer to town, there is a sand jetty dinghy landing. It's fairly shallow, so you may have to do a bit of wading at low water. *Note: North Creek is not a regular port of entry, so customs and immigration should be cleared before entering. At times, however, the harbormaster might allow you to clear at the government dock in North Creek, but do not attempt this without first talking with the harbormaster.* Normally you must clear at the commercial pier at Governor's Beach or off the town dock.

   If you should need emergency assistance in this area, contact the police vessel *Seaquest* or call *Delta Charlie* (Grand Turk police) on VHF 16.

   The town, generally referred to as Grand Turk although its real name is Cockburn Town, is a picturesque little outpost with Bermudian-style houses and buildings right on the waterfront and streets narrowly bounded by stone walls, with restored street lamps from another era. A few new modern buildings are vividly out of character. Also incongruous, at first, are the men trudging down the street in the noonday sun dressed in business suits complete with neckties, looking like they just arrived from London (which isn't far from the truth). For various reasons there is a large community of lawyers here, mostly British, and they dress the part. One who was building a new office described to us the extensive air-conditioning system he was installing so he could wear his jacket all day and maintain decorum. The people who live here are friendly and talkative and you'll not want for companionship. A pleasant spot to spend some time is the tiny town library, crammed with books and located across from the waterfront. No one should leave Grand Turk without visiting the remarkable Turks & Caicos National Museum on Front Street. This beautifully done showcase of artifacts and historical displays includes that of a 16th-century shipwreck that foundered on Molasses Reef, the oldest shipwreck discovered in the Americas. The recently added Natural History Room has exhibits about reef formation and ecology as well as the geology of the Turks and Caicos. Director Brian Riggs, whose fascination with his work is contagious, offers excellent tours for a $5 donation.

MPL Enterprises, a marine store, carries some supplies and outboard parts. They can repair outboards and will provide diesel and electrical service. Call *MPL* on VHF 16 and ask for Kirk.

There are several interesting places to stay, especially if you enjoy a Graham Greene type of atmosphere. The 150-year-old Salt Raker Inn, built by a Bermudian shipwright, has 12 rooms and cottages available and a garden restaurant and bar, with BBQ and sing-along nights weekly. Try to reserve one of the two pleasant rooms on the inn's second floor; they adjoin a large porch overlooking Front Street and the always uncrowded beach. Early one morning we saw from here a stately Turks Island woman standing barefoot in the sand,

Salt Raker Inn hallway leading to beachfront terrace. (Tropic Isle photo)

The Turks Head Inn, with the oldest pub on the island. (Tropic Isle photo)

wearing a flowered skirt and a "Party Naked" T-shirt. The Turks Head Inn, the oldest pub on the island, was built as a private mansion and was at one time the Governor's private guest house. The rooms are beautifully refurbished, using many original antiques. The Salt Raker and the Turks Head are popular stops for Grand Turk's eclectic happy-hour (and beyond) crowd. The Island House, on the ridge overlooking North Creek, has large suites with kitchens available. More conventional modern accommodations are available at the Guanahani Beach Resort, on the beach a bit out of town.

On Hospital Road, the Regal Beagal is "the best place for cracked conch in all the islands," according to one of our contributors. Another favorite spot to eat is Peanuts Butterfield's Pepper Pot restaurant. During the day you might find Peanuts at her other establishment, a seaside snack bar near the town pier. She'll likely be out back running conch through the grinder to make her famed

TURKS & CAICOS NATIONAL MUSEUM
At Guinep House, Grand Turk

■ View recovered artifacts from the Molasses Reef Wreck—the oldest European ship found in the New World
■ See photos and displays of local culture
■ Learn more about the history of the Turks and Caicos Islands
Hours: 10 a.m. to 4 p.m. M-F; 10 a.m. to 1 p.m. Sat.

Peanuts Butterfield, selling her Hot Rhythm Pills. (Tropic Isle photo)

conch fritter "rhythm pills," advertised with strong Jamaican beer: "DRAGON STOUT AND RHYTHM PILLS PUTS IT BACK." Madison Avenue doesn't know anything about selling a product that Peanuts hasn't figured out.

There are several well-stocked grocery, hardware, and dry-good stores. City Liquor will deliver beer and spirits to your boat. If you're interested in exploring the area's spectacular reefs, there are some good dive concessions in town.

The hospital at Grand Turk is equipped with x-ray facilities, operating theater, pathological laboratory, and an outpatient and dental clinic with medical officers and dentist in residence.

Salt Cay is a triangular-shaped island a little more than 2 miles on a side. A small, neat community of perhaps 200 people and the remains of some fine houses can be found on this island just 5.5 miles south-southwest of Grand Turk. Large salt ponds a few yards in from the shore are still pumped by wooden windmills over a hundred years old, a photographer's delight. The anchorage off the island's western shore is an open roadstead — close in, straightforward, and deep, but untenable in anything but prevailing weather. Ashore, horseback riding is a popular diversion, and some impressive bulls that wander the streets will definitely get your attention. The Mount Pleasant Guest House has rooms available, a good restaurant and bar, and dive facilities. The proprietor is Bryan Sheedy. Their dive boat is interesting — it's an old landing draft that can drop its bow ramp into the water so you can swim aboard instead of climbing a ladder. The Windmills is a beautiful, unusual resort with very expensive accommodations catering to guests who value their privacy, but if you aren't a guest you might be able to have dinner here with reservations 24 hours in advance.

Endymion Rock is barely submerged with about 4 feet on it and lies 5 miles and 224° from the south end of Sand Cay. It is surrounded by a cluster of rocky heads. It often does not break, so it mostly cannot be seen. It is especially dangerous when approaching from the south.

Mt. Pleasant Guest House, Salt Cay. (Tropic Isle photo)

Caicos Islands

D.M.A. Charts: 25720, 26260, 26261, 26268. British Admiralty Charts: 409, 1266. Tropic Isle Sketch Chart: L-1.

The **Caicos Bank** is more than 60 miles across and some 50 miles wide. It is surrounded by reefs and generously sprinkled with coral heads, rocks, and sandbanks. Yet this area offers a variety of delights to the cruising yachtsman. It abounds in reef harbors, small cays, and seemingly endless meandering inlets. Fishing is excellent almost everywhere. The northern perimeter of the bank, west through southeast, is bordered by the six largest islands in the group, and for most of the distance they are fringed with reef extending from a mile to several miles offshore. There are small settlements and some developments on all the major islands except East and West Caicos.

Yachts drawing 7 feet or less regularly cross the bank en route to or from Puerto Plata and down island. This should be done only in good light, as there are numerous isolated coral heads. Anchoring on the banks is safe at night and preferable to risking collision with a coral head. Many boats going south will leave Provo, spend a night on the banks, and then spend the next night at either Salt Cay or Sand Cay, leaving a better angle and straight deep-water sail to Puerto Plata. Be aware, however, that holding can be poor, and the banks can become choppy fast. Best to plan your trip so you complete the crossing before dark. Boats drawing more than 7 feet bound for South Caicos or Puerto Plata that are unable to cross the banks must either go around the north side of Provo or out Clear Sand Road and around French Cay. Those drawing 7 feet or under crossing the banks should sail 134°T for about 20 miles to a point southwest of the shoal at 21°30'N and 72°00'W (position taken from government charts, not a GPS reading), then 100°T for 22 miles, which will put them just south of Six Hill Cays. A good landmark is the microwave tower at Provo, which is 253 feet

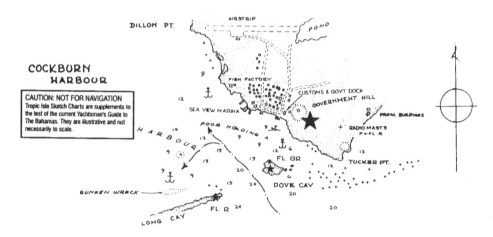

above sea level with a constant red light visible for miles.

South Caicos is 7 miles long with a ridge of hills forming a peninsula along its eastern shore. Very shallow banks lie on its western side, and an almost continuous reef extends along its eastern side. It may be approached only on the south end at Cockburn Harbour, through the wide channel between Dove Cay and Long Cay, as shown on the sketch chart of Cockburn Harbour. Flashing lights, red on Long Cay and Green on Dove Cay (old system) guide fishing boats in and out of the harbor in the dark. A handsome old plantation house stands prominently on a hill 2 miles east of the township of Cockburn Harbour. The headland south of this house should be given a wide berth of at least a mile because of the submerged reef. A new radio transmission tower on the northern tip of South Caicos rises to about 480 feet above sea level. It is topped by a red lights and presumably there are intermediate lights, but we've been unable to ascertain any of the flashing characteristics.

Cockburn Harbour is the only harbor on South Caicos, a port of entry for the Turks and Caicos Islands, and the largest harbor in the archipelago. It offers good protection from almost any weather. Though it is open to the west-northwest, very shallow banks give a good measure of protection in this direction. Strong southerly or southeasterly winds produce an uncomfortable swell in the harbor close to the town. This can be avoided by anchoring in the

SEA VIEW MARINA

For supreme service in South Caicos call on Sea View Marina. With over 20 years experience in shell products. Diesel fuel, gasoline and oils.

FUEL and GROCERIES • RESTAURANT • TELEPHONE • WATER

Free dockage overnight & marine facilities. Transportation & experienced mechanic. Marine products, outboard motors, and spare parts. Call on us anytime for reliable service. If your boat is too big for our dock we will serve you at the government dock. Our fuel truck carries 2,500 gals. Call on us on VHF channel 16

     Ask for Capt. Lewis Cox or Norman
Ph or Fax (649) 946-3219

Cockburn Harbour. (Tropic Isle photo)

lee of Long Cay, as indicated on the sketch chart.

Cockburn Harbour was once the main export point for the salt industry, but today the island's salt pans are abandoned and marked by a few tattered windmills. The town itself offers little in the way of diversion, but the area's reefs provide good fishing and diving, although there is no organized dive concession. Julius "Goo" Jennings is a locally recommended fishing guide. Long Beach, a few miles' taxi ride out of town, is pretty and good for beachcombing. (During the days after a rain, though, the beach and the path that leads to it swarm with the bloodthirstiest mosquitoes you'll ever meet, so don't let yourself get stranded out there.) There is a clinic, post office, telephone station, and some small

PINNACLE
FUEL SUPPLIERS LTD. & MARINA

Professional Refuellers Serving Yachtsmen Since 1962

*When Yachtsmen Want Reliable Service and
Quality Products They Call Us*

- We carry: No. 2 Diesel - Unleaded Gasoline - Oils.
- We supply speedy service with telephone calls, groceries, water, transportation, etc.
- We are always on VHF Channel 16, and are known by the call sign of "Charlie Alpha."
- We are proud of our reputation as the Yachtsman's friend and go out of our way to assist at any time of the day.

Phone: (649) 946-3283/3417 Fax: (649) 946-3377

Ask for Ken Lightbourne or Norman Saunders
E-mail: nbs@tciway.tc

grocery stores where frozen foods and staples might be purchased. The Club Caribe hotel has several rooms with ceiling fans, and has a restaurant with good food and a friendly bar, both with a panoramic view of the harbor. Next door, a marine biology school now occupies what used to be the Admiral's Arms Inn.

The Sea View Marina, run by Captain Lewis Cox, has Shell fuel and can serve you alongside their dock (if your boat has too much draft for their dock, they can meet you at the government pier). Facilities at the marina include water, groceries, a restaurant, and telephone. The services of a mechanic and some marine supplies are available. Call the marina on VHF 16. Pinnacle Fuel Suppliers will deliver Esso fuel at the government pier at this writing but plans to build a marina facility in the near future. Diesel, gas, oil, and water can be arranged, and American Express and Mastercard are accepted. Call on VHF 16 by calling *Charlie Alpha.*

The customs office is at the east end of town on the waterfront.

Ambergris Cays lie 15 miles south-southwest of Cockburn Harbour and have little to offer except a fine picnic or exploring area. Anchor between the two in 6 feet of water.

French Cay, low, scrubby, and uninviting, is very important as a reference point in crossing the bank. It lies 40 miles due west of Cockburn Harbour and serves as a base for Puerto Rican fishermen much of the year. The entire land area and surrounding 400 feet of sea is a sanctuary, and entry is by permit only. A line drawn between French Cay and Cockburn Harbour would determine the northern edge of the deeper areas on the bank.

West Caicos, a little over 60 feet high, bounds the bank on the west side. Extensive reefs lie north of it, but it is steep-to on the west. The greater part of the west coast of West Caicos is a National Park. At our publication deadline there was no designated anchorage in the West Caicos National Park, which precludes anchoring by any vessels over 60 feet in length. When rounding the southern point of West Caicos, stay about 500 yards off. In prevailing winds, anchorage may be had about 200 yards off the west side of West Caicos opposite the remains of houses. Remember to anchor only in clear sand. In a northerly an emergency anchorage can be had on the eastern side one mile northeast of the southern tip, close in. There are outstanding beaches on the eastern coast, which you'll have to dinghy into because the bottom slopes very gradually and it's shallow for a long way out. On the island are the interesting turn-of-the-century ruins of Yankee Town. A contributor who visited the ruins recently found huge bird nests, cotton growing wild, and a narrow railroad track running from the ruins across Lake Catherine to the east coast. Flamingos sometimes wade in Lake Catherine. The wall of the west side provides some of the best virgin diving in these islands. The water is so clear that the same contributor writes that "you can lay on the surface and identify species of fish as they swim by 60+ feet below." If approaching West Caicos from the west of north, you may first sight the remains of a grounded freighter on **West Reef**; the sea has pretty much had its way with this, and about all that remains above water is the stem and the bridge. It is approximately 1.6 miles north of Sand Bore channel. It should be noted that West Reef extends approximately one-half mile west-southwest of the stranded freighter.

Sand Bore Channel is a deep break in the reef approximately 2 miles north of the northwest point of West Caicos. It is approximately 15 feet deep, one-half mile wide, and easily visible. Its edge is marked on the northern side by the very extensive **West Reef,** which usually breaks and is then easy to distinguish both entering and leaving the bank aided by the contrasting water color on the northern edge. Don't look for a breaking reef to the south of Sand Bore Channel. It is a gradual drop-off and not a distinctive reef line. The passage from the bank is found by going southwest 2 miles from the anchorage off South Bluff and turning to steer about 278°. The bottom at the east end of the cut is rocky and there are spots to avoid, but the north side of the channel is clearly visible. It is not unusual to find small fishing smacks anchored here off to the north, in or behind reef outcroppings.

Approaching and traversing **Providenciales** on the south side from Sand Bore Channel as far as the Five Cays is straightforward for up to 8 feet draft, but should never be attempted at night. Steering 095° and keeping approximately one mile south of South Bluff (a readily discernible white cliff) and one-half mile south of Osprey Rock will bring you into Sapodilla Bay or South Dock. Take care, as there are several heads mainly west and south of Osprey Rock. Although many charts show an anchorage in prevailing winds west of South Bluff on Provo, it is impossible to get much more than 5 feet at low water in the lee of the bluff. There is a nice beach, but the anchorage is not recommended for more than a lunch stop. Also ashore is cave worth exploring. North of the beach, flamingos might be spotted wading in the water. That passage from the bank is

Caribbean Marine
& Diesel Ltd.

MARINE & DIESEL REPAIRS
SALES and PARTS

MOBILE WELDING	FULL
Aluminum & Stainless Steel Tower and Top Repairs	PROPELLER REPAIR

* Detroit Diesel * Westerbeke * ZF Transmissions
* Kilopak Generators * John Deere Marine * Perkins
Now located at Caicos Marina & Shipyard

PH. 649-941-5903 FAX 649-941-5902
Providenciales, Turks & Caicos Islands, BWI
Email: caribmarinediesel@tciway.tc

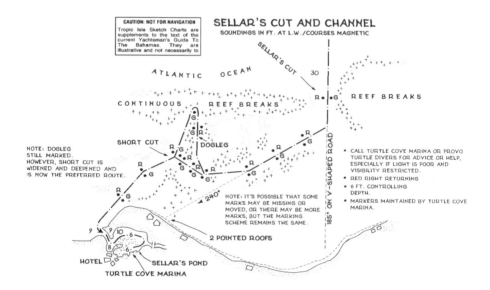

CAUTION: NOT FOR NAVIGATION
Tropic Isle Sketch Charts are supplements to the text of the current Yachtsman's Guide To The Bahamas. They are illustrative and not necessarily to

SELLAR'S CUT AND CHANNEL
SOUNDINGS IN FT. AT L.W./COURSES MAGNETIC

SELLAR'S CUT

ATLANTIC OCEAN

CONTINUOUS   REEF BREAKS   REEF BREAKS

SHORT CUT   DOGLEG

NOTE: DOGLEG STILL MARKED. HOWEVER, SHORT CUT IS WIDENED AND DEEPENED AND IS NOW THE PREFERRED ROUTE.

240°   NOTE: IT'S POSSIBLE THAT SOME MARKS MAY BE MISSING OR MOVED, OR THERE MAY BE MORE MARKS, BUT THE MARKING SCHEME REMAINS THE SAME.

2 POINTED ROOFS

HOTEL   SELLAR'S POND
TURTLE COVE MARINA

185° ON V-SHAPED ROAD

• CALL TURTLE COVE MARINA OR PROVO TURTLE DIVERS FOR ADVICE OR HELP, ESPECIALLY IF LIGHT IS POOR AND VISIBILITY RESTRICTED.
• RED RIGHT RETURNING
• 6 FT. CONTROLLING DEPTH.
• MARKERS MAINTAINED BY TURTLE COVE MARINA.

found by going 275° from a point one-half mile south of Osprey Rock.

If approaching West Caicos from the south or southeast, another easy entrance to the banks is through Clear Sand Road. This is a deep-water channel that will carry 13 feet at low water, used by ships and tankers that go to the new government dock at Gussy Point between Sapodilla Bay and Five Cays on the south side of Providenciales. Pass the south end of West Caicos approximately one-quarter mile off and steer 060°T, which will put you on a direct course to the government dock. You will first notice a crane at the dock and the buildings at Sapodilla Point. West Caicos as well as the Molassas Reef is the fishing ground for the extensive conch and lobster industry located on Providenciales.

Providenciales (Provo) is a large island, among the highest and prettiest in the group. A boom in tourist and building industries has brought several resort complexes to the island, including a Club Med and a Sandals. Turks and Caicos islanders along with Canadians, French, Americans, British, Germans, Haitians, Greeks, and other Europeans and South Americans, make up an unusually cosmopolitan community. Several dive operations serve those who want to explore nearby wrecks and reefs, and there is a recompression chamber.

Customs service for yachts is available at the Turtle Cove Marina, Sapodilla Bay, Caicos Marina and Shipyard, and Leeward Marina. On arrival at any of these, contact the harbormaster (customs) and an officer will come out to clear you in, but he can only give you 7 days to stay. After 7 days in the islands, yachtsmen reportedly may now apply for a cruising permit good for 3 months. Hours are 8:00 a.m. to 4:30 p.m. Monday through Thursday, and 8:00 a.m. to 4:00 p.m. Friday. Anything else is overtime, including the lunch hours 12:30 to 2:00. It is still necessary to obtain a transire to visit the other inhabited islands.

Turtle Cove Marina is located midway in the bight on the north shore. Excellent protection can be found here in 6 feet at dockside. Markers privately maintained by Turtle Cove Marina define the approach channel from **Sellar's**

Beautiful Provo beach. (Tropic Isle photo)

Cut. (The sketch chart depicts this entry as if all marks were present, but because these are vulnerable to the forces of nature, marks have been known to be missing or moved from time to time. Generally, the marking scheme remains the same, but be aware.) Management now informs us that the "short cut" has been widened and deepened, and is now the preferred approach, although the "dogleg" is still marked. When you arrive off Sellar's Cut, call ahead on VHF 16 to Turtle Cove Marina or Provo Turtle Divers for up-to-the-minute advice about this entry. Because of the profusion of coral heads in this approach, good light is a must. This is a complicated entrance, and we recommend that for your first entry here you arrange for the services of a pilot. (An experienced local captain on Grand Turk told us that this entrance is complicated enough that even though he was once based at Sellar's Pond, he'll hire a pilot for the first time in when he returns.) Water, electricity, and TV hookups are available at each slip at Turtle Cove Marina. At the fuel dock, diesel, gas, oil, water, and ice are available. An ambitious renovation includes the addition of a 650-foot land peninsula stretching out into the pond, and the rebuilding and addition of docks. Plans for the future include a commercial complex with marina office, condominiums, shops, and restaurants. Nearby are restaurants, hotels, boutiques, and a dive shop. The marina is home of the annual Caicos Cup sportfishing contest. The 1996 tournament included 29 boats with a new record of 111 blue marlin caught. All but four were released; only fish exceeding 300 pounds may be boated.

   Club Med Cut, between Sellar's and Leeward Cuts, is unmarked. Good light

The UNICORN Bookstore
The Market Place, Leeward Highway
Providenciales, TCI
• Current Best Sellers • Newspapers •
• Charts-Aerial & Nautical •
• Local Info & Publications •
Ph: 649-94-15458   E-Mail:unicorn@tciway.tc   Fax: 649-94-15510

is essential for staying in deep water as you pass through the break in the reef. The break is found by keeping the big stand of casuarina just east of the most westerly Club Med building in transit with the microwave tower behind it. The northeast reef is most abrupt and easy to see; the southwest is more gradual and not so obvious. Once through, you can continue inside the reef westward until in front of Le Deck, where you will find good day anchorage. A northeast current runs here.

Leeward Cut is marked by privately maintained marks placed by Leeward Marina. These define the entrance through the cut and show the route to follow between the sandbars forming off the southwest end of Little Water Cay and off Pelican Point, the northeast tip of Provo. Low water depths through here are about 7 feet, but these sandbars continue to shift, and depths can decrease or increase practically overnight, so it is advisable to call Leeward Marina on VHF 16 for advice or to request a guide. Good light is essential here. The Leeward Going Through itself has depths of 10 feet or better and offers protected anchorage. Leeward Cut is considered safe in moderate weather but, during strong northerly conditions or when a ground swell is running, it is safer to enter at Fort George's Cay, 3 miles to the northeast, to await better weather. Enter on 130° on the Meridian Club buildings to the anchorage inside, and from there navigate south inside the reef, using the eyeball method. A draft of 7 feet can be carried all the way.

Leeward Marina offers water, electricity (110/220), and cable TV hook-ups at each slip. It is advisable to call ahead for availability. The marina also has gasoline, diesel, oil, laundry, and telephone and fax service as well as 24-hour security. Very extensive development of the marine facilities here should begin in early 1999, including construction of a 100-berth marina. Gilley's restaurant serves excellent seafood and daily lunch specials. Leeward Marina is a port of entry and home to a number of sailing, boat charter, fishing, and diving operations. It is also a natural stepping stone to the cays and neighboring islands.

Sapodilla Bay, at the island's most southern point, just west of the government dock at Gussy Point, is a well-protected anchorage where boats drawing up to 5 feet can anchor fairly close in to the beach in good holding sand. Take care not to approach too close to the point, as there is a 65-foot wreck awash at low water about 75 yards north of the point. Sapodilla Bay is a port of entry. Call the harbormaster, headquartered at the government dock, on VHF 16 when you enter for instructions. Fuel is available at the government dock.

Government dock at Gussy Point and Sapodilla Bay. (Tropic Isle photo)

Sapodilla Bay is also a good place for careening boats; many island sloops periodically do their maintenance here. The anchorage here is about 4 miles from town — you can hail the Public Bus on VHF 70, which can take you into town for $2 per passenger, or you can contact a taxi on VHF 6. There's a government dumpster on the beach road. The Provo Aquatic Centre and the Mariner Hotel here are no longer in operation here.

Caicos Marina and Shipyard at **Long Bay** has dockage, duty-free fuel for transit vessels, water, electricity, and dry storage. A 75-ton travel lift with 25-foot beam is in operation, and there is a machine shop and woodworking shop, fiberglass repair facilities, restrooms, showers, washers and dryers. Call ahead here to confirm that the services or amenities you depend on will be available when you arrive; call 649-946-5600.) The entry channel is privately marked. Before you enter, contact the marina on VHF 16 or 72 for assistance regarding marks, depths, your draft, and possible channel obstructions. The marina is a port of entry.

Good hurricane holes on Provo are **Sellar's Pond** or the canals at Discovery Bay just east of Five Cays. As has been well demonstrated recently, a "good hurricane hole" is a relative term; even the best are no good if they receive a direct hit.

Provo has modern, well-stocked supermarkets, machine shops, international banks, a dry cleaner, and boutiques in the town area near the airport. There is a clinic with doctors and nurses as well as a doctor, dentist, and several veterinarians. The commercial fisheries by the government dock processes local

CMS

Caicos Marina & Shipyard Ltd.

MasterCard, VISA,
American Express Accepted

Located Halfway Between
Miami and the Virgin Islands
Providenciales,
Turks & Caicos Islands
Tel: 649 - 946 - 5600
Fax: 649 - 946 - 5390
VHF 16/72 SSB 4143.6

TRUMPORT

Mailing Address:
Caicos Marina & Shipyard
P.O. Box 24, Juba Point, Providenciales
Turks & Caicos Islands, B.W.I.

Yacht Carpentry • Fiberglass & Rigging • Port of Entry • Full Marina Services
75-Ton Traveling Boat Hoist with 25 ft. Beam • Fuel Service
Ice • Complete Machine Shop • Diesel, Gas & Electrical Repairs
30/50 AMP • Minor Electrical Repairs • Chandlery
Wash Down and R/O Water • USA Direct Phone and Fax Service
Dry Storage • Showers • Laundry • Car Rental Arranged
Federal Express and UPS Service • Mail Held or Forwarded

conch and lobster catch and will sell to the public. The new First Choice IGA Market on Leeward Highway offers free delivery to boats ordering $50 or more. Ice is available at First Choice, TC Trading, Carib West Liquors, Island Pride Grocery, and Hey Jose. S. Walkin and Son Marine is an authorized Johnson/ Evinrude dealer. Caribbean Marine & Diesel specializes in diesel marine repairs. NAPA Auto Parts has enlarged its stock of marine supplies. Marine supplies and fishing gear are also available in limited supply at Building Materials Ltd.'s Do-It Center, and Leeward Marina's office/shop.

Pleasant accommodations can be found at the Turtle Cove Inn. The Erebus Inn has several chalet-like cottages with terraces perched high on a bluff overlooking Sellar's Pond, and there's a good restaurant and congenial bar. In the evening there's often music and dancing.

Restaurants and shops seem to proliferate in Provo. In town, the Tasty Temptation bakery opens early for fresh-ground coffee and excellent pastries, serves lunch until 3 p.m., and will deliver to your boat orders of $20 or more. The Banana Boat's dockside bar and grill on The Pond serves lunch, dinner, and late-night snacks. The cheerful poolside Tiki Hut at the Turtle Cove Marina serves breakfast, lunch, and dinner. The Shark Bit Bar and Grill has a popular happy hour from 5-6 on Wednesdays, Thursdays, and Fridays. The Ports O' Call shopping center opposite the Allegro Resort has two popular delis, Barefoot Café and Angela's, as well as several good restaurants and bars. A rake-and-shake band plays on Friday nights. A block up form Ports O' Call is the China Restaurant for good Chinese food. Pizza Pizza on Leeward Highway will deliver. At Central Square on Leeward Highway, Hey Jose's is a boaters' favorite for fun, Mexican food, and pizza (also available for takeout). For island cooking, try Fast Eddie's on Airport Road or Dora's on Leeward Highway. Le Deck Hotel and Beach Club serves breakfast, lunch, and dinner. There's a beautiful beach. You can get a good hamburger at Gilley's Cafe at the airport. For conch, try Bonnie's Bistro & Bar on Le Deck Road. For elegance, try Anacaona at the Grace Bay Club or Draco's up on the hill overlooking Sellar's Pond. The Terrace at Turtle Cove Marina also serves exceptional meals.

At the Market Place, the Bamboo Gallery has Haitian and other Caribbean art. Maisson Creole, next to Caicos Cafe has nice crafts, and a local craft "village" up the road opposite China Restaraurant, has a wide variety of local crafts for sale.

The Island Sea Center, on the northeastern point of Provo at Leeward Going Through, is the world's first commercial sea farm for the queen conch. It produces millions of small conch yearly. Tours of the hatchery include a film and hands-on exhibits, and there's a gift shop. The Conch Bar serves conch dishes and refreshments. Dinghies may tie up at the Conch Farm dock. The Center's dolphin project, Into the Blue, has succeeded in releasing captive dolphins back into the wild after retraining them to feed themselves in the Conch Farm pasture, where the conch is raised. PRIDE, a marine research and education organization, is adjacent to the Conch Farm. You can get information about native shells and plants, as well as local National Parks and Land Reserves, at their information/conservation center.

Another interesting spot is Cheshire Hall, the ruins of an 18th-century

Loyalist plantation. The Caicos Cays link Providenciales to North Caicos. These cays are noted for magnificent beaches, but the deep channels that used to separate them have now, for the most part, filled in. **Pine Cay** has an inner anchorage on the inside of the north side of the island that is comfortable in any weather. Ashore, the Meridian Club is an immaculate vacation resort built along the dunes, easily recognized from seaward as the only two-story structure visible on Pine Cay. Call *Pine Cay* on VHF 16 for dinner reservations or information. Nearby creeks offer tarpon fishing, and reef trips and underwater excursions can be arranged. Just to the north, **Fort George Cay,** with its submerged cannon, is a National Park; no spearfishing or taking of live shells, please

North Caicos, the most fertile of the group, has interesting plantation ruins. The anchorage off the Prospect of Whitby hotel here can be approached by shoal-draft vessels through Clark's Cut to the east, which serves **Bottle Creek.** Best to negotiate this channel in favorable light on the cable houses, then follow the deeper water inside the reef west to Whitby. The elegantly casual accommodations are built of native stones, with pleasant patios and courtyards.

Grand Caicos and East Caicos. The north coast must be approached with great care and only in good light. It is easy to get too close in passing Haulover Point. In poor visibility with accompanying rain squalls it is also easy to mistake Haulover Point for Cape Comete, 15 miles to the east. When rounding the latter under good light conditions it is safe for small boats to pass inside Phillips Reef, which always breaks. In poor or questionable visibility it is recommended that all vessels stand off the coast at least 5 miles, thereby rounding Phillips Reef on the outside. There is a good anchorage under the lone cay inside Jacksonville Cut at the west end of East Caicos, but very good light and favorable sea conditions are required to enter.

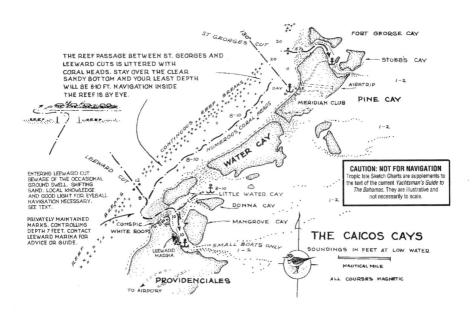

THE CAICOS CAYS

Tides in the Bahamas

Knowing the state of the tide helps anyone who runs a boat. It saves detours around sandbars, open coves and harbours shallow at the entrances, and allows you to work on your craft's bottom between tides. Should you run aground, you'll know what to do: hustle to get off on a falling tide or relax and float free on a rising tide.

The daily pattern of tides in the Bahamas is simple: two equal high waters and two equal low waters with roughly 6 hours from one change to the next. When the moon is full or new the tide is high at about 0800 and 2000. After that high water will be very roughly an hour later each day.

In Nassau the mean range of the tide is 2.6 feet. Neap tides, after the first and last quarters of the moon, rise half a foot less. Spring tides, after new and full moons, rise half a foot more. When the moon is nearest earth during spring tides, another half foot is added to the range.

In the following pages you will find a tide table for Nassau for the year. Eastern Standard Time is used. Daylight Saving Time tides will be one hour later. Midnight is shown as 0:00, noon as 12:00. When evening tide changes to morning tide, or the other way around, about once a week a tide is missing. This is shown by dashes. Heights of low and high waters are to be added to the depths given on you charts. They are in feet and tenths of feet. If you read inches for the tenths you won't be far off.

Winds upset all predictions. A strong wind drives water against the shore of away from it. A storm may change the tidal level by several feet. Also, in most cuts, bights and harbor the current will not slack and turn at the time of high or low water. It may keep running in what seems the wrong direction for several hours.

Difference on Nassau Time

Height: **Stations above the double line:** Range of tide 0.0-0.3 ft. less than range of same tide in Nassau.**Stations below the line:** Range 0.5-0.6 ft. less than same tide in Nassau.

Island or area	Station	Time (min.)
W. Edge of Gt. Bahama Bank	North Cat Cay	Later 30
Grand Bahama Island	West End	Later 25
Abaco	North Bar Channel	Later 30
Berry Islands	Whale Cay	Later 40
Andros	Fresh Creek	Same
Eleuthera	East Coast	Later 20
	The Bight	Earlier 2h 25
Cat Island	The Bight	Earlier 25
San Salvador	Cockburn Town	Same
Long Island	Clarence Town	Later 25
	Salt Pond	Later 2h 30
Exuma	Highborne Cay	Later 20
	George Town	Same
Acklins	Southwest Point	Earlier 10
Mayaguana	Abraham's Bay	Later 10
Great Inagua	Matthew Town	Later 20

JANUARY 1999 - Standard Time

Day		Time	Ht.	Time	Ht.	Time	Ht.	Time	Ht.
○ 1	F	20 L	0.0	654 H	3.8	1317 L	0.1	1915 H	3.1
2	Sa	112 L	0.0	745 H	3.8	1407 L	0.0	2006 H	3.1
3	Su	203 L	0.0	834 H	3.7	1455 L	0.1	2056 H	3.1
4	M	253 L	0.1	921 H	3.6	1542 L	0.1	2145 H	3.0
5	Tu	343 L	0.2	1007 H	3.4	1627 L	0.3	2233 H	3.0
6	W	433 L	0.4	1053 H	3.2	1712 L	0.4	2322 H	2.9
7	Th	523 L	0.6	1138 H	3.0	1756 L	0.5		
8	F	12 H	2.8	616 L	0.7	1225 H	2.8	1841 L	0.6
9	Sa	103 H	2.8	712 L	0.9	1315 H	2.7	1928 L	0.7
10	Su	157 H	2.8	810 L	0.9	1407 H	2.6	2017 L	0.7
11	M	251 H	2.9	908 L	1.0	1501 H	2.6	2107 L	0.7
12	Tu	344 H	2.9	1004 L	0.9	1555 H	2.6	2157 L	0.7
13	W	434 H	3.0	1056 L	0.9	1646 H	2.6	2245 L	0.6
14	Th	520 H	3.2	1143 L	0.8	1734 H	2.7	2331 L	0.6
15	F	604 H	3.3	1227 L	0.7	1820 H	2.8		
16	Sa	15 L	0.5	645 H	3.4	1309 L	0.6	1903 H	2.9
● 17	Su	58 L	0.4	726 H	3.5	1349 L	0.5	1945 H	2.9
18	M	140 L	0.4	806 H	3.5	1428 L	0.4	2027 H	3.0
19	Tu	224 L	0.3	846 H	3.5	1508 L	0.3	2110 H	3.1
20	W	308 L	0.3	929 H	3.5	1549 L	0.3	2155 H	3.1
21	Th	356 L	0.4	1013 H	3.4	1631 L	0.3	2242 H	3.1
22	F	448 L	0.4	1101 H	3.3	1718 L	0.3	2334 H	3.1
23	Sa	545 L	0.5	1154 H	3.1	1808 L	0.3		
24	Su	32 H	3.2	648 L	0.6	1252 H	2.9	1904 L	0.3
25	M	134 H	3.2	756 L	0.6	1356 H	2.8	2005 L	0.3
26	Tu	241 H	3.2	907 L	0.6	1504 H	2.7	2109 L	0.3
27	W	348 H	3.3	1014 L	0.5	1610 H	2.8	2212 L	0.2
28	Th	451 H	3.4	1115 L	0.4	1712 H	2.8	2312 L	0.1
29	F	549 H	3.5	1211 L	0.2	1809 H	2.9		
30	Sa	8 L	0.1	642 H	3.6	1302 L	0.2	1902 H	3.0
○ 31	Su	100 L	0.0	731 H	3.6	1349 L	0.1	1951 H	3.1

FEBRUARY 1999 - Standard Time

Day		Time	Ht.	Time	Ht.	Time	Ht.	Time	Ht.
1	M	150 L	0.0	817 H	3.5	1433 L	0.1	2037 H	3.1
2	Tu	237 L	0.1	900 H	3.4	1514 L	0.2	2121 H	3.1
3	W	322 L	0.2	941 H	3.3	1554 L	0.3	2203 H	3.1
4	Th	406 L	0.4	1020 H	3.1	1632 L	0.4	2245 H	3.0
5	F	451 L	0.5	1100 H	3.0	1711 L	0.5	2328 H	2.9
6	Sa	537 L	0.7	1141 H	2.8	1751 L	0.6		
7	Su	13 H	2.9	627 L	0.9	1226 H	2.7	1835 L	0.7
8	M	102 H	2.8	721 L	1.0	1315 H	2.6	1923 L	0.8
9	Tu	155 H	2.8	819 L	1.1	1410 H	2.5	2016 L	0.8
10	W	252 H	2.9	918 L	1.1	1508 H	2.6	2112 L	0.8
11	Th	349 H	3.0	1015 L	1.0	1606 H	2.6	2206 L	0.8
12	F	442 H	3.1	1107 L	0.9	1659 H	2.7	2258 L	0.6
13	Sa	531 H	3.3	1154 L	0.7	1749 H	2.9	2348 L	0.5
14	Su	616 H	3.4	1237 L	0.6	1836 H	3.0		
15	M	35 L	0.4	700 H	3.5	1319 L	0.4	1920 H	3.2
● 16	Tu	121 L	0.3	743 H	3.6	1400 L	0.3	2004 H	3.3
17	W	208 L	0.2	826 H	3.6	1441 L	0.2	2049 H	3.4
18	Th	255 L	0.2	911 H	3.6	1523 L	0.2	2135 H	3.5
19	F	344 L	0.2	957 H	3.5	1607 L	0.2	2223 H	3.5
20	Sa	436 L	0.3	1045 H	3.3	1654 L	0.2	2315 H	3.4
21	Su	533 L	0.4	1138 H	3.1	1746 L	0.3		
22	M	13 H	3.4	635 L	0.5	1237 H	3.0	1844 L	0.4
23	Tu	116 H	3.3	742 L	0.6	1341 H	2.8	1947 L	0.5
24	W	225 H	3.3	852 L	0.7	1450 H	2.8	2055 L	0.5
25	Th	335 H	3.3	1000 L	0.6	1559 H	2.8	2201 L	0.4
26	F	440 H	3.3	1101 L	0.5	1701 H	2.9	2302 L	0.3
27	Sa	537 H	3.4	1154 L	0.4	1757 H	3.0	2358 L	0.3
28	Su	629 H	3.5	1242 L	0.4	1847 H	3.1		

MARCH 1999 - Standard Time

Day		Time	Ht.	Time	Ht.	Time	Ht.	Time	Ht.
1	M	48 L	0.2	714 H	3.5	1326 L	0.3	1932 H	3.2
○ 2	Tu	135 L	0.2	756 H	3.5	1405 L	0.3	2014 H	3.3
3	W	218 L	0.3	835 H	3.4	1443 L	0.4	2053 H	3.3
4	Th	300 L	0.4	912 H	3.3	1518 L	0.5	2131 H	3.3
5	F	340 L	0.5	949 H	3.2	1553 L	0.6	2208 H	3.2
6	Sa	420 L	0.7	1025 H	3.1	1629 L	0.7	2246 H	3.2
7	Su	501 L	0.8	1103 H	2.9	1706 L	0.8	2326 H	3.1
8	M	545 L	1.0	1144 H	2.8	1747 L	0.9		
9	Tu	11 H	3.0	634 L	1.1	1231 H	2.7	1834 L	1.0
10	W	102 H	3.0	730 L	1.2	1325 H	2.7	1928 L	1.0
11	Th	200 H	3.0	830 L	1.2	1424 H	2.7	2028 L	1.0
12	F	301 H	3.1	930 L	1.1	1525 H	2.8	2129 L	0.9
13	Sa	400 H	3.2	1025 L	1.0	1623 H	2.9	2227 L	0.8
14	Su	454 H	3.3	1115 L	0.8	1717 H	3.1	2321 L	0.6
15	M	545 H	3.5	1201 L	0.7	1806 H	3.3		
16	Tu	12 L	0.5	632 H	3.6	1245 L	0.5	1853 H	3.5
● 17	W	102 L	0.3	719 H	3.7	1329 L	0.3	1940 H	3.7
18	Th	151 L	0.2	805 H	3.7	1412 L	0.2	2027 H	3.8
19	F	240 L	0.2	851 H	3.7	1457 L	0.2	2114 H	3.9
20	Sa	331 L	0.2	940 H	3.6	1543 L	0.2	2204 H	3.8
21	Su	424 L	0.3	1030 H	3.4	1633 L	0.3	2258 H	3.7
22	M	520 L	0 4	1124 H	3.2	1727 L	0.4	2356 H	3.6
23	Tu	621 L	0.6	1224 H	3.1	1827 L	0.5		
24	W	100 H	3.4	728 L	0.7	1330 H	3.0	1933 L	0.6
25	Th	209 H	3.3	836 L	0.8	1439 H	2.9	2043 L	0.7
26	F	319 H	3.3	941 L	0.8	1546 H	3.0	2150 L	∩.7
27	Sa	424 H	3.3	1039 L	0.7	1647 H	3.1	2251 L	0.6
28	Su	520 H	3.3	1131 L	0.6	1740 H	3.2	2345 L	0.5
29	M	608 H	3.4	1216 L	0.6	1826 H	3.3		
30	Tu	33 L	0.5	652 H	3.4	1256 L	0.6	1909 H	3.4
○ 31	W	117 L	0.5	731 H	3.4	1333 L	0.6	1947 H	3.5

APRIL 1999 - Standard Time

Day		Time	Ht.	Time	Ht.	Time	Ht.	Time	Ht.
1	Th	157 L	0.5	808 H	3.4	1409 L	0.6	2024 H	3.5
2	F	236 L	0.6	844 H	3.3	1443 L	0.7	2059 H	3.5
3	Sa	314 L	0.7	918 H	3.2	1517 L	0.8	2134 H	3.4
4	Su	352 L	0.8	954 H	3.1	1551 L	0.9	2209 H	3.4
5	M	430 L	0.9	1031 H	3.1	1628 L	1.0	2247 H	3.3
6	Tu	511 L	1.1	1110 H	3.0	1708 L	1.1	2329 H	3.2
7	W	556 L	1.2	1156 H	2.9	1754 L	1.1		
8	Th	17 H	3.2	648 L	1.2	1248 H	2.9	1848 L	1.2
9	F	114 H	3.1	745 L	1.3	1346 H	2.9	1950 L	1.2
10	Sa	215 H	3.2	844 L	1.2	1448 H	3.0	2054 L	1.1
11	Su	318 H	3.3	941 L	1.1	1548 H	3.1	2156 L	0.9
12	M	417 H	3.4	1033 L	0.9	1644 H	3.4	2255 L	0.7
13	Tu	511 H	3.5	1123 L	0.7	1736 H	3.6	2349 L	0.5
14	W	603 H	3.6	1210 L	0.5	1826 H	3.8		
● 15	Th	42 L	0.3	653 H	3.7	1257 L	0.3	1916 H	4.0
16	F	134 L	0.2	743 H	3.7	1344 L	0.2	2005 H	4.1
17	Sa	225 L	0.2	832 H	3.7	1432 L	0.2	2055 H	4.1
18	Su	317 L	0.2	923 H	3.6	1522 L	0.3	2147 H	4.0
19	M	411 L	0.3	1015 H	3.5	1615 L	0.4	2241 H	3.9
20	Tu	507 L	0.4	1111 H	3.3	1711 L	0.5	2340 H	3.7
21	W	607 L	0.6	1211 H	3.2	1813 L	0.7		
22	Th	43 H	3.5	709 L	0.7	1316 H	3.1	1919 L	0.8
23	F	150 H	3.3	813 L	0.8	1423 H	3.1	2028 L	0.8
24	Sa	257 H	3.2	914 L	0.8	1527 H	3.1	2134 L	0.8
25	Su	359 H	3.2	1009 L	0.8	1625 H	3.2	2233 L	0.8
26	M	453 H	3.2	1058 L	0.8	1716 H	3.3	2326 L	0.7
27	Tu	541 H	3.2	1142 L	0.7	1800 H	3.4		
28	W	12 L	0.7	623 H	3.3	1221 L	0.7	1841 H	3.5
29	Th	55 L	0.6	702 H	3.3	1259 L	0.7	1918 H	3.6
○ 30	F	134 L	0.7	739 H	3.3	1334 L	0.8	1954 H	3.6

MAY 1999 - Standard Time

Day	Time	Ht.	Time	Ht.	Time	Ht.	Time	Ht.
1 Sa	212 L	0.7	815 H	3.2	1409 L	0.8	2029 H	3.6
2 Su	250 L	0.8	851 H	3.2	1444 L	0.9	2103 H	3.5
3 M	326 L	0.9	926 H	3.1	1519 L	0.9	2138 H	3.5
4 Tu	404 L	0.9	1004 H	3.1	1556 L	1.0	2215 H	3.4
5 W	443 L	1.0	1043 H	3.0	1637 L	1.1	2256 H	3.3
6 Th	526 L	1.1	1128 H	3.0	1723 L	1.2	2343 H	3.3
7 F	613 L	1.1	1218 H	3.0	1817 L	1.2		
8 Sa	37 H	3.2	706 L	1.1	1314 H	3.0	1918 L	1.2
9 Su	136 H	3.2	802 L	1.1	1414 H	3.1	2024 L	1.1
10 M	239 H	3.3	858 L	0.9	1515 H	3.3	2129 L	0.9
11 Tu	341 H	3.3	953 L	0.8	1613 H	3.5	2230 L	0.7
12 W	439 H	3.4	1046 L	0.6	1708 H	3.8	2328 L	0.5
13 Th	535 H	3.5	1138 L	0.4	1801 H	4.0		
14 F	23 L	0.3	629 H	3.6	1229 L	0.3	1854 H	4.1
● 15 Sa	117 L	0.2	722 H	3.6	1319 L	0.2	1945 H	4.2
16 Su	210 L	0.1	814 H	3.6	1411 L	0.2	2037 H	4.2
17 M	303 L	0.2	907 H	3.5	1504 L	0.2	2130 H	4.1
18 Tu	356 L	0.2	1001 H	3.4	1558 L	0.4	2225 H	3.9
19 W	451 L	0.4	1057 H	3.3	1655 L	0.5	2322 H	3.7
20 Th	547 L	0.5	1156 H	3.2	1756 L	0.7		
21 F	22 H	3.4	645 L	0.6	1257 H	3.1	1901 L	0.8
22 Sa	123 H	3.3	742 L	0.7	1359 H	3.1	2006 L	0.9
23 Su	225 H	3.1	838 L	0.8	1500 H	3.2	2110 L	0.9
24 M	324 H	3.0	931 L	0.8	1555 H	3.3	2208 L	0.9
25 Tu	417 H	3.0	1019 L	0.8	1645 H	3.3	2300 L	0.8
26 W	505 H	3.0	1103 L	0.8	1729 H	3.4	2346 L	0.8
27 Th	549 H	3.0	1144 L	0.8	1810 H	3.5		
28 F	29 L	0.7	630 H	3.1	1223 L	0.8	1849 H	3.6
29 Sa	110 L	0.7	709 H	3.1	1301 L	0.8	1925 H	3.6
○ 30 Su	148 L	0.7	747 H	3.1	1338 L	0.8	2001 H	3.6
31 M	226 L	0.8	825 H	3.1	1415 L	0.9	2037 H	3.6

JUNE 1999 - Standard Time

Day	Time	Ht.	Time	Ht.	Time	Ht.	Time	Ht.
1 Tu	303 L	0.8	902 H	3.1	1452 L	0.9	2113 H	3.5
2 W	340 L	0.9	940 H	3.1	1531 L	1.0	2150 H	3.5
3 Th	419 L	0.9	1021 H	3.0	1613 L	1.0	2231 H	3.4
4 F	459 L	0.9	1104 H	3.0	1700 L	1.1	2316 H	3.3
5 Sa	543 L	0.9	1153 H	3.1	1753 L	1.1		
6 Su	8 H	3.3	632 L	0.9	1247 H	3.1	1854 L	1.0
7 M	105 H	3.2	725 L	0.9	1345 H	3.3	1959 L	1.0
8 Tu	206 H	3.2	820 L	0.8	1445 H	3.4	2105 L	0.8
9 W	309 H	3.2	917 L	0.6	1545 H	3.6	2209 L	0.7
10 Th	411 H	3.2	1014 L	0.5	1644 H	3.8	2309 L	0.5
11 F	511 H	3.3	1110 L	0.4	1740 H	4.0		
12 Sa	7 L	0.3	608 H	3.4	1205 L	0.2	1835 H	4.1
● 13 Su	102 L	0.2	703 H	3.4	1259 L	0.2	1929 H	4.1
14 M	155 L	0.1	757 H	3.4	1353 L	0.2	2022 H	4.1
15 Tu	247 L	0.1	851 H	3.4	1447 L	0.2	2114 H	4.0
16 W	339 L	0.2	944 H	3.4	1542 L	0.3	2207 H	3.8
17 Th	430 L	0.3	1038 H	3.3	1638 L	0.5	2300 H	3.6
18 F	521 L	0.4	1133 H	3.2	1736 L	0.6	2354 H	3.3
19 Sa	613 L	0.6	1230 H	3.2	1835 L	0.8		
20 Su	49 H	3.1	704 L	0.7	1327 H	3.2	1936 L	0.9
21 M	145 H	3.0	755 L	0.8	1423 H	3.2	2037 L	1.0
22 Tu	241 H	2.9	845 L	0.9	1517 H	3.2	2134 L	1.0
23 W	335 H	2.8	934 L	0.9	1607 H	3.3	2227 L	0.9
24 Th	425 H	2.9	1021 L	0.9	1654 H	3.4	2316 L	0.9
25 F	513 H	2.9	1105 L	0.9	1737 H	3.4		
26 Sa	1 L	0.9	557 H	2.9	1148 L	0.9	1818 H	3.5
27 Su	43 L	0.8	639 H	3.0	1230 L	0.8	1857 H	3.6
○ 28 M	123 L	0.8	720 H	3.1	1310 L	0.8	1935 H	3.6
29 Tu	201 L	0.8	800 H	3.1	1350 L	0.8	2012 H	3.6
30 W	239 L	0.8	839 H	3.1	1430 L	0.9	2050 H	3.6

JULY 1999 - Standard Time

Day	Time	Ht.	Time	Ht.	Time	Ht.	Time	Ht.
1 Th	316 L	0.8	918 H	3.1	1511 L	0.9	2128 H	3.5
2 F	353 L	0.8	958 H	3.2	1554 L	0.9	2209 H	3.5
3 Sa	432 L	0.8	1042 H	3.2	1641 L	0.9	2254 H	3.4
4 Su	515 L	0.8	1129 H	3.3	1734 L	1.0	2344 H	3.3
5 M	601 L	0.8	1221 H	3.3	1834 L	0.9		
6 Tu	39 H	3.2	653 L	0.7	1319 H	3.4	1938 L	0.9
7 W	140 H	3.1	749 L	0.7	1420 H	3.5	2046 L	0.8
8 Th	245 H	3.1	849 L	0.6	1523 H	3.7	2151 L	0.7
9 F	349 H	3.1	950 L	0.5	1625 H	3.8	2254 L	0.6
10 Sa	452 H	3.2	1050 L	0.4	1724 H	3.9	2352 L	0.4
11 Su	552 H	3.2	1148 L	0.3	1821 H	4.0		
● 12 M	47 L	0.3	648 H	3.3	1244 L	0.3	1915 H	4.0
13 Tu	139 L	0.2	742 H	3.4	1339 L	0.2	2007 H	4.0
14 W	229 L	0.2	834 H	3.4	1432 L	0.3	2057 H	3.9
15 Th	317 L	0.3	925 H	3.4	1525 L	0.4	2146 H	3.7
16 F	404 L	0.4	1015 H	3.4	1617 L	0.5	2234 H	3.5
17 Sa	449 L	0.5	1105 H	3.4	1710 L	0.7	2321 H	3.3
18 Su	535 L	0.6	1155 H	3.3	1804 L	0.9		
19 M	10 H	3.1	620 L	0.8	1246 H	3.3	1900 L	1.0
20 Tu	101 H	3.0	707 L	0.9	1338 H	3.2	1957 L	1.1
21 W	153 H	2.9	756 L	1.0	1432 H	3.2	2055 L	1.2
22 Th	248 H	2.8	847 L	1.0	1524 H	3.3	2150 L	1.2
23 F	342 H	2.8	938 L	1.1	1615 H	3.3	2241 L	1.1
24 Sa	434 H	2.9	1028 L	1.0	1702 H	3.4	2329 L	1.0
25 Su	523 H	3.0	1115 L	1.0	1747 H	3.5		
26 M	12 L	1.0	609 H	3.1	1201 L	0.9	1829 H	3.6
27 Tu	53 L	0.9	652 H	3.2	1244 L	0.9	1909 H	3.7
○ 28 W	133 L	0.8	733 H	3.3	1327 L	0.9	1948 H	3.7
29 Th	210 L	0.8	813 H	3.3	1409 L	0.8	2027 H	3.7
30 F	248 L	0.7	854 H	3.4	1452 L	0.8	2107 H	3.7
31 Sa	325 L	0.7	935 H	3.5	1537 L	0.8	2149 H	3.6

AUGUST 1999 - Standard Time

Day	Time	Ht.	Time	Ht.	Time	Ht.	Time	Ht.
1 Su	405 L	0.7	1019 H	3.5	1625 L	0.9	2234 H	3.5
2 M	447 L	0.7	1106 H	3.6	1719 L	0.9	2324 H	3.4
3 Tu	534 L	0.7	1159 H	3.6	1818 L	0.9		
4 W	19 H	3.3	626 L	0.7	1257 H	3.6	1922 L	1.0
5 Th	120 H	3.1	725 L	0.8	1400 H	3.7	2031 L	0.9
6 F	227 H	3.1	828 L	0.7	1506 H	3.7	2138 L	0.8
7 Sa	335 H	3.1	933 L	0.7	1611 H	3.8	2241 L	0.7
8 Su	440 H	3.2	1037 L	0.6	1712 H	3.9	2339 L	0.6
9 M	540 H	3.3	1137 L	0.5	1809 H	4.0		
10 Tu	32 L	0.5	635 H	3.4	1233 L	0.4	1901 H	4.0
● 11 W	121 L	0.4	727 H	3.5	1326 L	0.4	1950 H	4.0
12 Th	207 L	0.4	816 H	3.6	1416 L	0.5	2036 H	3.9
13 F	250 L	0.4	902 H	3.6	1505 L	0.6	2120 H	3.7
14 Sa	332 L	0.5	947 H	3.6	1553 L	0.7	2203 H	3.6
15 Su	413 L	0.7	1031 H	3.6	1640 L	0.9	2246 H	3.4
16 M	453 L	0.8	1115 H	3.5	1728 L	1.0	2329 H	3.2
17 Tu	534 L	1.0	1201 H	3.4	1819 L	1.2		
18 W	15 H	3.1	618 L	1.1	1249 H	3.4	1913 L	1.3
19 Th	106 H	3.0	706 L	1.2	1341 H	3.3	2010 L	1.4
20 F	201 H	2.9	759 L	1.3	1437 H	3.3	2108 L	1.4
21 Sa	259 H	2.9	855 L	1.3	1532 H	3.4	2203 L	1.4
22 Su	356 H	3.0	951 L	1.3	1624 H	3.5	2252 L	1.3
23 M	449 H	3.1	1043 L	1.2	1712 H	3.6	2338 L	1.1
24 Tu	537 H	3.3	1132 L	1.1	1757 H	3.7		
25 W	20 L	1.0	622 H	3.4	1219 L	1.0	1840 H	3.8
○ 26 Th	59 L	0.9	705 H	3.6	1304 L	0.9	1921 H	3.9
27 F	138 L	0.8	746 H	3.7	1349 L	0.8	2002 H	3.9
28 Sa	216 L	0.7	828 H	3.8	1434 L	0.8	2045 H	3.9
29 Su	256 L	0.7	911 H	3.9	1521 L	0.8	2129 H	3.8
30 M	337 L	0.7	956 H	3.9	1611 L	0.8	2215 H	3.7
31 Tu	421 L	0.7	1045 H	3.9	1705 L	0.9	2306 H	3.5

SEPTEMBER 1999 - Standard Time

Day		Time	Ht.	Time	Ht.	Time	Ht.	Time	Ht.
1	W	510 L	0.8	1139 H	3.9	1804 L	1.0		
2	Th	3 H	3.4	606 L	0.9	1239 H	3.8	1909 L	1.1
3	F	107 H	3.2	708 L	0.9	1345 H	3.8	2018 L	1.1
4	Sa	216 H	3.2	815 L	1.0	1454 H	3.8	2126 L	1.0
5	Su	325 H	3.2	924 L	0.9	1601 H	3.8	2228 L	0.9
6	M	431 H	3.3	1029 L	0.8	1702 H	3.9	2323 L	0.8
7	Tu	529 H	3.5	1129 L	0.7	1756 H	3.9		
8	W	13 L	0.7	622 H	3.6	1223 L	0.7	1845 H	3.9
● 9	Th	58 L	0.6	710 H	3.8	1313 L	0.7	1930 H	3.9
10	F	140 L	0.6	754 H	3.8	1359 L	0.7	2012 H	3.8
11	Sa	220 L	0.7	836 H	3.9	1444 L	0.8	2053 H	3.7
12	Su	257 L	0.8	916 H	3.8	1527 L	0.9	2131 H	3.6
13	M	334 L	0.9	955 H	3.8	1610 L	1.0	2210 H	3.4
14	Tu	411 L	1.0	1034 H	3.7	1653 L	1.2	2250 H	3.3
15	W	450 L	1.2	1115 H	3.6	1739 L	1.4	2333 H	3.2
16	Th	531 L	1.3	1200 H	3.5	1829 L	1.5		
17	F	22 H	3.1	619 L	1.4	1251 H	3.4	1925 L	1.6
18	Sa	116 H	3.0	713 L	1.5	1346 H	3.4	2023 L	1.6
19	Su	216 H	3.0	813 L	1.5	1445 H	3.5	2119 L	1.5
20	M	317 H	3.1	913 L	1.5	1542 H	3.6	2211 L	1.4
21	Tu	413 H	3.3	1010 L	1.4	1634 H	3.7	2258 L	1.2
22	W	503 H	3.5	1103 L	1.2	1722 H	3.8	2341 L	1.1
23	Th	550 H	3.7	1153 L	1.0	1808 H	3.9		
24	F	23 L	0.9	635 H	3.9	1241 L	0.9	1853 H	4.0
○ 25	Sa	103 L	0.8	718 H	4.1	1328 L	0.8	1937 H	4.0
26	Su	145 L	0.7	802 H	4.2	1416 L	0.7	2022 H	4.0
27	M	227 L	0.6	848 H	4.3	1505 L	0.7	2109 H	3.9
28	Tu	311 L	0.6	935 H	4.3	1556 L	0.8	2158 H	3.7
29	W	359 L	0.7	1026 H	4.2	1651 L	0.9	2252 H	3.6
30	Th	451 L	0.8	1122 H	4.1	1751 L	1.0	2351 H	3.4

OCTOBER 1999 - Standard Time

Day		Time	Ht.	Time	Ht.	Time	Ht.	Time	Ht.
1	F	550 L	0.9	1224 H	3.9	1856 L	1.0		
2	Sa	56 H	3.3	655 L	1.0	1331 H	3.8	2004 L	1.1
3	Su	207 H	3.3	806 L	1.1	1441 H	3.7	2110 L	1.0
4	M	316 H	3.3	916 L	1.0	1547 H	3.7	2210 L	1.0
5	Tu	420 H	3.4	1021 L	1.0	1646 H	3.7	2302 L	0.9
6	W	516 H	3.6	1119 L	0.9	1738 H	3.8	2349 L	0.8
7	Th	605 H	3.7	1210 L	0.8	1825 H	3.8		
8	F	32 L	0.8	649 H	3.9	1257 L	0.8	1907 H	3.7
● 9	Sa	111 L	0.8	730 H	3.9	1340 L	0.8	1946 H	3.7
10	Su	148 L	0.8	808 H	3.9	1421 L	0.9	2024 H	3.6
11	M	223 L	0.9	845 H	3.9	1501 L	1.0	2101 H	3.5
12	Tu	258 L	1.0	921 H	3.8	1541 L	1.1	2138 H	3.4
13	W	333 L	1.1	958 H	3.8	1621 L	1.2	2216 H	3.3
14	Th	411 L	1.2	1036 H	3.7	1703 L	1.4	2257 H	3.2
15	F	451 L	1.3	1117 H	3.6	1750 L	1.5	2344 H	3.1
16	Sa	537 L	1.4	1205 H	3.5	1841 L	1.5		
17	Su	36 H	3.0	631 L	1.5	1258 H	3.4	1936 L	1.5
18	M	135 H	3.1	732 L	1.5	1357 H	3.4	2032 L	1.5
19	Tu	236 H	3.2	835 L	1.5	1456 H	3.5	2125 L	1.3
20	W	334 H	3.3	937 L	1.3	1553 H	3.6	2214 L	1.1
21	Th	427 H	3.5	1034 L	1.2	1646 H	3.7	2301 L	1.0
22	F	517 H	3.8	1127 L	1.0	1736 H	3.8	2346 L	0.8
23	Sa	605 H	4.0	1218 L	0.8	1825 H	3.9		
○ 24	Su	30 L	0.6	652 H	4.2	1309 L	0.6	1913 H	3.9
25	M	115 L	0.5	739 H	4.3	1359 L	0.5	2001 H	3.8
26	Tu	201 L	0.4	827 H	4.4	1450 L	0.5	2051 H	3.8
27	W	250 L	0.4	917 H	4.3	1543 L	0.6	2143 H	3.6
28	Th	341 L	0.5	1010 H	4.2	1638 L	0.7	2238 H	3.5
29	F	436 L	0.7	1107 H	4.0	1737 L	0.8	2339 H	3.3
30	Sa	537 L	0.8	1209 H	3.8	1840 L	0.9		
31	Su	44 H	3.2	643 L	0.9	1315 H	3.7	1944 L	0.9

FOR THE FINEST SELECTION OF WINES & SPIRITS IN THE BAHAMAS FEATURING OVER 500 WINES FROM OVER 20 DIFFERENT COUNTRIES.

STORE HOURS:
10 a.m. – 8 p.m. Mon. – Sat.
Closed Sundays

GOING TO THE BAHAMAS!
NEED A MAIL DROP?
Address Your Correspondence
(Letters and Postcards only) To:

Name:
P.O. Box SS6218
c/o Harbour Bay
Liquors,
Nassau, Bahamas

MONITORING VHF
CHANNEL 6

RADIO CALL

"HAPPY HOUR"

Tel. 394-0630/1 • Fax 394-0632 • Harbour Bay, Nassau
Located across from the Nassau Harbour Club.

Yachtsman's Guide to the Virgin Islands

Over 300 pages of indispensable information including 16 pages of full color aerial photos.

Yachtsman's Guide to the Bahamas

Over 450 pages of indispensable information

- The most complete guides available for cruising the Bahamas and Virgin Islands.
- Profusely illustrated with our beautiful hand-drawn sketch charts, landfall sketches and photographs.
- Detailed island by island profiles and things to do ashore.

Sketch Charts also available separately in 11"x17" format. Call or use order form in the Guide.

Call (305) 893-4277

Or write to:
Tropic Isle Publishers
P.O. Box 610938
North Miami, FL 33261-0938

"Someday, Father, I shall write great guides for yachtsmen. Sailors like us will never wander aimlessly again. That is... if we ever get back. Sir, will we soon see land?"

NOVEMBER 1999 - Standard Time

Day		Time	Ht.	Time	Ht.	Time	Ht.	Time	Ht.
1	M	153 H	3.2	754 L	1.0	1422 H	3.5	2046 L	0.9
2	Tu	301 H	3.3	903 L	1.0	1526 H	3.5	2143 L	0.9
3	W	402 H	3.4	1007 L	1.0	1624 H	3.4	2234 L	0.8
4	Th	456 H	3.5	1103 L	0.9	1714 H	3.4	2320 L	0.8
5	F	543 H	3.7	1153 L	0.8	1800 H	3.4		
6	Sa	1 L	0.7	626 H	3.7	1238 L	0.8	1841 H	3.4
● 7	Su	39 L	0.7	705 H	3.8	1319 L	0.8	1919 H	3.4
8	M	116 L	0.8	742 H	3.8	1359 L	0.8	1957 H	3.3
9	Tu	151 L	0.8	817 H	3.8	1437 L	0.9	2033 H	3.3
10	W	227 L	0.9	852 H	3.7	1515 L	1.0	2110 H	3.2
11	Th	302 L	1.0	927 H	3.6	1554 L	1.1	2148 H	3.1
12	F	339 L	1.1	1004 H	3.6	1633 L	1.1	2228 H	3.0
13	Sa	419 L	1.2	1043 H	3.5	1715 L	1.2	2312 H	3.0
14	Su	503 L	1.3	1127 H	3.4	1801 L	1.3		
15	M	1 H	2.9	555 L	1.3	1217 H	3.3	1851 L	1.2
16	Tu	57 H	3.0	654 L	1.3	1313 H	3.3	1944 L	1.2
17	W	156 H	3.1	759 L	1.3	1412 H	3.3	2038 L	1.0
18	Th	255 H	3.2	903 L	1.1	1512 H	3.3	2130 L	0.9
19	F	351 H	3.5	1005 L	1.0	1610 H	3.4	2221 L	0.7
20	Sa	445 H	3.7	1102 L	0.7	1705 H	3.5	2311 L	0.5
21	Su	537 H	3.9	1157 L	0.5	1759 H	3.5		
22	M	0 L	0.3	628 H	4.1	1250 L	0.4	1851 H	3.6
○ 23	Tu	50 L	0.2	719 H	4.2	1343 L	0.3	1943 H	3.5
24	W	140 L	0.2	810 H	4.3	1435 L	0.2	2035 H	3.5
25	Th	232 L	0.2	902 H	4.2	1528 L	0.3	2129 H	3.4
26	F	326 L	0.3	956 H	4.0	1623 L	0.3	2225 H	3.3
27	Sa	422 L	0.4	1052 H	3.8	1719 L	0.4	2324 H	3.2
28	Su	522 L	0.6	1150 H	3.6	1817 L	0.5		
29	M	26 H	3.1	627 L	0.7	1251 H	3.4	1916 L	0.6
30	Tu	131 H	3.1	734 L	0.8	1354 H	3.2	2014 L	0.7

DECEMBER 1999 - Standard Time

Day		Time	Ht.	Time	Ht.	Time	Ht.	Time	Ht.
1	W	236 H	3.1	842 L	0.9	1455 H	3.1	2109 L	0.7
2	Th	335 H	3.2	944 L	0.8	1552 H	3.0	2159 L	0.7
3	F	429 H	3.3	1040 L	0.8	1643 H	3.0	2246 L	0.6
4	Sa	517 H	3.4	1130 L	0.8	1730 H	3.0	2328 L	0.6
5	Su	559 H	3.5	1215 L	0.7	1812 H	3.0		
6	M	8 L	0.6	639 H	3.5	1257 L	0.7	1852 H	3.0
● 7	Tu	46 L	0.6	716 H	3.5	1337 L	0.7	1931 H	3.0
8	W	124 L	0.6	752 H	3.5	1415 L	0.7	2009 H	3.0
9	Th	201 L	0.7	827 H	3.5	1452 L	0.7	2046 H	3.0
10	F	237 L	0.7	902 H	3.5	1529 L	0.8	2124 H	2.9
11	Sa	315 L	0.8	938 H	3.4	1606 L	0.8	2203 H	2.9
12	Su	354 L	0.9	1016 H	3.3	1645 L	0.9	2244 H	2.9
13	M	437 L	1.0	1057 H	3.3	1726 L	0.9	2330 H	2.9
14	Tu	526 L	1.0	1143 H	3.2	1811 L	0.9		
15	W	21 H	2.9	623 L	1.0	1236 H	3.1	1900 L	0.8
16	Th	118 H	3.0	726 L	1.0	1334 H	3.1	1953 L	0.7
17	F	217 H	3.1	832 L	0.9	1435 H	3.0	2049 L	0.6
18	Sa	318 H	3.3	938 L	0.7	1538 H	3.0	2145 L	0.4
19	Su	417 H	3.5	1040 L	0.5	1638 H	3.1	2241 L	0.2
20	M	514 H	3.7	1139 L	0.4	1736 H	3.2	2336 L	0.1
21	Tu	609 H	3.9	1234 L	0.2	1832 H	3.2		
○ 22	W	31 L	0.0	703 H	4.0	1328 L	0.1	1926 H	3.3
23	Th	124 L	-0.1	756 H	4.0	1420 L	0.0	2020 H	3.3
24	F	218 L	-0.1	848 H	3.9	1512 L	0.0	2114 H	3.2
25	Sa	312 L	0.0	941 H	3.8	1604 L	0.1	2208 H	3.2
26	Su	408 L	0.1	1033 H	3.6	1655 L	0.2	2304 H	3.1
27	M	505 L	0.3	1127 H	3.4	1748 L	0.3		
28	Tu	1 H	3.0	604 L	0.5	1222 H	3.1	1840 L	0.4
29	W	100 H	3.0	707 L	0.6	1318 H	2.9	1934 L	0.5
30	Th	200 H	3.0	810 L	0.7	1416 H	2.8	2027 L	0.6
31	F	259 H	3.0	912 L	0.8	1512 H	2.7	2118 L	0.6

Here's a selection of tasty recipes sent in by *Guide* contributors, many of them easy to prepare with standard provisions, and some using fish, fruits, and vegetables encountered in The Bahamas. Why don't you volunteer one of your galley masterpieces for our Galley Guide? If we use your recipe, we'll send you a complimentary *Yachtsman's Guide.* Send your recipe to the Editor, Yachtsman's Guide to the Bahamas, P.O. Box 15397, Plantation, FL 33318. Don't forget to include your name and address!

Scheel Sundowner
Contributed by Dave and Kathy Irwin, *Scheel Delight*
This drink tastes like a chocolate milkshake — but with quite a kick. Add equal parts of the following liqueurs to ice in a blender and blend until frothy.
- Baileys Irish Cream (or an equivalent cream liqueur)
- Frangelico
- Vodka
- Kahlua
- Chocolate liqueur

This is another great drink that can be adapted, based on which liqueurs you have aboard. But, beware — they are very potent and you won't know what hit you until the next morning!

Banana Muffins *Redjello*
Contributed by Mary Lou Tout, Yacht *Redjello*
This is a good recipe for boats without refrigeration as it doesn't require eggs or shortening. One 8-ounce jar of mayonnaise makes a double batch.
- 1/2 cup sugar (white or brown)
- 1/2 cup Miracle Whip mayonnaise (can use Light version)
- 1 large mashed banana
- 1 cup all-purpose flour
- 1 tsp. baking soda

Bake at 375° for 18-20 minutes. Makes 8 large muffins.

Papy's Rum Dolphin
(fish, not porpoise)
Contributed by Frank Papy
Cut dolphin fillets in 5-inch squares. Marinate 1/2 hour in lime juice, soy sauce, and one capful of dark rum. Cook in frying pan with butter and pepper

for 5 minutes with cover on. Then uncover and pour off all but a small amount of the juice. The butter, lime juice, soy sauce and rum form a delicious syrupy substance. Cook to a golden brown. The smell is almost as good as the taste. Serve with steamed rice or grits.

Grouper in Red Sauce
Contributed by Jane Billings, S/V *Magic*
Drizzle olive oil generously on the bottom of a shallow baking dish. Cover with fresh tomato slices, minced garlic, and minced hot red pepper. Place fish fillets on top and cover with more tomato slices. Drizzle olive oil lightly over all. Salt and pepper. Cover with foil and bake for approximately 20 minutes at 400°.

Ty's Winning Chicken
Contributed by T. W. Morrison, S/V *Blue Moon*
One pan has the potatoes, meat, and gravy. No muss, no fuss.
• 6 medium chicken pieces, boned (optional)
• 1 can cream of mushroom soup
• 1 can of cream of broccoli soup
• 1.5 lb. potatoes, red or other
• 1/2 can water
Place chicken in aluminum baking dish (throwaway). Mix both cans of soup with 1/2 can of water and pour over diced or halved potatoes and chicken. Cook for 60 minutes in tightly foiled baking tin at 250°. Poke some holes in the foil. One

Panton Cove Conch Chowder
Contributed by Debbie and Ed Miraglia, *Joan Debra II*
• Meat from large conch, pounded and chopped fine.
• Several bacon slices, cooked, drained, and chopped
• 1 or 2 cups chopped onions/celery
• 1 or 2 chopped garlic cloves
• 1 16-oz. can white potatoes drained and diced
• 1 14-1/2 oz. can tomatoes with liquid , coarsely chopped
• 1 tsp. Italian seasoning
• 1 tsp. Gravymaster or Kitchen Bouquet
• 1 bouillon cube, crumbled

Eating Your Catch:
Caution Regarding Ciguatera Poisoning

Please read the boxed information on page 34 of this Guide before eating any fish you catch. Ciguatera poisoning results in serious illness and can be fatal.

- 1 tbsp. cooking oil

Sauté onion/celery/garlic in oil several minutes until tender. Add remaining ingredients and cook/simmer until flavors meld (about 15-20 minutes_, adding water as necessary. Serves 2.

Debbie's Snapper "Omelette"

Contributed by Debbie and Ed Miraglia, *Joan Debra II*

Dip snapper fillets in flour, then in egg that has been beaten with one teaspoon water and sauté until brown and done. Variation: Beat egg with one teaspoon Worcestershire sauce instead of water.

Meatless Burgers

Contributed by Linda Chaffee, S/V *Argo*

- 1/2 cup ground nuts
- 1 cup uncooked oatmeal
- 2 eggs, beaten
- 1 tbsp. powdered milk
- 3 tbsp. water
- 1 tsp. dehydrated chopped onion
- 1 tsp. sage
- 1/2 tsp. salt
- 2-3 tbsp. cooking oil

Mix all ingredients except the oil and form into four patties. Cook for about 10 minutes in an oiled frying pan, turning to brown on both sides. This also can be used as "meatballs" for spaghetti and it is hard to tell the difference. Just cook in ball form before adding to sauce. Recipe can be doubled. Any nuts or combination of nuts can be used, but walnuts are best.

Margarita Pie

Contributed by Bill Billich, *Best Friend*

Crust:
- 1/2 cup butter
- 1 1/4 cup finely crushed pretzels
- 1/4 cup sugar

Filling:
- 14-ounce can condensed milk
- 1/2 cup lime juice
- 2-4 tablespoons tequila
- 2 tablespoons Triple Sec
- 1 cup *very firm* whipped cream

Mix pretzel crumbs and sugar with butter. Press into buttered pie shell and chill. Combine condensed milk, lime juice, tequila and Triple Sec. Mix well and fold in whipped cream. Pour into chilled crust, freeze for at least four hours. Top with lime or orange garnish.

LIGHT LIST

Important Notes and Additions

1. Remember that lighthouses and beacons are maintained by the Bahamas government. Due to the vastness of the area and the number of lights to be maintained, at any given time some (perhaps even most) lights will not be working or may have flashing patterns varying from those noted on sketch charts, government charts, or in this text. This list tells things as they are meant to be, but be prepared for something else, or nothing. See text as to conditions we've heard of at press time. Rather than noting that some lights are unreliable, we caution that all are unreliable.

2. Prior to our deadline, we receive from Batelco a current list of their communications towers throughout the Bahamas (this list appears on page 39. We are unable to plot many of these towers on our sketch charts and they are not included in this light list.

3. There is a radio transmission tower on the northwestern tip of South Caicos which tops out at about 480 feet above sea level. We've been unable to ascertain flashing characteristics of the red light at the top or of any intermediate lights.

4. For status of Northwest Channel Beacon, consult box on page 73. Russell and Sylvia Beacons are, as we go to press, replaced with buoys.

Key to abbreviations: LH/Lighthouse MTT/Missle Tracking Tower

Location	Characteristics	Height (ft)	Range(mi)	Remarks
LITTLE BAHAMA BANK				
Memory Rock	Fl W ev 3 secs	37	11	Steel twr
Little Sale Cay	Fl W ev 3 secs	47	9	Steel twr
Walker's Cay	Fl (airwarning) R Fx	250	20	Steel bayonet twr, R&W bands
Carter Cay	Fl (airwarning) R fixed	200	25	Steel bayonet twr, R&W bands
Crab Cay (Angelfish Pt)	Fl W ev 5 secs	33	8	Steel twr
Whale Cay	Fl W ev 5 secs	40	8	Black and aluminum
Man of War Cay	Qk W Fl	30	5	W pole
Elbow Cay (LH)	Gp Fl W (5) ev 15 secs	120	15	Stone twr, R&W bands
Little Harbour	Fl W ev 4 secs	61	10	Stone building
Hole in the Wall (LH)	Fl W ev 10 secs	168	19	Conical stone twr, lower part W, upper R
Rock Point (near Sandy Pt)	Fl W ev 6 secs	35	10	Steel twr
More's Island	Fl W ev 2.5 secs	32	6	Black iron twr
GRAND BAHAMA				
Sweetings Cay (SE Gr Bah)	Fl W ev 5 secs	23	8	W steel twr
Reef Buoy (Bell Ch)	Gp Fl W (2) ev 5 secs	6		Buoy
Bell Channel (S Gr Bah)	Fl W ev 3 secs	36	7	Black iron twr
Pinder Point Light	Gp Fl WR (3) ev 5 secs	64	12	Concrete twr B&W bands, R sector 255-301° W sector 301-114°
Riding Pt Twr (MTT)	Fl R (airwarning top) Fx	135	14	R sector 113°-133° W sector 133°-255°
Settlement Point	Fl W ev 4 secs	32	6	Gray framework
Indian Cay	Fl W ev 6 secs	40	8	Steel twr
Gold Rock Creek (MTT)	Fl W (airwarning) Fx	420	27	Steel bayonet twr, R&W bands
GREAT BAHAMA BANK				
Great Isaac (LH)	Fl W ev 15 secs	152	23	Steel twr, R&W bands
North Rock, 1 m N of N Bimini	Fl W ev 3 secs	40	8	W iron twr
Gun Cay	Fl W ev 10 secs	80	14	Twr, upper half R, lower W
Ocean Cay Range	Qk W Fl	35	7	2 iron twrs
	Occ W	50	9	
South Riding Rock	Fl W ev 5 secs	35	10	Steel framework
Russell Beacon	Fl W 4 secs	20	8	Pipe structure
Mackie Beacon	Fl W ev 2 secs	20	8	Pipe structure
Sylvia Beacon	Fl W ev 4 secs	20	8	Pipe structure
Northwest Shoal Buoy	Fl W ev 2 secs	12	5	R Buoy
NW Channel Beacon	Fl W ev 3 secs	33	8	Skeleton Twr, W, R & B
BERRY ISLANDS				
Great Stirrup Cay LH	Gp Fl (2) W ev 20 secs	82	22	Visible from 18° to 306°

Location	Characteristics	Height (ft)	Range(mi)	Remarks
				W twr
Bullock's Harbour	Fl W ev 6 secs	20	7	Iron twr
Little Harbour Cay	Fl W ev 2 secs	75	9	Iron twr, 23 ft
Chub Point	Fl R&W ev 10 secs	44	7	R from 233° to 140°, W from 140° to 233°

ANDROS

Location	Characteristics	Height (ft)	Range(mi)	Remarks
Bethel Channel Range	Fl W ev 5 secs (2 lights)	60-65	9	Two R & aluminum tripods
Staniard Rock	Fl W ev 4 secs	18	6	Pipe structure
Middle Bight	Fl W ev 5 secs	17	7	W twr
South Bight				
on Sirius Rock	Fl W ev 3 secs	29	7	
Duncan Rock	Fl W ev 3.3 secs	37	6	R top with blue base
Tinker Rock	Fl W ev 4 secs		8	

NEW PROVIDENCE ISLAND

Location	Characteristics	Height (ft)	Range(mi)	Remarks
Goulding Cay (W End)	Fl W ev 2 secs	36	8	Steel twr
Fort Fincastle	Fl W ev 5 secs	216	18	Gray concrete water twr, revolving W&W
Paradise Island	Fl W or R ev 5 secs	68	W10, R5	W stone twr Shows R when bar is dangerous. Obsc from 334° and 25°
Range Light (Front)	Fl G	37	7	
Range Light (Rear)	Fl G	61	7	151° from front light
The Narrows (between				
Athol I & Hog I)	Fl R ev 5 secs	12	2	Steel structure
Porgee Rocks	Fl W ev 3 secs	23	5	Pipe structure
East Point, N Providence	Fl W ev 6 secs	57	8	W square stone house
Chub Rock (Sandy Cay)	Fl W ev 5 secs	25	4	Steel twr

EXUMA CAYS & GREAT EXUMA

Location	Characteristics	Height (ft)	Range(mi)	Remarks
Beacon Cay (N. Rk)	Fl W&R ev 3 secs	38	8	Steel structure R from 292°
Ship Channel				to 303°
Elbow Cay	Fl W ev 2 secs	46	11	Steel structure
Staniel Rock	Fl W ev 2 secs	16	5	Iron twr
Harvey Cay	Fl W ev 3.3 secs	49	6	
Dotham Cay	Fl W ev 5 secs	36	8	Steel frame twr
Galliot Cut	Fl W ev 4 secs	50	7	Steel twr
George Town Hbr, Conch Cay	Fl W ev 5 secs	40	8	Steel twr
Green Cay	Fl W ev 3 secs	33	7	
Jewfish Cut	Fl W ev 2.5 secs	38	8	Steel twr
Hawksbill Rock	Fl W ev 3.25 secs		6	

ELEUTHERA

Location	Characteristics	Height (ft)	Range(mi)	Remarks
Powell Point	Fl W ev 3 secs	38	8	Steel twr
Poison Point	Fl W ev 15 secs	29	7	
Eleuthera Point	Fl W ev 4.5 secs	61	6	Frame structure
US Navy Buoy (Exuma Sound)	Fl W ev 4 secs			R buoy
Governor's Harbour	Fl W ev 4 secs	40	8	W frame twr
Hatchet Bay	Fl W ev 15 secs	57	8	Steel twr on N side of entrance
Hatchet Bay	2 R Fl			R lights in transit lead through entrance
Current Rock	Fl W ev 8 secs	41	7	Steel twr
Great Egg Island	Fl W ev 3 secs	112	12	Steel frame twr
Man Island (near Harbour Island)	Gp Fl W (3) ev 15 secs	93	12	Frame twr, W house nearby

Location	Characteristics	Height (ft)	Range(mi)	Remarks
LITTLE SAN SALVADOR	Fl W ev 2.5 secs	69	13	Steel twr
CAT ISLAND				
Bennett's Harbour	Fl W ev 4 secs	53	12	Gray structure, vis 350° to 130°
Smith's Bay	Fl W ev 4 secs	38	7	Steel twr
Devil Point	Fl W ev 5 secs	143	12	Steel twr
CONCEPTION ISLAND	Fl W ev 2 secs	84	6	Steel twr
LONG ISLAND				
Cape Santa Maria (N end)	Fl W ev 3.3 secs	99	14	Gray steel twr, obsc from 240° to 340°
Clarence Harbour (Booby Rocks)	Fl W ev 2 sec	41	8	Steel tower, R&W
South Point (S end)	Fl W ev 2.5 secs	61	12	
SAN SALVADOR				
Dixon Hill (LH)	Gp Fl W (2) ev 10 secs	163	19	W stone twr, partially obsc be tween 001°and 008°; 010° and 068°; 76° and 095°
CROOKED ISLAND				
Bird Rock (LH)	Fl W ev 15 secs	112	23	Conical stone twr
Atwood Harbour	Fl W ev 5 secs	20	8	Steel twr
Hell Gate (NE Pt Acklins Is)	Fl W ev 6 secs	56	10	W wooden structure
Windsor Point	Fl W ev 3 secs	35	8	
Castle Island (LH)	Gp Fl W (2) ev 20 secs	130	22	W conical twr
Hogsty Reef (NW Cay)	Fl W ev 4 secs	29	8	Steel twr, W&R bands
GREAT BAHAMA BANK (CONTINUED)				
Nuevitas Rocks on eastern Jumentos Cays	Fl W ev 4 secs	38	10	Steel twr
Flamingo Cay	Fl W ev 6 secs	138	8	Steel twr
Hawksbill Rocks	Fl W ev 33 secs	32	6	
Ragged Island	Fl W ev 3 secs	118	12	Black Col on W hut
Cay Santo Domingo	Fl W ev 5 secs	30	7	Aluminum & R horizontal stripes
Cayo Lobos (LH)	Gp Fl W (2) ev 10 secs	145	22	Circular iron twr
MAYAGUANA				
Guano Pt, Abraham's Bay	Fl W ev 3 secs	14	8	Steel twr
Northwest Point	Fl W ev 5 secs	70	12	Steel twr
GREAT INAGUA				
Southwest Point (LH)	Gp Fl W (2) ev 10 secs	120	17	W conical twr, partially obs between 165° and 183°
CAICOS ISLANDS	All lights are unreliable			
TURKS ISLANDS				
Grand Turk (LH)	Fl W ev 7.5 secs	108	16	W circular iron twr Signal station
Range, head of wharf, west side of island				
Front	2 Fl W & R ev 3 secs	20 & 30	3	Sychronized range lights 084°
Head of Wharf, Rear	Fl W ev 3 secs			
Sand Cay	Fl W ev 2 secs	85	15	W frame

INDEX

ADVERTISER INDEX

CHART INDEX

Did You Know

that Tropic Isle Sketch Charts are available in an easy-to-read 11" x 17" format?

These convenient easy-to-read sketch charts are 11"x17" enlargements of the sketch charts in your current *Yachtsman's Guide* and are intended to be used in conjunction with the current *Guide*. Sketch Charts may be purchased singly or in sets as described on the following pages. They are printed on heavy stock for durability and shipped flat.

Postage and Handling Charges - Inside the U.S.A.

Sketch Charts Ordered	Charges
1 - 20	$3.50
21 - 40	$5.00
41 or more	$6.50

For shipment outside the U.S. add $5.00 to above amounts. Florida residents add appicable sales tax. Sketch Charts are not refundable.

Please send the following:

QTY.	CHART NO. and TITLE	PRICE
	Clear Plastic Envelope @ 5.00 each	
	Postage Handling & Applicable Tax	
	TOTAL	

Send Check or Money Order to:
TROPIC ISLE PUBLISHERS, INC.
P.O. Box 610938 • North Miami, FL 33261-0938

NAME _____

ADDRESS _____

CITY, STATE, ZIP _____

THE BAHAMAS and TURKS & CAICOS
TROPIC ISLE SKETCH CHART CATALOG

These convenient, easy to read sketch charts are 11"x17" enlargements of the sketch charts in your current *Yachtsman's Guide* and are intended to be used in conjunction with the current *Guide*. Sketch charts may be purchased singly at $3.00 each or in sets as described below. They are printed on heavy stock for durability and shipped flat. Sketch charts are non-refundable.

Complete Set-72 sketch charts with 2 clear plastic envelopes
$195.00

19"x13" Clear Plastic Envelope $5.00 each

Postage and Handling Charges - Inside U.S.A.

Sketch Charts Ordered	Charges
1-20	$3.50
21-40	$5.00
41 or more	$6.50

For shipment outside the U.S. add $5.00 to above amounts. Florida residents add applicable sales tax. Sketch Charts are nonrefundable.

TROPIC ISLE PUBLISHERS, INC.
P.O. Box 610938 • North Miami, FL 33261-0938
(305) 893-4277

SKETCH CHARTS ARE NOT REFUNDABLE.

SINGLE TROPIC ISLE SKETCH CHARTS - $3.00 EACH (Not Shown)

39 – Approaches to the Bahamas
#41 – The Bahamas Islands
#42 – Little Bahama Bank
#43 – Bahamas Far Out Islands

Set "B" – 5 Sketch Charts - $14.00

B 1 Bimini - Cat Cay
B 2 West End, Grand Bahama
B 3 Freeport-Lucaya
B 4 Grand Lucayan Waterway
B 5 Hawksbill Creek

Set "C" – Berry Islands
4 Sketch Charts - $11.50

C 1 Northern Berry Islands
C 2 Central Berry Islands
C 3 Southern Berry Islands
C 4 Little Hbr. & Alder Cay Anch.

Set "D" – New Providence
5 Sketch Charts - $14.00

D 1 Appr. to New Providence & Nassau Hbr.
D 2 Nassau Harbour
D 3 Eastern Approaches to Nassau Hbr.
D 4 Rose Island
D 5 Western New Providence

Set "E" – Eleuthera
9 Sketch Charts - $25.00

E 17 Islands of North Eleuthera
E 18 Hatchet Bay
E 19 Governor's Harbour
E 20 Spanish Wells Harbour
E 21 Eleuthera Island
E 22 Powell Point to Rock Sound
E 23 Current Cut
E 24 Cays to Eleuthera
E 25 Spanish Wells to Harbour I.

Set "F" – Andros - 4 Sketch Charts - $11.50

F 1 Jouters Cays to Stafford Creek
F 2 Stafford Creek to North Bight
F 3 The Bights of Andros
F 4 South Bight to Hawksbill Creek

Set "H" – Abaco - 14 Sketch Charts - $38.75

H 1 Walkers Cay to Carter Cay
H 2 Carter Cay to Allan's Pensacola Cay
H 3 Allan's Pensacola Cay to Green Turtle Cay
H 4 Green Turtle Cay to Hope Town
H 5 Man of War Cay to Cherokee Sound
H 6 Green Turtle Cay
H 7 Man of War Cay
H 8 Marsh Harbour
H 9 Elbow Cay
H 10 North Bar Channel
H 11 Little Harbour
H 12 Bight of Abaco
H 13 Whale Cay Passage
H 14 Hub of Abaco

Set "J" – Exuma Cays
13 Sketch Charts - $36.00

J 35 Allan's & Highborne Cay
J 36 Annan's Cay Harbour
J 37 Staniel Cay
J 38 Sail Rocks to Cistern Cay
J 39 Cistern Cay to Bitter Guana Cay
J 40 Bitter Guana Cay to Bock Cay
J 41 Bock Cay to Channel Cay
J 42 Elizabeth Hbe. to Hog Cay
J 43 Pipe Creek
J 44 Elizabeth Harbour
J 45 Hog Cay Cut
J 46 Farmer's Cay-Galliot Cut
J 47 Central Bahamas

Set "K" – Long Islands
3 Sketch Charts - $8.50

K 1 Long Island
K 2 Long Island, North End
K 3 Long Island, East Coast Hbrs.

Set "L" – Turks and Caicos
1 Sketch Chart - $3.00

L 1 Turks & Caicos Islands

Set "M" – Cat Island
3 Sketch Charts - $8.50

M 1 Cat Island, Little San Salvador
M 2 Cat Island, Harbours & Creeks
M 3 Little San Salvador

Set "N" – Crooked Island
3 Sketch Charts - $8.50

N 1 Crooked Island
N 2 Crooked-Acklins Islands
N 3 French Wells & Turtle Sound

Set "O" – Ragged Island
1 Sketch Chart - $3.00

O 1 Jumentos Cays and Ragged I. Hbr.

Set "P"
3 Sketch Charts - $8.50

P 1 San Salvador
P 2 Conception Islands
P 3 Rum Cay

Sketch Charts may be ordered singly – $3.00 each

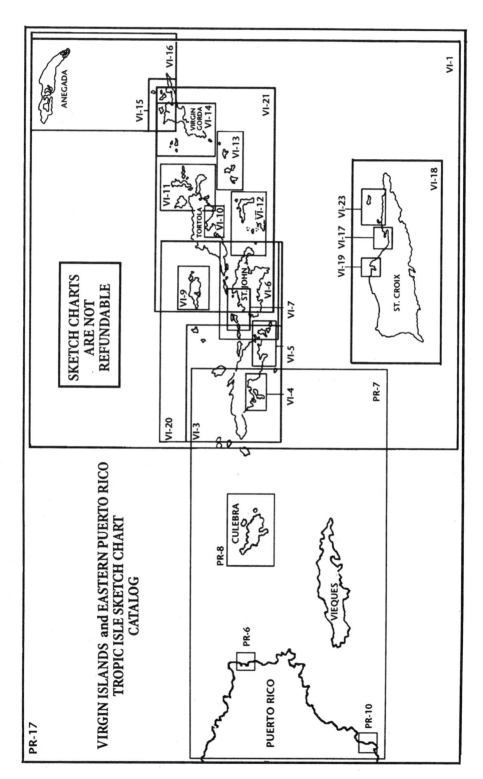

VIRGIN ISLANDS and EASTERN PUERTO RICO
TROPIC ISLE SKETCH CHART
CATALOG

SKETCH CHARTS
ARE NOT
REFUNDABLE

**Complete Set - 22 U.S.V.I. and B.V.I. Sketch Charts
with 1 clear plastic envelope $65.00**

U.S. VIRGIN ISLANDS
Set "USVI" – 12 Sketch Charts -$33.00

VI 1 Virgin Islands
VI 2 Approaches to the Virgin Islands
VI 3 St. Thomas
VI 4 St. Thomas Harbour
VI 5 Southeastern St. Thomas
VI 6 St. John
VI 7 Northwestern St. John
VI 17 Christiansted Harbour
VI 18 St. Croix
VI 19 Salt River Bay, St. Croix
VI 20 U.S. Virgin Islands
VI 23 St. Croix's Northeast Shore

BRITISH VIRGIN ISLANDS
Set "BVI" – 10 Sketch Charts -$27.50

VI 8 West End of Tortola
         and Jost Van Dyke
VI 9 Jost Van Dyke
VI 10 Road Harbour
VI 11 Eastern Tortola
          and Adjacent Islands
VI 12 Norman and Peter Islands
VI 13 Salt, Cooper, Ginger Islands
VI 14 Virgin Gorda
VI 15 Approaches to Gorda Sound
VI 16 Anegada and Gorda Sound
VI 21 British Virgin Islands

EASTERN PUERTO RICO
Set "PR" – 5 Sketch Charts -$13.75

PR6 East Coast Harbours and Marinas
PR7 Vieques Sound
PR8 Culebra
PR10 Palmas Del Mar
PR17 Virgin Islands and
          Eastern Puerto Rico

```
SKETCH CHARTS
ARE NOT
REFUNDABLE
```

Sketch Charts may be ordered singly - $3.00 each
19"x13" Clear Plastic Envelope - $5.00 each

Postage And Handling Charges - Inside U.S.A.

Sketch Charts Ordered	Charges
1 - 20	$3.50
21-40	$5.00
41 or more	$6.50

For shipment outside the U.S.A. add $5.00 to the above amounts.
Florida residents add applicable sales tax.

These convenient, easy to read sketch charts are 11"x17" enlargements of the sketch charts in your current *Yachtsman's Guide* and are intended to be used in conjunction with the current *Guide*. Sketch charts are printed on heavy stock for durability and are shipped flat.

TROPIC ISLE PUBLISHERS, INC.
P.O. Box 610938
North Miami, FL 33261-0938
(305) 893-4277

Cruising Log

Suggestions for next year's Guide?
We'd like to hear them! Send your notes to the Editor, Yachtsman's Guide to the Bahamas, P.O. Box 15397, Plantation, FL 33318 before June 1999. Please include your name and address. Thanks!

Cruising Log

Suggestions for next year's Guide?

We'd like to hear them! Send your notes to the Editor, Yachtsman's Guide to the Bahamas, P.O. Box 15397, Plantation, FL 33318 before June 1999. Please include your name and address. Thanks!

Cruising Log

Suggestions for next year's Guide?

We'd like to hear them! Send your notes to the Editor, Yachtsman's Guide to the Bahamas, P.O. Box 15397, Plantation, FL 33318 before June 1999. Please include your name and address. Thanks!

Cruising Log

Suggestions for next year's Guide?

We'd like to hear them! Send your notes to the Editor, Yachtsman's Guide to the Bahamas, P.O. Box 15397, Plantation, FL 33318 before June 1999. Please include your name and address. Thanks!

Cruising Log

_____

_____

_____

_____

_____

_____

_____

_____

_____

_____

_____

_____

_____

_____

_____

_____

_____

_____

_____

_____

_____

_____

_____

Suggestions for next year's Guide?

_We'd like to hear them! Send your notes to the Editor, Yachtsman's
Guide to the Bahamas, P.O. Box 15397, Plantation, FL 33318 before
June 1999. Please include your name and address. Thanks!_

Cruising Log

Suggestions for next year's Guide?

We'd like to hear them! Send your notes to the Editor, Yachtsman's Guide to the Bahamas, P.O. Box 15397, Plantation, FL 33318 before June 1999. Please include your name and address. Thanks!

FREE CHART OFFER

Please take a few minutes to fill out this Reader Survey Form. You'll help us improve our *Guide* and you'll get a FREE CHART for yourself (select one chart from the sketch chart catalog on preceding pages). Please use this original reader survey form (no photocopies), tear it out, and mail it to:

TROPIC ISLE PUBLISHERS, INC.
P.O. Box 610938 • North Miami, FL 33261-0938

YES, I'd like a FREE CHART ... please send Chart No. _____

Chart Title _____

NAME: _____

ADDRESS: _____

CITY, STATE, ZIP: _____

1. Occupation
- ☐ Executive/Management
- ☐ Professional/Technical
- ☐ Sales/Service
- ☐ Business Owner
- ☐ Student
- ☐ Other _____

2. Which group best describes your family income? Married __ Single __
- ☐ Under 20,000
- ☐ $20,000-$40,000
- ☐ $40,000-$60,000
- ☐ $60,000-$80,000
- ☐ $80,000-$100,000
- ☐ Over $100,000

3. What type of boat do you own?
- ☐ Inboard cruiser ☐ Diesel ☐ Gas _____ Length.
- ☐ Sailboat ☐ w/auxillary ☐ Diesel ☐ Gas _____ Length.
- ☐ Trawler ☐ Diesel ☐ Gas _____ Length.
- ☐ Other _____

4. Do you plan to purchase a boat within the next 12 months?
☐ Yes, ☐ No, ☐ Maybe.

5. In the last 12 months were you asked for ...
Advice on which boat to buy
☐ Yes ☐ No
Advice on which equipment to buy
☐ Yes ☐ No

6. How frequently do you cruise the Bahamas?
- ☐ Once a year ☐ Twice a year.
- ☐ Occasionally ☐ Other _____
- ☐ I spend about $ _____ on each cruise.
- ☐ Number of persons aboard is usually _____

7. My copy of this Guide came from ...
- ☐ Purchased in Marine store
- ☐ Purchased in Bookstore
- ☐ Mail order
- ☐ Other _____

8. I purchase a new Guide ...
- ☐ Every year. ☐ Every other year.
- ☐ Only when I plan a cruise.
- ☐ Other _____

9. In addition to myself _____ other persons read this Guide.

10. I'd rate the importance of the following sections of the Guide as follows ...
Skipper Should Know ☐ Very, ☐ Somewhat, ☐ No.
Bahamas Holidays ☐ Very, ☐ Somewhat, ☐ No.
Wind & Weather ☐ Very, ☐ Somewhat, ☐ No.
Radio Facilities ☐ Very, ☐ Somewhat, ☐ No.
Cruising Facilities ☐ Very, ☐ Somewhat, ☐ No.
Diving Section ☐ Very, ☐ Somewhat, ☐ No.
Tide Tables ☐ Very, ☐ Somewhat, ☐ No.
Galley Guide ☐ Very, ☐ Somewhat, ☐ No.
Light List ☐ Very, ☐ Somewhat, ☐ No.
Advertisements ☐ Very, ☐ Somewhat, ☐ No.
Index ☐ Very, ☐ Somewhat, ☐ No.

THIS OFFER EXPIRES OCTOBER 31, 1999

If you have additional comments to make about any part of our *Guide* (good or bad), please jot them down on the back of this survey and they will be forwarded to the editor.

Allow 3-4 weeks for delivery of your charts. Charts will be folded to fit a 9x12 envelope. If you wish to frame your chart, please add $3.50 for special handling so chart can be shipped flat. Whatever information you choose to give us in sections 1-10 will be kept strictly confidential. The purpose of this reader survey is to determine a reader profile and provide us with demographic figures useful in determining the effectiveness and appropriateness of our editorial and advertising content